# The American
# Socialist Movement
# 1897-1912

# The American
# Socialist Movement
# 1897-1912

*by*

## IRA KIPNIS

GREENWOOD PRESS, PUBLISHERS
NEW YORK                    1968

*for Jake*

# Acknowledgments

THE CONTRIBUTIONS made by one's associates during the long process which finally culminates in the publication of a book can perhaps be acknowledged only in generalizations. However, the usual thanks would not begin to express my gratitude for the considerable and generous assistance of professors Bessie Louise Pierce, Kermit Eby, and Walter Johnson, all of the University of Chicago. Professor Pierce's detailed criticism of the first five chapters did much to alter, and, I hope, improve the remainder of the work. Professor Eby read the entire manuscript, and his experience and concern with the problem of factionalism were invaluable. To Walter Johnson should go much of the credit for whatever worth this study may have. He first called my attention to the need for an investigation of the role of the Socialist Party during the era of the Progressive Movement, and throughout the period of research and writing gave generously of his time, knowledge, and penetrating interest in all phases of historical inquiry. Unfortunately, there is a limit to the aid which even the most able and liberal scholars can provide. For such shortcomings as this study reveals, therefore, I alone am responsible.

IRA KIPNIS

*February 21, 1952.*

# Contents

# I

# Introduction

AMERICAN CAPITALISM has been praised for many virtues. Its supporters have credited the unrestricted operation of the "free enterprise" system with extending the national boundaries from coast to coast, developing an enormous productive plant, rewarding the industrious, encouraging the poor, bringing prosperity to all, and providing the only environment for a society dedicated to freedom, democracy, and social justice.

Yet, throughout our history many Americans have found that what was praised in theory did not work in practice. Negro slaves, indentured servants, debt-ridden farmers, propertyless workers, ambitious professionals, and hard-pressed businessmen have all concluded at one time or another that society would benefit from some more or less basic changes in the operation of the American economy. Comparatively few ever went so far as to suggest that capitalism itself be eliminated. But many held that if they were to have the opportunities assumed to be available to all under a competitive system, the activities of those who had clawed their way to positions of economic power would have to be regulated and restricted.

Most American reformers have continued to seek ways to compel the free enterprise system to operate equitably. But the hardships and dislocations caused by the impact of industrial capitalism on America's relatively egalitarian agrarian society caused the ideology of European utopian socialism to be greeted with considerable enthusiasm before the Civil War. The new working class of the 1820s was discovering that the Declaration of Independence needed restating to meet the problems created by industrial capitalism.[1] Middle-class social reformers were in search of a program

---

[1] See, for example, the "Preamble of the Mechanics' Union of Trade Associations,

that would stop deepening class division and growing class conflict. To these, co-operative communities seemed a simple and logical means of escaping the increasing economic, social, and moral disorganization of American life. In the 1820s and 1830s some nineteen co-operative colonies were founded under the direct or indirect inspiration of Robert Owen. And in the 1840s, Fourier's American disciple, Albert Brisbane, saw the hopeful beginning and dismal ending of more than forty Fourierist phalanxes.[2]

Co-operative colonies were not the only utopian solutions attempted by dissatisfied members of society. Producers' and consumers' co-operatives flourished sporadically for over forty years as utopian alternatives to the production and distribution relations of capitalism. With every new industrial crisis, with every failure of the trade unions to alter materially the conditions of labor and the standard of living in pre- and post-Civil War America, farmers and workers turned anew to co-operatives as a way to beat the capitalists at their own game. While some co-operatives were successful for short periods, none succeeded in freeing its members from the web of capitalist wages, prices, and depressions.[3]

The utopian socialists did their best to point up the need for drastic remedies in an industrial society which they accused of causing the creator of wealth to lose more and more of his just reward. But the building of socialist islands in capitalist oceans did little to enable labor to keep all it produced. The utopians saw no need to fight for immediate gains within the existing economic system. Therefore, the trade union movement was neglected. Socialism was to be achieved by withdrawing from contact with the evils of society. Therefore, there was no reason to engage in political activity to change that society. Thus, while the utopians spotlighted the shortcomings of capitalism they actually weakened the day-to-day struggles of the unions and radical political parties. The utopian socialists saw no relation between the development of capitalism, the

---

1827," in John R. Commons, ed., *A Documentary History of American Industrial Society* (Cleveland, The Arthur Clark Co., 1910), V, 84–90.

[2] Commons, *et al., History of Labour*, I, 491–506; Mary Beard, *A Short History of the American Labor Movement* (New York, The Macmillan Co., 1940), pp. 60–61.

[3] Commons *et al., History of Labour*, I, 506–21, II, 110–12, 430–38; Anthony Bimba, *The History of the American Working Class* (New York, International Publishers, 1927), pp. 108–14, 162–63; Mary Beard, *A Short History of the American Labor Movement* (New York, The Macmillan Co., 1940), pp. 65–75, 124–26.

growth of the working class, the daily class struggle, and the winning of socialism.

Economic and social conditions even before the Civil War had been such as to bring forth proposals for a complete overhauling of the economy. But the domestic conflicts which followed the war made ante-bellum America seem in retrospect a land flowing with milk and honey for all. While production expanded at an unprecedented rate in the thirty-five years following the abolition of slavery, competing small-scale manufacture rapidly gave way to noncompetitive giant industrial enterprise. The small manufacturer's vision of limitless opportunities for expansion in a slaveless America vanished in the struggle to maintain a precarious business position against increasing monopoly pressure. The farmer's hope for endless prosperity inspired by the prospect of free land and adequate transportation disappeared in a flood of mortgages, high freight rates, falling prices, and vanishing frontiers. The worker's dream of job security, a rising standard of living, and escape into farming or even business ownership in an expanding economy turned into a nightmare of depressions, wage cuts, and unemployment.

In this atmosphere of ruined hopes and lost fortunes, of jobless workers and factoryless businessmen, of land-poor farmers and farmless laborers, the schemes for alleviating hardship and returning to the more or less imaginary "good old days" of competition and equality through government intervention were legion. Farmers' granges and alliances, producers' and consumers' co-operatives, antimonopoly, union labor, and People's parties all sought to break the trusts' tightening stranglehold on the nation's economic life. Each in turn disappeared, victim of monopoly's tremendous strength, shaky theoretical assumptions, and an inability to unite farmer, worker, and small businessman against the common enemy.

But attempts to return to more competitive conditions or to escape into co-operative colonies or factories were no longer the only alternatives offered those who believed there was too much opportunity for Satan in America's "devil take the hindmost" economy. Marxian socialism was first advocated in the United States in the 1850s, and political parties based on the social analysis of Karl

Marx and Frederick Engels were organized on a national basis
almost immediately following the end of the Civil War. By 1900,
Marxian or scientific socialism was the ideology of almost all American movements designed to eliminate the inequities of capitalism by
replacing it with socialism. "The socialism that inspires hopes and
fears to-day is the school of Marx," wrote Thorstein Veblen in
1907. "No one is seriously apprehensive of any other so-called socialistic movement, and no one is seriously concerned to criticise
or refute the doctrines set forth by any other school of socialists." [4]

Despite the decline of economic opportunity and the murderous
ferocity which greeted labor's efforts to organize, socialist progress was difficult in America. The fable of rags to riches had had
a core of truth in the days of Jacksonian democracy. And while it
continued to be far more popular than its actual incidence war-
ranted, there were still many examples of rapid capital accretion in
the last third of the nineteenth century. Immigrants poured into
America as the land of opportunity, and it took considerable experience to convince them that they or their children were not some
day destined to repeat the great American success story.

Bolstering the tradition of economic opportunity were the democratic political forms developed during periods when comparative
economic democracy through widespread land ownership was the
rule. While the growth of monopoly corrupted these democratic
forms, the shell and tradition remained. Free elections, free speech,
and a free press cloaked government strike-breaking and business
subsidies. And it was difficult for the socialists to expose the "capitalist state" as nothing but an instrument of the bourgeoisie when
every male adult had the theoretical right to participate in the
election of government officials.

These obvious objective difficulties faced by advocates of socialism, together with the still more obvious fact that the United States
has not replaced its capitalist economy with a socialist one, have
encouraged American historians to dismiss the socialist movement
in the United States as an aberration. Such studies of American
socialism as do exist are limited to its utopian phase. Aside from
the chapters devoted to the Socialist Party in Nathan Fine's *Labor
and Farmer Parties in the United States, 1828–1928*, there have

---

[4] Thorstein Veblen, "The Socialist Economics of Karl Marx and His Followers,"
*Quarterly Journal of Economics*, XXI (Feb., 1907), 299–300.

been almost no investigations of the American socialist movement during the period when it was at the height of its activity—1897–1912.[5] As far as this author has been able to determine, there have been only two articles in the last thirty years in scholarly publications on the socialist movement in America.[6] In contrast, articles on "communism" as practiced by the Incas of Peru were published almost every year.

The American Socialist Party cannot be so easily dismissed. At the height of its power it had over one hundred and fifty thousand dues-paying members, published hundreds of newspapers, won almost a million votes for its presidential candidate, elected more than one thousand of its members to political office, secured passage of a considerable body of legislation, won the support of one third of the American Federation of Labor, and was instrumental in organizing the Industrial Workers of the World. A study of the Socialist Party is essential if we are to understand such American developments as industrial unionism, national and municipal ownership of public utilities, socialized Christianity, restrictions on immigration, women's rights, labor legislation, municipal reform, and the general attack on privilege and corruption known as the Progressive Movement.

Finally, the Socialist Party should be studied both as a political party and as a social movement in order to discover the reasons for its limited success and general failure. To dismiss the advocates of socialism simply as helpless victims of an environment that had no need for them is to ignore the great social unrest of the early twentieth century and the real gains made by their party. Surely the activities of the Socialists themselves had something to do with the nature of the results they achieved. If not, history must be merely the record of the movements of human puppets pulled by invisible strings. And if this be the case, historians had best turn their attention to discovering the nature and intentions of the puppeteer.

[5] Two exceptions are Cox, *The Socialist Party in Indiana since 1896,* published in 1916, and Wachman, "History of the Social-Democratic Party of Milwaukee, 1897–1910," written in 1943, an unpublished thesis. Note the paucity of secondary source material listed in the bibliography.

[6] Howard H. Quint, "Julius A. Wayland, Pioneer Socialist Propagandist," *Mississippi Valley Historical Review,* XXXV (March, 1949), 585–606; David A. Shannon, "The Socialist Party Before the First World War: an Analysis," *Mississippi Valley Historical Review,* XXXVIII (Sept., 1951), 279–88.

# II

# The Socialist Labor Party

Marxian socialism came to America with the German immigrants of the 1850s. Among these immigrants were men who had worked and corresponded with Marx in the European socialist movement. Once in America they became active in the German-American labor movement,[1] and Americans familiar with socialism only as a colonial withdrawal from a wicked society [2] began to be bombarded with calls to end capitalism through organized activity within that economy.

Outstanding among these early disseminators of Marxism was Joseph Weydemeyer, who as newspaper editor and union organizer worked not only to strengthen American trade unionism but also to educate its members on the importance of political action.[3] Weydemeyer held that "there should be no division between economics and politics." [4] The proletariat should not limit its activities to demands for higher wages and shorter hours. Trade union activity, although of great importance, could not in itself end exploitation. Nor could the proletariat escape the tornado of capital accumulation merely by building storm cellars labeled producers' and consumers' co-operatives. "The accumulation of capital is not harmful to society; the harm lies rather in the fact that capital serves the interests of the few. If the bourgeoisie has fulfilled the first task [of accumulating capital], it is the task of the proletariat to put an end to this state of affairs which has ended in chaos." [5] Weydemeyer and other German-American Marxists worked to unite native and foreign-born, skilled and unskilled workers into an or-

[1] Commons, et al., History of Labour, II, 204.
[2] Ely, Recent American Socialism, pp. 9–16.
[3] Commons, et al., History of Labour, I, 617–19, II, 204; Pierce, History of Chicago, II, 186–87.
[4] Joseph Weydemeyer in Die Reform, May, 1853.
[5] Joseph Weydemeyer in the New York Turn Zeitung, Aug. 1, 1852.

ganization which combined trade union and political activity.[6]

American socialists supported the Civil War in the belief that it was the only way to eliminate slavery. They held that as long as the nation was half slave, there could be no hope of moving it from the comparative freedom of capitalism to the greater freedom of socialism. Weydemeyer rose to the rank of colonel and was assigned by Lincoln to the post of commander of the military district of St. Louis.[7] After chattel slavery was abolished, the socialists returned to the organization of the proletariat for the abolition of wage slavery.

Before the Civil War, German-American socialists had formed Communist Clubs. When the first international organization of labor was formed in September, 1864,[8] Marx sent Weydemeyer four copies of his Address and Provisional Rules.[9] After the Civil War, American socialists began to organize sections of the International Working Men's Association. By 1872 there were about thirty sections with five thousand members of the First International in the United States.[10]

While few trade unions affiliated with the International in America, the socialists exerted considerable influence among unorganized workers. This was particularly true during the depression which followed the Panic of 1873. The great movement of the unemployed of 1873–1874 was led by socialists. Early demonstrations were impressive, and for a time it appeared that the socialists would establish firm roots among the working class. But the American socialist movement was torn by dissension, and by 1874 was so split on principles and tactics that the unemployed were left to shift for themselves.[11]

American socialists were divided into Lassalleans and Marxists. The former accepted Ferdinand Lassalle's belief in the "iron law of wages," agreeing that since there was always a surfeit of labor

[6] Obermann, *Joseph Weydemeyer*, pp. 55–93.        [7] *Ibid.*, pp. 114–33.

[8] Letter from Karl Marx to Karl Klings, Oct. 4, 1864, *Founding of the First International*, p. 45; letter from Karl Marx to Frederick Engels, Nov. 4, 1864, *Selected Correspondence*, pp. 159–63.

[9] Letter from Karl Marx to Joseph Weydemeyer, Nov. 29, 1864, *Founding of the First International*, pp. 51–52.

[10] Hillquit, *History of Socialism*, pp. 194–97; Commons, *et al.*, *History of Labour*, II, 206–14.

[11] Commons, *et al.*, *History of Labour*, II, 219–21.

under capitalism, wages were always forced down to minimum
levels. Therefore, any economic action by labor aimed at raising
wages or shortening hours was futile. The disintegration of the
unions in 1873 and the great number of unemployed bolstered the
American Lassalleans in their determination not to waste their
time in foredoomed union organizations and demonstrations by the
unemployed. The German Lassallean goal of universal male suffrage was already achieved in the United States. So the American
Lassalleans devoted themselves exclusively to the next step in the
program—the formation of workers' political parties and the use
of the ballot to obtain state credits for producers' co-operatives.[12]
Thus, as far as the Lassalleans in the American socialist movement
were concerned, socialist activity was to consist of appeals to the
workers to vote for state credits for co-operatives.

The Marxists were not opposed to political activity. In fact, they
held that every class struggle was a political struggle. But they
insisted it was impossible in the 1870s to form a workers' party
strong enough to influence elections. Political action was broader
than parliamentary activity. The revival and building of trade
unions and mass demonstrations of the unemployed, the Marxists
held, were the proper functions of the socialist movement. These
activities would not only alleviate workers' hardships but would
also develop class consciousness. This, in turn, would open the way
for still greater political action.[13]

But it was far easier to appeal for votes than to engage in the
day-to-day grind of building unions. In 1874 the Lassalleans
formed the Social-Democratic Party of North America with
Adolph Strasser as head of its executive board. The new party ran
candidates for local office, but the results were discouraging. The
influence of the Marxists again began to be felt, and the Social-
Democratic Party moved gradually toward an acceptance of the

[12] Karl Marx, *Critique of the Gotha Program* (New York, International Publishers, 1938); Commons, *et al., History of Labour*, II, 205–6, 226–29; Foner, *History
of the Labor Movement*, pp. 447fn., 448–49. It is difficult to determine to what extent the American Lassalleans were merely reflections of their recent German contacts, and to what extent they were part of or influenced by the Greenback movement which had as part of its program the building of producers' co-operatives with
government paper money.

[13] Saposs, *Left Wing Unionism*, pp. 16–17; Commons, *et al., History of Labour*,
II, 217–19.

Marxian principles of the First International.[14] By 1876, rank and file pressure on the leadership of the party was so great that the executive board agreed to meet with nineteen American sections of the International to discuss merger. The 1876 conference resulted in formation of the Working Men's Party of the United States with a platform which emphasized trade union activity and called for delay in election activities until the party "was strong enough to exercise perceptible influence." [15]

The Marxists won the platform, but the Lassalleans won a majority of the seats on the national executive committee and their leader, Philip Van Patten, was elected national secretary. True to their assumptions, the party leadership refused to participate actively in the great strikes of 1877. Instead, mass meetings were held at which strikers and the unemployed were instructed in "the futility of planless revolts" and in the necessity of voting for their emancipation.[16]

When the strikes were crushed, the Lassallean executive committee dropped all pretense of following the party platform. P. J. McGuire, later to become general secretary of the "pure and simple" United Brotherhood of Carpenters, insisted that trade unionism was of questionable utility during prosperity and futile during depressions. Besides, if unions could really be of service to the workers, of what use was the Working Men's Party? [17] The executive committee ruled that since the government officials who ordered the use of police and troops against the strikers and the unemployed could not be removed through trade union action, unions were useless. Only independent political action at the ballot box could aid labor.[18]

At the December, 1877, convention of the Working Men's Party, the Lassalleans, their prestige enhanced by an increased socialist vote in the recently concluded elections, won complete control of the party. The constitution and platform were overhauled, and

[14] Hillquit, *History of Socialism*, pp. 449–50.

[15] *Labor Standard*, Aug. 12, 1876; Workingmen's Party of the United States, *Proceedings of the Union Congress;* Hillquit, *History of Socialism*, pp. 208–10; Commons, *et al., History of Labour*, II, 269–70.

[16] Hillquit, *History of Socialism*, pp. 223–25; Commons, *et al., History of Labour*, II, 269–70.

[17] *Labor Standard,* Jan. 6, 13, 1877.

[18] *Ibid.,* July 14, 1877.

party activity was directed exclusively to mobilization of workers for action at the polls. The socialist movement was to be based on the slogan, "Science the Arsenal, Reason the Weapon, the Ballot the Missile." To emphasize the changed character of the organization, the name too was altered, and the Working Men's Party of the United States became the Socialist Labor Party of North America.[19]

For the next few years the increased socialist vote and the election of a number of aldermen and state legislators convinced the Socialists that they were about to duplicate the phenomenal success of the German Social Democratic Party. Party membership jumped from about three thousand in 1876 to some ten thousand in 1878. The Socialists were organized in one hundred party sections in twenty-five states. The success, however, was short-lived. The increased vote brought no improvement in wages, hours, and working conditions. Lectures on the glorious life to be achieved after socialism was voted in failed to mobilize workers between elections. And with the return of prosperity, problems other than the election of Socialists occupied the minds of most Americans. By 1881 party membership had dwindled to an optimistically estimated 2,600,[20] and the socialist movement was again split wide open over principles and tactics.

The meager socialist forces divided themselves into three groups: the vote-conscious Socialist Labor Party; the wages and hours-conscious craft unions; and the more or less bomb-conscious Social Revolutionary Clubs. The Socialist Labor Party's concentration on parliamentary action to the exclusion of all other types of activities had failed to improve workers' conditions. Many socialists concluded that political action was a waste of time and proposed trade union work for immediate economic reforms as the only correct socialist activity. Other socialists agreed with the Lassalleans that "pure and simple" unionism would not end the exploitation of labor. But they considered the ballot too puny a weapon to cope with the explosive weapons employed by the capitalist state against

[19] *Socialistische Arbeiter-Partei, Platform, Constitution und Beschlusse;* Commons, *et al., History of Labour,* II, 271–79; Saposs, *Left Wing Unionism,* pp. 17–18; Hillquit, *History of Socialism,* pp. 208–10, 216–17.

[20] Hillquit, *History of Socialism,* pp. 226–30, 259–65, 267–69; Commons, *et al., History of Labour,* II, 279–90, 300.

the proletariat. The "propaganda of the deed" was to be substituted for the propaganda of the ballot.[21]

The arrival in the early 1880s of German revolutionaries fleeing the Anti-Socialist Exception laws swelled the anarchist movement in America. Few American workers were complete anarchists, but growing numbers of militant trade unionists accepted portions of anarchist theory as the only answer to what they considered an ineffectual ballot, corrupt politicians, and the use of police, troops, and *agents provocateurs* against the labor movement.[22] In 1883 the scattered social revolutionary and anarchist clubs united to form the loosely coordinated International Working People's Association. Section after section of the Socialist Labor Party seceded and joined the more militant Association. Both organizations had their main base among German immigrants and where one grew the other failed. By the end of 1883 the Party had dropped to 1,500 members, while by 1885 the Association boasted a membership of 7,000.[23]

In a desperate attempt to stop the drain of its members, the Socialist Labor Party at its December, 1883, convention made concessions to its Marxist members. It adopted a proclamation declaring politics to be only a means of propaganda and conceding that the privileged classes would surrender their privileges only when compelled to do so by force.[24] In spite of their considerable contribution to labor's eight-hour day struggle, the growth of the International Working People's Association was short-lived. The intrinsic weakness of the anarchist position and the hysteria created after the Haymarket bombing combined with the now more militant position of the Socialist Labor Party to re-establish that party as the leading revolutionary organization in America.

The strength that the I.W.P.A. had gained through its work among the unions convinced at least some of the Socialist leadership that the Marxist emphasis on union work was tactically cor-

[21] Ely, *Recent American Socialism*, pp. 21–46; Saposs, *Left Wing Unionism*, pp. 17–21; Hillquit, *History of Socialism*, pp. 217–18.

[22] Henry David, *The History of the Haymarket Affair* (New York, Farrar and Rinehart, 1936).

[23] *Ibid.*, pp. 82–105.

[24] *Platform und Constitution der Sozialistischen Arbeiter-Partei, December, 1883* (Herausgegeben von dem National Executive Committee, 1885).

rect. While some Socialists had already abandoned the struggle for more rewarding positions in the American Federation of Labor, those who had remained true to the socialist cause now began to work within the "pure and simple" unions. They did not seek to lead the unions in their everyday campaigns for higher wages and shorter hours. All they really wanted was a resolution from each local, central, and national union endorsing in general terms the desirability of socialism. They hoped to get these endorsements by devoting their union activities to an educational campaign among union members.[25]

The Socialist Labor Party had failed to grasp the real reason for the influence of the International Working People's Association in the unions. The Association had not devoted itself exclusively to propagation of its theories through lectures and literature, but had also assumed leadership in the fight for the eight-hour day. But the Socialists, with rare exceptions, refused to "interfere" in purely "trade union" concerns. They limited their activity to propaganda for socialism and attacks on union leaders who opposed the endorsement of socialism. That they met with any success at all is an indication of the tremendous discontent which was sweeping the ranks of labor in the tumultuous eighties and nineties.

The Socialist Labor Party had its main strength in the labor movement in the German-American trade unions, and especially in the United German Trades of New York City. The Jewish Socialists of New York became the recognized leaders of the United Hebrew Trades when they temporarily abandoned their exclusive devotion to propaganda and led the Jewish workers in the sweated tailoring industry to victory in the strikes of the 1890s.[26] By 1893, 16 central labor bodies recognized delegates from the Socialist Labor Party, and the party was in control of the 72 trade unions united in the powerful Central Labor Federation of New York.[27]

In 1890 the Socialist Labor Party recruited a Columbia University lecturer in international law, who was to assume almost immediate leadership of the socialist movement in America. Daniel

[25] Henry Kuhn, "Reminiscences of Daniel De Leon," in *Daniel De Leon,* pp. 6–7; Fine, *Labor and Farmer Parties in the United States, 1828–1928,* pp. 140–46; Hillquit, *History of Socialism,* pp. 240–43.

[26] Hillquit, *History of Socialism,* pp. 286–89.

[27] *Ibid.,* pp. 284–86; Saposs, *Left Wing Unionism,* p. 22.

De Leon was born in the Dutch West Indies and educated in Dutch and German universities and the Columbia Law School. He first participated in politics in the Henry George campaign of 1886, and by 1890 was soap-boxing for the Socialist candidate for mayor of New York. He was received with great enthusiasm by the New York party and within a year the Columbia University lecturer in international law was the acknowledged intellectual leader of the American socialist movement and editor of its new English language weekly, *The People*.[28]

De Leon brought new vigor to the party's program of trying "to inoculate the trade unions of the land with Socialist revolutionary principles by means of a method designated in those days as boring from within." [29] The party redoubled its efforts to convince local unions and central labor bodies, and, through these, the national conventions of the A.F. of L. and the Knights of Labor of the necessity of endorsing the principles of socialism.[30] By 1893 it had made such inroads that the Federation convention agreed, 2,244 to 67, to submit to the membership for referendum an eleven-plank program introduced by the Chicago Socialist, Thomas J. Morgan. The program, after advocating political action to win the standard trade union demands of compulsory education, employer liability, and the eight-hour day, moved to municipal ownership of public utilities and culminated in Plank Ten calling for "the collective ownership by the people of all means of production and distribution." [31]

It is probable that a majority of the Federation members instructed their delegates to adopt the platform at the 1894 convention. At any rate, so the Socialists insisted. But the conservative leadership was not to be instructed by its more radical rank and file. They introduced a substitute for Plank Ten which called for "abolition of the monopoly system of land holding and the substitution therefor of a title of occupancy and use only," and brought pressure upon enough delegates to violate their instructions to

[28] Coleman, *Debs*, pp. 189–90; Fine, *Labor and Farmer Parties*, pp. 148–49; Hillquit, *Loose Leaves*, p. 45.

[29] Henry Kuhn, "Reminiscences of Daniel De Leon," in *Daniel De Leon*, pp. 6–7.

[30] *Ibid.*, p. 7.

[31] *Report of Proceedings of the Thirteenth Annual Convention of the American Federation of Labor Held at Chicago, December 11th to 19th, Inclusive, 1893*, pp. 31, 37–38.

carry the substitute.[32] The Socialists struck back by helping to defeat Gompers and electing opportunist John McBride of the mine workers to the presidency of the Federation.[33] De Leon hailed the victory in his usual biting fashion:

*The People* of Sunday, April 12, 1891, consoled itself over the then recent decease of the Great American Humbug and king of circus shows, with the reflection: "Barnum is dead, but Gompers is alive." That consolation proved short-lived. In the light of recent events and the election returns, there is no consolation left. Barnum is dead and so is Gompers.[34]

De Leon held his wake for Gompers prematurely. At the 1895 Federation convention Gompers was back in the saddle, intent upon revenge. He left the Socialists in no doubt as to who had the whip hand when the convention elected him president and refused to seat the regularly elected Socialist delegate of New York's Central Labor Federation, Lucien Sanial.[35] The Socialists were outnumbered three to one, and De Leon concluded that not only were the Federation leaders "labor fakirs" "doing picket duty for capitalism," [36] but that craft unions as a whole were little more than a "conspiracy of the capitalists and conservative labor leaders against the working class." [37] Besides, there was no point in capturing a union that was "at best a cross between a windbag and a rope of sand." [38] De Leon ordered the Socialists to abandon the American Federation of Labor to the sure death which awaited it under the command of the labor fakirs.

While the Socialists in the Federation had been attempting to "kick the rascals out," [39] De Leon had given his personal attention to the rapidly declining Knights of Labor. Supported by the Ger-

---

[32] *Proceedings of the Fourteenth Annual Convention of the American Federation of Labor Held at Denver, Colorado, December 10 to 18, 1894,* pp. 38–43.

[33] *Ibid.,* pp. 41–42; Saposs, *Left Wing Unionism,* pp. 22–26; Hillquit, *History of Socialism,* pp. 299–301; Coleman, *Debs,* p. 191; Commons, *et al., History of Labour,* II, 513.

[34] Quoted in Coleman, *Debs,* p. 191.

[35] *Report of the Proceedings of the Fifteenth Annual Convention of the American Federation of Labor 1895,* p. 69; Carrol, *Labor and Politics,* pp. 37–39; Henry Kuhn, "Reminiscences of Daniel De Leon," in *Daniel De Leon,* p. 7; Saposs, *Left Wing Unionism,* p. 26; Hillquit, *History of Socialism,* p. 301.

[36] Bloor, *We Are Many,* p. 55; Fine, *Labor and Farmer Parties,* pp. 152–53.

[37] Foster, *From Bryan to Stalin,* p. 35.

[38] *The People,* Dec. 24, 1893.          [39] *Ibid.,* Oct. 8, 1893.

man, Jewish, and other non-English speaking Socialist-led unions of New York, the S.L.P. won the leadership of the Knights' most powerful New York body, District Assembly 49. The Socialists then went into the 1893 national convention, allied themselves with J. R. Sovereign, a Populist, and ousted Terrence V. Powderly from his fourteen-year sinecure as Grand Master Workman.[40] But the alliance of Sovereign and De Leon was in reality only a truce. The 1893 Socialist convention had denounced the People's Party as being as "fully as antagonistic to the interests and aims of the proletariat as the rule of the plutocracy." Grand Master Sovereign obtained Socialist support in 1894 only by promising to appoint Lucien Sanial editor of the *Journal of the Knights of Labor*, a promise on which he reneged after his re-election. De Leon declared war. Sovereign countered by packing the 1895 convention and refusing to seat De Leon as the delegate from District Assembly 49.[41] The party leadership concluded "that the whole fabric of the organization was rotten to the core and nothing could be gained by capturing what had been reduced to a nest of crooks." [42] The Socialist-led unions accordingly withdrew their 13,000 members from the Knights and left the remaining 17,000 to find their own way to oblivion.[43]

De Leon immediately prepared to implement his conception of Marxian principles and tactics by organizing a new revolutionary union. He followed the principles of the early American Marxists in his emphasis on the necessity of building the trade union movement. But unlike these early Marxists, De Leon did not plan to have the party lead the unions in their day-to-day struggles. All attempts to improve conditions under capitalism were doomed to defeat, he argued. De Leon's lieutenant, Sanial, informed a labor conference in 1894 that strikes and boycotts had no chance of success in industries with considerable capital concentration.[44] And

[40] Knights of Labor, *Proceedings,* pp. 39–40, 55–56; Powderly, *The Path I Trod,* pp. 265–66; Commons, *et al., History of Labour,* II, 494–95, 519.

[41] New York *Daily Tribune,* July 30, 1894; *Journal of the Knights of Labor,* Nov. 14, 21, 28, 1895; Commons, *et al., History of Labour,* II, 519; Fine, *Labor and Farmer Parties,* pp. 153–57; Saposs, *Left Wing Unionism,* pp. 26–27; Hillquit, *History of Socialism,* pp. 292–94.

[42] Henry Kuhn, "Reminiscences of Daniel De Leon," in *Daniel De Leon,* p. 8.

[43] Hillquit, *History of Socialism,* pp. 293–94; Fine, *Labor and Farmer Parties,* pp. 151–52.

[44] Fine, *Labor and Farmer Parties,* pp. 151–52.

even if such tactics occasionally succeeded, De Leon insisted that "concessions" won by the unions were only "banana peelings under the feet of the proletariat." [45] "The program of . . . [the] revolution . . . demands the unconditional surrender of the capitalist system. . . . Nothing short of that—whether as a first, temporary, or any other sort of step can at this late date receive recognition in the camp of the modern revolution." [46]

De Leon believed that the unconditional surrender of capitalism was to be secured by organizing workers in a revolutionary, industrial union. The Socialist Labor Party was to function as an educational and electoral body, but the real fighting organization of the working class was to be its revolutionary union.[47] The party's experiences with the Federation and Knights convinced De Leon that there was no hope of converting those "capitalist traps" into revolutionary bodies. Only a new union, pure in theory and uncorrupted in practice from the very start, could fulfill the revolutionary needs of the proletariat.

There were, however, many Socialists in the party who insisted on continuing to bore from within the Federation to obtain the passage of resolutions sympathetic to socialism. De Leon, therefore, did not precipitate a quarrel within the party over the question of forming a dual union. Instead, in December, 1895, he had New York District Assembly 49 issue a call to all progressive bodies interested in establishing a national union based on the class struggle.[48] With this District Assembly 49 and the New York Central Labor Federation as its nucleus, various Eastern central labor bodies, German and Jewish unions, and singing, athletic, and burial

---

[45] Foster, *From Bryan to Stalin*, p. 34.

[46] De Leon, *Reform or Revolution*, p. 19.

[47] Foster, *From Bryan to Stalin*, p. 34. The exact relation of elections and revolutionary union activity in De Leon's system was not clarified until ten years later. In 1904, in *The Burning Question of Trades Unionism*, De Leon announced that if the capitalists refused to acknowledge the majority vote for socialism, then the revolutionary industrial unions would force that acknowledgment by locking out the employers. The industrial unions were also to form the basis of the new socialist society. Of course, it was just a step from De Leon's emphasis on revolutionary industrial unionism and depreciation of party activity in the 1890s to the syndicalism of the Industrial Workers of the World in the early 1900s. While De Leon never accepted the logical conclusions drawn from his premises by the syndicalists, there can be little doubt that he was the intellectual fount of American syndicalism.

[48] Selig Perlman and Philip Taft, in Commons, *et al.*, *History of Labour*, IV, 221; Saposs, *Left Wing Unionism*, p. 28; Fine, *Labor and Farmer Parties*, p. 160.

societies on the periphery, and the De Leon group in control, the Socialist Trade and Labor Alliance was launched as a revolutionary, industrial union designed to lead the working class in its historic mission of destroying capitalism.[49]

When the 1896 Socialist Labor Party convention was held, De Leon and his lieutenants, Lucien Sanial and Hugo Vogt, introduced the Socialist Trade and Labor Alliance as a revolutionary union whose main purpose was to organize the unorganized. The true dual union purpose of the Alliance was further hidden by the passage of the classic socialist resolution urging all Socialists "to join the organizations of the trades to which they respectively belonged." With the smoke screen thus well laid, De Leon then introduced a resolution endorsing the "revolutionary spirit" of the Alliance and urging all Socialists to carry that spirit into all workers' organizations. The Alliance booby trap was endorsed 71 to 6.[50] Within three years it had blown the Socialist Labor Party apart.

The Socialist Trade and Labor Alliance began its stormy career with a membership of about fifteen thousand, mainly from the New York area. Almost at once the Alliance began to call on class-conscious workers to desert their craft unions and join the new industrial union.[51] De Leon turned the full power of his vitriolic pen to the task of exposing "the [A.F. of L.] 'leaders' who are essentially hired men of the capitalist class," [52] "the politicians who were sent to keep the toilers in line." [53] From the implied purpose of organizing the unskilled whom the Federation considered beyond the pale, the Alliance moved rapidly to an open attempt to destroy the A.F. of L. and place "the economic movement of Labor upon a proper Labor basis." [54] The craft unions were accused of betraying labor by grounding their economic organization upon capitalist interests. The sole purpose of the Federation was the emasculation

[49] New York *Daily Tribune,* June 30, July 2, July 5, 1896; Henry Kuhn, "Reminiscences of Daniel De Leon," in *Daniel De Leon,* pp. 10–12; Selig Perlman and Philip Taft, in Commons, *et al., History of Labour,* IV, 221–22.

[50] Socialist Labor Party, *Proceedings of the Ninth Annual Convention,* pp. 25–32.

[51] "Statement of the National Executive Committee [Henry Slobodin, Secretary] to the Members of the Socialist Labor Party, July 16, 1899," *The Workers' Call,* Sept. 23, 1900; "Report of the Delegates of the ["united"] S.D.P. to the International Socialist Congress at Paris, September, 1900," *The Workers' Call,* Sept. 23, 1900; Bloor, *We Are Many,* p. 54; Coleman, *Debs,* p. 191.

[52] *The People,* Jan. 15, 1899.          [53] *Ibid.,* Jan. 22, 1899.

[54] *Ibid.,* Jan. 15, 1899.

of the labor movement. "As no reform is any longer possible from within, the gangrene having gone too far, the Alliance was set up. . . . The Alliance proceeds from the obvious principle that, despite everything, economic uprisings of the proletariat are inevitable; if the field is left free to the labor fakir, these uprisings will be regularly run into the ground." [55]

The Alliance sailed in with fists and pens flying in an effort to destroy the Federation lightning rod. De Leon's incisive exposures of the opportunist "labor fakirs" and "labor skates" who preyed upon the craft unions aroused a secret admiration among the Federation's frustrated rank and file. Union members who found they had less and less to say about the policies of their organization snickered at De Leon's description of "the Cattle-Market, Miscalled A.F. of L. Convention." [56] And, although the Alliance was small, the Federation leadership was hard put to answer its charges, and, at times, to fight off its raids.[57] In the three years following its launching on an uneasy union sea, the Alliance issued 228 charters,[58] and collected a crew of 30,000.[59]

But while its membership doubled in three years, the Socialist Trade and Labor Alliance was never a serious threat to the American Federation of Labor. American workers needed leadership in their everyday activities, not merely biennial calls to the ballot box. The dual union raids of the Alliance interfered with the day-to-day work of the craft unions and antagonized many workers.[60] The desertion to the Alliance of many Socialist leaders weakened the craft unions' fighting power and left the "labor fakir" without effective opposition. The reluctance of the Alliance to fight for "sops" and "concessions" disgusted many of the unions which had affiliated with the socialist union; by the end of 1898 more than half of them had torn up their charters. With the withdrawal of the New York Central Labor Federation shortly after the 1898 convention, the Alliance was reduced to a few thousand members, for

[55] Ibid.          [56] Ibid., Jan. 22, 1899.          [57] Coleman, Debs, p. 192.
[58] Hillquit, History of Socialism, pp. 303–4.
[59] "Report of the General Executive Board of the Socialist Trade and Labor Alliance to the Third Annual Convention, Buffalo, July 4, 1898," The People, July 3, 1898.
[60] "Report of the Delegates of the ["united"] S.D.P. to the International Socialist Congress at Paris, September, 1900," The Workers' Call, Sept. 23, 1900; Bloor, We Are Many, p. 57.

the most part Socialist "leaders"—a sectarian and impotent letter-head organization.[61]

De Leon's union program was being pushed with the object of perfecting a socialist fighting organization. But the "educational organization," the Socialist Labor Party itself, was growing at a snaillike pace. Socialist progress in America was difficult, of course, because of objective conditions within the country. But the existence of a measure of economic and political democracy was not the only, or perhaps even the primary, reason for the slow growth of the socialist movement. The American Socialist Labor Party was made up almost exclusively of recent immigrants, for the most part Germans, with a scattering of Jews, Poles, Bohemians, and Italians. It was estimated that at no time during the nineteenth century did native Americans make up more than 10 percent of the party membership.[62] The immigrants who made up the socialist movement were chiefly skilled workers who made great sacrifices to spread the doctrine of socialism in what to them was a politically backward America. But they were separated from the American workers by tradition, language, and experience, and the gulf between them and the masses they sought to reach seemed to widen even as they struggled to bridge it.

After their early failures at the polls, the Socialists recognized in theory the necessity of "Americanizing" the movement. But Americanization did not progress much beyond the discussion stage. Indeed, having paid lip service to the necessity of bringing socialism to the American workers, the German-American Socialists seemed to draw still closer together and virtually excluded all who could not speak their language or recite the dogma by rote. Frederick Engels wrote bitterly to Frederick Sorge of the American S.L.P. that

the Germans have not understood how to use their theory as a lever which could set the American masses in motion; they do not understand the theory themselves for the most part and treat it in a doctrinaire and dogmatic way, as something which has got to be learnt off by

---

[61] *Ibid.;* Commons, *et al., History of Labour,* II, 519; Hillquit, *History of Socialism,* pp. 303–4; Fine, *Labor and Farmer Parties,* p. 165; Saposs, *Left Wing Unionism,* pp. 28–29.

[62] Hillquit, *History of Socialism,* pp. 213–14; Henry Kuhn, "Reminiscences of Daniel De Leon," in *Daniel De Leon,* pp. 4–5.

heart but which will then supply all needs without more ado. To them, it is a *credo* and not a guide to action. Added to which they learn no English on principle.[63]

And Philip Van Patten, in retirement in Texas, complained that the German leadership of the party did not "seem to care to make Americans understand them—they act as though *they don't have to* explain." [64]

By 1888 the party had become Americanized to the extent of publishing one English-language weekly, the New York *Workmen's Advocate*, with a circulation of fifteen hundred mainly among German-Americans. A few years later an "American section" of the party was organized in New York City. But Alexander Jonas agreed to run for mayor of New York in 1888 only after repeated assurances that a knowledge of English was not a constitutional requirement for office.[65] And in 1891 only two members of the national executive committee could speak English.[66]

The Socialists expended far more effort in obtaining native-American votes for Socialist candidates than in recruiting American members for the party. During the death struggle with the anarchists, political action had been more or less abandoned. But the S.L.P. returned to politics in 1886 when it played a leading part in the Henry George campaign for mayor of New York.[67] The next year, however, the single-taxers in the United Labor Party, moved to desperation by biting attacks on their theories, obtained a convention ruling enforcing the constitutional prohibition of or-

[63] Letter from Frederick Engels to Frederick Sorge, Nov. 29, 1886, in Marx and Engels, *Selected Correspondence,* pp. 449–50.

[64] Letter from Philip Van Patten to George A. Schilling, April 11, 1893, Labadie Collection.

[65] Hillquit, *Loose Leaves,* pp. 44–45.

[66] Henry Kuhn, "Reminiscences of Daniel De Leon," in *Daniel De Leon,* pp. 4–5. Kuhn estimates that in 1891, 99 percent of the party membership was foreign-born and could speak no English. This estimate appears far too high.

[67] Frederick Engels was delighted that the American socialist movement had at last taken steps to break through their sectarianism. "The first great step of importance for every country newly entering into the [socialist] movement is always the organization of the workers as an independent political party, no matter how, so long as it is a distinct workers' party. . . . The masses must have time and opportunity to develop and they can only have the opportunity when they have their own movement—no matter in what form so long as it is only *their own* movement—in which they are driven further by their own mistakes and learn wisdom by hurting themselves." (Letter from Frederick Engels to Frederick Sorge, Nov. 29, 1886, in Marx and Engels, *Selected Correspondence,* p. 450.)

ganized parties within the coalition, and the S.L.P. as a party was expelled.[68]

The Socialists then decided that there was no point in working in a United Labor Party founded on a false theoretical base.[69] They determined to force the correct platform "down people's throats" and let them digest it at their leisure. When the United Labor Party nominated Henry George for governor in 1887, the Socialists did not imitate Engels and refrain from speaking "out fully and exhaustively" in the interest of consolidating a national labor party. Instead, they formed a new labor party, the Progressive Labor Party, on "scientific" principles and ran a candidate in opposition to George. When this party polled only 5,000 votes, the S.L.P. concluded that all attempts to build a labor party were futile and in reality a betrayal of the movement for socialism.[70] Just as the only real labor union was a socialist union, so the only real labor party was the Socialist Labor Party.

In 1888 a full Socialist slate was put forward in New York. It received 3,000 votes. By 1891 the New York vote had climbed to

[68] Hillquit, *History of Socialism,* pp. 275–79.

[69] Frederick Engels's warning to them at the conclusion of the 1886 George campaign was ignored: "What the Germans [in America] ought to do is to act up to their own theory—if they understand it, as we did in 1845 and 1848—to go in for any real general working-class movement, accept its *faktische* starting points as such and work it gradually up to the theoretical level by pointing out how every mistake made, every reverse suffered, was a necessary consequence of the original programme; they ought, in the words of *The Communist Manifesto,* to represent the movement of the future in the movement of the present. But above all give the movement time to consolidate, do not make the inevitable confusion of the first start worse by forcing down people's throats things which at present they cannot properly understand, but which they will soon learn. A million or two of workingmen's votes next November [1887] for a *bona fide* workingmen's party is worth infinitely more at present than a hundred thousand votes for a doctrinally perfect platform. The very first attempt—soon to be made if the movement progresses—to consolidate the moving masses on a national basis will bring them all face to face, Georgites, K. of L., Trade Unionists and all; and if our German friends by that time have learnt enough of the language of the country to go in for a discussion, then will be the time for them to criticise the views of the others and thus, by showing up the inconsistencies of the various standpoints, to bring them gradually to understand their own actual position, the position made for them by the correlation of capital and wage labor. But anything that might delay or prevent that national consolidation of the workingmen's party—no matter [on] what platform—I should consider a great mistake, and therefore I do not think the time has arrived to speak out fully and exhaustively either with regard to H.G. or the K. of L." (Letter from Frederick Engels to Florence Wishnewetsky, Jan. 27, 1887, in Marx and Engels, *Selected Correspondence,* pp. 454–55.)

[70] *Socialist Almanac,* p. 225; Hillquit, *History of Socialism,* pp. 280–81.

14,561 and the S.L.P. began to think of itself as a mass labor party. In 1896, 20 states gave the Socialist candidate for President 36,275 votes. After the defeat of Bryan in that year, many socialists and semi-socialists outside the party [71] began throwing their support to party political candidates, and the 36,000 votes of 1896 leaped to 55,550 in 1897 and 82,204 in 1898.[72]

While the Socialist vote had increased thirtyfold in 10 years, party membership only doubled during the same period. In 1889 the 3,000 members were organized in 70 sections concentrated in a few large cities—New York, Brooklyn, Philadelphia, Boston, and Chicago. In 1898 the 6,000 members were still concentrated in the large Eastern cities, but there were strong sections in Ohio, Illinois, and California.[73] Most of the new recruits continued to be immigrants,[74] and the organization of an English-speaking "American branch" was still sufficiently rare to cause jubilation.[75] It was particularly difficult to organize sections in the small towns where lack of English-speaking organizers and public hostility raised havoc with efforts of hardy Socialist pioneers.[76]

The failure of the nonsocialist reform movements to change materially the economic and social inequalities of the 1890s, together with the defeat of Bryan, did bring a trickle of American reformers into the Socialist Labor Party. The increasing radicalism of the new socialist converts reflected the rising bitterness of farmers, workers, and small businessmen against the swelling monopolies. Some discovered that "socialism is [a] more extensive reform than Populism." [77] One Indiana Socialist started as a Prohibitionist in 1888 and

wade[d] thro' . . . the different stages of morals and economics until I have reached the only solution of the ills that beset the produc-

---

[71] See Chapter IV.    [72] Hillquit, *History of Socialism,* pp. 252–59.

[73] *Socialist Almanac,* pp. 225–66; Fine, *Labor and Farmer Parties,* p. 180.

[74] Letter from Fred E. Martin of the National Executive Committee, Socialist Labor Party, to the organizer of Section New York, Feb. 2, 1895, De Leon Collection.

[75] Letter from B. Reinstein, Buffalo, N.Y., to Daniel De Leon, Jan. 17, 1898, and letter from William Edlin, Syracuse and Rochester, N.Y., to Daniel De Leon, Feb. 7, 1898, De Leon Collection.

[76] Letter from C. R. Davis, Brighton, Ill., to Daniel De Leon, Jan. 11, 1898, and letter from M. Rosenblatt, Paducah, Ky., to Henry Kuhn, April 9, 1898, De Leon Collection.

[77] Letter from Vincent J. Stedry, Broken Bow, Nebr., to Daniel De Leon, Feb. 22, 1898, De Leon Collection.

ing classes; the utter abolition of the private ownership of the means of life, land and capital, the establishment of practical Socialism . . . it is useless for me, in the light of current events, political as well as industrial, to allign [*sic*] myself to parties or measures [i.e., the Populists] that would simply act as a "plaster on a wooden leg." [78]

The old-timers in the party viewed this influx with mixed feelings. At last, real, English-speaking Americans were joining the party. But what Socialists! The newcomers "will sign the application and come into the section and think they are Socialists but they bring in more fool ideas than would 'patch hell a mile' all of which patches must be raped [*sic*] off." [79] San Francisco Socialists scored an average of 18 percent on the simplest kind of socialist test.[80] The American reformers "don't know any more about socialism than a Bull Frog knows of high glory." [81]

The party leadership was far more concerned with keeping the organization untainted with unscientific ideas than in leading and teaching the great body of American workers. They labored not to lead in the building of a better America but to maintain themselves free from the corruption sure to come through association with less advanced segments of the working and middle classes.[82] The party's bureaucratic leadership was quick to expel any member who strayed from the path of truth and virtue. [83] "The only perfectly safe socialist is one who is a constant reader of our . . . organ The People." [84] The capitalists, the reactionary middle-class reformers,[85] and the corrupt craft unions were already in an advanced stage of decay. The task of the Socialist Labor Party was to maintain its purity while that decomposition took place. Let the party stand by, ready to sound the call for socialism.

By the time the "aroma" of the decomposing body of pure-and-simple fakirdom will sufficiently fill the nostrils of . . . [the] working

---

[78] Letter from C. Y. Edkins, Greensburg, Ind., to Captain C. C. Bryant, March 29, 1898, De Leon Collection.

[79] Letter from F. J. Dean, Washington State Organizer, to Henry Kuhn, Jan. 3, 1898, De Leon Collection.

[80] Letter from Edel Hecht, San Francisco, Calif., to Daniel De Leon, Feb. 12, 1898, De Leon Collection.

[81] Letter from F. J. Dean to Henry Kuhn, Jan. 3, 1898, De Leon Collection.

[82] De Leon, *Reform or Revolution*, p. 28.

[83] *The People*, 1897–1899; Hillquit, *History of Socialism*, p. 323.

[84] Letter from F. J. Dean to Henry Kuhn, Jan. 3, 1898, De Leon Collection.

[85] *The Workers' Call*, April 1, 1899.

people the . . . socialists will be ready to step into the field, strong, young and healthy, to bury the corpse and to lead the onslaught on both—republican highway robbers and popocratic sneak thieves.[86]

Frederick Engels, noting the hopeless sectarianism of the American Socialist Labor Party, concluded as early as 1890 that

the decay of the specifically German party [in America], with its absurd theoretical confusion, its corresponding arrogance and its Lassalleanism, [would be] a real piece of good fortune. Not until these separatists are out of the way will the fruits of your [Frederick Sorge] work come to light again. The [German Anti-] Socialist Laws were a misfortune, not for Germany, but for America to which they consigned the last *Knoten*.[87]

---

[86] Letter from B. Reinstein to Daniel De Leon, Jan. 17, 1898, De Leon Collection.

[87] Letter from Frederick Engels to Frederick Sorge, Feb. 8, 1890, Marx and Engels, *Selected Correspondence*, pp. 468–69. By "Knoten" Marx and Engels meant the German handicraftsmen who maintained a petty-bourgeois attitude in a period of rising capitalism.

# III

# The "Rochester" Socialist
# Labor Party

MEMBERS of the Socialist Labor Party all agreed that America was destined to go socialist. But they did not agree on the part they were to play in the fulfillment of that destiny. Party members, leaders, sections, and press engaged in endless wrangles over the merits of independent socialist political action, feasibility of reform within a capitalist framework, desirability of supporting reform parties, the value of trade unions, the role of the trade unions, the need for a socialist trade union, party work in the unions, direct action, indirect action, propaganda of the word, propaganda of the deed—in short, over every conceivable principle and tactic. No step, no matter how simple or how urgent, could be taken without month-long, year-long, and even decade-long debates. Party leaders increasingly turned to intraparty intrigue to secure adoption of their policies, and every major policy decision was accompanied or followed by suspensions, expulsions, and secessions.

When Daniel De Leon took over leadership of the party in 1891–1892, the simmering pot of dissension boiled. It took De Leon only three years of active participation in the socialist movement to hammer out what seemed to him Marxian solutions to all the problems that had plagued the party since its founding. Having hardened Marxian theory into a fixed dogma, De Leon was not one to tolerate the "unscientific" speculations of those who differed with him. Members and organizers unable to agree with the principles and tactics of *The People's* editor found themselves the public objects of De Leon's biting sarcasm and fertile invective. As dissatisfaction with the party's growing sectarianism increased, party

activity came to center almost exclusively around heresy-hunting
in its own ranks.[1]

By 1897 party leaders who followed De Leon were devoting most
of their energies to expelling heretics, suspending and reorganizing
mutinous sections, and destroying socialist newspapers. Only *The
People* and *Vorwaerts* were considered reliable and scientific. Much
of the party strength, in fact, the largest part of its working class
support, had come from the German and Jewish unions in New
York City. But by 1897 De Leon had broken with both groups.[2]
The Socialist Labor Party was soon so honeycombed with intrigue,
conspiracy, and counter-conspiracy, that the National Executive
Committee was forced to reach and carry out its decisions as though
it were an underground faction working within the party.[3]

The conspiratorial formation of the Socialist Trade and Labor
Alliance in December, 1895, by De Leon and Hugo Vogt precipitated the controversy which blew the socialist movement apart. In
spite of the overwhelming endorsement which the 1896 S.L.P. convention gave the "revolutionary spirit" of the Alliance, it soon became clear that there was a considerable difference of opinion as
to what that endorsement meant. De Leon's group insisted that the
endorsement was given with the "clear understanding . . . that
it meant a declaration of war against the 'pure and simple' trade
unions of the land, typified by the American Federation of
Labor." [4] Therefore, all Socialists who refused to support the Alliance, and certainly all those who continued to work within the
A.F. of L., were traitors guilty of giving aid and comfort to the
enemy. The "boring from within" group, on the other hand, protested that the Alliance endorsement had been obtained "on the

[1] *The People*, 1895–99; letter from Fred E. Martin to the organizer of Section
New York, S.L.P., Feb. 2, 1895, De Leon Collection. Martin resigned from the National Executive Committee and the party in 1895 in protest against the dictatorial,
sectarian policies of De Leon and his "secret clique, known to those outside the
charmed circle as the 'Triangle.'"

[2] New York *Daily Tribune*, Aug. 2, 1897.

[3] Minutes of the National Executive Committee, S.L.P., 1896–99, minutes of the
National Board of Appeals, Cleveland, 1896–99, in *The People*, 1896–1899; letter
from Barney Berlin to Daniel De Leon, Oct. 10, 1897, De Leon Collection; letter
from Fred E. Martin to the organizer of Section New York, Feb. 2, 1895; *Social
Democracy Red Book*, p. 51; Henry Kuhn, "Reminiscences of Daniel De Leon,"
in *Daniel De Leon*, p. 17; Hillquit, *History of Socialism*, pp. 322–25; Fine, *Labor
and Farmer Parties*, pp. 171–74; Coleman, *Debs*, p. 193.

[4] Henry Kuhn, "Reminiscences of Daniel De Leon," in *Daniel De Leon*, p. 15.

express promise given by its founders that it would not interfere with the existing trade unions, but would devote itself to organizing the unorganized workers." [5] They pointed out that nothing had been said at the 1896 convention about destroying the A.F. of L. and other craft unions. Therefore, party leaders engaged in that nefarious enterprise were in reality defying the will of the 1896 convention.

The German and Jewish unions of New York refused to sit idly by while their own political party sought to destroy them. Nor would S.L.P. leaders outside New York who had reached positions of financial and political power within the A.F. of L.—union organizers and editors like Max Hayes and Gustave Hoehn of the Typographical Union and J. Mahlon Barnes of the Cigarmakers —permit De Leon and his lieutenants to withdraw the socialist support which had enabled them to win leadership in their unions.[6] By 1897 the party war against "pure and simpledom" had been turned into a party civil war with De Leon's opponents determined to replace the party leadership with men sympathetic to the American Federation of Labor.[7]

The struggle raged in every Section and in every state, but the decisive battles were fought in New York City. There, Morris Hillquit prepared to do battle with De Leon.[8] The two were well matched. De Leon had an incisive mind, a flare for oratory, and few equals in the art of invective. Hillquit, a Russian-born attorney who was to show a remarkable skill at combining well-mannered attacks on capitalism with the successful practice of corporation law, was a skillful debater, a competent organizer, and a past master at manipulating issues and personalities so as to appear neutral while creating majorities and knifing unsuspecting allies.[9]

[5] "Report of the Delegates of the ["united"] S.D.P. to the International Socialist Congress at Paris, September, 1900," *The Workers' Call,* Sept. 23, 1900.

[6] New York *Daily Tribune,* Aug. 2, 1897.

[7] Rudolph A. Katz, "With De Leon since '89," in *Daniel De Leon,* pp. 59–63.

[8] Hillquit, *Loose Leaves,* p. 47; Rudolph A. Katz, "With De Leon since '89," in *Daniel De Leon,* p. 71; Fine, *Labor and Farmer Parties,* p. 196; Coleman, *Debs,* p. 204.

[9] One of the reasons why the Right wing of the Socialist Party so consistently outmaneuvered the Left wing was the latter's persistent refusal to recognize the fact that Hillquit, while continuing to give verbal support to revolutionary socialism, was actually allied with the Right to crush the "revolutionaries." As late as July, 1908, Herman F. Titus, leader of the party's Left wing in the state of Washington, insisted that Hillquit was the one revolutionary member on the National Executive

Hillquit's opposition to De Leon's policies was heightened, perhaps, by the fact that "Pope" De Leon stood in the way of his ambition to be a power in the Socialist Labor Party. Moreover, Hillquit's personal vanity was lacerated by the open contempt with which the party executive treated him. To De Leon, Hillquit was nothing but a pettifogging lawyer who sought to use the socialist movement to advance his legal practice.[10] To Hillquit, De Leon was a petty tyrant who sought as much omnipotence in the socialist movement as the Pope held in the Catholic Church, and whose every action was part of a conspiracy to betray the socialist movement.[11] In Hillquit's drive to unseat the De Leon organization and in the latter's "reign of terror" attempt to wipe out its dangerous opposition, no tactic was deemed too unworthy, no slander too false, and no fraud too great.

Hillquit recognized that the first step in overthrowing the well-entrenched machine of De Leon, Kuhn, Sanial, and Vogt must be the formation of an equally efficient counter organization. Starting with a handful of personal contacts among disgruntled leaders, the Hillquit machine spread into the local organizations and from there into Section New York. Once in the Section, it began undermining the De Leon administration by stalling any and every action with acrimonious debate and time-consuming referendums, until at the end of 1898 the opposition fire which had been creeping through the walls of the party burst out in the party press.[12]

In 1898 there were three leading socialist newspapers in New York, all of national importance—the daily *New Yorker Volkszeitung* [13] and the weeklies *Vorwaerts*[14] and *The People*.[15] Shortly

Committee of the Socialist Party. (Herman F. Titus, "Executive Partisanship," *The Socialist*, Seattle, July 25, 1908.)

10 *The People*, 1897–99; Rudolph A. Katz, "With De Leon since '89," in *Daniel De Leon*, p. 37.

11 "Report of the Delegates of the S.D.P. to the International Socialist Congress at Paris, Sept. 1900," *The Workers' Call*, Sept. 23, 1900; *The Workers' Call*, Oct. 28, 1899; *The People* (Williams St.), July–Dec., 1899; Hillquit, *History of Socialism*, pp. 323–25.

12 Hillquit, *Loose Leaves*, p. 47; Henry Kuhn, "Reminiscences of Daniel De Leon," in *Daniel De Leon*, pp. 16–17, 20.

13 The *New Yorker Volkszeitung* began publication in 1878. In 1884 its circulation was 11,600. By 1898 it was a four-page daily with a circulation of 18,000. Its subscription price was $6.00 a year. Its circulation began a slow decline after 1900, and in 1912 it was down to 14,000. (N. W. Ayer and Son, *American Newspaper Annual*, for 1884, 1898, 1900, 1903, 1912.)

14 *Vorwaerts* began publication in 1892. Its circulation in 1895 was only 2,000.

after the Socialist Labor Party was formed in 1877, German socialists in New York City determined that the party should have
a daily paper. Since New York laws made it impossible for the
party itself to publish such a paper, some of its members formed
the Socialistic Co-operative Publishing Association for the purpose
of owning and publishing a German-language daily, the *New
Yorker Volkszeitung*.[16] By 1891 the socialist movement had become sufficiently "Americanized" to require an English-language
weekly. It was arranged that the S.C.P.A. should undertake publication of an official party organ, *The People*, with the editor to be
named by the party National Executive Committee.[17] *Vorwaerts*
was published as the Sunday edition of the *Volkszeitung*, but it too
was an official party organ, published by the Association and edited
by an N.E.C. appointee.[18] De Leon was editor of *The People* and
his aide, Hugo Vogt, was in charge of *Vorwaerts*.

The Socialist press wielded great power in the movement. It was
through the press that ideological battles were fought and members
informed or misinformed as to the conditions within the party.
Therefore it was of utmost importance to the success of De Leon's
opponents that they obtain control of as much of the socialist press
as possible. Fortunately for Hillquit, De Leon virtually handed
him one of the papers and also the entire publishing association.
From its founding, the *Volkszeitung* had exerted considerable influence in the party,[19] and its editors and supporters did not take
it kindly when De Leon's *People* supplanted it as the leading social-

---

But by 1898 it was an eight-page weekly with a circulation of 10,000 and a subscription price of $1.50 a year. In 1912 its size had increased to ten pages and its
circulation climbed to 15,000. (N. W. Ayer and Son, *American Newspaper Annual*,
for 1895, 1898, 1900, 1903, 1912.)

15 *The People* was a four-page weekly selling at one dollar a year. In 1895 its
circulation was 4,500, and in 1898, 10,000. In 1900, after the major split of the
Socialist Labor Party, the De Leon-edited *People* claimed a circulation of 13,500.
Circulation dropped sharply, thereafter, and by 1903 the paper was refusing to
give publication figures and had been forced to raise its price to $3.50 a year. (N. W.
Ayer and Son, *American Newspaper Annual*, for 1895, 1898, 1900, 1903.)

16 "The Situation in New York, Statement of the National Executive Committee,
Socialist Labor Party, to the Party Membership and to Voters of the S.L.P. Ticket
throughout the Land," *The People*, May 1, 1899.

17 Hillquit, *History of Socialism*, pp. 325–26.

18 "The Situation in New York, Statement of the National Executive Committee,
Socialist Labor Party, to the Party Membership and to Voters of the S.L.P. Ticket
throughout the Land," *The People*, May 1, 1899.

19 Hillquit, *History of Socialism*, pp. 227–28, 256–58, 269–70, 282; Fine, *Labor and
Farmer Parties*, pp. 38, 116–17, 137.

ist paper. The Hillquit machine therefore found it easy to win the allegiance of the leaders of the Socialistic Co-operative Association.[20] Since for all practical purposes the powerful *Volkszeitung* was not bound by party decisions, it was in an excellent position to use its circulation, prestige, and semiofficial character to build up the anti-De Leon opposition and to attack all party decisions and activities.

The launching of the Socialist Trade and Labor Alliance had not been greeted with any great enthusiasm by the *Volkszeitung*. But so long as the German and Jewish unions, and particularly the Central Labor Federation, remained in the Alliance, disapproval was confined to omission of favorable reference to the Alliance's crusade against the "capitalist conspiracy" known as the American Federation of Labor.[21] By 1898, however, the German and Jewish unions had broken with the Alliance and the Central Labor Federation had withdrawn in disgust. The Hillquit faction then prepared for its big push.

The four-to-one defeat which Socialists who had remained in the Federation suffered at the December, 1898, A.F. of L. convention was used as the excuse for the opening shot in the battle. On December 14, 1898, the *Volkszeitung* published a biting attack on the Socialists who had chosen to lead "a separate existence, of doubtful success" outside the Federation, and held them responsible for the easy "Gompersite" victory. For the next five months the *Volkszeitung* laid down a deadly rolling barrage which began by accusing the dual union party policy of retarding the "flow of the Socialist current," [22] and which culminated by announcing that the *Volkszeitung* could not permit the party to continue its suicidal "rival union" policy.[23]

*The People* answered the attack in terms which could not be misinterpreted. The Socialist opponents of the Alliance had sold out to the capitalists. They had traded their socialist principles for soft trade-union berths formerly reserved for nonsocialist "labor

[20] Henry Kuhn, "Reminiscences of Daniel De Leon," in *Daniel De Leon*, p. 17; Hillquit, *History of Socialism*, p. 325.

[21] *New Yorker Volkszeitung*, 1897–98; "The Situation in New York, Statement of the National Executive Committee, Socialist Labor Party, to the Party Membership and to Voters of the S.L.P. Ticket throughout the Land," *The People*, May 1, 1899.

[22] *New Yorker Volkszeitung*, Dec. 19, 1898.

[23] *Ibid.*, April 4, 1899.

fakirs" and "labor skates." They could either submit to party discipline and support the Alliance or they could get out of the party.[24] And since the Hillquit faction showed no sign of leaving the party of their own accord, the National Executive Committee backed up its verbal barrage with a growing number of suspensions and expulsions.[25]

The Hillquit group countered by publishing a "Monthly Edition of the New Yorker Volkszeitung," devoted exclusively to attacks on party leadership and policy, and mailing it to all subscribers of *The People* and *Vorwaerts*.[26] When the N.E.C. protested the use of party mailing lists for anti-party propaganda, the Socialistic Co-operative Publishing Association coolly announced that "our Association has always been and now is a sole owner of both *The People* and the *Vorwaerts* and everything connected with them including the mailing list as well as the right of issuing the said organs in any form it may desire, and with or without a supplement, as it may think best." [27]

The party leadership was now in an untenable position. Its dual union policies had alienated a good part of its New York trade union support. And the *Volkszeitung* was using the party press and mailing lists to cut away its non-union base. They had to act before the opposition obtained a majority in New York. On May 31, 1899, the National Executive Committee ordered a referendum of party members on a resolution severing all party relations with the S.C.P.A. and calling upon the Association to surrender possession of *The People* and *Vorwaerts*.[28] The vote was to close August 1, but the N.E.C. had delayed too long. Hillquit was already preparing his coup d'état.

[24] "Sign-Posts That Will Have to Guide the Party for the Safe-Keeping of a Daily People," *The People*, April 2, 1899; "The Situation in New York, Statement of the National Executive Committee, Socialist Labor Party, to the Party Membership and to Voters of the S.L.P. Ticket throughout the Land," *The People*, May 1, 1899; *The People*, Dec. 25, 1898–July, 1899.

[25] Fine, *Labor and Farmer Parties*, p. 168; Hillquit, *History of Socialism*, p. 325.

[26] Letters from the National Executive Committee of the Socialist Labor Party to the Socialistic Co-operative Publishing Association, May 15, 24, 1899, *The People*, June 11, 1899.

[27] Letter from the Socialistic Co-operative Publishing Association to the National Executive Committee, Socialist Labor Party, May 27, 1899, *The People*, June 11, 1899.

[28] "Proceedings of the National Executive Committee, Socialist Labor Party, May 31, 1899," *The People*, June 11, 1899.

The National Executive Committee and the National Secretary of the S.L.P. were elected by the General Committee of Section New York.[29] Therefore, whoever controlled that local General Committee controlled the national party and its publications. Early in July, 1899, New York held its semiannual election of delegates to the Section's General Committee. Both the De Leon and Hillquit factions accused each other of stuffing ballot boxes and voting "paper" assembly districts, and both came to the General Assembly meeting of July 8 determined to eliminate the opposition for all time.[30]

Section Organizer Abelson, a De Leonite, called the meeting to order and the floor was opened to nominations for the office of chairman. The De Leonites nominated Arthur Keep. Hillquit countered by nominating Richard Bock. A quarrel over election procedure immediately broke out. Since debate seemed unable to settle the controversy, Keep sought to prove himself qualified to chair unruly socialist meetings by swinging at Hillquit's nose. He failed the test, his punch merely grazing Hillquit's chest. The vote for Keep was called, and 32 hands were raised—less than a majority of those claiming to be bona fide delegates. The vote for Bock was demanded by the opposition, but instead of counting the vote, the Chair entertained a motion challenging the credentials of all newly-elected delegates. The Hillquit faction objected. The Chair insisted. The two factions simultaneously concluded that it was a matter of principle which could be settled only on the field of honor, and the meeting ended in a free-for-all. After most of the furniture and a number of heads had been broken, a corporal's guard of the anti-De Leon faction found themselves in possession of the hall. They took advantage of this doubtful triumph to send forth a call for a special meeting of the General Committee to be held on July 10 "for the purpose of reorganizing the Committee and to take action upon the conduct of our officers, and in regard to the situation in our Section." [31]

29 This election procedure had been adopted at the 1896 national convention, ostensibly to permit the National Executive Committee to meet with a minimum of expense.

30 *The People,* June 26, July 2, 9, 1899; *New Yorker Volkszeitung,* June 26–July 8, 1899.

31 New York *Daily Tribune,* July 10, 1899; *The People,* July 16, 1899; Rudolph

De Leonites boycotted the July 10 meeting on the ground that it had not been called by the section organizer. The unopposed Hillquit faction proceeded to make short work of reorganizing the party. The state committee and the executive committee of Section New York were suspended for willfully neglecting "to make an effort toward preventing the struggle of factions that rend the Sections of the State of New York. . . ." The National Executive Committee was suspended for encouraging factionalism and attempting "to lay down fundamental principles of Socialist economics and declare them binding upon the membership. . . ." Henry Kuhn was suspended from his position as National Secretary on general principles. New officers for the Section, State, and national party were selected, and the new National Secretary, Henry Slobodin, was instructed to take immediate possession of the party's property at National Headquarters.

Slobodin called for volunteers and marched them over to 184 Williams Street to install the new revolutionary administration. On his arrival he found that while the Hillquit forces had been busy with suspensions and elections, the De Leonites had barricaded themselves in the party offices. Slobodin's volunteers broke down the door and attacked the entrenched De Leon regulars, and Williams Street was soon ringing with smashed beer bottles, windows, and noses. At the height of the battle, police arrived, separated the warriors, discovered that Kuhn paid the office rent, and cleared out the insurgents. The next morning the De Leonites, still under police protection, withdrew all files and furniture to prepared positions in new offices on Beekman Street and left Slobodin in possession of what might or might not be the national office of the Socialist Labor Party.[32]

By July 15 the old National Executive Committee had recovered sufficiently to meet and suspend all party members who supported the N.E.C. elected by the Hillquit faction. The next day a De Leon-edited *People* appeared, and the civil war was resumed.[33]

A. Katz, "With De Leon since '89," in *Daniel De Leon*, II, 66–67; Hillquit, *History of Socialism*, pp. 325–26; Fine, *Labor and Farmer Parties*, pp. 174–75.

[32] New York *Daily Tribune*, July 11, 1899; *The People*, July 16, 1899; Hillquit, *History of Socialism*, p. 326; Fine, *Labor and Farmer Parties*, pp. 175–78.

[33] New York *Daily Tribune*, July 14, 1899; *The People* (Beekman St.), July 23, 1899.

To the rank and file members of the New York party the internal situation was far from clear. There were two National Headquarters (the Hillquit faction at Williams Street and the De Leon faction at Beekman Street), two National Secretaries (Henry Slobodin and Henry Kuhn), two National Executive Committees, two Sections New York, and two editions of *The People*. Both editions of *The People* came out on the same day under the same masthead, were printed with the same make-up, and carried the same features. To add to the confusion, the De Leon *People* ran brilliant burlesques of the Hillquit *People's* columns, and signed them with the same pen names used by the insurgents' authors.

If the New York party members were confused, Socialists away from the scene of battle were dumbfounded.[34] In spite of growing unrest among many leaders of Sections throughout the country,[35] there was no nationally organized opposition, and the scattered opposition leaders seldom took the rank and file into their confidence. As a result, the New York anti-De Leon faction had little national support. On August 13 the new N.E.C. submitted a referendum to the membership on the question of permanently suspending the old N.E.C. By September the vote was in—790 to 12 for permanent suspension.[36] But the total of 802 votes which were cast represented only eleven per cent of the party membership. Section Chicago, where dissatisfaction with the De Leon regime was strong,[37] estimated that six weeks after the attempted suspension of the N.E.C. less than 20 percent of the national membership had taken sides in the controversy.[38]

While few rank and file Socialists felt that the issues were clear enough to justify a break with the De Leon N.E.C., many party leaders outside of New York and almost the entire socialist press quickly concluded that the time had arrived to shake off the De

[34] Letter from Thomas J. Morgan to Henry Demerest Lloyd, July 18, 1901, Henry D. Lloyd Papers.

[35] Dietzgen, *Lese Majesty and Treason to the "Fakirs"*; letter from Barney Berlin to Daniel De Leon, Oct. 10, 1897, and letter from Henry J. Poelling to Hugo Vogt, Jan. 30, 1898, De Leon Collection.

[36] *The People* (Williams St.), Sept. 10, 1899.

[37] Letter from Barney Berlin to Daniel De Leon, Oct. 10, 1897, De Leon Collection.

[38] "Statement to the Members by the Central Committee of Section Chicago," *The Workers' Call*, Aug. 26, 1899.

Leon yoke. In official explanations which the Hillquit faction issued to socialists all over the world, the split of the Socialist Labor Party was laid entirely at the door of dual union tactics practiced by De Leon's administration.[39] While the Socialist Trade and Labor Alliance was unquestionably the main bone of contention, the personality and leadership conflicts caused by De Leon's dictatorial and sectarian regime cannot be ignored. In some cases, vigorous supporters of the Alliance nevertheless took the lead in bringing their sections into the anti-De Leon camp.[40] Consequently, as soon as reports of the New York revolution began to trickle in, state and section leaders who had felt the lash of De Leon's scorn began to pass resolutions calling for removal of the N.E.C. to another city and for the immediate convening of a national convention.[41] Party newspapers whose growth had been stunted by a jealous De Leon threw their pages open to endless attacks on the "Pope." [42] All attempts by rank and file Socialists to uncover the real issues in the controversy were drowned in a flow of invective.

Since the overwhelming majority of party members either favored the De Leon administration or maintained a wavering neutrality, anti-De Leon leaders and press outside New York decided to delay an open break. They set up liaison with the new N.E.C., refused to send funds to Henry Kuhn because of the "confused situation," and limited official statements to viewing with alarm the civil war in New York. But as the reams of invective against De Leon began to have effect, and as the old N.E.C. undiplomatically expelled all who even queried the status of the opposition,

[39] "Report of the Delegates of the ["united"] S.D.P. to the International Socialist Congress at Paris, September, 1900," The Workers' Call, Sept. 23, 1900.

[40] In Chicago, for example, Thomas J. Morgan, who had a national reputation for his leadership in the S.T. and L.A. and who daily "wipetet [sic.] the floor with the pure and Simple unions and all the Labor fakirs," was instrumental in swinging Section Chicago against De Leon (letter from John Collins to Daniel De Leon, Oct. 10, 1897, De Leon Collection; letter from Thomas J. Morgan to Henry D. Lloyd, July 18, 1901, Henry D. Lloyd Papers).

[41] "Resolutions of the Central Committees of Sections Chicago, Los Angeles, San Francisco, Cleveland, and Philadelphia," The Workers' Call, July 22, Aug. 5, 1899.

[42] Among the papers which De Leon and the old N.E.C. had attacked were the Chicago Workers' Call, the Cleveland Citizen, the San Francisco Class Struggle, the Danish Arbeideren, the Minneapolis Tocsin (which was forced to combine with The Workers' Call), the Lima, Ohio, Advocate, and the Lima, Ohio, Proletarian (The Workers' Call, Aug. 26, 1899).

anti-De Leon leaders became bolder.[43] Technical neutrality gave
way to open allegiance to the new N.E.C. Protest against the
wholesale expulsions conducted by the De Leonites turned into
expulsion of all who continued to side with the old regime.[44]

With each side expelling its opposition, there were soon two
Socialist Labor Parties in place of one, each insisting that the
other had neither legal title nor members. Moreover, the Hillquit
faction illogically implied that the De Leon regime in its efforts to
"Americanize" the party had alienated the immigrant socialists
and that the new administration therefore had the allegiance of all
foreign-born socialists,[45] while at the same time it held that the
new N.E.C. was supported in the main by native Americans and
that De Leon was left with only a handful of sections, "the German
and foreign element of the party." [46] In reality, the two factions
were made up of the same national grouping and were of about
equal strength, the new N.E.C. having won the allegiance of approximately forty-five percent of the party's seven thousand members by October, 1899.[47]

With an actual membership of some three thousand, and a
claimed membership of seven thousand, the Hillquit-led faction of
the Socialist Labor Party set out to correct the De Leon theories

[43] "Statement of the Illinois State Committee," *The Workers' Call,* Dec. 16, 1899.

[44] "Resolutions of Section Chicago, September 12, 1899," and "Resolutions of
Section San Francisco, September 9, 1899," *The Workers' Call,* Sept. 16, 1899; *The
Workers' Call,* Oct. 28, 1899; "Report of the National Executive Committee to the
Tenth National Convention, S.L.P., Rochester New York, January 29, 1900," *The
People* (Williams St.), Feb. 4, 1900.

[45] *The People* (Williams St.), Nov. 12, 1899.

[46] "Socialist Prospects," *The Independent,* LII (April 5, 1900), 800. It was
conveniently forgotten that the leadership of the new N.E.C. had its base in the
German Socialist Co-operative Publishing Association and the *New Yorker Volkszeitung.*

[47] This estimate of comparative strength is calculated from the total vote cast
on referendums submitted by the two national executive committees. On July 10,
1899, the total S.L.P. membership was placed at 7,000. In a September referendum
the old N.E.C. received a vote of confidence totaling 2,861. In an October referendum
the new N.E.C. received a vote of confidence totaling 2,487. Neither committee's
opposition participated in the other's referendum. (*The People* [Williams St.],
Oct. 8, 1899.) At the Rochester S.L.P. convention, Jan. 29, 1900, the new N.E.C.
revised the total S.L.P. membership before the split down to 5,500, and claimed
the early allegiance of 4,000 of these. ("Report of the National Executive Committee
to the Tenth National Convention, S.L.P., Rochester, New York, January 29, 1900,"
*The People* [Williams St.], Feb. 4, 1900.) There seems to be little basis for these
January, 1900, figures. The new N.E.C. certainly did not have the support of almost
four fifths of the total party membership.

and tactics which it blamed for the slow growth of socialism in America. The party under De Leon, it was charged, had exchanged the scientific socialism of Marx for the alchemy of revolutionary dual unionism.[48] The new party leaders explained that it was not the task of the unions to fight for socialism. The function of the union was to win concessions from employers so as to maintain present standards of living.[49] It was senseless for the party to weaken existing unions by attempting to build a socialist union. Furthermore, by building rival unions the party lost the numerical and financial support of already established craft unions.[50] Therefore, the Socialist Labor Party henceforth would look with equal favor on all economic organization of labor designed to improve the living standards of the working class. All Socialists were to join the organization of their trade and participate in their union's activities.[51]

But while all party members were to be active union members, they were to recognize that the economic activities of their unions could not bring an end to capitalist exploitation.[52] Indeed, the increased use of easily replaced unskilled labor made questionable the utility of the strike even to achieve the limited ends of higher wages and shorter hours.[53] Since economic activity by unions was of such limited value, there was little reason for Socialists in the unions to devote the major part of their energies to building and leading those unions. Rather, their major task in the unions was to "propagate the ideas of Socialism among the workingmen." [54]

Already, it was claimed, the policies of the American Federation of Labor were showing the effect of socialist propaganda. The rank

[48] Letter from Eugene Dietzgen to the Grievance Committee of Section Chicago of the Socialist Labor Party, March 3, 1899, in Dietzgen, *Lese Majesty and Treason to the "Fakirs."*

[49] " 'Resolution on Trade Unions,' Unanimously Adopted at the Tenth National Convention of the S.L.P., Rochester, January 30, 1900," *The People* (Williams St.), Feb. 4, 1900.

[50] "Statement of the National Executive Committee to the Members of the Socialist Labor Party, July 14, 1899," *The People* (Williams St.), July 16, 1899.

[51] " 'Resolution on Trade Unions,' Unanimously Adopted at the Tenth National Convention of the S.L.P., Rochester, January 30, 1900," *The People* (Williams St.), Feb. 4, 1900.

[52] *Ibid.*          [53] Simons, *Socialism*, p. 10.

[54] "Report of the National Executive Committee to the Tenth National Convention, S.L.P., Rochester, New York, January 29, 1900," *The People* (Williams St.), Feb. 4, 1900.

and file were increasingly scornful of Gompers' policy of "begging capitalist legislative bodies to pass laws for the benefit of labor." [55] At the December, 1899, Federation convention, the delegates not only recommended that local labor bodies consider using the ballot along independent lines, but also called for the study of trusts and monopolies so as to permit an intelligent stand on nationalization. "This call practically places the A.F. of L. in the position of endorsing the collective ownership of the means of production. It opens the door to socialism." [56]

Now that union leaders had generously, if unconsciously, opened the door to socialism, it was necessary to convince the workers that they must cross the threshold. The Hillquit N.E.C. explained that the daily class struggle which unions carried on against capitalists tended to develop a sense of solidarity and political independence in the workers.[57] But this sense of solidarity which came from the involuntary, unconscious participation in class struggles would not in itself bring a recognition of the necessity of socialism. Such recognition would come only with conscious, articulate understanding of "the fact of the class struggle." And such understanding would come only through educational activities of socialist members of the unions.[58]

But after workers had been educated into a state of class consciousness, then what? How was recognition of "the fact of the class struggle" to bring about the overthrow of capitalism and the building of socialism? The answers provided by the Hillquit S.L.P. were incomplete and contradictory. The party emphasized on every possible occasion that it was a revolutionary organization. But it was always quick to explain that revolution did not mean a violent struggle with the capitalists. It meant only that the party was not interested in superficial reforms aimed at correcting some outward manifestations of an internally rotten system. The term "revolutionary" was emphasized so as to distinguish the S.L.P. from reform movements whose limited aims were to end drink, prostitution,

[55] The People (Williams St.), Dec. 31, 1899.

[56] The People (Williams St.), Dec. 24, 31, 1899; Max S. Hayes, "Trades Unions and Socialism," International Socialist Review, I (July, 1900), 51.

[57] " 'Resolution on Trade Unions,' Unanimously Adopted at the Tenth National Convention of the S.L.P., Rochester, January 30, 1900,"The People (Williams St.), Feb. 4, 1900.            [58] The People (Williams St.), Jan. 21, 1900.

corrupt politics, and trusts. Social cancers would be cured not by treating the symptoms which seemed to call for reform, but through a revolutionary change in the economic structure of society—complete elimination of capitalism and complete triumph of socialism.[59] Thus, Socialists were educating the workers for revolutionary change but not for the violent overthrow of capitalism.

The Hillquit-led S.L.P. also spoke of organizing "the working class in its struggles against capital." [60] But since it was futile to work for social and economic reforms within a capitalist framework, since the day-to-day struggles of the unions were of doubtful value and could not lead to the end of capitalism, and since such day-to-day struggles as did happen to be led by the party were not destined to lead directly to the overthrow of capitalism, the party was somewhat at a loss to explain what was meant by effective "struggles against capital." This difficulty was consciously or unconsciously recognized, and the phrase was soon dropped from party literature.

Party leaders generally agreed that having eliminated all direct relationship between daily economic conflicts and achievement of socialism the only remaining weapon was "political action." [61] But political action did not mean to the new S.L.P. what it had meant to the early German-American Marxists—leadership and participation in all struggles by the workers against capitalism and the capitalist state. To Hillquit and the new National Executive Committee political action meant only the attempt to elect Socialists to public office.[62]

The role to be played by the Socialists once they were elected to office was undefined. The party was not interested in capturing the state. The capitalist state was described as nothing more than the "greatest of business corporations." Its functions were threefold: preservation of order through the repression of the workers; waging war on behalf of one national group of capitalists against another national group; and conducting certain large business enter-

[59] *The People* (Williams St.), May 20, 1900.

[60] "Report of the National Executive Committee to the Tenth National Convention, S.L.P., January 29, 1900," *The People* (Williams St.), Feb. 4, 1900.

[61] Simons, *Socialism*, p. 13.

[62] "Report of the National Executive Committee to the Tenth National Convention, S.L.P., January 29, 1900," *The People* (Williams St.), Feb. 4, 1900.

prises which could not be entrusted to individual corporations. Therefore, socialism could not be built through the existing state. And the Socialist Labor Party, unlike the "State Socialists"—the Bellamys, Fabians, and Joneses—did not intend further to strengthen this state by extending its functions. Under socialism this state was to disappear.[63] The party was to participate in elections primarily to propagate its ideas and to record its increasing influence among workers. If Socialists were elected to office they might use that office to pass some labor legislation and further propagate socialist doctrines. But socialism was not to be achieved by gaining control of a government whose sole object was maintenance of class rule.[64] "We participate in politics only to agitate against the system on which politics rests. We enter into the State only to destroy it." [65] How the Socialists were to destroy the state once they had gained entrance was not explored. Thus, according to the self-acclaimed new leaders of the Socialist Labor Party, socialism was to be won through political action, and political action meant nothing more than election of Socialists to public office. However, socialism could not be achieved through reforms or revolutionary changes obtained by controlling the capitalist state and its capitalist government. The contradictions in this position were never officially recognized by the party. In practice, the contradictions were resolved by ignoring the theory.

The party continued to insist that one of the functions of the class state was to conduct businesses too large and important to entrust to individual corporations, and that Socialists would have nothing to do with increasing the power of that state by increasing the number of businesses it operated. But the Socialists at the 1899 A.F. of L. convention worked day and night to obtain a halfway endorsement of the nationalization of the trusts, and then hailed that endorsement as a step which virtually placed the "Federation in the position of endorsing the collective ownership of the means of production and distribution." [66]

The party also maintained that socialism was to be achieved not

---

[63] *The People* (Williams St.), Nov. 26, 1899.

[64] "Report of the National Executive Committee to the Tenth National Convention, S.L.P., January 29, 1900," *The People* (Williams St.), Feb. 4, 1900.

[65] *The People* (Williams St.), Nov. 26, 1899.

[66] *Ibid.*, Dec. 24, 1899.

through the use of the ballot but through some sort of revolutionary activity on the part of the class-conscious proletariat.[67] Participation in elections was for propaganda only. Yet the Socialist platform and all Socialist publicity was increasingly concentrated on winning office for Socialist candidates. Gradually the sugar-coating of "elections for purposes of propaganda" wore thin, and it became tacitly understood, if still openly denied, that election of Socialists and the achievement of socialism were synonymous.[68] Socialist theories already showed signs of giving way to an opportunism which was to make election to office and reform of capitalist "excesses" the only goals of the Socialist Party.

De Leon's faction of the party, however, threatened to put an end to the Hillquit faction's political ambitions before the latter could run even one campaign. Both factions of the party nominated slates for the November, 1899, New York elections, and both slates were put forward under the name of the Socialist Labor Party. The dispute was taken to court, and the court ruled that the De Leon-led National Executive Committee was the only legally elected executive of the party. The Hillquit faction was now faced with the probability of being served with injunctions forbidding its use of the party name and literature.[69] To meet this threat, the now legally nonexistent N.E.C. finally bowed to demands of Sections Chicago and San Francisco [70] and called for a party convention to meet in Rochester, New York, on January 29, 1900.[71]

Fifty-nine delegates assembled in Rochester to hold what they stubbornly insisted was the Tenth National Convention of the Socialist Labor Party. They quickly repudiated the Socialist Trade and Labor Alliance, and after prolonged discussion adopted a platform and resolutions in keeping with Hillquit's conception of Marxism.[72] Then, in line with their real if not avowed conception

[67] "Report of the National Executive Committee to the Tenth National Convention, S.L.P., January 29, 1900," *The People* (Williams St.), Feb. 4, 1900.

[68] "Platform of the Socialist Labor Party, adopted at Rochester, N.Y., Feb. 2, 1900," *The Workers' Call*, Feb. 10, 1900; *The People* (Williams St.), July 16, 1899–March, 1900; *The Workers' Call*, July 22, 1899–March, 1900.

[69] Hillquit, *History of Socialism*, pp. 327–28.

[70] "Resolutions of Section Chicago, September 12, 1899," and "Resolutions of Section San Francisco, September 9, 1899," *The Workers' Call*, Sept. 16, 1899.

[71] *The People* (Williams St.), Nov. 12, Dec. 24, 1899.

[72] *Ibid.*, Feb. 4, 11, 1900.

of the function of a socialist party, the delegates got down to what is the main business of any American political convention, the nomination of candidates for President and Vice President of the United States. After almost no open debate it was agreed that Job Harriman, a San Francisco attorney who had led the fight against De Leon in California, and Max Hayes, editor of the Cleveland Federation of Labor's Cleveland *Citizen*, would bear the Socialist standard in the 1900 campaign.[73]

The convention did not really intend to run both Harriman and Hayes for office. Despite their apparent defiance of the court decision depriving them of the name of Socialist Labor Party, delegates were aware that they could not hope to continue as a fraction of the original party. The real purpose of the convention was not to hammer out the party ideology or even to nominate a complete slate for public office, but to begin proceedings looking to a merger of the Hillquit faction of the S.L.P. with the other local and national socialist organizations which had recently sprung up in the United States. Hillquit's goal was the amalgamation of his party fraction and the new Social Democratic Party, led by Victor Berger of Milwaukee and having as its spokesman the country's most popular labor leader and socialist, Eugene V. Debs.[74]

Nomination of candidates was therefore followed by passage of a resolution calling for unification of the two parties and appointment of a committee of nine to meet with such representatives as it was hoped the Social Democratic Party would appoint. The committee on unity was authorized to prepare a "treaty of Union" and select candidates for public office, the "treaty" to be submitted to the membership of the two parties for ratification. Having nominated their presidential and vice-presidential candidates, one of whom they expected to withdraw in favor of a S.D.P. nominee, and having elected their committee of nine to undertake unity discussions, the Rochester Convention of the Socialist Labor Party adjourned *sine die*, confident that within two months they would have a new, united socialist party, a fitting rival to the famous and successful German Social Democratic Party.[75]

[73] *The People* (Williams St.), Feb. 11, 1900.
[74] *Ibid.* See also Hillquit, *History of Socialism,* pp. 328–33.
[75] *The People* (Williams St.), Feb. 11, 1900.

# IV

# The Social Democracy
# of America

FEWER THAN fifteen thousand Americans had enrolled
in the organized socialist movement by 1898, and fewer than one
hundred thousand had ever voted for a socialist candidate in any
single election.[1] But farmers, workers, and little businessmen did
organize granges, alliances, trade unions, antimonopoly and People's parties, and the progressive movement, in desperate attempts
to reverse the direction of post-Civil War social and economic development.

The American Marxists in the Socialist Labor Party made no
effort to organize this widespread discontent into the broad alliance
essential to a successful antimonopoly movement. The Socialist
Labor Party under De Leon refused to endanger its political
chastity through association with a doomed middle class. Middle-class reform, the party held, would not end wage slavery. America
could be saved only through socialism, and socialism could be won
only through the election of candidates running on a straight socialist ticket. The sooner middle-class reform movements were defeated and destroyed, the sooner the working class would recognize
the necessity of voting the straight socialist ticket. The Socialist
Labor Party, therefore, far from attempting to build the antitrust
and reform movements of the 1890s, devoted its slowly growing
influence among the workers to the discouragement of any attempt
to fight monopoly outside the sectarian circle of socialist politics.[2]

Although the Socialist Labor Party was the leading socialist
organization in America, not all Marxian socialists were members

---

[1] The Socialist Labor Party vote in 1898 was 82,204, an increase of 27,000 over
the 1896 vote.
[2] *The People,* 1892–99.

of that party, and not all American socialists were Marxists. The innumerable expulsions and splits of the party had resulted in the formation of many independent local socialist clubs. And depressions and the growth of monopoly had given new vigor to utopian socialism in America. The search for reforms designed to restore prosperity, security, and morality to American life led many writers to rediscover the obvious solution of replacing an unsatisfactory system with its opposite, of replacing competition with co-operation and private ownership with social ownership. Some forty utopian socialist novels painted vivid murals of the consummate life awaiting all Americans if only they would will a co-operative society. Edward Bellamy's *Looking Backward* was a literary and social sensation, and 162 Nationalist Clubs were formed to teach Americans that the wish was father to the fact.[3] Ministers and professors, led by William D. P. Bliss, George D. Herron, and Richard T. Ely, formed the Society of Christian Socialists to bring all social, political, and industrial relations into harmony with "the fatherhood of God and the brotherhood of man, in the spirit and according to the teachings of Jesus Christ." [4] When the forced resignation of Herron from his chair of applied religion at Iowa College brought activities of the Society to an end, Bliss sought to gain socialism and yet avoid the class struggle by founding the short-lived American Fabian Society.[5]

Far more influential than the Christian Socialist and Fabian movements, and, indeed, more influential than Daniel De Leon's *People*, were the journalistic activities of Julius A. Wayland, a publisher determined singlehandedly to "Yankeefy" the American socialist movement.[6] Beginning as an unsuccessful Indiana small town newspaper editor, and then achieving some success as a job printer in Pueblo, Colorado, Julius Wayland finally stumbled onto the real estate speculation which by 1890 had made him a small fortune.[7] In that year a Pueblo shoemaker, probably a Fabian so-

---

[3] Schlesinger, *Rise of the City*, pp. 261–62, 426; *Social Democracy Red Book*, p. 42; Chester McArthur Destler, "Western Radicalism, 1865–1901: Concepts and Origins," *Mississippi Valley Historical Review*, XXXI (Dec. 1944), 350–51. Daniel De Leon continued his political development after the Henry George New York mayoralty campaign of 1886 by contributing to the *Nationalist Magazine*.

[4] Hillquit, *History of Socialism*, pp. 319–21.

[5] *Social Democracy Red Book*, p. 51.      [6] Bloor, *We Are Many*, p. 67.

[7] Wayland, *Leaves of Life*, pp. 7–23; Howard H. Quint, "Julius A. Wayland,

cialist, saw in Wayland's sympathy for striking railroad workers a base on which he could build a socialist edifice. The speculator emerged from the protracted debates with the shoemaker with a strong if somewhat hazy conviction that socialism must replace capitalism. He immediately closed his real estate office and gave full time to "trying to get my neighbors to see the truths I had learned." [8] Wayland had absorbed enough socialist theory, however, to conclude that the American economy was about to go through another crisis, and in 1892 he began to turn his property into cash. Always a hard-headed businessman, he accepted nothing but gold and government bonds from the banks, insisting that they "were gold standard men and should be given a taste of their own medicine." [9] The panic of 1893 found socialist speculator Wayland with eighty thousand dollars in gold cached away in safety deposit boxes, ready to begin his career as a socialist publisher.[10]

During the election campaign of 1892 Wayland had undertaken the publication of a local labor paper. Within three months he had boosted its circulation from a few hundred nonpaying to 2,700 paying subscribers. In February, 1893, he moved to Greensburg, Indiana, where he established *The Coming Nation*, a socialist weekly which had its largest circulation among left-wing Western Populists.[11] *The Coming Nation* was an immediate success, and by July, 1894, Wayland was ready to take the next step in the classical utopian pattern, the founding of a co-operative colony. Ruskin Colony, established in Tennessee City, had as its main enterprise the publication of the *Coming Nation*. Although the paper continued to thrive, the colony was soon torn by the dissension accompanying most utopian ventures. Within a year Wayland had packed and left, leaving the colony his paper and press.[12] A month later the first issue of his new paper, the *Appeal to Reason*, was

---

Pioneer Socialist Propagandist," *The Mississippi Valley Historical Review*, XXXV (March, 1949), 585–606.

[8] Wayland, *Leaves of Life*, p. 24.          [9] *Ibid.*, p. 25.

[10] A. W. Ricker in Wayland, *Leaves of Life*, p. 28.

[11] *Ibid.*, pp. 29–30. *The Coming Nation* was a four-page weekly selling at a subscription price of fifty cents a year. No figures are available on its circulation. N. W. Ayer and Son's *American Newspaper Annual* for 1895 (p. 189) describes its political position as "Nationalist," not as "Socialist."

[12] *Social Democracy Red Book*, pp. 50–51.

mailed from Kansas City, and a few months later the *Appeal* was established in its permanent home in Girard.[13] From that small Kansas town its pointed paragraphs, easy style, and constantly reiterated message were to make it the trail blazer of the socialist movement throughout the country.[14] With a circulation that in a decade grew to 260,000, the reform socialism of the *Appeal* did much to set the tone of the American socialist movement.[15]

Wayland's publications were the most widely read of the "step-at-a-time" socialist papers. But it was a 35-year-old public school teacher who was to become the leading proponent of the socialism-through-reform-and-public-ownership school in America. Victor L. Berger was born into a well-to-do Austrian family. He was educated mainly by private tutors and attended the universities of Budapest and Vienna. When his parents lost their fortune, he emigrated with them to America where for a time he earned his living by doing odd jobs. Finally settling upon Milwaukee as the setting for his future activities, he taught school there until 1892 when he assumed the editorship of the local German-language daily of the Socialist Labor Party.[16] Within a few months, Berger, who was never to show great tolerance for socialist views at variance with his own, led a split in the Milwaukee party. When the National Executive Committee refused his faction a charter, he and what he now considered his personal newspaper established an independent socialist party in that city.[17]

Berger's Social Democratic Society soon allied itself with both the Milwaukee People's Party and the trade unions, in which organizations it carried on tireless and successful propaganda for Berger's concepts of Marxian socialism—government ownership

[13] Ricker, in Wayland, *Leaves of Life*, p. 31.

[14] Letter from Eugene V. Debs to J. A. Wayland, June 6, 1899, in Wayland, *Leaves of Life*, p. 38.

[15] During the first few years of its publication, Wayland said that the purpose of the *Appeal* was to break ground for more advanced scientific publications like *The People* (letter from J. A. Wayland to J. C. Butterworth, Jan. 17, 1898, De Leon Collection). But Wayland was never more than a reform socialist, albeit a militant one. The *Appeal* was a four-page weekly with a subscription price of twenty-five cents a year. By 1912 its circulation had grown to over 600,000 (N. W. Ayer and Son's *American Newspaper Annual*, Philadelphia, 1903, 1905, 1908, 1912). For further information on the *Appeal* see below, pp. 248–50.

[16] *Social Democracy Red Book*, p. 107.

[17] F. G. R. Gordon, "History of the Milwaukee Social Democratic Party," *Social-Democratic Herald*, March 3, 1900; *Social Democracy Red Book*, pp. 55–56.

of public utilities, better schools, and public baths.[18] From its stronghold in Milwaukee, the Berger brand of "scientific" socialism, peculiarly similar to the antimonopoly and good government reform theories of the middle-class Progressives, spread throughout the growing socialist movement in America, shaping its ideology and sapping its vitality.

Berger's most vaunted convert in the 1890s, though the importance of Berger's contribution to the conversion is subject to question, was Eugene V. Debs, president of the American Railway Union. It is difficult to determine when Debs, long a militant fighter against oppression, became a Marxian socialist, and impossible to discover when he first decided that capitalism would have to be replaced with some sort of co-operative society. In his testimony before a Senate Investigating Committee in August, 1894, months before he began his prison term for defying the blanket injunction which broke the Pullman strike, Debs informed the Senators that he believed "in a co-operative commonwealth as a substitute for the wage system." [19]

At Woodstock prison Debs was flooded with literature describing cures for capitalist ills, and the socialists were not hesitant in furnishing him with their prescriptions. Perhaps it is true, as Debs once generously wrote,[20] that Berger, when visiting the American Railway Union prisoners at Woodstock in 1895, first taught him the rudiments of Marxian socialism. At any rate, on September 4, 1895, Debs joined J. Keir Hardie, head of the British Independent Labour Party, who had also visited Debs, and Thomas J. Morgan of the Chicago Socialist Labor Party, to form the International Bureau of Correspondence and Agitation, designed to bring "into active and harmonious relation all organizations and persons favorable to the establishment of the Industrial Commonwealth founded upon collective ownership of the means of production and distribution." [21] The Bureau did nothing toward uniting the perpetually divided socialists. And three months after its formation, Debs con-

---

[18] See sources cited in Note 17.

[19] U.S. Congress, Senate, *Report on the Chicago Strike,* Senate Executive Documents, 53d Cong., 3d Sess., Appendix A (Washington, Government Printing Office, 1894), p. 170.

[20] Eugene V. Debs, "How I Became a Socialist," *The Comrade,* I (April, 1902), 147–48.

[21] Manuscript, Thomas J. Morgan Collection.

tinued to refuse to permit Thomas Morgan to publicize its existence.[22]

On his release from Woodstock, Debs told the thousands who had
gathered in Chicago to pay him tribute that only through socialism
could the workers win their liberty.[23] The next day the *Coming
Nation* carried a letter from Debs calling on all workers to use their
ballots to establish the co-operative commonwealth.[24] But Debs
did not mean that the workers should mark their ballots for a
straight socialist ticket. Debs and almost all the other independent
socialists, whether utopian or Marxian, were convinced in 1895
that the workers could begin to "vote their way from slavery to
emancipation" by marching to the polls in support of the People's
Party.[25]

The People's Party had been founded in 1892 by the Northern
and Southern Farmers' Alliances with some labor support, and was
the culmination of a 25-year fight to break through monopoly en-
circlement.[26] The new People's Party based itself on a broad anti-
trust program which called for government ownership of railroads,
telegraph, and telephone, a subtreasury produce storage plan, a
graduated income tax, and higher prices for farm products
through currency inflation—the free and unlimited coinage of
silver. In an effort to win the alliance of organized labor, the new
party demanded shorter hours for labor and the destruction of the
union-breaking Pinkerton Detective Agency. In spite of its failure
to win the labor vote in the 1892 campaign, the People's Party
polled over a million votes, 9 percent of the total cast.[27]

The depression and strikes of the next two years won the People's
Party thousands of adherents from the farm, labor, and middle
classes.[28] The Christian Socialists, Fabians, Nationalists, Social
Democrats, and even some sections of the Socialist Labor Party,
became active in the Populist movement.[29] But neither the socialists

[22] Ginger, *The Bending Cross*, p. 174.     [23] *Social Democracy Red Book*, p. 51.
[24] *The Coming Nation*, Nov. 23, 1895.
[25] Eugene V. Debs in the *Railway Times*, Sept. 2, 1895.
[26] Chester McArthur Destler, "Western Radicalism, 1865–1901: Concepts and
Origins," *Mississippi Valley Historical Review*, XXXI (Dec., 1944), pp. 353–54.
[27] Hicks, *The Populist Revolt;* Fred A. Shannon, *The Farmer's Last Frontier*,
pp. 317–23.
[28] Fred A. Shannon, *The Farmer's Last Frontier*, pp. 322–23.
[29] Letter from Philip Van Patten to George A. Schilling, July 2, 1893, Labadie

nor the labor leaders who now participated in the People's Party stressed labor's part in the Populist coalition, nor did they seem aware of the increasing emphasis which many Populist leaders were placing on free silver to the exclusion of all other antimonopoly planks.[30] In 1892 the demand for nationalization of the railroads and abolition of corporate land ownership in excess of actual needs had been the most popular planks. By 1896, however, the prolonged deflation of prices brought on by the depression of 1893 and per- haps aggravated by Cleveland's monetary policies furnished the environment for an inflationary craze which saw in free silver and free silver only the solution to all the economic and social problems which beset the nation.[31] By the time the socialists, labor leaders, and "middle-of-the-road" [32] or left-wing Populists awoke to the changing Populist emphasis, they found themselves at the 1896 convention faced with a demand for fusion with the Democratic Party on the ground that that party had adopted one plank of the People's Party's many-sided 1892 antimonopoly program—the free coinage of silver.[33]

At the Populist convention, the "middle-of-the-roaders," under Victor Berger's leadership, secured 412 written pledges from the 1,300 delegates to oppose fusion under the candidacy of William Jennings Bryan and to support the nomination of Eugene V. Debs for President of the United States.[34] But the antifusionists had de- layed too long. Feeling for a free silver coalition was so high that the left feared that insistence on the nomination of Debs would split the People's Party.[35] Henry D. Lloyd therefore read a telegram

---

Collection; letter from Henry D. Lloyd to C. Harrow, November 23, 1894, Henry D. Lloyd Papers; F. G. R. Gordon, "History of the Milwaukee Social Democratic Party," *The Social-Democratic Herald,* March 3, 1900; *Social Democracy Red Book,* p. 53.

[30] James Peterson, "The Trade Unions and the Populist Party," *Science and Society,* VIII (Spring, 1944), 146–48.

[31] Fred A. Shannon, *The Farmer's Last Frontier,* pp. 323–24.

[32] "Middle-of-the-road" because they favored a policy of steering clear of both the Republican and Democratic parties.

[33] Harlan R. Crippen, "Conflicting Trends in the Populist Movement," *Science and Society,* VI (Spring, 1942), 142–43.

[34] *Social Democracy Red Book,* p. 54. In 1895, Indiana Populists had talked of nominating Debs for governor (New York *Daily Tribune,* Nov. 26, 1895).

[35] Henry D. Lloyd, "The Populists at St. Louis," *Review of Reviews,* XIV (Sept., 1896), 299.

from Debs declining to be a candidate, and the People's Party chose Bryan, fusion, and oblivion.[36]

In the ensuing campaign Debs toured the country speaking for Bryan and free silver as "the only solution to the problem now staring us in the face as to how to open the mills and factories to the workingmen." [37] Eight months later Debs explained that he supported free silver only because it provided labor with a rallying cry and "afforded common ground upon which the common people could unite against the trusts, syndicates, corporations, monopolies—in a word, the money power." [38] At any rate, the failure of the free silver campaign of 1896 convinced Debs and many wavering independent socialists that labor could not depend upon the middle class and middle-class panaceas. Labor would have to build its own political organization and campaign on the only program designed to free the working class—socialism.[39]

The January 1, 1897, issue of the American Railway Union's *Railway Times* announced a new Debs position. In a signed editorial Debs insisted that it had been a correct policy to support Bryan despite the weakness of the free silver issue because a Democratic triumph might have blunted "the fangs of the money power." But now it was clear that American workers could escape from the "cannibalistic" American economy based on robbery only by following "the pathways mapped out by the socialists." The issue was "Socialism vs. Capitalism" and Debs was for socialism because he was for humanity. Henceforth, Debs informed the members of the American Railway Union, he was going to devote all his energy to hastening the coming triumph of the co-operative commonwealth.[40]

Early in January, 1897, some leaders of Bellamy's Nationalist Movement, a handful of utopian socialists like Henry D. Lloyd, and a few independent socialists like Jesse Cox joined with Ruskin Colony's *Coming Nation* to form the Brotherhood of the Co-

[36] *Social Democracy Red Book*, p. 54.     [37] *Railway Times*, Nov. 2, 1896.
[38] *Ibid.*, June 15, 1897.
[39] James Peterson, "The Trade Unions and the Populist Party," *Science and Society*, VIII (Spring, 1944), 147; letter from Thomas I. Kidd to Henry D. Lloyd, Sept. 16, 1895, and letter from Paul Ehrman to Henry D. Lloyd, Dec. 3, 1896, Henry D. Lloyd Papers.
[40] Eugene V. Debs, "Present Conditions and Future Duties," *Railway Times*, Jan. 1, 1897.

operative Commonwealth.[41] The Brotherhood planned to build a socialist America by combining the techniques of colonization and voting. Socialist colonies would be established in some sparsely populated Western state. As soon as the colonial socialists outnumbered the nonsocialists in that state, they would vote in a socialist constitution and elect socialist officials. From this one socialist state the new technique would permeate the country until all the United States were socialist.[42] The Brotherhood convinced Debs that he could best serve the socialist movement by spreading the good tidings of this new technique. Debs became an organizer for the Brotherhood,[43] and the *Railway Times* became one of its most enthusiastic supporters.

On May 1 the independent socialist press carried the text of a telegram from Debs to the New York *Journal* which set forth the plans for the coming special convention of the American Railway Union. The union realized, said Debs, that another strike at this time would be hopeless. Therefore, the American Railway Union would throw its weight behind the Brotherhood plan of colonizing a Western state and using the ballot to make it the first co-operative commonwealth.[44] Debs followed this announcement with an extensive correspondence with the leaders of the independent socialist parties.[45] These socialists attempted to convince him that colonial ventures were futile, and that the union should become the base for a national socialist political party. Debs conceded the desirability of a new party, but continued to insist that colonies were necessary as a means of immediate relief for the unemployed.[46]

When the last convention of the remnants of the once powerful American Railway Union met in Chicago on June 15, 1897, it was immediately besieged by church reformers, Christian Socialists, silver leaguers, economic clubs, single taxers, anarchists, and Marxian socialists.[47] The first three days of the convention were devoted

[41] Letters from Barney Berlin to Daniel De Leon, Jan. 1, 6, 1897, De Leon Collection; Hillquit, *History of Socialism*, p. 351.

[42] *Social Democracy Red Book*, p. 56.

[43] Painter, *That Man Debs*, p. 80.

[44] Eugene V. Debs to the New York *Journal*, April 16, 1897.

[45] *Social Democracy Red Book*, p. 55.

[46] Debs's address to the delegates of the American Railway Union Convention, June 15, 1897, *Railway Times*, June 15, 1897.

[47] *The Social Democrat*, July 1, 1897; Chicago *Tribune*, June 16, 1897.

to winding up the affairs of the A.R.U. and changing its name to
the Social Democracy of America. The Social Democracy in turn
adopted a declaration of principles which began with an analysis
of the development and contradictions of capitalism, called on all
workers to unite to win the co-operative commonwealth, recommended immediate public ownership of all trusts, mines, and systems of transportation, suggested the inauguration of a system
of public works to provide work for the unemployed, and recommended the establishment of postal savings banks and adoption of
the initiative, referendum, and recall. The doors of the convention
were then thrown open to the myriad of reformers who were now
permitted to participate as accredited delegates of the new Social
Democracy.[48]

Although the Declaration of Principles had called for the colonizing of a Western state to secure immediate relief for the unemployed, the Social Democracy had yet to determine how large a
part colonization was to play in its activities. The convention settled down to a four-day battle between the political-action-only
socialists (led by Victor Berger, Jesse Cox, Seymour Stedman,
Charles Martin, and Frederic Heath) and the conglomeration of
reformers who all managed to see in colonization the working-out
of their favorite panaceas.[49] Debs and the Railway Union delegates
shrank back while the battle raged. Finally, a theoretical compromise was reached. The Social Democracy was to engage in political
activity in *all* states with the aim of electing public officials. But
at the same time, a colonization commission was to be appointed to
plan and lead the occupation of a Western state.[50] The Railway
Union was now again pushed to the fore, and an executive board
of five former A.R.U. officials, all veterans of Woodstock prison,
was elected, with Debs as chairman and Sylvester Keliher as
secretary-treasurer. The *Railway Times* became the *Social Demo-*

---

[48] *The Social Democrat,* July 1, 1897; Chicago *Tribune,* June 17, 18, 19, 1897.

[49] *Social Democracy Red Book,* p. 56.

[50] The utopian nature of this colonization scheme is illustrated by a letter Debs
wrote to John D. Rockefeller on June 9, 1897, during the convention. Debs appealed to Rockefeller as a "Christian gentleman . . . widely known for your bene-
factions" to aid the unemployed by making a contribution to the proposed colonial
movement "in which there are no class distinctions. Rich and poor are equally welcome to aid in dethroning gold and exalting humanity." (Letter from Eugene V.
Debs to John D. Rockefeller, Chicago *Tribune,* June 20, 1897.)

*crat*, and the delegates departed, each convinced that the Social Democracy had pledged itself to the one technique which in a few years could convert America into a co-operative commonwealth.[51]

The compromise between the political actionists and the colonists, of course, settled nothing. Organization to win socialism through political action and publicity for achieving socialism through migration were not compatible. And even if they were, the Social Democracy had neither the resources nor the organization to be able to devote itself to both activities. The membership was organized into local branches, state unions, a national council, and a five-man executive board. But most of the branches were just the old intellectual reform clubs with new names.[52] These were interested only in the colonial scheme, and their activities were largely limited to drawing up elaborate plans for a colonial way of life. The colonization commission was appointed by the Executive Board shortly after the convention and consisted of Richard J. Hinton of Washington, D.C., W. P. Borland of Bay City, Michigan, and Cyrus Field Willard of Chicago.[53] The plans of the commission received the major share of the publicity in the *Social Democrat*, and the effort to raise funds to implement those plans engaged the attention of the Social Democracy for the next year.

The plans of the commission and its supporters were ambitious indeed. Even before the convention Debs had outlined the scheme in detail.[54] All members of the Social Democracy would be expected to contribute according to their means to a general fund for the use of the commission. Recruiting offices would be established to examine volunteers for the first colony, and only those volunteers fully conversant with the philosophy and ideals of the organization would be accepted. The first contingents would probably march under strict discipline to the chosen Western state. Since the Social Democracy would quickly attract a membership of 100,000 to contribute monthly a sum of $25,000, the pioneers would have no diffi-

[51] *Social Democracy Red Book*, pp. 56–58; *The Social Democrat*, July 1, 1897; Chicago *Tribune*, June 22, 1897.

[52] *The Social Democrat* of July 15, 1897, boasted that the New York City branch was made up of the following "class-conscious" socialists—two lawyers, five physicians, one dentist, three druggists, and two editors.

[53] *The Social Democrat*, Aug. 12, 1897.

[54] Eugene V. Debs to the New York *Journal*, May 30, 1897.

culty in providing themselves with land, agricultural machinery, and factories. In a few months the colony would be self-sufficient.

By the time of the next state election, the colonists would sweep the state, call a constitutional convention, inaugurate public ownership of all the means of production and distribution, and solve the money question through use of labor exchanges. Of course, the Federal Constitution would prescribe limitations, but the other states would be inspired by the success of the first, and soon the entire nation would be socialist.

In the national campaign of 1900 the new movement will be a factor in the election. Its political principles will be those of the Socialist Labor Party and its political battles will, doubtless, be fought under the banner of that party.[55] In that election two million votes should be polled and in the national campaign of 1904, the great co-operative party . . . should carry the country, and the co-operative commonwealth will be fully established.[56]

While the daily press in general condemned the plan for failing to recognize competition as the only reliable stimulus to "the really highest qualities of man," [57] and felt pity for the fools who would follow the leadership of a convict like Debs,[58] the Populist press and some of the journalists who were soon to become the muckrakers of corruption found much in the plan worthy of support and even conceded that it might well be successful.[59]

The colonization commission "with a devotion to principles that laughs at death and a will that cannot be broken or turned aside" set out at once to acquire the money and land for the first colony.[60]

---

[55] Clearly, the anti-S.L.P. socialists led by Berger could never accept this proposal. To the political-action socialists it indicated that the colonists had no intention of building a socialist political party.

[56] This contradiction is typical of Debs's position in 1897–1898. On the one hand, socialism was to come through colonization of state after state. On the other hand, it was to be won in two national elections. In June, 1897, Debs said that the socialist state would use its power of taxation to eliminate "syndicates and land sharks" (New York *Daily Tribune,* June 25, 1897).

[57] *The State Register* (Des Moines), cited in *The Literary Digest,* XV (July 3, 1897), 276.

[58] *The Mail and Express* (New York), cited in *ibid.,* p. 277; Chicago *Tribune,* June 16, 22, 1897.

[59] *The News* (Denver), cited in *The Literary Digest,* XV (July 3, 1897), 276; Ray Stannard Baker, "The Debs Co-operative Commonwealth," *The Outlook,* LVI (July 3, 1897), 538–40.

[60] *The Social Democrat,* Aug. 12, 1897.

The number of branches and members was growing rapidly—300 applications for charters by July 1,[61] 25,000 members in 19 states by the middle of August.[62] The members demanded action.

The commission began its money-raising activity in September by requesting twenty dollars from each local branch.[63] A week later it gave an impatient membership an analysis of the problem and the proposed solution. It carefully pointed out that "our work is reconstruction rather than revolution." The colonies were to be "home-making and protective in character and plan." The states of Washington and Idaho were considered ideal for the "large beginnings" of the first colonies. They had rich resources, sparse population, and were "in friendly hands." In fact, the population was so friendly toward the co-operative commonwealth that most of the first five thousand colonists would probably come from within the borders of the chosen states.[64] Colonies would probably be limited in size to five hundred settlers. Their economic activity would be primarily agricultural, with small settlements operating in timber camps, cattle ranges, coal and other mines, and manufacturing, trade, and exchange. It was now just a matter of the commission's selecting the most suitable site.[65]

The next week Washington and Idaho were forgotten in the enthusiasm for another plan—the building of 75 miles of railroad for the city council of Nashville, Tennessee, in exchange for

[61] *The Social Democrat,* July 1, 1897.

[62] "Recent Socialistic Experiments," *Gunton's Magazine,* XIII (Sept., 1897), 205; *The Social Democrat,* Aug. 12, 1897. Illinois led in the number of branches, followed by Wisconsin, New York, Indiana, and Texas.

[63] Circular letter from Eugene V. Debs and Sylvester Keliher to all Local Branches of the Social Democracy of America, *The Social Democrat,* Sept. 23, 1897.

[64] "First Report of the Colonizing Commission of the National Executive Board of the S.D. of A.," *The Social Democrat,* Sept. 30, 1897. Debs had claimed during the June, 1897, S.D. of A. convention that he could mobilize a "peaceful army" of 10,000 unemployed in Chicago within ten days. He had written to the Union Pacific Railroad asking for land in the state of Washington in line with grants the railroad had given to other colonies. His army would be ready to march to Washington in 30 days. The railroad, however, viewed Debs's request as falling into a different category than earlier colonial ventures. (New York *Daily Tribune,* June 16, 1897.) Some members of the Social Democracy had long-range plans for converting their states to socialism. Kansas Social Democrats, for example, planned to get themselves employed in the state school systems and thus eventually convert the younger generation. (New York *Daily Tribune,* Oct. 14, 1897.)

[65] "First Report of the Colonizing Commission of the National Executive Board of the S.D. of A.," *The Social Democrat,* Sept. 30, 1897.

$300,000 worth of city bonds.[66] By the end of October, while still insisting that the railroad deal was going through, the commission left on a tour of the West to look over possible sites.[67] In December it was decided to spend the winter months in preparations that would permit the establishment of the first colony in the spring.[68] When spring arrived the only preparations completed were plans for the issuance of $2,500,000 worth of bonds in ten-dollar denominations to finance a new colonial corporation to be organized under the laws of Kansas.[69] The sum of $1,600,000 was to be used to purchase land, and the remaining $900,000 was to furnish the operating costs until the colonies became self-sustaining.[70]

Meanwhile, criticism of the colonizing commission was mounting. In response, the commission issued glowing but vague generalizations; every week it announced that the good news of the completed plans would be published in another week, or in two weeks at the most. But until the plans were ready, absolute secrecy was necessary in order to frustrate fanatical capitalist opposition to them. In May, the commission was again forced to admit that final plans had yet to be made. But, they insisted, colonies "will sooner or later" be established in Tennessee, Washington, and Colorado "as parts of a great plan in which the strategic importance of all the states outside the plutocratic states have been duly considered." Loyal citizens of Idaho and Kansas were reassured with the information that these socialistically inclined states might well be added to the list after colonies were under way in the first three states. The membership, warned the commission, must not ask for the revelation of the master plan until the time was ripe. "Open and secret attack have been made not only by capitalistic influences, but also by those masquerading under the name of socialist." These subversive elements must not be given the opportunity to destroy the Social Democracy of America.[71]

While hundreds of humanitarians and the members of the commission were combing the country for the site of the new utopia, "those masquerading under the name of socialist," the political action socialists, devoted their energies to the fall and spring elec-

[66] The Social Democrat, Oct. 7, 21, 1897.
[67] Ibid., Oct. 21, 1897.    [68] Ibid., Dec. 23, 1897.    [69] Ibid., April 28, 1898.
[70] Ibid., May 12, 1898.    [71] Ibid., May 5, 1898.

tions. Since the Social Democracy had not had time to get a ticket in the field for the 1897 fall elections, Debs urged all members to forget personal differences and vote on principle for the candidates of the Socialist Labor Party.[72] In the spring municipal elections of 1898, the Milwaukee Social Democrats put forward a complete slate of candidates. The platform was largely Populist reform, ranging from city operation of public utilities to equalization of water rates and monthly city-sponsored symphony concerts. After a vigorously conducted campaign the Socialists polled some twenty-five hundred votes, 6 percent of the total cast.[73] To the political actionists the vote was "the beginning of the end" for capitalism. To the colonizers, it was nothing less than sabotage of the important work of the colonizing commission.[74]

The political actionists picked up their main strength in 1898 from rebellious members of the Haverhill, Massachusetts, Socialist Labor Party. In December, 1897, the Haverhill S.L.P. had elected James F. Carey to the city council. Within a month the party was split over the question of supporting the reform measures advocated by Carey. The party ideology as laid down by Daniel De Leon held that all reforms were devices to prolong the life of the fatally ill capitalist system. When Carey was chosen president of the Common Council in January, 1898, the leaders of the party closest to De Leon concluded that he had sold out for political advancement. It was charged that Carey had "as much class consciousness as an oyster," [75] seemed inclined to go "Debsward," and probably was not accountable for his actions because he was "in the last stages of consumption." [76] In March, Debs and Sylvester Keliher visited the very much alive Carey and brought him and the main body of Haverhill socialists into the Social Democracy of America.[77]

Outside of Milwaukee and Haverhill, with scattered support in Chicago and St. Louis, the political actionists had their main base in New York's East Side. There, the Jewish socialists had broken

---

[72] Letter to *The Social Democrat*, Oct. 21, 1897.
[73] *The Social Democrat*, Feb. 10, April 4, 1898; *Social Democracy Red Book*, p. 60.
[74] *The Social Democrat*, April 14, 1898.
[75] Letter from Arthur Keep to Henry Kuhn, Jan. 8, 1898, De Leon Collection.
[76] Letter from Fred M. Drither to Henry Kuhn, Jan. 9, 1898, De Leon Collection.
[77] *Social Democracy Red Book*, p. 60.

with De Leon in 1897 and founded their own daily Jewish language newspaper, the *Forward*. Abraham Cahan, Meyer London, and Isaac Hourwich obtained an endorsement of the Social Democracy from the 200 members of the Forward Association, and the *Forward* became an invaluable socialist propagandist on New York's East Side, recruiting unattached socialists and detaching members of the S.L.P. and transferring them into the political action wing of the Social Democracy.[78]

While the political actionists were slowly building the political machine which they saw as the basis of the socialist movement, they became increasingly aware that the Social Democracy was a hindrance rather than a help to their plans. The colonizing commission's incessant demands for money, and its directives to the organization to concentrate on propaganda favoring the coming march to utopia prevented effective propaganda on the socialist triumph sure to follow a concerted march to the polls.[79] Although Debs, when speaking to the Milwaukee socialists, had insisted that colonization was only a subordinate and temporary relief phase of the Social Democracy,[80] a majority of the branches and the *Social Democrat* acted as though it were the sole purpose of the organization. While Debs participated in labor organization, particularly in the miners' strike of 1897,[81] the colonizers sneered at strikes for the eight-hour day,[82] and condemned socialist labor agitators as opportunists seeking to line their own pockets.[83] And while the political actionists made periodic condemnations of the threatened war with Spain,[84] the colonizers refused to permit themselves to be diverted from their one important job. In the early months of the Social Democracy, even the members of the colonizing commission went out of their way to insist that they were part of a class-

[78] George Seldes, *Lords of the Press* (New York, Blue Ribbon Books, 1941), pp. 103–4; Coleman, *Debs,* pp. 193, 195. In 1908 the *Forward* was an eight-page daily with a circulation of 52,000 and a subscription price of $3.50 a year. By 1912 the circulation had climbed to over 120,000. (N. W. Ayer and Son, *American Newspaper Annual,* for 1903, 1905, 1908, 1912.)

[79] Letter from the Boston Branch of the Social Democracy of America to *The Social Democrat,* Oct. 14, 1897.

[80] Milwaukee *Daily News,* reprinted in *The Social Democrat,* July 15, 1897.

[81] *Social Democracy Red Book,* pp. 58–60.

[82] *The Social Democrat,* Feb. 17, 1898.

[83] *Ibid.,* June 16, 1898.

[84] *Ibid.,* March 10, 1898; letter from Debs to *The Social Democrat,* May 14, 1898.

conscious movement.[85] But by the June, 1898, convention, class consciousness was being denounced by the colonizers as an un-American "fatal German theory" which ignored the "organic unity of society." [86]

The growing conflict between the utopians and the political actionists came to a head on June 2, 1898, five days before the delegates to the first national convention assembled. Unable to float the $2,500,000 bond issue, having collected not $25,000 every month as expected but only $2,400 in a year, and having spent the $2,400 in "prospecting," the colonization commission decided to raise the money necessary for its ventures by buying a Colorado gold mine. The purchase required a $5,000 down payment, and a $95,000 mortgage. The commission, apparently convinced that it would be easier to sell stock in a gold mine than in a nonexistent $2,500,000 farm, planned to float $200,000 worth of bonds. The hundred thousand not needed for the purchase price would be used for developing the mine and marching the first contingent of colonists West.[87]

The anticolonists stormed at this new "gold-brick" scheme. Protests had poured into the National Headquarters against the attempts to solicit money for a project that would probably never exist. These protests were now redoubled.[88] When the national convention assembled on June 7, it was clear to all the delegates that the Social Democracy would have to decide between colonization and political action. It would never again be able to choose both.[89]

The outcome of the convention was determined by the method of representation. Each branch, regardless of size, was entitled to one vote. The seventy delegates who gathered at what was to be the first and last convention of the Social Democracy represented 94 branches.[90] It is impossible to determine which of the two factions was the larger. But there is no question as to which was organized into the greatest number of branches. Although the political actionists had been picking up strength from dissident members

---

85 Letter from C. F. Willard to Daniel De Leon, Aug. 11, 1897, De Leon Collection.
86 Laurence Gronlund in *The Social Democrat*, June 23, 1898.
87 *The Social Democrat*, June, 1898.
88 *Social Democracy Red Book*, pp. 64–65; Bloor, *We Are Many*, p. 53.
89 Hillquit, *History of Socialism*, pp. 331–32.
90 *The Social Democrat*, June 16, 1898.

and even entire sections of the Socialist Labor Party,[91] they could never hope to equal the colonizers in the number of local organizations. The colonizing faction included dozens of varieties of reformers, ranging from prohibitionist to anarchist.[92] Each variety was convinced that its own brand of reform could be best achieved through a co-operative colony; under no circumstances would one group of reformers join with others who sought to use the colony for their own nefarious ends. Consequently, each clique had a chapter of its own, sometimes with a total membership of five or six; [93] each of these chapters was entitled to a vote at the convention. Forty of the seventy delegates came from Chicago reform clubs, and these forty, together with a handful from Georgia, Kansas, Pennsylvania, New York, and Colorado, controlled the convention.[94]

No sooner had Debs let his gavel fall to declare the first annual convention in session than Secretary Keliher, of the political actionists, rose to accuse the colonizers of organizing five paper branches in Chicago three weeks earlier in an attempt to pack the convention. Keliher announced that he had refused to issue charters to these chapters and that they were therefore not entitled to representation. The entire first day was spent in bitter debate over this point, and that night the National Executive Board ordered Keliher to issue the charters.[95]

The next day the political actionists scored their only convention victory when they elected Victor Berger and Margaret Haile of Massachusetts to the three-man platform committee. Berger and Haile made one last attempt to compromise with the utopians by offering to list as one of the Social Democracy's demands the grant of land by a state to be used for a colony for relief of the unemployed. The offer was rejected.[96] The political actionists then decided: to have their committee majority report a platform completely rejecting colonization; debate the platform in the plenary

[91] Hillquit, *History of Socialism*, pp. 331–32.

[92] Shortly after the Social Democracy was organized, Johann Most instructed all readers of his *Freiheit* to join the organization (*Social Democracy Red Book*, p. 59). At the 1898 convention, the anarchists were led by Emma Goldman (Goldman, *Living My Life*, I, 220).

[93] Sylvester Keliher in the *Social Democratic Herald*, July 9, 1898.

[94] Frederic Heath in *ibid.*

[95] The Chicago *Tribune*, June 8, 1898; *Social Democracy Red Book*, p. 65.

[96] Margaret Haile in the *Social Democratic Herald*, July 16, 1898.

session; and, then, after they had lost the vote, to abandon the convention and start a new party.[97] The colonizers, equally desirous of a showdown, issued a minority report which stressed the use of colonies as the means of introducing the co-operative commonwealth; they recommended political action only where there was no other party in the field supporting policies which might lead to increased "socialization." The platform debate lasted all day Friday, and not until three in the morning was the vote taken. The minority report was adopted 52 to 37. Isaac Hourwich jumped on a chair and shouted that all delegates who opposed the minority report would meet across the street at Revere House at eight o'clock.[98]

The next morning the Social Democracy convention concluded its business and adjourned, convinced that "American Socialist Methods" had triumphed over "the old German Socialist methods, with its 'class consciousness' club tactics." [99] There was no issue of the *Social Democrat* on June 9. On June 16 the paper again appeared, featuring convention reports, sneers at the bolters as a pack of foreigners, glowing promises from the colonizing commission, and the good news that in two weeks $170 worth of bonds of the needed $200,000 for the gold mine had been purchased. The long-unpaid printer saw to it that this was the last issue of the *Social Democrat*. Two small colonies with a total membership of 110 were eventually established in the state of Washington. The remainder of the Social Democracy of America broke up into its component parts.[100] But the torch of American social democracy was picked up by the 33 bolting political actionists who, while the colonizers were still celebrating the convention victory which was to lead to their extinction, met across the street to organize a new party based on the principles of International Socialism.

[97] *Social Democracy Red Book*, p. 65.
[98] The Chicago *Tribune*, June 11, 12, 1898; *The Social Democrat*, June 16, 1898.
[99] *The Social Democrat*, June 16, 1898.
[100] Fine, *Labor and Farmer Parties*, p. 194.

# V

# The Social Democratic Party

THE THIRTY-THREE DELEGATES who bolted the convention of the Social Democracy of America did not wait until eight o'clock to organize their new party. At three in the morning of their convention defeat, with Frederic Heath presiding and F.G.R. Gordon of New Hampshire acting as secretary, the delegates adopted the name Social Democratic Party, accepted the majority platform that Berger and Haile had written for the Social Democracy, and issued an address to the members explaining the reason for the split. Then they went to bed.[1]

They reassembled five hours later at Hull House, Chicago, adopted a constitution differing very little from that of the Social Democracy, and elected an executive board consisting of Jesse Cox and Seymour Stedman of Illinois, Eugene Debs of Indiana,[2] and Victor Berger and Frederic Heath of Wisconsin. Chicago was chosen as the site of National Headquarters, and Theodore Debs, Eugene's brother, was chosen national secretary at $75 a month, if he could raise it. After instructing the new executive board to revise and edit the constitution and by-laws, and declaring their intention to nominate candidates in the fall elections in every district where the party had a foothold, the delegates adopted the

[1] "Address to the Members of the Social Democracy of America," June 16, 1898, *Social Democratic Herald,* July 9, 1898; Chicago *Tribune,* June 12, 1898; New York *Daily Tribune,* June 12, 1898.

[2] Eugene Debs, who became ill during the Social Democracy convention, did not attend either the meeting at Revere House or the later meeting at Hull House. Although in his opening remarks to the convention Debs had insisted that he favored both colonization and political action, he became convinced during the proceedings that he had had "all the experience along that line [of colonization] my constitution can stand." (Letter from Eugene V. Debs to the Social Democratic Party, *Social Democratic Herald,* July 16, 1898.) Debs's name was signed to the "address" issued by the bolters.

motto "Pure Socialism and No Compromise" and adjourned.[3]

To the Social Democrats, "Pure Socialism" carried connotations quite different from those ascribed to it by either the De Leon or Hillquit faction of the Socialist Labor Party. Both factions of the S.L.P. emphatically rejected the extension of government ownership under capitalism as the means of achieving socialism. While the Social Democrats did not formulate their theories with any clarity in 1898–1899, government ownership and socialism were linked in all their philosophical discussions and tactical decisions.

In keeping with the Populist and Nationalist backgrounds of many of its members, the new Social Democratic Party placed main emphasis on the growing power of trusts in American life. But, unlike the Populists, the Social Democrats insisted that there was no hope of returning to the by-gone days of small-scale production. "In economic evolution there is no retrogression." [4] Even if the trusts could be dissipated, the result would be economically reactionary, they said. Society would lose the increased efficiency which came with large-scale production, while small capitalists would continue to exploit labor in much the same manner as the large ones had.[5] Economic evolution could no more be stopped than could natural evolution. The only solution of the trust problem was continuous economic evolution until the contradictions between social production and private appropriation were resolved.[6] The Social Democrats argued that the rise of the trust meant that America's economy had become a "plutocratic socialism"—socialism for the benefit of the few. If America was to free herself of depressions and exploitation, she must develop plutocratic socialism into democratic socialism, an economy in which the trusts would be owned by and operated for the benefit of all.[7]

The Social Democrats were not content with mere protest against the attempted dissolution of the trusts. Not only should the existing trusts be preserved, they held, but the growth of new trusts should

[3] "Address to the Members of the Social Democracy of America," June 16, 1898, *Social Democratic Herald*, July 9, 1898; Social Democratic Party, "Report of the Secretary of N.E.B. of the S.D.P., June, 1898–January, 1900," typescript, John Crerar Library, Chicago; Chicago *Tribune*, June 12, 1898.

[4] Vail, *Scientific Socialism*, pp. 24–25.

[5] *Social Democratic Herald*, June 24, Aug. 5, 1899.

[6] Vail, *Scientific Socialism*, pp. 26–28; *Social Democratic Herald*, June 24, 1899.

[7] Charles H. Vail in the *Social Democratic Herald*, June 10, 1899.

be encouraged.[8] Every trust was ready for democratic socialization; [9] the greater the number of trusts, the closer the country to
complete socialism. The Socialists admitted it would be extremely
difficult, even undesirable, for the government to take over hundreds
of thousands of small businesses; but, they declared, the government could easily appropriate a few large trusts. Achievement of
socialism was simply a matter of extending the principle underlying
government ownership of the post office to all industry which had
reached the level of development which necessitated trusts and
monopolies.[10] After the nation had declared a trust to be its property, the original board of directors would continue to operate the
trust as before, but would now act in the interest of all the people.[11]

Complete socialism required the public ownership of all the
means of production and distribution. To this end much could be
done on a local basis.[12] The municipal socialism program of the
Social Democrats aimed at extending the powers of the municipality to ownership of all public utilities, particularly gas and
electric lighting plants, street railways, and telephones.[13] It would
seem, therefore, that the Social Democrats envisioned a gradual
socialization of America through piecemeal nationalization of
trusts and municipal ownership of public utilities.

As "scientific socialists" the Social Democrats did not expect
to obtain government ownership of the trusts through appeals to
the innate reasonableness or kindliness of all citizens of the United
States.[14] Socialism was a working-class movement,[15] and American
socialism would be won through the class struggle.[16] The Social
Democrats held that society was divided into two classes: a capitalist class which owned the means of production, and a working class
whose access to those means was dependent upon the will of the

---

[8] *Social Democratic Herald,* Aug. 5, 1899.

[9] Victor L. Berger, "American Socialism," *Social Democratic Herald,* July 9,
1898. The *Herald* every week joyously printed a list of recently-formed trusts—a
herald of the coming triumph of socialism.

[10] Vail, *Modern Socialism,* pp. 11–12.

[11] *Ibid.,* p. 28; Vail, *Scientific Socialism,* p. 28.

[12] Jesse Cox in the *Social Democratic Herald,* April 15, 1899.

[13] John C. Chase, "Municipal Socialism in America," *The Independent,* LII (Jan.
25, 1900), 249–51.

[14] Noyes, *Evolution of the Class Struggle,* p. 15.

[15] Vail, *Scientific Socialism,* p. 230.

[16] Victor L. Berger, "American Socialism," *Social Democratic Herald,* July 9,
1898.

capitalist class. The working class, unlike the middle class, did not seek to limit mass production through trust-busting, but increasingly sought to obtain equitable distribution of the goods it produced.[17] The capitalist class naturally insisted on retaining its private appropriation, and, therefore, the interests of the working and capitalist classes were irreconcilably antagonistic.[18] "Only the self-righteous and misinformed who seek to arrive at the social millennium by retaining the system that makes classes inevitable, who browse in the region of fancy and vainly imagine that pink teas will solve the problem, are unconscious of the class struggle."[19] The mission of the Social Democratic Party was to end the class struggle through resolution of the contradiction between socially organized production and private ownership under the co-operative commonwealth.[20]

The Social Democrats were convinced that their crusade to end the class struggle would end on the electoral battlefield. Class interests, they maintained, were always expressed in class politics. The capitalists already had two political armies in the Democratic and Republican parties. The workers must also have a political party, so that through an intelligent use of the ballot they might gain control of the governing power and institute public ownership of the trusts.[21] While in the past the class struggle had taken only the economic form of strikes, boycotts, and lockouts, in the future it would be a political struggle between opposing political parties. Socialism would be gained when the working class united under the banner of the Social Democratic Party and voted that party's candidates into office.[22] Socialists were to devote all their energies to winning a maximum vote in every election "for straight and uncompromising socialism."[23]

The Social Democrats recognized, however, that the working class did not understand the necessity of striking at the ballot box.

---

[17] Noyes, *Evolution of the Class Struggle*, p. 25.

[18] "Report of the National Executive Board to the S.D.P. Convention, March 6, 1900," *Social Democratic Herald*, March 17, 1900.

[19] *Social Democratic Herald*, Dec. 9, 1899.

[20] "Report of the National Executive Board to the S.D.P. Convention, March 6, 1900," *Social Democratic Herald*, March 17, 1900.

[21] Vail, *Scientific Socialism*, pp. 230–31.

[22] "Report of the National Executive Board to the S.D.P. Convention, March 6, 1900," *Social Democratic Herald*, March 17, 1900.

[23] *Social Democratic Herald*, Sept. 16, 1899.

The main task of the party, therefore, was "by patient but power-ful agitation and propaganda to convince and organize the masses." [24] All Socialists must join existing unions and support the unions' economic activities. But under no circumstances were they to attempt to engage the union in political action. Working-class politics was the exclusive property of the Social Democratic Party. Socialists in the unions were to work for the unity of the workers on the economic field and, far more important, educate union mem-bers on the need to join and vote for the S.D.P.[25]

The avowed Marxian nature of the Social Democratic Party made imperative its theoretical emphasis on *working-class* political activities. The party was careful to point out editorially that the middle class alone had neither the desire nor the ability to bring socialism to America. Even if it should become aware of its pre-carious position in the monopoly capitalist economy, the true mid-dle class, the small businessmen and not the growing number of salaried employees, was growing so weak that it could not institute the changes necessary to end capitalism.[26] The only hope for the middle class was to throw its support to the working-class movement and thus help usher in the new social order which would benefit all, worker and small employer alike.[27]

But as was to be expected in a party which emphasized working-class activity but was itself largely middle class in composition, the program advocated by the Social Democratic Party was largely Populist in content and middle-class reform in appeal. The plat-form adopted at the June 11, 1898, Hull House meeting pointed out that capitalism was impoverishing the working class and called for establishment of a co-operative commonwealth. Then, "as steps

24 "Report of the National Executive Board to the S.D.P. Convention, March 6, 1900," *Social Democratic Herald,* March 17, 1900.

25 "Resolution on Trade Unions," adopted at the S.D. of A. Convention and re-adopted by the bolters at Hull House, June 11, 1898 (*Social Democratic Herald,* July 9, 1898); "Resolution on Trade Unions," adopted at the S.D.P. Convention, March 8, 1900 (*Social Democratic Herald,* March 17, 1900). There were already those who considered it futile for the working class to battle the capitalists on the economic field where the latter always had more powerful weapons. These socialists insisted that only on the electoral field where working-class votes outnumbered capitalist votes could the workers hope to be successful (Vail, *Scientific Socialism,* p. 32).

26 *Social Democratic Herald,* July 16, 1898.

27 "Platform of the Social Democratic Party, June 11, 1898," *Social Democracy Red Book;* Vail, *Scientific Socialism,* p. 230.

in this direction," it laid out a twelve-point program of constitutional revision, public ownership of railways, mines, and telegraph,
reduction of hours of labor, and institution of political reforms
lifted almost bodily from the middle-class platform of the Populists and the developing municipal reform parties. Emphasizing
the agrarian background of the socialist program were the special
demands for leasing of public land to farmers "in small parcels of
not over six hundred and forty acres"; construction of grain elevators, magazines, and cold storage buildings to be rented to farmers at cost; unification of railroad, telegraph, and telephone systems; uniform rates for transportation of all agricultural products
on all railroads; and issuance of public credit to counties and towns
for improvement of roads and soil and for irrigation and drain-
age.[28]

The *Social Democratic Herald*, party pamphlets, and political
speeches always devoted some space and time to the exploitation
of labor. But all reserved their sharpest barbs to impale capitalism
for its corruption of middle-class morals. The elimination of prostitution, crime, and insanity, the restriction of divorce, the stabiliza-
tion of the home, the encouragement of temperance and vegetarian-
ism, of democracy, personal liberty, and simplicity in government,
the establishment of equal rights for women and equality of all
before the law, all these reforms dear to the heart of liberal middle-
class America were the real benefits to follow hard on the heels of
the co-operative commonwealth.[29]

Socialism was to come as a blessing to the small producer and
large capitalist alike. It would end the anguish suffered by every
capitalist in his struggle to prevent other capitalists from appropriating his capital. "The mental suffering of many of the capitalist class is continually underestimated." And socialism would do
more than bring economic security to the embattled capitalist: it
would eliminate the personal danger which he and his family underwent when compelled to go forth into a world peopled by embittered

[28] "Platform of the Social Democratic Party, June 11, 1898," *Social Democracy
Red Book,* pp. 132–33.
[29] *Social Democratic Herald,* July, 1898–Jan., 1900; Wood-Simons, *Woman and
the Social Question;* Vail, *Scientific Socialism;* H. T. Hicocks in the *Commonwealth
Magazine,* reprinted in the *Social Democratic Herald,* May 27, 1899; Frederic Heath
in *The Vegetarian,* reprinted in the *Social Democratic Herald,* Jan. 28, 1899.

victims of social injustice. "Why the average capitalist should wish a continuance of this barbaric struggle for existence is beyond comprehension, and can only be accounted for by his prejudice against and ignorance of Socialism." [30] The new socialist party resolved to remove the veil of ignorance and prejudice from the eyes of the mentally anguished and personally endangered owners of the tools of production. With the noble objective of saving the middle and capitalist classes from themselves through the class struggle, political reform, and public ownership, the Social Democratic Party set out to organize locals and elect candidates who would permit the "resistless thirst, . . . the inherent impulse, that drives men forward" to be quenched.[31]

Few American political parties ever started so ambitious a program with smaller financial and numerical support. While there were hundreds and even thousands of non-Socialist Labor Party socialists in America, they were either affiliated with jealously independent local and state organizations, or saw no need to belong to any organized socialist body. Only in Milwaukee, St. Louis, and Massachusetts, where strong branches of expelled members of the S.L.P. existed, did the Social Democratic Party have any real organized support.[32] The five-man executive board elected by the S.D. of A. bolters had confined its first efforts to adopting a program, authorizing the publication of a weekly newspaper, and appointing Theodore Debs national secretary-treasurer.[33] Chicago, the location of the new national headquarters, had only fifteen active party members who could be called on to help establish a national office. Between them they raised $75, rented an office across the street from the city hall at $10 a month, and began to organize to sweep the country in the next two national elections.[34]

Within a month the party was penniless. Seymour Stedman, who was combining the practice of law and the secretaryship of the N.E.B., staved off bankruptcy by borrowing $200 from Eugene Dietzgen, a Chicago businessman who belonged to the anti-De Leon faction of the S.L.P. and whose father, Joseph, had had some asso-

---

[30] Vail, *Scientific Socialism*, pp. 95–97.    [31] *Ibid.*, pp. 174–75.

[32] *Social Democracy Red Book*, pp. 68–69.

[33] Social Democratic Party, "Report of the Secretary of N.E.B. of S.D.P., June, 1898–January, 1900," typescript, John Crerar Library, Chicago.

[34] Coleman, *Debs*, pp. 199–200.

ciation with Karl Marx. When this money evaporated, Theodore Debs pawned his watch for $40—the first trip of a procession which was to wear a path to the pawnbroker's shop—and then, on Christmas eve, spent his last quarter on a lottery ticket which brought the party a windfall of $125. While the days were devoted mainly to letter-writing and raising money to pay postage and rent, evenings were spent by Debs, Keliher, and Heath in pasting socialist stickers on the El in the Loop and in making the windows of the State Street department stores billboards of socialist propaganda.[35] The party staff obtained its office equipment through Berger, at a discount and on time payments,[36] and took its meals at the free lunch counters of the city saloons.[37] An English socialist, Alfred S. Edwards, was appointed editor of the eight-page *Social Democratic Herald*, and after a few months he and the paper were forced to move to Belleville, Illinois, to cut publishing costs.[38]

Although the decision to move the *Herald* to Belleville was the only concrete action taken by the Board in its biweekly meetings through November, 1898, by the first of September the party had active branches in 12 states—the result of the personal letters and solicitations of Eugene Debs.[39] With Debs on the road speaking almost nightly for socialism,[40] and with the receipts of these meetings bolstering the finances of the national office enough to prevent foreclosure on what little property the office could boast,[41] the Social Democratic Party considered itself to be on a sound enough basis to indulge in a little internal wrangling.

Ideologically, the first intraparty fight took place over the Special Demands for Farmers which the bolters had included in the Platform adopted at Hull House in June. Constitutionally, the dispute raged about the National Executive Board whose members had been chosen by the 33 bolting delegates of the Social Democracy and who came from the three Midwestern states of Wisconsin, Illinois, and Indiana. The other state organizations, and particu-

[35] *Ibid.*, pp. 200–202.
[36] Social Democratic Party, "Report of the Secretary of N.E.B. of S.D.P., June, 1898–January, 1900," typescript in John Crerar Library, Chicago.
[37] Coleman, *Debs*, pp. 200–202.
[38] *Social Democracy Red Book*, pp. 68–69.
[39] *Social Democratic Herald*, Sept. 3, 1898.
[40] *Social Democratic Herald*, Dec. 3, 1898.
[41] Coleman, *Debs*, p. 202.

larly that of Massachusetts (which by June, 1899, represented 1,200 members in 33 branches—50 percent of the total national membership) strongly resented the attempts of the National Board to enforce the constitutional right, drawn up by them, to "determine the policy and do all other things required to carry out the general objects of the organization." [42]

The increasingly bitter year-long quarrel over the demands for farmers which began almost immediately after the Hull House Meeting was the first skirmish in the twenty-year civil war between the Left and Right factions, which was to end only with the final expulsion of the Left in 1919 and the formation of the Communist Party. A majority of the National Executive Board—Berger, Heath, and Stedman—insisted that the Demands for Farmers were not only in keeping with the principles of International Socialism, but, still more important, were indispensable if the S.D.P. was to win the farmer vote. Without that vote it would be impossible to carry out a program of municipal ownership.[43] The farmer, they maintained, was more intelligent than the city worker, and, given a program designed to back his fight to keep his farm, would vote overwhelmingly for socialism. The party might well devote more time to propagandizing farmers than attempting to educate the urban proletariat. Already 140,000 Kansas citizens had "cast a vote for reforms—Socialistic planks—and nine-tenths of them were farmers." [44]

To the majority of the Board, talk of socializing the farms was ridiculous. There was no sign of an economic evolution leading to the formation of farm "trusts," they said.[45] Socialism had no such goal as appropriation of either the small farm or the small business.[46] The way to win the farmer was to present him with a program of government grants of land, government-operated grain elevators, and nationalization of railroads, telegraph, and telephone. With his support the 1908 elections would usher in a socialist America.[47]

[42] Social Democratic Party, "Report of the Secretary of N.E.B. of S.D.P., June, 1898–January, 1900," typescript, John Crerar Library, Chicago.
[43] Seymour Stedman in the *Social Democratic Herald*, July 9, 1898.
[44] F. G. R. Gordon to the *Social Democratic Herald*, July 9, 1898.
[45] Frederic Heath to the *Social Democratic Herald*, April 29, 1899.
[46] Victor Berger in the *Social Democratic Herald*, Aug. 6, 1898.
[47] F. G. R. Gordon to the *Social Democratic Herald*, April 22, 1899.

The Left, whose experiences with the Populist Party had made it suspicious of anything that hinted at "trading" with nonworking class forces, saw in the Demands a compromise of socialist principles designed to trade the co-operative commonwealth for a mess of middle-class pottage. The Left pointed out that, according to the Socialist platform, society was divided into two classes, the capitalists and the dispossessed workers. These two classes were engaged in a never-ending struggle which could cease only with the establishment of socialism. Therefore, it was inconsistent with the aims of International Socialism to tack on at the end of a class-struggle platform a series of demands designed to ameliorate the hard-pressed group of small capitalists known as farmers.[48]

The Left admitted that farmers were being attacked by the trusts. But so were the small manufacturers. It was not the purpose of the Social Democratic Party to prolong the capitalist system by preserving a class doomed by economic evolution to extinction.[49] Measures such as the leasing of land and construction of grain elevators would only give the farmers an illusory hope of continued economic well-being under capitalism. The Left said, moreover, that wealthy farmers would use devices like grain elevators to store their crops against a rise in the market.[50] This would mean the further degradation of the working class, which would have to pay still higher prices for food.[51] As for poor farmers, they would gain nothing from such halfway measures. They would have to support the Social Democratic Party on a simple statement of the objects of the socialist movement, and in the knowledge that under capitalism they faced nothing but extinction, while under socialism they, like all mankind, would lead a better and richer life.[52]

American farmers, the argument continued, had been driven to desperation by domestic and foreign competition and by the exploitation of trusts and absentee landlords and were now ready for straight socialist propaganda.[53] They had no further use for middle-class Populism. The great danger threatening the Socialist Party was that it might compromise its principles, that it might

---

[48] Charles R. Martin in the *Social Democratic Herald*, April 8, 1899.
[49] Charles R. Martin in the *Social Democratic Herald*, May 6, 1899.
[50] Rosa Proletaire in the *Social Democratic Herald*, May 13, 1899.
[51] Charles R. Martin in the *Social Democratic Herald*, May 6, 1899.
[52] W. Roper in the *Social Democratic Herald*, May 27, 1899.
[53] Jesse Cox in the *Social Democratic Herald*, Sept. 9, 1898.

gain victory by winning the support of small capitalists who had
been promised ameliorative measures designed to preserve their
status as independent businessmen.[54] Every progressive party of
the past 35 years—the Greenback Party, the Union Labor Party,
and the People's Party—had been

disrupted by the prostitute of American politics, the democratic
party . . . unless the S.D.P. builds on sharp, clearly defined, class
conscious lines, with compact disciplined organization, the old hag
will don a new dress, paint her cheeks a catchy red and once more be-
guile those in a hurry to "win." . . . When development and education have reached the proper stage, winning will take care of itself.
The danger is abortion.[55]

By February, 1899, opposition to the Demands for Farmers
and criticism of the Board (which seemed inclined to perpetuate
itself in office without even the formality of promising a forthcoming party convention) had grown to such a pitch that the Board
recognized that some action would have to be taken to prevent a
general exodus from the Party.[56] At the March 6 meeting, therefore, the Board graciously passed a resolution declaring it "desirable that the members of the N. Ex. Board should at all times be
in accord with the majority of the party and subject at all times
to its will." In keeping with this desire, the Board called on each
state to send two delegates to a conference to be held on the third
and fourth days of June, 1899, to frame proposals to submit to
a referendum vote of the party membership, and also to set a date
for a national convention.[57]

When the conference finally assembled in July, 1899, it found
that it had been boycotted by the powerful Massachusetts party,
which considered the conference a waste of money and looked
toward a convention to settle its problems.[58] Indeed, besides the
members of the Board, the only additional delegates were one each

---

[54] C. W. Herwitt in the *Social Democratic Herald*, June 24, 1899.

[55] Charles R. Martin in the *Social Democratic Herald*, June 3, 1899. (Unfortunately for those who desired a socialist America, the Left's incessant fear of abortion frequently prevented any attempt at conception.)

[56] "To the Members of the Social Democratic Party from the National Executive
Board," *Social Democratic Herald*, Feb. 18, 1899; Eugene V. Debs in the *Social
Democratic Herald*, Aug. 5, 1899; Margaret Haile to the *Social Democratic Herald*,
Aug. 5, 1899.

[57] Social Democratic Party, "Report of the Secretary of N.E.B. of S.D.P., June,
1898–January, 1900," typescript, John Crerar Library, Chicago.

[58] John C. Chase to the *Social Democratic Herald*, July 29, 1899.

from the states of Missouri, Indiana, and Wisconsin. After prolonged debate the conference decided to submit to a referendum vote the question of continuing the existent constitution until the national convention—set conveniently ahead to March, 1900. This bitter pill was sweetened by permitting disgruntled members to vote on the Demands for Farmers. The membership voted 478 to 81 to eliminate these, but agreed to continue under the constitution until the March convention.[59] With a year in office behind it and nine more months of undisputed command ahead, the Board, which had been appointed by 33 members at the time the party was formed, settled down to strengthen the established lines of party work in unions and elections and to build their personal local and national support in the socialist movement.

The Social Democratic trade union policies were first put into effect at the December, 1898, A.F. of L. convention. In November the National Executive Board wrote to Samuel Gompers, president of the Federation, and begged him to work for an endorsement of socialism and the S.D.P. at the coming convention.[60] Gompers was unmoved. At the December 4 meeting of the Board, Berger and Stedman were instructed to attend the convention in the role of observers, and to direct the campaign aimed at securing the desired endorsements.[61]

When Berger and Stedman arrived in Kansas City on December 13, they found that the Social Democrats and the anti-De Leon Socialist Laborites had already mapped out a two-pronged campaign strategy. On one front they were organizing for the defeat of Gompers and all other "pure and simple" union leaders who, under the guise of pleading the cause of labor before such sympathetic politicians as Tom Reed, were actually associating "with the capitalist class for the interests of themselves." [62] On a second front, a series of resolutions had been introduced endorsing the Social Democratic Party and calling for "class conscious propaganda for abolition of the wage system." [63]

---

[59] Social Democratic Party, "Report of the Secretary of N.E.B. of S.D.P., June, 1898–January, 1900," typescript, John Crerar Library, Chicago.
[60] *Ibid.*                                 [61] *Ibid.*
[62] *Ibid.;* letter from Ernest W. Timson to the *Social Democratic Herald,* Jan. 14, 1899.
[63] *Report of Proceedings of the Eighteenth Annual Convention of the American Federation of Labor, 1898,* pp. 40–41, 65; *Social Democratic Herald,* Dec. 24, 1898.

Stedman and Berger immediately took charge of the socialist delegates. Viewing the socialist role in the trade union movement to be primarily one of getting union votes for Socialist candidates,[64] and inspired by the recent abstract endorsement of socialism by the British Trade Union Congress,[65] Stedman and Berger insisted that any involvement in internal union controversies would only weaken attempts at socialist propaganda. Accordingly, the socialist opposition to Gompers was dropped, and the socialist delegates accepted the positions of eunuchs in the "pure and simple" harem. The strategists from the Socialist national office then called to pay their respects to Gompers, whose opposition to the socialist resolution they considered "unintentional." Gompers refused to be swayed by Berger's logic, insisting that leaders must not get ahead of members in philosophical matters.[66]

Convention debate on the socialist resolution was vigorous, but the Gompers machine's opposition was decisive. The Socialists, however, were able to muster an impressive show of strength, the final vote being 493 for the resolution, 1,971 against.[67] The party leaders were torn between disappointment at their failure to win Gompers and their delight in collecting more than one fifth of the vote in spite of his opposition. They concluded that within two years the American Federation of Labor would take the same "advanced ground for Socialism" as had their brothers in the British Trade Union Congress.[68] This conviction was reinforced when, according to Berger, Gompers told him after the adjournment of the convention: "I have read Karl Marx; I am as much a Socialist as you and I will vote the Social Democratic ticket and advise trade unionists to do so." [69]

Aside from their "victory" at the Federation convention, socialist work among the unions in the first year and a half of party ac-

[64] *Social Democratic Herald,* Dec. 24, 1898.

[65] *Social Democracy Red Book,* p. 69.

[66] Social Democratic Party, "Report of the Secretary of N.E.B. of S.D.P., June, 1898–January, 1900," typescript, John Crerar Library, Chicago; *Social Democratic Herald,* Dec. 24, 1898.

[67] *Report of Proceedings of the Eighteenth Annual Convention of the American Federation of Labor, 1898,* p. 104; *American Federationist,* V (Jan., 1899), 219, 220; *Social Democracy Red Book,* p. 71.

[68] *Social Democratic Herald,* Dec. 24, 1898.

[69] Social Democratic Party, "Report of the Secretary of N.E.B. of S.D.P., June, 1898–January, 1900," typescript, John Crerar Library, Chicago.

tivity was confined to expressions of sympathy to the working class, the printing of a boycott notice for the Brewery Workers (the notice was withdrawn under threat of criminal prosecution), and appearances by a number of Socialist speakers before local unions. The National Executive Board of the party was so encouraged by these strides and by the prospect of still more trade union doors "being opened to our agitators," that they confidently informed the first party convention that the "near future" would see a mass movement of trade unionists into the ranks of the Social Democratic Party.[70]

The party leaders were equally pleased with the victories won on the political field. The eagerly awaited elections came five months after the split of the Social Democracy in June, 1898. Socialist city and state tickets were put forward in Massachusetts, Missouri, Wisconsin, Indiana, New York, Maryland, and New Hampshire.[71] Twelve thousand votes were polled, over half coming from Massachusetts, which sent two Socialists to the state assembly.[72] The *Social Democratic Herald* saw in this victory the pattern of the coming of socialism to America.[73] And when in January, 1900, the National Executive Board reported that the party had already elected 20 of its members to offices ranging from school committeeman to mayor, there were few Social Democrats who were not convinced that the triumph of socialism was less than a decade away.[74]

By far the most impressive socialist victories in 1898 and 1899, and the ones most shocking to editors satisfied that socialism was a foreign plant incapable of growth on free American soil, were scored in the normally Republican town of Haverhill, Massachusetts. Haverhill, a shoe manufacturing community with a native-American population of 21,000 and an immigrant population of only 6,000,[75] had been the scene of a series of strikes precipitated by cuts in the already low wages paid the shoe workers. The strikes had been directed by a socialist union leader, James F. Carey, and

[70] *Ibid.*

[71] *Social Democratic Herald,* Oct. 22, 1898.

[72] *Ibid.,* Nov. 12, Dec. 17, 1898.       [73] *Ibid.,* Nov. 12, 16, 1898.

[74] Social Democratic Party, "Report of the Secretary of N.E.B. of S.D.P., June, 1898–January, 1900," typescript, John Crerar Library, Chicago; *Social Democratic Herald,* June 10, 1899; *Social Democracy Red Book,* pp. 69, 75.

[75] Leonard D. Abbott, "The Socialist Movement in Massachusetts," *The Outlook,* LXIV (Feb. 17, 1900), 410.

in 1897 the disgruntled workers had elected Carey to the Common
Council of Haverhill. By November, 1898, Haverhill was torn by
another strike, this time on the town's street railways. The Lowell,
Lawrence, and Haverhill Street Railway Company had insisted
that their employees bond themselves against losses suffered by the
company due to "negligence or misconduct" on the part of employees. The railway workers struck, and the shoe workers, again
led by Carey, organized a boycott of the railway company. When
the November elections were held, the workers elected Carey of the
shoe workers and a fellow Socialist, Louis Scates, a striking railway
worker, to the State Assembly.[76]

The following month Massachusetts received still another shock.
Haverhill elected as its first socialist mayor John Chase, and also
filled three of the Common Council's 21 seats with Socialists. Chase
had campaigned on the Social Democratic ticket, on the issue not
of socialism but public ownership of the electric light and street
railway utilities.[77] Chase was re-elected in 1899 over the fusion
candidate of the combined Republican and Democratic parties, in
large part thanks to the refusal of the state gas commission to bring
into court the sworn returns of the local gas company.[78] The party
was jubilant, and the socialist movement took on some of the religious fervor of the pre-Civil War reform movements, the temperance pledges taken by known tipplers on joining the party receiving more publicity than work among unionists. The success was
short-lived. The failure of the Socialist administration to bring
either municipal ownership or higher wages needed only a slight
local depression, brought on by the refusal of wholesalers to buy
shoes manufactured in a socialist town, to bring about a decisive
defeat for Chase in 1900.[79]

The Haverhill Socialists set the pattern for and met the fate of
almost all Socialists later elected to public office. Elected on a platform of public ownership of public utilities, Chase found himself
in no position to implement this pledge so long as the state refused

[76] Calvin M. Clark, "A Socialist Mayor in Haverhill, Mass.," *The Independent,* L
(Dec. 29, 1898), 1926–27.

[77] "The Socialist Mayor's Inaugural," *The Outlook,* LXI (Jan. 14, 1899), 99.

[78] "Two Socialist Mayors in Massachusetts," *The Outlook,* LXIII (Dec. 16, 1899),
904; Leonard D. Abbott, "The Socialist Movement in Massachusetts," *The Outlook,*
LXIV (Feb. 17, 1900), 412.

[79] "The Socialist Defeat at Haverhill," *The Outlook,* LXVI (Dec. 22, 1900), 958.

to grant home rule to Haverhill. Other platform planks, such as requiring the union label on government printing and using union labor on city projects, were put into effect with little difficulty.[80] But these accomplishments were not great enough to maintain political enthusiasm at a high pitch over any length of time. The Republican and Democratic parties in Haverhill quickly made public ownership part of their own program.[81] Middle-class voters, discouraged by the inability of the Socialists to carry out their pledges, returned to the old parties, who, they reasoned, had the strength to carry out the public-ownership pledges they had now been forced to make. Moreover, having tasted political victory, the Socialists abandoned their militant trade union activity. Since Socialist election successes did little to increase wages, and since the Socialists were too busy with municipal socialism to bother with the "economic struggle," the workers joined the middle class in abandoning Socialist candidates to the inadequate support of loyal party members. But the Socialists were not discouraged. The Haverhill pattern of victory and failure was to be repeated many times throughout the country in the next twelve years.

The successful campaigns in Haverhill in 1898 and 1899 convinced the Socialist leaders that the Social Democratic Party, as an independent political organization, could win easy and rapid victories at the polls. Since their conception of political action was exclusively electoral, it followed that the party could maintain its political independence only through refusal to "fuse" with other parties during elections. Their bitter experience with the Populist Party, which they had seen destroyed as an effective independent organization after its fusion with the Democratic Party in the election of 1896, made them peculiarly sensitive to any combination, no matter how tenuous, with other groups on coalition tickets.

The National Executive Board insisted that independent Socialist slates be put forward at every opportunity, regardless of the possibility of forming broad coalitions around progressive candidates and issues.[82] Support of candidates like John Peter Altgeld

[80] "The Socialist Mayor's Inaugural," *The Outlook*, LXI (Jan. 14, 1899), 99.
[81] "Two Socialist Mayors in Massachusetts," *The Outlook*, LXIII (Dec. 16, 1899), 904.
[82] "Report of the National Executive Board to the S.D.P. Convention, March 6, 1900," *Social Democratic Herald*, March 17, 1900.

for mayor of Chicago would be a betrayal of principle. And while the immediate results of an "independent" role would not be as startling as the support of a coalition, it would show reformers that the Social Democrats were in earnest and would soon lead to clear-cut socialist election victories.[83] Consequently, at their March 26, 1899 meeting, the National Executive Board adopted a formula for application for membership in the S.D.P. which compelled the applicant not only to subscribe to the principles of the party, but pledged him to sever all connections with other political organizations, never to consent to the fusion or alliance of the Social Democratic Party with any other political party, and to agree that if ever he were chosen as a party candidate for public office, he would not accept the endorsement of any other political party.[84]

The first Socialists to challenge this edict were members of branches in the weak New York area.[85] The Brooklyn trolley strike of 1899 had convinced many trade unionists that they must elect their own leaders to public office if they were to win economic justice. Early in the fall of 1899 they issued a call for a political convention designed to form an Independent Labor Party. The New York Socialists were invited to attend. They accepted and sent delegates who participated in the formation of the I.L.P. and in the nomination of a slate for the November elections.[86]

The S.D.P. Board acted with a speed reserved for instances of intraparty deviation. To the New York branches' plea that the I.L.P. was a trade union party and that all Socialists were pledged to support the unions, the Board replied that "the trades union movement [was] an economic movement only for the purpose of maintaining and possibly elevating the standard of living of the wage workers." And since the unions were made up of members of all political parties and could not lead the proletariat politically,

[83] *Social Democratic Herald,* April 15, 1899.

[84] Social Democratic Party, "Report of the Secretary of N.E.B. of S.D.P., June, 1898–January, 1900," typescript, John Crerar Library, Chicago.

[85] The New York S.D.P. received only 1,245 votes in the November, 1898, elections —one tenth the total S.D.P. vote cast in the seven states which advanced S.D.P. tickets. The Socialist Labor Party completely dominated the socialist movement in New York. (*Social Democratic Herald,* Dec. 17, 1898.)

[86] *Social Democracy Red Book,* p. 75; Social Democratic Party, "Report of the Secretary of N.E.B. of S.D.P., June, 1898–January, 1900," typescript, John Crerar Library, Chicago.

"the trades unions must be supplanted in the political field by the Social Democratic Movement." The Board ruled that members of the S.D.P. could not be permitted to follow the unions' zigzag course on the political field. The Independent Labor Party was a capitalist trick designed to confuse the workers so as to prevent them from supporting the only party organized to emancipate the proletariat from wage slavery. All branches in New York were to recall their delegates from the I.L.P. convention and sever all connections with that party or stand suspended.[87] The New York branches capitulated. The I.L.P. was abandoned as a snare for unsuspecting workers, and the S.D.P. did not put forward a slate in the New York 1899 elections.[88]

In spite of the inactivity of Social Democrats on a national scale, the party grew rapidly after the first year. It is impossible to estimate what percentage of those who joined were new converts to socialism, and what percentage had already been through the mill of Socialist Labor Party conversion and expulsion. Since the Social Democrats had no paid national organizers, they depended on the *Social Democratic Herald* and on the speaking and organizing activities of Eugene Debs to bring in new branches and to hold the party together. The weekly *Herald* was sent free to all dues-paying party members, and sold to all prospective members at fifty cents a year. Its circulation grew from 3,000 in 1898 to 8,000 by the end of 1899.[89] Debs, who was speaking almost nightly throughout the country, convinced unorganized socialists in town after town to affiliate with the S.D.P. In addition, he brought in the independent socialist parties of Texas, Tennessee, and Arkansas, giving the party a toehold in the South.[90] By March, 1900, the Social Democratic Party claimed the support of 25 socialist papers,[91] and boasted a dues-paying membership of 4,636 in 226 branches,

[87] Social Democratic Party, "Report of the Secretary of N.E.B. of S.D.P., June, 1898–January, 1900," typescript, John Crerar Library, Chicago.

[88] *Social Democracy Red Book,* p. 75.

[89] "Report of the National Executive Board to the S.D.P. Convention, March 6, 1900," *Social Democratic Herald,* March 17, 1900.

[90] Eugene V. Debs to the *Social Democratic Herald,* June 3, 1899; W. E. Farmer, President, Socialist Party of America (Texas), to the *Social Democratic Herald,* June 11, 1899.

[91] "Report of the National Executive Board to the S.D.P. Convention, March 6, 1900," *Social Democratic Herald,* March 17, 1900.

organized in 32 states. And almost a thousand of these 4,600 had joined in the two months preceding the March, 1900, convention.[92]

The National Executive Board of the S.D.P., therefore, went into the first party convention with confidence in the party's future and in their ability to continue in control of its policies. For while the growth of the S.D.P. was not the product of their activities, they were still titular heads of an organization that had made impressive gains in the first year and a half of its existence. The party was far from wealthy, or even solvent, but the days of pawning the secretary-treasurer's watch were over. Twenty Socialists had been elected to public office. Membership roles were growing rapidly. And the S.D.P.'s great rival, the Socialist Labor Party, whose vote was watched with greater jealousy than that of the Republican or Democratic parties,[93] had recently split in two. Already, disgruntled members of the S.L.P. were swelling the ranks of the Social Democrats. It seemed only a matter of months before the Social Democrats would gain some five thousand ex-members of the S.L.P.[94]

The majority of the S.D.P. Board were determined to acquire the Socialist Labor Party membership on an individual basis, and thus not be forced by amalgamation proceedings to relinquish their grip on the party machinery. But when the 67 delegates representing 2,136 members assembled in Indianapolis on March 6, the plans of the National Executive Board collided head-on with the desire of a majority of the membership for immediate organic unity with the anti-De Leon wing of the Socialist Labor Party. This collision of the irresistible membership and the immovable Executive Board resulted in an eighteen-month factional fight from which the finally united Socialist Party never wholly recovered.

[92] "Report of the National Secretary-Treasurer of the S.D.P. to the First National Convention, March 6, 1900," *Social Democratic Herald*, March 17, 1900.

[93] In the early years the S.D.P. always compared its election returns with those of the S.L.P. and seemed to consider a vote larger than that of the S.L.P. almost as good as victory. (*Social Democratic Herald, passim.*)

[94] *Social Democracy Red Book*, pp. 72–73.

# VI

# Formation of the
# Socialist Party

IMMEDIATELY FOLLOWING the November, 1899 elections, the rank and file of both the Social Democratic and the anti-De Leon Socialist Labor parties began to demand organic unity of their two organizations. The Brooklyn branches of both parties held a joint meeting, called attention to the virtual identity of the two party platforms, and urged the National Executive Board of the Social Democrats to send negotiators to the forthcoming Socialist Laborite convention in Rochester.[1] The Cleveland branches of the two parties met separately, noted that the Social Democrats had repealed the "reactionary" Demands for Farmers, that the Socialist Laborites had sloughed off De Leonism, and called for immediate unity.[2] Feigenbaum of the S.L.P. wrote to Carey of the S.D.P. asking him to explain certain of his actions as a member of the Haverhill Common Council. When Carey did so in the interest of an "honorable union," both letters were published in the socialist press.[3]

Leaders of the Social Democracy, alarmed by these growing demands for unity, warned that the Socialist Labor Party was plotting to destroy the Social Democratic Party which, it claimed, had made greater progress in the one and a half years of its existence than the S.L.P. had in an entire decade. The National Executive Board of the S.D.P. issued a manifesto forgiving all Socialist Laborites who had been misled into attacking the Social Democrats,

[1] *The Workers' Call*, Dec. 2, 1899; *Social Democratic Herald*, Dec. 9, 1899.
[2] *Social Democratic Herald*, Dec. 2, 1899.
[3] Letter from B. Feigenbaum (of the *New Yorker Volkszeitung*) to James F. Carey, and letter from James F. Carey to B. Feigenbaum, Nov. 14, 1899, *Social Democratic Herald*, Dec. 2, 1899.

and inviting them to leave their present organization and join the Social Democracy.[4] Eugene Debs published a letter expressing a desire for unity, but holding that such unity was impossible as long as the S.L.P.'s official organ, *The People*, "continues to retail malicious libels respecting our party and its comrades." [5]

During December and early January the press of both parties was flooded with letters demanding unity and urging the National Executive Board of the S.D.P. to send representatives to the January anti-De Leon S.L.P. convention in Rochester. But the Board chose to send a letter instead of delegates. The letter extended "a hearty invitation to your convention, as well as to all members of your party, to join the Social-Democratic party in the struggle to emancipate humanity from class rule and the slavery of capitalism by the establishment of the Co-operative Commonwealth." [6]

Morris Hillquit replied for the convention. He insisted that if any of the three socialist parties could exist without amalgamation it was the "Rochester" Socialist Labor Party; that the convention "finds itself unable to grasp the exact import of the invitation extended by you"; that the S.L.P. was naturally willing to co-operate in order to establish the Co-operative Commonwealth, but that it did not believe the rank and file of Social Democracy would support the Board's dishonorable proposals to a "self-respecting socialist party." After making this reply a part of the public record of the convention, the delegates then modified it to a return of greetings and a promise of further communications.[7] These further communications took the form of an executive committee report hailing the evolution of the S.D.P. into "a true Socialist

[4] Statement of the National Executive Board, Nov. 24, 1899, "issued in view of the S.L.P. controversy," "Report of the Secretary of N.E.B. of S.D.P., June, 1898–January, 1900," typescript, John Crerar Library, Chicago.

[5] Letter from Eugene V. Debs to the *Social Democratic Herald,* Jan. 20, 1900. Debs's charge of "malicious libels" was somewhat unfair. While many leaders of the anti-De Leon wing of the S.L.P. considered the S.D.P. opportunist, and while the Chicago *Workers' Call* had referred to the "muddled socialism of the Social Democracy" before the S.L.P. split (*The Workers' Call,* March 25, 1899), *The People* (Williams St.) was careful not to attack the S.D.P. with which it sincerely desired organic union. The S.D.P. was attacked in six letters opposing union published by *The People,* but the paper also published 22 letters favoring union. Moreover, *The People* disclaimed responsibility for the opinions expressed in its letter columns.

[6] *Social Democratic Herald,* Feb. 3, 1900.

[7] *The People* (Williams St.), Feb. 4, 1900.

party," [8] a resolution in favor of immediate organic unity, and the appointment of a committee of nine to negotiate a treaty of union. Representatives of the committee were to attend the S.D.P. convention to tender the S.L.P. communication in person.[9]

The National Executive Board of the Social Democracy found itself temporarily outmaneuvered. It made the best of the situation by informing its membership that the S.L.P. representatives would be welcomed at the party's Indianapolis convention, scheduled for March 7, 1900, and the *Social Democratic Herald* expressed the pious hope "that the work of the joint committee on union may in due season be crowned with success." [10]

The Social Democratic convention greeted the S.L.P. delegates —Hillquit, Harriman, and Max Hayes—with "tumultuous and long-continued applause." They spoke on unity from the platform, and were promptly seated as delegates with voice but not votes.[11] Eugene Debs moved the appointment of a committee to bring in a report on the conduct of unity negotiations. His motion was adopted without open opposition.[12] The next day the committee brought in a majority and minority report, and what was to prove to be the apple of discord—the future name of the united party—was officially thrown in for the first time. As the clamor for unity had grown in the ranks of the S.D.P., the leadership of the party had given ground, but on each occasion had insisted that any unity moves would have to be postulated on the retention of the name "Social Democratic Party." Only by keeping that name, they claimed, could the identity and ideals of the party be preserved from destruction by the Socialist Labor Party. [13]

The majority report of the convention committee called for appointment of a committee of nine to negotiate a treaty of union, but instructed that committee to "stand" for the name Social Democratic Party. The minority report provided only that the committee "urge" retention of that name. Victor Berger warned the delegates that adoption of the minority report would destroy all

[8] "Report of the N.E.C. to the Tenth National Convention, S.L.P. Rochester, New York," *The People* (Williams St.), Feb. 4, 1900.

[9] *The People* (Williams St.), Feb. 4, 1900.

[10] *Social Democratic Herald,* Feb. 10, 1900.

[11] *Ibid.*, March 17, 1900.                    [12] *Ibid.*

[13] *Ibid.*, Dec. 16, 1899, Jan. 6, 1900.

the work he and his colleagues had done to build the S.D.P. Others warned that loss of the name would end the movement which was making socialism respectable in America. Hillquit was asked for his party's attitude toward the two reports. After consulting with Harriman and Hayes he replied that while they had no fetish about names, the S.L.P. committee was uninstructed and desired to meet the S.D.P. committee on equal ground. Therefore, if the majority report was adopted, his committee would be forced to withdraw from further negotiations. The convention thereupon adopted the minority report by a vote of 1,366 to 770.[14]

The delegates then turned to nomination of candidates for President and Vice President of the United States. Eugene Debs was immediately nominated for President but declined for reasons of health; representatives of the S.L.P. at the convention urged him to accept, but he remained adamant.[15] Two other nominations were likewise declined. James F. Carey then rose and nominated Job Harriman, the S.L.P. presidential candidate. There were cheers and seconds, whereupon William Mailly of New York nominated Max Hayes for Vice President. Thus the only two names placed in nomination by the Social Democratic Party convention were the nominees of the Rochester faction of the Socialist Labor Party, and it seemed that they were about to be accepted by acclamation.[16]

The convention was in an uproar. Members of the National Executive Board made points of order, claiming that the convention could not nominate men who were not even members of the party. Delegates shouted that they would nominate whomever they pleased. In the midst of the turmoil someone shouted for adjournment, and the grateful chairman immediately declared the session adjourned.[17]

F.G.R. Gordon and William Mailly then urged Hillquit to consent to a conference of some of the leaders to attempt to reach a compromise.[18] Hillquit agreed, and Gordon then cornered Berger. Berger at first refused, saying that he feared trickery, but finally

---

[14] *The People* (Williams St.), March 18, 1900.
[15] *Social Democratic Herald*, March 17, 1900.
[16] *The People* (Williams St.), March 18, 1900.
[17] *Ibid.*
[18] Frederic Heath later explained that it was necessary to call the caucus because the S.D.P. was splitting into two factions over the majority and minority reports of the committee on union. (*Social Democratic Herald*, May 12, 1900.)

consented to attend.[19] The ten socialist leaders who gathered in a room in the Occidental Hotel consisted of seven members of the S.D.P., and Hillquit, Harriman, and G. B. Benham of San Francisco for the S.L.P.[20]

Gordon started the discussion by pointing out that the convention seemed intent upon nominating Harriman and Hayes, and that if that were done, the Socialist Labor Party should give some assurance that it would accept "Social Democratic Party" as the future united party name. The three S.L.P. members at once pledged their support for the name if the two Socialist Laborites were nominated.

Berger then said that he had been on his way to a meeting of some of Debs's oldest friends for the purpose of urging him to accept the nomination. He asked whether the pledge to support the name of Social Democracy would stand if he were able to convince Debs to accept the nomination. Hillquit and Harriman renewed their pledges, but Benham said he would go along only if the candidates were Harriman and Hayes. The caucus broke up after agreeing to meet again at 11:30 that night, when Berger would have Debs's decision.[21]

As the delegates were leaving the room they met three of the Socialists who had been in conference with Debs. They announced the good news that Debs had agreed to run. The caucus was somewhat taken aback, for Berger had assured it that he might need two hours to convince Debs to run. The S.L.P. members and some of the Social Democrats demanded to know whether the whole caucus was staged just to obtain pledges for the name Social Democrat. They were assured it was not, and since Debs was now a candidate the 11:30 meeting was canceled.[22] As for the status of the pledges on the party name, it soon developed that there was considerable difference of opinion.

[19] "Affidavit of F. G. R. Gordon, April 2, 1900," *Social Democratic Herald*, April 7, 1900.

[20] "Affidavit of A. S. Edwards, April 2, 1900," *Social Democratic Herald*, April 7, 1900.

[21] "Affidavit of F. G. R. Gordon, April 2, 1900," and "Affidavit of A. S. Edwards, April 2, 1900," *Social Democratic Herald*, April 7, 1900.

[22] Statement of William Butscher in the *Social Democratic Herald*, April 28, 1900; "Affidavit of F. G. R. Gordon, April 2, 1900," and "Affidavit of A. S. Edwards, April 2, 1900," *Social Democratic Herald*, April 7, 1900.

The next morning Debs and Harriman were nominated by acclamation,[23] the convention adjourned, and members of both parties awaited only the formality of ratifying a treaty which everyone claimed to favor.[24]

The Joint Committee on Unity met in New York City on Sunday, March 25, sixteen days after adjournment of the Indianapolis convention. The make-up of the committee indicated that all was not as harmonious as official press releases predicted. For one thing, a majority of the Social Democratic Party delegates to the committee had spoken and voted for the Indianapolis convention majority report which had insisted on the name Social Democratic Party.[25] Perhaps more significant than the make-up of the S.D.P. delegation was the fact that Victor Berger, although an elected delegate, did not attend. Nor did he inform his alternate, Charles R. Martin of Ohio, an outspoken advocate of unity, of his intention to be absent.[26]

After the election of a chairman and vice-chairman, the committee held a five-hour discussion on the future party name. "Social Democracy" was discussed from the viewpoints of history, etymology, and philology. After four hours of this, Frederic Heath, Berger's right-hand man in the Wisconsin movement, announced that he wished to speak openly on the subject, but for the honor of the Socialist Labor delegates, could only speak in executive session. When the room was cleared, Heath, on the basis of the secret caucus held in the Occidental Hotel, charged that the Socialist Labor Party had broken its pledges to support the name Social Democratic. Heath apparently failed to convince the other members of the S.D.P. delegation, and the committee adjourned.[27]

The next morning John C. Chase, for the Social Democrats, proposed that for the sake of unity two names be submitted to the referendums of the two parties. The Socialist Laborites submitted "United Socialist Party," and the Social Democrats naturally proposed "Social Democratic Party." Since the two party conven-

---

[23] *Social Democratic Herald*, March 17, 1900.

[24] *The Workers' Call*, March 24, 1900.

[25] *The People* (Williams St.), March 18, 1900.

[26] Margaret Haile, "The Union Conference," *Social Democratic Herald*, April 7, 1900; "Resolution Adopted by the St. Louis Branches of the Social Democratic Party in Joint Meeting, April 10, 1900," *The Workers' Call*, April 21, 1900.

[27] G. B. Benham in *The People* (Williams St.), April 1, 1900.

tions had provided that all proposals of the treaty of union be ratified by the two parties concurrently, Chase also proposed for the Social Democrats that the following question be submitted to referendum: "In case the party name voted for by you fails to obtain the concurrent majority of both parties, shall the name receiv[ing] the majority of the total vote of both parties be adopted?" The Socialist Laborites accepted the proposal, and Frederic Heath promptly left the conference to return to Milwaukee where he reported to Berger.[28]

Other provisions of the "Treaty of Union'' were agreed upon more quickly. There was to be no official party newspaper, but since the *Social Democratic Herald* had been operating on the basis of a subsidized party press sent free to every dues-paying member, the united party would pay its operating deficits up to sixty dollars a week for six months. All party members were to pay ten cents quarterly in exchange for a subscription to any one newspaper to be selected by them from a list to be furnished by the national executive committee.

Springfield, Massachusetts was chosen as the site of party headquarters as a compromise between New York City and Chicago. A national council consisting of a representative elected from each state and meeting annually was to be the supreme governing body. This council was to nominate a slate of fifteen from which the party membership in turn would elect seven by referendum vote to make up the national executive committee of the party. Until the council was established, a temporary executive committee was to be elected by each party's nomination of four socialists from New York, four from Massachusetts, and two from Connecticut. In the referendum vote on unity each party was to elect five members of the temporary ten-member executive committee.[29]

[28] Margaret Haile, "The Union Conference," *Social Democratic Herald*, April 7, 1900; G. B. Benham in *The People* (Williams St.), April 1, 1900.

[29] The selection of Springfield, Massachusetts, was a bad tactical blunder on the part of the pro-unity forces. Or, perhaps, it was a deliberate attempt to exclude certain S.D.P. leaders from leadership in the united party. In either case, it lessened the chance for a united party. Since the members of the temporary executive committee were to be chosen from the states near the party headquarters so that they could meet with a minimum of expense, the selection of Springfield automatically meant that the executive committee would be chosen largely from New York and Massachusetts. It was inconceivable that Milwaukee and Chicago leaders of the S.D.P., who were at best reluctant to form a united party, would permit

The party platform and constitution were settled by the simple expedient of combining the existing documents of the two parties. Debs and Harriman were to be the united party's nominees for President and Vice President. A sop was thrown to the Midwest by providing that Chicago should elect a committee to run the Presidential campaign. And Eugene Dietzgen was chosen as the united party representative to the coming Paris Congress of the Second International.[30]

The delegates of the Socialist Labor Party concluded that "it was all over but the shouting." "The vote in favor of unity seems a forgone conclusion." [31] On March 31, five days after the conclusion of the committee meeting, while the committee officials were still preparing their report and the referendum ballot, the *Social Democratic Herald* was already listing *The People* and the Chicago *Workers' Call* among the papers supporting the Social Democratic Party. Two days later the "Treaty of Union" was turned into a declaration of war.

On April 2 the National Executive Board of the Social Democratic Party issued a "manifesto" charging the S.L.P. delegates to the committee on union with trickery, treachery, and double-dealing. For the first time it was revealed that a caucus had been held the second night of the Indianapolis convention. At that caucus, claimed the manifesto, Harriman, Hillquit, and Benham had promised to support the name Social Democratic Party if the Presidential ticket consisted of Harriman and Hayes; Hillquit and Harriman had agreed to support that name if the ticket were made up of Debs and Harriman. The manifesto included sworn affidavits by F. G. R. Gordon and A. S. Edwards describing the convention "peace conference" and claiming that Hillquit and Harriman had given their unconditional support to the desired name. Furthermore, the manifesto said that on the floor of the convention the next day, Max Hayes, who had not attended the "peace conference,"

---

themselves to be eliminated from the executive committee. It is significant that Margaret Haile of Massachusetts and Seymour Stedman of Chicago, both of the S.D.P., insisted on Chicago during the discussion and so voted when the decision was made.

[30] Margaret Haile, "The Union Conference," *Social Democratic Herald*, April 7, 1900; G. B. Benham in *The People* (Williams St.), April 1, 1900.

[31] G. B. Benham in *The People* (Williams St.), April 1, 1900; Hillquit, *History of Socialism*, pp. 335–36.

pledged his support and the support of his paper, the Cleveland *Citizen*, to the name Social Democratic Party.

But, continued the manifesto, at the New York conference on unity all the S.L.P. delegates except Hayes broke their pledges and unanimously opposed the name. And Max Hayes did not even attend the conference discussion. The Indianapolis convention had provided that all questions, including that of party name, be accepted by the concurrent majorities of both parties. Yet the ballots being prepared by the joint committee on unity gave voters the opportunity to override this proviso by asking them if they would accept the combined majority vote of the two parties on the question of name.

Therefore, concluded the manifesto, it was the painful duty of the National Executive Board to point out that unity could not be built upon deceit, but only upon "unsullied honor and integrity." "It may be asked why has the national executive taken immediate action and before reading the official report. In reply we say that promptness on our part will alone save disintegration and disastrous disaffection . . . the spirit of revolt is already thundering at our doors." The Board asked all Social Democrats to vote "yes" or "no" on the following question: "Is union between the Social Democratic party and the Socialist Labor party faction desirable?" Ballots were to be in by May 7.[32]

The Board's manifesto aroused a storm of protest within the ranks of the party. Without waiting for answers to the charges made against members of the Socialist Labor Party, Social Democratic branches denounced their Board and its manifesto. They contended that the caucus at which the pledges allegedly were made was not authorized by the convention and had no binding force. They held that the committee on unity was acting democratically when it gave each party the right to vote on whether it

[32] "Manifesto of the National Executive Board of the Social Democratic Party, April 2, 1900," *Social Democratic Herald,* April 7, 1900. The manifesto was signed by four of the five-man N.E.B.—Jesse Cox, Victor L. Berger, Frederic Heath, and Seymour Stedman. The fifth member, Eugene Debs, the manifesto stated, while agreeing with that document on the evidence presented, withheld his signature until he received the majority report of the joint committee on unity. (The minority report, which was really expressed only in the manifesto, was apparently that of Berger, who did not attend the committee meetings, Heath, who walked out early in the meeting, Haile, who did not sign the manifesto since she was not a member of the N.E.B., and Stedman.)

was willing to be bound by a straight instead of a concurrent majority.

The Board issued its manifesto without having seen the report of the committee on union, and without even hearing from a majority of the S.D.P. delegates to that committee. Therefore, charged the pro-unity Social Democrats, the Board had betrayed its trust. "The N.E.B. is manifestly opposed to union upon any terms except such as may redound to the glory of the four signers of the manifesto; . . . the Board seems afraid to allow the membership to vote on the questions submitted by the Joint Committee." Berger, continued the protests, did not even attend the committee meetings. The Board is in contempt of the national convention. The Board "has made the official organ of the party a personal circular letter and has disseminated at the expense of the party the most infamous and treasonable utterances against it and its candidates, against its welfare and its aspirations." The Board must be recalled. The need for union transcends individuals. All party branches and members are urged to vote "yes" on the Board's referendum.[33]

The replies to the manifesto by the S.L.P. representatives at the Indianapolis convention, which appear irrefutable, were accepted by every attending member of the joint committee on unity except Heath. Harriman and Hillquit had agreed to support the name Social Democratic Party only in exchange for the nomination of Harriman and Hayes, or to enable Berger to persuade Debs to accept the nomination. This is borne out not only by the statements of Harriman, Hillquit, and Benham, but also by the affidavits of Gordon and Edwards upon which the Board manifesto was based, and by the testimony of William Butscher of the Brooklyn S.D.P., who also participated in the secret caucus. Since the ticket was not Harriman and Hayes, and since Berger had nothing to do with the decision of Debs to run, the pledges were void.[34]

---

[33] "Resolutions Adopted by the St. Louis Branches of the Social Democratic Party in Joint Meeting, April 10, 1900," *The Workers' Call,* April 21, 1900; circular letter from Massachusetts Branch 16, S.D.P. Haverhill, to the members of the S.D.P. and the S.L.P., April 11, 1900, *The Workers' Call,* April 21, 1900; "Resolution of Branch 2, S.D.P., Seattle, Washington, April 12, 1900," *The Workers' Call,* April 21, 1900; editorial from *Public Ownership* (Erie, Pa.), reprinted in *The Workers' Call,* April 21, 1900.

[34] Circular letter from Morris Hillquit and Job Harriman to the Socialist press,

Everyone agreed that Benham had refused to pledge support for "Social Democratic" unless the ticket were Harriman and Hayes. Max Hayes had promised to support the name unconditionally. He had done so in public meetings and in the Cleveland *Citizen,* and said he would continue to do so. He had not participated in the discussions on party name at the meetings in New York because on both occasions he had been asked by local Socialists to address the Central Federated Union and the striking cigarmakers.[35] As for the proposed alternative method of voting on two party names in the referendum, that solution had been advanced by the Social Democrats, not by the Socialist Laborites, at the New York meeting.[36]

The evidence seems to indicate that from the time unity first began to be discussed in the fall of 1899, a majority of the National Executive Board of the S.D.P. conducted itself in a manner designed to frustrate the organic union of the two parties. Jesse Cox, the chairman of the Board, made no secret in top party circles of his opposition to union.[37] Victor Berger's German-language Milwaukee newspaper, *Wahrheit,* ran articles bitterly attacking union almost up to the convening of the Indianapolis convention.[38] Frederic Heath of Milwaukee was Berger's alter ego. Stedman at best was lukewarm for union. Debs played little part in determining Board policy.[39] William Butscher of the S.D.P. correctly stated the situation when in answer to the manifesto he charged that "some of the N.E. Board were strongly opposed to a unification of the S.L.P. and S.D.P., and were it not for the overwhelming majority and sentiment of the delegates at the convention who came in-

*Social Democratic Herald,* April 21, 1900; letter from G. B. Benham to *The Workers' Call,* April 21, 1900; affidavits of Edwards and Gordon, in the *Social Democratic Herald,* April 7, 1900; letter from William Butscher to the *Social Democratic Herald,* April 28, 1900.

[35] Letter from Max Hayes to *The Workers' Call,* April 14, 1900.

[36] Margaret Haile, "The Union Conference," *Social Democratic Herald,* April 7, 1900.

[37] Letter from Jesse Cox to the National Board of the Social Democratic Party, April 11, 1900, *Social Democratic Herald,* April 21, 1900.

[38] Letter from E. Val Putnam (Secretary, City Central Committee, St. Louis S.D.P.) to the *Social Democratic Herald,* April 21, 1900.

[39] Social Democratic Party, "Report of the Secretary of N.E.B. of S.D.P., June, 1898–January, 1900," typescript, John Crerar Library, Chicago. Board decisions were frequently made without consulting Debs. Debs's function was to use his personal popularity to gain support for Board decisions and actions.

structed to work for union, negotiations to that effect would have been prevented at that time." [40]

Perhaps the basis of some of the party leaders' opposition to unity was correctly analyzed by the executive committee of the Washington state S.D.P. when it accused them of favoring a policy designed to attract "all the 'Reformers' . . . [who] are 'Socialistically inclined.' With the magic name of Debs at the head of the ticket, that policy may win votes, but they will not be Socialist votes." [41] Berger, at any rate, in an editorial against union, attacked the S.L.P. for its faith in Marxism. [42]

Berger's attacks in *Wahrheit* on those who favored union (Harriman was "a Tammany politician of the seventeenth degree"; Hillquit was "a thorough class conscious lawyer of New York," a "Polish apple Jew," a "Moses Hilkowitz from Warsaw," a "rabbinical candidate"; and James F. Carey, of Berger's own party, was a "ward politician" [43]) probably had little effect other than to make clear to the tightly organized party of Wisconsin that they were to vote against unity. But Debs's letter to the *Herald* carried great weight. He opposed immediate union with a party "trained in the bitter school of bigotry and intolerance." But he favored eventual union, and believed its "consummation will not be deferred long after the national election." Debs suggested that formal union now would destroy the possibility of real unity. In the meantime, let both parties present a united front in the coming Presidential campaign. [44]

The vote on the referendum sent out by the Board of the S.D.P. was announced on May 12. Almost half of the claimed membership had participated. The final vote stood: for union, 939; against union, 1,213. [45] Most of the states with "heavy" Socialist member-

[40] Letter from William Butscher to the *Social Democratic Herald*, April 28, 1900.

[41] "Statement of the Executive Committee of the Social Democratic Party of Washington, June 12, 1900," *The Socialist*, Oct. 23, 1909.

[42] Berger in the *Social Democratic Herald*, April 28, 1900. Debs, however, insisted that the S.D.P. was "not a reform party, but a revolutionary party. . . . It refuses to be flattered, bribed, stampeded or otherwise deflected from the straight course mapped out for it by Marx and Engels, its founders." (Eugene V. Debs in the New York *Journal*, reprinted in the *Social Democratic Herald*, June 9, 1900.)

[43] Quoted in circular letter from Hillquit and Harriman, *Social Democratic Herald*, April 21, 1900.

[44] Letter from Debs to the *Social Democratic Herald*, April 21, 1900.

[45] *Social Democratic Herald*, May 12, 1900.

ship split fairly evenly, making Berger's Wisconsin vote of 366 to 8 against union decisive.[46]

During the month of April, while the Board of the S.D.P. was polling its membership on whether to go ahead with the referendum on the treaty of union, the secretaries of the Joint Committee on Union sent out their ballots to the two national headquarters.[47] The Board of the S.D.P. refused to send the "treaty" ballots to its locals. Consequently, John Chase, of the S.D.P., as chairman of the Joint Committee, called that committee to reconvene in New York and asked Debs to attend.[48]

With the exception of Benham and Heath, but including Debs, all members of the committee assembled on May 20. Seymour Stedman immediately announced that as a result of the vote recently taken by the S.D.P. the joint committee no longer had a legal existence and that the meeting was only an "informal conference of former members of the committee." Berger and Haile agreed with this analysis. The other five Social Democrats present, however, insisted that the committee was still in legal existence. Berger, Haile, Stedman, and Debs then offered to discuss "political union" on candidates, but not organic union. Cornered by Hillquit, Stedman was forced to admit that if the committee was illegal, it could not discuss candidates with any authority.

Hillquit then launched a blistering attack on the S.D.P. dissenters. They had rejected unity on the ground that Socialist Laborites were unfit for comradeship. Yet now that they realized they did not have sufficient strength to get on the ballot in such key states as New York, Pennsylvania, Ohio, and California, they were willing to let the S.L.P. wage its campaign for them. This, said Hillquit, "we must respectfully decline."

A motion was made that the committee was a committee on unity and had authority to discuss nothing else. On a roll call vote the motion was carried. Berger, Haile, and Stedman voted no, and

[46] *Ibid.*, May 19, 1900. The accuracy of the vote is subject to some question. The Washington S.D.P., for example, which was strongly for immediate organic union, has a recorded vote of nine against and zero for union. The St. Louis branches had not only combined to condemn the Board's manifesto, but took steps to organize the entire state, yet the vote from Missouri is reported as 18 for and 16 against.

[47] *The People* (Williams St.), May 20, 1900.

[48] Margaret Haile in the *Social Democratic Herald*, June 2, 1900; *The People* (Williams St.), May 27, 1900.

promptly withdrew. The committee then provided for a statement on the unity situation and ordered ballots for the unity referendum sent to the locals of their respective parties.[49] The problem of the opposition of the National Executive Board of the S.D.P. was thus solved by by-passing it. Even while the vote was being taken in June, and tabulated in July, Socialist Laborite and Social Democratic branches in sixteen states held joint conventions, declared themselves united, and nominated slates for the fall elections.[50]

On July 9, the S.L.P. vote was announced. About 2,500 members of the "Rochester" faction of the Socialist Labor Party participated, and voted on an average of 2,450 to 100 for all the unity proposals.[51] About 1,100 members of the Social Democratic Party participated, and voted an average of 1,050 to 50 for the various unity proposals.[52]

The comedy of what was to be the party's name had a fitting conclusion. The Social Democrats voted 993 to 81 for retention of their old name. The Socialist Laborites voted 2,227 to 326 for "Social Democratic Party." [53] So much for nine months of alleged Socialist Labor "plots" to destroy the nature of the Social Democratic Party by sending its good name into oblivion.

It could not be said that the picture of socialist party organization was now clearer than it had been before the referendum. There were no longer two Socialist Labor parties, but only one, that led by Daniel De Leon. But instead of one Social Democratic Party there were now two, one with headquarters in Chicago, and the "united" one with headquarters in Springfield, Massachusetts.

On July 13, the National Executive Committee of the "Rochester" faction of the S.L.P. held its last meeting in New York City and turned over its books and powers to the "united" Social Demo-

49 Margaret Haile in the *Social Democratic Herald,* June 2, 1900; *The People* (Williams St.), May 27, 1900; *The Workers' Call,* June 2, 1900; New York *Daily Tribune,* May 21, 1900.

50 *The Workers' Call,* June 6, 23, July 14, 21, Aug. 4, 1900. The states were New York, Minnesota, Missouri, Illinois, Maryland, Ohio, Washington, Pennsylvania, Texas, Kentucky, Vermont, Connecticut, Massachusetts, Michigan, Oklahoma, and California.

51 "Report of Secretaries of Unity Conference to N.E.C., S.L.P., July 9, 1900," *The People* (Williams St.), July 15, 1900.

52 *The People* (Williams St.), July 22, 1900. The S.D.P. defeated one proposal—it refused to subsidize the *Social Democratic Herald.*

53 *The People* (Williams St.), July 15, 22, 1900.

cratic Party.[54] The next day the newly elected provisional executive committee held its first meeting in Springfield.[55] William Butscher of the old Brooklyn S.D.P. was elected national secretary at a salary of twenty dollars a week. Plans were laid for making the paper party organization a reality, and for hiring Socialists for agitation and organization tours. Debs and Harriman were formally notified of their nominations and a call was issued for contributions to a national campaign fund.[56] Debs accepted the nomination and the campaign was launched.[57]

William Jennings Bryan's support of the treaty with Spain had enabled him to make America's newborn imperialism an issue of the 1900 campaign. But to the Social Democrats of both parties, imperialism was no issue at all. They held it was a bone of contention between large and small capitalists, but of no concern to the working class. Imperialism is simply the capitalist drive for more markets, the Socialists explained. Under the wage system the product of labor is divided into two nearly equal parts—half to the workers in the form of wages, and half to the capitalists in the form of profits. Since workers could only buy back half of what they produced, and since capitalists could not consume all of the other half, the great trusts were forced to seek markets abroad.[58] Debs quoted Senator Chauncey Depew to the effect that the United States already had 5 percent of the markets of the Orient and that she needed 50 percent. Commented Debs: "The getting of the other 45 percent constitutes the white man's burden at the present time." [59]

In the present campaign, continued the Socialist analysis, the three political parties stand for the three economic classes of American society: the Republican Party represents the large capitalist

[54] *The Workers' Call*, July 28, 1900.

[55] The members of the executive committee were William Lonergan and William E. White of Connecticut; John C. Chase, S. M. Jones, Charles Fenner, and Morris Kaplan of Massachusetts, and Morris Hillquit, Henry Slobodin, William Butscher, and I. Phillips of New York. When Butscher was elected national secretary, Leonard D. Abbott of New York was selected to take his place on the committee.

[56] *The Workers' Call*, July 28, 1900.

[57] Letter from Eugene V. Debs to William Butscher, July 31, 1900, *The Workers' Call*, August 11, 1900.

[58] Charles H. Vail in the *Social Democratic Herald*, Aug. 18, 1900.

[59] Campaign speech by Eugene V. Debs, Central Union Hall, Chicago, September 29, 1900, *The Workers' Call*, Oct. 6, 1900.

class, the Democratic Party represents the middle class of small capitalists, and the Social Democratic Party represents the proletariat or wage-working class.[60] Both the Republican and Democratic parties stood for preservation of capitalism. The Democratic Party opposed imperialism for two reasons: small capitalists had no surplus capital to invest abroad, and imperialism strengthened the trusts which were crushing the small capitalists.

Social Democrats said that the working class had no cause to help preserve the dying middle class and therefore had no reason to fight imperialism. "The Socialist is not an expansionist like the republican nor an anti-expansionist like the democrat—he merely points out the facts." [61] The real issue of the campaign was not imperialism, it was socialism versus capitalism. The only concern of the working class was to institute the collective ownership of the means of production, and only through control of the government by Social Democrats could the goal of the working class be attained.[62]

Of course, the Social Democrats realized that neither the working class nor the capitalist classes, whose ultimate interests also lay with socialism,[63] as yet understood that their future was tied up with the co-operative commonwealth. The campaign, therefore, was conducted as a sort of socialist Chautauquan circuit, designed to inform Americans on the facts of twentieth century economic and political life. The success of this educational campaign was to be measured by the vote polled by Socialist candidates in the November elections.

The two media of socialist education were literature and public speaking. Of primary importance, at least in the eyes of their editors, were the twenty-odd English and foreign-language socialist weekly newspapers.[64] But during the campaign, special pamphlets equaled, if they did not replace, the socialist press in importance as a propaganda medium. The "united" S.D.P. distributed 350,000

---

60 *Ibid.;* Charles H. Vail in the *Social Democratic Herald,* Aug. 18, 1900.

61 Charles H. Vail in the *Social Democratic Herald,* Aug. 18, 1900.

62 Debs, Chicago campaign speech, Sept. 29, 1900.

63 Charles H. Vail in the *Social Democratic Herald,* Aug. 18, 1900.

64 "Report of the N.E.C. of the ["united"] S.D.P. to the Delegates in Convention Assembled at Indianapolis, Ind., July 29, 1901," in "Proceedings of Socialist Unity Convention, 1901," typescript in Harper Library, University of Chicago, pp. 86–87.

leaflets through its local organizations,[65] and the locals of the S.D.P. with Chicago headquarters disposed of 105,000 foreign-language and over a million English-language leaflets.[66] That the campaign was not a mere "get out the socialist vote" drive is shown by the titles of some of these pamphlets: "An Open Letter to the Average American Workingman"; "Machine Production, Where the Profits Go"; and "Industrial Crises—Cause and Cure." In addition, the two parties distributed between them about 17,000 lithographs and 21,000 campaign buttons. Of the two parties, the organization with headquarters in Chicago excelled by far in the quantity of its campaign pamphleteering.[67]

When it came to personal campaigning, however, the "united" Social Democrats came into their own. No less than 16 orators were sent out by the Springfield headquarters to educate the workers in "the principles of Revolutionary, Scientific Socialism." No section of the country was neglected by these tireless agitators.[68] When to these national speakers are added the hundreds of Socialists throughout the country who spoke nightly at neighborhood street-corners, the tours of Debs (whose speaking load during campaigns was staggering) and Harriman (whose health had not yet collapsed), the number of persons reached through direct appeal becomes impressive indeed.[69]

Downtown Chicago, for example, had dozens of street meetings every Sunday night.[70] The weekend activities of one small group of Chicago campaigners are typical: They stationed themselves at the corner of 111th Street and Michigan Avenue on Saturday night and waited until the Salvation Army "got thro their devotions." Then, taking advantage of the crowds already gathered, "we got a barrel and from the head of that we dispensed the gospel of so-

[65] *Ibid.*

[66] "Report of the National Campaign Committee of the S.D.P. [Chicago]," *Social Democratic Herald*, Dec. 1, 1900.

[67] *Ibid.;* "Report of the N.E.C. of the ["united"] S.D.P. to the Delegates in Convention Assembled at Indianapolis, Ind., July 29, 1901," in "Proceedings of Socialist Unity Convention, 1901," typescript in Harper Library, University of Chicago.

[68] "Report of the N.E.C. of the ["united"] S.D.P. to the Delegates in Convention Assembled at Indianapolis, Ind., July 29, 1901," in "Proceedings of Socialist Unity Convention, 1901," typescript in Harper Library, University of Chicago.

[69] *The People* (Williams St.), Oct. 28, 1900.

[70] *The Workers' Call*, Sept. 15, 1900.

cialism for two hours amid intermittent yells of Bryan-McKinley from youthful partisans of the old parties." The next day, Sunday, they stationed themselves in the middle of a parade of Bohemians at 50th and Lincoln and spoke "from a wagon on the prairie on the relationship of the Rep., Dem., and Socialist parties to the humble foreigner who had selected this country from all the nations of the earth as his home." By eight o'clock they had hurried down to Chicago and Halsted to speak on the evolution of the United States from colonial days when Americans had objected to King George helping himself to the products of their labor, down to the present when King George had been replaced by Rockefeller. When a speaker was dragged from the platform by the police, another stepped into his place.[71]

On July 22, the Socialists of Chicago took over the corner of State and Quincy and held forth from 3 P.M. to 11 P.M. By eight o'clock, when Job Harriman spoke, 10,000 Chicagoans had gathered to hear "his masterly analysis of the profit system." [72] When Debs and Harriman appeared in New York City on October 30, they packed Cooper Union's 9,000 seats, filled the aisles, and held an overflow meeting attended by an additional 500.[73]

Campaign work among the unions apparently was not very vigorous. The "united" S.D.P. reported that it had sent one organizer to agitate for socialism in the Pennsylvania coal fields when a strike broke out there in the midst of the campaign.[74] And Edward Boyce, president of the Western Federation of Miners, came out for Debs and Harriman in the *Miners' Magazine*. Boyce admitted that he had his doubts whether the Republic could be preserved by political methods alone. But he agreed that it was worth a try, especially since Debs and Harriman had shown by their support of the W.F. of M. in the past that they stood for principles designed to "free the people from the grasp of the profitmongers." [75] But aside

[71] Letter from Thomas J. Morgan to Henry D. Lloyd, Oct. 29, 1900, Henry D. Lloyd Papers.

[72] *The Workers' Call,* July 28, 1900.

[73] New York *Times,* Oct. 21, 1900; *Social Democratic Herald,* Nov. 10, 1901.

[74] "Report of N.E.C. of the ["united"] S.D.P. to the Delegates in Convention Assembled at Indianapolis, Ind., July 29, 1901," in "Proceedings of Socialist Unity Convention," typescript in Harper Library, University of Chicago.

[75] Edward Boyce in the *Miners' Magazine,* Oct., 1900, reprinted in *The People* (Williams St.), Oct. 21, 1900.

from these two instances, the record of the 1900 campaign is conspicuous for its silence on trade union work and support.

Relations between the two Social Democratic parties during the early stage of the campaign were a bit strained. Debs refused to confer directly with the national office's campaign committee at Springfield, and suggested negotiations between the two parties.[76] Not until September did the *Social Democratic Herald* even mention the fact that Job Harriman was the Vice Presidential candidate for the party. Finally, on September 1 the *Herald* announced the "National Ticket" of Debs and Harriman, and suggested the use of the following inspired cheer:

> Debs and Harriman, rah, rah, rah!
> Debs and Harriman, rah, rah, rah!
> Hoo-rah! Hoo-rah!
> Socialists candidates,
> Rah, rah, rah!

Despite the reluctance of top-level Socialist leaders to cooperate, local Socialists showed considerable ability to deal with the facts of American political life. By September, the Social Democratic parties had managed to get themselves on the ballot in 25 states,[77] and by November voters had the opportunity of casting their ballots for Socialist candidates in at least 30 states.[78] As the campaign reached its climax, the *Herald* was seeing "Enthusiasm Paralleling Abolitionist Days," with the Socialist vote "SURGING ONWARD, UPWARD, FORWARD!!"[79]

When the vote was finally tabulated, it showed Debs and Harriman polling 96,918 votes, and the Socialist Labor Party's candidates, 33,450 votes.[80] To show what great strides socialism had made since the formation of the S.D.P., the Social Democrats com-

[76] Letter (unsigned) from Thomas J. Morgan to Eugene V. Debs and letter from Eugene V. Debs to Thomas J. Morgan, Aug. 14, 1900, Thomas J. Morgan Collection.

[77] Max S. Hayes, "The World of Labor," *International Socialist Review*, I (Sept. 1, 1900), 189.

[78] *The People* (Williams St.), Oct. 28, 1900.

[79] *Social Democratic Herald*, Nov. 3, 1900.

[80] *The People* (Williams St.), Jan. 20, 1901. The largest S.D.P. votes were in New York, 12,869; Massachusetts, 9,761; Illinois, 9,687; California, 7,572; Wisconsin, 7,095; and Missouri, 6,182. New Jersey, Ohio, and Pennsylvania had over four thousand votes each, and Minnesota had over three thousand. (*The People* [Williams St.], Dec. 30, 1900.)

pared their 1900 vote with the 36,000 votes polled by the Socialist Laborites in 1896, conveniently ignoring the 82,000 votes cast for the S.L.P. in 1898.[81] But even compared to the 1898 vote, the more than 50 percent gain in total socialist vote in two years was impressive.

It is impossible to estimate exactly how many votes the Social Democrats expected to poll. They made few election predictions. Debs summed up the general feeling: "The figures are smaller than most of us expected, but we are satisfied . . . the showing, if not inspiring, has at least nothing discouraging in it." [82] This lack of enthusiasm over a vote which had quadrupled in four years can probably be explained only in terms of the conviction running through all Social Democratic literature since the formation of the Social Democracy of America in 1897 that the co-operative commonwealth was only four to eight years away. Seen in that light, a total vote of 130,000 was indeed "not inspiring."

Even before the final returns were in, the S.D.P. with headquarters in Chicago blamed the unsatisfactory vote on its enforced alliance with a clique which had stolen its name and which showed "only a surface earnestness for a large vote . . . in certain quarters." [83] But the Chicago group's attacks on the "united" party were no longer effective. The united local efforts necessitated by the campaign increased the demands for socialist unity. And since it was the Springfield headquarters which stood for unity, the strength of that party grew rapidly.

A permanent national organizer, the Reverend Charles H. Vail, was hired by the Springfield office at $2,000 a year. George D. Herron made an extended "agitational tour" of the Northeastern states.[84] In the spring of 1901, "open air circuits" were organized in fifty Northeastern cities and towns which scheduled regular open air meetings for a series of speakers sent out by the Springfield headquarters.[85] Of the score of socialist weekly papers, only the *Herald* and Berger's *Wahrheit* continued to support the Chicago

81 *The People* (Williams St.), Dec. 30, 1900.
82 Letter from Eugene V. Debs to the *Social Democratic Herald,* Dec. 1, 1900.
83 *Social Democratic Herald,* Nov. 10, 1900.
84 "Report of the N.E.C. of the ["united"] S.D.P. to the Delegates in Convention Assembled at Indianapolis, Ind., July 29, 1901," in "Proceedings of Socialist Unity Convention," typescript in Harper Library, University of Chicago.
85 *Ibid.*

headquarters.[86] During the last five months of 1900 the "united" party issued charters to 97 locals with 1,046 members. In the first six months of 1901 it issued 40 additional local charters for 445 members, some of whom were new recruits, but many of whom had formerly owed allegiance to the Chicago group.[87]

For the first few months after the "united" party set up its national office in Springfield, the Social Democratic Party with headquarters in Chicago whistled to keep up its courage. For the benefit of its own dwindling membership it made a few transparent calculations. Since, explained the *Herald*, only 2,500 Socialist Laborites and 1,100 Social Democrats had voted for union, that meant that the "united" party only had 3,600 members. The Chicago national office, boasted the *Herald*, had 6,000 members on its books even after deleting the 1,100 who had voted for unity.[88] But it took no mathematical skill to notice that if one applied the *Herald's* method of computing the "united" party's strength to the Chicago headquarter's party, that party had only 1,213 members—the total number voting against union.[89]

During the 1900 election campaign the Chicago headquarters was forced to issue a stream of press releases explaining that despite the fact that the two parties had the same name, candidates, and platform, they were separate parties, with Chicago the only true headquarters.[90] In September, even before the campaign was concluded, the "united" Social Democratic Party's delegates to the International Socialist Congress in Paris were confidently predicting the speedy completion of union.[91] In fact, "united" S.D.P. leaders generally were convinced that they had backed the Chicago headquarters faction into an untenable position.[92]

[86] "Report of the Delegates of the ["united"] S.D.P. to the International Socialist Congress at Paris, September, 1900," *The Workers' Call*, Sept. 23, 1900.

[87] "Report of the N.E.C. of the ["united"] S.D.P. to the Delegates in Convention Assembled at Indianapolis, Ind., July 29, 1901," in "Proceedings of Socialist Unity Convention," typescript in Harper Library, University of Chicago.

[88] *Social Democratic Herald*, Aug. 4, 1900.

[89] In view of the number of Chicago-led Social Democrats represented at the Socialist Unity Convention held in July, 1901, this method of calculation would not have been too inaccurate for 1901.

[90] *Social Democratic Herald*, July–Aug., 1900.

[91] "Report of the Delegates of the ["united"] S.D.P. to the International Socialist Congress at Paris, September, 1900," *The Workers' Call*, Sept. 23, 1900.

[92] Letter from Thomas J. Morgan to Henry D. Lloyd, Oct. 25, 1900, Henry D. Lloyd Papers.

The final "combination" which was to lead to the checkmating of
the Chicago National Executive Board opened with a mass meeting
held in Boston by both Social Democratic parties one week after
the November election. The rally demanded an immediate call for a
national convention to unite all socialist groups in the United
States.[93] This was followed six days later by an all-day rally in
Chicago called by the joint party campaign committee which had
managed the Chicago campaign. Almost six hundred socialists
turned out to demonstrate for union.[94]

The Chicago rally cut into the heart of the very groups Berger
and Stedman had counted on to build their party. Taking part in
it were the socialist "independents"—the Christian Socialist
League, the Federation of Social Justice, and the Social Crusade.
After spending twelve hours listening to speeches by George D.
Herron and the Reverends Strickland, Wise, and Stitt Wilson, the
meeting unanimously passed resolutions in favor of union and for
the calling of a city convention to nominate a slate for the spring
mayoralty election.[95]

Within a week the Chicago Board attempted to counter this move
by holding a closed meeting of Chicago Social Democrats opposed
to union. The meeting issued a call for a party convention to be
held at the Chicago headquarters on January 15 to lay plans for
"a vigorous campaign of agitation, education, and organization."
To show it had no intention of capitulating to unity demands, the
Board planned to run its own slate in the Chicago spring elections.[96]

The Springfield Committee replied by publishing a blistering
letter to the Chicago Board accusing it of plotting to frustrate the
declared wishes of its own party membership.[97] Resolutions from

[93] *The Workers' Call,* Nov. 24, 1900.

[94] *Ibid.*

[95] *Ibid.;* letter from Thomas J. Morgan to Henry D. Lloyd, Dec. 3, 1900, Henry D.
Lloyd Papers.

[96] Letter from Thomas J. Morgan to Henry D. Lloyd, Dec. 3, 1900; "Call for
Special Convention by the N.E.B. of the S.D.P. [Chicago]," *Social Democratic
Herald,* Dec. 1, 1900. When the vote for mayor of Chicago was counted in April,
1901, the united Socialist ticket, running under the name "Socialist Party," polled
5,384 votes, as against 2,043 for the Chicago Board's candidate, and 649 for the Socialist Laborites (*The Workers' Call,* April 20, 1901).

[97] Letter from the N.E.C., ["united"] S.D.P. to the Chicago N.E.B., Theodore
Debs, Secretary, December 13, 1900, *The People* (Williams St.), Dec. 23, 1900.

committees and unity mass meetings continued to pour into both headquarters through December.[98] On December 31 the Springfield Committee issued ballots to its adherents for a vote on whether to call a unity convention of all socialists.[99]

The Chicago Board reported to its convention on January 15, 1901, with its defenses crumbling. The Springfield Committee was about to appeal over the heads of the Chicago Board, and their unity convention was sure to cut away a good part of the Board's support. The *Social Democratic Herald* was in heavy financial difficulties—two and a half months later it ceased publication without notice.[100] The 89 delegates from 19 states who were attending the convention represented only 1,400 members, compared to the 2,136 members represented at the Indianapolis convention only nine months before.[101] The Board put the best possible face on an impossible situation. A communication from the Springfield Committee requesting a unity convention was read to the delegates.[102] The Board reported to the convention that it had always stood for honorable union, even with the "harassers" and "obstructors" of the Springfield faction.[103] Eugene Debs moved that the membership be polled on the desirability of calling a unity convention. The motion was carried, 1,400 to 4, and the convention adjourned.[104]

The membership of both parties voted overwhelmingly for holding the convention.[105] After three months of negotiations, the two

[98] Resolutions received from: Local Chicago; Iowa State Committee; Connecticut State Committee; Seattle, Tacoma, Buckley and Benton, Washington; Erie, Pennsylvania; Nashville, Tennessee; Tiffin and Dayton, Ohio; Saginaw, Michigan; Ticonderoga, New York; Bridgeport, Connecticut; Haverhill, Massachusetts; Bowling Green, Kentucky; State Committee of Ohio; and State Committee of California (Minutes of National Executive Committee, ["united"] S.D.P., Dec. 29, 1900, *The People* [Williams St.], Jan. 6, 1901).

[99] "Report of the N.E.C. of the ["united"] S.D.P. to the Delegates in Convention Assembled at Indianapolis, Ind., July 29, 1900," in "Proceedings of Socialist Unity Convention," typescript in Harper Library, University of Chicago.

[100] The last issue was dated March 30, 1901.

[101] *The People* (Williams St.), Jan. 27, 1901.

[102] *Ibid.*

[103] "Report of the [Chicago] National Executive Board of the S.D.P. to the Special Convention, January 15, 1901," *Social Democratic Herald,* Jan. 26, 1901.

[104] *The People* (Williams St.), Jan. 27, 1901.

[105] The Springfield-led party voted roughly twenty-seven hundred to one hundred, and the Chicago-led party sixteen hundred to one hundred in the affirmative. ("Minutes of the Provisional N.E.C. of the ["united"] S.D.P., March 9, 1901," *The People* [Williams St.], March 17, 1901; *Social Democratic Herald,* March 23, 1901.)

committees finally agreed to hold the convention at Indianapolis on July 29, a date early enough to enable them to enter the fall elections as a united party.[106]

Representation at the convention was on the basis worked out by the Chicago headquarters S.D.P. for its Indianapolis convention in 1900. Any member of any socialist organization could attend the convention, and cast a vote for himself and one vote for every socialist signature he had appended to his credential.[107] The Springfield-led party was represented by 70 delegates from 15 states and one territory with 4,798 votes; the Chicago Board by 47 delegates from 12 states with 1,396 votes; and three independent socialist state organizations, Iowa, Kentucky, and Texas, by eight delegates with 352 votes—a total of 125 delegates representing 6,546 socialists.[108] The claim was made by the convention that it represented 12,000 active socialists,[109] but Hillquit later admitted that this figure was "born somewhat more of our enthusiasm than of actual fact." [110]

There was considerable contrast between this convention and the conventions of the Socialist Labor Party in the 1890s in the age and place of birth of the delegates. Delegates past middle age were the exception, and most of the delegates were in their twenties and thirties. Even more striking was the claim that at least four fifths of the delegates were American-born.[111] The days of organizing a special English-speaking branch of the socialist movement in America were over.

The debate on a name for the united party was refreshingly reasonable. Berger argued for "Social Democratic" as a matter of principle: it "explained clearly what the party stood for—so-

[106] Letter from Theodore Debs to William Butscher, March 28, 1901, *The Worker* (New York), May 5, 1901; letter from William Butscher to Theodore Debs, April 18, 1901, *The Worker*, May 5, 1901; letter from William Butscher to Theodore Debs, May 15, 1901, *The Worker*, May 21, 1901; letter from Theodore Debs to William Butscher, May 17, 1901, *The Worker*, May 21, 1901; *The Worker*, June 2, 1901.

[107] "Proceedings of Socialist Unity Convention, 1901," typescript in Harper Library, University of Chicago, pp. 5–6.

[108] *Ibid.*, p. 28.

[109] *Ibid.*

[110] Socialist Party, *Proceedings of the National Convention, 1912*, p. 4.

[111] *The Worker*, Aug. 11, 1901; Hillquit, *History of Socialism*, p. 339.

cialism economically and democracy politically." [112] And Hillquit
was willing to accept that name since another change would com-
pound confusion.[113] But most of the delegates were convinced when
Gustave Hoehn and others pointed out that state legislators were
already striking at the Social Democratic parties by passing laws
forbidding third parties "the right to use all or part of the name
of any of the existing parties." Therefore, "Democratic" would
have to be eliminated.[114] By a vote of 79 to 19 the question was
settled once and for all in favor of "Socialist Party." [115]

St. Louis, Missouri, was chosen for party headquarters when
all delegates opposed to Chicago—"they [socialists] are continually at war in Chicago"—united to defeat that city's adherents
3,517 to 3,096.[116] The constitution was modeled on that of the
"united" party. A National Committee comprised of one member
elected from each state was to meet annually and supervise the
work of the national secretary, represent the party in national
and international affairs, call party conventions, and submit referendums to the membership. The National Committee was to
select a "Local Quorum" of five from those of its members who
lived in the region of party headquarters. The Local Quorum was
to assist the national secretary.[117] Both the national secretary and
the quorum were subject to removal by the National Committee.
But all actions of the National Committee were subject to referendum by the party membership. Each state committee was to pay
five cents a month into the national treasury for each member in
good standing.[118]

One result of the two years of bitter wrangling which preceded
the formation of the Socialist Party was the high degree of autonomy won by each state organization. The Chicago Board and
the Wisconsin delegates led the fight for a minimum of national
party control, but all local leaders seemed anxious to have a mini-

[112] "Proceedings of Socialist Unity Convention, 1901," typescript in Harper Library, University of Chicago, pp. 435–36.
[113] *Ibid.,* pp. 446–47.          [114] *Ibid.,* p. 441.          [115] *Ibid.,* p. 448.
[116] *Ibid.,* pp. 581–91.
[117] Perhaps the defeat of Chicago as headquarters was aimed at the Wisconsin
and Chicago opponents of union who were thus automatically eliminated from the
Local Quorum.
[118] "Constitution of the Socialist Party," *The Worker,* Aug. 11, 1901.

mum of "outside interference." [119] The constitution, therefore, provided that

the state or territorial organization shall have the sole jurisdiction of the members residing within their respective territories, and the sole control of all matters pertaining to the propaganda, organization, and financial affairs within such state or territory, and the National Executive Committee [National Committee] and sub-committee [Local Quorum] or officers thereof shall have no right to interfere in such matters without the consent of the respective state or territorial organizations.[120]

Leon Greenbaum of St. Louis, who had joined the socialist movement only the year before,[121] and who was unique in that he had not taken an active part in interparty squabbles, was elected national secretary at a salary of $1,000 a year, if he could raise it.[122] The Socialist Party was starting its career with an indebtedness of $1,700.[123]

The unity of the two Social Democratic parties was assured when Berger informed the convention just before adjournment that if it were legally possible, which it was not, he would be willing to dispense with requiring confirmation of the union by a referendum of his party.[124] Two months later the membership of the Chicago headquarters party was informed that union had been ratified without a dissenting vote, and the Socialist Party was launched on its stormy career.[125]

[119] "Proceedings of Socialist Unity Convention, 1901," typescript in Harper Library, University of Chicago, pp. 511–23; *Social Democratic Herald,* Aug. 17, 1901.

[120] Constitution of the Socialist Party, *The Worker,* Aug. 11, 1901.

[121] Letter from Gustave A. Hoehn to *The Worker,* Jan. 24, 1904.

[122] "Proceedings of Socialist Unity Convention, 1901," typescript in Harper Library, University of Chicago, p. 729; Hillquit, *History of Socialism,* p. 338.

[123] "Proceedings of Socialist Unity Convention, 1901," typescript in Harper Library, University of Chicago, pp. 90–93, 97.

[124] *Ibid.,* p. 728.

[125] Letter from the Committee on Arrangements for the Unity Convention to the State and Local Organizations of the Social Democratic Party with Headquarters at Chicago, Illinois, October 23, 1901, *The Missouri Socialist,* Nov. 2, 1901.

# VII

# Socialist Ideology
# 1901-1904

THE NEW SOCIALIST PARTY was united structurally
by a loose party federation. Ideologic␣lly, however, there were few
signs of unity. Almost all party leaders gave lip service to the
philosophy of scientific socialism as expounded by Marx and
Engels. In 1901 even the more conservative party papers reprinted
excerpts from Marxian "classics" and ran articles on various phases
of Marxian economics.[1] But when party leaders attempted to apply
Marxism to twentieth century America, considerable disagreement
appeared among the "scientists."

By the 1904 Socialist convention the party had already divided
into three loose factions—Right, Center, and Left.[2] In personnel,
the Right at first consisted largely of those members of the Social
Democratic Party who had held out against unity, while the Center
and Left were drawn from the Social Democratic Party which had
its national headquarters in Springfield, Massachusetts. Debs, however, belonged to the Left.[3] In the party's first two or three years
of activity, the Center and Left were almost indistinguishable as
far as public pronouncements of doctrine were concerned. Distinction between them during this period is perhaps attributable more
to historical hindsight than to differences recognized by the members themselves. This Center-Left coalition constituted an overwhelming majority of the party membership and leadership, and

---

[1] *Missouri Socialist,* Feb. 2, 1901 to June 29, 1901; *Social Democratic Herald,*
Nov. 24, 1900 to March 31, 1901.

[2] Algernon Lee in *The Worker,* May 15, 1904.

[3] As early as March, 1899, Debs announced that he had tried "step-at-a-time"
reforms and other forms of "opportunism" and that they always ended in the
continuation of "wage-slavery." (New York *Daily Tribune,* March 23, 1899.)

was opposed only by a comparatively small group under the guidance of Victor Berger and the Milwaukee branch of the Socialist
Party. Much of the Center-Left Socialist theory was accepted by
the Right wing in the early years of the party. The important
differences will be discussed after an exposition of the ideology of
the majority coalition.[4]

The Center-Left theory which guided the Socialist Party for
the first four or five years of its existence looked upon socialism
as a phase of the many-sided revolutionary movement produced
by changing economic conditions. Socialism was the natural transformation and development of society to its next political and
economic system. It was a philosophy, a process, and a type of social organization.[5]

The Center-Left explained that the science of socialism was
based on the "economic interpretation of history," or as Marx "unfortunately" called it, the "materialist conception of history."
They considered Marx's name for his theory "unfortunate" because it tended to inject historical materialism into the conflicting ideologies of philosophic materialism and idealism. These
theories, said the American Marxists, had nothing to do with the
important theory of economic determinism.[6] Economic determinism, they held, was the recognition of the fact that man is governed
by his economic needs and interests, and that society was divided
into economic classes based on relationship to the means of production. The ruling class in each social organization determined the
form of government, set the moral standards, and exercised all
forms of social control.[7]

Feudal society, continued the analysis, had given way to capitalism when changing methods of production and commerce had produced a capitalist class unable to advance its interests under feudal
restrictions.[8] Capitalism was an economy in which the means of
production—factories, railroads, mines, land—were owned by
private individuals, the capitalists. The working class—those who

[4] In the following section, Right-wing Socialists are cited along with Center-Left
theorists when both groups are in fundamental agreement.

[5] Simons, *Philosophy of Socialism*, p. 4; *The People* (Williams St.), June 17, 1900.

[6] Ghent, *Mass and Class*, pp. 8–9.

[7] *Ibid.*, p. 40; Simons, *Philosophy of Socialism*, pp. 6–7; Ernest Untermann, "The
Materialist Conception of History," *Appeal to Reason*, Sept. 19, 1903.

[8] Simons, *Philosophy of Socialism*, pp. 8–12.

produced all the goods of society—were forced to share their products with the capitalists because the latter controlled the means of production.[9] The goods used by society were now produced by men working together in mines and factories. However, ownership of those goods, explained the Socialists, was not in the hands of those who produced them, but of those who owned the tools. Production was social, but appropriation was individual. This contradiction within the capitalist system was at the root of all modern society's shortcomings.[10]

The Center-Left Socialists held that

society should be so organized, in its economic foundation and political forms as to promote liberty, equality, and fraternity, to secure to the greatest possible number of people the greatest possible amount of leisure, the greatest possible share of material well-being, and the greatest possible enjoyment of the pleasures of civilization. Our present industrial and political system signally fails in all these things.[11]

Liberty, they charged, was destroyed in the increasing subordination of the workers to the economic domination of the capitalists.[12] Natural inequalities were increased through private ownership and inheritance, and through the inequitable administration of justice. Fraternity could not exist where men were engaged in a never-ending struggle for existence and power.[13] Justice, integrity, and democracy in government were impossible so long as the wealthy few could amass still greater wealth through the systematic corruption of government.[14] Material well-being and leisure could not be attained by the working class under capitalism because wages in a profit economy could never be great enough to enable the purchase of all the goods produced. Therefore, overproduction, depressions, and unemployment were the only fruits of increased production.[15]

[9] The People (Williams St.), Oct. 7, 1900.

[10] Simons, Philosophy of Socialism, pp. 12–15.

[11] The People (Williams St.), Oct. 7, 1900.

[12] Ibid.; Walter Thomas Mills, Struggle for Existence, pp. 20, 207–8.

[13] Socialist Campaign Book of 1900, pp. 119–29; The People (Williams St.), Oct. 7, 1900; Hitchcock, Ethics of Socialism, pp. 2–12.

[14] Ghent, Mass and Class, pp. 229–30; Social Democratic Herald, March 22, 1902; The People (Williams St.), Aug. 26, 1900; Walter Thomas Mills, Struggle for Existence, pp. 512–13, 530–37.

[15] James Oneal, "The Absurdity of Capitalism," The Worker, April 28, 1901.

Since the Socialists held that production under capitalism always outstripped the economic ability to consume, it followed that businesses were forced to fight for the limited market. And since large corporations were more efficient producers and distributors than small businesses, trusts and monopolies were rapidly displacing competitive enterprise. But while great corporations were able to produce more economically, they used their monopoly position to raise prices and cut still further the living standards of the majority of Americans. Furthermore, in their efforts to find greater and greater markets, they engaged in imperialist wars which were of no benefit to the working class.

The Center-Left Socialists had nothing against trusts in themselves. They believed trusts were to be welcomed as a natural development of society's ability to produce. But private ownership of these trusts increased all the exploitation, crime, and corruption inherent in capitalism. The trusts could not and should not be destroyed: their destruction would decrease production. Nor could they be controlled by the government, because the government was controlled by them. Therefore, the only solution to the trust problem and to all the other problems brought by capitalism was confiscation of the trusts by a people's government. Only when the people owned the means of production would the material conditions prerequisite to the attainment of a peaceful, prosperous, and democratic way of life exist in America.[16]

The Socialists insisted that capitalism had already outgrown its usefulness. Soon its giant combines would find all the world markets glutted. Then, with unemployment and starvation marking the death of capitalism, society would have to move on to the next social order—socialism. The task of the Socialist Party was to hasten the end of capitalism and "to make easier the passage to a new and better system." [17]

At the heart of Center-Left theory on the role of the party was

[16] *The Workers' Call*, Oct. 7, 1899; *The People* (Williams St.), June 17, Oct. 7, 14, 1900; "Roosevelt and the Trusts," *The Chicago Socialist*, July 12, 1902; Eugene V. Debs, "Why There Are Trusts," *Social Democratic Herald*, June 13, 1903; Walter Thomas Mills, *Struggle for Existence*, pp. 469-72; *Social Democratic Herald*, Aug. 4, 1900; *Socialist Campaign Book of 1900*, pp. 22-44; Morris Hillquit, "Patriotism and Socialism," *La Vie Socialiste*, reprinted in *The Worker*, Aug. 5, 1905; Simons, *Philosophy of Socialism*, pp. 15-16; Hagerty, *Economic Discontent*, pp. 8-9, 26-31.

[17] *The People* (Williams St.), Oct. 7, 1900; Walter Thomas Mills, *Struggle for Existence*, p. 279.

the concept of the class struggle. In capitalist America, it was explained, there were two classes, capitalist and proletariat. The capitalist class consisted of the owners of the great trusts and monopolies and of the small businessmen who favored a competitive economy. These middle-class small businessmen were organized in the Democratic Party in order to capture the government and use it for the "reactionary" purpose of destroying or controlling the monopolies. The owners of monopolies controlled the Republican Party which, in turn, used the government to foster and protect corporations and to win foreign markets.[18] The proletariat was always engaged in a struggle with its employers for possession of the goods it produced. The moment when individual members of the proletariat realized that their battle for higher wages and better working conditions was part of a general class struggle, they would have become class conscious.[19] Then the class-conscious working class would join the Socialist Party in order to do battle with the political parties of capitalists, large and small.[20]

The American Socialists of the Center-Left coalition agreed with the 1893 International Socialist Congress that the state and its governmental machinery was an instrument valuable to its possessor. At the 1893 Congress Wilhelm Liebknecht had replied to the Dutch socialists' charge of opportunism by saying that "just as tactics in themselves are neither revolutionary nor reactionary, so the state machine is not in itself reactionary. It is nothing but an instrument for exercising power, a sharp and powerful weapon." [21] American Socialists believed that workers must be taught that the United States government, instead of being the government of the people, was being used by the capitalist class to aid in the exploitation of the proletariat. To drive the ruling class from power, it was necessary only to capture the already existing machinery of government and use it "to make the instruments of wealth production the common property of all." [22]

[18] Clarence Meily, "Economic Classes and Politics," *International Socialist Review*, V (July, 1904), 21–28.

[19] Letter from A. M. Simons to Henry D. Lloyd, May 14, 1903, Henry D. Lloyd Papers; Ghent, *Mass and Class*, pp. 56–61; Walter Thomas Mills, *Struggle for Existence*, pp. 269–77.

[20] Eugene V. Debs, "The Inevitable War of the Classes," *Social Democratic Herald*, June 21, 1902.

[21] Quoted in Lenz, *Rise and Fall of the Second International*, pp. 34–35.

[22] William Mahoney, "The Functions of Government," *The Worker*, April 28,

Nor was the task a difficult one, they said. Once the workers, who far outnumbered the capitalists, learned to transfer the economic class struggle to the political field and struck at the ballot box, the battle for socialism would be won. "When ten million American citizens will quietly drop a demand for the means of production and distribution into the ballot box, the capitalist army will have no foe but themselves, and their riot bullets will be as harmless as children's marbles." [23]

At the same time, the Center-Left coalition insisted that the Socialist Party was a revolutionary party, if one understood the true meaning of the word: "revolution" was nothing more than a decisive forward step in evolution. Productive forces were undergoing constant change. With the development of large-scale production, the social organization of society found itself in conflict with its industrial organization. When that social organization had been changed to bring it in line with the new industrial conditions, a revolution would have occurred.

Revolution, to the Center-Left theorists, was nothing more than thorough reform. Changed economic conditions made its occurrence inevitable. But revolution did not necessarily mean violence and bloodshed. When the organized working class won control of the government through an election victory, the socialist revolution would have established the co-operative commonwealth. Socialists, they admitted, "are not making the Revolution. It would be nearer the truth to say that Morgan and Rockefeller are making it. The work of Socialists is to explain it; to prepare the people for it, to help it along, to enable it to come as speedily and as easily as possible." [24]

1901; Spargo, *Socialism*, pp. 159–60; Walter Thomas Mills, *Struggle for Existence*, pp. 297–98.

[23] Ernest Untermann, *Sparks of the Proletarian Revolution* (Girard, Kansas, J. A. Wayland, 1904; Wayland's Monthly No. 47), p. 21; Simons, *The American Farmer*, p. 171; Wilshire, *Why a "Workingman" Should Be a Socialist;* Wilshire and Seligman, *Debate on Socialism;* Cline, *Socialist Catechism*, p. 11; Hanford, *Labor War in Colorado*, pp. 46–48; Eugene V. Debs, "What Socialism Proposes," *Metal Worker,* reprinted in *Social Democratic Herald,* Sept. 23, 1904; Upton Sinclair, "The Socialist Party," *The World's Work,* XI (April, 1906), 7432; Spargo, *The Socialists,* pp. 73–74; "The Principles of Socialism Briefly Explained," *The Worker,* April 29, 1905.

[24] "What We Mean by Revolution," *The Worker,* April 28, 1901; Simons, *Philosophy of Socialism,* pp. 17–26. This definition of "revolution" as a "radical change

The Center-Left Socialists informed the workers that until such time as they had won local and national political power nothing was to be gained from municipal and public or government ownership of utilities. There was no "public" under capitalism. There was only a capitalist class and a working class. Since the capitalist class controlled the national government, and since the municipality was virtually a capitalist corporation, public ownership on either the national or local level was merely a further development of capitalism. And state or municipal capitalism was not socialism.

The Center-Left held that the proletariat had little to gain by cheaper gas rates or lower streetcar and railroad fares. Government workers were exploited as heavily as those employed by private industry. The operation of the United States Post Office and the treatment of workers in cities with municipal ownership like Glasgow and in countries with government ownership like Germany and Italy showed that public ownership provided no relief for the proletariat. Furthermore, public ownership meant that the working class would receive low wages so as to enable payment of interest on the bonds floated to finance public purchase. Socialism would reclaim the industries, created by labor and stolen by the capitalists, through confiscation, not purchase.

The Center-Left considered agitation for public ownership the product of the drive for further concentration of industry and of middle-class struggle against monopoly. It was not the concern of the working class to perfect the development of capitalism or to fight the battles of the middle class. "Socialists are not opposed to municipal ownership nor are they wasting their energy in advocating it." Let the capitalists solve their own problems. If Socialists obtained control of a city before they won the entire country, they would use their power to aid and strengthen the working class through an improved educational and health system, regulation

---

of things" was considered too loose and pointless by some Socialists even in 1901. This "floating with the tide" kind of revolution advocated or accepted by the Center was soon to lead to a split of the Center-Left coalition. One Socialist criticized the Center definition in 1901 and insisted that revolution meant "a radical overturning of things ACHIEVED BY A MILITANT CLASS IN OPPOSITION TO THE CONSERVATIVE RULING POWER, in the firm conviction that it is, and until the final decision must and will continue to be, a matter of MIGHT AGAINST MIGHT." (Letter from B. Feigenbaum to *The Worker,* May 26, 1901.)

of working conditions, construction of decent housing, and preven-
tion of police interference with strikes. Only when the entire
country had been won for the working class, only when the capitalists had lost all political power, could the gradual inauguration
of co-operative and true public ownership begin.[25]

As part of the international socialist movement, the Center-Left
believed the purpose of the American Socialist Party was to drive
the capitalist class from power and establish the classless co-
operative commonwealth. This was to be done through independent
working-class political action organized in the Socialist Party.
When members of the Socialist Party, running on that party's
ticket, won a majority of the elective offices in the United States,
all that remained in order to establish socialism would be confiscation of the privately owned means of production by the socialist
government. Thus, the immediate, and indeed sole, goal of the Socialist Party was "to organize the slaves of capital to vote their
own emancipation." [26] Socialist progress was to be measured almost exclusively by the size of the Socialist vote and the number
of Socialist candidates elected to office.[27]

Therefore, the time and energy of the Socialist Party should be
devoted to convincing the American people they should vote the
Socialist ticket. This was not quite so easy as persuading them to
vote Democratic or Republican. It meant that the party must be
organized to explain the entire social process, ranging from the
class struggle to the relation of drink and capitalism. The job be-

[25] "The Socialist Party and Municipal Ownership," *The Chicago Socialist*, Nov.
28, 1903; Simons, *The American Farmer*, p. 174; Courtenay Lemon, "Government
Ownership and Class Rule," *The Worker*, April 6, 1902; Ernest Untermann, "An
Appeal to Reason," *The Chicago Socialist*, April 19, 1902; *The Chicago Socialist*,
June 14, 1902; "The Socialist State," *The New Time*, Sept. 20, 1902; *The Miner's
Magazine*, II (November, 1902), 38; Untermann, *How to Get Socialism*, p. 47;
Untermann, *The Municipality*, pp. 2–25; George D. Herron, "The Social Opportu-
nity," *International Socialist Review*, IV (April, 1904), 589–90; Eugene V. Debs,
"The Social Revolution," *Appeal to Reason*, July 8, 1905; Simons, *What the So-
cialists Would Do*, pp. 9–10, 12–23; Spargo, *The Socialists*, pp. 94–97; "The Socialist Movement: What It Is and What It Seeks to Accomplish," *The Worker*,
April 25, 1906; "Confiscation," *The Worker*, July 5, 1903; "The Confiscation Question," *American Labor Union Journal*, reprinted in *The Socialist*, June 21, 1903.
[26] "Socialist Organization," *The Socialist* (Seattle), April 3, 1904; "Socialism and
Public Ownership," *The Worker*, May 1, 1902; Herman F. Titus, "ABC of Socialism," *The Socialist* (Toledo), April 8, 1905; "The Socialist Party," *The Chicago Socialist*, Dec. 1, 1906.
[27] *The Worker*, May 1, 1903.

tween elections was to proselyte, and that could be done only through the written and spoken word. Friends were to be visited, street corner crowds harangued, classes and lectures organized, and union members educated. But the most effective way to make converts, agreed the Socialists, was to distribute literature and to sell subscriptions to the socialist press. For only through study could one acquire the knowledge necessary to understand the social process. And if the task seemed difficult at first, the Center-Left theorists reassured each other that economic development made understanding and success inevitable. The ground for socialist theory was becoming ever more fertile. The Socialist Party could not appeal to the "ignorant vote"; but "it is the conviction of all socialists that the presentation of the facts of our economic and industrial conditions is sufficient in itself to expose the uselessness and falsity of the capitalist parties." [28]

Socialists saw the revolutionary movement as forming three concentric circles. The outer ring consisted of those Americans imbued with a "dim, nebulous something called radicalism." The middle ring was made up of those who accepted socialism as the coming social order and who voted the Socialist ticket. At the center of these two rings lay the organization which educated the radicals so they would join the middle circle, and which conducted the election campaigns—the Socialist Party.[29] In addition to winning Socialist votes, the party sought to increase its dues-paying membership by recruiting into its ranks those it had persuaded to vote the Socialist ticket.[30] Prospective recruits were urged to join so that their dues would furnish the funds for electioneering and propaganda, so that they might proselyte with greater effectiveness, and so that they might participate in the selection of candidates and the election of party officers.[31]

[28] *Socialist Campaign Book of 1900,* Preface; "Socialist Organization," *The Socialist* (Seattle), April 3, 1904; Ernest Untermann, "Final Stages of Capitalism," *The Chicago Socialist,* April 5, 1902; Walter Thomas Mills, *How to Work for Socialism,* pp. 13–19; Patterson, *The Socialist Machine,* pp. 18–21; Leffingwell, *Easy Lessons,* pp. 14–16; Benson, *Socialism Made Plain,* pp. 41–42; Spargo, *Forces That Make for Socialism,* pp. 10–28.

[29] "The Socialist Party," *The Chicago Socialist,* Dec. 1, 1906; Patterson, *The Socialist Machine,* pp. 18–21.          [30] See sources cited in Note 29.

[31] Charles H. Kerr: "The Socialist Party," *The Chicago Socialist,* July 22, 1905; *Why Join the Socialist Party?* (Chicago, C. H. Kerr and Co., 1902); Spargo, *The Socialists,* pp. 135–37; *The Worker,* June 23, 1906.

The Center of the Center-Left coalition was anxious to have anyone in the party who professed willingness to support the interests of the working class. The Center faction divided possible recruits into three groups—manual labor, brain labor, and capitalists. Few capitalists would be recruited, it granted, but both manual and brain laborers belonged to the proletariat. However, because of their environment, brain workers would be somewhat more difficult to convince than manual workers. But the development of capitalism was rapidly ending all differences between "college lads" and manual workers, and both groups would form the backbone of the Socialist Party.[32] This conception of the essential class identity of "brain workers" and manual workers was to be expected from the Center, for its leaders and supporters were drawn from professionals and the middle class.

The Left of the Center-Left coalition was far more concerned than the Center about the class make-up of the party. It did not attempt to disguise the growing influence of the middle class in the workers' party by describing that class as proletarian "brain workers." It held that members of the middle class were unreliable, that at best they were seldom more than "reformers," that they constantly sought to use the working class for their own ends. "The Socialist party can perhaps assimilate a few middle-class people, but if many were to join its ranks, they would emasculate the movement, first because they are reactionary and secondly because there can be no real unity of action when there is not an identity of interest." [33] The greatest danger facing the party, the Left warned, was the inundation of the working-class movement by middle-class recruits. Equally disastrous would be election victories gained through middle-class votes. The Left granted that the working class did not as yet constitute a majority of the voting population, but held the party had no alternative but to "wait until the percentage increased over 50 per cent, as it soon will." [34]

The relative ideological unity of Left and Center did not last many years. The Center soon showed that it was willing to forget early "revolutionary" ideological indiscretions when they inter-

[32] The Worker, July 21, 1901.      [33] Beresford, Tactics and Strategy.
[34] Ibid.; "Socialist Organization," The Socialist (Seattle), April 3, 1904; A. A. Lewis in The Socialist (Seattle), April 26, 1903.

fered with electoral growth at the polls. And the Left did not long accept a definition of revolution and class struggle which limited itself to between-election talk and pamphleteering while strikes were broken, union leaders imprisoned, and workers' organizations destroyed.

The Right wing of the Socialist Party agreed with much of the early Center-Left theory. On such matters as the failure of capitalism, the futility of trust-busting and regulation, and especially the need to capture the government through the election of Socialists to public office, there was little that distinguished the three party factions.[35] But there were sharp differences on other matters. And before many elections had gone by, the Center accepted more and more of the Right analysis as more "practical" for a party devoted to success at the polls.

The American Right wing made no secret of the source of its ideology. The rise of the relatively privileged leadership of the craft unions and of the new middle class—professionals and relatively high-paid salaried employees—had been accompanied by attempts to revise Marxian teachings to meet their needs and ambitions. The most famous and influential of these revisions was published in 1899 by Edward Bernstein, a leader of the German Social Democratic Party.[36] Victor Berger, ideological and political leader of the American Socialist Right wing, had worked out a rather crude version of many of Bernstein's revisions some years before the publication of the latter's *Evolutionary Socialism*.[37] But their formalization by a leading theoretician of the most successful of the world's socialist parties, notwithstanding their formal rejection by that party in 1901, gave them heightened standing among the more conservative of American Socialists.[38]

Berger's *Social Democratic Herald*, which had moved from Chicago to Milwaukee after the 1901 unity convention, outlined Bernstein's theories in June of that year: Bernstein had challenged Marx's theories of historical materialism, dialectics, value, and

---

[35] Thompson, *Principles and Program of Socialism*, pp. 25–32.

[36] *Die Voraussetzungen des Sozialdemokrat und die Aufgaben der Sozialdemocratie* (Stuttgart, Germany, J.H.W. Dietz Nachf., 1899).

[37] Walling, *Socialism as It Is*, p. 179.

[38] Victor L. Berger, "To Understand the Party News from Germany," *Social Democratic Herald*, Oct. 5, 1901.

historical role of the proletariat; had held that the number of capitalists was increasing, that capital was decentralizing through
widespread stock ownership, that small business could thrive along-
side trusts, and that democratic organization of giant industry in
any form of economy was impossible. He had insisted that depressions could always be overcome through world markets, that there
was no such thing as a proletariat of identical class interests, and
that the proletariat was becoming and should continue to become
more nationalistic; and finally, that permeation of the state and
industrial body with democratic convictions rather than the dictatorship of the proletariat should be the goal of proletarian politics.[39]

Berger answered the rejection of Bernstein's theories by the
German Social Democratic Party by insisting that "the tactic of
the American Socialist Party, if that party is to live and succeed—
can only be the much abused and much misunderstood Bernstein
doctrine." [40] Berger set himself the task of hammering Bernstein's
revisions into the American socialist program.[41] And by 1905 he
could boast that he was "rather proud of being called the 'American Bernstein.' " [42]

The Center-Left theorists devoted themselves to tactics aimed
at winning election majorities on all government levels so that socialism could be inaugurated after the working class had gained
complete political power. But the Right considered such theory
utopian and unscientific. They held that it ignored the evolutionary
nature of social change. Socialism was not going to be inaugurated
after political victory. Socialism was partially here now, and more
of it was coming every day.[43] Some examples of socialism in the
United States which the Right cited were limitations on dividends
of public service corporations, the police department, the post
office, and municipal ownership of street railways.[44] Socialism was

[39] *Social Democratic Herald*, June 1, 1901.
[40] Berger in the *Social Democratic Herald*, Oct. 12, 1901.
[41] *Ibid.*, Sept. 21, 1901; "The Bernstein Doctrine for America," *Social Democratic
Herald*, Oct. 12, 1901.
[42] Berger, "Not 'Revolutionary' Humbugs," *Social Democratic Herald*, April
22, 1905.
[43] Ladoff, *The Passing of Capitalism*, pp. 138–40; "How It Will Probably Come,"
*Social Democratic Herald*, Jan. 4, 1902.
[44] Benson, *Socialism Made Plain*, pp. 124–30. The *Social Democratic Herald* re-

to replace capitalism by a gradual process of growth. It was to permeate and transform the capitalist system.[45] For Berger the era of the complete establishment of socialism was of no importance. "The MOVEMENT is of ALL IMPORTANCE to ME. And by the term movement I understand not only the general movement of society, i.e., social progress, but also the political and economic agitations, for effecting this progress." [46]

While the Center-Left theorists were indifferent to government ownership, regarding it as nothing but an extension of capitalism, the Right viewed it as a step toward the establishment of socialism.[47] Berger wanted the Socialist Party to put itself at the head of the antitrust movement with a demand for nationalization of the trusts.[48] Gaylord Wilshire, "the millionaire socialist," held that government ownership was socialism,[49] and in 1902 the Wisconsin Socialist platform, to the disgust of the Center-Left, called for government purchase of the railroads.[50] *Appeal to Reason* cited the $23,000,000 profit of the government-owned Australian railroads as proof of the benefits flowing from nationalization or socialism.[51]

But even nationalization was really too big a "socialist step" for the Right wing. Economic justice, like charity, began at home, they explained. And home was the municipality. The Socialist Party should go into each city election with a platform advocating home rule, municipal ownership of public utilities, better schools and hospitals, and civil service reform. The Right explained that this platform would differ from that of reform parties because the latter were interested in municipal ownership only in order to lower

---

peatedly referred to this exposition of "police department socialism" as the "best propaganda book since [Robert Blatchford's] *Merrie England.*"

[45] Ladoff, *The Passing of Capitalism,* p. 151.

[46] Berger, "Edward Bernstein," *Social Democratic Herald,* Oct. 19, 1898.

[47] Letter from Henry D. Lloyd to Mrs. L. Pass Christian, Henry D. Lloyd Papers; Davis, *Public Ownership of Railroads,* p. 68; J. A. Wayland, *Why Railroad Men Should Be Socialists,* Girard, Kansas, J. A. Wayland, 1902 (Studies in Socialism No. 19), pp. 1–7; Francis M. Elliot, "Socialism and Public Ownership," *International Socialist Review,* VI (June, 1906), 732–35.

[48] Victor L. Berger, "The Trust Problem, as Socialists See It," *Social Democratic Herald,* May 17, 1902.

[49] Gaylord Wilshire, *Why a "Workingman" Should Be a Socialist,* Wilshire Leaflet No. 1, 1903.

[50] *The Worker,* Nov. 23, 1902.          [51] *Appeal to Reason,* Jan. 20, 1906.

taxes, while the Socialists wanted to use the profits to aid the workers.[52] Of course, said the Right wing, such measures could not be understood in cities like New York, "that Babel of sin and deviltry. There can be no doubt that even Socialism and Socialists will become corrupted—or rather poisoned—in that sea of evil." [53] And Chicago and Philadelphia, also centers of Center-Left socialist theory, were little better. Consequently, insisted the Right, the hope of socialism lay in the smaller cities like Milwaukee and San Francisco where wickedness and corruption were less intense.[54]

There seems little doubt that only a soul free of "corruption" could have produced the pamphlet on *How to Inaugurate Socialism* which flooded relatively sin-free San Francisco in 1902. If the people of San Francisco would only elect members of the Socialist Party in the forthcoming elections, announced this pamphleteer for freedom, the city would serve as the base for the spread of socialism all over the United States. By floating $50,000,000 in bonds, the socialist city could erect banks, "many stories high," factories, "many stories high," and "tenements," "all many stories high." The idea would spread from city to city, and soon the nation would be socialist. Then the socialist nation could print greenbacks and buy up all giant industry. The author held that confiscation would not be equitable; but justice could be served through purchase with paper money, followed by a proclamation declaring the money worthless. Labor checks would then be used for all goods bought. "We want to impress upon every town, village and city the necessity of at once beginning social or universal co-operative clubs, by sending at once to the headquarters of the Socialist party . . . for a charter." [55]

Berger's Right wing had completed the circle. It had helped split the Social Democracy of America in 1898 for advocating colonization and the conquest of the nation state by state. Now the conquest was to come city by city. Instead of trekking across the country, Socialists were to stay at home and till their own back yards.

The Right-wing Socialists usually claimed that they "believed"

[52] Ladoff, *The Passing of Capitalism,* pp. 138–40; Walter Thomas Mills, *Struggle for Existence,* p. 523.
[53] "As to Municipal Elections," *Social Democratic Herald,* Nov. 16, 1901.
[54] *Ibid.*
[55] DeWitt Clinton, *How, When and Where to Inaugurate Socialism,* pp. 4–14.

in the existence of classes in America, and in the class struggle.[56] They neither created nor desired class conflict. They merely recognized it as a fact. And class conflict did not mean "class hatred." It simply meant that capitalism unfortunately divided society into two classes, and that these two classes should express their conflict at the ballot box.[57] Socialism, assured the Right, was not a class movement, it was a race movement. All human beings were willing to sacrifice their individual interests for the race. And since socialism would benefit the whole race, capitalists would soon support the Socialist Party.[58] Berger held that the threat of epidemics, mob violence, and mass starvation under capitalism were conditions "civilized white men cannot and will not endure." Socialism was a movement not just for the working class, but for all mankind.[59]

Moreover, the Right warned that if socialism were just a proletarian movement it could have no hope for success. The proletariat was not "ripe for socialism." [60] The masses of mankind were stupid, indolent philistines. Social progress was not carried by the workers but by the intellectual "cranks" of all classes who saw clearly that they must lead.[61] "Class consciousness is the idol of narrow-minded, dogmatic, pseudo scientific Socialists of the orthodox type." [62] Unless there were intelligent men to guide the socialist movement, the ignorant and desperate workers would try to obtain socialism through force and bloodshed. The rich owed a duty to their wives and children to join the Socialist Party and help prevent violence by working for the gradual inauguration of socialism.[63] And the middle class, unless misled as to their true

[56] Victor L. Berger, "Classes in Free America," *Social Democratic Herald*, Jan. 13, 1906.

[57] Leon Greenbaum in a speech delivered to the Populist Conference, Dec. 29, 1900, *Missouri Socialist*, Jan. 12, 1901; Ladoff, *The Passing of Capitalism*, pp. 72, 74; Walter T. Mills, quoted in the *Colorado Socialist*, June 5, 1903; Joseph Medill Patterson in the Chicago *Record Herald*, July 17, 1906.

[58] Gaylord Wilshire, "Class vs. Class: Resultant," *Wilshire's Magazine*, VI (Nov., 1904), 3–4.

[59] Victor L. Berger, "A Word to the Rich," *Social Democratic Herald*, Aug. 8, 1903; *Social Democratic Herald*, May 6, 1905.

[60] Victor L. Berger, "Moving by the Light of Reason," *Social Democratic Herald*, April 15, 1905.

[61] Isador Ladoff, "Some Thoughts on the Crank in History," *Social Democratic Herald*, June 28, 1902.          [62] Ladoff, *Passing of Capitalism*, p. 72.

[63] Leffingwell, *Easy Lessons*, pp. 24–25; Joseph M. Patterson in an address at St. Louis, quoted in *Wilshire's Magazine*, X (Oct., 1906), 10.

economic interests, would join the party because in reality "they belong to the working class." [64]

The Right granted that this was not a "revolutionary" program. But it held that society did not advance by revolution or "catastrophe." The Socialist Party must not follow the path of the fanatical abolitionists who rejected Henry Clay's "wise proposals" to end slavery gradually through purchase. The choice was that of evolution through right reason, or of disaster through violence. Working-class revolution would lead not to socialism, but to the dictatorship of a Caesar.[65] The Socialist Party "ought to make a clean sweep of stupid phrases and senseless catchwords" like "social revolution." [66] The party should work for class "understanding" through the development of mutual "class respect." If Socialists devoted themselves to the support of all reforms, in thirty years America might advance to the point where nationalization of monopoly would be established government policy. This was all that could be hoped for.[67]

The Right readily conceded that this was not Marxian Socialism, but answered that it did "not care a ————" [68] The less said about *The Communist Manifesto*, the better.[69] The Right claimed that its socialism was the only socialism that would work. Critics did not seem to realize that never before in history had "the ruling and ruled classes . . . stood on exactly the same footing before the law . . . wage workers in progressive countries have the same political rights as capitalists." The Socialist Party had one job— to convince workers that they must use the ballot to better their conditions.[70]

All factions of the party agreed that the best, if not the only, way to make Socialists was through personal or soapbox appeals

[64] Walter Thomas Mills, *Struggle for Existence*, pp. 467–68.

[65] Victor L. Berger, "Do We Want Evolution or Revolution? *Social Democratic Herald*, June 28, 1902; *Social Democratic Herald*, Aug. 24, 1901.

[66] Victor L. Berger, "The Mistake in Belgium," *Social Democratic Herald*, June 14, 1902.

[67] "What We Anticipate," *Social Democratic Herald*, Dec. 21, 1901; *Social Democratic Herald*, Aug. 24, 1901.

[68] "Our View of the Situation," *Social Democratic Herald*, Jan. 18, 1902.

[69] Letter from Charles R. Martin to *The Worker*, Aug. 12, 1905. Martin points out that Berger refused to sign the 1904 Socialist platform unless all reference to *The Communist Manifesto* was deleted. It was.

[70] "Timely Thoughts on the Ballot," *Social Democratic Herald*, May 3, 1902.

and distribution of literature.[71] Between 1898 and 1903 the number of socialist pamphlets and leaflets published increased from about a dozen to over five hundred.[72] In 1898 the total circulation of the socialist press was probably about twenty-five thousand. By 1903 there were over one hundred English-language socialist weeklies and monthlies. The *Appeal to Reason* alone had a circulation of 50,000, and *Wilshire's Magazine,* from its Canadian refuge where it had been driven by U.S. postal authorities, sold 100,000 copies monthly.[73]

At least for the official record, propaganda among the trade unions was considered by all Socialists the most important party work. Trade unions were viewed as a product of the class struggle. The unions fought within the framework of capitalism for higher wages and better working conditions on the economic field. The Socialist Party, also a product of the class struggle, fought for workers' rights on the political field, through the ballot.[74] The Center-Left held that Socialist votes would eventually bring the workers an economic system in which they would get not just a slightly higher wage, but everything they produced. In the meantime, the very threat of socialism, together with the aid of Socialists elected to office, would obtain passage of legislation of benefit to labor.[75] The Right held that strikes were too costly at best, and hopeless at worst. Labor support of Socialist candidates, on the other hand, would enable the only party really interested in the passage of legislation to benefit labor—sick benefits, old age pensions, accident and unemployment insurance—to gain office and supplement such work as the unions could do in the economic field.[76]

[71] Patterson, *The Socialist Machine,* pp. 20–21; *The Workers' Call,* March 9, 1901; *Social Democratic Herald,* Aug. 9, 1902, Dec. 2, 1905; Carl D. Thompson, "The Power of the Personal Appeal," *Social Democratic Herald,* Aug. 16, 1902.

[72] A. M. Simons, "The Socialist Movement in America," *The World To-Day,* V (July, 1903), 940.

[73] *Ibid.,* pp. 938–39; Hillquit, *History of Socialism,* pp. 244–46.

[74] *Socialist Campaign Book of 1900,* pp. 11–21; "The Socialist Party and the Trade Unions," *The Worker,* Dec. 14, 1902; Victor L. Berger, "Party Politics and the Trade Unions," *Social Democratic Herald,* Dec. 13, 1902; A. M. Simons, "Socialist Movement in America," *The World To-Day,* V (July, 1903), p. 935.

[75] Eugene V. Debs quoted in the Chicago *Record Herald,* Dec. 7, 1903; "The Socialist Party and the Trade Unions," *The Worker,* Dec. 14, 1902; "Socialist Progress in the United States," *The Worker,* May 1, 1903.

[76] Victor L. Berger, "Party Politics and the Trade Unions," *Social Democratic Herald,* Dec. 13, 1902; "To the Bitter End," *Appeal to Reason,* August 6, 1904.

The Socialist Party pledged itself to give moral and financial support to the unions in all their economic struggles. In addition, all party members were instructed to join the union of their trade.[77] But the Socialists added that trade union members also had obligations. They had to realize that a worker who scabbed at the ballot box by voting for a capitalist party was a greater scab than one who crossed a picket line: "he is not in fact a union man at all who, although a member of the union on the economic side, is a non-unionist on the political side; and while striking for, votes against the working class. . . . The fully developed labor-unionist uses both his economic and political power in the interest of his class."[78] Socialist members of unions were to devote themselves to educating their brothers to the need for voting Socialist. This was to be done through general discussions at union meetings, introduction of socialist resolutions in city federations and national A.F. of L. conventions—either for working class political action or for "socialistic" reforms—the distribution of socialist pamphlets, and the sale of socialist papers to union members.[79]

While emphasizing the need for working-class political action, the Socialists tirelessly warned the unions of the danger and futility of union labor parties.[80] The Socialists insisted the only possible basis for labor politics was recognition of the class struggle and the need for socialism. Labor parties which failed to recognize this principle were merely unwitting tools of the capitalists.[81] Moreover, there was no need to form a new labor party on the basis of

[77] "Trade Union Resolution," "Proceedings of Socialist Unity Convention, 1901," typescript in Harper Library, University of Chicago, pp. 529–30; Daniel Lynch (President, Union No. 11, Boston, Brotherhood of Painters and Decorators of America), *Socialism and Trade Unionism,* pp. 4–17.

[78] Debs, *Unionism and Socialism,* pp. 23–24; *The Capitalist's Union or Labor Unions: Which?* pp. 11–12, 15, 27–28.

[79] Max S. Hayes, "The Attack on the Trade Unions," *The Worker,* May 1, 1903; John Spargo, "Shall the Unions Go into Politics," *The Worker,* Nov. 15, 1903; Lynch, *Socialism and Trade Unionism;* Berger, "Party Politics and the Trade Unions," *Social Democratic Herald,* Dec. 13, 1902; "Trade Unionism," *The New Time,* Dec. 13, 1902; *Social Democratic Herald,* Aug. 9, 1902.

[80] "The Socialist Party and the Trade Unions," *The Worker,* Dec. 14, 1902.

[81] A. M. Simons, "Trade Unions and the Socialist Party," *International Socialist Review,* III (Jan., 1903), 427; "Manifesto of Local San Francisco, October, 1903," *The Socialist* (Seattle), Oct. 18, 1903; "To Trade Unionists," *The Workers' Call,* Dec. 7, 1901; *The Workers' Call,* Nov. 23, 1901; Victor L. Berger, "As to American Labor Parties," *Social Democratic Herald,* Sept. 1, 1902.

the irreconcilable interests of labor and capital. Such a party already existed, the Socialist Party. And just as the Socialist Party respected the unions' exclusive rights in the field of economic organization, so the unions should recognize that party's exclusive rights in the field of political or electoral action.[82]

The Socialist Party absolutely refused to support any attempts by unions to form local or national political parties around the issues of injunctions, labor legislation, political corruption, and municipal ownership. "The Social Democratic party fuses, trades, combines, co-operates, works with, coalesces or unites with no political party that does not favor, believe in and work for the substitutions of social ownership of the means of production in place of private ownership." [83] The party considered independent Socialist political campaigns as "the most vital principle" of the socialist movement.[84] Union labor parties were traps designed by the capitalists to stop the growing vote of the Socialist Party.[85] A vote for a labor party was a vote for capitalism.[86] All locals of the Socialist organization were told to nominate a full slate of candidates in every local and national election. If for any reason the local branch or state organization could not make such nominations, it was ordered to boycott the election. No member of the party was ever to support or vote for the candidates of any other party.[87]

Socialists who violated this fundamental principle were suspended or expelled. Locals that participated in "fusion" had their charters revoked.[88] Socialist Party candidates even refused to accept the endorsement of union labor parties, since that would imply

[82] "Resolution of National Committee of the Socialist Party," adopted unanimously, Jan. 30, 1903, *The Worker*, Feb. 8, 1903; Robert Hunter, *Labor in Politics* (Chicago: The Socialist Party, 1915), pp. 178–79; Berger, "As to American Labor Parties"; "To Trade Unionists," *The Workers' Call*, Dec. 7, 1901.

[83] *Social Democratic Herald*, Dec. 23, 1899.

[84] "National Committee Resolution No. 8, 1905," *The Socialist Party Official Bulletin*, May, 1905.

[85] Thompson, *Principles and Program of Socialism*, pp. 33–35; "That New 'Labor' Party," *The Worker*, July 28, 1906; "A Peep Behind the Scenes," *The Workers' Call*, Dec. 7, 1901.

[86] "Manifesto of Local San Francisco, October, 1903," *The Socialist* (Seattle), Oct. 18, 1903.

[87] "National Committee Resolution No. 8, 1905," *The Socialist Party Official Bulletin*, May, 1905.

[88] *The Socialist Party Official Bulletin*, July, 1905.

recognition and respect for a capitalist tool.[89] And no Socialist could accept an appointment from a nonsocialist government except under regular civil service procedure.[90]

Party opposition to "rival" labor parties was not limited to discipline of its own membership. Socialists, wherever possible, prevented formation of labor parties. When Chicago unions attempted to form a party in December, 1901, two hundred Socialists packed the meeting. As soon as it was called to order, the Socialist majority secured passage of a resolution declaring "that the laborers of Chicago do not need the help of a gang of grafters meeting in the wine room of a saloon to organize a Labor Party for them." They then adjourned the meeting.[91]

In strike-torn Colorado, at a three-day conference of four hundred labor leaders to discuss the advisability of independent labor political action, the Socialist delegates defeated the motion for a union labor party.[92] In St. Louis, the Socialist-controlled Central Trade and Labor Union rejected local union demands for a broad labor party.[93] Job Harriman was asked to go to Arizona in 1910 and help destroy the newly formed labor party there, thus duplicating "the splendid work the Los Angeles comrades have done in averting the formation of a labor party as a rival to the Socialist Party." [94] Left-wing Socialists never relaxed their opposition to the formation of labor parties. Right-wing leaders abandoned their opposition to all labor parties only once, after their election setback in 1908. And they toyed with the labor party idea only for a little over a year, until the increased Socialist vote in 1910 again convinced them that "fusion was betrayal." [95]

The approach of the Socialist Party to the middle class was compounded equally of jealousy of rival parties and desire for

[89] Letter from W. H. Dettrey to A. R. Meluish, Aug. 7, 1906; letter from A. R. Meluish to H. B. Ringler, Aug. 12, 1906; letter from P. F. R. East to A. R. Meluish, Aug. 15, 1906, all in *The Worker*, Sept. 8, 1906.

[90] Socialist Party, *Proceedings of the National Convention, 1904*, p. 50.

[91] Chicago *Tribune*, Dec. 8, 1901; "A Still-Born Child," *The Workers' Call*, Dec. 14, 1901.

[92] *The Worker*, Jan. 31, 1904.

[93] *The Chicago Socialist*, June 30, 1906.

[94] "Minutes of the National Executive Committee Meeting, August 8, 1910," *Socialist Party Weekly Bulletin*, Sept. 3, 1910.

[95] See below, pp. 228–31.

middle-class votes.[96] The Socialists could not lecture little business-men and professionals, as they could trade unions, that their field was economic struggle and not politics. Instead, they told them that all their efforts to win "progressive" reforms through reform parties were doomed to failure because they were a dying class.[97] Party papers pointed with delight to the defeats of Bryan in 1900 and Tom Johnson of Cleveland in 1902, and to the decayed state of the Populist Party.[98]

Socialist propaganda aimed at middle-class audiences stressed that only a working-class party had the strength to obtain lasting reforms under capitalism. Concessions were won from the capitalist class by the threat of an increased Socialist vote. Ultimately, the Socialists insisted, small businessmen must become either manual workers or professionals. Both the Center and Right told profes-sionals that they were "brain workers." Therefore, if the middle class wanted to preserve democracy and win progressive reforms, it must recognize that socialism was inevitable—eventually—and it must therefore join the only party with a future.[99]

Although the Socialists could not agree on the farmer's place in the American class structure, they were agreed that for him, as for the middle class, the only hope lay in the Socialist Party.[100] Many Right-wing Socialists believed that the Socialist Party's only hope lay in winning the farm vote. Otherwise, with 40 percent of the population living on farms, it would be impossible to carry out the municipal reforms leading to socialism.[101] Berger warned that since the farmers were already armed their support must be won

[96] La Monte, *Science and Socialism*, pp. 26–27; "Report of the Delegates of the Social Democratic Party to the International Socialist Congress at Paris," *The Worker*, Sept. 22, 1900; William J. Ghent, "Why Socialists Are Partisans," *The Independent*, LIX (Oct. 26, 1905), 967–71.

[97] A. M. Simons, "Socialist Tactics," *International Socialist Review*, I (June, 1900), 822–23; Ghent, "Why Socialists Are Partisans," *The Independent*, LIX (Oct. 26, 1905), 970–71.

[98] "Lessons from the Election," *The New Time*, Nov. 15, 1902; *Social Democratic Herald*, Aug. 23, 1902.

[99] *Missouri Socialist*, Jan. 5, 1901; "The Populist Conference," *Missouri Socialist*, Jan. 12, 1901; Ghent, "Why Socialists Are Partisans," *The Independent*, LIX (Oct. 26, 1905), 969–70.

[100] *Socialist Campaign Book of 1900*, pp. 45–57.

[101] Speeches by A. M. Simons, Victor L. Berger, and Seymour Stedman, "Pro-ceedings of Socialist Unity Convention, 1901," typescript in Harper Library, Uni-

or they could slaughter an unarmed pro-Socialist working class.[102]

Glowing pictures of life under socialism were painted for the farmers. Mortgages on small farms would be canceled.[103] But the higher returns which workers received on the efficient co-operative farms set up on government-owned land would convince most farmers that they should give up their individual holdings.[104] They would live in cities and be whisked to their farms by electric cars and automobiles. Machinery would cut the workday to three or four hours. And beautiful homes, schools, libraries, lectures, and theaters would enable them to become truly independent citizens.[105]

But there was some question whether an analysis of farm exploitation under monopoly capitalism coupled with odes to socialist farming would win the farm vote. Some Left-wing Socialists argued that despite the difficulty of this approach, farmers could not be appealed to on any other basis. They admitted that the farmer would benefit from "populist" reforms if those reforms were won by the Socialist Party. But such reforms would be of little benefit to the proletariat, they insisted. And victories won on the basis of a Socialist-Populist ideological alliance would cripple the Socialist Party. The Left held that the party must remain an uncompromising working-class organization, one which welcomed middle-class allies, but only as allies who accepted a straight socialist program.[106]

Some members of the Center and Right wings of the party insisted that farmers had exactly the same interests as workers.[107]

---

versity of Chicago, pp. 350, 358-60, 381-86; Simons, *The American Farmer,* pp. 165-66.

[102] Speech by Victor L. Berger, "Proceedings of Socialist Unity Convention, 1901," typescript in Harper Library, University of Chicago, p. 361.

[103] *Appeal to Reason,* Jan. 24, 1903.

[104] Simons, *The American Farmer,* pp. 207-12.

[105] Green, *Why Farmers Should Be Socialists,* pp. 3-12; Walter Thomas Mills, *Struggle for Existence,* pp. 449-50; *Appeal to Reason,* Jan. 24, 1903; Simons, *The American Farmer,* pp. 178-214.

[106] Herman F. Titus in *The Socialist* (Seattle), March 8, May 17, June 14, July 12, 1903; speeches by F. G. Spring, James Carey, and Frank Silverman, "Proceedings of Socialist Unity Convention, 1901," typescript in Harper Library, University of Chicago, pp. 257, 363-66, 372-74.

[107] Speech by A. M. Simons, "Proceedings of Socialist Unity Convention, 1901," typescript in Harper Library, University of Chicago, pp. 346-50. Ernest Untermann, acknowledged by most party members in 1903 as one of the leading "revolutionary" theoreticians, insisted that the small farmer, the "rural proletariat,"

Both were exploited under capitalism, and both sold only their labor power. To the charge that the farmers were also interested in exploiting their laborers, these Socialists replied that farm prices were so low that it was impossible for farmers to extort surplus value from their workers. They held that farm tenancy and mortgages were not increasing and that farming would not become a corporate enterprise. Therefore, the party would have to formulate a program appealing to the immediate interests of the independent farmers.[108]

At the Socialist Unity Convention in 1901, Algie Simons, who viewed himself as the farm expert of the party, introduced a plank into the draft platform reiterating that the interests of farmers and workers were identical. Some of the delegates advocated a series of "immediate demands" for farmers along the line of the familiar "populist" proposals. But opposition by delegates from Right, Center, and Left was so vigorous that all mention of the farmer was deleted from the platform.[109] Instead, a special farm resolution was adopted telling the farmer that the development of machinery had made him little more than a wage slave and that socialism alone would win for him the full product of his labor.[110]

Berger charged that this resolution was "meaningless," and that the farmer was too important "to be dismissed with such a bundle of strips . . . [torn] out of the old platform." [111] There was almost no socialist propaganda among farmers during the first five years of party activity. And while Berger might consider the farm vote too important to dismiss in a few stereotyped phrases, the Wisconsin party limited itself to passing out leaflets at the Wisconsin state fair.[112]

---

constituted the most uncompromising revolutionary class in America and should form the backbone of the Socialist Party (Untermann: "The Farmer's Struggle for Liberty," *Appeal to Reason,* Jan. 24, 1903; "The American Farmer and the Socialist Party," *The Socialist* [Seattle], July 12, 1903; "Omaha, Our New Headquarters," *Appeal to Reason,* Feb. 14, 1903).

108 Speeches by A. M. Simons, Victor L. Berger, and Seymour Stedman, "Proceedings of Socialist Unity Convention, 1901," typescript in Harper Library, University of Chicago, pp. 346–50, 358–61, 381–86; letter from A. M. Simons to Herman F. Titus, May 21, 1903, *The Socialist* (Seattle), May 31, 1903.

109 "Proceedings of Socialist Unity Convention, 1901," typescript in Harper Library, University of Chicago, pp. 345–95.

110 *Ibid.,* p. 539.                    111 *Ibid.,* pp. 540, 543.

112 *Social Democratic Herald,* Sept. 23, 1905.

Besides labor, the middle class, and the farmer, the Socialist Party in its early years discussed only two other groups as possible objects of propaganda—the foreign-born and Negroes. Although the socialist movement in America had originally been developed by immigrants, and although a good percentage of its membership at the time of its formation were foreign-born, the party showed little concern for their rights. They were not encouraged to join the party, and socialist agitation among them was carried on by independent national socialist organizations which had little contact with the Socialist Party until 1910–1912. The only official statement on the rights of the foreign-born was one passed by the party's national committee in 1907. It urged Socialists to stand for equal civil and political rights for all residents regardless of race or nativity.[113] Nothing was ever done to implement this resolution. And the immigration controversy which developed in 1907 and continued through 1912 indicated that a good proportion of the party, anxious to win the support of A.F. of L. leaders, had no desire for immigrants in the country, much less in the party.[114]

The Negro received greater attention than the immigrant, but most of that attention was not directed toward Negro equality. There were three Negro delegates to the Socialist Unity Convention.[115] At the insistence of one of these delegates, William Costley of San Francisco, a resolution was finally passed declaring the party's sympathy for the Negro and urging him to join the socialist movement and vote his way to emancipation. The resolution was adopted, however, only after repeated revisions and reintroductions had wearied delegates who expressed their indifference by passing numerous motions to table.[116] This was the only resolution for Negro rights ever passed by a national socialist body from 1901 through 1912.[117]

But this by no means exhausted party discussion of the place of the Negro in American society. In September, 1903, the Socialist locals in Louisiana met to form a state organization. They adopted

---

[113] "Resolution No. 6, 1907," *The Socialist Party Official Bulletin*, April, 1907.
[114] See below, pp. 276–88.    [115] *The Worker*, Aug. 4, 1901.
[116] "Proceedings of Socialist Unity Convention, 1901," typescript in Harper Library, University of Chicago, pp. 125–32, 134–43, 560–69, 695–96.
[117] Except, of course, for the resolution on equal rights for all regardless of race or nativity, mentioned above.

a platform advocating the "separation of the black and white races into separate communities, each race to have charge of its own affairs." The party National Committee, then under Center-Left control, demanded an explanation from the Louisiana Socialists.[118] They replied that race instincts would never permit intermingling; that the Democratic Party was already accusing the Socialists of favoring social equality; and that steps had to be taken to prevent the swamping of the Socialist Party by Negroes who had no other party to join.[119]

The National Committee voted to withhold Louisiana's charter until the "negro clause" was deleted.[120] Party officials explained that the organization could not have such statements in its official documents. The question of segregation could be taken up after socialism was achieved. In the meantime, the party should concentrate on economic equality only.[121] Louisiana capitulated.[122]

Party leaders differed in their analysis of the causes of race prejudice. The Center and Left laid the blame on deliberate incitement by capitalists who created Negro-white antagonism the better to exploit both.[123] The Right, however, declared that the whites disliked the Negroes because Negroes were inferior, depraved degenerates who went "around raping women [and] children." [124] Berger declared "that the free contact with the whites has led to the further degeneration of the negroes." [125] White girls who were "depraved" enough to associate with Negroes only did so because

[118] "Report of the National Secretary of the Socialist Party, November, 1903," The Worker, Nov. 15, 1903; letter from National Secretary William Mailly to P. Aloysius Molyneaux, Oct. 16, 1903, The Worker, Nov. 8, 1903.

[119] Letter from Louisiana State Secretary P. Aloysius Molyneaux to William Mailly, Oct. 20, 1903, The Worker, Nov. 8, 1903.

[120] "Report of the National Secretary of the Socialist Party, December, 1903," The Worker, Dec. 27, 1903.

[121] A. H. Floaten in the Socialist Party Weekly Bulletin, Dec. 17, 1903; letter from Caroline Pemberton to The Worker, Nov. 15, 1903; "The Race Question in the Party," The Worker, Dec. 6, 1903.

[122] Eraste Vidrine, "Negro Locals," International Socialist Review, V (Jan., 1905), 389.

[123] Charles H. Vail, "The Negro Problem," International Socialist Review, I (Feb., 1901), 468–70; A. M. Simons, "The Negro Problem," International Socialist Review, I (Oct., 1900), 208–10; letter from Eugene V. Debs to the Indianapolis World, May 23, 1903, reprinted in The Worker, June 28, 1903.

[124] Social Democratic Herald, Sept. 14, 1901.

[125] Victor L. Berger, "The Misfortune of the Negroes," Social Democratic Herald, May 31, 1902.

capitalism prevented them from earning a living "in a natural way." Socialism would end such degeneration.[126]

The indifference of the party toward violence against Negroes brought an inquiry in 1903 from the International Socialist Bureau, with which the American party was affiliated, as to its attitude toward lynching. The executive board of the party, the National Quorum, informed the Bureau that economic conditions under capitalism fostered brutal instincts leading to crime. These same brutal instincts caused the injured members of society to punish those crimes with lynching.

The Socialist Party points out the fact that nothing less than the abolition of the capitalist system and the substitution of the Socialist system can provide conditions under which the hunger maniacs, kleptomaniacs, sexual maniacs and all other offensive and now lynchable human degenerates will cease to be begotten or produced.[127]

Apparently the International Socialist Bureau was content with this explanation.

Despite differences of opinion as to the causes of race hatred, both Center and Right agreed that socialism was exclusively an economic movement and had nothing to do with social equality. The party would insist that under socialism both Negro and white workers received all they produced. But that did not mean that the two races would work in the same factories or even live in the same cities. Center and Right-wing Socialists explained that Negroes and whites did not want to associate. It was capitalism that forced them to live and work together. Socialism would solve the race question in the only possible manner—complete segregation.[128] Until socialism was achieved there was no objection to separate Negro communities, schools, and Socialist locals.[129] There were no

[126] "White Girls, Black Troopers," *The New Time*, May 14, 1904.

[127] "Report of the Meeting of the National Quorum of the Socialist Party, November, 1903," *The Chicago Socialist*, Nov. 28, 1903.

[128] Letter from John Chase to *The Worker*, April 2, 1903; *The Worker*, May 1, 1903; "The Negro and Socialism," *Appeal to Reason*, April 25, 1903; *Appeal to Reason*, Dec. 31, 1904; Walter Thomas Mills, *Struggle for Existence*, pp. 544–54; E. F. Andrews, "Socialism and the Negro," *International Socialist Review*, V (March, 1905), 524–26.

[129] Letter from G. F. Bentley to J. Mahlon Barnes and a letter from Algernon Lee to J. Mahlon Barnes, both printed in *The Socialist Party Official Bulletin*, April, 1907; "The Race Question in the Party," *The Worker*, Dec. 6, 1903. Gaylord Wilshire

Negroes in southern Socialist locals,[130] but the Center and Right-wing Socialists insisted that this was not discrimination. Jews also lived apart from gentiles, and "no one will claim that there is, in any civilized community deserving the name, any vestige of ill-will between the two peoples." [131]

There is no record that the party ever actively opposed discrimination against Negroes from 1901 to 1912. Only one resolution on the subject was offered to the National Committee. In 1906 President Roosevelt dismissed without trial and apparently without justification three companies of Negro troops in connection with a riot at Brownsville, Texas.[132] A member of the Socialist National Committee moved that the committee condemn Roosevelt's action. The Right and Center objected to this "attempt to inject the negro question into the Socialist Party." The Left objected because the army was a "capitalist tool" and Socialists were not interested in army justice. The motion was defeated, 28 to 4, with 25 abstentions.[133]

The party Left wing had no use for distinctions between economic, political, and social equality. Debs opposed all discrimination and toured the South calling on the Negro to reject the false doctrines of "meekness and humility." Only through organized struggle in the labor and socialist movement, said Debs, would the Negro win equality.[134] The Left held that the South should not be permitted to build segregated locals. Southern Socialists should work to wipe out race prejudice and discrimination.[135] The party

---

suggested that since the Negro could not respect property he should be disenfranchised at once ("Reno and the Negro Problem," *Wilshire's,* XIV [August, 1910], 6–7).

[130] Eraste Vidrine, "Negro Locals," *International Socialist Review,* V (Jan., 1905), 389.

[131] E. F. Andrews, "Socialism and the Negro," *International Socialist Review,* V (March, 1905), 525.

[132] Pringle, *Theodore Roosevelt,* pp. 458–64.

[133] *The Socialist Party Official Bulletin,* January, 1907. In 1902 when a Negro was nominated for Congress by one district of the Socialist Party of Indiana, the non-Socialist press considered it an act sufficiently rare to dismiss it as an "eccentricity." (The *Springfield Republican,* quoted in the New York *Daily Tribune,* Oct. 16, 1902.)

[134] Letter from Debs to the Indianapolis *World,* May 23, 1903; Coleman, *Debs,* pp. 215–16. But Debs himself did nothing to mobilize the Socialist Party to fight for Negro rights.

[135] Letter from Edwin Arnold Brenholtz (Texas) to Herman F. Titus, *The Socialist* (Seattle), Jan. 17, 1904.

must engage in active propaganda and organization among Negroes.[136] As the years passed with no organized work among Negroes and with race prejudice apparently increasing among Socialists, some members of the Left became increasingly bitter in their criticism of party chauvinism.[137] But despite their theoretical stand for Negro equality, the Left made virtually no effort to use the party in a struggle for Negro rights. Those Socialists who felt the urgency of work among minorities turned more and more to the Industrial Workers of the World as the organization that was not afraid to fight.[138]

From these conflicting conceptions of socialist theory, organization, and activity it is not possible to generalize with certainty on what the Socialist Party as a party thought it was doing or accomplishing. At best it can be said that from 1901 through 1904 most Socialists considered socialism a science whose leading expounders had been Karl Marx and Frederick Engels. This science showed that new industrial techniques were rendering obsolete the capitalist form of production and distribution. Economic law made the transition to socialism inevitable. The Socialist Party was to be exclusively a political or electoral organization for which workers and farsighted farmers and members of the middle class would cast their votes. Socialism would be ushered in either after the national and local electoral triumph of the party (Center-Left position) or as the almost unnoticed culmination of a long series of reforms (Right-wing position). Participation in the problems of minority groups or in the economic struggles of labor was at most of secondary importance. The major concern of the party was education leading to votes for Socialist candidates. And that meant speeches and distribution of literature.

Few Socialists were willing to speculate on the nature of the society which would be built once a majority of the American people had been talked or pamphleteered into voting the Socialist ticket. It was considered utopian to speculate on the details. They would have to be worked out by the people through their experiences with

[136] Herman F. Titus in *The Socialist* (Seattle), Oct. 24, 1904.

[137] I. M. Robbins, "The Economic Aspects of the Negro Problem," *International Socialist Review*, X (June, 1910), 1006–17.

[138] Brissenden, *The I.W.W.*, pp. 84, 208.

a new form of society.[139] But the need to document the superiority of socialism, and to answer the charges of a hostile press that socialism would divide the wealth, end liberty, equality, and democracy, break up the family, destroy the home, crush individuality, and kill incentive necessitated the formulation of at least a few generalizations about life in the future state.[140]

Under socialism, the party explained, all means of production (private ownership of which enabled the few to exploit the many) would be owned by the people. Ownership would be incorporated in the national, state, or local governments, depending on the scope of the enterprise. Items of personal use, such as clothing, would remain private property.[141] All physically capable citizens would be required to work, in so far as possible at jobs of their own choosing, or they would not eat.[142] Wealth would probably be distributed on the basis of the social contribution made, but with a tendency toward equalization of reward.[143] For the more unpleasant tasks, payment would be higher and hours of labor shorter.[144] The "low" incentive of pecuniary gain would be replaced by the desire for recognition of social contribution.[145]

Much of the state apparatus would be discarded because government would no longer be concerned with maintaining an exploitative economy or with settling quarrels between capitalists over division of the spoils stolen from labor. In addition to ownership of the natural monopolies, such as raw materials and railroads, the national government would be little more than a giant information bureau.[146] The fight among political parties for spoils would dis-

---

[139] Josephine Conger, "Theories of Socialists," *Appeal to Reason,* Sept. 3, 1904; Spargo, *Socialism,* p. 213.

[140] "A Propaganda of Socialism," *The Nation,* LXXXI (Oct. 5, 1905), 272–73; "Better than Socialism," *The Outlook,* LXX (Jan. 25, 1900), 213–14; *The Worker,* Oct. 27, 1906.

[141] Spargo, *Socialism,* pp. 220–27; Simons, *The American Farmer,* pp. 173–74; *Social Democratic Herald,* Aug. 31, 1901.

[142] Spargo, *Socialism,* pp. 227–30.

[143] Morris Hillquit, "The Socialist 'Plan' of Wealth Distribution," *Putnam's Magazine,* IV (April, 1908), 56–57; Spargo, *Socialism,* p. 233.

[144] *The People,* Nov. 4, 1900; *The Worker,* June 30, 1906; Spargo, *Socialism,* pp. 230–33.

[145] Hillquit, *Socialism in Theory and Practice,* pp. 125–26.

[146] Simons, *The American Farmer,* pp. 172–73; Hillquit, *Socialism in Theory and Practice,* pp. 30–32; Spargo, *Socialism,* pp. 222–27.

appear. The government would truly represent all the people. Equality of opportunity and freedom of speech and religion would be realities for the first time, since there would no longer be a class interested in suppressing them.[147] An end to poverty and insecurity would enable the development of true individualism and a warm family life.[148] Freed from the profit motive, science and education would make great progress,[149] and art and beauty would permeate all of mankind's endeavors.[150]

The ideals of socialism were not just the achievement of economic well-being.

When the bread-and-butter problem is settled and all men and women and children the world around are rendered secure from dread of war and fear of want, then the mind and soul will be free to develop as they never were before. We shall have a literature and an art such as the troubled heart and brain of man never before conceived. We shall have beautiful houses and happy homes such as want could never foster or drudgery secure. We shall have beautiful thoughts and sentiments, and a divinity in religion, such as man weighted down by the machine could never have imagined.[151]

---

[147] Hillquit, *Socialism in Theory and Practice*, pp. 33–34; Ladoff, *Passing of Capitalism*, pp. 71–72; Spargo, *The Substance of Socialism*, pp. 30–31; Eugene V. Debs, "Socialist Ideals," *The Arena*, XL (Nov., 1908), 432; *The People* (Williams St.), Jan. 17, 1900; "Socialism and Liberty," *The Worker*, Sept. 16, 1905; *Social Democratic Herald*, Aug. 24, 1901, June 10, 1905.

[148] "Socialism and Personal Liberty," *The Worker*, May 1, 1904.

[149] *The People* (Williams St.), Jan. 20, 1901; Walter Thomas Mills, *Struggle for Existence*, p. 429.

[150] Leonard D. Abbott, "Socialism and Art," *The People* (Williams St.), March 3, 1901; Sinclair, *Our Bourgeois Literature*, pp. 30–31; Walter Thomas Mills, *Struggle for Existence*, pp. 398–99; Ladoff, *Passing of Capitalism*, p. 65.

[151] Eugene V. Debs, "Socialist Ideals," *The Arena*, XL (Nov., 1908), pp. 433–34.

# VIII

# The Greenbaum and Mailly

# Administrations

# 1901-1904

T HE TASK OF DEVELOPING twenty-three jealous
state organizations into a united party was almost impossible under
the loose national structure of the Socialist Party. Six months
after the unity convention of 1901 the national secretary, Leon
Greenbaum, was complaining that only seven states had paid their
full quota of national dues.[1] On the first anniversary of the unity
convention the membership was informed that the treasury was
empty, and the party almost twenty-four hundred dollars in debt.[2]
There were disquieting reports that the membership of ten thousand claimed when the party was organized was rapidly declining.[3]
And five state organizations were split by bitter factional fights.[4]

One national party organizer was in the field, Charles H. Vail,
who had been carried over from the old "united" Social Democratic
Party. In 1901 Vail gave 241 public lectures in 24 states, before
an average attendance of 214.[5] But even this lone national representative was too much for some of the jealous state organizations.[6]

[1] "Report of National Secretary Greenbaum to the National Committee, Socialist
Party, February, 1902," *Missouri Socialist,* Feb. 22, 1902.

[2] "Semi-Annual Report of the National Committee of the Socialist Party to the
Membership, September 12, 1902," *The Worker,* Sept. 28, 1902.

[3] "Greenbaum's Queer Report," *Social Democratic Herald,* Feb. 7, 1903.

[4] "Semi-Annual Report of the National Committee of the Socialist Party to the
Membership, September 12, 1902," *The Worker,* Sept. 28, 1902.

[5] "Report of National Organizer Charles H. Vail to National Secretary, Socialist
Party, January, 1902," *Missouri Socialist,* Jan. 25, 1902.

[6] "Report of National Secretary Greenbaum to National Committee of Socialist
Party, January, 1902," *Missouri Socialist,* Jan. 25, 1902.

The Illinois state executive complained that the national office was violating the constitution by contracting local engagements for Vail over the heads of the state committee, although that committee had refused to respond to queries from the national office.[7] Each state organization jealously guarded its membership files, and each state duplicated for itself all organizational procedures.[8]

The Wisconsin organization even refused to apply for a national party charter. The application blank gave the national committee the authority to recall the charter for cause, so Wisconsin insisted that she be given a charter without applying for one. That would make the Wisconsin charter irrevocable. When Secretary Greenbaum refused, Wisconsin simply remained in the party without a charter until 1905 as a party organization with all of the privileges and none of the obligations.[9]

Despite its lack of funds or authority, the national office entered at once into kinds of activity which became characteristic of the party during its first twelve years. National Secretary Greenbaum had hardly opened his office in St. Louis when the Amalgamated Association of Iron, Steel and Tin Workers asked for Socialist support for its August, 1901, strike. The Socialist press responded at once with appeals for funds. The Local Quorum called for organization of Socialist strike aid committees and advised them that it would be "eminently proper . . . to call the attention of the strikers to the fact that ELECTIONS ARE IMMINENT." When the strike was called off in September, Greenbaum could report that the party had received excellent publicity in the ironworkers' press, and that the *Amalgamated Journal* had even published an editorial "warning its members against bourgeois public ownership." [10]

[7] "Proceedings of Illinois Executive Committee, March 4, 1902," *The Chicago Socialist,* March 15, 1902; letter from Seymour Stedman to *The Workers' Call,* March 8, 1901; letter from Leon Greenbaum to *The Chicago Socialist,* March 22, 1902.

[8] "Semi-Annual Report of the National Committee of the Socialist Party to the Membership, September 12, 1902," *The Worker,* Sept. 28, 1902.

[9] Letter from Victor L. Berger (for Organization Committee, Social Democratic Party of Wisconsin) to Leon Greenbaum, Sept. 18, 1901; letter from Elizabeth H. Thomas, Secretary, Organization Committee of Wisconsin, to Leon Greenbaum, Oct. 4, 1901; letter from Victor L. Berger to Leon Greenbaum, Oct. 24, 1901; all letters in the *Socialist Party Official Bulletin,* Aug., 1905.

[10] "Letter of Appeal and Advice to the State, Territorial and local organizations composing the Socialist Party from the Local Quorum," *The Workers' Call,* Aug.

Union work during the rest of 1901 was limited to sending telegrams of greeting to the conventions of various national A.F. of L.
unions.[11] The first four months of 1902 apparently offered no opportunities for socialist work among the unions. But in May the
great anthracite strike began. The Pennsylvania Socialist state
committee immediately sent a letter to the chairman of every United
Mine Workers' local advising him that a solid vote for public ownership of the mines would force the operators to arbitrate.[12] The
Pennsylvania committee also appealed to the national membership
to contribute funds to enable it to send speakers and Socialist organizers into the struck fields.[13]

At first the national office agreed with the Pennsylvania Socialists that the party job was to organize Socialist locals among the
striking miners.[14] But by July the Local Quorum had changed its
mind, and insisted that all money raised should be used exclusively
for relief. Organization of Socialist locals would only distract the
strikers from their real struggle.[15] The Pennsylvania committee
proved stubborn, however, and kept four full-time Socialist organizers in the field throughout the strike in addition to distributing strike relief. The Pennsylvania Socialists reported phenomenal
success. Each of the four organizers was establishing Socialist
locals at the rate of one a day. The membership of these locals sky-
rocketed from about 25 to 340 each, within a matter of weeks.[16]

---

24, 1901; "Report of National Secretary Greenbaum to National Committee of
Socialist Party, January 24, 1902," *The Workers' Call*, Feb. 1, 1902.

[11] "Report of National Secretary Greenbaum to National Committee of Socialist
Party, January 24, 1902," *The Workers' Call*, Feb. 1, 1902.

[12] Letter from Pennsylvania Socialist State Committee to Chairman of U.M.W.
Locals, May 11, 1902, *The Chicago Socialist*, May 24, 1902.

[13] "Circular Letter from Pennsylvania State Committee of Socialist Party to All
Members of Socialist Party, May 11, 1902," *The Chicago Socialist*, May 24, 1902.

[14] "Letter from Leon Greenbaum, National Secretary, to All State Secretaries of
the Socialist Party, June 21, 1902," *The Worker*, July 6, 1902; Leon Greenbaum,
"Appeal for Strike Propaganda Fund," *Missouri Socialist*, June 14, 1902.

[15] "The Socialist Duty," *Missouri Socialist*, July 26, 1902; "Annual Report of
National Secretary Greenbaum to the National Committee of the Socialist Party,
January 29, 1903," *The Worker*, Feb. 15, 1903.

[16] "Reports of Pennsylvania State Committee, Socialist Party, July 21, 1902,"
*The Chicago Socialist*, July 9, 1902; "Proceedings of Pennsylvania State Committee,
Socialist Party, Philadelphia, July 28, 1902," *The Chicago Socialist*, Sept. 13, 1902;
letter from Miners' Socialist Propaganda Fund Committee, Philadelphia, Pennsylvania, to *The Worker*, Aug. 17, 1902.

The Socialist organizers "preached the necessity of Solidarity and explained the industrial situation so that the miners could not help but become imbued with an increased faith in themselves." [17] In the meantime, the national office raised and contributed $9,000 for strike relief.[18] As a result of this combined activity, and political discontent fostered by the strike, the Socialist vote in Pennsylvania increased almost 400 percent, from 4,800 in 1900 to 22,000 in 1902.[19]

Socialist Party leaders bent over backwards to refrain from participating in the strike itself. That was exclusively the area of the union. Secretary Greenbaum attended the United Mine Workers convention in July, 1902, but refused an invitation to address the delegates. He "did not wish to raise any question before the convention other than that for which it had been called"—relief for the miners.[20] When the miners were debating in that same month on whether to call a general coal strike, the party took no official position. In fact, it could not have done so, since the party was unofficially split. Greenbaum and the Local Quorum, which had close ties with the A.F. of L. leadership, agreed with the Federation officials who opposed a general strike as a "breach of contract." [21] Debs and most of the Center-Left press held that only a general strike could lead to victory, but that it was not their business to tell the union what to do.[22] Greenbaum used his influence among the Socialist delegates to the U.M.W. convention to help defeat the proposed general strike.[23]

Much of the Socialist press virtually ignored the strike. The *Social Democratic Herald*, for example, carried only one item during the entire seven-month strike, an article by Berger recommending public ownership of the mines.[24] And the Milwaukee party re-

[17] William Mailly, "The Anthracite Coal Strike," *International Socialist Review,* III (Aug., 1902), 83–84.

[18] *The Worker,* Nov. 16, 1902; *The Miners' Magazine,* II (Dec., 1902), 5.

[19] *The Worker,* Feb. 22, 1903.

[20] "Will Be No General Strike," *Missouri Socialist,* July 26, 1902.

[21] *Ibid.*

[22] "The Miners' Convention," *The Chicago Socialist,* July 19, 1902; Eugene V. Debs, "The Anthracite Arbitration," *American Labor Union Journal,* Jan. 8, 1903.

[23] "Will Be No General Strike," *Missouri Socialist,* July 26, 1902.

[24] Victor L. Berger, "More Facts About the Anthracite Strike," *Social Democratic Herald,* Oct. 11, 1902.

fused to distribute the strike-relief subscription blanks because "the state was in the midst of an important campaign . . . and it would not have been good generalship to have distracted their attention from the battle." [25]

Party publications showed far more concern with annual American Federation of Labor conventions than with strikes and day-by-day work in the unions. Socialists at the 1900 Federation convention concentrated on two resolutions. Max Hayes, of the Cleveland typographers, introduced a demand for nationalization of the trusts. The convention, however, adopted, 4,552 to 349, a substitute calling for study of the trust problem.[26] John Slayton of the Pennsylvania carpenters then proposed a resolution favoring the collective ownership of the means of production and distribution. The debate lasted an entire day. Again a substitute was adopted, welcoming the support of all reformers, including "the greater body of Socialists," and favoring the discussion of all political questions in the unions. The vote was 4,169 to 689 for the substitute.[27] Max Hayes concluded it was only a question of a year or two before the Federation went on record for socialism.[28]

Socialist activity at the 1901 Federation convention was similar to that in 1900. Twelve "socialistic" resolutions were introduced, but an all-day debate resulted in the passage of virtually the same substitute resolutions on trust nationalization and collective ownership.[29] But at the 1902 convention, when the resolution committee again moved to substitute welcome of Socialist support and political discussion for statements in favor of collective ownership, Max Hayes was ready with an amendment. Since, said Hayes, it was the duty of the unions to protect labor from all exploitation, he moved that the Federation go on record as advising all workers "to or-

[25] "Greenbaum's Queer Report," *Social Democratic Herald*, Feb. 7, 1903.

[26] *Report of Proceedings of the Twentieth Annual Convention of the American Federation of Labor, 1900*, pp. 131–32; Max S. Hayes, "American Federation of Labor Convention," *International Socialist Review*, I (Jan., 1901), 419–21; *The People* (Williams St.), Dec. 23, 1900.

[27] *Report of Proceedings of the Twentieth Annual Convention of the American Federation of Labor, 1900*, pp. 132–34.

[28] Max S. Hayes, "American Federation of Labor Convention," *International Socialist Review*, I (Jan., 1901), 421.

[29] American Federation of Labor, *Report of Proceedings of the Twenty-First Annual Convention, 1901* (Washington, Globe Printing Co., 1901), pp. 89, 92, 107, 119, 120, 125, 128, 129, 133, 134, 234–35, 240.

ganize their economic and political power to secure for labor the full equivalent of its toil and the overthrowal of the wage system and establishing an industrial co-operative democracy." This did not constitute an endorsement of the Socialist Party, Hayes explained, but was simply a declaration recognizing the principles of the class struggle and socialism.[30]

In an attempt to gain an inch if a mile was unobtainable, Hayes accepted an amendment which deleted all reference to overthrowal of the wage system and the institution of co-operative democracy.[31] The debate was long and full of personal recriminations, with special reference paid to the dual-union activities of the Socialist Labor Party. The miners, carpenters, and brewers supported the resolution, and it was defeated only by the comparatively narrow margin of 4,744 to 4,344.[32]

Socialist strength in the A.F. of L., of course, did not approximate the strength this vote might seem to indicate. The resolution meant different things to different men,[33] particularly since no trade unionist, no matter how conservative his analysis, could object to activity aimed at securing labor "the full equivalent of its toil." Berger claimed that at least one delegate from the Mine Workers union considered the resolution an endorsement of the Democratic Party. Furthermore, said Berger, national endorsement of even a clear socialist resolution would bring few additional votes. The Federation's conservatism was shown by the defeat, 90 to 85, of Berger's resolution on old-age pensions. Berger concluded that Socialists should work not to pass resolutions but to make personal converts in the unions.[34]

Although the National Secretary and the Local Quorum objected to all criticism of the leadership of the A.F. of L., the Center-Left press held that "sympathy and co-operation with the trades

---

[30] *Report of Proceedings of the Twenty-Second Annual Convention of the American Federation of Labor, 1902* (Washington, D.C., The Law Reporter Co., 1902), pp. 86, 111, 118, 122, 125, 178.        [31] *Ibid.*, p. 179.

[32] *Ibid.*, pp. 179–84; "Federation Convention," *The Worker*, Nov. 30, 1902; "A Surprising Vote," *Social Democratic Herald*, Nov. 29, 1902.

[33] *Report of Proceedings of the Twenty-Second Annual Convention of the American Federation of Labor, 1902* (Washington, D.C., The Law Reporter Co., 1902), pp. 180–84.

[34] Victor L. Berger, "The A.F. of L. and Socialism," *Social Democratic Herald*, Dec. 6, 1902.

unions" did not mean support of "the traitors to the working class who are wrecking the unions." [35] A *Chicago Socialist* cartoon caricatured Gompers as a dog with a dollar sign for a tail blocking the bridge leading to socialism.[36]

While some Socialists were attacking Gompers's leadership of the A.F. of L., Western Socialists were concluding that the entire Federation was too corrupt to be reformed. The Western Federation of Miners had been organized in 1893 as an A.F. of L. union of workers in the metalliferous mines and smelters.[37] When the national Federation refused to aid the W.F.M. during the long and bloody Leadville strike in 1896, the miners determined to keep their money for their own defense in the future and thereupon quit the A.F. of L.[38] The Western Federation hailed the formation of the Socialist Party in 1901 [39] and endorsed the principles of socialism.[40] Its two top leaders, Edward Boyce and William D. (Big Bill) Haywood, joined the party immediately after the unity convention.[41]

In 1898, the Western Federation, together with a number of small Western unions, formed the Western Labor Union,[42] "an industrial, educational, and political organization, uncompromising in policy." [43] At the June, 1902, convention of the Western Labor Union in Denver, representatives of the A.F. of L. executive appeared and threatened to destroy it unless it immediately affiliated with the A.F. of L.[44] The threat was particularly pointed since the A.F. of L. was at that very moment scabbing on a building-

[35] "We Are Still Unrepentant," *The Chicago Socialist*, Sept. 20, 1902.

[36] *The Chicago Socialist*, Aug. 30, 1902.

[37] Perlman, *History of Trade Unionism*, p. 213.

[38] "Origins of American Labor Union," *American Labor Union Journal*, Sept. 3, 1903; Eugene V. Debs, "The Western Labor Movement," *International Socialist Review*, III (Nov., 1902), 258; Gompers, *Seventy Years of Life and Labor*, I, 421–24.

[39] *The Miners' Magazine*, II (Nov., 1901), 10.

[40] Haywood, *Bill Haywood's Book*, p. 95.

[41] *Ibid.*

[42] "Origins of American Labor Union," *American Labor Union Journal*, Sept. 3, 1903.

[43] Clarence Smith, "Wanted—Real Hard Work by Every Friend of Western Unionism," *The Miners' Magazine*, II (Feb., 1901), 31–32. Correction of typographical errors, *ibid.*, II (March, 1901), 21.

[44] See sources cited in Note 43; Eugene V. Debs, "The Western Labor Movement," *International Socialist Review*, III (Nov., 1902); letter from F. W. Ott to A. M. Simons, July 14, 1902, *International Socialist Review*, III (Aug., 1902), 107–8; Gompers, *Seventy Years of Life and Labor*, I, 421–24.

trades strike in Denver led by the W.L.U.[45] The mine delegates were furious, and called on Eugene Debs, a convention guest, to answer the A.F. of L. threats. Debs declared that he, too, was in favor of labor unity, but not unity at the cost of principle. When the A.F. of L. had recalled its leaders from the Civic Federation, and when it had recognized the need for political action, then would be the time for unity.[46]

The Western Labor Union rejected the demand for amalgamation. It prepared to meet A.F. of L. raids by changing its name to the American Labor Union, thus making itself a national union, declared for political action, and adopted as its program the platform of the Socialist Party.[47] By June, 1903, the American Labor Union claimed a dues-paying membership of 100,000.[48]

Socialist Party leaders were far from enthusiastic in their reception of the American Labor Union.[49] While they welcomed the "unsolicited" endorsement of socialism, they "regretted" the decision of the union to maintain a dual existence.[50] But these polite regrets of the Socialist press were as nothing compared with the denunciations which flowed from the National Secretary and the Local Quorum. Greenbaum refused to give an A.L.U. organizer power to organize Socialist locals, because he held such a dual capacity might be misunderstood by organized labor.[51] Greenbaum, himself, was both National Secretary of the Socialist Party and an organizer for the A.F. of L.[52] The Local Quorum instructed all

[45] Letter from F. W. Ott to A. M. Simons, July 14, 1902, *International Socialist Review*, III (Aug., 1902).

[46] *American Labor Union Journal*, Dec. 11, 1902.

[47] Western Federation of Miners of America, *Proceedings of the Tenth Annual Convention*, pp. 83, 86–87, 93–95; "Origins of American Labor Unions," *American Labor Union Journal*, Sept. 3, 1903; Eugene V. Debs, "The Western Labor Movement," *International Socialist Review*, III (Nov., 1902), 261–62.

[48] "Report of Secretary-Treasurer Clarence Smith to the Convention of the American Labor Union, June 1, 1903," *American Labor Union Journal*, June 10, 1903.

[49] Eugene V. Debs, "The Western Labor Movement," *International Socialist Review*, III (Nov., 1902), 257–58.

[50] "The American Labor Union," *The Worker*, June 15, 1902; A. M. Simons, "Socialism and the Trade Union Movement," *International Socialist Review*, III (July, 1902), 46–49.

[51] "Annual Report of National Secretary Greenbaum to the National Committee of the Socialist Party, January 29, 1903," *The Worker*, Feb. 15, 1903.

[52] "Greenbaum's Queer Report," *Social Democratic Herald*, Feb. 7, 1903.

Socialists to recognize the error of the A.L.U.'s ways and help bring that union into the A.F. of L.[53]

This was too much for the influential New York *Worker,* which editorially informed the Quorum that it was not the business of the party to tell unions how to organize.[54] The *Social Democratic Herald,* angry over Greenbaum's refusal to give Wisconsin a party charter without receipt of an application, demanded to know by what right Greenbaum pronounced the A.F. of L. "the established trade union movement?" [55] Debs, who seldom participated in policy matters, suggested that those who had damned the A.L.U. with faint praise had apparently decided that "it was wiser policy to curry favor with numbers than to stand by principles." [56] He asked why, if unity at all costs was so important, the A.F. of L. had not amalgamated with the Knights of Labor, or why the Socialist Labor Party had been split? The A.L.U. would serve to inspire all workers who favored industrial unionism, socialism, and political action. Debs said that the A.L.U. was not organized to fight the A.F. of L. It had already offered to join a general mine strike to support the anthracite strikers. But the reactionary A.F. of L. unions refused. "There is one way and one way only to unite the American trades-union movement," Debs declared. "The American Federation of Labor must go forward to the American Labor Union; the American Labor Union will never go back to the American Federation of Labor. Numbers count for nothing; principle and progress for everything." [57]

It was not a dispute over the principles of union organization alone that led to the downfall of Greenbaum and the Local Quorum, but an uproar over election tactics. To the surprise of the Socialists,[58] their vote in the Congressional elections of 1902 increased

---

[53] "Resolutions of the Local Quorum of the National Committee of the Socialist Party on the Attitude of the Socialist Party towards the American Labor Union, St. Louis, August 2, 1902," *The Worker,* Aug. 10, 1902.

[54] "The Western Labor Movement," *The Worker,* Dec. 21, 1902.

[55] "Greenbaum's Queer Report," *Social Democratic Herald,* Feb. 7, 1903.

[56] Eugene V. Debs, "The Western Labor Movement," *International Socialist Review,* III (Nov., 1902), 260–61.

[57] Eugene V. Debs, "The Western Labor Movement," *International Socialist Review,* III (Nov., 1902), 258–63; Eugene V. Debs, "An Up-to-Date Labor Class Movement," *Social Democratic Herald,* Aug. 23, 1902.

[58] Hillquit, *History of Socialism,* pp. 341–42.

over that of 1900 by more than 125 percent, from 97,000 to 227,000.[59] But the California vote increased by only 25 percent.[60] San Francisco had been torn by a series of strikes after the 1900 presidential elections. Out of these strikes had been born the Union Labor Party. The San Francisco Socialists had attacked the U.L.P. in the 1901 elections as a "scab," "reform," and "capitalist" party, and the Socialists had lost two thirds of their 1900 vote.[61]

When the state election approached in the fall of 1902, the San Francisco and Los Angeles Socialists decided not to run candidates for the offices of justices of the peace, superintendent of schools, state assemblymen and state senators. The Socialists announced that they did not endorse the U.L.P. ticket, but that they "simply stood aside and let them prove their claims if they could." [62] However, the slate did become popularly known as the Socialist-Union Labor Party fusion ticket.[63]

*The Worker* began denouncing the California "fusion" as soon as the election returns were in.[64] But four members of the five-man Local Quorum [65] and National Secretary Greenbaum immediately sent letters to the Socialist press defending the action of the California Socialists, and suggesting that other state and local organizations might well adopt similar tactics. Local St. Louis answered these suggestions with a resolution calling for the resignation of Greenbaum and the offending members of the Local Quorum.[66]

The National Committee, with one delegate from each of 22 states, met in St. Louis on January 29, 1903.[67] By a vote of 16 to 6 it summarily removed the Local Quorum and National Secretary Greenbaum. No explanation was given for the removal, but it was

[59] *The Worker*, Feb. 22, 1903.        [60] *Ibid.*

[61] Letter from Job Harriman to *The Worker*, Feb. 8, 1903.

[62] *Advance*, (San Francisco), Dec. 20, 1902.

[63] "Resolution of Local St. Louis, January 5, 1903," *The Chicago Socialist*, Jan. 24, 1903.

[64] *The Worker*, Nov.–Dec., 1902, Jan., 1903.

[65] E. Val Putnam, James S. Roche, William Brandt, and M. Ballard Dunn. Quorum member Gustave Hoehn did not participate in the dispute. (*The Worker*, Feb. 8, 1903.)

[66] "Resolution of Local St. Louis, January 5, 1903," *The Chicago Socialist*, Jan. 24, 1903.

[67] "National Committee, Report of Proceedings at St. Louis," *The Worker*, Feb. 8, 1903.

understood by all that the major crime had been the stand for "fusion." [68] The committee unanimously passed a resolution declaring that the party would not take sides in purely trade union disputes, and that the Socialist Party would under no circumstances "fuse, combine or compromise" with any other political party.[69]

It took three ballots to elect a new national secretary. But the Center-Left finally won with the election of William Mailly of Massachusetts.[70] When the committee voted to choose a new site for national headquarters, the states of the Missouri Valley united. Because the vote of Kansas was equal to that of New York or Illinois, it was possible to designate Omaha, Nebraska, as the heart of the proletarian movement and to stipulate that the local Quorum would be made up of one member from each of the states of South Dakota, Nebraska, Iowa, Kansas, and Missouri.[71]

The Center-Left press immediately called for a referendum, pointing out that, whereas the Socialist Party was supposed to be a workers' movement, the new center of control for the party was in an agricultural area. It was also charged that the Right-wing National Committeeman from Kansas, Walter Thomas Mills, had maneuvered the Omaha deal after failing to get headquarters located in his "socialist school" in Kansas City.[72] The *Appeal to Reason* replied that the East was conservative; the West was the

[68] *Ibid.;* Victor L. Berger, "Review of National Committee Meeting," *Social Democratic Herald,* Feb. 14, 1903. All members of the committee were for removal, but the six who voted against the motion for removal did so because the members of the Quorum were not given a chance to defend themselves (*ibid.*). Greenbaum left the Socialist Party at once, and helped bolster Gompers' charge that the party favored the A.L.U. and opposed the A.F. of L. (Letter from Gustave A. Hoehn to *The Worker,* Jan. 24, 1904.)

[69] "National Committee, Report of Proceedings at St. Louis," *The Worker,* Feb. 8, 1903; "Annual Report of the National Secretary of Socialist Party, 1903," *The Worker,* March 27, 1904.

[70] "National Committee, Report of Proceedings at St. Louis," *The Worker,* Feb. 8, 1903.

[71] *Ibid.;* letter from Morris Hillquit to *The Worker,* Feb. 2, 1903, *The Worker,* Feb. 8, 1903; Victor L. Berger, "Review of National Committee Meeting," *Social Democratic Herald,* Feb. 14, 1903; "Where We Stand Now," *The Socialist* (Seattle), Feb. 15, 1903.

[72] Letter from Morris Hillquit to *The Worker,* Feb. 2, 1903; "The National Headquarters," *The Worker,* Feb. 8, 1903; "Classes, Not Individuals," *The Worker,* March 22, 1903; "Where We Stand Now," *The Socialist* (Seattle), Feb. 15, 1903.

true home of revolution.[73] At the same time, Ernest Untermann, of the new Local Quorum, informed the party membership that he was not a farmer but an "intellectual proletarian." [74]

A national referendum in May, 1903, on the motion to move the party headquarters to Chicago was defeated by 43 votes: 3,527 to 3,484. But a motion to select the Local Quorum from the states of Illinois, Wisconsin, Indiana, Iowa, and Kentucky was carried by 3,848 to 2,965. The membership, by a vote of 4,195 to 1,180, confirmed the action of its National Committee in removing the St. Louis Local Quorum.[75] Even the supporters of Omaha understood, however, that the 1904 party convention would move the party headquarters to Chicago.[76]

In William Mailly the party at last had a national secretary capable of turning chaos into order. In 1903, 22 organizers and lecturers were sent out from the national office for varying periods at a salary of $3 a day.[77] Fifty to one hundred "soap-boxers" were continually in the field, earning only what they received from the sale of socialist pamphlets, books, and newspaper subscriptions.[78] State committees were encouraged to conduct their own organizational and propaganda campaigns, with the national office defraying part of the cost and serving as general co-ordinator.[79]

There were still complaints against the threat of party discipline and demands for greater state autonomy.[80] But Mailly was diplomatic enough to co-ordinate party operations and still leave the extreme states' rights leaders with the illusion that they were as

[73] A. W. Ricker, "National Committee Meeting," *Appeal to Reason,* Feb. 14, 1903.
[74] "Resolution and Statement of Majority of Local Quorum," *The Worker,* March 22, 1903.
[75] "The Vote on Headquarters," *The Worker,* May 31, 1903.
[76] *Appeal to Reason,* Feb. 14, 1903.
[77] "Semi-Annual Report of the National Secretary of the Socialist Party, Omaha, Nebraska, July 14, 1903," *The Worker,* Aug. 9, 1903; "Annual Report of the National Secretary of the Socialist Party, 1903," *The Worker,* March 7, 1904; letter from William Mailly to Howard H. Caldwell, Dec. 23, 1903, *The Socialist* (Seattle), Jan. 10, 1904.
[78] A. M. Simons, "Socialist Movement in America," *The World To-Day,* V (July, 1903), 939.
[79] "Semi-Annual Report of the National Secretary of the Socialist Party, Omaha, Nebraska, July 14, 1903," *The Worker,* Aug. 9, 1903; A. M. Simons, "Socialist Movement in America," *The World To-Day,* V (July, 1903), 939–40.
[80] W. G. Critchlow, State Secretary, Ohio, "State Autonomy," *The Socialist* (Seattle), Jan. 18, 1903; Victor L. Berger, "Review of National Committee Meeting," *Social Democratic Herald,* Feb. 14, 1903.

independent as ever. The party membership, an optimistically estimated 10,000, had remained stationary during Greenbaum's nineteen months as secretary. By the end of 1903, dues payments indicated that the "average membership" had increased to 16,000.[81] The national office had paid off its debts, and was operating on a national budget of over $14,000.[82]

While Mailly was busy welding the Socialists into a real national organization, party activities continued to follow the pattern of literature and lectures laid out by state leaders during the Greenbaum administration. Socialist delegates at the 1903 A.F. of L. convention again offered their resolutions on the need for labor to use its economic and political power along class lines to secure the full product of its toil. This resolution had been sufficiently innocuous to win the support of the miners in 1902. But the settlement of the coal strike, and perhaps the Socialist criticism of the nature of the settlement, had swung the mine leaders to the right.[83] The delegates rejected the Socialists' compromise motion, 11,282 to 2,145.[84]

The organization of the American Labor Union gave some life to the lukewarm support of Socialist convention delegates for industrial unionism.[85] They spoke on the advantages of industrial organization during the jurisdictional disputes at the 1902 and 1903 A.F. of L. conventions. And they were at least partly responsible for the convention decision to substitute interunion negotiations for executive council adjudication in jurisdictional controversies.[86]

In the meantime, the American Labor Union had increased its membership from 18,000 direct and 70,000 affiliated in 1902, to

[81] "Annual Report of the National Secretary of the Socialist Party, 1903," *The Worker*, March 7, 1904.        [82] *Ibid.*

[83] Eugene V. Debs, "The Anthracite Arbitration," *American Labor Union Journal*, Jan. 8, 1903; "John Mitchell's Ingratitude," *Social Democratic Herald*, Jan. 31, 1903; "The Coal-Strike Decision," *The Worker*, April 5, 1903; Eugene V. Debs in the *Social Democratic Herald*, Dec. 5, 1903.

[84] *Proceedings of the American Federation of Labor, 1903* (Bloomington, Illinois, Pantagraph Printing and Stationery Co., 1906), pp. 100, 120, 126, 127, 131, 132, 137, 138, 139, 143, 147, 151, 152, 188–99, 212; "Federation Convention," *The Worker*, Nov. 29, 1903.

[85] "The A.F. of L. Convention," *Missouri Socialist*, Dec. 21, 1901.

[86] *Proceedings of the American Federation of Labor, 1903* (Bloomington, Illinois, Pantagraph Printing and Stationery Co., 1906), pp. 72, 116, 217, 218, 253; Max S. Hayes, "The A.F. of L. Convention," *International Socialist Review*, III (Dec., 1902), 371, 373.

70,000 direct and 200,000 affiliated in June, 1903.[87] The union continued to give unqualified endorsement and publicity to the Socialist Party, and participated indirectly in the elections which sent five Socialists to the Montana legislature and swept the Anaconda municipal elections.[88]

Socialist support of Western miners' strikes, however, was not quite so enthusiastic. The great Cripple Creek strike had broken out in Colorado in 1903 in an attempt to enforce the eight-hour day. An amendment to the state constitution in 1902 had overridden a court decision declaring the eight-hour day unconstitutional. But, despite the election promises of both Democratic and Republican parties, neither the governor nor legislature took any action to implement the amendment. The strike was fought bitterly on both sides, with police and militia ignoring all guarantees of civil liberties.[89]

Socialist members of the Western Federation of Miners later charged that Right-wing Socialists looked on the strike as a "border feud" of little importance to the party.[90] At any rate, the action taken by the Socialist Party in Colorado struck the union and Left-wing Socialists as leaving much to be desired. The party leadership in Colorado issued a statement listing the legal violations committed by state authorities representing the mine owners—murders committed without punishment, strikers arrested without warrant and held in military prisons, writs of habeas corpus denied, armed invasion of courts, unlawful search and seizure, and military censorship of the press. The Socialist leaders then called on all their followers to point out to the strikers that the capitalist parties could not be trusted. But, declared the Socialist state committee, Socialists must not attempt to organize protests to force an end to the terror. Instead, they should "pursue relentlessly the policy of stat-

[87] "Address of Charles Moyer (President) to Annual Convention of Western Federation of Miners," *The Chicago Socialist,* June 23, 1903; John M. O'Neill, "Western Federation of Miners," *American Labor Union Journal,* Sept. 3, 1903; D. C. Coates, "The Struggle in Colorado," *American Labor Union Journal,* Sept. 3, 1903.

[88] A. M. Simons, "Socialist Movement in America," *The World To-Day,* V (July, 1903), 937.

[89] Selig Perlman and Philip Taft, in Commons, *et al., History of Labour,* IV, 194–207; Langdon, *The Cripple Creek Strike.*

[90] Haywood, *Bill Haywood's Book,* p. 108.

ing and re-stating the facts of the actual situation, realizing that
no accusation is so strong as a temperate, manly statement of the
truth." Finally, Socialists should warn the strikers of the danger
and futility of union labor parties.[91] Aside from half a dozen protest meetings held in Denver, there is no evidence that the party, as
an organization, violated the state committee's edict.[92]

In addition to instructing its strikers on how to vote, the only
time Socialist leaders mentioned the American Labor Union was in
an occasional editorial advising them to go into the A.F. of L.[93]
In return, A.L.U. leaders, after early denials that they had formed
a dual union,[94] became increasingly bitter toward Socialists who
criticized them and defended A.F. of L. leaders.

The gigantic intellect [Gustave Hoehn] which control[s] St. Lous
[*sic.*] Labor sees no inconsistency in giving aid, comfort, support and
per capita tax to a person ["Slimy Sam Gompers"] who has shown
himself as antagonistic to working class interests as any capitalist in
the land. There is about as much consistency in Editor Hoehn's position as there is in that of the pure and simple union man who votes the
bosses ticket.[95]

Debs told the Socialist leaders who devoted themselves to A.F. of L.
convention politics that they might as well "orate to a lot of wooden
Indians as seek to change the controlling clique of the convention." [96] Debs warned that only work among the rank and file and
support of the A.L.U. would win support for socialism among trade
unionists.[97]

The spring and fall elections of 1903 seemed to indicate that
additional work was necessary if more Socialist votes were to be attracted. The party did succeed in consolidating its position in a

[91] "Statement of the Local Quorum of the State Committee of Colorado," *The
Chicago Socialist*, Jan. 30, 1904.

[92] *The Chicago Socialist*, July 2, 1904.

[93] Max S. Hayes, "The World of Labor," *International Socialist Review*, IV
(July, 1903), 51.

[94] Speech by David C. Coats (Vice-President of the A.L.U.) delivered in Brick-
layers' Hall, Chicago, Oct. 27, 1903, *The Chicago Socialist*, Oct. 31, 1903.

[95] *American Labor Union Journal*, May 5, 1904; *American Labor Union Journal*,
April 28, May 12, 1904.

[96] Eugene V. Debs in the *Social Democratic Herald*, Dec. 5, 1903.

[97] *Ibid.;* Eugene V. Debs, "An Up-to-Date Labor Class Movement," *Social
Democratic Herald*, Aug. 23, 1902.

number of towns and villages, to the extent of electing some one
hundred councilmen, assistant assessors, and school board members.[98] But in many state elections the Socialist vote dropped
sharply. Party leaders were particularly concerned over such
symptoms as a 30 percent loss in Massachusetts and a 40 percent
loss in Pennsylvania, both states formerly the leading examples of
socialist progress.[99] The reduced vote can probably be explained
in part as due to a combination of the loss of middle-class support
in cities where campaigns were conducted on strict working-class
lines,[100] and the tendency elsewhere for party leaders to forget
all about socialism and the working class in their efforts to
strengthen their own political fortunes. It was even charged by
sympathetic non-Socialists that the party had already "degenerated into a sort of Socialistic Tammany." [101]

The question of how to win votes for socialism had been discussed at great length at the Socialist Unity Convention in 1901
in the two-day debate over the "Immediate Demands." Platforms
of both the Springfield and Chicago headquarters Social Democratic parties included a list of twelve "immediate demands" for
public ownership of monopolies and public utilities, woman suffrage, initiative and referendum, old age, accident, and unemployment insurance, and abolition of war.[102] They were originally
drafted by the Chicago Board, but were accepted by the anti-De
Leon S.L.P. when it made its first attempts at unity with the Social
Democrats.

At the 1901 Unity Convention, however, the difference in the
approach of the Center-Left and that of the Right toward the
"Immediate Demands" was brought into sharp focus. The Right,
with its conception of socialism as the ultimate product of a series
of reforms, considered the demands as "steps" along the road
to socialism; the Center-Left viewed them merely as measures
to ameliorate suffering until socialism was ushered in by the complete electoral triumph of the Socialist Party. Many members of

98 "Socialist Progress in the United States," *The Worker,* May 1, 1903; Hillquit,
*History of Socialism,* p. 343.
99 "The Year's Progress," *The Worker,* May 1, 1904.
100 "Recent Elections," *The Socialist* (Seattle), Dec. 13, 1903.
101 "The Socialist Reverses," *The Independent,* LV (Nov. 26, 1903), 2823.
102 "Social Democratic Party Platform," *The Workers' Call,* Oct. 20, 1900.

the Center-Left feared that the Right would make the demands and not the electoral "revolution" the be-all and end-all of the socialist movement. They insisted, therefore, that the party platform delete all immediate demands and consist simply of the generally acceptable eight-paragraph summary of scientific socialism. The Right protested that this was anarchism, and that every socialist party in the world had immediate demands in its platform.

Finally, George D. Herron, who personally inclined toward elimination of the demands, worked out a compromise. The demands were to be included, although they now emphasized better wages and hours, as well as public ownership, greater democracy in government, and greater state aid to education. But the seven demands concluded with a statement that all promises of capitalist public ownership parties were "for the purpose of obtaining greater security in the exploitation of other industries, and not for the amelioration of the condition of the working class." The Right-wing protested, but since it was clear that unless they accepted this last paragraph, all the demands might be eliminated, they agreed to go along. The platform, demands and all, was adopted with just one dissenting vote.[103]

But Right-wing Socialists did not feel themselves bound by the national platform's approach to reform when it came to municipal elections. In Milwaukee and in Spokane, Washington, where the Right was in control, the 1902 and 1903 Socialist platforms gave a quick nod in the direction of socialism, and then proceeded to lay out general demands for an end to private franchises for public utilities, abolition of the contract system on public works, and the forcing of large corporations to pay their share of taxes. Milwaukee also included a demand for monthly symphony concerts.[104] The Olathe, Kansas, socialist platform consisted of only one demand—homeowners to have the option of using *either* sidewalk brick or cement.[105] As the 1904 national Socialist convention

[103] *Proceedings of Socialist Unity Convention, 1901,* typescript in Harper Library, University of Chicago, pp. 157–430.

[104] "Milwaukee Municipal Platform, Social Democratic Party," *Social Democratic Herald,* March 15, 1902; "Spokane Socialist Platform," *The Socialist* (Seattle), Feb. 8, 1903.

[105] "A New Socialist Issue—Brick or Cement?" *The Socialist* (Seattle), Oct. 4, 1904.

approached, Berger suggested that the convention not waste its time discussing socialist principles: "All this convention ought to do . . . is to formulate a working program for the present national campaign, and working programs for the coming state and municipal elections." [106]

This tendency on the part of the Right to concentrate on the immediate issues, which were to form the heart of the "progressive movement," gave birth to a typical Socialist reaction—"impossibilism." [107] The term "impossibilist" was later applied by the Right to all Socialists who opposed their program of "step-at-a-time" socialism. But in 1903–1905, the impossibilists were a sect criticized by Left and Right alike.[108] The impossibilists held that all activity other than circulation of propaganda for the immediate inauguration of socialism was a waste of time. There was only one proper immediate demand, the one calling for achievement of the co-operative commonwealth.[109] Some of those who toyed with impossibilism reacted to Right "appeasement" of the A.F. of L. leadership with a theory that considered all union activity as an attempt to benefit the individual at the expense of the entire proletariat.[110]

The impossibilists admitted that some Socialists might be elected to office before the party had complete control of the government. So they included in all their platforms the following:

The Socialist party, when in office, shall always and everywhere, until the present system of wage slavery is utterly abolished, make the answer to this question its guiding rule of conduct; will this legislation advance the interest of the working class and aid the workers in their class struggle against capitalism? If it does, the Socialist Party

[106] Victor L. Berger in *Social Democratic Herald*, April 23, 1904.

[107] Perhaps the term originated as the conscious contrast of this policy with that of the anti-Marxian French "Possibilists" formed by Paul Brousse in the 1880s (Kirkup and Pease, *A History of Socialism*, p. 327).

[108] Herman F. Titus, "Shall We Condemn the Unions?" *The Socialist* (Seattle), April 10, 1904; statement by Herman F. Titus in Socialist Party, *Proceedings of the National Convention, 1904*, p. 211; *The Socialist* (Seattle), April 8, 1905; Ernest Untermann, "The Trade Union Resolution and the Working Program," *American Labor Union Journal*, May 19, 1904.

[109] "Proceedings of the State Convention of Illinois Socialists, Peoria, Illinois, July 4, 1902," *The Chicago Socialist*, Aug. 2, 1902; Morris Kaplan in *The Chicago Socialist*, Jan. 16, 1904; "The Duty of the Hour," *The Chicago Socialist*, May 4, 1904.

[110] Robert Rives LaMonte, "Socialism and the Trade Unions," *International Socialist Review*, V (July, 1904), 12–17; Morris Kaplan in the *Chicago Socialist*, Jan. 16, 1904.

is for it; if it does not, the Socialist Party is absolutely opposed to it.[111]

Ironically, it was Herman F. Titus, leading theoretician of the Left and an implacable enemy of impossibilism, who originally wrote this statement for the 1902 Seattle platform. It was to be followed by a list of "immediate demands." But the impossibilists at the Seattle convention, temporarily in control, adopted the phrase and then deleted all the demands.[112]

The impossibilists, most of whose supporters were professionals and small businessmen,[113] explained that it was not feasible to write a series of immediate demands which would benefit both labor and the middle class. They added that labor needed the support of the middle class to win the election. And, they concluded, the minimum program about which support could be rallied was immediate establishment of socialism.[114]

By the fall of 1903, the Socialist Party was so split over Socialist theory that the National Committee adopted by a vote of 14 to 7 a motion to abandon the project for a "campaign book" for the 1904 election.[115] "The campaign book would infallibly contain statements to which each of us would take exceptions. Nevertheless, we would be bound by these statements. . . . The whole project is therefore impracticable and unwise." [116]

In February, 1904, William Mailly had been re-elected National Secretary, receiving 21 of the 22 votes cast, eight national committee members abstaining.[117] In April a national referendum moved the party headquarters from Omaha to Chicago.[118]

On May 1, 183 delegates from 36 states met in Brand's Hall on

[111] "Platform of Seattle Socialist Party, June 29, 1902," *The Socialist* (Seattle), Feb. 8, 1903; "Platform of Cincinnati Socialist Party, 1903," *The Socialist* (Seattle), March 29, 1903; "Platform of Kentucky Socialist Party, 1903," *The Socialist* (Seattle), April 12, 1903; "Cook County Socialist Platform, 1904," *The Chicago Socialist,* March 19, 1904.

[112] Statement by Herman F. Titus in Socialist Party, *Proceedings of the National Convention, 1904,* pp. 259–60.

[113] Socialist Party, *Proceedings of the National Convention, 1904,* pp. 22–26, 243–76.

[114] Morris Kaplan in *The Chicago Socialist,* May 4, 1904.

[115] *Socialist Party Weekly Bulletin,* Nov. 7, 1903.

[116] Letter from John M. Work to William Mailly, Oct. 12, 1903, *Socialist Party Weekly Bulletin,* Oct. 14, 1903.

[117] *The Worker,* Feb. 14, 1904.

[118] "Report of National Secretary of Socialist Party, April, 1904," *The Worker,* April 24, 1904.

the corner of Clark and Erie streets, Chicago, for the first regular convention of the party.[119] One hundred and twenty of the delegates were American-born; the 19 delegates of German extraction were the largest group of foreign-born. The occupations of the delegates showed a characteristic which was to become more pronounced with passing years: twenty editors of socialist newspapers comprised the largest group; then came fifteen lawyers, seven professional lecturers, seven teachers, five physicians, and five paid party organizers. The remainder of the delegation was made up largely of craft workers, professionals, and small businessmen. Seventy-eight were members of trade unions, but this included the twenty editors, who held cards in the typographical union.[120]

William Mailly gave his report as National Secretary. In the fifteen months since he had taken office the party had grown from a doubtful 10,000 occasional dues-payers to 22,000 regular contributors.[121] But Mailly warned that there was great need to tighten up the party organization. "Of the writing of books, the making of speeches, and the editing and publishing of papers, there is no end, but there is an appreciable lack of application to the executive branches of our party work." Too many leading Socialists, Mailly complained, wanted paid jobs with the national office which would allow them to travel around the country giving lectures. Too many state leaders placed their state organization above the national party. Too many local party bosses sounded the slogans of democracy and state autonomy but really practiced extreme individualism and interference in the affairs of other states. If the party was to take advantage of growing "socialist sentiment" in America, its organization must be revised and its leaders must stop seeking personal prestige and begin co-operating with one another.[122]

The Center and Right-wing leaders were furious. Led by Berger, and with the co-operation of the session's chairman, Frank Siever-

[119] *Social Democratic Herald,* May 7, 1904; Socialist Party, *Proceedings of the National Convention, 1904,* p. 16.

[120] From data compiled by Charles R. Martin, published in the Cleveland *Citizen,* May 21, 1904.

[121] "The Year's Progress," *The Worker,* May 1, 1904.

[122] "Report of the National Secretary to the 1904 Socialist Party Convention, May 1, 1904," in Socialist Party, *Proceedings of the National Convention, 1904,* pp. 56–60.

man of New York, the party heads among the delegates attacked Mailly as a bureaucrat, a dictator who sought to control the party for his own ends, a miser who was interested in socialism only because of his salary. Mailly replied that the delegates would have his resignation by the end of the convention.[123]

The delegates mulled this over for two days and finally realized that without Mailly an effective national Presidential campaign would be virtually impossible. Debs and Ben Hanford, who had been selected as the party's candidates, insisted that Mailly continue as National Secretary through the campaign. Sieverman apologized for the manner in which he had handled the session at which Mailly was attacked. George Herron moved that Mailly be asked to withdraw his resignation, or at least postpone it until after the election. Berger was compelled to second it. The motion was passed, and Mailly agreed to postpone his resignation until after the election.[124]

The convention tried to give the party a more truly national character through the adoption of a new constitution. The new charter called for a National Committee to consist of one delegate from each state, plus an additional delegate for every thousand party members or major fraction thereof. This committee was to elect an executive committee of seven members who were to serve for one year. The executive committee was to meet at least once a quarter, transact all business of the national office, and supervise the work of the national secretary under the direction of the National Committee. The National Committee, except for a meeting held in even-numbered years in which there were no Presidential elections, would conduct its affairs by mail. The state organizations of the party continued to have "sole jurisdiction" over members residing in their states, but the National Secretary was to have control of national lecture and literature bureaus and have authority to deal directly with party locals. The National Secretary was to issue an official bulletin to all party organizations, but the national office was not to publish an official party newspaper.[125]

The question of party attitude toward labor unions was the subject of a very confused debate. The resolutions committee consisted

<hr>

123 Socialist Party, *Proceedings of the National Convention, 1904*, pp. 129–37.
124 *Ibid.*, pp. 279–81.          125 *Ibid.*, pp. 310–14.

overwhelmingly of A.F. of L. members.[126] The supporters of industrial as against craft organization had expected to discuss the subject fully during the debate on the resolution, but had not considered it necessary to prepare for that debate.[127] The Committee's resolution recognized trade unions as a product of class struggle, and called on all Socialists to aid unions in their economic battles. It warned unionists that only political action leading to socialism could help them in the long run. Then the resolution concluded with what was to become the bone of contention: "Neither political nor other differences of opinion justify the division of the forces of labor in the industrial movement." [128] This sentence seems to have been introduced to force the Socialist-led American Labor Union to disband and join the A.F. of L. For it was just these "political" and "other differences"—industrial rather than craft organization—which furnished the basis for the A.L.U.[129]

The resolution was no sooner read than it was attacked by the impossibilists on the ground that unions were merely reform organizations and the Socialist Party should have nothing to do with reform. Those who favored the resolution were able to hold the floor and confine their defense to answering the impossibilists. The number of speakers was limited by convention rules. There was no mention of the real issues—dual unionism, craft vs. industrial unionism, A.F. of L. vs. A.L.U.—until the last speaker, Malcolm O'Malley of Montana, managed to get the floor.[130] He charged that those who favored the A.F. of L. were using their superior parliamentary knowledge "to hide behind the trades union movement as a general proposition, in endeavoring to force through this organization a specious endorsement of one kind of unionism." He warned that before those who stood for industrial unionism and political action would capitulate to those who were "playing into the hands of the capitalists" they would tell the "convention to go to hell. (Loud applause.)" [131]

126 *Ibid.*, p. 41.
127 Ernest Untermann, "The Socialist Party and the Trade Unions," *The Worker*, May 5, 1906.
128 Socialist Party, *Proceedings of the National Convention, 1904*, p. 206.
129 Statement of Gustave Hoehn, quoted by William E. Trautmann in *The Socialist Party Official Bulletin*, April, 1905.
130 Socialist Party, *Proceedings of the National Convention, 1904*, pp. 177–212.
131 *Ibid.*, p. 212.

The debate was closed. Those who favored industrial unionism were faced with the dilemma of voting with the impossibilists against any endorsement of union work, or voting for a resolution they suspected to be aimed at industrial unionism.[132] They divided, and the resolution was adopted, 107 to 52.[133]

Despite Right-wing caucuses designed to gain control of key committees,[134] the platform committee was overwhelmingly Center-Left in outlook.[135] The committee made a determined effort to present the party's analysis of scientific socialism in terms traditional in American political life.[136]

The Socialist Party makes its appeal to the American people as the defender and preserver of the idea of liberty and self-government, in which the nation was born; as the only political movement standing for the program and principles by which the liberty of the individual may become a fact; as the only political organization that is democratic, and that has for its purpose the democratizing of the whole society.

While the platform, written by George D. Herron and edited by Herman Titus,[137] did not quite accomplish its purpose, it was a far cry from the clichés which characterized the 1900 platform.

The question of "immediate demands" was settled by including them in the body of the platform, but not under a separate heading. The platform warned, however, that "such measures of relief as we may be able to force from capitalism are but a preparation of the workers to seize the whole powers of government, in order that they may thereby lay hold of the whole system of industry, and thus come into their rightful inheritance." [138]

---

[132] John M. Work, "The Trade Union Resolution," *American Labor Union Journal*, June 2, 1904; Ernest Untermann, "The Trade Union Resolution and the Working Program," *American Labor Union Journal*, May 19, 1904.

[133] Socialist Party, *Proceedings of the National Convention, 1904*, pp. 214–15.

[134] Herman F. Titus, "The Working Class Convention," *The Socialist* (Seattle), May 15, 1904.

[135] Eugene V. Debs, chairman, George D. Herron, Ben Hanford, William Mailly, Herman F. Titus, G. H. Strobell, Thomas E. Will, Victor L. Berger, and M. W. Wilkins.

[136] Statement of Eugene V. Debs in Socialist Party, *Proceedings of the National Convention, 1904*, p. 254.

[137] "Official Report of H. F. Titus, Delegate-at-Large from State of Washington, May 22, 1904," *The Socialist* (Seattle), May 29, 1904.

[138] Socialist Party, *Proceedings of the National Convention, 1904*, pp. 306–9.

The committee on "State and Municipal Program" brought in a list of reform measures for Socialists to advocate and support in local elections and in local governing bodies. The impossibilists opposed the program as a series of proposals torn from the back page of the Hearst *Chicago American*.[139] The Right-wing delegates refrained from speaking, except for Seymour Stedman who suggested that reforms were steps leading to socialism.[140] The Center-Left held that the "program" and the "platform" were two different things. The party would campaign on the platform, but would work for the measures listed in the program as long as capitalism lasted. When the Socialists won complete control of the government, they would inaugurate socialism, as outlined in the platform.[141] All factions, except the impossibilists, finally agreed to refer the State and Municipal Program back to committee for reworking.[142] The 34 planks of this program were adopted in 1906 by party referendum, 4,000 to 150 [143]—an indication that impossibilism had virtually disappeared.

The impossibilists attempted a rally to defeat the 1904 platform in the referendum vote that followed the convention. On May 8, two days after adjournment, the Cook County (Chicago) Central Committee, under impossibilist leadership, passed a resolution condemning the platform as opportunist.[144] They appointed a committee which wrote and circulated a platform which secured some support in Washington, Idaho, and Nebraska.[145] The back of the movement was broken, however, when on May 15 the anti-impossibilist forces in Chicago obtained control of the county central committee, removed impossibilist officers, expelled the two largest impossibilist ward branches, put their representatives in charge of the *Chicago Socialist*, and endorsed the convention plat-

---

139 *Ibid.*, pp. 24, 243–44, 246–47, 257, 266.    140 *Ibid.*, p. 258.

141 *Ibid.*, pp. 249, 250, 258–62.

142 *Ibid.*, pp. 271–76.

143 *The Socialist Party Official Bulletin*, April, 1906.

144 Letter from A. M. Simons to *The Worker*, May 17, 1904, *The Worker*, May 29, 1904; "Statement of the Executive Committee to the members of the Socialist Party in Cook County," *The Worker*, May 29, 1904; "Statement of New Cook County Executive Committee," *The Chicago Socialist*, May 21, 1904.

145 D. M. Smith, "An 'Impossibilist' Position," *International Socialist Review*, V (July, 1904), 46–48; "Resolution of Local Omaha, Nebraska, June 1, 1904," *The Worker*, June 12, 1904; "Resolution of Nebraska Socialist Party State Convention, July 4, 1904," *The Worker*, July 24, 1904.

form.[146] The national party referendum adopted the platform accepted by the convention by a vote of 5,776 to 549.[147]

The developing Left-wing of the party [148] won its major convention victory in the unanimous nominations of Eugene Debs and Benjamin Hanford for President and Vice President of the United States.[149] Debs had voted against the trade union resolution because he considered it an attack on industrial unionism and the American Labor Union, and that fact was stressed in the nominating and seconding speeches.[150] Hanford, of the New York typographers' union, creator of the mythical "Jimmie Higgins," the rank-and-file Socialist who did all the work while party leaders took all the credit, was nominated by Herman Titus who said he did so in the face of remarks by some delegates that a "nonworker" should be chosen.[151]

Debs, speaking for the Center and Left, set the tone for the election campaign when he declared for "the overthrow of the capitalist system and the emancipation of the working class from wage-slavery. The capitalists may have the tariff, finance, imperialism and other dust-covered and moth-eaten issues entirely to themselves." [152] Whatever the inclinations and efforts of the party Right to conduct the campaign exclusively on a local reform basis, Debs, Hanford, and the national office, together with the great majority of the local organizations, devoted themselves to exposition of capitalism's evils and socialism's benefits.

The Republican and Democratic parties were both attacked as tools of the capitalist class.[153] Their labor planks were "interchangeable and non-redeemable." [154] It was pointed out that

[146] "Statement of New Cook County Executive Committee"; letter from W. Harry Spears to *The Worker*, July 23, 1904, *The Worker*, May 14, 1904; handbill issued by "Revolutionary Socialists of Cook County" (impossibilist), May, 1904, in Wisconsin State Historical Library, Socialist Pamphlet Box; the Chicago *Record Herald*, May 23, 1904.

[147] "Monthly Report of National Secretary of Socialist Party, July, 1904," *The Worker*, July 31, 1904.

[148] See below, pp. 175–98.

[149] Socialist Party, *Proceedings of the National Convention, 1904*, pp. 219–23.

[150] *Ibid.*, pp. 219–20.          [151] *Ibid.*, pp. 221–23.

[152] *Opening Campaign Speech of E. V. Debs, Indianapolis, September 1, 1904* (Chicago, National Headquarters, Socialist Party, 1904).

[153] "Of Two Evils Choose Neither," *The Worker*, Aug. 21, 1904.

[154] *Opening Campaign Speech of E. V. Debs, Indianapolis, September 1, 1904* (Chicago, National Headquarters, Socialist Party, 1904).

Alton B. Parker had secured the Democratic nomination through the aid of August Belmont and other millionaires. And as a judge, Parker had declared the New York eight-hour law unconstitutional.[155] Theodore Roosevelt, warned Debs, was nothing but a clever representative of capitalism. He had enthusiastically supported Cleveland when the latter broke the Pullman strike. "How impressive to see the Rough Rider embrace the Smooth Statesman! Oyster Bay and Buzzard's Bay!" [156] Roosevelt's cabinet appointees included such enemies of labor as "Injunction Bill" Taft and Paul Morton who had broken the Chicago, Burlington and Quincy and the Santa Fe strikes. His friends included such men as General Sherman Bell, "the military ferret of the Colorado mine owners." The Republican Congress under his administration suppressed all pro-labor legislation.[157] "Between Two Evils—Choose Neither." [158]

The 1904 Socialist campaign was conducted on a far more ambitious scale than that of 1900. Debs spoke in every state in the union, sometimes delivering six to ten speeches a day.[159] Debs's campaign expenses were covered by the unusual practice of charging admission to hear his speeches. Yet the halls were always packed, and by the end of his tour it was claimed that Debs had addressed some 250,000 people.[160] The national Socialist office spent $32,700 on the election,[161] almost nothing compared to the millions expended by the Republicans,[162] but a substantial sum for the recently bankrupt Socialist Party. In addition, the state organizations conducted vigorous campaigns. That of Illinois, for example, kept 45 speakers continuously in the field and distributed half a million pieces of literature.[163]

The press and both the Republican and Democratic parties showed some concern over indications of growing support for the

---

[155] Ibid.
[156] Ibid.
[157] Ibid.
[158] The Worker, Aug. 21, 1904.
[159] Karsner, Debs, p. 182.
[160] Upton Sinclair, "The Socialist Party," The World's Work, XI (April, 1906), 7431.
[161] Ibid.
[162] U.S. Congress, Senate, Privileges and Elections Committee, Hearings Before a Sub-Committee on Campaign Contributions, 62nd Cong., 3rd Sess., 1913 (Washington, Government Printing Office, 1913), pp. 1073–90.
[163] Upton Sinclair, "The Socialist Party," The World's Work, XI (April, 1906), 7431.

Socialist Party.[164] The 1904 vote caused most political commentators to exclaim over Theodore Roosevelt's thumping 2,000,000 majority, and over the Socialist Party's 408,000 votes. The Socialists had polled more than four times their 1900 vote, and almost twice their 1902 total. A party which seemed destined to double its electoral support every two years could not be ignored.[165]

Party leaders were jubilant. They claimed that the Socialist vote indicated their arrival as a third party. Little consideration was given to the likelihood that part of their increased vote represented dissatisfaction with Democratic abandonment of liberal leadership and enthusiasm for Socialist Party immediate demands rather than for the future co-operative commonwealth. The Socialists held that the Democratic defeat meant that there would soon be only two parties, Republican and Socialist, and then the class struggle would be plain for all to see.[166] Furthermore, they calculated Socialist strength at much higher than 400,000. Many voters, they reasoned, had been converted to socialism but had not voted the Socialist ticket under the mistaken notion that a vote for the Socialist Party was a vote thrown away. All that was necessary to increase Socialist strength was to teach these voters that the only way to waste votes was to vote for something they did not want. A few more elections and the victory of the Socialist Party would be complete. And then the building of the co-operative commonwealth could begin.[167]

[164] The Chicago *Record Herald,* Aug. 28, 1904.

[165] W. J. Ghent in *The Worker,* Feb. 19, 1905; Coleman, *Debs,* p. 223.

[166] Gaylord Wilshire, "The Death of the Democratic Party," *Wilshire's,* VI (December, 1904), 3; Coleman, *Debs,* p. 224.

[167] Spargo, *Forces That Make for Socialism,* pp. 9–10; Ernest Untermann, *Sparks of the Proletarian Revolution* (Girard, Kansas, J. A. Wayland, 1904; Wayland's Monthly No. 47), pp. 9–12.

# IX

# The End of the
# Center-Left Coalition
# 1905-1906

IN THE LAST THREE MONTHS of William Mailly's administration, November, 1904–January, 1905, the party was reorganized to conform with the new constitution. The 54-man National Committee set basic party policy. In 1905, for example, the committee voted on 35 referendums covering 43 motions. These ranged from recall of a member of the Executive Committee and rejection of applications for positions as party speakers to policy decisions on independent political action and revision of the proposed municipal program.[1]

The National Executive Committee, which by a constitutional amendment in December, 1905, was to be elected by a national party referendum,[2] functioned chiefly as an administrative agency of the National Committee and exerted little influence in policy matters.[3] When Mailly insisted upon carrying through his resignation in January, 1905, the National Committee elected as National Secretary J. Mahlon Barnes, a member of the cigarmakers' union and Socialist Party state secretary in Pennsylvania.[4] Barnes

[1] *Socialist Party Official Bulletin*, Jan., 1906.

[2] *Ibid.*, Dec., 1905.

[3] Members of the National Executive Committee for 1905 were Victor Berger (Wisconsin), Barney Berlin (Illinois), Robert Bandlow (Ohio), William Mailly (Ohio), Stephen Reynolds (Indiana), Henry Slobodin (New York), and John Work (Iowa). The influence of the N.E.C. was so limited in 1905 that Berger declined to stand for re-election. The 1906 N.E.C. consisted of Robert Bandlow, A. H. Floaten (Colorado), Charles G. Towner (Kentucky), Charles H. Kerr (Illinois), William Mailly, A. M. Simons (Illinois), and John Work. (*Socialist Party Official Bulletin*, April, 1905, Feb., 1906.)

[4] *Socialist Party Official Bulletin*, Jan., 1905.

was re-elected every year until a combination of Left-wing opposition and charges of immorality brought about his removal in 1911.[5]

The national office operated on a budget of $17,000 in 1905, and $31,000 in 1906, although half of the increase was money raised for the specific purposes of aid to the Western Federation of Miners and relief for Russian revolutionaries after the 1905 revolution.[6] In addition to the National Secretary, the party headquarters employed an office force of five—a bookkeeper, a clerk in charge of routing speakers, a clerk in charge of literature, and two stenographers.[7] Expenditures were largely for clerical work, speakers, and printing and distributing literature.[8]

The national headquarters maintained twenty-odd lecturers and organizers in the field constantly. Thanks to the practice of charging admissions at some meetings and selling literature at all, the total annual cost to the national office was only about $3,000.[9] The office staff was fond of tracing party strength and growth on maps. For each state there was a separate map transfixed with varicolored pins denoting county organizations, locals, members, sympathizers, and speaker assignments. Elaborate files were maintained on each community with at least one sympathizer, whose name was usually first obtained when he wrote for information or literature. Organizers sent to a community were furnished with data on the character of the population, its attitude toward socialism, the arguments which seemed likely to be most effective, the type of literature which sold best, the addresses of party members and sympathizers, and a rating of the hotels and boarding houses.[10]

---

[5] See below, pp. 379–80.

[6] "Annual Report of the National Secretary of the Socialist Party, January 1, 1905 to December 31, 1905," *Socialist Party Official Bulletin,* Jan., 1906; "Annual Report of the National Secretary of the Socialist Party, January 15, 1907," *Socialist Party Official Bulletin,* Jan., 1907.

[7] "Report of Committee on Finances of the National Executive Committee, March 30, 1906," *Socialist Party Official Bulletin,* Jan., 1907.

[8] "Annual Report of the National Secretary of the Socialist Party, January 1, 1905 to December 31, 1905," *Socialist Party Official Bulletin,* Jan., 1906; "Annual Report of the National Secretary of the Socialist Party, January 15, 1907," *Socialist Party Official Bulletin,* Jan., 1907.

[9] See sources cited in Note 8.

[10] Patterson, *The Socialist Machine,* pp. 17–18, 21–24; Upton Sinclair, "The Socialist Party," *The World's Work,* XI (April, 1906), 7431.

The organization of the larger city locals of the party resembled that of the national office.[11] Most socialist locals continued to implement the national office's conception of proper local activity: sell books and newspaper subscriptions; distribute leaflets; hold business meetings twice a month; hold public meetings and an occasional "social session"; recruit new members; and, of course, get all Socialist sympathizers to the polls and keep a committee at the polls until all the votes were counted.[12]

Measured by the increasing publication and circulation of socialist literature, party activity flourished along the accepted lines of propaganda. Most of the books and pamphlets were published by the *Appeal to Reason* and Charles H. Kerr and Company of Chicago. But during campaigns, state and local organizations entered the publishing field. It was estimated that from 1904 to 1907 these latter printed and distributed more than one hundred million pieces of propaganda.[13]

Unfortunately for Socialist plans and dreams, however, political events in America were making it increasingly difficult to win elections merely through wide distribution of socialist analyses of capitalist shortcomings. The opposition organized by farmers against growing corporate power in America's economic and political life had spread to the cities, where hard-pressed businessmen, professionals, and white collar workers viewed the elimination of corruption in government as their road to security and prosperity. Reform and municipal ownership leagues mushroomed in the early 1900s. And in those communities where at least one of the major parties declined to give even lip service to municipal reform and public ownership of utilities, new parties appeared to carry the battle for honest government, fair taxes, and elimination of vice.[14]

The Socialists found themselves competing for votes in municipal and state elections with powerful, "respectable" parties,

---

[11] *Sunday Record Herald* (Chicago), April 2, 1905.

[12] *How a Socialist Local or Branch Should Be Conducted.*

[13] International Socialist Congress, *Recent Progress of the Socialist and Labor Movements in the United States*, p. 11.

[14] Faulkner, *The Quest for Social Justice*, pp. 81–109; Steffens, *Autobiography*, pp. 365–488; Chamberlain, *Farewell to Reform*, pp. 199–202.

whose platforms incorporated most of the immediate demands contained in Socialist platforms. Electors could cast their ballots for municipal ownership of public utilities, the ending of graft, the initiative and referendum, and municipal home rule by voting for either the Socialist Party or for one of the major or reform parties. Faced with these alternatives, most voters chose to vote for the party which had a chance of winning the current election and which required no future acceptance of a new social order.

In cities and states where the Center-Left factions controlled the Socialist Party, campaign platforms and literature curtsied in the direction of International Socialism, and then insisted that only the Socialist Party would bring the kind of municipal ownership which would benefit the working class. Middle-class municipal ownership, they said, was designed to reduce taxes, not to raise workers' standards of living.[15] In communities where the Left was more influential than the Center, the platforms and campaigns tended to stress the eventual goal of socialism and legislation for shorter hours and better working conditions more often than in those where the Center set the line.[16] Both Center and Left agreed, however, that no good could be expected from municipal ownership unless it was carried out under a Socialist administration.[17]

The Center-Left Socialists distributed millions of pieces of propaganda during 1905 and 1906 trying to convince voters of the reasonableness of the Socialist position.[18] But the electorate seemed increasingly difficult to convince. The Ohio reform move-

[15] "Platform of the Chicago Socialist Party, 1905," *The Chicago Socialist,* March 25, 1905; "Platform of the Springfield, Massachusetts Socialist Party, 1906," *The Worker,* Dec. 2, 1905; "Municipal Platform of the New York Socialist Party, 1905," *The Worker,* June 3, 1905; "Socialism in the New York Campaign," *The Outlook,* LXXXIV (Nov. 3, 1906), 541–42; *The Hearst Ticket* (New York, New York Socialist Party, 1906).

[16] "State Platform of the Ohio Socialist Party, 1905," *The Socialist* (Toledo), June 3, 1905.

[17] "Platform of the Chicago Socialist Party, 1905," *The Chicago Socialist,* March 25, 1905; "Platform of the Springfield, Massachusetts Socialist Party, 1906," *The Worker,* Dec. 2, 1905; "Municipal Platform of the New York Socialist Party, 1905," *The Worker,* June 3, 1905; "State Platform of the Ohio Socialist Party, 1905," *The Socialist* (Toledo), June 3, 1905.

[18] "Socialism in the New York Campaign," *The Outlook,* LXXXIV (Nov. 3, 1906), 541–42; *The Sunday Record Herald* (Chicago), April 2, 1905; "The Use of Literature in Our Campaign," *The Worker,* Aug. 19, 1905.

ment cut the 1905 vote of the Toledo, Cincinnati, and Cleveland Socialist parties 50–85 percent below that of 1904.[19] The two Hearst municipal ownership campaigns of 1905 and 1906 dropped the New York Socialist vote to a third its 1904 total.[20] And in the 1907 Chicago elections, Judge Edward F. Dunne, Democratic candidate for mayor on a municipal ownership platform, cut the Socialist vote in half.[21]

The Milwaukee Socialist Party was highly critical of Center-Left election tactics.[22] They considered the rising tide of middle-class reform a sign of awakening social conscience. Socialists should put themselves at the head of this movement because municipal ownership and honest government were steps toward socialism.[23] Gaylord Wilshire argued that the only reason for voting Socialist instead of for Hearst was that socialism would come quicker through straight party votes.[24]

Berger and the Milwaukee party were convinced that a "realistic" approach to the middle class was all that was needed to bring a Socialist victory in Milwaukee in 1906.[25] Milwaukee provided a unique opportunity for Socialists to act as a municipal reform party. The Democratic machine was notoriously corrupt. And the Republican Party in Milwaukee was the stronghold for the anti-La Follette movement in Wisconsin.[26] Of course, Berger considered Robert La Follette nothing but an "unqualified humbug," [27] but in principles and tactics the Milwaukee Social-Democratic Party closely resembled the La Follette progressive movement.

For the 1906 municipal campaign, Milwaukee Socialists adopted a platform and campaign arguments which were to become stand-

[19] Social-Democratic Herald, Nov. 18, 1905.

[20] "The Result in New York City," The Worker, Nov. 11, 1905; The Worker, Nov. 10, 1906.

[21] A. M. Simons, "The Chicago Elections," International Socialist Review, VII (April, 1907), 623–24.

[22] Victor L. Berger, "Socialist Lessons in the Hearst Campaign," Social-Democratic Herald, Nov. 18, 1905.

[23] Ibid.; Social-Democratic Herald, May 20, 1905.

[24] Gaylord Wilshire, "Hearst and Socialism," Wilshire's Magazine, IX (Dec., 1905), 8.

[25] Marvin Wachman, "History of the Social-Democratic Party of Milwaukee, 1897–1910," Urbana, University of Illinois, 1943; abstract of thesis.

[26] La Follette's Autobiography, pp. 249–54.

[27] Victor L. Berger, "Let the Nation Own the Trusts," Social Democratic Herald, Oct. 25, 1902.

ard for the party Right wing. The platform began by announcing that "the Social-Democratic party is the American expression of the international movement of modern wage-workers for better food, better houses, sufficient sleep, more leisure, more education, more culture." There was no longer any mention of socialism as the ɔnly form of society in which these goals could be achieved in plenty. The platform continued with a list of immediate demands: gas regulation, an end to corruption, public baths, free school-books, and a public holiday on election day. The demands also included a plank which Berger, in a special editorial, described as "another step forward in our municipal platform." [28] This was the substitution of a request for "fair terms" for franchises granted by the city in place of the standard Socialist demand for an end to all franchises.[29]

The Milwaukee platform showed little resemblance to the "revolutionary socialist" platform of the 1901 and 1904 conventions, and the Milwaukee campaign bore even less relationship to Debs's 1904 campaign. The Socialist candidate for mayor, William A. Arnold, declared that "the business interests of Milwaukee will be safer in the hands of an administration made up of Social Democrats than they have been under the Republican and Democratic administrations." Arnold assured the voters that he was a property holder and taxpayer himself, so obviously he had no desire to harm the city's business. An end to graft and corruption would bring new prosperity to Milwaukee business. "Our party believes in all things that are for the business life of the city." [30]

Berger personally assured the city's industrialists that a vote for the Social Democratic Party was a vote against strikes. He explained that Social Democrats understood the industrial system. They realized that since capitalists were bound by that system they found it very hard to pay higher wages or permit shorter hours. Milwaukee had had fewer strikes in the past six or seven years than any city one-half its size. Berger said this was due to Socialist influence in Milwaukee unions. "I can say from actual experience that

[28] Victor L. Berger, "Looking Further Forward," *Social-Democratic Herald,* Jan. 27, 1906.

[29] "Municipal Platform of the Milwaukee Social-Democratic Party, 1906," *Social-Democratic Herald,* Feb. 3, 1906.

[30] The Milwaukee *Journal,* Feb. 17, 1906.

the Social-Democrats in this city have opposed almost every strike that has ever been declared here." [31] Big business and little business, alike, need have no alarm. Only thieves, said Berger, need fear a Social Democratic administration.[32]

Despite repeated assurances and tempting promises, Milwaukee's voters continued distrustful. The Socialists barely held their own in the 1906 election, polling 16,500 votes against 21,000 for the Democrats and 23,000 for the Republicans.[33] But even the ability to hold its earlier vote was an outstanding electoral triumph when compared with the losses suffered in areas where the party was led by the Center-Left.[34]

The party received yet another blow to its electoral hopes in 1906. It had confidently predicted the election of a number of Congressmen, including Morris Hillquit from New York's ninth district.[35] But when the ballots were counted, Socialists could claim no Congressional victories, and their total vote was a disappointing 281,000, a 30 percent drop from the 1904 total of 408,000.[36]

The declining Socialist vote enabled Right-wing Socialists to redouble their attacks on the Center-Left coalition.[37] The Left replied that "if the Socialist Party . . . was merely a municipal ownership party and not a revolutionary party it would be a good enough party for middle class reformers and opportunists to support." [38] The Left rejected the concept of a party "broad" enough to gain capitalist support. It warned that Berger and his supporters were pursuing a policy of compromise which, if successful, would destroy the revolutionary character of the Socialist Party.[39]

---

[31] Victor L. Berger, "Who Is Afraid of the Social-Democratic Victory in Milwaukee?" *Social-Democratic Herald,* March 24, 1906.

[32] *Ibid.*

[33] *Social-Democratic Herald,* April 7, 1906.

[34] Herman F. Titus, "Revolutionary Socialism and Reform Socialism," *The Socialist* (Toledo), Jan. 7, 1906.

[35] "The Socialist Party," *The Worker,* Oct. 27, 1906.

[36] *The Worker,* May 11, 1907; New York *Daily Tribune,* Oct. 8, 1906.

[37] Victor L. Berger, "Are We for Public Ownership?" *Social-Democratic Herald,* July 8, 1905; Gaylord Wilshire: "Another Impossibilistic Crotchet," *Social-Democratic Herald,* July 8, 1905; "The Policy of the Socialist Party," *Wilshire's Magazine,* VIII (July, 1905), 8; "Hearst Socialism," *Wilshire's Magazine,* IX (Dec., 1905), 8; "Millionaire Socialists," *Wilshire's Magazine,* X (April, 1906), 6; *Social-Democratic Herald,* Nov. 11, 1905; *Appeal to Reason,* Feb. 10, 1906.

[38] *The Socialist* (Toledo), Nov. 25, 1905.

[39] *Ibid.*

The Center, however, did not reject the Right-wing criticisms. In fact, during the 1906 New York "Socialism and Hillquit for Congress" campaign, the Center gave strong indications that it had decided that the Right's theories on political campaigning were correct. Socialism was played down and the business integrity and stability of an attorney already worth $100,000 were emphasized.[40] The Center had placed so much of its emphasis on winning socialism by electing Socialist candidates that it could not pass lightly over electoral results which indicated that the party was a long way from victory at the ballot box. While Center explanations of election defeats stressed the competition of reform parties and the need for a more efficient Socialist political machine, their spokesmen and papers were soon engaged in phrasing Right-wing theories in Center "revolutionary" language.[41]

The death of the Center-Left coalition and the rapprochement of Center and Right, while beginning to exist on a theoretical level even before the 1904 elections, became a reality during 1905 and 1906. Berger's anatomical curiosity of a "two-armed labor movement" in which each party member devoted one arm to union work on the economic field and the other arm to political work through the Socialist Party, with neither arm "interfering" with the other,[42] became accepted theory for the Center.[43] The Center also adopted the Right theory [44] that economic development would teach union members to vote Socialist,[45] and that strikes were futile.[46] The Center agreed that Socialists in the unions must now de-

[40] M. Baranoff in *Freiheit*, reprinted in *Social-Democratic Herald*, Dec. 8, 1906.

[41] International Socialist Congress, *Recent Progress of the Socialist and Labor Movements in the United States*, pp. 5–12; *The Worker*, Nov. 10, 1906; Upton Sinclair, "The Socialist Party," *The World's Work*, XI (April, 1906), 7431; A. M. Simons, "Need of Organization," *International Socialist Review*, VII (Nov., 1906), 302–4; Hillquit, *History of Socialism*, 1910 ed., p. 348.

[42] Victor L. Berger, "Labor Learns in the School of Experience," *Social-Democratic Herald*, Dec. 2, 1905.

[43] International Socialist Congress, *Recent Progress of the Socialist and Labor Movements in the United States*, pp. 17–18; *The Chicago Socialist*, Nov. 25, 1905; George D. Herron, "The Social Opportunity," *International Socialist Review*, IV (April, 1904), 590–91.

[44] Victor L. Berger, "Labor Learns in the School of Experience," *Social-Democratic Herald*, Dec. 2, 1905.

[45] Spargo, *Socialism*, pp. 152–53; International Socialist Congress, *Recent Progress in the Socialist and Labor Movements in the United States*, p. 23.

[46] "The Chicago Strike," *Appeal to Reason*, May 13, 1905; *Appeal to Reason*, May 19, 1906; "Is the Strike Played Out?" *The Worker*, Oct. 2, 1904.

vote themselves almost exclusively to educating workers in the benefits to accrue from an intelligent use of the ballot.[47]

The Center-Right Socialists in the A.F. of L. abandoned their efforts to get the Federation's national convention to endorse political action.[48] Instead, they secured adoption of resolutions recommending discussion of economic and political subjects in local meetings.[49] The policy of noninterference in union "internal affairs" and education for votes for socialism was implemented by almost complete cessation of agitation for union organization along industrial lines.[50] Berger continued to introduce resolutions for old-age pensions and a military system along the lines of Switzerland's.[51] Max Hayes, having been elected a Fraternal Delegate to Great Britain, decided that it did not "matter much to the trade unionists of the country who are chosen to transact the Federation's business." [52] Both Berger and Hayes agreed that it was pointless to fight the Federation leadership,[53] and the Socialist press began to admit that Socialists were playing an ever-smaller role in the Federation.[54]

[47] *Appeal to Reason*, March 3, 1906; *The Chicago Socialist*, Nov. 25, 1905.

[48] International Socialist Congress, *Recent Progress of the Socialist and Labor Movements in the United States*, pp. 17–18; Max S. Hayes, "The World of Labor," *International Socialist Review*, V (Dec., 1904), 375; *Report of Proceedings of the Twenty-Fifth Annual Convention of the American Federation of Labor, 1905* (Washington, D.C., The Law Reporter Printing Co., 1905), pp. 92, 109, 110, 239.

[49] *Report of Proceedings of the Twenty-Fourth Annual Convention of the American Federation of Labor, 1904*, pp. 138, 204; *Report of the Proceedings of the Twenty-Sixth Annual Convention of the American Federation of Labor, 1906*, pp. 31–35, 63, 76–82, 89, 115, 119, 130, 155, 158, 163, 183–206.

[50] *Report of Proceedings of the Twenty-Fourth Annual Convention of the American Federation of Labor, 1904*, pp. 133, 175, 176; *Report of Proceedings of the Twenty-Fifth Annual Convention of the American Federation of Labor, 1905* (Washington, D.C., The Law Reporter Printing Co., 1905), pp. 158, 180; *Report of the Proceedings of the Twenty-Sixth Annual Convention of the American Federation of Labor, 1906*, pp. 148, 149, 176.

[51] *Report of Proceedings of the Twenty-Fourth Annual Convention of the American Federation of Labor, 1904*, pp. 133, 204, 205; *Report of Proceedings of the Twenty-Fifth Annual Convention of the American Federation of Labor, 1905* (Washington, D.C., The Law Reporter Printing Co., 1905), 156, 157, 179; *Report of the Proceedings of the Twenty-Sixth Annual Convention of the American Federation of Labor, 1906*, pp. 148, 234, 235; *Social Democratic Herald*, Nov. 26, 1904; *The Chicago Socialist*, Nov. 25, 1905.

[52] Max S. Hayes in the Cleveland *Citizen*, Dec. 10, 1904.

[53] Victor L. Berger, "No Golden Anniversary for the American Federation of Labor," *Social-Democratic Herald*, Dec. 9, 1905.

[54] *The Chicago Socialist*, Nov. 25, 1905; *The Socialist* (Toledo), Dec. 9, 1905; *The Worker*, Dec. 2, 1905; Max S. Hayes, "The World of Labor," *International Socialist Review*, VI (Feb., 1906), 592–93.

As it joined the Right in soft-pedaling criticism of A.F. of L. leaders and policies, the Center began to emphasize theories and propaganda palatable to a middle class already exposed to anti-trust agitation. In its early days the Center had rejected graft exposure as of no importance to the working class. Now it announced that "the Socialists are always the most implacable foes of corruption and graft." [55] The Center also discovered that "attempts to develop the class consciousness of the workers" were "not of themselves manifestation of [class] hatred." [56]

The Center assured prospective middle-class voters that Socialists did not intend to socialize all property, but only great corporate wealth. Individual small businesses were to be of no concern to the socialist state.[57] Finally, the Center attempted to quiet middle-class fears of revolution by explaining, as the Right had been doing for years, that "revolution" simply meant a long series of reforms which would eventually change the social order. No Socialist, they emphasized, worked for or expected violence or a sudden transition to socialism.[58] And until socialism finally arrived, the Center Socialists granted employers who joined the party an indulgence permitting them to destroy labor unions. They explained that in voting for socialism, a capitalist was contributing all that could be expected of him. He had a perfect right to join an employers' association for the purpose of fighting his fellow-Socialists' unions.[59]

If the Center's new line was designed to attract middle-class and even upper-class membership to the Socialist Party, it succeeded admirably. J. G. Phelps Stokes, a reformer and philanthropist who had been active in the Hearst Municipal Ownership campaign in 1905 and who was a member of one of New York's most aristocratic and wealthy families, discovered that Socialists did not really feel "intense bitterness and ill-will . . . toward nearly all persons who approve and support the capitalist system," and joined the party

[55] Spargo, *The Socialists*, pp. 9–10.

[56] Ghent, *Mass and Class*, pp. 66–67.

[57] Spargo, *The Socialists*, pp. 80, 85; "What Socialism Is Not," *The Independent*, LIX (Dec. 21, 1905), 1488.

[58] Herbert N. Casson, "Socialism, Its Growth and Its Leaders," *Munsey's Magazine*, XXXIII (June, 1905), 295; letter from Jack London to Gaylord Wilshire, *Wilshire's Magazine*, X (April, 1906), 6; Spargo, *Forces that Make for Socialism*, pp. 30–31.

[59] *The Worker*, July 29, 1905.

in 1906.[60] In Chicago, William Bross Lloyd, another millionaire philanthropist, decided that since America was "absolutely controlled" by one hundred men, everyone else was a member of the working class. He, too, joined the Socialist Party.[61]

But the greatest victory for American socialism in 1906, according to the Center, was millionaire Joseph Medill Patterson's letter of resignation to Chicago's reform mayor Edward Dunne. Patterson wrote that he was resigning as Commissioner of Public Works because he now realized that the municipal ownership platform upon which Dunne had been elected could not in itself remove the source of the "many ills under which the nation suffers." Since money was essential to satisfy all man's needs, Patterson could not "see why money, which is the greatest thing in life, should not be more or less evenly distributed, just as the ballot is." This could be accomplished only through common ownership of the means of production and distribution. Patterson, therefore, was offering his support to the Socialist Party.[62]

Center and Right-wing party leaders were jubilant. The National Committee, by a vote of 21 to 16, ordered Patterson's letter printed for mass distribution.[63] And state and local party conventions sought vainly for means to avoid the constitutional restrictions which prevented them from immediately giving Patterson high rank in the party as well as nomination for public office.[64]

The conversion of Stokes, Lloyd, and Patterson was accompanied by a drive to recruit reformers and muckrakers like Robert Hunter and Charles Edward Russell,[65] as well as lesser lights from among middle-class leaders of the surging progressive movement.[66] At the 1907 International Socialist Congress, Morris Hillquit

[60] Letter from J. G. Phelps Stokes to the Executive Committee of the Independence League, July, 1906, *The Worker*, July 14, 1906; New York *Daily Tribune*, July 13, Sept. 16, 1906.

[61] Letter from William Bross Lloyd to the Chicago *Daily Journal*, March 29, 1906, printed in *The Chicago Socialist*, April 7, 1906.

[62] Letter from Joseph Medill Patterson to Mayor Edward F. Dunne, Feb. 28, 1906, printed in *The Chicago Socialist*, March 10, 1906.

[63] *The Socialist Party Official Bulletin*, April, 1906.

[64] Chicago *Record Herald*, Aug. 21, 1906.

[65] Hillquit, *Loose Leaves*, pp. 56–60.

[66] *Ibid.*, pp. 55–56; New York *Daily Tribune*, March 4, 1906; William Hard, "The Making of a Socialist," *The World To-Day*, XI (Aug., 1906), 851–55.

could boast that "in the United States, probably more than any-where else, socialism is recruiting adherents from the better situ-ated classes of society." [67] Some observers believed that wage earn-ers constituted a minority in the Socialist Party,[68] and even an occasional Center leader "viewed with alarm" the tendency of party leadership and control to fall increasingly into the hands of the middle class.[69]

Although the party was attracting proportionally more mem-bers from the middle class, its rate of membership growth declined. Party enrollment had swelled from 15,975 in 1903 to 20,763 in 1904, an increase of c.4,800. In 1905, membership rolls increased by only 2,500, and in 1906 by 3,400.[70] Actually, far more than three thousand Socialists were recruited every year. But thousands signed cards, attending a few meetings, and were never heard from again.[71] Party activity declined between elections, and lack of So-cialist participation in the everyday problems and struggles of the working class was reflected in a declining vote at the polls.[72]

As long as middle-class Socialists grouped in the party Center gave lip-service opposition to policies and tactics advocated by Berger's Right wing, the party Left remained nascent. There were, of course, occasional warnings against what seemed an increasing tendency to stress "palliatives" rather than the class struggle and socialism.[73] The bitter January, 1903, National Committee meet-ing which removed the National Secretary and Local Quorum brought attacks on Hillquit by Western Socialists who accused him of being a "smooth" and "slippery" manipulator "who always had a 'job' or 'trick' to spring on the meeting." [74] Further, the national

[67] International Socialist Congress, *Recent Progress of the Socialist and Labor Movements in the United States*, p. 11.

[68] "The Socialists," *The Independent*, LVII (Nov. 17, 1904), 1165–66.

[69] A. M. Simons, "Socialists and Government Ownership," *International Socialist Review*, VI (Jan., 1906), 495–96.

[70] The 1905 membership averaged 23,347, and that for 1906, 26,784 ("Annual Re-port of the National Secretary of the Socialist Party, January 15, 1907," *The So-cialist Party Official Bulletin*, Jan., 1907).

[71] E. S. Egerton, "The New Member," *The Worker*, Aug. 19, 1905.

[72] "The Tendencies of the Times," *The Chicago Socialist*, July 22, 1905; "The Year That Has Passed," *The Worker*, April 28, 1906.

[73] Letter from Louis Marcus to *The Chicago Socialist*, Feb. 25, 1902, *The Chicago Socialist*, April 19, 1902.

[74] Clarence Smith, "Impressions at St. Louis," *American Labor Union Journal*, Feb. 12, 1903.

committeeman from Washington charged that the middle-class members of the National Committee had organized to elect opportunists to the Executive Committee.[75] Local Toledo spelled out the charge by circulating a letter among Ohio locals accusing Walter Thomas Mills, national committeeman from Kansas, of going "before the national committee with a scheme for organizing a secret society within the Socialist Party, with a view to keeping control of it. This was set down good and hard, but it shows the bent." [76] The early division over labor policy has already been discussed in Chapter VIII.

These differences indicate definite disagreements within the Center-Left coalition. But there were few open conflicts, particularly when compared with what was to follow. This would seem to show that it was the comparatively sudden influence acquired by the step-at-a-time Socialists within the party, due to the rapprochement of Center and Right between 1904 and 1906, which precipitated the appearance of the militant, articulate, and increasingly sectarian Left. While the Center was adding and emphasizing one immediate demand after another in an effort to stop the municipal reform parties from "stealing their thunder" and their votes, the Left was welcoming the chance to distinguish between adherents of revolutionary socialism and reform or municipal-ownership socialism. "Just as the colonization split saved the Social Democratic Party in 1898 by freeing it from dreamers and Utopians, so now the best thing that can happen to the Socialist Party is the departure of those who, though with us, are not of us." [77]

Early in 1905, shortly after his resignation as National Secretary, William Mailly joined forces with Herman Titus to publish a newspaper intended to stand for uncompromising revolutionary socialism. Titus, a Seattle physician who had devoted increasing portions of his time since 1900 to publishing the Seattle *Socialist*, moved his paper to Toledo, Ohio. Mailly and Titus chose Ohio be-

[75] George E. Boomer, "Thoughts by Your Uncle," *The Socialist* (Seattle), Feb. 15, 1903.

[76] Circular letter from T. F. Keogh for Local Toledo to the members of the State Committee and locals of the Socialist Party of Ohio, Sept. 14, 1903, *The Socialist* (Seattle), Oct. 4, 1903.

[77] *The Socialist* (Seattle), April 24, 1904; E. B. Ault, "A Reply to Comrade Wilshire," *The Socialist* (Toledo), Feb. 17, 1906.

cause of its central geographic location and also because of its growing industrial importance.[78] Under their coeditorship during 1905 and 1906, the Toledo *Socialist* became the national organ of the developing Left wing of the party, serving to restate and publicize the Center-Left theory of the party's first years.

The most complete exposition of Left Socialist ideology before the development of "industrial socialism" [79] was made by Titus in a series of articles entitled "Revolutionary and Reform Socialism" published in his paper between January and March, 1906. The arguments were much the same as those developed by the Center-Left in 1901 and 1902. Now, however, the Center no longer accepted its early analysis.

Titus contended that there were only two kinds of socialism, reform and revolutionary. Fabian, Christian, utopian, state, and municipal socialism were all forms of reform socialism. They were products of middle-class struggle against monopoly, and not of working-class struggle against capital.[80] Revolutionary socialism was based on scientific method and the recognition of certain scientifically determined facts.[81] Titus found three key facts prerequisite to an understanding of the social process: (1) that the workers did not receive the products they created, but only a subsistence upon which they might live; [82] (2) that capital and labor were engaged in a class struggle which would continue as long as capitalism existed; [83] and (3) that the government was an organ of capitalist rule.[84]

Titus held that these facts demonstrated that the working class need have no concern with the various reform movements and measures which were the product of the quarrel between big and little capital as to who should have the privilege of robbing the working class.[85] The Socialist Party organization must be based on class struggle so that all powers of government may be won through working-class activity at the polls. When the working class, through the Socialist Party, had swept the country in the national

[78] *The Socialist*, May 27, 1905.        [79] See below, pp. 312–17.
[80] Herman F. Titus, "Revolutionary Socialism and Reform Socialism," *The Socialist* (Toledo), Jan. 7, 1906.
[81] *Ibid.*, Jan. 20, 1906.        [82] *Ibid.*, Feb. 3, 1906.        [83] *Ibid.*, Feb. 17, 1906.
[84] *Ibid.*, March 3, 1906.        [85] *The Socialist* (Seattle), Oct. 11, 1903.

elections, it would use the power of government to end capitalism and institute socialism.[86]

The Left argued that the working class would not elect the candidates of a revolutionary Socialist Party until they had a scientific understanding of society. "We fear our comrades of Milwaukee and Maine [87] will fail in their somewhat questionable effort to bring about the social revolution by stealth, while people are not looking. Notwithstanding how it is sugarcoated, Socialism will not go down the throats of the working class until they thoroughly understand what it is and that they want it." [88] Failure to base all party activity on recognition of the class struggle would cause the Socialists to go the way of the Populists.[89] The Socialist Party, therefore, should devote itself to educating the working class and the members of its own party in principles of scientific socialism.[90]

The Left said that the division into one faction for reform and one for revolution was characteristic of the socialist movement in every country. It was caused by a class division within the international socialist movement. Middle-class members sought to use the party to obtain reforms they thought would strengthen their class in its defense against the attacks of monopoly. Proletarian members sought to keep their parties on the path of revolutionary, scientific socialism. The Left welcomed middle-class converts to socialism, but insisted that they support a working-class program. The socialist movement could not be both reform and revolutionary.[91]

As the Center moved to take positions which in the eyes of the Left were increasingly opportunistic, the Left countered with bitter attacks on party leadership and policy. Eugene Debs, always part of the Left despite his reluctance to participate in party fac-

[86] Herman F. Titus, "Revolutionary Socialism and Reform Socialism," *The Socialist* (Toledo), Jan. 7, March 31, 1906.

[87] The Maine Socialist Party had adopted a platform based on that prepared by the Milwaukee Socialists for the 1906 municipal election ("Platform of the Maine Socialist Party, 1906," *The Socialist* [Toledo], Feb. 24, 1906).

[88] *The Socialist* (Toledo), Feb. 24, 1906.

[89] *Ibid.,* June 5, 1904.

[90] *The Socialist* ran an essay contest in 1905 on the subject, "What Is the Greatest Necessity of the Socialist Party?" Almost all contestants agreed that education of party members in the principles of Marxist revolutionary socialism should be the area of concentration. (*The Socialist* [Toledo], Sept. 16–Oct. 14, 1905.)

[91] Herman F. Titus in *The Socialist* (Toledo), Feb. 16, 1907.

tionalism, charged New York Socialist leaders with responsibility for the poor showing the party had made in the 1905 campaign. He accused them of compromising their principles to obtain the support of corrupt "pure and simple" union leaders.

The pure and simple unionism of New York . . . smiled like a prostitute upon the Socialist party until the horn of Hearst was blown and sounded the campaign slogan of "Graft and Boodle," and then the whole mercenary gang who want "no politics in the union" rushed to the Hearst camp and there remained steadfast and true while there was a dollar in sight or a pocket to pick.[92]

The Left grew restive at such signs of party "respectability" as the excitement which greeted Joseph Medill Patterson's conversion,[93] and the tendency to use middle-class reformers as the party's main speakers at mass meetings.[94] It warned that it did not intend to turn the party over to reformers who had come to socialism via the "kid glove route" and who still carried unconscious capitalist prejudices.[95] Party organizers who belonged to the Left refused to follow suggestions that they tone down their remarks so as not to antagonize the community's "best people." [96] They accused party moderates of "everlastingly adulterating our clear proletarian bugle calls by their hybridization of bourgeois and proletarian ideas." [97] And they warned that "the class struggle is not a contest between incense and rosewater. Drop that sprayer and get a weapon worth the game." [98]

Factional fights on a national level did not reach a high pitch until the N.E.C. election of January, 1907. But internecine warfare on a state level began with the organization of the Socialist Party. By 1903 Socialist civil wars in states and locals had reached

[92] Eugene V. Debs in the *New York Zeit-Geist,* reprinted in *The Chicago Socialist,* Jan. 6, 1906.
[93] "Minutes of the Local Quorum of the State of Washington, April 22, 1906," *The Socialist Party Official Bulletin,* May, 1906; Alfred Wagenknecht, "To the Members of the Socialist Party," *The Socialist* (Toledo), March 24, 1906; *The Socialist* (Toledo), March 31, 1906.
[94] Letter from W. B. Killingbeck to *The Worker,* Feb. 3, 1905.
[95] "About Impossibilists," *American Labor Union Journal,* May 26, 1904.
[96] M. W. Wilkins, "Notes from a Veteran," *The Socialist* (Toledo), Aug. 5, 1905.
[97] Ernest Untermann, "Marxism and Eclecticism," *International Socialist Review,* VI (April, 1906), 1597.
[98] M. W. Wilkins in *The Socialist* (Toledo), Aug. 23, 1905,

the stage where Right-wing speakers and organizers sent out by states and locals under Right-wing control were touring the country to participate in the fratricidal strife.

One of the most vigorous of these representatives was Walter Thomas Mills, sometime minister, evangelist, and temperance lecturer who had come to the Socialist Party by way of the Democratic Party and a series of co-operative ventures of doubtful legality.[99] His trail in the socialist movement, which leads from Chicago to Australia, is strewn with charges of immorality, dishonesty, and fraud.[100] In 1903, after the failure of a series of socialist schools, from which, however, he apparently succeeded in extracting a fair profit,[101] Mills began to use his position as national committeeman from Kansas as a credential for renting himself at fifteen dollars per day to local party organizations and dissident socialist propaganda clubs for the purpose of factional activity.

After a more or less successful beginning in Ohio, where Right-wing leaders prevented the engagement of Ben Hanford, Socialist Vice Presidential candidate in 1904,[102] Mills moved on to Nebraska. There, under the auspices of a Right-wing group which had withdrawn from the party and organized the Socialist Propaganda Club, Mills joined Carl D. Thompson of Wisconsin and toured the state in an effort to build a Right-wing caucus within the state organization. In this they succeeded to the degree that Nebraska Socialists were soon so busy expelling each other that they had time for little else.[103]

Colorado, with its strong Left-wing base in the Western Federation of Miners, was a tougher nut for the Right to crack. Instead

[99] Letter from Thomas J. Morgan to Erwin B. Ault, printed in *The Socialist* (Seattle), Nov. 2, 1907; *The Socialist* (Seattle), April 14, 1907.

[100] See sources cited in Note 99; circular letter from T. F. Keogh for Local Toledo to the members of the State Committee and locals of the Socialist Party of Ohio, Sept. 14, 1903, *The Socialist* (Seattle), Oct. 4, 1903; "Resolution of Local Omaha, May 14, 1903," *Socialist Party Weekly Bulletin*, [May, 1903].

[101] Walter Thomas Mills, *How to Work for Socialism*, p. 29.

[102] Circular letter from T. F. Keogh for Local Toledo to the members of the State Committee and locals of the Socialist Party of Ohio, Sept. 14, 1903, *The Socialist* (Seattle), Oct. 4, 1903.

[103] "Resolution of Local Omaha, Nebraska, May 6, 1903," letter from J. Alfred LaBelle to Walter T. Mills, April 24, 1903, letter from Walter T. Mills to J. Alfred LaBelle, April 25, 1903, all in *Socialist Party Weekly Bulletin* [May, 1903]; Resolution of Nebraska State Committee, May 14, 1903, *Socialist Party Weekly Bulletin* [May, 1903]; *Appeal to Reason*, Oct. 10, 1903.

of bringing in just one or two outside organizers, the Right sent to Colorado an entire committee, "The Social Crusade." The leaders were the Reverends Winfield Gaylord and Carl Thompson of Wisconsin and J. Stitt Wilson of California.[104] The Crusaders had the full co-operation of Local Denver which had gone "right" when its predominantly middle-class membership adopted the practice of permitting entrance to paid workers in the Democratic and Republican parties. They toured the state showing lantern slides of "Our Martyred President William McKinley," and giving lectures on "The Life ⸳ Message . . . Health . . . Happiness . . . and a more harmonious Inner Life." In those counties where farming rather than mining was the major economic activity, the Crusaders organized Socialist locals of four or five farmers, and thus gained temporary control of the state committee, since each county was entitled to one delegate. Rightists in Colorado adopted political principles and tactics similar to those of Milwaukee, and branded Socialists in the Western Federation of Miners as impossibilists.[105]

The Colorado miners who made up the Left-wing Socialist faction were engaged in bitter strikes. They were not disposed to take kindly to the efforts and tactics of the Social Crusade or Local Denver, neither of which gave more than token assistance to the Western Federation of Miners.[106] In 1903, after two years of acrimonious factionalism, the Teller County–Cripple Creek locals of the Socialist Party withdrew their support of the state organization and issued a pamphlet asking other Colorado locals to join them in setting up a new state committee.[107]

The Teller County Socialists charged that capitalism, in an effort to stop the socialist movement, had "fostered in her lap a great brood of conscienceless political coyotes whom she has quartered on us." These "capitalist class decoys" within the party were accused of advocating class harmony and subverting working-class interests to middle-class aspirations. The "cockroach element" of Local Denver, according to the insurgent group's pamphlet,

<hr>

[104] Thompson, *Principles and Program of Socialism;* on the cover is a list of members of the Social Crusade.

[105] *Social Democratic Herald,* Oct. 7, 1905; letter from Former Member of the Colorado Socialist Party, *Social-Democratic Herald,* Nov. 4, 1905; *Address by Teller County Locals,* pp. 7–8.

[106] See above, pp. 150–51.       [107] *Address by Teller County Locals,* p. 3.

stood for: the social crusaders . . . ; sentimental slush for literature; voted to retain all the capitalist politicians who had already
sneaked into the party and to allow the backdoor open for all other
comers of the same stripe; advocated a loose, tapeworn form of organization; stood for privately owned press, with which irresponsible
careerists might from time to time club your party into submission;
stood for clownish jolliers as agitators.[108]

The factional fight in Colorado continued for years, although by
1905 the Left had regained control of the state organization.[109]

Party factionalism reached new heights in 1905. With the Center
moving toward agreement with the Right, there were full-scale
ruptures in Minnesota, Nebraska, California, Ohio, Washington,
and Kansas, to say nothing of minor disputes in virtually every
state.[110] Indicative of the changes brought forth by the realignment
were the first real efforts to use the national organization to aid
one or the other factions in a state controversy.

In 1905 the Minnesota state executive committee revoked the
charter of Local Minneapolis, whose 400 members made up more
than half the total party strength of the state. The executive committee took this step after Local Minneapolis had initiated a state
referendum for removal of the state secretary and National Committeeman for condoning fusion during elections.[111] The National
Committee defeated nine motions asking for an investigation of the
Minnesota situation and favoring recognition of the new state secretary selected by Local Minneapolis and a majority of the other
major Minnesota locals.[112] Thus, despite admitted violation of the

[108] *Ibid.*, pp. 4–20.
[109] Letter from Former Member of Colorado Socialist Party to the *Social Demo-
cratic Herald*, Nov. 4, 1904.
[110] Letter from John Work, National Committeeman from Iowa, to National
Secretary J. Mahlon Barnes, *Socialist Party Weekly Bulletin*, Sept. 13, 1905.
[111] Open letter from Theodore Richeter, Chairman, and Mrs. Martin Hanson,
Secretary, Local Minneapolis, "To the Comrades of Minnesota and Members of
Local Minneapolis of the Public Ownership Party," July 16, 1905, letter from
Harriet Birnbaum-Hanson, Recording Secretary, Local Minneapolis, to J. Mahlon
Barnes, Aug. 1, 1905, letter from Frank Hick, Financial Secretary, Local Minne-
apolis, to J. Mahlon Barnes, Aug. 4, 1905, letter from William Mailly to J. Mahlon
Barnes, Aug. 24, 1904, all in the *Socialist Party Official Bulletin*, Sept., 1905; letter
from J. E. Nash, State Secretary, Minnesota, to members of National Committee,
Socialist Party, *Socialist Party Weekly Bulletin*, Sept. 16, 1905.
[112] Motions 31–39, *Socialist Party Weekly Bulletin*, Sept. 13, Oct. 5, Nov. 15, 1905;
"Protest of Wisconsin State Committee," *Socialist Party Weekly Bulletin*, Sept.
16, 1905. The Minnesota locals supporting the position of Local Minneapolis in-

national Socialist constitution by officials of the Minnesota party, and despite opposition to those officials by well over half the Minnesota Socialists, the Right, with Center support, was able to maintain those officials in power. The National Committee simply refused to instruct the National Secretary, himself a member of the Center-Right, to stop recognizing the old state secretary and conducting all party business through him.[113]

In 1905 the Left made a belated attempt to stop the growing tendency of Right-wing Socialists, led by Wisconsin, to honor the party constitution and platform largely in the breach. The Wisconsin state organization had never applied for a national charter,[114] and while the state insisted on the privilege of participating in all party decisions, it did not feel obliged to carry out those decisions. When attacked for open violation of basic party tenets, Berger would reply that since Wisconsin was virtually the only state in the country "where the Socialists have grown to be a real party," Wisconsin Socialists had to deal with problems in a manner that differed from the rest of the country.[115] The Wisconsin party had gained a reputation both inside and out of the socialist movement of being "boss-ridden." Berger boasted that he made all major decisions on policy and tactics, and those who disagreed found themselves outside the party.[116]

When it came time for the Milwaukee Socialists to nominate candidates for the 1905 judicial elections, Berger decided not to put forth a Socialist ticket. Instead, in an editorial in *Die Wahrheit*, he urged Socialist voters to throw their support to the Republican candidate because he was "a liberal, upright man." [117] The New York *Worker* immediately accused Berger and the Wisconsin party of violating the national constitution by urging support for a "capitalistic candidate." [118] Local Crestline, Ohio, then called for

cluded Locals St. Paul, Duluth, Carmody, and Deerwood (*Socialist Party Weekly Bulletin*, Oct. 7, 28, Nov. 24, 1905).

[113] *Socialist Party Weekly Bulletin*, Nov. 15, 1905.

[114] See above, p. 138.

[115] Victor L. Berger in the *Social-Democratic Herald*, April 8, 1905.

[116] Herbert N. Casson, "Socialism, Its Growth and Its Leaders," *Munsey's Magazine*, XXXIII (June, 1905), 296–97; letter from Barney Berlin to J. Mahlon Barnes, Aug. 2, 1905, the *Socialist Party Official Bulletin*, Aug., 1905; letter from Charles R. Martin, Aug. 5, 1905, *The Worker*, Aug. 12, 1905.

[117] Victor L. Berger in *Die Wahrheit*, March 18, 1905.

[118] "Bad News from Milwaukee," *The Worker*, April 1, 1905.

a national referendum on its resolutions to remove Berger from the National Executive Committee and to bar Wisconsin from all participation in national party affairs until it applied for and received a charter.[119] By July 1 the Crestline resolutions had been seconded by the requisite number of locals and were submitted to a national referendum.[120] While seconds were coming in in support of the Crestline resolutions, the National Committee, by a vote of 24 to 17, with nine abstentions, removed Berger from the executive committee.[121]

The Left, however, had begun its offensive against the Right too late. Morris Hillquit, who was already leading a large segment of the New York Center into closer relations with the Right, immediately came to Berger's defense. Hillquit claimed that he was "unalterably opposed to any compromise of socialist principles," but at the same time he advocated "a spirit of tolerance." He then bitterly attacked his former allies, William Mailly and Herman Titus, who were leading the fight against Berger.[122] Mailly replied that Berger, at the last executive committee meeting, had warned that if the constitution were construed against his views, "there would soon be three Socialist parties in this country." Mailly further pointed out that if opportunism were not stopped, its opponents would react by turning to policies correctly characterized as "impossibilism." [123] To confirm Mailly's charge, Berger's *Wahrheit* warned that a hostile national vote on the Crestline resolutions would cause the Wisconsin party to take the lead in forming a new socialist organization.[124]

The vote on the Crestline resolutions was completed in September. The motion to remove Berger from the National Executive Committee was defeated, 4,718 to 4,215. The motion to force Wisconsin to apply for a charter was carried, 4,518 to 4,496.[125] Thus,

---

119 Resolution adopted by Local Crestline, Ohio, April 20, 1905, the *Socialist Party Official Bulletin,* July, 1905.
120 The *Socialist Party Official Bulletin,* July, 1905.
121 *Ibid.,* May, 1905.
122 Morris Hillquit, "Moderation, Comrades!" *The Socialist* (Toledo), May 6, 1905; William Mailly and Herman Titus, "At the Parting of the Ways," *The Socialist* (Toledo), April 8, 1905.
123 William Mailly, "Shield No One," *The Socialist* (Toledo), May 6, 1906.
124 *Die Wahrheit,* Aug. 5, 1905.
125 *The Socialist Party Official Bulletin,* Sept., 1905.

the refusal of the Center, particularly that of New York, to insist on what it still claimed to be the inviolable principles of international socialism,[126] combined with National Secretary Barnes's refusal to permit the 400-strong Left-wing local of Minneapolis to vote,[127] defeated the Left's attempt to stop the Right-wing offensive against Center-Left locals, theories, and tactics. The National Committee reinstated Berger on the executive committee,[128] and Barnes, violating the Crestline resolutions, sent Wisconsin a charter without waiting for the application which would have committed that state's party to accepting national party decisions.[129]

The Left, supported by part of the Center, then initiated a referendum calling for a national party convention in 1906. The convention was to tighten internal party organization and put a stop to "campaigns for votes upon . . . questions affecting immediate [and] frequently middle class interests instead of educational campaign [based on] the principles of Socialism." [130] The Right opposed the convention, charging that "enemies of the party" would be delegates and use the convention to gain control of the organization.[131] The main argument used by the Right, however, was that the convention would cost too much money, money that could be used for the 1906 campaign. The ballots sent out by Barnes played up the estimated $15,000 cost by preceding the motion with a special call for funds if the motion were passed. The special call was unnecessary, since convention fund-raising was already provided for in the constitution. The motion for a special convention was defeated, 4,252 to 2,992.[132]

The National Executive Committee elections which took place in January, 1907, were the first in which factional struggle for

[126] "Our Ideal of Democracy," *The Worker*, May 1, 1904; *The Socialist* (Toledo), Nov. 18, 1905, reprinted in *The Worker*, Nov. 25, 1905.

[127] *The Socialist Party Official Bulletin*, Sept., 1905.

[128] *Ibid.*, Oct., 1905.

[129] Letter from Elizabeth H. Thomas, State Secretary, Wisconsin, to J. Mahlon Barnes, Sept. 30, 1905, *The Socialist Party Official Bulletin*, Sept., 1905; "Resolutions of the State Committee of Washington," *The Socialist Party Official Bulletin*, Oct., 1905.

[130] *The Socialist* (Toledo), March 31, 1906; *The Chicago Socialist*, Oct. 7, 1905; A. M. Simons, National Committeeman from Illinois, to *The Chicago Socialist*, Nov. 11, 1905.

[131] *Social-Democratic Herald*, Feb. 3, 1906.

[132] *The Chicago Socialist*, March 17, 1906; *The Socialist* (Toledo), March 31, 1906.

control of the committee was brought into the open. Officers of the Wisconsin party organization sent letters on official stationery to leading members of Socialist locals throughout the country presenting them with a slate of "constructive" candidates. These included the controversial Right-wing state secretary of Minnesota, Gustave Hoehn of Missouri, Seymour Stedman of Illinois, and three members of the Wisconsin party, headed by Berger. For balance, the Wisconsin Socialists suggested that Ben Hanford of New York might be elected "as one who might represent the other wing of the party." [133]

The election revealed a weakness of the Left which it did not begin to overcome until 1910—it had no nationally known leaders outside of Eugene Debs. And Debs persistently refused to run for party office. One hundred and twenty-eight candidates were nominated for the seven-man committee. Each party member was entitled to vote for seven. Faced with a slate of more than one hundred candidates, most Socialists voted for the one or two local leaders they knew, and then voted for the "big names"—the lecturers, writers, and middle-class converts.[134]

This characteristic of executive committee elections, admitted by all leaders of the party, is clearly shown in the 1907 vote. Some 9,200 Socialists voted. Ben Hanford, nationally known as lecturer and Vice Presidential candidate, and somewhat nebulously attached to what remained of the old Center-Left coalition, received the highest vote, 4,203—less than a majority. Berger, an editor and acknowledged leader of the Right, was second with 4,197 votes. After him came editor and writer A. M. Simons, of the Center; Morris Hillquit, lecturer, of the Center; Joseph Medill Patterson, millionaire convert of the Right; Ernest Untermann, writer, of the Center-Left; and John Work, lecturer, of the Right. The only member of Wisconsin's recommended slate to get elected was Berger. No member of the new committee received even half of the total

[133] Circular letter from Carl D. Thompson to members of the Socialist Party, Dec. 29, 1906, circular letter from Elizabeth H. Thomas, State Secretary of Wisconsin, to members of the Socialist Party, letter from Ferdinand Ufert to J. Mahlon Barnes, letter from Elizabeth Thomas and Carl D. Thompson to J. Mahlon Barnes, all in *Socialist Party Weekly Bulletin,* Jan. 12, 1907.

[134] Letter from Robert Hunter to the *Social-Democratic Herald,* Dec. 9, 1911.

vote, and Untermann and Work were elected with less than one fourth.[135]

Also characteristic was the re-election of J. Mahlon Barnes as National Secretary with a 5,000 plurality over his nearest opponent.[136] During the period under study, no National Secretary ever won a campaign for re-election by less than a five to one margin. And no National Secretary ever lost a campaign.

One reason for the Left wing's rapid loss of power in the Socialist Party between 1904 and 1907 was that while denouncing "reformist vote-getting" tendencies of the Center-Right leadership, the Left rapidly relegated most party political work to a role of minor importance. Instead, the Left turned its attention almost exclusively to union organization, declaring that the decisive battle for socialism would be fought not at the ballot box but at the factory gate. The formal democratic political rights already possessed by America's working class encouraged the development of syndicalist theory which considered the cause and solution of all working-class problems to rest solely in economic relationships and struggles. The growth of syndicalism was further encouraged by the apparent failure of an alternative theory, the use of political, or rather, electoral rights to solve economic problems. Neither reform legislation nor votes for socialism seemed to make much headway in gaining socialism or immediate benefits for workers. Therefore, abandon politics and build the revolutionary labor union.[137]

In the fall of 1904 the *American Labor Union Journal* began to set forth the theory which in nine months became the philosophical basis of the Industrial Workers of the World. The first article, published in October, was comparatively moderate. It pointed out that many Socialists who called for working-class unity at the ballot box were themselves guilty of supporting craft unionism, which divided the workers every day except election day. Socialism was primarily an economic movement, and in order for the party

[135] *Supplement to the Socialist Party Official Bulletin,* Jan., 1907.
[136] *Ibid.*
[137] Brooks, *American Syndicalism,* pp. 56–59; John Strachey, *What Are We to Do?* (New York, Random House, 1938), pp. 99–100; Foster, *From Bryan to Stalin,* pp. 42–46.

to win at the polls it must be backed by industrial unity as well as political class consciousness.[138]

The December *Journal* went a little farther. It charged that it was hopeless to attempt to convert the A.F. of L. into a militant, class-conscious industrial union. Right-wing Socialists, the organ of the American Labor Union sneered, were transforming the Federation at a rate comparable to the growth of a coral reef: "the American Federation of Labor is to the workingman industrially what the Demo-Republican party is to him politically; the former is the union of his craft, while the latter is the party of his graft." The *Journal* said that industrial organization was the core of the socialist movement. The political party "is simply the public expression at the ballot box." Socialists must organize the workers in industrial unions which approximated the departments of production and distribution into which the co-operative commonwealth would be divided.[139]

The *Voice of Labor*, published by the A.L.U. in Chicago from January to June, 1905, while preparations were being made for the convention which would launch the Industrial Workers of the World, continued the theoretical development of American syndicalism. The "industrial" Socialists, announced the *Voice*, were not opposed to political action. But they recognized that industrial organization must keep pace with political activity. Industrial unionism and political action were *equally* necessary in order to emancipate the working class. Moreover, the *Voice* charged, the vote polled by the Socialist Party in the 1904 election was in large part made up of the ballots cast by discontented middle-class reformers. The only Socialist votes which had "vital meaning" were those cast by workers organized in industrial unions.[140] Even Father Thomas J. Hagerty, who was shortly to become one of the severest critics of political action as a means of achieving socialism, wrote that the purpose of industrial economic organization was to build a disciplined, class-conscious force, "capable of taking over and collectively administering the tools of industry which they shall

---

[138] "Scabbing after Election," *American Labor Union Journal*, Oct., 1904.

[139] "A Pickwickian Socialist," *American Labor Union Journal*, Dec., 1904. The "Pickwickian Socialist" referred to was Max Hayes.

[140] *Voice of Labor*, Jan., 1905.

replevy from the capitalist class through the ballot box." [141]

Some members of the Center, like A. M. Simons, while they did not go along with the theory of a labor union state, agreed that the A.F. of L. was hopelessly out of step with the times, and urged Socialist support for the move to form a new industrial union.[142] Left and Center supporters of the new industrial unionism agreed that the Socialist Party, as the organized political expression of the socialist movement, could not tie itself to any particular labor union. But it must declare in favor of industrial unionism.[143] "Any other procedure is mere vote-getting subterfuge and compromise." [144]

At the end of June, 1904, the American Labor Union transferred its headquarters eastward to Chicago, from which base it planned to organize all workers into one industrial union.[145] That fall, six members of the Socialist Party and the American Labor Union sent a letter inviting some thirty Socialists and union leaders to join them in a secret conference at Chicago on January 2, 1905, to discuss means of uniting workers on revolutionary principles. The letter asserted that only through correct political and industrial organization could the workers establish the co-operative commonwealth. Correct industrial organization meant organization along syndicalist lines—"a labor organization builded as the structure of socialist society, embracing within itself the working class in approximately the same groups and departments and industries that the workers would assume in the working-class administration of the Co-operative Commonwealth." [146]

Of those invited, only Victor Berger and Max Hayes did not attend the January conference.[147] The Socialist Labor Party was

---

141 Thomas J. Hagerty, "The Function of Industrial Unionism," *Voice of Labor,* III (March, 1905).

142 A. M. Simons, "The Chicago Conference of Industrial Unions," *International Socialist Review,* V (Feb., 1905), 496–99.

143 *Ibid.,* p. 499; "Time Serving Diplomacy," *Voice of Labor,* Feb., 1905.

144 "Time Serving Diplomacy," *Voice of Labor,* Feb., 1905.

145 *American Labor Union Journal,* July 5, 1904.

146 Letter signed by William E. Trautmann, George Estes, W. L. Hall, Eugene V. Debs, Clarence Smith, and Charles O. Sherman, printed in Industrial Workers of the World, *Proceedings of the First Convention,* pp. 82–83; Haywood, *Bill Haywood's Book,* p. 174; Commons, *et al., History of Labour,* IV, 230–32, 236; Brissenden, *The I.W.W.,* pp. 58 n.

147 Commons, *et al., History of Labour,* IV, 230–31.

represented in the person of Frank Bohn of Michigan who had recently become active in that party, and who was soon to become one of the leaders of the Left in the Socialist Party.[148] The conference issued a manifesto containing a blistering attack on craft unionism as a form of labor organization fostered by capitalism to divide the working class. It called for formation of a new industrial union which would recognize the solidarity of all labor, the class struggle, and the need to abolish wage slavery. All workers who agreed with these principles were invited to meet in Chicago on June 27 to organize a new all-embracing industrial union.[149] Secretaries were elected, and 200,000 copies of the Manifesto were distributed.[150]

When the convention which was to form the Industrial Workers of the World assembled in Chicago it was immediately clear that early hopes that a number of A.F. of L. national unions would join the new industrial organization in a body were to be disappointed.[151] Among the 203 delegates present, only sixteen A.F. of L. locals were represented, and only five of these were prepared to affiliate.[152] Sixty-one of the delegates represented only themselves, and 72 others came as sympathetic observers from organizations not willing to affiliate at once. Only 70 delegates representing 51,000 union members, of whom more than half belonged to the Western Federation of Miners, were authorized to join the new organization.[153] Nevertheless, the convention scoffed at the idea that they were setting up a rival union. Debs rejected the charge that they were assembled to disrupt the union movement, commenting that when workers were ordered to scab on each other by the A.F. of L. the movement was already disrupted.[154] Bill Haywood, chairman of the convention, opened the proceedings by saying, "It has been said that this convention was to form an organization rival to the A.F. of L. This is a mistake. We are here for the purpose of forming a labor organization." [155]

[148] Henry Kuhn, "Reminiscences of Daniel De Leon," in *Daniel De Leon,* p. 49.
[149] *The Chicago Socialist,* Jan. 14, 1905.
[150] Haywood, *Bill Haywood's Book,* p. 179.
[151] Brissenden, *The I.W.W.,* pp. 66–67.        [152] *Ibid.,* pp. 71–72.
[153] A. M. Simons, "Industrial Workers of the World," *International Socialist Review,* VI (Aug., 1905), 66; Brissenden, *The I.W.W.,* p. 74.
[154] Haywood, *Bill Haywood's Book,* p. 183.
[155] Industrial Workers of the World, *Proceedings of the First Convention,* pp. 1–2.

Every officer of the I.W.W. elected at the convention, and almost all the leading participants, were members of the Socialist Party.[156] De Leon's defunct Socialist Trade and Labor Alliance had only 1,450 members and therefore only 1,450 votes. Yet the economic and political theories adopted by the I.W.W. were basically those of De Leon and Thomas Hagerty, rather than of Debs, Simons, Charles Moyer, and Ernest Untermann.[157]

The preamble of the I.W.W. constitution did recognize the need for political action, but in a somewhat ambiguous form: "Between these two classes a struggle must go, until all the toilers come together on the political as well as on the industrial field, and take and hold that which they produce by their labor, through an economic organization of the working class without affiliation to any political party." [158] This sentence certainly does not make clear for what purpose the workers were to unite on the political field. Since the workers were to gain all that they produced through their economic organization, political endeavor seemed pointless. The ambiguity of the preamble seems to reflect the lack of clarity in

[156] Haywood, *Bill Haywood's Book*, pp. 182, 186; Brissenden, *The I.W.W.*, p. 109.

[157] One result of the co-operation of Left-wing members of the Socialist Party with the Socialist Labor Party in forming the I.W.W. was a series of attempts to unify the two socialist parties. Conferences were held by those favoring unity between September 10, 1905, and March 4, 1906, in various New Jersey cities. The two major items discussed were party attitudes towards unions and ownership of the socialist press. On the latter question, the conferences recommended party ownership. (*The Worker* answered by quoting from Milton's "Areopagitica," and Mills' "Essay on Liberty" [*The Worker*, April 7, 14, 1906].) The conferences recognized "the usefulness of the Industrial Workers of the World to the proletarian movement" and condemned the A.F. of L. "as an obstacle to the emancipation of the working class." (New Jersey Socialist Unity Conference, *Proceedings, 1905–1906*.)

Nothing came of these first conferences, but in January, 1908, the Socialist Labor Party acted on the 1907 International Socialist Congress' recommendation and asked the Socialist Party to appoint a committee of seven to meet and work out terms of union to be submitted to a referendum vote. The National Committee of the Socialist Party rejected the overture, 44 to 11. (*The Socialist Party Official Bulletin*, Jan., Feb., 1908.)

The 1908 Socialist Party convention voted down a resolution calling for national unity and one calling for unity on the state level of the two parties where the local organizations so desired. This latter resolution was favored by Michigan and Minnesota where the two parties were working in close co-operation. Instead, the convention chose "to invite all members of the Socialist Labor Party who so desire to become members of the Socialist Party. (Socialist Party, *Proceedings of the National Convention, 1908*, pp. 123–35.)

[158] Industrial Workers of the World, *Proceedings of the First Convention*, pp. 220–21.

De Leon's own analysis. During the convention De Leon stated that "the political expression of labor is but the shadow of the economic organization," [159] an emphasis on the militant role of the unions and the educational role of the political party that dated back to the formation of the Socialist Trade and Labor Alliance in 1896.[160]

Perhaps Thomas Hagerty's analysis came closest to what was in the minds of the writers of the preamble, if indeed there was some clear ideology rather than merely an attempt to reconcile the theories of syndicalism and the Socialist and Socialist Labor parties. Hagerty's thesis maintained that the I.W.W. would participate in politics, but that politics had nothing to do with political parties. Political ends would be gained through economic action. Thus, Russian workers were engaging in politics through their revolutionary strikes. Hagerty said the I.W.W. would welcome workers who belonged to no party, and he for one did not believe that the working class needed any particular political party to win its freedom. "The ballot box is simply a capitalist concession. Dropping pieces of paper into a hole in a box never did achieve emancipation for the working class, and to my thinking it never will achieve it." [161]

Whatever the preamble may have meant, the I.W.W. president, Charles Sherman, and the members of the all-powerful General Executive Board were all Socialists with long records of advocacy of political action of the type espoused by the Socialist Party. Bill Haywood, who was to become the most effective organizer of the Industrial Workers, had written a leaflet for the party during the 1904 campaign in which he urged the ballot as the way to end "rascally government, poverty and crime" and to achieve collective ownership of the means of production and distribution.[162]

The Left wing of the Socialist Party was generally enthusiastic in its support of the new industrial union.[163] Unity on the economic

[159] *Ibid.*, pp. 225–28, 231–32.       [160] See above, pp. 15–16.
[161] Industrial Workers of the World, *Proceedings of the First Convention*, pp. 220–21, 233, 244, 245, 246.
[162] William Haywood, *The Wolf* (Detroit, Socialist Party, 1904), p. 1.
[163] Some Left-Wing leaders showed concern over the influence of Daniel De Leon in the I.W.W., and the already noticeable tendency of I.W.W. leaders to sneer at the "Slowcialist Party" and all electoral activity (circular letter from Local San Francisco to the Socialist Press, *The Socialist* [Toledo], April 8, 1905);

field would lead to working class unity on the political field, and that meant electoral support for the party.[164] Furthermore, revolutionary industrial unionism prepared the workers for the administration of industry under socialism,[165] and gave the party an organization whose strikes could force the capitalist class to respect a Socialist mandate at the polls.[166] Debs summed up the Left's attitude on the need for a new union: "To talk about reforming these rotten graft-infested [A.F. of L.] unions, which are dominated absolutely by the labor boss, is as vain and wasteful of time as to spray a cesspool with attar of roses." [167]

While a minority of the Left wingers advocated immediate endorsement of the I.W.W. by the party,[168] the majority held to established Socialist theory that the party had no right to tell labor what organization to support. But the Left insisted that the party was duty-bound to endorse industrial as opposed to craft unionism. This, coupled with its almost unanimous condemnation of efforts to reform the A.F. of L., meant that for all practical purposes the party Left was casting its lot with the Industrial Workers of the World.[169] Debs went East to organize for the I.W.W.[170] Party leaders of the Center and Right were quick to note and

---

William Mailly, "The Industrial Union Launched," *The Socialist* (Toledo), July 8, 1905.

[164] Ernest Untermann, "The Socialist Party and the Trade Unions," *The Worker*, May 5, 1906; Eugene V. Debs, "The Socialist Party and the Trade Unions," *The Worker*, July 28, 1906.

[165] Letter from Eugene V. Debs to *The Chicago Socialist,* Dec. 23, 1905.

[166] Letter from Emil Herman to *The Socialist* (Toledo), Dec. 30, 1905.

[167] Letter from Eugene V. Debs to *The Chicago Socialist,* Dec. 23, 1905.

[168] Examples of these demands are "Resolutions of Pottawatomie County, Oklahoma Territory, Socialist Party," *Socialist Party Official Bulletin,* June, 1906; "Resolutions of New Orleans Socialist Party, July 11, 1906," *Socialist Party Official Bulletin,* July, 1906; letter from Emil Herman to *The Socialist* (Toledo), Dec. 30, 1905; *Social Democratic Herald,* June 9, 1906. The New Orleans resolution of July 11, 1906 received only nine seconds, eleven short of the minimum required for a national referendum (*Socialist Party Official Bulletin,* Jan., 1907).

[169] "Resolution of Local Portland [Oregon], *Social Democratic Herald,* Oct. 21, 1905; Alfred Wagenknecht in *The Socialist Party Official Bulletin,* Oct., 1906; Ernest Untermann, "The Socialist Party and the Trade Unions," *The Worker,* May 5, 1906; Charles L. Breckon, "The Socialist Party and the Trade Unions," *The Worker,* May 19, 1906; Eugene V. Debs, "The Socialist Party and the Trade Unions," *The Worker,* July 28, 1906; William Mailly, "The Industrial Union Convention," *The Socialist* (Toledo), July 15, 1905.

[170] Letter from Eugene V. Debs of Joseph A. Labadie, December 12, 1905, Labadie Collection.

complain that "active workers in the Socialist party all over the country have suddenly grown lukewarm in the effort to build up a political organization and are enthusiastically proclaiming the advantages of 'industrialism.' " [171]

The Party Right wing was virtually unanimous in its condemnation of the I.W.W. from the start.[172] It echoed charges made by A.F. of L. leaders that the new industrial union was nothing but a plot by certain Socialist leaders to destroy the Federation and save the American Labor Union.[173] The Right, ignoring the fact that they virtually had ceased to agitate for industrial unionism at Federation conventions, insisted that the A.F. of L. had been about to adopt the industrial form of organization, but that the formation of the I.W.W. had killed the industrial movement in the Federation.[174]

Having attacked the Left for ruining the chance for immediate conversion of the A.F. of L. to industrial unionism, the Right went on to say that industrial unionism versus craft unionism was not an issue "worth quarreling about." [175] American industry had not yet consolidated to the point where socialism was an issue, explained the Right. And when industry had so consolidated, socialism would come gradually through reforms won at the polls, and not through industrial violence. Socialist Party activity in the unions, meaning American Federation of Labor unions, should be solely the educational task of teaching workers to vote Socialist.[176]

---

[171] Max S. Hayes, "The World of Labor," *International Socialist Review*, VI (April, 1906), 631; letter from H. C. Terline (Memphis, Tennessee) to the *Social-Democratic Herald*, June 9, 1906.

[172] An interesting exception was Joseph Gilbert, Right-wing national committeeman from Utah, who immediately became a strong proponent of the I.W.W. Gilbert held that the Socialist Party should remain an opportunist political party while the I.W.W. carried on the "revolutionary struggle." (Joseph Gilbert, "The Socialist Party and the Trade Unions," *The Worker*, June 2, 1906.)

[173] Hugh McGregor, "Words of Warning," *American Federationist*, XII (June, 1905), 354; *American Federationist*, XII (August, 1905), 514–15.

[174] *Social-Democratic Herald*, Feb. 18, 1905.

[175] Max S. Hayes, "The Socialist Party and the Trade Unions," *The Worker*, May 12, 1906.

[176] Victor L. Berger, "A Timely Warning against Unwise Action," *Social-Democratic Herald*, Jan. 21, 1905; Victor L. Berger, "The Fight against Sectarianism," *Social-Democratic Herald*, April 8, 1905; Victor L. Berger, "No Golden Anniversary for the A.F. of L.," *Social-Democratic Herald*, Dec. 9, 1905; Max S. Hayes, "The World of Labor," *International Socialist Review*, V (Feb., 1905), 501–2; Max S. Hayes, "The World of Labor," *International Socialist Review*, VI (April, 1906),

The Right, which when in the minority had always opposed party discipline and insisted upon absolute freedom of opinion and action for all in the Socialist Party regardless of the accepted platform or theory,[177] now took advantage of its growing alliance with the Center to move against those Socialists who were active in the I.W.W. Left-wing Socialists who supported the Industrial Workers were accused of "party treachery." [178] William Trautmann, the Socialist national committeeman from Ohio and editor of the United Brewery Workers' *Brewers' Journal*, was chosen as an example of what would happen to other Socialists whose jobs depended on Socialist-led Federation unions. Trautmann had no sooner participated in calling the June, 1905, I.W.W. convention than Gompers demanded action against him. The Brewery Workers' union was one of the so-called "socialist unions." Guided by Gustave Hoehn of St. Louis and Victor Berger, the Right-wing Socialists managed to scrape up a bare majority and Trautmann was removed from the executive board of the union and fired from his position as editor of the *Journal*.[179] When Left-wing Socialists attempted to retaliate by removing Berger from the executive committee of the party for advocating fusion, the Center threw enough support to Berger to defeat the move.[180]

Although some members of the Center faction of the Socialist Party defended the Industrial Workers and even attacked "those editors of socialist papers and officials of the Socialist Party who have organized unions for the purpose of getting themselves elected to national conventions and posing as trade union leaders," [181] most Center leaders went along with the Right wing in attacking the I.W.W. without reservation.[182] They vociferously protested their belief in the superiority of industrial as compared to craft

---

631–32; Thomas J. Morgan, "The Socialist Party and the Trade Unions," *The Worker,* May 19, 1906.

[177] W. G. Critchlow (State Secretary of Ohio Socialist Party), "State Autonomy," *The Socialist* (Seattle), Jan. 18, 1903.

[178] *Social-Democratic Herald,* Jan. 20, 1906.

[179] *The Socialist Party Official Bulletin,* March, April, 1905; *The Worker,* April 22, May 13, 1905; "The Trautmann Case," *Voice of Labor,* June, 1905.

[180] See above, pp. 183–85.

[181] A. M. Simons, "Industrial Workers of the World," *International Socialist Review,* VI (Aug., 1905), 76.

[182] Hillquit, *Loose Leaves,* p. 96; Coleman, *Debs,* p. 230.

organization, but insisted that industrial unionism could not be imposed from above by a "junta" of A.L.U. officers, "three or four editors, an ex-priest, some deposed union officers, and some other individuals, acting solely on individual responsibility, or irresponsibility, as the case may be." [183] The A.F. of L. was moving in its own way toward an industrial form of organization. Besides, "the Socialist Party is not responsible for what happens within the unions." [184] Finally, no type of economic organization could solve labor's problems. Socialism could come only through the winning of elections. And Socialist participation in forming the I.W.W., charged the Center, had antagonized the craft unions and was responsible for the drop in the Socialist vote in the 1905–1906 elections.[185]

If the Socialist Party was divided in its attitude toward the Industrial Workers of the World in 1905, the split over personalities and to some extent, principles, which occurred at the 1906 I.W.W. convention and which resulted in the withdrawal of the Western Federation of Miners,[186] drew the lines hard and fast. Center Socialists like A. M. Simons turned from support of the Industrial Workers to bitter attack.[187] The Center and Right socialist press echoed and reechoed with "I told you so's," and prophecies of the imminent dissolution of the new union.[188]

It now became clear that the Socialist division over the Industrial Workers was not a simple matter of whether industrial labor organization could best be achieved by "boring from within" or by building a new union. The Center-Right Socialists began to distinguish between themselves and those Socialists who supported the I.W.W. not on the basis of approach to industrial unionism, but on the question of peaceful transition through political action or revolution through conflict, struggle, and violence.[189]

---

[183] "The Industrial Reorganizationists Convention," *The Worker*, June 24, 1905.

[184] *Ibid.;* "The Industrial Organization Manifesto," *The Worker*, Jan. 29, 1905; *The Worker*, April 1, 15, 1905; *The Chicago Socialist*, July 8, 15, 1905; A. W. Mance, "Labor's Internal Struggles," *The Chicago Socialist*, Dec. 23, 1905.

[185] W. J. Ghent, "The Socialist Vote," *The Worker*, May 11, 1907.

[186] Brissenden, *The I.W.W.*, pp. 136–53; Haywood, *Bill Haywood's Book*, p. 204.

[187] A. M. Simons in the *International Socialist Review*, VII (Oct., 1906), 243.

[188] "To Take and to Hold," *The Chicago Socialist*, Oct. 13, 1906; *The Worker*, Oct. 20, 1906; Max S. Hayes, "The Voice of Labor," *International Socialist Review*, VII (Nov., 1906), 311–12.

[189] Spargo, *Socialism*, p. 152.

The Left Socialists maintained that they were not opposed to political action. In fact, Bill Haywood ran for governor of Colorado on the Socialist ticket in 1906, and the Nevada Socialist ticket was made up almost exclusively of members of the I.W.W.[190] But the Left insisted that a political party could not fight the everyday battles of the workers against the capitalists. Nor could a political party "wrest control of the industries from the exploiting master class, give them over to the workers and protect the workers in possession of them." All the political phase of the socialist movement could do, concluded the Left, was to take the lead in educating and agitating for socialism, register the increasing support for socialism at elections, and show that all responsibility for violence belonged to the capitalist class if that class "should refuse peacefully to turn over to the workers the things they should vote to take possession of." [191]

The now rapidly forming Center-Right coalition did its best to discredit and eliminate supporters of the Industrial Workers from the party. William Trautmann, who had become secretary-treasurer of the I.W.W., and Alfred S. Edwards, editor of the *Social Democratic Herald* in its early days and now editor of the *Industrial Worker*, were expelled from the party by their locals for "treasonable conduct." [192] Even Eugene Debs was not immune. Although Debs left the I.W.W. in 1906 because he believed they were putting too little emphasis on political activity, his place in the party continued to be with the Left. Debs was far too popular with the rank and file of the party and with the electorate to be attacked openly. The Center-Right leaders were forced to confine themselves to spreading stories to the effect that his heart was in the right place, but that really he was little more than an "orator." [193] Friction between Debs, who symbolized the party, and the real party bosses like Hillquit, Berger, Spargo, and Barnes increased over the years.[194] By 1912, when party factionalism and

[190] *Miners' Magazine*, VIII (July 26, 1906), 13.

[191] "Political Power Alone Not Sufficient," *Voice of Labor*, June, 1905, pp. 12–13.

[192] *Social-Democratic Herald*, Oct. 27, 1906.

[193] Victor Berger, quoted by Lincoln Steffens in "Eugene V. Debs on What the Matter Is in America and What to Do About It," *Everybody's Magazine*, XIX (Oct., 1908), 462.

[194] Hillquit, *Loose Leaves*, pp. 49, 51; Coleman, *Debs*, pp. 220–22, 230–31; Bloor, *We Are Many*, p. 59; Madison, *Critics and Crusaders*, pp. 499–500.

the Presidential campaign were in full swing, Berger announced publicly that "many intelligent Socialists have long known that Gene suffers from an unduly exaggerated ego . . . after the 5th of November some plain words will be addressed to him." [195]

It was, perhaps, some consolation to the Left to be able to reply that Center-Right leaders opposed the I.W.W. because there was no place in it for small capitalists, lawyers, and ministers.[196] But such countercharges alone were not sufficient to stop the growing control which Center-Right leaders exercised in the determination of national and local Socialist policies and activities.

[195] Victor L. Berger in the *National Socialist,* quoted in "This Thing Must Be Settled," *International Socialist Review,* XIII (Sept., 1912), 276–77.
[196] Macy, *Socialism in America,* 163–64.

# X

# The Stagnant Years
## 1907-1908

IT IS IMPOSSIBLE to analyze the character of the Socialist Party membership with any degree of accuracy. The party itself made only one attempt to investigate the nature of its dues-paying support, and the results were inconclusive. Less than one sixth of the membership answered the questionnaire sent out by the national office early in 1908. The returns were so scattered and uneven that they cannot be used as the basis for an accurate evaluation of the party make-up. Yet, since no other such analysis exists, it is summarized here for whatever it may be worth.

Sixty-three hundred dues-paying Socialists answered the 1908 questionnaire—6,000 men and 300 women. Of these, more than two thirds were over 30 years old, and almost one third were over 45. American birth was claimed by 71 percent, German birth by 8.5 percent, Scandinavian by 5 percent, English by 4 percent, and Finnish by 2 percent.[1] The occupations of the party members were broken down into broad categories: "craftsmen" made up 41 percent of the respondents; "laborers," 20 percent; farmers, 17 percent; "commerce," 9 percent; professional 5 percent; transport 5 percent; and housewives 3 percent.

The previous political affiliations of those who returned the questionnaire were rather evenly divided between Republican and Democratic, 35 percent for the former and 40 for the latter. In addition, 15 percent had come to the socialist movement by way of the Populists, 4 percent from the Prohibitionists, and 6 percent had been independents. Of converts to the party, 39 percent came

[1] By 1912, approximately 10 percent of the Socialist membership belonged to the party through the Finnish Socialist Federation. See below, pp. 273-74.

through reading periodicals, 19 percent through discussion, 13 percent through books, and the rest through street meetings, lectures, leaflets, and "study." Two thirds of those who answered subscribed to the *Appeal to Reason*, although almost all were subscribers to one or more local or factional Socialist periodicals.[2]

Even if the questionnaire reflected the character of the total membership as of 1908, it did not reveal the nature of the recruits who had joined the party since 1905–1906, when the Center joined the Right in appealing chiefly for middle-class and farm support. National Secretary Barnes claimed in 1908 that for the previous two years a large proportion of recruits were farmers.[3] Robert Hunter, a writer and municipal reformer who had married into the Stokes family and joined the party in 1907,[4] rising rapidly to a place on the National Executive Committee, boasted that the party was now drawing its strength from university circles, professionals, the clergy, farmers, and businessmen.[5]

If the questionnaire's figures as to craftsmen, laborers, and transport workers were accurate, the working-class majority of the party was most definitely not represented on the National Executive Committee (which had replaced the National Committee as the seat of power). The seven members elected to the executive committee in February, 1908, were Victor Berger, A. H. Floaten, Morris Hillquit, A. M. Simons, J. G. Phelps Stokes, Carl D. Thompson, and John Work.[6] The working-class was led by two lawyers, two editors, one well-to-do merchant, one millionaire reformer, and one minister.

The rate of growth in party membership continued to decline, party enrollment increasing by only 2,000 in 1907.[7] Organizational techniques remained the same as in the days of more success-

2 "Minutes of the National Executive Committee Meeting, April 10, 1909," the *Socialist Party Official Bulletin*, April, 1909.

3 J. Mahlon Barnes quoted by Ernest Poole, "Harnessing Socialism," the *American Magazine*, LXVI (Sept., 1908), 428.

4 *The Worker*, Jan. 19, 1907.

5 Robert Hunter, "The Socialist Party in the Present Campaign," the *American Review of Reviews*, XXXVIII (Sept., 1908), 297–98.

6 *Socialist Party Weekly Bulletin*, Feb. 18, 1908; *Supplement to the Socialist Party Official Bulletin*, Feb., 1908.

7 Total strength for 1907 was 28,679 (letter from J. Mahlon Barnes to the National Committee and State Secretaries, *The Socialist Party Official Bulletin*, Jan., 1908).

ful recruiting,[8] and indeed thousands of new members continued to apply for admission every year. But militancy seemed to have left the party. In fact, the Center gave up all claim of favoring a fighting political organization. Socialist locals were told to limit their activity to the sale of newspaper subscriptions, leaflets, and books, raising funds for educational work, and getting out the vote on election day.[9] As one Center analyst proudly observed, "The Socialist Party is not so much a party militant as an organization for the study of political economy and the teaching of a true political economy to the masses. It is a party of [social] interpretation." [10]

Newly recruited members found little to do in this "party of interpretation," and they dropped out almost as fast as they entered. Between 1904 and 1908 it was estimated that Local Cook County (Chicago) had from 6,000 to 10,000 new recruits, but less than a thousand of these had continued their membership.[11] New York City received a thousand applications for membership annually, but New York state's strength remained stationary at about 2,600.[12] Ninety-five percent of the new subscriptions obtained by the New York *Worker* were lost within a few months.[13] All factions agreed "that there is something weak about the Party." [14]

The recognition of a growing lethargy among party members did not cause Center leaders to reconsider their rapprochement with the admittedly opportunist Right wing. Center leaders still attacked Right-wing "bosses" on occasion. The *Social-Democratic Herald*, for example, was denounced as "the most inaccurate and sloven periodical in America." [15] But such recriminations were no

[8] J. Mahlon Barnes quoted by Ernest Poole, "Harnessing Socialism," the *American Magazine*, LXVI (Sept., 1908), 427–28; Robert Hunter, "The Socialist Party in the Present Campaign," the *American Review of Reviews*, XXXVIII (Sept., 1908), 296–97.

[9] "Suggestions for Socialist Locals," *The Worker*, Oct. 26, 1907.

[10] Ellis O. Jones, "Some Unique Features of the Socialist Party," *The Arena* XXXVIII (Oct., 1907), 423.

[11] Letter from Guy Williams to J. Mahlon Barnes, June 1, 1908, *Socialist Party Weekly Bulletin*, June 13, 1908.

[12] Letter from "Vulcan" to *The Worker*, June 8, 1907; letter from T. J. Lloyd to *The Worker*, June 15, 1907.

[13] Letter from T. J. Lloyd to *The Worker*, June 15, 1907.

[14] A. M. Simons, "Looking Forward and Backward," *International Socialist Review*, VIII (Jan., 1908), 431.

[15] Letter from W. J. Ghent, Secretary, Rand School of Social Science to Elizabeth H. Thomas, Secretary of the Wisconsin Social Democratic Party, Feb. 7, 1907, *The Worker*, Feb. 16, 1907.

longer based primarily in principle. Rather they were a continuation of the bitter personal antagonisms built up some five years before when both Center and Left regarded the opportunism of the Right as the greatest threat facing the Socialist Party.

In the two years between the 1906 and 1908 elections, the Center continued to embrace theories held by the Right from the formation of the party. Center theoreticians began to correct what they considered Marx's lapses into "utopianism" and to suggest that it was time that Marx was brought up to date. One month before the panic of 1907, Algie Simons informed party members that trusts and monopolies had eliminated the planlessness of competition and could always invest all the surplus value they took from labor. Therefore, reasoned Simons, it was quite likely that there would be no more depressions.[16]

John Spargo and Morris Hillquit devoted themselves to correcting those Socialists who still did not understand that Marx had "lapsed at times into the Utopian habit of predicting the sudden transformation." [17] Hillquit said flatly, "so far as we Socialists are concerned, the age of physical revolution . . . has passed." [18] Socialism was to come gradually. In fact, it was now in the process of coming into being. Spargo was so convinced that his analysis of step-at-a-time socialism was the only scientifically reasonable one, that he insisted "no Socialist whose works have any influence in the movement believes that there will be a sudden, violent change from capitalism to Socialism." [19]

Along with acceptance of a gradualist theory of the coming of socialism, the Centerists naturally became ardent advocates of nationalization of public utilities.[20] Since the Center had long insisted that government was a capitalist tool, it was forced to add one temporary variation to the Right's explanation of how national

[16] A. M. Simons, "Some Problems of the Trust," *International Socialist Review,* VIII (Oct., 1907), 240–43.

[17] John Spargo, "The Means of Realization," stenographic report of an address delivered to some students of socialism, New York, Oct., 1907, reprinted in Spargo, *Socialism,* 1913 ed., p. 324.

[18] Morris Hillquit, "A Reply to Mr. Mallock," *The Worker,* March 9, 1907.

[19] Spargo, "The Means of Realization," in Spargo, *Socialism,* 1913 ed., pp. 325–26.

[20] E. Backus, Member of the State Committee of the California Socialist Party, "Industrial Evolution and Socialist Tactics," *International Socialist Review,* VII (Jan., 1907), 411–14; "The Federation Convention," *The Worker,* Nov. 30, 1907.

and municipal ownership would lead inevitably to socialism. Center theoreticians explained that if the capitalist government used its power to oppress workers in the newly nationalized utilities, these workers would then realize the futility of voting for the old political parties. And once they used their ballots to put Socialists into office, the nationalized trusts automatically would be socialized.[21]

The Center was now careful to point out that the party favored nationalization only of those industries "made ready" for socialization "by a degree of monopolization." "Non-productive wealth" in the form of savings, no matter how large, and small businesses would not be touched. "By means of such measures as the Initiative and Referendum, and election of judges by the people, the sovereignty of the people will be established," Spargo declared.[22]

The Center continued to point to the increasing number of Socialist recruits from the ranks of the middle and capitalist classes as proof of the correctness of their analysis and tactics. Furthermore, they saw the enlistment of these "parlor socialists" into the ranks of the party as an indication that the movement was being "Americanized." [23] The non-Socialist reform press, on the other hand, welcomed "parlor socialists" into the Socialist Party as moderate men who would see to it that the socialist movement pursued a reasonable reform course.[24]

When working-class members of the party protested against what seemed to them the conversion of the party into an organization for radical middle-class reform, the Center promptly replied that the "uninstructed proletariat . . . is the sport and plaything of its economic masters." The "chumps" and "demagogs" in the party who insisted that the working class could furnish its own leaders were blamed for failure of the party to increase its vote.[25] The Center held that the "intellectuals" in the party, those whose

[21] E. Backus, Member of the State Committee of the California Socialist Party, "Industrial Evolution and Socialist Tactics," *International Socialist Review*, VII (Jan., 1907), 411–14; Morris Hillquit, "Declaration of Principles," *The Worker*, March 7, 1908.

[22] Spargo, "The Means of Realization," in Spargo, *Socialism*, 1913 ed., pp. 329–37.

[23] Ellis O. Jones, "The Parlor Socialists," *International Socialist Review*, VIII (Oct., 1907), 212–14.

[24] "Parlor Socialist," *The Independent*, LXIV (April 9, 1908), 821.

[25] Letters from W. J. Ghent to *The Worker*, Nov. 23, Dec. 14, 1907; letter from Morris Hillquit to *The Worker*, March 14, 1908.

wealth had enabled them to secure a college education and the leisure to study social questions objectively, were the only ones fit to lead. Workers were "incompetent mentally" and therefore unfit to steer the party through the intricacies of step-at-a-time socialism.[26] "The intelligence that certain men bring to the movement is the social force that wins thousands of workmen, previously unenlightened, to our cause," announced W. J. Ghent, head of the Socialist Rand School. "This intelligence should be rewarded, as it almost invariably is rewarded, thruout the International Socialist movement, with the responsibility of leadership, no matter what the demagogs say." [27]

As the 1908 convention approached, the three factions flooded the socialist press with their analyses of the Socialist Party's proper role. The Right wing struck the first blow with publication of a draft platform drawn up by John Work of the National Executive Committee.[28] Work's proposed platform condemned capitalism as a "nuisance" responsible for drink, crime, poverty, and prostitution. Work wrote that socialism would nationalize those giant industries which prevented the worker from receiving the full product of his labor. Other businesses and small farms would be retained by their present owners. According to Work, capitalists who performed useful labor were not really capitalists. Finally, Socialists did not teach class hatred, but asked all members of society to support the evolutionary movement and the twenty-odd immediate demands of the Socialist Party which would lead to socialism.[29]

Hillquit immediately replied for the Center. He criticized the "primer style affected by Comrade Work" and held that the platform should be "addressed to intelligent and reasoning men." Furthermore, said Hillquit, the concept that the socialist state would

[26] Ellis O. Jones, "The Parlor Socialists," *International Socialist Review*, VIII (Oct., 1907), 212.

[27] Letter from W. J. Ghent to *The Worker*, Nov. 23, 1907.

[28] Work offered the platform as a member of the platform committee appointed by the National Committee in the summer of 1906. He charged that other members of the committee had refused to co-operate. (Letter from John Work to J. Mahlon Barnes, *Socialist Party Weekly Bulletin*, Jan. 18, 1908.) The publication of Work's draft, however, galvanized Hillquit, also a member of the platform committee, into action.

[29] *Socialist Party Weekly Bulletin*, Jan. 18, 1908.

be organized to secure every man "the full product of his labor" was no longer accepted as sound socialist principle. In the collective state, those unable to produce would have to be provided for, so no one would receive the full value of his individual labor.[30] In place of the Work platform, Hillquit offered his own "Declaration of Principles," a platform which put Work's reform proposals in the "revolutionary" phraseology of the international socialist movement.[31]

Herman Titus, for the Left, criticized Hillquit's draft platform as a compromise "prudently omitting what might be objected to by anybody on either side, but not constituting a militant proletarian educational instrument." Titus charged that the Hillquit Declaration carefully ignored the central thesis of the socialist movement, the exploitation of labor. It was all very well to call attention to the evolutionary movement toward socialism, but unless "wage exploitation" was made the heart of the Socialist platform, middle-class public ownership would swamp the socialist movement.[32]

The Left, however, still reserved its sharpest barbs for the party Right wing. Work's platform proposals were an "idiotic conglomeration of single tax phraseology, capitalist reform and Hearst Socialism." [33] While the Left granted that the party did not "create" the conditions responsible for class hatred, it insisted that the party most certainly did teach the working class to hate its enemy. The Left said the proletariat could not concern itself with the metaphysical problem of separating the capitalist from his system. Nor could the working class ignore the class struggle and repudiate scientific socialism in order to join Bryan and Theodore Roosevelt in crying "down with the trusts!" [34]

The Left held that all wage labor was exploited, and it did not matter to the proletariat whether surplus value was extracted by trusts, little business, or government. "The Socialist Party will

[30] Letter from Morris Hillquit to J. Mahlon Barnes, Feb. 20, 1908, *The Socialist* (Seattle), March 7, 1908.

[31] Morris Hillquit, "Declaration of Principles," *The Worker*, March 7, 1908.

[32] Herman Titus in *The Socialist* (Seattle), March 7, 1908.

[33] Tom Sladden (Secretary, Socialist Party of Oregon), "Mixers," *Socialist Party Weekly Bulletin*, Feb. 8, 1908.

[34] *Ibid.;* Herman F. Titus, "What the Socialist Party Stands For," *The Socialist* (Seattle), March 7, 1908; letter from Emil Herman to J. Mahlon Barnes, Jan. 31, 1908, *Socialist Party Weekly Bulletin*, Feb. 8, 1908.

gain the respect and be the Party of the working class, and that is the class that works for wages, only by forgetting all other classes, and fighting for its own," said Tom Sladden, secretary of the Oregon Socialist Party. "Volunteers may come to aid us but they must carry our banner and leave theirs at home." [35] The Left insisted that the 1908 Socialist convention must decide whether the party was to be proletarian or petty bourgeois. [36]

The Right wing replied that all criticism of Work's draft platform came from "a few misplaced De Leonites in the party." [37] Berger held that the convention should draw up a platform which ignored theoretical analysis and limited itself to the "questions of the day." He said the convention was being held to formulate a program for the coming national election campaign, and such a program should center around the issues of nationalizing the trusts, relief for farmers, and restriction of immigration. [38]

The delegation which assembled for the May, 1908, party convention contained few representatives of the working class. This was due in part to the fact that the delegates, unlike those to the 1904 convention, were not provided with living expenses for the trip and eight-day session. [39] Far more than at the 1904 convention, the socialist movement was represented by lawyers, small businessmen, editors, farmers, politicians, professional organizers and agitators, and ministers and ex-ministers of the gospel. [40] These delegates were easy targets for party Right-wing arguments, especially those of the Wisconsin delegation which could boast of having lost the Milwaukee election by only two thousand votes after an eight-year campaign for honest government. [41]

[35] Tom Sladden, "Mixers," *Socialist Party Weekly Bulletin,* Feb. 8, 1908.

[36] *The Socialist* (Seattle), April 11, 1908; Herman F. Titus, "The Socialist Party National Convention," *The Socialist* (Seattle), May 3, 1908.

[37] *Social-Democratic Herald,* March 14, 1908.

[38] Victor L. Berger, "And the Victory Will Be Ours," *Social-Democratic Herald,* May 9, 1908.

[39] "Minutes of National Executive Committee of Socialist Party, July 18, 1908," the *Socialist Party Official Bulletin,* July, 1908; letter from Herman F. Titus to Richard Krueger, April 30, 1908, *The Socialist* (Seattle), May 3, 1908. Titus, who had bankrupted himself in supporting *The Socialist,* was unable to afford to attend the convention.

[40] Robert F. Hoxie, "The Convention of the Socialist Party, 1908," the *Journal of Political Economy,* XVI (July, 1908), 442.

[41] *Ibid.,* pp. 442–43; Robert Hunter, "The Socialist Party in the Present Campaign," the *American Review of Reviews,* XXXVIII (Sept., 1908), 295–96; Char-

The convention platform committee brought in some twenty immediate demands to form the basis of the party campaign. The Left managed to amend the first demand to include a proposal for nationalization of all land. But after that early victory, they failed in all their efforts to direct the demands away from municipal reform and toward legislation of immediate benefit to labor.[42]

The debate on the party's relations with labor organizations again brought factional divisions into the open. The Left managed to get the name of the committee and its resolution changed from "Trades Unions" to "Address to Organized Labor," despite Berger's threat to bolt the party.[43] But the resolution itself consisted of nothing but platitudes on the importance of unions and the need for labor to vote the Socialist ticket. The Left then introduced an amendment stating that it was the duty of the Socialist Party "to point out to the workers that the industrial form of organization is best suited to developing the working class solidarity necessary to the success of organized labor under the present methods of production." The Right replied with its familiar analogy of the "two-armed labor movement," but with the two arms completely independent of each other. The amendment was defeated, 138 to 48.[44]

For the first time factional divisions in the party entered the question of who should be nominated as candidates for President and Vice President. The Right wing, supported by some Center leaders, made a concerted effort to prevent the nomination of Debs. The fact that failure to nominate him might destroy all Socialist enthusiasm for the coming campaign did not deter Right-wing leaders. Negotiations were started to prevent the nomination of "certain ignorant, doctrinaire, ultra-revolutionary, semi-anarchistic element[s] represented by such men as Bill Haywood and certain individuals connected with such sheets as the *Appeal to Reason* [Eugene V. Debs]." [45]

Haywood, an organizer for the I.W.W. and a member of the

lotte Teller, "The National Socialist Convention," *The Arena*, LX (July, 1908), 26–28.

[42] Socialist Party, *Proceedings of the National Convention, 1908*, pp. 167–229.

[43] *Ibid.*, pp. 25–33.          [44] *Ibid.*, pp. 94–102.

[45] Robert F. Hoxie, "The Convention of the Socialist Party, 1908," the *Journal of Political Economy*, XVI (July, 1908), 446. Debs was the only nationally prominent staff contributor to the *Appeal*.

party Left wing, had leaped into prominence as a result of the Moyer-Haywood-Pettibone kidnapping and trial of 1906–1907.[46] However, he quickly made it clear that he was not a candidate and urged the nomination of Debs.[47] The Right wing then turned its fire on Debs, for whom, they admitted, there was "some sentiment" at the convention. The Right sought to counter this "sentiment" by insinuating that his connection with the organization of the Industrial Workers of the World had ended his effectiveness as a campaigner.[48]

When the convention floor was thrown open to nominations, Debs was immediately proposed, John Spargo seconding the nomination for the entire New York delegation.[49] Spargo's seconding speech, despite its emphasis on Debs's "human mistakes" and its damning with faint praise, ended Right-wing hopes that they could swing the entire Center against Debs. Seymour Stedman of Chicago then arose and to the accompaniment of hisses and cries of "no" informed the convention that Debs had recently undergone a throat operation and would be unable to campaign. He therefore offered the convention the name of Algie M. Simons. Since Simons was an excellent speaker, explained Stedman, the party would have the benefit of his oratory and also that of the noncandidate (and apparently miraculously cured) Debs.[50]

Ben Hanford of New York answered Stedman by reading a letter from Debs in which Debs explained that the operation and his year of absence from speaking had resulted in a complete recovery. Hanford sarcastically pointed out that Stedman had read this letter before nominating Simons.[51] Victor Berger then announced that it seemed to be his fate "to do unpopular things." He explained that until two or three years before there had been few friendships as close as his and Debs. In fact, he still loved him. But he loved

---

[46] See below, pp. 323–31.

[47] Haywood, *Bill Haywood's Book*, p. 230; *The Socialist* (Seattle), May 16, 1908; Robert F. Hoxie, "The Convention of the Socialist Party, 1908," the *Journal of Political Economy*, XVI (July, 1908), 447.

[48] Frederic Heath, "National Socialist Convention," *Social-Democratic Herald*, May 16, 1908. The Party Right meant, although they would not dare state it openly, that Debs support of industrial unionism would cost the party the support of A.F. of L. leaders.

[49] Socialist Party, *Proceedings of the National Convention, 1908*, pp. 146–48.

[50] *Ibid.*, pp. 148–50.                    [51] *Ibid.*, pp. 151–52.

the socialist movement more. He granted that if Debs were nominated he and the Wisconsin party would "do our duty." But the party should select "a man who stands for constructive work such as is being done in Wisconsin." He therefore placed in nomination the man for whom the Right wing had been caucusing for months, Reverend Carl D. Thompson of Wisconsin.[52]

There were immediate protests that Thompson had participated in so many state factional fights that he could not possibly get the wholehearted support of all Socialists.[53] The Right then sought to split the Left and Center vote by nominating James F. Carey of Massachusetts.[54] Alfred Wagenknecht of the Washington Left wing seconded Carey's nomination, and then informed him that of course he could decline to run.[55] The Massachusetts delegation announced that Carey refused to be used as a candidate against Debs and therefore withdrew.[56]

After a number of other nominations and withdrawals had been made for purposes of lining up votes, the chairman announced that only three candidates remained: Debs (Left wing), Simons (Center), and Thompson (Right wing). The vote was decisive—for Carey (despite his withdrawal), 16; for Thompson, 14; for Simons, 9; and for Debs, 159.[57]

Right-wing leaders were able to do little better in the contest for the Vice Presidential nomination. Ben Hanford, a member of the Center faction and the candidate of both the Left and most of the Center, won easily over five Center and Right-wing candidates, 106 votes for Hanford against a total of 79 for his five opponents.[58]

Each of the three party factions hailed the convention as victory for its principles. As proof that "the Proletarians were in control of the Socialist National Convention," [59] the Left made four points: the platform statement that the struggle between "wage workers and capitalists" was increasing in intensity; the trade union resolution which did not single out the American Federation of Labor for exclusive support; the defeat of the "populistic" farmers' planks; and the nomination of Debs and Hanford.

52 *Ibid.*, pp. 152–53.          53 *Ibid.*, pp. 153–55.          54 *Ibid.*, pp. 155–56.
55 *Ibid.*, p. 160.          56 *Ibid.*          57 *Ibid.*, pp. 160–61.
58 *Ibid.*, pp. 161–64.
59 Herman F. Titus, "One Thing Settled," *The Socialist* (Seattle), May 30, 1908; *The Socialist* (Seattle), May 16, 1908; Haywood, *Bill Haywood's Book*, p. 230.

The Left optimistically predicted that its "triumph" at the convention would bring an end to "silly jeers at 'Skyentific' Socialism or jokes about the 'Prowling Terriers' or flings at 'R-r-r-evolutionary' doctrines or loud boasts about 'Constructive Socialism.' " [60]

The Center and Right wings were also convinced that the 1908 convention had settled once and for all the question as to whether the party was to be revolutionary or constructive. They admitted they had won only by uniting eloquence with adroitly worded resolutions, delay with superior parliamentary manipulation, and reform measures with revolutionary protestations. They further admitted that Debs had been nominated despite the fact that "it was clearly understood that Debs has no longer mind nor character for party leadership and that neither of the candidates really represent the dominant trend in the party policy." [61]

But the Center and Right insisted that their victories had been decisive. Adoption of immediate demands, refusal to endorse industrial unionism, passage of a resolution favoring the restriction of immigration,[62] and of a constitutional amendment restricting party membership to those who advocated political action [63] were considered of fundamental importance.[64] The Center boasted that the Right-wing Wisconsin delegation had exercised great influence at the convention.[65] And to leave no doubt as to where the party stood, the Center and Right delegates who made up the "committee on style" [66] for the party platform boldly changed that document's wording after the convention so that instead of reading that the working class could not expect adequate relief "from any reform of the present order *or* from the dominant class of society,"

[60] Herman F. Titus, "One Thing Settled," *The Socialist* (Seattle), May 30, 1908.

[61] Robert F. Hoxie, "The Convention of the Socialist Party 1908," the *Journal of Political Economy,* XVI (July, 1908), 443–47.

[62] See below, pp. 279–82.

[63] See below, p. 403.

[64] Victor L. Berger, "Impossibilism to the Rear," *Social-Democratic Herald,* May 23, 1908; W. J. Ghent, "A Few Words on the Convention," *New York Socialist,* May 23, 1908; Robert F. Hoxie, "The Convention of the Socialist Party, 1908," the *Journal of Political Economy,* XVI (July, 1908), 442–50; Frederic Heath, "The National Convention," *Social-Democratic Herald,* May 13, 1908.

[65] Robert Hunter, "The Socialist Party in the Present Campaign," the *American Review of Reviews,* XXXVIII (Sept., 1908), 295–96.

[66] The members of the Committee on Style were Victor Berger, Algernon Lee, and A. M. Simons (Socialist Party, *Proceedings of the National Convention, 1908,* p. 229).

it now read "from any reform of the present order *at the hands of* the dominant class." [67]

The nonsocialist press agreed that the party had given up revolution for reform, and that it was doubtful whether the party would ever push its reforms all the way to socialism.[68] And the party "moderates" themselves conceded that even if the entire program of immediate demands incorporated in the party platform were enacted, a feat which would take years to accomplish, the country would still be a long way from socialism. Therefore, they assured potential middle-class supporters, joining and voting for the Socialist Party did not mean a drastic change in America's social and political organization. "The party," said Robert Hunter, "sees for years to come it must work steadily at democratizing our political institutions and altering the present industrial system so as to make conditions more equitable for the workers." [69]

Since all factions seemed convinced that they now controlled the party, they all threw themselves into the Presidential campaign with an enthusiasm for party work which had not been shown since the 1904 election. But even the effort to achieve a maximum vote exposed the widening gap in Socialist ranks. Debs toured the country appealing for a million Socialist votes. He said the capitalists understood only one language, that of power. A million votes for socialism would frighten the capitalist parties into granting concessions to labor—an end to injunctions, and the enactment of eight-hour laws, liability acts, and safety regulations. Ultimately, Debs explained, independent working-class political action would develop sufficient strength to end exploitation and usher in socialism.[70]

The party Center and Right wings, on the other hand, directed their appeals almost exclusively to the middle class. The national campaign committee, headed by Joseph Medill Patterson, devoted itself to explaining that socialism did not destroy incentive, stand

[67] *The Socialist* (Seattle), July 3, 1908. Italics mine.

[68] "The Moderate Socialists," *The Nation*, LXXXVII (Sept. 24, 1908), 580-81; Robert F. Hoxie, "The Convention of the Socialist Party, 1908," the *Journal of Political Economy*, XVI (July, 1908), 449.

[69] Robert Hunter, "The Socialist Party in the Present Campaign," the *American Review of Reviews*, XXXVIII (Sept., 1908), 293-95.

[70] Eugene V. Debs, "What a Million Votes for the Socialist Party Will Mean," *Socialist (Perpetual) Campaign Book*, pp. 5-9.

for "dividing up," or advocate "free love." When it was not defending the party from such ancient charges, the campaign committee launched counterattacks consisting of quotations from Senator Robert La Follette's indictment of Morgan and Rockefeller for precipitating the panic of 1907, and denunciations of monopoly as the cause of prostitution, child labor, and destruction of little business.[71]

If Socialist votes had varied in direct proportion to Socialist campaign literature and speeches, the party would have trebled or quadrupled its 1904 vote of four hundred thousand. The national office printed and distributed three and a quarter million copies of eight pamphlets outlining the Socialist position on questions of the day.[72] State and local organization printed and disposed of at least an additional ten million pieces.[73]

The Debs campaign was epoch-making even in a country of fabulous political campaigning. A special train, the "Red Special," was chartered, and Debs and his managers spent the time between August 31 and the election touring 33 states. The train consisted of a locomotive, an observation coach, a sleeper, and a baggage car packed with literature. For 65 straight days Debs spoke from six to ten times a day, addressing crowds from the train and "monster rallies" in the major cities. It was estimated that in all he addressed over eight hundred thousand persons.[74] When Samuel Gompers, who had thrown official A.F. of L. backing to the Democratic candidacy of William Jennings Bryan, accused the Republican Party of financing Debs's "Red Special," [75] the Socialist Party replied by printing the names and addresses of the 15,000 subscribers whose pennies, dimes, and dollars had paid the train's cost of $35,000.[76]

While the Milwaukee Socialists sneered at the "Red Special" as

71 Socialist (Perpetual) Campaign Book.

72 Letter from J. Mahlon Barnes to the National Executive Committee, Oct. 24, 1908, Socialist Party Weekly Bulletin, Oct. 24, 1908.

73 Hillquit, History of Socialism, 1910 ed., p. 350.

74 "Minutes of the National Executive Committee Meeting, July 10, 1908," the Socialist Party Official Bulletin, July, 1908; Coleman, Debs, pp. 245–48; Karsner, Debs, pp. 191–96.

75 Samuel Gompers, "Debs, the Apostle of Failure," American Federationist, XV (Sept., 1908), 737.

76 The Socialist Party Official Bulletin, Sept.–Nov., 1908.

a toy for those enamored with red fires and brass bands and held that the national party should pour its funds into the Milwaukee campaign to assure election for a couple of congressmen,[77] many Socialists still maintained the party's job was educational and not the winning of a few political offices.[78] The enthusiasm aroused by the campaign brought many into the party who had been hanging on the outskirts. In a few months dues-paying membership jumped from 30,000 to 46,000.[79]

No matter what the various factions thought of the campaign, all seemed to agree that this year the Socialist vote would grow to someplace between one and a half and two million.[80] And the Republican Chicago *Tribune* conceded at·least a million votes to the Socialist Party.[81] But when the vote was counted the Socialists found they had increased their vote not by over one million, but by an insignificant thirteen thousand, polling a total of 421,000.[82]

[77] *Social-Democratic Herald,* Oct. 10–Nov. 21, 1908. Debs ran fifteen hundred votes behind local Socialist candidates in Milwaukee in 1908 (*Social-Democratic Herald,* Nov. 7, 1908).

[78] Letter from Lyn D. Joseph, Green Bay, Wisconsin, *Social-Democratic Herald,* Nov. 21, 1908.

[79] Circular letter from J. Mahlon Barnes, *Social-Democratic Herald,* Oct. 31, 1908.

[80] Hunter, "The Socialist Party in the Present Campaign," p. 299; Victor L. Berger, "Impossibilism to the Rear," *Social-Democratic Herald,* May 23, 1908.

[81] The Chicago *Tribune,* Oct. 15, 1908.

[82] Morison and Commager, *Growth of the American Republic,* II, 741.

# XI

# The Amalgamated Center
# and Right Wings
## 1909-1912

Party LEADERS had many explanations for the stunning defeat of 1908. After a time, however, the explanations boiled down to three: the reform campaign waged by both Democrats and Republicans as contrasted to the conservative Democratic campaign of 1904; the endorsement of Bryan by the A.F. of L. executive committee; and the depression which caused many workers to lose their eligibility to vote when they left their homes to look for work.[1] But these leaders assured their followers that in the 1908 campaign "the alleged radical democratic candidate was making his last stand." Next time, things would be different.[2]

Despite public expressions of confidence in the ability of the Socialist Party to replace radical Democrats, Socialist leaders were badly shaken by their party's poor showing in 1908 and in the local elections which took place the following spring.[3] It was clear that the party could not hope to achieve electoral success while suspended between the poles of revolution and reform. The Left wing, headed by Debs, demanded that the party stop pursuing the will-o'-the-wisp of political office and return to its role as the organization of the working class. But the Center was convinced that

[1] "Report of the National Secretary to the National Congress of the Socialist Party, May 15, 1910," in Socialist Party, *Proceedings of the First National Congress, 1910*, p. 30; Hillquit, *History of Socialism*, 1910 ed., pp. 348–49.

[2] "Report of the National Secretary to the National Congress of the Socialist Party, May 15, 1910," in Socialist Party, *Proceedings of the First National Congress, 1910*.

[3] Hughan, *American Socialism*, p. 247; Madison, *Critics and Crusaders*, p. 455.

the only way to get Bryan's supporters to beat a quick path to the Socialist Party's door was to build an organization which promised to out-reform the liberal Democrats.[4]

Center leaders like Hillquit, Spargo, and Hunter lost no time in concluding an alliance with such Right-wing leaders as Berger and Work, and in opening a campaign to eliminate the Left-wing leaders and ideology which stood in the way of their plans for a bigger and broader political organization.[5] Since the leaders of the old Center and Right wings already held the key national and state offices of the party, it was comparatively simple for what was now the new amalgamated party Right wing to formulate and carry through its reform policies.[6] The theories and practices of step-at-a-time and reform socialism which had been in various stages of development in the old Center and Right-wing factions were brought to completion between 1909 and 1912 and made the official line of the American Socialist Party.

One indication of how rapidly the old Center and Right factions united to make a clean break with the party's semirevolutionary past after the 1908 election was the abandonment of a Karl Marx memorial day. In February, 1908, the party's National Committee voted 48 to 4, with 11 abstentions, to designate March 14 as a day for nation-wide rallies commemorating the life, labor, and death "of the greatest economist known to the modern world." [7] At the May, 1908, Socialist national convention, portraits of Marx and Engels draped with the American flag decorated the hall.[8] But within a month after the November, 1908, elections, the National Committee defeated by 44 to 13 the motion to designate March 14, 1909, as Karl Marx Memorial Day. John Spargo for the old Center opposed the motion because he held that "nothing could do us more harm than the cultivation of a fetish worship of Marx." And Victor Berger accompanied his negative vote with the comment that

[4] See sources cited in Note 3.

[5] Hughan, *Facts of Socialism,* p. 145; John Spargo, "What Is the Matter with the Socialist Party," *New York Call,* Nov. 13, 1909; Spargo, *Sidelights on Contemporary Socialism,* pp. 72–73; letter from William J. Ghent to *New York Call,* Nov. 28, 1909.

[6] Skelton, *Socialism,* pp. 303–4.

[7] *Socialist Party Official Bulletin,* March, 1908.

[8] Frederic Heath, "National Socialist Convention," *Social-Democratic Herald,* May 16, 1908.

"if I wanted any saints I would prefer to join the Roman Catholic church and get them wholesale." [9]

In hammering out an ideological line designed to attract the support of those Americans who were backing the progressive movement in the Democratic and Republican parties and the soon-to-be-formed Progressive Party itself, the leaders of the amalgamated Socialist Right wing were forever plagued with the problem of distinguishing between the political and economic reforms they were proposing and those advocated by the "capitalist parties." Robert Hunter conceded that it was well-nigh impossible to keep details of Socialist immediate demands in advance of legislation proposed or passed by the bourgeois parties.[10] Socialist resentment of what they considered the raiding tactics of reform parties reached its height when Theodore Roosevelt's Progressive Party adopted a platform in 1912 which virtually duplicated a good portion of the immediate demands of the Socialist Party. William Ghent bitterly charged that "the new party, which goes boldly forth to its first campaign with the inscription on its banners, 'Thou Shalt Not Steal!' begins its career with the brazen theft of half the working program of the Socialist party." [11]

Morris Hillquit formulated the distinction which the Socialists sought to sell the public. The reform platforms of the old parties, explained Hillquit, resembled a menu à la carte, put together to please a variety of tastes, but with no cohesion. By contrast, the Socialist platform was a table d'hôte dinner, each of the courses forming part of a well-planned and well-balanced meal. Hillquit added that the disconnected reforms advocated by the progressive movement were designed either to fulfill the reactionary purpose of restoring competition, or to ameliorate suffering through charity and the elimination of corruption. Socialist reforms, taken in a body, meant eventual inauguration of the socialist state.[12]

The socialist state which these reforms were to introduce, however, was not the co-operative commonwealth which the party had worked for in its first campaigns. Socialism could no longer be de-

[9] *Socialist Party Official Bulletin*, December, 1908.

[10] Hunter, *Socialists at Work*, pp. 178–79.

[11] W. J. Ghent in the *Social-Democratic Herald*, Sept. 28, 1912.

[12] Hillquit, *Socialism in Theory and Practice*, pp. 207–13; Hillquit, *Socialism Summed Up*, pp. 60–61, 75.

fined simply as the collective ownership and democratic management of the means of production and distribution. The Right-wing
party leadership now held that distinctions must be drawn between
various kinds of production. Socialism, they granted, still intended
to do away with all forms of exploitation. But exploitation was no
longer defined in terms of wage-labor and surplus value. "Now it is
pretty generally understood and admitted," wrote Carl Thompson, "that unearned income arises from one or another sort of
monopoly privilege." And, continued Thompson, in the final analysis all monopoly privilege rests "upon some form of private ownership of some form of public utility." Socialism, therefore, would
be achieved when public utilities were publicly owned.[13]

According to the new Socialist analysis, profits made by small
capitalists were not a product of exploitation of the working class.
They were a result of the labor of the small capitalist himself, and
these profits, therefore, were really wages.[14] Since the small capitalist had now been revealed in his true garb as a wage worker, and
since socialism did not have as its object the confiscation of the little
property yet possessed by any worker, it was clear that socialism
would not interfere with the activities of the competitive producer.
According to Right-wing theoreticians, there were to be three types
of property under socialism: first, public ownership of the great
utility trusts; second, ownership of certain industries by private
co-operative societies; and third, private ownership of competitive
industry.[15] So as to remove all fears from the minds of possible
Socialist supporters among antimonopoly small businessmen, the
1910 Socialist Congress deleted the words "capitalist class" from
the party constitution and substituted the term "propertied
classes"—which term permitted distinctions among various types
of producers for purposes of the coming socialist state.[16]

The meaning of socialism for farmers also underwent revision.
The national organization of the Socialist Party paid little attention to the organization of farmers, and increased recruiting

[13] Carl D. Thompson, "A Socialist's Definition of Socialism," *The Arena,* XXXIX
(May, 1908), 565.

[14] Benson, *Truth about Socialism,* pp. 47–48.

[15] Hillquit, *Socialism in Theory and Practice,* pp. 113–18; Carl D. Thompson, "A
Socialist's Definition of Socialism," *The Arena,* XXXIX (May, 1908), 569.

[16] Socialist Party, *Proceedings of the First National Congress, 1910,* pp. 238–39.

among farmers was the product of the activities of state party leaders like Oscar Ameringer of Oklahoma.[17] But the national Right-wing leadership was determined that the national platform should attract the maximum farm vote.[18] At the 1908 convention the delegates, led by those who were themselves farmers, had overwhelmingly rejected the farm planks proposed by the nonfarmer convention committee as "too Populistic." The farm delegates insisted that those farmers who opposed "straight socialism" and public ownership of land were not "farmers who farmed the soil" but landlords who "farmed the farmer." [19]

However, within ten months of the 1908 election, a national referendum of the party membership deleted the platform demand calling for collective ownership of "all the land" by a vote of 5,382 to 3,117.[20] At the 1910 convention the party Right led by Algie Simons and Victor Berger again tried to secure adoption of a series of farm demands based largely on the 1892 Populist Party platform, but without the free silver plank. The proposals were attacked as a middle-class panacea which ignored the lot of the farm laborer, and the convention instructed its farm committee to think it over for another two years.[21]

At the 1912 convention Simons again brought in a series of farm demands. After a bow in the direction of farm tenancy by pledging the party's sympathy and support to attempts by renters to better their lot, the demands continued in the familiar vein of demanding public ownership of transportation and storage plants "when such means are used for exploitation," insurance against disease and national calamities, and publicly owned farms for experimental and educational purposes. After a twelve-hour debate the Farmers' Demands were adopted. Convention chairman James Carey, formerly of the Center and now of the amalgamated Right wing, refused to permit Left-wing leader Charles Ruthenberg of Ohio to introduce an amendment which described the demands as an "im-

17 "The Oklahoma Encampment," *International Socialist Review*, X (Sept., 1909), 278–79; "The Oregon-California Encampment," *International Socialist Review*, XI (Aug., 1910), 107–9.
18 Socialist Party, *Proceedings of the National Convention, 1908*, p. 15.
19 *Ibid.*, pp. 13–16, 178–86.
20 *Socialist Party Weekly Bulletin*, Sept. 11, 1909.
21 Socialist Party, *Proceedings of the First National Congress, 1910*, pp. 212–35.

mediate program" and affirmed party backing for "the ultimate collective ownership of all the land used for productive purposes." On appeal, the chair was upheld, 167 to 93, the vote being on strict Right-Left factional lines.[22]

The Socialist Party picked up considerable farm support, and in the 1910 and 1912 Congressional and Presidential elections several agricultural states numbered among those having the largest percentage of the Socialist vote.[23] Socialist propaganda in farm communities was distributed in mammoth Socialist encampments [24] and by Socialist drummers, country doctors, and farmers.[25] The Populist attack on privilege and monopoly which had been so effective in 1892 and 1896 was revived by the Socialists, who developed further the Populist program of government aid to farming.[26] Ernest Poole interviewed a Socialist Party farm organizer at the 1908 Socialist convention:

"You city people don't realize how deep the old passion for democracy still is in the country region," said the Socialist organizer. "He sees that democracy is going; he sees the power converging into that Wall Street group. And he has about made up his mind that the only way to get that power back is by government ownership of the trusts and railroads. He showed it by his vote for the populist party. That party sold him out. And now he is coming our way."

"But," I argued, "as far as I can find, you people want not only the trusts but every man's private business, give it all to the politicians. How about the farmer's vote then?"

"That's way off in the future," he said. "We're busy these days with a string of concrete issues. Times have changed. We're getting votes. And the farmer agrees to enough."

" 'First,' said one old codger, 'I don't want every blamed thing put under the government, but I do like the idea of Uncle Sam bein' the big dog again an' Wall Street bein' the pup. Second, I don't believe in

---

[22] Socialist Party, *Proceedings of the National Convention, 1912*, pp. 67–85, 192–93.

[23] *American Labor Year Book*, 1916, pp. 97–98.

[24] "The Oklahoma Encampment," *International Socialist Review*, X (Sept., 1909), 278–79; "The Oregon-California Encampment," *International Socialist Review*, XI (Aug., 1910), 107–9.

[25] Ernest Poole, "Harnessing Socialism," the *American Magazine*, LXVI (Sept., 1908), 428.

[26] *Ibid.*, pp. 428–29; Cox, *The Socialist Party in Indiana*, p. 122.

this here class struggle if you mean only them union strikes. But if you mean the democracy agin the men who are stealing its independence, then I'm with you hard.' "

"You took him in on that basis?" I asked. He nodded. "Isn't that stretching Marx a bit?"

"Let him stretch," said the socialist stoutly. "Stretching means growth, doesn't it? On the road I'm always picking up rattling good points from new kinds of recruits." [27]

In addition to modifying their conception of the nature of socialist society, the consolidated party Right wing adopted without qualification Berger's hypothesis of step-at-a-time socialism. The leaders of what had formerly been the Center abandoned their argument that socialism could be built only after the Socialist Party had swept a majority of national and local elections. Hillquit found the "Socialist state" even now "persistently filtering into the present order," and American society being permeated with socialist institutions at an ever-accelerating pace; as compared to the status a century earlier, the America of today could be described as semisocialist, and Americans as "already living at least in the outskirts of the 'Socialist state.' " [28]

The constructive or step-at-a-time Socialists believed socialism was coming of its own accord. Every extension of government intervention into the economic life of the nation, every social and political reform that improved the lot of the average American, was not only an involuntary step in the *direction* of socialism, but was in itself the *addition* of a bit of socialism to the economy.[29] And as Hillquit explained socialist reform to Samuel Gompers before a Congressional committee: "If I have set out to earn a hundred dollars, and if I had done part of my work and earned ten dollars, I

[27] Ernest Poole, "Harnessing Socialism," the *American Magazine,* LXVI (Sept., 1908), 429.

[28] Hillquit and Ryan, *Socialism: Promise or Menace?* p. 240.

[29] Victor L. Berger, "Socialism in Brief," *Socialist Campaign Book,* 1912; Ernest Poole, "Harnessing Socialism," the *American Magazine,* LXVI (Sept., 1908), 431–32; "Step at a Time," *The Party Builder,* Oct. 16, 1912; Gaylord, *Socialism Is Coming—Now,* p. 7. The very fact that Berger was selected to write the article defining socialism in the party's official publication for the 1912 campaign is a good indication of the extent to which the party had shifted from its early self-described "revolutionary position" to its later theories of "reform" and "gradualism."

would not consider that as makeshift or patchwork, but would consider it as a part realization of my ultimate object." [30] Since socialism arrived so gradually, there was no longer any question of a sudden or violent revolution.[31] In fact, Jack London found himself the object of severe censure by Socialists for daring to suggest at a University of California lecture that good Socialists closed their letters with the phrase, "Yours for the Revolution." [32]

In the spring of 1909 the *Saturday Evening Post* asked ten leading members of the Socialist Party [33] what steps they would take to establish the co-operative commonwealth if their party were to win the Presidency and a majority in Congress. The great majority of the replies were prefaced with a declaration that socialism would not come via a Socialist Party sweep of political offices. Rather, they said, it was now coming through those reforms which were making the country's political life more democratic, and through an extension of municipal and government regulation and ownership.

All the Socialists who answered the *Post's* questionnaire, with the exception of Eugene Debs, went on to say that if the Socialist Party were suddenly to win public office it would continue development of the co-operative commonwealth already taking place through the gradual purchase of the major trusts at full value. Debs held that if the party won complete victory it would "doubtless proceed by legal and orderly means to abolish the capitalist political state and establish an industrial democracy—that is to say, they will supplant the capitalist government of men with the democratic administration of things." The new Socialist society would then take over as rapidly as possible the essential means of social production, beginning with the monopolies. Debs did not specify the means by which the monopolies would become public

[30] Hillquit in Hillquit, Gompers, and Hayes, *Double-Edge of Labor's Sword*, pp. 33–34. To Gaylord Wilshire the financial and technical aid which the British government gave to the Cunard Line in the building of the S.S. Lusitania made that vessel a "Socialist ship." (*Wilshire's Magazine*, XI [Oct., 1907], 15.)

[31] Hunter, *Socialists at Work*, pp. 153–56.

[32] *Social-Democratic Herald*, May 2, 1908.

[33] The Socialists queried were Eugene V. Debs, Victor Berger, Gaylord Wilshire, Upton Sinclair, Bernard Berlin, John C. Chase, William Mailly, Robert Hunter, A. M. Simons, and J. Mahlon Barnes.

property, but his position on that subject was well known—confiscation.[34] The answers furnished by the Socialist leaders and printed by the *Post* were of a nature which permitted that magazine to comment: "We leave it to our readers to judge whether the preachers of this new gospel have a cure for social ills which they or anyone else can apply practically." [35]

The building of the co-operative commonwealth through purchase of certain key trusts, particularly in the public utility field, became one of the cardinal principles of the Socialist Party under leadership of the Right. Emphasis on socialization by purchase and forthright denial of such "reckless, visionary and impracticable theories" as confiscation [36] increased as proposed solutions of the "trust problem" were advanced in Theodore Roosevelt's "New Nationalism," Robert La Follette's progressivism, and Woodrow Wilson's "New Freedom." Hillquit expressed the official party theory when he praised trust organization for decreasing the "chaos and anarchy of the competitive system," curbing waste and overproduction, and diminishing the evil of depressions. But Hillquit admitted that along with these benefits the trusts had brought a number of disadvantages: overcapitalization meant that workers paid an annual tribute to holders of watered stock; lack of competition meant that trusts could dictate terms of employment; monopolization meant power to fix prices. "But more baneful even than the economic evils of the trusts," concluded Hillquit, "are their corrupting effects on the public and political life of the country." [37]

During Victor Berger's first term in Congress, 1911–1912, he introduced a bill empowering the government to purchase, at a cash value price to be determined by a committee of fifteen experts, all trusts controlling as much as 40 percent of an industry. Payment was to be made in government bonds bearing 2 percent interest; the bonds were to be repurchased through a 50-year sinking fund. A Bureau of Industries established within the Department

[34] Lincoln Steffens, "Eugene V. Debs on What the Matter Is in America and What to Do About It," *Everybody's Magazine*, XIX (Oct., 1908), 461–62.

[35] " 'Practical' Socialism, Is There Any Such Thing?" the *Saturday Evening Post*, CLXXXI (May 8, 1909), 8–9, 55.

[36] Spargo and Arner, *Elements of Socialism*, p. 350.

[37] Hillquit, *Socialism Summed Up*, pp. 18–19.

of Commerce and Labor was to operate all government-owned industries.[38] Berger also introduced a bill for repeal of the Sherman Antitrust Act, since "the Socialists are not in the business of busting trusts." [39] It was suggested by party supporters of these proposals that government bonds be repurchased out of profits made by the government-operated trusts.[40]

In addition to reform, regulation, and nationalization (which was leading an apparently unsuspecting nation toward socialism), Right-wing Socialist leaders discovered between 1910 and 1912 another development within capitalism—the co-operative movement. Before 1910 the Socialist Party did not recognize any possible relationship between consumers', distributors', and producers' co-operatives and the coming of socialism. Carl Thompson, one of the ideological leaders of the Wisconsin party, had written his master's thesis at the University of Chicago in 1902 on the co-operative movement. But he had concluded that co-operatives were of value only as a means of "social amelioration" and as an educational device.[41]

In 1910, however, the International Socialist Congress at Copenhagen reversed its previous position on co-operatives, and assigned to those bodies the task of "helping to prepare in making production and exchange democratic and socialist." [42] The 1912 American Socialist Party convention advanced the role of co-operatives another notch. The convention resolution on co-operatives held that labor unions fought for "industrial self-control" for the workers, while the Socialist Party fought for their "political self-control." The labor and Socialist movements worked together to secure their "intellectual self-control." And the co-operative movement led the fight for the workers' "economic self-control." [43]

It only remained for Winfield Gaylord, party organizer for Wis-

[38] Benson, *Truth About Socialism*, p. 65.
[39] Victor L. Berger in Hillquit, Gompers, and Hayes, *Double-Edge of Labor's Sword*, p. 192.
[40] Allan L. Benson, "How the People Will Buy the Trusts and Become Free," *Pearson's Magazine*, reprinted in *Social-Democratic Herald*, Aug. 31, 1912.
[41] Carl D. Thompson, "The Need of Cooperation of the Rochdale Type in and about Chicago" (unpublished master's thesis, The University of Chicago, 1902), pp. 26–29.
[42] Lenz, *Rise and Fall of the Second International*, pp. 107–8.
[43] Socialist Party, *Proceedings of the National Convention, 1912*, p. 194.

consin, to tie these various "socialistic tendencies" into one package, and the theory of step-at-a-time socialism was complete. Gaylord declared in 1912 that socialism was developing in three ways—through co-operatives, trade unions, and political action. Wherever human beings were securing control over means of production and distribution through co-operatives, over their hours, wages and conditions of their work through trade unions, and over the "laws of property" through their political party, "to that extent," announced Gaylord, "the principles of the co-operative commonwealth are being practiced now." [44]

In the days when official party declarations avowed that socialism would come as a clean break with the past after a sweeping victory at the polls, it was possible for party leaders to evade questions about the political structure of the co-operative commonwealth. But when the party analysis turned to descriptions of the gradual infiltration of socialism into the capitalist economy, it became necessary to make at least a few generalizations about the structure of the developing socialist society. In keeping with its conception of the role then being played by the state in transformation of the nation from capitalism to socialism, the party abandoned its earlier position that there could be no such thing as a "socialist state" since there would be no class to oppress. Party theoreticians now talked in terms of three types of states—the extinct capitalist state, the existent transitional or reform state, and the future socialist state.[45]

Morris Hillquit predicted that the American socialist state would most likely be a democratic, federal republic, divided into its present 48 states. Its central government would be concerned with those economic and political affairs of the country which were national in scope. Congress would probably continue to be divided into two houses, the House of Representatives to have charge of political problems (foreign affairs, national defense, treasury, justice, education, insurance, fine arts), and the Senate to control those economic functions which were national in character (post office, railroads, mines, public works, and the trusts).

Hillquit explained that the government would be far less central-

[44] Gaylord, *Socialism Is Coming—Now*, pp. 9, 13–14, 18, 27, 38–39.
[45] Hillquit, *Socialism in Theory and Practice*, pp. 96–98, 103–4.

ized in the socialist state than in the capitalist. Most political and economic operations would be handled by the states and municipalities. In fact, the city was to become by far the most important governmental unit.[46] The industrial affairs of the nation, however, would not be administered by men popularly chosen to office, but rather by experts selected by each separate trade. The socialist state would be "a classless state of co-operative producers and its government must be a 'committee for the managing of the common affairs' of the members of that state. . . . It will be a democratic state." [47] Since the present American state was already well into its "transitional" form, and since the future socialist state would use much of the transitional apparatus, it followed that the Socialists were interested in "overthrowing" not the government but "the capitalist system, with its profits, interest and rent." [48]

Although Right-wing leaders were agreed that it was the "system" and not the government which was to be gradually eliminated, there seemed to be some disagreement as to the importance of the part the Socialist Party was to play in the process of elimination. Joseph Wanhope of New York, for example, declared that the party could contribute virtually nothing. Socialism was coming by itself, the product of economic forces beyond the realm of conscious human influence. The only reason people joined the Socialist Party, according to Wanhope, was because "when I sit down on a tack—and Capitalism is that tack—I can't sit quiet and be comfortable." [49]

Hillquit, on the other hand, agreed that no system could be changed until it was "ripe for the transformation," a stage reached without human effort. But once that level of development was reached, qualified Hillquit, then a majority of the population must act to produce the transformation. Therefore, Hillquit said, the function of the party was to prepare the people, through propaganda and education, so that they would be able to take the steps

---

[46] This concept of the importance of the municipality in the organization of the "socialist state" of course parallels the emphasis the Socialist Party was placing on municipal elections and municipal reform. See below, pp. 231–34.

[47] Hillquit, *Socialism in Theory and Practice*, pp. 131–42.

[48] *Appeal to Reason*, Jan. 29, 1910.

[49] Charlotte Teller, "The National Socialist Convention," *The Arena*, XL (July, 1908), 33.

necessary gradually to transform capitalism into socialism, when the economic system had matured sufficiently to warrant the change.[50]

Victor Berger agreed with Wanhope that the "transition is coming quite of itself." [51] The Socialists, "with the exception [of] certain fanatical impossibilists," said Berger, did not expect to "make history" by bringing socialism to America. All the Socialists did, he explained, was study history and economics. This enabled them to recognize the direction civilization was taking, and thus they were able to put themselves "in line with the march of civilization, so that civilization will carry us, instead of crushing us." [52]

Just why, in Berger's analysis, it should be of importance for the party to organize to win elections on the city, state, and national level, was not made clear. There would seem to be two possible explanations. One, that having recognized the direction of the march of civilization, it was only natural for intelligent men to take advantage of their discovery by reaping the political rewards of their insight. The other, perhaps more in keeping with the mechanistic nature of these Right-wing socialist theories, is that party members and leaders, in running for office, were merely carrying out the automatic and unconscious will of the material forces of society. At any rate, the policies pursued by the party seemed to be compounded of Hillquit's and Berger's theories, with but few members willing to accept in its entirety the completely automaton concept of history advanced by Wanhope.

Having agreed that the Socialist Party's function was to create a public sympathetic to socialist ideas, elect as many Socialists to office as possible, and help inaugurate political and economic reforms in step with "the march of civilization," [53] the next question facing the Right-wing leaders was who to educate. The answer continued to be "the proletariat." But proletariat now meant to the

50 Hillquit, Socialism Summed Up, pp. 44–49.

51 Victor L. Berger, "How to Make the Change," Social-Democratic Herald, Nov. 27, 1909.

52 Victor L. Berger, "Can We Make Common Cause with 'Reformers?'" Social-Democratic Herald, May 29, 1909.

53 Gaylord, Socialism Is Coming—Now, p. 38; Hillquit, Socialism Summed Up, pp. 76, 80–83, 85–94; Victor L. Berger, "Socialism, the Logical Outcome of Progressivism," the American Magazine, LXXV (Nov., 1912), 20–21; Spargo, Common Sense of Socialism, pp. 170–72.

amalgamated Right wing what it had always meant to the Wisconsin Socialists—skilled craftsmen, small farmers, intellectuals, and small producers and merchants. At times, "proletariat" even included the capitalist class, that is, the class of great industrialists and financiers which had furnished the socialist movement with "some of the brightest minds, the noblest hearts, and the cleanest souls of the age in which we live." [54]

Indeed, it seemed to be the wage-working members of the "proletariat" who gave the party leaders most difficulty because of their uncleanliness, backwardness, and stupidity.[55] Party leaders warned each other that a socialist movement consisting of and led by unskilled workers, the "product of the gutter and the slums," could not gain victory because it could never enlist the support of enough voters. And even if such a rabble-led party were to slide into power, it would not have the intelligence to administer the cooperative commonwealth.[56] Left-wing Socialists were lectured on the evils of "class jingoism," and warned that there was no distinction between national and class jingoism.[57] They were reminded that class hatred was "a monstrous thing . . . to be abhorred by all right-thinking men and women." [58]

It was only natural therefore, that the chairman of the Committee on Organization, John Work of Iowa, should report to the 1910 National Socialist Congress that the major task of the party was physical and intellectual uplift of the "booze-fighting" rabble who were members of the party and of the working class. "Under the mentally stifling pressure of capitalism," Work informed the Congress,

millions of people are constantly poisoning themselves, depleting their brain power, and destroying their resisting power, by the use of liquor, tobacco, patent medicines, confectionery, soda counter abominations, unwholesome diet, excessive sexual intercourse, lack of venti-

[54] Carl D. Thompson, "Who Constitute the Proletariat?" *International Socialist Review,* IX (Feb., 1909), 603–11.

[55] Spargo, *The Substance of Socialism,* pp. 112–14, 140–42; "Class Hatred and Class Consciousness," *New York Call,* Aug. 18, 1912.

[56] Carl D. Thompson, "Who Constitute the Proletariat?" *International Socialist Review,* IX (Feb., 1909), 611–12.

[57] Ghent, *Socialism and Success,* pp. 168–69.

[58] Spargo, *The Substance of Socialism,* pp. 112–14, 140–42; *New York Call,* Aug. 18, 1912.

lation, unsanitary homes, ignorance of the requirements of their bodies, etc.

Since millions of workers were below the minimum intellectual plane, he added, leisure to them was synonymous with dissipation. And once socialism gave them added leisure, they would become complete degenerates. Work recommended that the party immediately instruct its organizers that their first task was to form classes for presentation of "theoretical and practical" lectures on health, hygene, sanitation, and physical development." [59]

Left-wing delegates to the Congress immediately denounced the report as an insult "to the laboring men" of the party. Winfield Gaylord, one of the ministerial leaders of the Wisconsin party, demanded to know why the report was considered an insult. He was promptly informed that "booze-fighters" were more reliable in the battle against capitalism than "gospel sharks." Many Right-wing leaders thereupon attacked the opponents of the report as "impossibilistic anarchists." But Work's proposals were too much even for some of the Right to swallow. John Spargo and Robert Hunter, who as conservative leaders of the National Executive Committee had commissioned Work to make the report, suggested that the proposals might be distributed "as curiosities· of Socialist literature," and that Work might join the antitobacco league. The report was finally buried in committee.[60] However, the rejection of so blatant a program did not mean that the philosophy behind it was rejected. In fact, within a year John Work was to become national secretary of the Socialist Party.

Right-wing Socialist leaders were now in general agreement as to the manner in which socialism was coming, and as to the nature of their public appeal. But they had yet to settle on the organization which was to be the vehicle for winning political office. This was true despite the fact that ever since the removal of the first Local Quorum in 1903 for advocating fusion, the one tenet on which all party factions were agreed was that the Socialist Party was the only true labor party and that co-operation or fusion with any other party meant the immediate expulsion of the offending mem-

[59] Socialist Party, *Proceedings of the First National Congress, 1910*, pp. 38–43.
[60] *Ibid.*, pp. 49–58.

ber. In January, 1910, the *International Socialist Review* broke
to a virtually uninformed membership the news that a majority of
the members of the National Executive Committee favored party
support of a Union Labor Party if the American Federation of
Labor should decide upon such an organization. In that case, the
Socialist Party was to bear the same relationship to the labor party
that the Independent Labour Party in England bore to the British
Labour Party.[61]

The *Review* story consisted of a series of letters exchanged by
party leaders and the answers to questionnaires the *Review* had
subsequently sent to all candidates for the National Executive
Committee then being elected. The letters indicate that at the
N.E.C. meeting in the fall of 1909, Victor Berger had pointed to
the success of the British Labour Party and to the growing desire
for political activity among leaders of the A.F. of L. He therefore
recommended that the Socialist Party support a labor party if one
were formed.[62] Although a majority of the executive committee,
including Hillquit, Hunter, Spargo, and Simons, agreed with Berger, the proposal was withdrawn when J. G. Phelps Stokes warned
that it would create a "public scandal." [63]

In November, 1909, Algie Simons, who was attending the To-
ronto convention of the A.F. of L., wrote to William English Walling asking the latter's support for a movement to reform the Socialist Party along labor party lines. In his letter Simons warned
of the growing strength of the Industrial Workers of the World
in the Socialist Party, and declared that the A.F. of L. "comes
much nearer representing the working class than the Socialist
Party." Walling showed the letter to Stokes and others, and then
sent a circular letter to party leaders informing them of Simons's
program and interpreting Simons's phrase, "we [the National Executive Committee] would not surrender" to mean that if the pro-
labor party members of the executive committee were defeated in
the current elections they would "attempt to take possession of the

[61] "A Labor Party," *International Socialist Review*, X (Jan., 1910), 594–606.

[62] Letter from J. G. Phelps Stokes to Morris Hillquit, Dec. 2, 1909. This letter,
and other correspondence referred to concerning the formation of a labor party are
printed in the *International Socialist Review*, X (Jan., 1910), 656–62.

[63] *Ibid.*

party machinery and the party press, or, failing that, to attempt the organization of an 'Independent Labor' or 'Social Democratic party.' " [64]

Hillquit demanded an explanation from Stokes for what he called Stokes's connection with Walling's distorted construction and unfair publication of Simons's private letter.[65] Stokes replied by repeating the "pro-labor party" charges against a majority of the executive committee. Letters flew back and forth, and the *Review* published the entire exchange for the edification of its forty thousand readers. Meanwhile, Walling and Simons were exchanging insults in the letter columns of the *New York Call.*[66] Any hope of keeping the changed attitude among certain Right-wing Socialist leaders toward a labor party a secret until the membership had been gently brought around vanished in a storm of charges and countercharges.

That most Socialists still considered their party as the only real labor party is shown by the more than two dozen replies the *Review* received from candidates for the N.E.C. The only ones who refused to condemn for all time any possible support to a labor party were those members of the N.E.C. whose position had already been exposed, and they reneged to the extent of saying that they hoped a labor party would not be formed, and would only support it after its formation because nothing else could be done.[67]

It is unknown whether it was opposition from the rank and file, or failure of the A.F. of L. to form a national labor party, or the sharp increase in the Socialist vote in 1910, or a combination of all three that killed further speculation on possible future relations with a union labor party. At any rate, the controversy died as suddenly as it had risen. Within the year Victor Berger, who had precipitated the discussion, was able to dismiss the possibility of a

[64] Letter from Morris Hillquit to J. G. Phelps Stokes, Nov. 30, 1909; letter from Stokes to Hillquit, Dec. 2, 1909; letter from Hillquit to Stokes, Dec. 3, 1909; letter from Stokes to Hillquit, Dec. 11, 1909; letter from Stokes to Hillquit, Dec. 13, 1909; letter from Hillquit to Stokes, Dec. 14, 1909; letter from Stokes to Hillquit, Dec. 15, 1909.

[65] Letter from Morris Hillquit to J. G. Phelps Stokes, Nov. 30, 1909.

[66] *New York Call,* Dec., 1909–Jan., 1910.

[67] "A Labor Party," *International Socialist Review,* X (Jan., 1910), 594–606, 609, 654.

labor party as though no one had ever given it serious consideration. "It is not the business of the trade union as such to go into
politics," he wrote. "The union has to take care of the economic
field, while it is the mission of the Socialist Party of America, as in
every other country, to express the demands of the working class
in the political field." [68]

Socialist Party leaders pointed out that political activities of
the members of the working class—be they craftsmen, professionals, or little businessmen—were of necessity largely confined
to the cities. For that reason the party must be primarily a city
party; and since it would have "to grow in the soil of the cities,"
its first task must be to prepare the soil. "If this soil is absolutely
spoiled and made barren by corruption, Social-Democracy cannot
grow." Right-wing party leaders therefore insisted that the Socialist Party should concentrate on ending corruption in city government. [69]

Milwaukee Socialists, who had furnished the core of the Right
wing in the hard days when national leadership was in the hands
of the Center-Left coalition, again took the lead by showing how
to win control of a large city. The Democratic Party had won the
Milwaukee government in 1900 from the Republican city machine
which furnished the heart of opposition to Robert La Follette's
fight to turn the Wisconsin Republican Party into an organization
for progressive reform. Re-elected for four succeeding terms, the
Democratic mayor was generally accused of betraying his election
promises of municipal ownership of public utilities and an end to
graft and corruption. For eight years Milwaukee Socialists placed
increasing stress on their claim to be the only party really opposed
to corruption in government. They declared that an end to graft,
coupled with the refusal of Socialist-led unions to put pressure on

[68] Victor L. Berger, "We Must Present a Solid Front to the Enemy," *Social-
Democratic Herald*, Dec. 3, 1910.
[69] Victor L. Berger, "High Prices, Peaceful Progress and Thoro House Cleaning the Issue," *Social-Democratic Herald*, April 2, 1910. In 1913, Morris Hillquit
credited honest socialist administration in cities as the most important "concrete"
achievement of the Socialist Party. "Milwaukee, Schenectady, and Berkeley have
established standards of municipal administration which are rapidly beginning to
force other cities into the path of social progress." (*Socialism Summed Up*, pp.
76–94.)

capitalists who were victims of their own system, would lead to better business for all Milwaukee entrepreneurs.[70]

In the municipal campaign in the spring of 1910, the Milwaukee Socialist Party, which had by far the best organized political machine in the socialist movement,[71] distributed three quarters of a million pieces of literature denouncing crime and corruption. For five weeks preceding the election the party claimed to have put its literature in every home on every Sunday.[72] The Socialist platform, which in Milwaukee had devoted less and less space to socialism each year, in 1910 occupied three quarters of a newspaper page listing demands which ranged from home rule and fair corporate taxes to street water closets and suppression of vice. Only the last sentence mentioned that adoption of these planks would be a step toward socialism and the emancipation of mankind.[73] Many Milwaukee citizens apparently were convinced that neither the Republicans nor the Democrats had any intention of keeping their campaign promises, and many of the biggest Milwaukee businessmen, including at least two of the brewers, "expressed themselves privately in admiration of Mr. Berger and his purposes." [74] The final count showed 27,622 for the Socialists, 20,513 for the Democrats, and 11,262 for the Republicans.[75]

After the first shock of victory had worn off, Victor Berger rushed into print to set the political line for the victorious Milwaukee Socialists: "The very next question before us is that of applying the international Socialist philosophy to present conditions and to Milwaukee . . . we want to show our comrades all

70 Victor L. Berger, "Who Is Afraid of the Social Democratic Party?" *Social-Democratic Herald*, March 19, 1910.

71 Wachman, "History of the Social-Democratic Party of Milwaukee, 1897–1910," Urbana, University of Illinois, 1943; abstract of thesis.

72 Victor L. Berger, "High Prices, Peaceful Progress and Thoro House Cleaning the Issue," *Social-Democratic Herald*, April 2, 1910.

73 "Platform of the Milwaukee Social Democratic Party," *Social-Democratic Herald*, March 5, 1910.

74 New York *Journal*, April 22, 1910; "The Socialist Rule of Milwaukee," *The Independent*, LXIX (July 21, 1910), 148–49; John Collier, "The Experiment in Milwaukee," *Harper's Weekly*, LV (Aug. 12, 1911), 11.

75 *Social-Democratic Herald*, April 9, 1910. The Milwaukee party polled an extremely high straight vote. Its lowest candidate received only 1,100 votes less than its highest. In addition to electing most of the major city officials, it won absolute control of both the city council (21 seats out of 35) and the County Board (11 seats out of 16). (*Socialist Party Weekly Bulletin*, April 9, 1910; *Social-Democratic Herald*, April 9, 1910.)

over the country that our principles will lose nothing of their revolutionary energy by being thus applied to a local situation." Of course, added Berger, we must not expect a sudden growth in union strength. And socialism cannot be established in one stroke nor capitalism abolished in one city. Since capitalism was bound to continue in Milwaukee for some time, it was the duty of the Social-Democratic administration to improve the city's credit by turning out the "few dozen grafters" and giving "this city the best kind of an administration that a modern city can get under the present system and the present laws." [76] For the next two years Milwaukee Socialists flooded the nonsocialist press and their own with stories of diminished property taxes, increased city trade and manufacturing, and the scarcity of strikes since Socialist-led workers had learned to depend on political instead of economic action.[77]

The Socialist victory in Milwaukee and the growing number of Socialists elected to city and state government offices convinced party leaders that greater emphasis and study must be given to the specific measures that the new officials should favor: "There is nothing more vital to the socialist movement than its constructive program. To be able to point out in definite terms and in concrete measures the actual steps by which the goal of socialism may be reached is not only of great interest—it is an absolute necessity." [78] This program could be developed only through years of study and research.[79] The first step was a conference in Milwaukee of all Socialists elected to public office. The conference assembled in August, 1911, and under the slogan, "We'll Milwaukeeize Our Own Town," discussed tax reform, municipal ownership, and home rule.[80] On recommendation of the conference, the party set up an "Information Bureau" headed by Milwaukee's Carl D. Thompson. The bureau was to serve as a research agency and clearing house for Socialist administrative and legislative experience and practice.[81]

[76] Victor L. Berger, "We Will Apply the Philosophy of International Socialism to a Local Situation," *Social-Democratic Herald*, April 9, 1910.

[77] *Socialist Party Weekly Bulletin*, 1910–11.

[78] Ethelwyn Mills, *Legislative Program of the Socialist Party*, pp. 3–4.

[79] *Ibid.*

[80] *New York Call*, Aug. 20, 1911.

[81] "Minutes of the National Executive Committee, Sept. 17, 1912," *Socialist Party Monthly Bulletin*, Sept., 1912; *Socialist Party Monthly Bulletin*, Oct., 1912; Ethelwyn Mills, *Legislative Program of the Socialist Party*, pp. 3–4.

The emphasis on municipal reforms which would eventually lead to socialism compelled the party's national organization to revise its attitude toward the commission form of government. At the 1908 convention the party had announced unqualified opposition to commission government because the appointment rather than the election of officials and the use of nonpartisan ballots would in effect eliminate third parties from the ballots. The convention stated that the only intent of commission government was to further limit the already limited participation of the working class in the affairs of government: "This so-called non-partisan movement is one of the many schemes of the capitalist class to confuse the workers and obscure the class struggle and give the capitalist class a stronger hold upon the law-making power." [82]

By the 1910 convention, however, the delegates decided that many features of commission government "are not only not objectionable from the Socialist point of view, but are actually elements in the Socialist program." While still opposing nonpartisan nominations and elections, and city-wide balloting in place of ward representation, as methods designed to cut down Socialist victories, the party ruled that since the "Initiative, Referendum and Recall are . . . well-known Socialist principles" the commission form of government could no longer be opposed. Nevertheless, overwhelming defeat was accorded an attempt by the convention committee on commission government to get the party to permit Socialists to support a non-Socialist candidate in run-off elections after the Socialist candidate had been eliminated.[83] At the 1912 convention the delegates voted to grant individual Socialist city and state organizations the right to determine their respective attitudes and practices toward commission government.[84]

The increasing moderation of their platforms and activities brought the Socialist movement a proportionate increase in respect and sympathy from non-Socialist reformers. *The Nation*, which in the past had bitterly condemned the Socialist Party, noted that "parlor socialism" was replacing "revolutionary socialism," and congratulated the Socialists for accepting "things as they are to

[82] Socialist Party, *Proceedings of the National Convention, 1908*, pp. 311–12.
[83] Socialist Party, *Proceedings of the First National Congress, 1910*, pp. 291–301.
[84] Socialist Party, *Proceedings of the National Convention, 1912*, pp. 179–91.

the extent that they can see how essentially weak is man and how powerful are the circumstances that shape him." [85] The *American Magazine* accepted an article from Berger entitled "Socialism, the Logical Outcome of Progressivism," and referred to Berger as "the sanest and most influential socialist in the country," a "superprogressive" who "commands respect everywhere for his honesty and common sense." [86] *The Outlook*, which was soon to add Theodore Roosevelt to its editorial board, while continuing to oppose collective ownership and the attempt "to abolish the checks and restraints on the power of majorities," gave "full credit to the motives of the Socialists" and welcomed their support of specific reforms which *The Outlook* had "long advocated." [87]

John B. Clark, Professor of Economics at Columbia University, advised all reformers, and particularly those who favored social reforms for Christian reasons, to join the Socialist Party. Clark declared that the Socialists hoped to achieve the co-operative commonwealth through a "conservative line of action" consisting of many intermediate reforms. Until those reforms reached the stage where capitalism might be eliminated, insisted Clark, there was no reason why non-Socialist reformers should not support the Socialist Party. "What the reformers will have to do," Clark advised, "is to take the socialistic name, to walk behind a somewhat red banner and be ready to break ranks and leave the army when it reaches the dividing of the ways." [88]

With their plans for winning the votes of non-Socialist reformers apparently well on the way to success, party leaders turned with renewed vigor to the task of gaining electoral support from organized workers. To Right-wing Socialists, "organized workers" meant the American Federation of Labor. But Samuel Gompers, leader of the federation of national craft unions, viewed Socialists as men of warped minds or intellectual instability and regarded all Socialist activity as a series of machinations designed "to undermine trade unionism in order to get votes for 'The Party.'" [89]

[85] "Cheerful Destroyers," *The Nation*, LXXXIII (May 27, 1909), 527–28.
[86] The *American Magazine*, LXXV (Nov., 1912), 20.
[87] "The Socialist Platform," *The Outlook*, LXXXIX (Aug. 25, 1908), 976.
[88] John B. Clark in the *Congregationalist and Christian World* (May 15, 1909), pp. 995–96.
[89] Gompers, *Seventy Years of Life and Labor*, I, 383. Some twenty-five years

Right-wing party leaders agreed that Gompers' opposition to the
Socialists had been justified in the past. They accused old-time
Marxists of having believed that every success of the trade unions
retarded the coming of socialism by making the workers content
with their lot under capitalism. They conceded that the organization of such unions as the Socialist Trade and Labor Alliance and
the Industrial Workers of the World as rivals of the A.F. of L. had
rightly antagonized Federation officers. But Socialist leaders insisted that in recent years party representatives on city councils
and in state legislatures had worked to enact measures supported
by the trade unions, and the effectiveness of the "other arm of the
labor movement" should prove that the electoral aims of the party
and the economic aims of the unions were not antagonistic.[90]

In order to remove any remaining doubts in the minds of A.F.
of L. officials as to the intentions of their party, the Right-wing
Socialists emphasized again and again that they no longer sought
endorsement of their party by any union, national or local.[91] Moreover, Socialists disclaimed any interest in the internal affairs of
the unions. The party held that activities of trade unions in their
capacity as the economic organization of the working class were
the concern of the socialist movement only to the extent that the
unions deserved the sympathetic approval of the Socialists. One
arm of the labor movement should not interfere with the other.[92]

The major concession made by Right-wing party leaders in the
area of noninterference in internal union affairs was the abandonment of the fight for industrial unionism. Before the 1908 elections
Right-wing Socialists had attacked the Industrial Workers of the
World but had professed support in principle for the industrial in
contrast to the craft form of organization. But at the January,

---

later Morris Hillquit wrote that Gompers "was inherently class-conscious to the
point of religious fervor" (Hillquit, *Loose Leaves*, p. 95).

[90] Gaylord, *Socialism Is Coming—Now*, pp. 22–25.

[91] "Report of Victor L. Berger on the 'Socialist Party and the Trade Unions,'
to the National Executive Committee of the Socialist Party, January 22, 1909" and
"Minutes of the National Executive Committee, January 22, 1909," the *Socialist
Party Official Bulletin*, Jan., 1909; Hunter, *Labor in Politics*, pp. 33–34. Berger's
report was adopted.

[92] "Report of Victor Berger on the 'Socialist Party and the Trade Unions,' to
the National Executive Committee of the Socialist Party, January 22, 1909," the
*Socialist Party Official Bulletin*, Jan., 1909.

1909, National Executive Committee meeting, the committee adopted Berger's recommendation that Socialists as Socialists should not only abstain from participation in interunion struggles, but should also refuse to participate in organizational and tactical differences within any union. Since noninterference in the matter of industrial unionism still might not go far enough to reassure craft union officials as to the sincerity of Socialist intentions, Berger's report, which the executive committee adopted as the party line, concluded by identifying noninterference with support of craft unionism: "Our motto must be under all circumstances, join the union of your *craft* and the party of your class." [93]

Even before the disappointing 1908 national election, Max Hayes, a leading member of both the Socialist Party and the International Typographers Union, as well as editor of the Cleveland *Citizen* (official organ of the city's Central Labor Union) had suggested that, while industrial was preferable to craft unionism in principle, "it has weaknesses innumerable." Since Hayes was sure the "labor problem" was going to be settled "politically," "it is absurd for Socialists to waste a lot of valuable time in splitting hairs over the question of industrial organization." [94] With each passing year Hayes receded from his position that industrial unionism was preferable in principle even if unimportant in practice. By 1914, a little more than a year after he had received one third of the national A.F. of L. convention vote as Socialist candidate for president of the Federation, Hayes was insisting that the craft unionism of "the American Federation of Labor is the logical economic organization for this country." [95]

J. Mahlon Barnes, national party secretary and a leader in the A.F. of L. Cigarmakers Union, reported to the 1910 national Socialist convention that the older craft unions were the best recruiting grounds for Socialist votes. These craft unions, he said, had already won their victories and achieved their maximum strength in the economic field. Since they could advance no further through union organization, they were ripe for conviction as to the gains

[93] *Ibid.* Italics added.

[94] Letter from Max S. Hayes to J. Mahlon Barnes, April 5, 1907, printed in *The Socialist Party Official Bulletin*, April, 1907.

[95] Max S. Hayes, "Socialists in the Unions," reprinted in W. J. Ghent (ed.), *Appeal Socialist Classics* (Girard, Kansas, Appeal to Reason, 1916), pp. 36-37.

that could be made if union members voted the Socialist ticket.[96]

The Committee on Labor at the 1910 Socialist congress brought in a resolution "that the party has neither the right nor the desire to interfere in any controversies which may exist within the labor-union movement over questions of form of organization or methods of action in the industrial struggle." [97] A minority report by the two Left-wing members of the nine-man labor committee "recommended" the organization of labor along "industrial lines based on the recognition of the irrepressible class conflict in society," adding that "we do not oppose labor in any form of organization in its struggles against the capitalist class." [98]

Two other Left-wing Socialists, Frank Cassidy of New York and James Maurer of Pennsylvania, both members of the American Federation of Labor, offered a substitute resolution. Quoting the 1907 Stuttgart International Socialist Congress resolution which condemned class collaborationist craft unions, they averred that the American party could not be neutral on this question without betraying the working class and rendering itself impotent. Their resolution, while reiterating the party's desire to assist all forms of unions, as well as all unorganized workers in their struggles to improve working conditions, "endorses Industrial Unionism as a principle and as an indispensable part of the class struggle, without endorsing any particular organization." The resolution concluded by instructing all party organizers, editors, writers, and members not to limit themselves to propagandizing union members on the general principles of socialism "but also to carry them the message of *common action against the common enemy* and of Industrial Unionism generally." [99]

The debate on the various resolutions lasted all morning. Despite repeated assertions by their supporters that neither the minority nor the substitute resolutions endorsed the Industrial Workers of the World, Right-wing attacks on these resolutions stressed the evils of the I.W.W. and the correctness of a policy of noninterference in union affairs.[100] Quotation of condemnation of craft

[96] "Report of the National Secretary to the National Congress of the Socialist Party, May 15, 1910," Socialist Party, *Proceedings of the First National Congress, 1910*, pp. 34–35.
[97] Socialist Party, *Proceedings of the First National Congress, 1910*, p. 277.
[98] *Ibid.*, p. 278.        [99] *Ibid.*, p. 278.        [100] *Ibid.*, pp. 279–87.

unionism by the Stuttgart Socialist Congress was answered by the insistence that condemnation might be justified in Europe, but "conditions are entirely different here." [101] On a roll-call vote, the substitute resolution was defeated 58 to 23, and the minority report was defeated 54 to 29. The majority report was adopted by a voice vote.[102]

To Right-wing Socialists, noninterference in union activity came to mean more than refusal to throw their weight behind industrial unionism. Morris Hillquit testified that the party did not "engage in the economic struggles of the workers, except where such struggles assume a political or general aspect. . . . We would consider it meddling." [103] Socialists in the unions were to concentrate on programs capable of fulfillment only through legislative action.[104] They were to distribute literature, sell socialist newspaper subscriptions, and carry on a general agitation to convince trade union members of the importance of such legislative measures as old age pensions and judicial reform—measures which could be made into law if workers voted the straight Socialist ticket. As Berger never tired of repeating, "We must make the trade unionist constantly feel that the Socialist Party is the political complement—the other half—of the economic organization." [105]

The general socialist program advanced by the Right wing constituted no small deviation from the theories developed by Karl Marx and Frederick Engels. Socialist publicists recognized this growing divergence, and rarely cited the writings of Marx and Engels, whose books all but disappeared from party lists of basic works on socialism.[106] But the party had been founded only some ten years before as a political organization based on the teachings of Marx. During the first four years of the party's existence almost all of its literature had quoted Marx and Engels extensively, and its press had devoted major space to reprinting portions of their writings. Right-wing Socialist theoreticians realized that if they

101 *Ibid.*, p. 286.                    102 *Ibid.*, pp. 288–89.
103 Hillquit, in Hillquit, Gompers, and Hayes, *Double-Edge of Labor's Sword*, p. 29.
104 Saposs, *Left Wing Unionism*, p. 35.
105 "Report of Victor Berger on the 'Socialist Party and the Trade Unions,' to the National Executive Committee of the Socialist Party, January 22, 1909," *Socialist Party Official Bulletin*, Jan., 1909.
106 Hughan, *The Facts of Socialism*, pp. 102–3,

were to defend their program against Left-wing attacks on the one hand, and the criticism of moderate reformers and conservatives on the other, Marx and Engels could not simply be ignored. They would have to be interpreted and modified to suit the party program.

In an answer to charges from critics reared in the Christian-idealist philosophical tradition that socialism was a materialist philosophy holding that only matter exists, Morris Hillquit replied with a blanket denial. He insisted that Marx's materialist conception of history, on which, he said, the materialist charge was based, was no more than a theory of "social evolution" and had nothing to do with philosophic materialism or philosophic idealism. "It does not attempt to deal with the nature or function of the human mind or with the ultimate questions of existence. Socialism as such is neither materialistic nor dualistic. It is not committed to any school of philosophy and still less does it seek to advance a philosophic system of its own." [107]

Since the party wanted electoral support from small businessmen, and since in Marxist theory the small manufacturer was as guilty as the large of making profit by keeping the surplus value produced by his workers, the theory had to be revised. The concept of surplus value received its first major attack in the socialist press in January, 1908, when an article printed in the then Right-wing *International Socialist Review* stated that surplus value had nothing to do with the cause of depressions. The author held that since capitalists reinvested their profits, the accumulation of profits could not cause overproduction. The real cause of depressions, it was held, was the planlessness of capitalist economy which resulted in overproduction in some areas. The problem of surplus value, therefore, could be ignored. [108]

The leading Right-wing Socialist theoretician to devote himself to fitting Marx into the new socialist ideology was John Spargo. [109] The attack in 1908 on the importance of the theory of surplus value

---

[107] Hillquit and Ryan, *Socialism: Promise or Menace?* pp. 236–37.

[108] George W. Downing, "Planlessness of Production the Cause of Panics," *International Socialist Review*, VIII (Jan., 1908), 414–15.

[109] Victor Berger, of course, had revised Marx some fifteen years before (see above, pp. 117–18). But by 1910 Berger had passed beyond the need for further revision of Marxist theory. He simply dismissed Marx as hopelessly out of date.

may have been daring for an American Socialist. But by 1910 Spargo had advanced to the point of rejecting Marx's entire theory of value. Marx had held that value was measured by the average amount of socially necessary labor time that went into the production of a commodity. Spargo argued that in a monopoly economy the value of many commodities was determined "by their marginal utility, quite irrespective of the social labor actually embodied in them or necessary to their reproduction." [110]

Spargo also found Marx wrong in his "exclusive" emphasis on the role of the proletariat in the achievement of socialism, and in his prediction of the disappearance of the small farmer, merchant, and manufacturer. To Spargo the modern socialist movement in the United States recognized that the working class constituted a minority of the population and therefore appealed to the middle class as well as to the proletariat.[111] The critique concluded that Marx and Engels "lapsed occasionally into Utopianism"; this was particularly noticeable in their theory of the increasing misery of the proletariat and in their prediction "that an economic cataclysm must create the conditions for a sudden and complete revolution in society." [112]

Having denied that Marx and Engels were concerned with any philosophy, much less that of dialectical materialism, and having "corrected" such fundamental Marxist theories as the nature of value and surplus value, class make-up of capitalism, cause of depressions, role of the working class, growing contradictions of capitalism, and the necessity for socialist revolution, party Right-wing theoreticians were naturally somewhat hard-pressed to explain what contribution, if any, Marx and Engels had made to the socialist movement. Spargo advanced an ingenious solution to this problem: Marx was wrong in many of his theoretical formulations, but correct in his tactics.[113] The basis of Marxist tactics was opportunism. "Marx was nothing if not an opportunist." Since

[110] John Spargo, "The Influence of Karl Marx on Contemporary Socialism," *American Journal of Sociology*, XVI (July, 1910), 37.

[111] *Ibid.*, pp. 37–39.

[112] Spargo, *Socialism*, 1913 ed., p. 232. It is interesting to note that the first edition of this book, published in 1906, does not find Marx and Engels guilty of this "utopian" lapse.

[113] John Spargo in his introduction to Hughan, *American Socialism of the Present Day*.

the socialist movement now concerned itself in the main with social reforms, "palliative measures for the amelioration of the victims of the social struggle, within the existing order," Socialists were actually returning to the "most important teachings of Marx." [114]

So far as Spargo could see, only the investigation and rejection of Marx's theories by modern Socialists had enabled the socialist movement to rediscover the opportunist truths which had been obscured by mistaken principles. "Now that critical examination has forced the abandonment of some of his theories, and the modification of some others, Marx the leader, the tactician, the statesman, is taking the place of Marx the theorist to some extent." [115] The socialist movement was developing in "that broad spirit of opportunism which Marx himself so well and so bravely exemplified." [116]

[114] John Spargo, "The Influence of Karl Marx on Contemporary Socialism," *American Journal of Sociology*, XVI (July, 1910), 33.
[115] *Ibid.*, pp. 39–40.        [116] *Ibid.*, p. 37.

# XII

# Socialist Propaganda

# 1909-1912

THE TACTICS of Socialist opportunism called for enactment of social reforms designed to improve the conditions of the
working and middle classes under capitalism and move society step
by step down the road toward socialism. The party role was to secure passage of these reforms through election of Socialist officials
to government positions. These officials, when they became numerous enough, would pass reform legislation themselves. In the meantime, the growing Socialist vote would frighten elected representatives of the Republican and Democratic parties into adopting some
social legislation. The way to get Socialist votes was to carry on
ceaseless propaganda.

The basic party unit assigned the task of carrying on the propaganda campaign was the town or ward local, which was to organize
the activity of its members. Members were to devote an hour or two
a month to distributing socialist literature from door to door, selling newspaper subscriptions, holding public meetings, and recruiting other members for the same tasks.[1]

Apparently the locals showed little enthusiasm for handing out
pamphlets and bringing potential converts to meetings addressed
by national and local party leaders. In fact, almost all Right-wing
locals, restricting themselves to these activities, found that in between elections their organization "languished." Party leaders
placed the blame on what they described as a lack of imagination

---

[1] William H. Leffingwell, "The Socialist Local," *Wilshire's Magazine,* XIII
(March, 1909), 15; Edward Slade, "Propaganda Suggestions," *Social-Democratic
Herald,* June 1, 1907; Carl D. Thompson, "System Needed by Socialists," *Social-
Democratic Herald,* June 5, 1909; *Appeal to Reason,* Dec. 7, 1907.

in finding ways and means of carrying on propaganda.[2] They suggested that each local appoint a standing committee to organize the work so that literature was distributed from house to house, letters about socialism were written to newspapers, bookstands established on street corners and at fairs, party literature mailed to farmers, high school and college students encouraged to write and debate about socialism, newspaper subscriptions sold, and public meetings held.[3]

But despite repeated appeals for greater enthusiasm and more widespread participation in the propaganda campaign, Socialist leaders continued to complain that "the Socialists of America . . . seem to have gone to sleep just at the beginning of the battle of the votes." [4] Algie Simons reported that at the 1907 International Socialist Congress the United States delegates were treated more as "guests" than as members. The other delegates "seemed to act as though we Americans meant well—but we were not 'doing things.' And since thinking it over, I rather believe they were right." [5]

Distribution of socialist leaflets, pamphlets, and books had always played a major role in socialist propaganda. But when the 1908 election was followed by virtual amalgamation of the party Center and Right wings and consolidation of this new Right wing's control of the national as well as most state organizations, overwhelming emphasis was placed on the distribution of literature and the circulation of the socialist press. In reply to a request from a working-class local for advice on more effective means of Socialist activity, Gaylord Wilshire wrote, "No other method of making Socialist propaganda has been as yet devised, than the distribution of literature and the holding of meetings." [6] National Secretary Barnes reported that "the spread of the printed word has come

2 W. R. Shier, "Why Locals 'Languish,'" *New York Call*, Aug. 21, 1910; William H. Leffingwell, "The Socialist Local," *Wilshire's Magazine*, XIII (March, 1909).

3 Edward Slade, "Propaganda Suggestions," *Social-Democratic Herald*, June 1, 1907; Carl D. Thompson, "System Needed by Socialists," *Social-Democratic Herald*, June 5, 1909.

4 *Wilshire's Magazine*, XI (Oct., 1907), 3; William H. Leffingwell, "The Socialist Local, *Wilshire's Magazine*, XII (March, 1909).

5 Letter from A. M. Simons to Gaylord Wilshire, *Wilshire's Magazine*, XI (Oct., 1907), 3.

6 *Wilshire's Magazine*, XII (Feb., 1908), 7.

to be recognized as the most important means of propaganda," [7] and Victor Berger pointed out after the 1910 Socialist victory in Milwaukee that literature distribution was the only propaganda device that had been used. [8]

In April, 1910, Barnes reported to the National Executive Committee that inasmuch as seventeen states maintained a full-time secretary and most states kept one or more organizers in the field, the national office should dispense with its paid organizers and devote its resources to "a systematic distribution of literature." [9] Shortly thereafter the national office recalled its last organizer from the field. [10] Eighteen months later the new national secretary, John Work, recommended that henceforth the national office function in the main as a "publisher and disseminator of Socialist literature." In keeping with this program, Work suggested that the office absorb the privately owned publishing houses and become the largest, and perhaps the only, publisher of socialist propaganda. [11]

Leaders who supported the propaganda program claimed that approximately 60 percent of all converts had been made through the printed word. [12] It was only necessary to urge socialism on farmers, professionals, and little businessmen, and explain it to workers; its essential truths were quickly grasped by all these groups. Obviously, "slum proletarians" could not be expected to understand the written word; it must be directed at the more intelligent of organized labor—the members of the American Federation of Labor. [13]

The quantity of literature sent out by the national office for distribution by the local organizations reached enormous proportions

[7] "Annual Report of the National Secretary of the Socialist Party, January 1, 1910 to December 31, 1910," *Socialist Party Official Bulletin*, Jan., 1911.

[8] Victor L. Berger, "What Is the Matter with Milwaukee?" *The Independent*, LXVIII (April 21, 1910), 841.

[9] "Report of National Secretary Barnes to the National Executive Committee, April 9, 1910," *Socialist Party Weekly Bulletin*, April 28, 1910.

[10] Letter from J. Mahlon Barnes to the National Executive Committee, April 28, 1910, *Socialist Party Weekly Bulletin*, April 28, 1910.

[11] "Annual Report of the National Secretary of the Socialist Party, January 1 to December 31, 1911," *Socialist Party Monthly Bulletin*, Jan., 1912. Of course, this would eliminate the press of the Left-wing opposition.

[12] Cox, *The Socialist Party in Indiana*, p. 126.

[13] "Report of the Committee on Propaganda, Morris Hillquit, Chairman, to the 1910 Socialist Congress," Socialist Party, *Proceedings of the First National Congress, 1910*, pp. 62–63.

in 1911—37 different leaflets and pamphlets totaling almost five million pieces. In addition, the national office considered that it had made an important contribution to socialist propaganda by printing and distributing 800,000 copies of Victor Berger's Congressional speech on the tariff and 200,000 copies of his speech on old-age pensions.[14] There is no way of knowing how much additional literature was printed and distributed by state and local organizations. In the first four months of 1912 three and a half million items were sent out, and the 1912 election campaign had yet to get under way.[15]

The subject matter covered a wide range: official documents like the party platform and explanations of Socialist Party organization (*Why Socialists Pay Dues*) ; arguments for political reform (*Government by Commission* and *A Municipal Program*) ; outlines of labor legislation (*Workmen's Compensation*) ; muckraking and exposés of the Republican and Democratic parties (*Our Political Parties*) ; an *Address to Organized Labor;* and appeals to different social and economic groups (*To the Working Woman,* and *A Plea to Club Women*).[16] The increased importance of all this is shown by the revenue received by the national office from sales: in 1909, $1,714 ; in 1910, $5,777 ; in 1911, $7,967.[17]

It was to be expected that a political organization whose press was largely privately owned and which stressed propaganda by the printed word would find its work and policies greatly influenced by the owners and editors of its newspapers. During the first few years of the party's existence, when policy was largely determined by a Left-Center coalition, the Left wing took cognizance of the fact that most Socialist newspaper owners and editors belonged to the middle class and tended to publicize theories and policies of a non-Marxist, reformist character.

[14] "Annual Report of the National Secretary of the Socialist Party, January 1 to December 31, 1911," *Socialist Party Monthly Bulletin,* Jan., 1912.

[15] "Report of National Secretary John Work to the 1912 Socialist Party Convention," Socialist Party, *Proceedings of the National Convention, 1912,* p. 218.

[16] "Annual Report of the National Secretary of the Socialist Party, January 1 to December 31, 1911," *Socialist Party Monthly Bulletin,* Jan., 1912; Socialist Party pamphlet collections in Harper Library of the University of Chicago, Wisconsin State Historical Library, Labadie Collection, University of Illinois Library, and John Crerar Library, Chicago.

[17] "Annual Report of the National Secretary of the Socialist Party, January 1 to December 31, 1911," *Socialist Party Monthly Bulletin,* Jan., 1912.

At the 1904 Socialist convention, the Left-wing San Francisco local moved the establishment of an official daily or weekly party paper. Left-wing delegates supported the motion on the ground that it was ridiculous to have the party publicize dozens of different interpretations as to the meaning of its program. They charged that papers like the *Appeal to Reason* were in a position to determine party policy by influencing its readers. Furthermore, they pointed out that many of the larger papers in the Middle West and East were little better. The Center, however, did not want to weaken the influence of such powerful representatives of its position as the *New York Worker* and the *Chicago Socialist;* it opposed an official party press on the ground that its editor would be able to dictate party policy.[18] Not only was the San Francisco motion defeated, but a constitutional provision was adopted forbidding the National Committee to publish or designate an official party organ.[19] Five years later, however, when the party organization was controlled by a Center-Right coalition, the Left wing helped block establishment of a party-owned press, holding that it would permit a small group of leaders to dominate the party.[20]

The number of Socialist newspapers and periodicals was always surprisingly large. In 1904, when the party had twenty thousand members, it had about forty daily, weekly, and monthly papers and magazines.[21] In 1912, with membership climbing over the one hundred thousand mark, the party boasted no fewer than 323 papers and periodicals—five English and eight foreign-language dailies, 262 English and 36 foreign-language weeklies, ten English and two foreign-language monthlies.[22] The national office sent out weekly mimeographed "propaganda articles" to 400 Socialist, union, and other papers which agreed to print at least one article a week, and in 1911 it began to keep a press representative in Washington during Congressional sessions.[23] The total circulation of the Socialist press is impossible to estimate. In 1908 Hunter

---

[18] Socialist Party, *Proceedings of the National Convention, 1904,* pp. 85–96.

[19] *Ibid.,* pp. 118–20.

[20] "A Party Owned Press," *International Socialist Review,* X (July, 1909), 68–70.

[21] Hillquit, *History of Socialism,* 1910 edition, p. 352.

[22] "Report of National Secretary John Work to the 1912 Socialist Convention," Socialist Party, *Proceedings of the National Convention, 1912,* p. 221.

[23] "Annual Report of the National Secretary of the Socialist Party, January 1 to December 31, 1911," *Socialist Party Monthly Bulletin,* Jan., 1912.

claimed that the pro-party press reached "not less than a million voters." [24] And when it is noted that in that year the *Appeal to Reason* alone had a weekly circulation of almost four hundred thousand and the monthly *Wilshire's Magazine* had a circulation of two hundred and seventy thousand,[25] it is not difficult to accept Hunter's estimate as reasonably accurate.

The vast majority of the weekly papers were privately owned; only a minority were published by local party organizations. Usually the subscription price was fifty cents a year. With the exception of the *Appeal*, all operated with a deficit, which was covered, when it was covered, by appeals to party membership in the city or town where the paper was published.[26] In communities where party membership was small or poor, and where factional disputes divided support, there were frequent lapses in publication.[27]

Without question the most successful of Right-wing,[28] and, in fact, of all the socialist papers was Julius Wayland's *Appeal to Reason*. Simple and direct in style, sensational and muckraking in approach, with a subscription price of twenty-five cents a year, the *Appeal* maintained a circulation that usually varied between 300,000 and 500,000. As a promoter of newspaper circulation Wayland had few equals. The low price coupled with contests for steam yachts, trips to Europe, bonuses, and commissions enabled him to organize tens of thousands of *Appeal* readers and most party organizers into an "Appeal Army" perpetually engaged in selling subscriptions. For, as the "Appeal Army" was informed, socialism could not be won through violence but only through "the Book and the Ballot." [29] Special exposé issues, such as that of December, 1905, on trusts, sometimes sold as many as three million copies. Orders for bundles of hundreds and thousands would pour in for weeks before publication, and virtually the entire adult popu-

---

[24] Robert Hunter, "The Socialist Party in the Present Campaign," *The American Review of Reviews*, XXXVIII (Sept., 1908), 299.

[25] N. W. Ayer and Son, *American Newspaper Annual*, for 1908, pp. 293, 615.

[26] On a few occasions the national office gave financial support to the *New York Call*, *Chicago Daily Socialist*, and the Milwaukee *Social-Democratic Herald* (Hughan, *American Socialism of the Present Day*, p. 11).

[27] *Social-Democratic Herald*, May 12, 1906.

[28] The two most important Left-wing publications, the *International Socialist Review* and the Seattle (and sometimes Toledo) *Socialist* will be discussed in Chapter XIV.

[29] *Appeal to Reason*, Dec. 7, 1907.

lation of Girard, Kansas, would be engaged in wrapping and mailing.

In his use of the paper as a source of advertising revenue, Wayland was unscrupulous.[30] The faith of its readers in the *Appeal* was enormous, and Wayland did not hesitate to claim that he had investigated and found valid virtually every enterprise which took a full-page advertisement. *Appeal* readers were told, indeed, guaranteed, that the purchase of advertised gold stocks, patent medicines, and farm co-operatives were sure escapes from the trials of wage slavery. Thus, a typical advertisement trumpeted in two-inch letters that took up the entire back page of one issue:

DON'T BE A WAGE SLAVE
WHILE YOU MAY EARN FROM $3,000.00 TO $5,000.00 A YEAR
SIMPLY SEND THE COUPON FOR THIS FREE BOOK—
"HOW TO BECOME A MECHANO-THERAPIST."
BE INDEPENDENT. THROW OFF THE BONDS OF SLAVERY.
YOU HAVE BUT YOUR CHAINS TO LOSE—YOU HAVE
AN HONORABLE AND PROFITABLE CAREER TO GAIN.[31]

The *Appeal* was ably edited by Fred D. Warren, who continued to publish the paper after Wayland committed suicide in 1912. The first page, when not devoted to some particularly colorful exposé of corruption rampant in trustified America, was made up of an article by Eugene Debs and a series of one- and two-paragraph observations on happenings of the week and the obvious advantages of socialism. Thus, "You think the right to vote for public officers enlarges your liberty and makes you a sane man, and also that to vote on who shall be your boss at the shop, what hours you should work and what should be done with the earnings, would curtail your liberty and put you on a level with your employer. You certainly have a great mind." [32] And, "Industry is in the hands of the workers and out of the hands of the capitalists now. All that stands between the workers and industrial freedom are paper walls known as titles." [33]

The inside pages were devoted to descriptions of how socialism

---

[30] In 1906 the *Appeal* had an income of $10,000 a month (Upton Sinclair, "The Socialist Party," *The World's Work*, XI [April, 1906], 7431–32).

[31] *Appeal to Reason*, Oct. 17, 1908.          [32] *Appeal to Reason*, July 20, 1907.

[33] *Ibid.*, July 27, 1907.

would benefit the farmer, worker, small businessman, professionals, women, and children, including detailed descriptions of life in the new society. In addition to pictures of the good life to come for all as soon as socialism was voted in, inside pages also carried muck-raking articles and prepublication serialization of such books as Upton Sinclair's *The Jungle* and Gustavus Myers's *History of the Great American Fortunes* and *History of the Supreme Court of the United States*. The socialism of the *Appeal* was largely "constructive" or "step-at-a-time." Its motto was "Public Ownership of Monopolies," and its program and appeal, except for predictions of the nature of society in the distant future, were not too different from those of the old middle-of-the-road Populists.

Despite its wide circulation and its notable success in giving publicity to the socialist movement, the *Appeal* was sharply attacked by other socialist papers of all factions.[34] No doubt this was due at least in part to jealousy, for struggling socialist papers with a circulation of a few hundred to a few thousand and a price two to four times that of the *Appeal* found that paper formidable competition in the struggle for existence. But the *Appeal* was also criticized for its lack of publicity of the Socialist Party,[35] its "ultra-capitalistic business methods," its use of the party to build the *Appeal* instead of vice versa,[36] its reformist approach to socialism,[37] and its employment of salesmen who brought the socialist movement into disrepute.[38] The criticisms were frequently justified, but no other paper brought the first inkling of socialism to so many,[39] or mobilized party members in as many campaigns against labor frame-ups and government and business corruption.[40]

[34] W. J. Ghent, " 'The Appeal' and Its Influence," *The Survey,* XXVI (April 1, 1911), 24–28.

[35] *The Worker,* March 15, 1903.        [36] *Ibid.,* Jan. 29, 1905.

[37] *The Socialist* (Seattle), Jan. 18, 1903.

[38] In one case, the *Appeal* hired as a subscription salesman a "socialist" who combined his soap-box orations on socialism with the announcement, "Jesus Christ now addresses you through this instrumentality." (Letter from Charles R. Martin, Toledo, Ohio, to Herman F. Titus, July 4, 1903, *The Socialist* [Seattle], July 19, 1903.)

[39] In the 1910 Congressional election, the five states which polled the high Socialist vote of 47,000 to 60,000 each also had *Appeal* circulations which ranged from 24,000 to 41,000 (W. J. Ghent, " 'The Appeal' and Its Influence," *The Survey,* XXVI [April 1, 1911], 25).

[40] W. J. Ghent, " 'The Appeal' and Its Influence," *The Survey,* XXVI (April 1, 1911), 27–28.

Next to the *Appeal*, the most important Right-wing publication
in terms of circulation was *Wilshire's Magazine*, published and
edited by "millionaire socialist" Gaylord Wilshire. Its motto was
"Let the nation own the trusts," and in make-up it was modeled
after the popular monthlies of the day. At ten cents a copy its
circulation in 1910 was 200,000.[41] Like the *Appeal*, *Wilshire's
Magazine* engaged in some rather questionable financial transac-
tions. In the fall of 1906, Wilshire informed his readers that there
was only one business safe from the curse of overproduction—gold
mining. He then announced the good news that he now controlled
"the World's Greatest Gold Mine" and offered to let his readers in
on this depression-proof twenty billion dollar venture at the bar-
gain price of one dollar a share.[42] From then to 1911, when Wilshire moved his publishing ventures to London, the magazine
bombarded its readers with the advantages of this golden opportunity which was always about to begin declaring dividends. One
critic estimated that Wilshire invested a total of $100,000 in the
mine and sold from half a million to a million dollars' worth of
stock.[43] In England, Wilshire demonstrated the affinity between
right opportunism and left sectarianism by abandoning step-at-a-
time socialism for syndicalism and publishing a magazine for English syndicalists.[44]

While *Wilshire's Magazine* and the *Appeal* were the most important Right-wing organs of general propaganda, that faction's
leading papers which engaged in intraparty as well as public agitation were the *New York Worker* (later, the *New York Call*), the
Milwaukee *Social-Democratic Herald*, and the *Chicago Socialist*.
*The Worker* was originally published by Hillquit's faction of the
Socialist Labor Party as *The People*. When the New York courts
awarded Daniel De Leon's faction the party organization, Hillquit's group changed its paper's name to *The Worker*.[45] During

[41] N. W. Ayer and Son, *American Newspaper Annual*, for 1910, p. 672.
[42] *Wilshire's Magazine*, X (Sept., 1906), 3.
[43] Henry L. Slobodin, "Get-Rich-Quick-Schemes," *International Socialist Review*,
XI (Feb., 1911), 486–87.
[44] Gaylord Wilshire, "The Evolution of Parliament," *Wilshire's*, XV (March,
1911), 1; Gaylord Wilshire, "The London Dock Strike and Syndicalism," *Wilshire's*
(Sept., 1911), pp. 1–3; Gaylord Wilshire, "Vote-Chasing and the Revolution,"
*Wilshire's*, XVI (June–July, 1912), 4.
[45] *The People* (Williams St.), April 21, 1901.

its first years *The Worker* devoted most of its four pages to party news and long theoretical articles on scientific socialism. The theoretical articles were gradually replaced with news stories designed to increase the Socialist vote. By 1908 when the New York state organization took over the paper it was selling 32,000 copies weekly at an annual subscription rate of fifty cents.[46] Its weekly deficit of $90 to $100 was made up through contributions from individuals and local Socialist bodies.[47] The name was changed to the *New York Socialist* in 1908. The next year, after a long period of money-raising activity, the *New York Call* appeared as a six-page socialist daily. By 1912 it had a circulation of 32,000.[48]

When the *Social-Democratic Herald* moved from Chicago to Milwaukee after the Socialist Party's formation, Victor Berger took over the editorship. From the beginning of its Milwaukee career the *Herald* devoted itself to advancing the cause of step-at-a-time socialism and to winning votes for socialism in Milwaukee by exposing graft and corruption. There was no change in the paper's policies when Berger resigned as editor in 1902 "in order to devote more time to his German papers and to the difficult task of making a living while also agitating for socialism." [49] Frederic Heath, Berger's right hand man in the Wisconsin party, took over the editorship, and Berger each week contributed a long, signed front page article devoted to party policy and appeals to Milwaukee voters for electoral support. Until the Socialist victory in that city in 1910 the *Herald's* circulation fluctuated between twelve and fifteen thousand. By 1912 it had soared to sixty thousand.[50]

No other Socialist paper had so stormy a career as the *Chicago Socialist*. Established in 1899 as *The Workers' Call*, a supporter of the Socialist Labor Party, it quickly claimed a circulation of 25,000.[51] It played a leading role in the Socialist Labor Party factional fights which led to the formation of the Socialist Party, and in 1902 changed its name to *The Chicago Socialist*. In 1904 the Chicago Center faction overthrew the "impossibilist" control of

46 N. W. Ayer and Son, *American Newspaper Annual*, for 1908, p. 615.
47 *The Worker*, Aug. 3, 1907, April 28, 1908.
48 N. W. Ayer and Son, *American Newspaper Annual*, for 1912, p. 630.
49 *Social Democratic Herald*, May 10, 1902.
50 N. W. Ayer and Son, *American Newspaper Annual*, for 1905, 1908, 1910, 1912.
51 A. M. Simons in *The Workers' Call*, March 2, 1901.

the county board machinery and placed its representatives on the board of the *Socialist*. The next year it reported a circulation of 14,000, but from then until its demise in 1912 it refused to report its circulation.[52] After two years of preparation,[53] the board of the *Socialist* finally arranged to issue a six-page daily paper for the last two weeks of the 1906 Congressional campaign.[54] The daily was put on a permanent basis after the election and in 1907 the weekly *Chicago Socialist* was abandoned.[55]

From that point on the history of the *Chicago Daily Socialist* is replete with recriminations, accusations, and counteraccusations. The paper was published by a private corporation, but met its ever-mounting financial deficit through use of the Chicago party organization.[56] The Chicago Socialist movement was usually in the midst of factional struggle, and all factions sought to gain control of the paper for their own ends. Even on those occasions when the paper's board of directors and the Cook County Executive Committee belonged to the same faction, the board and the committee were engaged in a perpetual struggle to determine who should control the party organization and the party treasury.[57]

Under the editorship of A. M. Simons, the *Daily Socialist* played to the hilt its role as a proreform, pro-American Federation of Labor paper. It led the publicity fight to prevent imprisonment of Teamsters Union officials, attacked police brutality, exposed the use of debt peonage in Chicago by a branch of the Standard Oil Company, and aroused opposition to attempts by the federal government to return a Russian revolutionary to Tsarist Russia.[58] By 1909 it had settled down to concentrating its fire on "the hideous graft conditions that today are shaking the very foundations of Chicago's institutions." [59]

[52] N. W. Ayer and Son, *American Newspaper Annual,* for 1903, 1905, 1908, 1910, 1912.

[53] *Chicago Socialist,* Nov. 19, 1904; *Chicago Record-Herald,* Jan. 23, 1905.

[54] *Chicago Socialist,* Aug. 4, 1906.          [55] *Chicago Socialist,* April 6, 1907.

[56] Letter to Socialist Party membership from Board of Directors of the *Chicago Daily Socialist,* March 23, 1909, Thomas J. Morgan Collection.

[57] Letter from the Executive Committee, Local Cook County, to members of the National Committee, September, 1907, *Socialist Party Official Bulletin,* Sept., 1907.

[58] *Chicago Daily Socialist,* 1907–9; letter from the *Chicago Daily Socialist* to the *Appeal to Reason,* Nov. 13, 1909; Ernest Poole, "Harnessing Socialism," *The American Magazine,* LXVI (Sept., 1908), 430.

[59] Letter from the *Chicago Daily Socialist* to the *Appeal to Reason,* Nov. 13, 1909.

In 1910 another factional fight coupled with bitter personal antagonism brought about the resignation of Simons.[60] The paper continued its former policies, although its support of American Federation of Labor officials in union factional fights became more noticeable. In the 1910 garment workers' strike, for example, the party Left-wing charged that the *Socialist* suppressed news of calls for a general strike and fired its strike reporter for urging the workers to continue to refuse the weak settlement proposed by the Chicago Federation of Labor.[61] By 1912 the *Daily Socialist* was in deeper financial difficulties than ever. The Chicago pressmen's strike in that year proved too great a temptation for the shaky paper. Since the *Daily Socialist* was not struck, it changed its name to the *Chicago Evening World* and almost overnight increased its circulation to 300,000. The *World* found itself with a payroll of $8,000, and despite financial appeals to its readers and to the party National Executive Committee was unable to raise the money.[62] If that were not enough, a $35,000 bond issue came due on December 1, and the paper was unable to meet it. With debts of $120,000, and overdue notes of $18,000, the creditors foreclosed on December 3, and Chicago was without a socialist paper.[63]

Although the Right wing of the party considered literature and public meetings the two main forms of socialist propaganda, they placed less and less emphasis on street meetings.[64] In fact, the *Social-Democratic Herald* decided that they were "freakish" and "of doubtful value." [65] New York party leaders issued a list of instructions for street-corner speakers: Do not advocate or oppose any religious belief; Make clear that the party does not align itself with one type of unionism against another; "Do not class all capitalists as thieves, blacklegs, scoundrels, etc. Remember that it is the system that creates capitalists"; Do not attack or abuse the po-

60 *Chicago Record-Herald*, Aug. 2, 1910.

61 Robert Dvorak, "The Garment Workers Strike Lost, Who Was to Blame?" *International Socialist Review*, XI (March, 1911), 550–56; "The Daily Socialist and the Garment Workers," *International Socialist Review*, XI (March, 1911), 558–59.

62 *Socialist Party Monthly Bulletin*, Aug., 1912; *Chicago Record-Herald*, Dec. 5, 1912.

63 *Chicago Record-Herald*, Dec. 5, 1912.

64 "Report of the Committee on Propaganda, Morris Hillquit, Chairman, to the 1910 Socialist Congress," Socialist Party, *Proceedings of the First National Congress, 1910*, p. 66.

65 *Social-Democratic Herald*, March 14, 1908.

lice unnecessarily, for they are members of the working class and "we should have their good will"; The first speaker should begin by 8:15 P.M. and limit himself to one hour.[66]

When Right-wing Socialists mentioned the importance of propaganda meetings, they referred not to street-corner rallies addressed by members of the rank and file, but to carefully organized assemblies addressed by reliable speakers from the national office, which kept a list of about fifty speakers available for work through state organizations. The usual arrangement provided that the state organization and its locals paid about three fifths of the $5 cost per day per speaker, and the national office underwrote the difference.[67] In July, 1911, the National Secretary announced formation of a Socialist Lyceum Bureau. Any local could subscribe to the course of five lectures to be given by a speaker sent out by the Bureau. The local was to underwrite the cost of the series by selling $300 worth of books and newspaper subscriptions. The national office was to get the commissions on these sales, but the local was to be allowed to keep all money raised at the lectures from the collection and from book sales.[68]

The Lyceum's first season began in the fall of 1911. Four hundred and forty-two locals agreed to undertake the series, and tried to meet the Lyceum's terms by sale of books and subscriptions before the lectures and by a 25-cent admission charge, entitling the buyer to that amount of credit toward a subscription to any socialist paper. Three hundred locals were able to carry the program through, resulting in a total of 1,500 lectures. The Lyceum Bureau reported that during the first season audiences averaged 300, that 2,000,000 pieces of advertising were distributed and $100,000 worth of newspaper subscriptions sold, that 112 locals reported recruitment of 2,000 new members, and that 8,000 inches of publicity on the lectures were obtained from "capitalist papers"— "perhaps the most valuable feature of the entire work." [69] The

---

[66] Instructions adopted at meeting of Local New York, July 24, 1910, *New York Call*, July 31, 1910.

[67] Letter from National Secretary J. Mahlon Barnes to State Secretaries, Feb. 17, 1909, *Socialist Party Official Bulletin*, Feb., 1909.

[68] Letter from National Secretary J. Mahlon Barnes to the locals of the Socialist Party, July 8, 1911, *Socialist Party Official Bulletin*, July, 1911.

[69] "Annual Report of the National Secretary of the Socialist Party, January 1 to December 31, 1911," *Socialist Party Monthly Bulletin*, Jan., 1912; "Socialist

Lyceum had operated on a $76,000 budget, and ended "in the black." [70]

All was not enthusiasm for the Lyceum, however. Local Toledo, Ohio, charged that the Right-wing National Executive Committee had established the lecture bureau in order to tighten their machine control of the party.[71] Local Duluth, Minnesota, protested that too many of the lecturers were ministers, lawyers, and writers who looked upon socialism as a reform movement that could be used to their personal profit.[72] The state secretary of Minnesota, T. E. Latimer, complained to the National Executive Committee that the 16 Lyceum advance salesmen, equal in number to the lecturers, had persuaded many locals to undertake the series when they were in no position to do so. As a result, a "good many locals went broke on the proposition." Furthermore, charged Latimer, the nature of the program and the lecturers meant that only " 'respectable' elements" were reached. And in Minnesota, those who attended the lectures and were not "respectable" were already members of the party.[73]

Although the party leadership directed most of its energies toward bringing the printed and spoken word to adult males with electoral privileges, some attempt was made to reach those who would eventually have the vote. A number of locals feared that the public grammar school system "glorifies the competitive idea" and that their children would become "prejudiced against Socialism." [74] They therefore attempted to establish Socialist Sunday Schools designed to teach "the value of the Socialist spirit and cooperative effort." However, the Sunday Schools suffered from a lack of qualified teachers [75] and from the difficulties of curriculum

---

Prospects," *Appeal to Reason*, Jan. 27, 1912; "Report of L. E. Katterfield, Chairman of the Lyceum, to the National Executive Committee, Minutes of the National Excutive Committee, March 10, 1912," *Socialist Party Monthly Bulletin*, April, 1912; *The Party Builder*, Aug. 28, 1912.

[70] *Socialist Party Monthly Bulletin*, Jan., 1913.

[71] "Resolution of Local Toledo, Ohio, July 15, 1912," *Socialist Party Monthly Bulletin*, Aug., 1912.

[72] "Resolution of Local Duluth, Minnesota, December 19, 1911," *Socialist Party Monthly Bulletin*, Jan., 1912.

[73] "Minutes of the Meeting of the National Executive Committee, May 13, 1912," *Socialist Party Monthly Bulletin*, June, 1912.

[74] *American Labor Year Book*, 1916, p. 153.

[75] "Report of the Committee on Propaganda, Morris Hillquit, Chairman, to the

construction for the young.[76] Certain party leaders viewed the whole school idea "with some suspicion," and the national organization of the party refrained from giving it a blanket endorsement.[77]

In 1909 one Sunday School enthusiast boasted an enrollment of one thousand children in the New York schools,[78] but the 1912 *Socialist Campaign Book* claimed active Sunday Schools in only four large cities.[79] The "Red Sunday Schools" achieved some notoriety when the nonsocialist press publicized the action of Omaha students who replaced ("tore down," said the press version) a picture of Theodore Roosevelt in their classroom with that of Mother Jones, veteran mine worker organizer.[80] No figures are available on the total number of Sunday Schools or their enrollment, and Socialist efforts in that direction were admitted to be "spasmodic." [81]

In 1905 Mrs. George D. Herron came into control of a $200,000 trust fund created by her mother, Carrie Rand, "to carry on and further the work to which I have devoted the later years of my life." Mrs. Herron agreed to use the fund to endow a school designed to become "an intellectual center for the Socialist movement in the United States." [82] The trust provided a gradually diminishing income of about six thousand dollars a year, and with that money Mrs. Herron and Morris Hillquit, whom she named as cotrustee, organized the Rand School of Social Science.[83] The trustees planned to include courses on a "wide range of cultural sub-

---

1910 Socialist Congress," Socialist Party, *Proceedings of the First National Congress*, p. 69.

76 *American Labor Year Book*, 1916, pp. 153–54.

77 Spargo and Arner, *Elements of Socialism*, p. 301.

78 Letter from Edwin James Ross to the *New York Call*, Sept. 30, 1909.

79 *Socialist Campaign Book*, p. 39. The "cities" listed were New Jersey, Los Angeles, New York City, and Rochester, New York.

80 " 'Red' Sunday-Schools and Child Socialists," *The American Review of Reviews*, XXXVIII (July, 1908), 112–13.

81 *American Labor Year Book*, 1916, p. 153.

82 *Chicago Socialist*, Oct. 30, 1905.

83 Hillquit, *Loose Leaves*, p. 64. The board of directors named in the certificate of incorporation included George D. Herron, Morris Hillquit, Carrie Herron, Algernon Lee, Job Harriman, Benjamin Hanford, William Mailly, Leonard D. Abbott, and Henry Slobodin. An advisory committee made up of Charles A. Beard, Dr. P. A. Levine of the Rockefeller Institute, and Herman Schlueter, editor of the *New Yorker Volkszeitung*, was also appointed (*ibid.*, pp. 65–66).

jects" as well as on socialism, and the school soon advertised a curriculum which included courses on psychology, popular science, literature, music, foreign languages, and the drama.[84] By 1909 the school had an average annual enrollment of two hundred.[85]

The early years of the Rand School were not entirely harmonious. Its endowment revived the virulent press criticism of the Herrons. George Herron was compelled to issue a statement in which he denied that he had been left $11,000,000 by Carrie Rand to be used to destroy religion and the family; that their farm in New Jersey was a colony which practiced these doctrines; and that, to further the same end, he was writing a book to be translated into all languages. "For the millionth time, it is reported that Mrs. Herron and I took each other as 'companions,' nearly four years ago, and that we were not duly and legally married. This again is unqualified and malign invention." [86] No denials could stop the American press, however, and the Herrons were forced to leave for Italy where they spent the remainder of their lives.[87]

Criticism of the school also came from within the party. The *Social-Democratic Herald*, which had yet to make its peace with the Center faction which controlled the school, saw no reason for its establishment. Socialism, said the *Herald*, was a "phase of civilization, not a theology. We have no Socialist catechism that requires a school to teach" it. Social science, continued the *Herald*, was a branch of political economy that could be studied in any university, and since there were already a great many publications that made available the truths of socialism, there was no need for "this new school, that fairly waddles in money that somebody must help use up." [88]

In 1909, William J. Ghent, the school's administrative secretary, resigned while under attack for using the institution for factional purposes and because the institution was not making a large enough contribution to the socialist movement. Ghent explained the small enrollment and the minor contribution Rand School graduates made to the party on grounds of lack of funds, the low

[84] Rand School of Social Science, *Second Year Bulletin for Second Term*, (December 25, 1907), in the Labadie Collection; Hillquit, *Loose Leaves*, p. 67.

[85] W. J. Ghent, "The Rand School," *New York Call*, Nov. 28, 1909.

[86] *Chicago Socialist*, Oct. 30, 1905.          [87] Hillquit, *Loose Leaves*, pp. 63–64.

[88] *Social-Democratic Herald*, Oct. 21, 1905.

calibre of the students, the inability to enforce a planned curriculum, and the time it took to produce results in the field of education.[89] Algernon Lee, former editor of the *New York Socialist*, succeeded Ghent as secretary and continued as head of the Rand School for some years.[90]

Right-wing party leaders considered socialist propaganda in the schools and colleges to be "especially valuable . . . for it is not true that most college students are sons of wealthy."[91] In 1905, Upton Sinclair, then still a year away from the fame that publication of *The Jungle* was to bring him, obtained the signatures of ten leading reformers and Socialists to call for the formation of the Intercollegiate Socialist Society.[92] The increasing Socialist vote and sentiment, said the organizers of the Society, indicated that "educated men and women" could no longer remain uninformed. The principles and aims of socialism provided the remedy for "many far-reaching economic evils," and they therefore invited high school and college students, graduates, and teachers to join them in forming a society devoted to the study of socialism. Membership in the Socialist Party was not to be a prerequisite to membership in the Society.[93]

The organizing meeting was held in New York in September, 1905. Jack London was elected president, and Upton Sinclair and J. G. Phelps Stokes were elected vice presidents.[94] Not until 1908 did the Society show real signs of growth,[95] although London devoted much time lecturing before meetings called by college chapters of the Society in its first few years of existence.[96] By 1910 it was engaged in holding lectures and discussions and distributing socialist literature through its chapters in fifteen universities,[97]

---

[89] W. J. Ghent, "The Rand School," *New York Call*, Nov. 28, 1909.

[90] *Ibid.;* Hillquit, *Loose Leaves,* p. 67.

[91] "Report of the Committee on Propaganda, Morris Hillquit, Chairman, to the 1910 Socialist Congress," Socialist Party, *Proceedings of the First National Congress, 1910.*

[92] *The Worker,* Sept. 9, 1905; Hillquit, *Loose Leaves,* p. 60. The sponsors of the plea were J. G. Phelps Stokes, Thomas Wentworth Higginson, Charlotte Perkins Gilman, Clarence S. Darrow, Oscar Lowell Triggs, B. O. Flower, William English Walling, Leonard D. Abbott, Jack London, and Upton Sinclair. The last three listed were the only ones who at that time were members of the Socialist Party. (*The Worker,* Sept. 9, 1905.)

[93] *The Worker,* Sept. 9, 1905.          [94] *Ibid.,* Sept. 16, 1905.

[95] Hillquit, *Loose Leaves,* pp. 61–62.          [96] Foner, *Jack London,* pp. 77–78.

[97] Hillquit, *History of Socialism,* 1910 ed., p. 355.

and by 1912 it reported 43 chapters, an increase of 200 percent in less than two years.[98]

If Right-wing Socialist leaders showed intermittent interest in Socialist Sunday Schools and considerable enthusiasm for the Intercollegiate Socialist Society, they manifested complete unconcern for any youth organization not directly connected with an educational institution. As early as 1903 young Socialists in New York formed a Junior Socialist Club. The club received no support or encouragement from the New York party and died in a few years. In 1907 it was followed by the Young Friends Socialistic Literary Circle, which inspired the formation of a number of similar groups in New York. The party continued to ignore them.[99] Young Socialists attempted to form clubs outside the party in a number of other cities, most successfully in Chicago.[100] These clubs, as their names suggest, engaged mainly in discussion of literary and socialist works and did not participate in party activity.[101] By October, 1911, only about eight hundred young Socialists were organized in their own clubs throughout the country, and these clubs had no fraternal connections with each other.[102]

The attitude of most Socialist leaders toward the question of equal rights for women bore a striking resemblance to their approach to the question of Negro equality. It was readily granted that neither group had been granted full equality in American society.[103] The Negro was informed that his status was part of the general "labor problem," and that under socialism he would achieve complete equality together with complete segregation. Women were informed that the "woman question" was part of the "labor question," [104] and that capitalism, by forcing women to work, paying their husbands low wages, and causing unemployment, inadequate housing, starvation, divorce, prostitution, illegitimacy, suicide, and a high death rate, was breaking up the home.[105] Of course, said these Socialists, they had no intention of restricting women to the role of homemakers, but they knew that once the need to supplement

98 *Social-Democratic Herald,* May 11, 1912.
99 Letter from Edwin James Ross to the *New York Call,* Sept. 30, 1909.
100 *Socialist Party Weekly Bulletin,* Sept. 10, 1910.
101 Louis Wirtz, "The Young Socialist Movement," *International Socialist Review,* XII (Jan., 1912), 417–19.      102 *New York Call,* Oct. 15, 1911.
103 *The People,* Dec. 17, 1899.      104 *The Worker,* April 28, 1901.
105 May Walden Kerr, *Socialism and the Home,* p. 29.

the husband's earnings was eliminated, "ninety-nine women out of every hundred would choose the lot of wife and mother." [106] Under capitalism, continued the Socialist analysis, legal compulsion was used to keep women in the home at the same time that economic pressure was forcing her out. "Socialism would put an end to the economic compulsion, and that would make the legal compulsion quite unnecessary." [107]

The next question was how women themselves could contribute to building this new social order which would keep them in the home without the use of legal compulsion. Since they could not vote, they were asked to create "a sentiment" in favor of establishing the co-operative commonwealth. In Sunday schools they were to search out the capitalist ethics in the lessons and discover means to supplant them with socialist ethics. Those among them who were Christian Scientists were to help "create harmony among the workers." As housekeepers, "too worried and busy to find room for a new thought," they were to "simplify" their work, ask a friend about socialism, and then invite in their neighbors and "repeat the facts you have learned." As clerks, bookkeepers, and factory workers they were to talk about the identity of workers' interests, and point out that workers should "neither scorn nor envy" each other. And as teachers they were to "teach that a good character is more to be desired than great riches," and "arouse a sentiment" among other teachers for free text books, transportation, lunches, and clothing, less wasteful methods of education, and consolidated schools for rural districts.[108]

Even this minor role assigned women in the socialist movement was considered too great by many of their male comrades. In 1904 *The Worker* pointed out that too many men in the party, "good Socialists in most respects . . . look with disapprobation or with more irritating contempt on any participation by women in the affairs of our movement." The reason for this attitude, said *The Worker*, was that women were considered inferior to men in their organizational ability, were uninterested in improving their position because they were happy in it, and were "dominated by strictly personal preferences and narrow views." *The Worker* conceded

106 *The Worker*, April 28, 1901.          107 *Ibid.*
108 May Walden Kerr, *Socialism and the Home*, pp. 30–31.

that all these charges were justified and "that most thoughtful women will admit [their] truth." But *The Worker* held that when women, despite these handicaps, attempted to make some contribution to the socialist movement, the men should not discourage them.[109]

By 1908 the male superiority complex in the Socialist Party apparently had increased considerably. Although the party platform demanded complete political and economic equality for women, equality was to come as a gift presented by man to woman out of his infinite generosity. Party propaganda and organization paid little attention to the possibility that women might fight for their own freedom, and when they were "tolerated" in Socialist locals, they were not treated as equals, but "regarded . . . as useful only to make cakes for tea-parties or 'fancy things' to sell at fairs for raising funds." [110] Party meetings were frequently held in saloons where the few women members would not attend, and when women were used as propagandists, they were used as "attractions" to appeal to the masculine vote.[111] Moreover, what four years before had been described as woman's lack of organizational talent and unfortunate satisfaction with her inferior status had been developed into the "scientific discovery" that women were nearer to the "child" and "savage" than man.[112] It is not surprising, therefore, that some party members refused to sign petitions favoring suffrage extension to these "lower creatures" and argued that Socialist principles did not entail equal rights for women.[113] Of the 50,000 dues-paying Socialists in 1909, only 2,000 were women. A large proportion of party members apparently had not considered it worth their time to recruit even their wives and sisters.[114]

Resentment and organized opposition to this attitude and treat-

[109] "Women in the Party," *The Worker,* April 24, 1904.

[110] John Spargo, "Women and the Socialist Movement," *International Socialist Review,* VIII (Feb., 1908), 450-52.

[111] *Ibid.,* p. 452.

[112] Joseph Cohen, "Socialist Sociology," *International Socialist Review,* X (Aug., 1909), 874-75.

[113] Theresa Malkiel, "Where Do We Stand on the Woman Question?" *International Socialist Review,* X (Aug., 1909), 159; Socialist Party, *Proceedings of the National Convention, 1912,* pp. 118-19.

[114] Theresa Malkiel, "Where Do We Stand on the Woman Question?" *International Socialist Review,* X (Aug., 1909), 162.

ment grew rapidly among women Socialists.[115] By 1905 some of them were proposing establishment of a separate socialist party for women,[116] and by 1908 women members of the Socialist Party had formed federations, clubs, and leagues in New York, Chicago, St. Louis, Kansas City, Philadelphia, California, and many other cities and states.[117] Three months before the May, 1908, party convention, John Spargo, who had been approached a number of times on the question by leading women Socialists, wrote a biting indictment of the belief in male superiority in the Socialist Party. It was published by the Left-wing *International Socialist Review*,[118] which magazine provided the medium for the expression of the women's growing resentment at their treatment.

Spargo charged the party with giving nothing but lip service to the cause of equality for women, of treating women as inferiors within the party, of confining socialist propaganda among women to utopian pictures of community kitchens, and assuming

that any other employment for women than househould [*sic*] and maternal duties must be considered abnormal and wrong. Who is there in our movement that is not familiar with the promise that Socialism will do away with "unnatural labor" for women and enable them to stay at home; said unnatural labor being anything except house-wifery and maternity; the endless chain of sweeping, washing, mending, scrubbing, cooking, child-bearing and nursing. . . . It is not for man to set metes and bounds for woman's freedom.[119]

Spargo proposed the establishment of a National Woman's Committee within the party with responsibility for developing propaganda among women and for organizing the attack upon male superiority among Socialists.[120]

At the 1908 party convention, a committee of five women was

---

115 *Ibid.*, pp. 159–62; Lida Parce, "Woman and the Socialist Philosophy," *International Socialist Review*, X (Aug., 1909), 125–28; John Spargo, "Woman and the Socialist Movement," *International Socialist Review*, VIII (Feb., 1908), 452.

116 John Spargo, "Woman and the Socialist Movement," *International Socialist Review*, VIII (Feb., 1908), 452; Jessie M. Molle, "The National Convention and the Woman's Movement," *International Socialist Review*, VIII (May, 1908), 690.

117 Jessie M. Molle, "The National Convention and the Woman's Movement," *International Socialist Review*, VIII (May, 1908), 688–89.

118 John Spargo, "Woman and the Socialist Movement," *International Socialist Review*, VIII (Feb., 1908), 449–55.

119 *Ibid.*, p. 454.          120 *Ibid.*, p. 453.

elected to take charge of propaganda among women, and it was agreed that the National Committee would employ a full-time organizer for that work.[121] The Woman's Committee was instructed to recruit women into the party, agitate for women's suffrage, and increase the usefulness of the Socialist Sunday Schools. During 1908 the committee did what it could with limited resources to get people to visit the wives of party members, secure petitions for extension of the suffrage, and speak on the suffrage question at street-corner and party local meetings.[122] In December, 1908, the National Executive Committee acceded to the request of the Woman's Committee for some action on woman suffrage by recommending that all locals put that subject on the agenda for their May Day meetings in 1909.[123] During 1909 the New York Woman's Committee played an active part in support of the shirtwaist makers' strike.[124] Early in 1910 the national office again took notice of its Woman's Committee. For the first time the committee was permitted to use the national office to facilitate its correspondence,[125] and the National Executive Committee requested all locals to set aside February 27 for propaganda for extension of the suffrage and recruitment of women into the party.[126]

At the 1910 national party congress, the delegates spent almost an entire day debating the proposal of Ella Reeve Bloor of Connecticut that Socialist women devote some time to work in the general suffrage movement. Opponents of the proposal argued that it emphasized "sex consciousness" instead of "class consciousness." Women Socialists were instructed to work for their enfranchisement only through their own party.[127] However, the congress did create the post of general correspondent of the Woman's National Executive Committee with the task of implementing all the committee's decisions. During the remainder of 1910 the general cor-

---

121 Socialist Party, *Proceedings of the National Convention, 1908,* pp. 41, 62, 300–306.

122 May Wood-Simons in the *Socialist (Perpetual) Campaign Book,* pp. 91–93.

123 "Minutes of the National Executive Committee, December 19, 1908," *Socialist Party Weekly Bulletin,* Dec. 21, 1908.

124 "Report on Propaganda among Women," Socialist Party, *Proceedings of the First National Congress, 1910,* p. 179.

125 *Ibid.*

126 *Socialist Party Weekly Bulletin,* Feb. 5, 1910.

127 Socialist Party, *Proceedings of the First National Congress, 1910,* pp. 181–211.

respondent succeeded in organizing women's committees in 156 locals, and state committees in five states.[128] From then on the National Woman's Committee devoted itself to increasing the number of its local and state committees, obtaining woman's state correspondents, sending out propaganda for monthly entertainments, circulating petitions for extension of suffrage, and securing publication and distribution of leaflets and articles on woman's economic position, suffrage, war, boy scouts, child slavery, alcoholism, and white slavery.[129]

There is little question that with the formation of the Woman's Committee the Socialist Party began to devote more time to the subject of equal rights for women. But while there was a marked decrease in the Socialist press of references to the "inferior" sex, women Socialists seem to have carried on the fight for equal rights with little aid from the male members of the party.

[128] "Report of the General Correspondent of the Woman's National Committee to the National Executive Committee, December 12, 1910," *Socialist Party Official Bulletin*, Dec., 1910.

[129] "Annual Report of the National Secretary of the Socialist Party, January 1 to December 31, 1911," *Socialist Party Monthly Bulletin*, Jan., 1912; *Socialist Party Weekly Bulletin*, Sept. 30, 1911.

# XIII

# Christianity and
# Immigration

THE SOCIALIST PARTY gave far more attention to winning the support of Protestant ministers than it gave either to youth or women. During the days of the two Social Democratic parties, 1900–1901, both organizations conceded that individual Christians might recognize socialism as the essence of the Golden Rule.[1] But after granting that concession to the few Socialists who saw the co-operative commonwealth as the material expression of the teachings of Christ, the two Socialist parties concentrated on warning their followers that all organized religion was "based upon and [stood] for the present capitalist order." [2]

Organized religion was considered harmful to the working class movement for socialism because of

its hollowness and soullessness; its petrification and false pretenses; its fostering of prejudices, superstition and narrow sectarian exclusiveness; its intolerance and bigotry; its tendency to side with the powerful and strong and preach slavish virtues to the "humble and lowly" proletarians; its blasphemous attempts to sanctify the crying injustices of the social institutions of their time and country.[3]

Furthermore, Socialists must beware of churchmen who would "emasculate Socialism" to the point where it was nothing but another "muddle-headed" reform movement.[4] Finally, while there

---

[1] Isador Ladoff, secretary of the National Executive Board of the Social Democratic Party with headquarters in Chicago, in the *Social Democratic Herald*, Feb. 16, 1901; *The People* (Williams St.), June 10, 1900.

[2] *The People* (Williams St.), June 10, 1900.

[3] Isador Ladoff in the *Social Democratic Herald*, Feb. 16, 1901.

[4] *Ibid.*

would be complete liberty of conscience in a socialist society, still it must be remembered that the religion of slavery was paganism, of serfdom, Catholicism, of capitalism, Protestantism, and that of socialism would be humanism.[5]

It was George D. Herron who made the first real attempt to resolve the contradictions between Christianity and Marxian socialism, and Center and Right-wing party leaders were quick to grasp the electoral advantage that Herron's answer could bring. In April, 1901, Herron, then playing a major role in bringing unification of the two Social Democratic parties, wrote an article for *The Worker* in which he held that God worked through "economic fact and development. . . . The working class socialist philosophy of history alone gives the account of life and labor out of which a new religious synthesis can be woven." Herron said that God had united economic and spiritual life. The present crisis in religion was caused by the church's attempt to divorce them for the sake of "capitalistic influence and money." A new religious synthesis could be achieved only with the coming of socialism. "The sources of life which [Marxian socialism] discloses are identical with the spiritual forces which Jesus revealed; but the identity is unrecognized because Socialism has come to us in the scientific terms of class-struggle philosophy." Economic propaganda alone, continued Herron, would not be enough to win the co-operative commonwealth. "Socialism must become a religion, a spiritual as well as an economic ideal. . . . Not a letter of the economic philosophy or historic interpretation need be sacrificed in order for Socialism to avow itself as the historic approach to an ideal reaching away beyond itself." [6]

Other "Socialist Christians" [7] were quick to translate Herron's somewhat esoteric language into effective Socialist propaganda. Capitalism was the enemy of religion because it corrupted morals, established mastery and servitude, enforced injustice, and robbed the masses of time and strength for religious duties.[8] Socialism was the "logic of Christianity," representing the ideals of brotherhood,

[5] *Social Democratic Herald,* Oct. 26, 1901.

[6] George D. Herron, "The Socialist Disclosure of Spiritual Sources," *The Worker,* April 28, 1901.

[7] Webster, *The Kingdom of God and Socialism,* p. 23.

[8] Walter Thomas Mills, *The Struggle for Existence,* pp. 416–17.

justice, and love, "the Kingdom of God on earth." [9] Herron's thesis that Christian Socialists had no need to modify the principles of scientific socialism was rejected. Socialism was to come not through the class struggle, but because "God wills it." It was He who was responsible for the economic changes which were bringing socialism. "His Holy Spirit is in the great world-movement. And so by the power and wisdom and love of God, both the rich and the poor will simply *have* to accept the Kingdom by and by." [10]

This theory was good enough to convince a growing body of Protestant ministers, but the Catholic Church was not so easy to convert. Bishop Quigley of Buffalo, New York, informed all Catholics in his diocese that socialism was a recent importation from Europe that "denies the existence of God, the immortality of the soul, the right of private ownership, the rightful existence of our present social organization, and the independence of the church as a society complete in itself and founded by God." Therefore, no Catholic could join the Socialist Party or support any of its activities.[11] The growing moderation of the Socialist program brought an occasional suggestion in a Catholic publication that economists, psychologists, and theologians be consulted to determine whether or not socialism was really opposed to private property, the home, church, government, and order.[12] But most Catholic leaders continued to agree with the characterization of Father Sherman of the Society of Jesus: "Socialists are Hell's lowest vomit!" [13] The Socialists replied that the Catholic Church opposed socialism because Catholic dogmas could not bear scientific analysis, because it feared loss of its wealth and power, and because Socialists stood for the separation of church and state.[14]

The Socialists, however, devoted little time to attacking Catholicism. They apparently reasoned that they had more to gain by concentrating their propaganda on winning over the Protestant majority than on the difficult task of converting the Catholic minority.

[9] Thompson, *Principles and Program of Socialism*, pp. 6–7.

[10] Webster, *The Kingdom of God*, pp. 20–21.

[11] "Bishop Quigley's Attack upon Socialism," *The Literary Digest*, XXIV (April 12, 1902), 508.

[12] William J. Kerby, "Aims in Socialism," *The Catholic World*, LXXXV (July, 1907), 500–511.

[13] Quoted in the *Social-Democratic Herald*, Aug. 8, 1908.

[14] Thomas McGrady, "The Catholic Church and Socialism," *The Arena*, XXXVIII (July, 1907), 18–27; "Why the Catholic Church Opposes Socialism, by a Leading Socialist," *The Arena*, XXXVII (May, 1907), 520–24.

The Socialists utilized every opportunity to instruct the ministerial profession that they must work within the framework of a God-given economic determinism to make operative their Christian ideals.[15] The ministers were told that socialism sought "economic freedom as the only means whereby spiritual freedom can be secured." [16] Nonsocialist ministers testified to the effectiveness of Christian Socialist propaganda:

The Socialists made a better use of the New Testament for the purposes of moral appeal . . . than do the majority of the ministers of the gospel. The present writer has heard a dozen impassioned Socialists . . . make a finer, a more effective, a more dramatic, a more moral use of figures, the illustrations, and the moral teaching of the gospels, in a single evening, than he haş heard from any dozen preachers in a month in the last twenty years.[17]

In June, 1906, Christian ministers and laymen organized the Christian Socialist Fellowship

to carry to churches and other religious organizations the message of socialism; to show the necessity of socialism to a complete realization of the teachings of Jesus; to end the class struggle by establishing industrial and political democracy; and to hasten the reign of justice and brotherhood upon earth.[18]

Unlike the Christian Socialist movement of the 1890s, based almost exclusively on ethical concepts and without relationship to the Socialist Labor Party, the Fellowship endorsed the principles and program of the Socialist Party which it was organized to support.[19] As has been noted, there was considerable difference of opinion in the party as to just what constituted the principles of socialism. Since the Christian Socialists based their analysis on the brotherhood of man rather than on the class struggle, they aligned themselves with the opportunist rather than the revolutionary wing of the party.[20]

At a Christian Socialist Congress held in New York City in May,

[15] Vida D. Scudder, "Socialism and Sacrifice," *The Atlantic Monthly* CV (June, 1910), 1836–49; "The Church and Socialism," *The Arena*, XL (Sept., 1908), 243.

[16] Spargo, *The Substance of Socialism*, pp. 63–64.

[17] Reverend A. A. Berle, quoted in "The Church's Growing Sympathy with Socialism," *Current Literature*, XLIII (Nov., 1907), 537–38.

[18] Quoted by Hillquit, *History of Socialism*, 1910 ed., p. 257.

[19] *Ibid.; Christian Socialist* June 15, 1907; Hughan, *The Facts of Socialism*, p. 148; *American Labor Year Book*, 1916, p. 157.

[20] Hughan, *American Socialism of the Present Day*, pp. 223–24.

1908, it was claimed that more than three hundred American clergymen were members of the Socialist Party.[21] In 1909 the Fellowship changed its name to the Christian Socialist League of America. By that year the Christian Socialists were publishing two weekly papers and one monthly magazine,[22] and could point to an increasing number of articles sympathetic to socialism appearing in church publications of many denominations.[23]

Despite the activities of the Christian Socialists, the charge that socialism was atheistic and immoral continued to be used with telling effect against the party.[24] At the 1908 Socialist convention, therefore, the platform committee introduced a plank in the Immediate Demands stating "that religion be treated as a private matter—a question of individual conscience." [25] Morris Hillquit proposed that this plank be deleted and the following be inserted in the Declaration of Principles: "The Socialist movement is primarily an economic and political movement. It is not concerned with the institutions of marriage and religion." [26]

Both the committee proposal and the Hillquit substitute came under immediate fire from the Left and a majority of the Center on the grounds of inaccuracy and opportunism. It was pointed out that religion was not an individual but a social question, that Socialists could not be scientists in economics and theologians in philosophy, and that religion was used by the capitalist class to convince the workers that their place in society was God given. It was charged by James Carey, who was a member of the platform com-

21 "The Church and Socialism," *The Arena,* XL (Sept., 1908), 243. That all difficulties between Marxian and Christian socialism had not been resolved to the satisfaction of every member is indicated in a letter on the stationery of the *New York Call* arranging for a meeting of the literature committee for the 1908 Christian Socialist Congress. The committee chairman called the meeting to arrange for literature distribution, and to make sure that "wholesome scientific Socialist literature—debarring any having the least atheistic tint"—was selected. (Letter from J. Chant Lepes, chairman, to members of the literature committee, Brooklyn, May 18, 1908, Labadie Collection.)

22 Hillquit, *History of Socialism,* 1910 edition, p. 357. The most important of the papers was *The Christian Socialist,* published in Chicago. In 1913 it claimed a circulation of 19,205 at a subscription of fifty cents a year (N. W. Ayer and Son, *American Newspaper Annual,* for 1913, p. 173).

23 "The Church's Growing Sympathy with Socialism," *Current Literature,* XLIII (Nov., 1907), 538.

24 Boyle, *What Is Socialism?* p. 189.

25 Socialist Party, *Proceedings of the National Convention, 1908,* p. 191.

26 *Ibid.,* pp. 191–93, 194–97, 200–201, 202–4.

mittee, that the religious plank had been introduced by party intellectuals over the protests of the working class members.[27] Elliot White, an Episcopalian minister from Massachusetts, held that Christianity in its present organized form would have "to go under," and suggested that the only appropriate Socialist plank on religion would be one protesting Christian discrimination against "atheists and infidels." [28] Finally, it was charged that the proposal was another fence-straddling, vote-getting maneuver.

. . . when we talk of educating mankind and when we talk of raising mankind above the level in which he is, then we have got to throw from his arms those crutches that bind him to his slavery, and religion is one of them. Let it be understood that the moment the Socialist Party's whole aim and object is to get votes, we can get them more quickly by trying to please the religionists and those whose only ambition is to pray to God and crush mankind. . . . To spread forth to the world that religion is the individual's affair and that religion has no part in the subjection of the human race, we lie when we say it. (Great Applause.) The Socialist party has reached a stage where it has come to the turnpike, and will either have to stand for the truth or declare for opportunism of the barest kind and invite anybody and everybody to give us their vote, irrespective of the importance of the views they hold on economic slavery.[29]

The party Right wing and its Center supporters replied on contradictory grounds: the Center conceded that religion and "materialist dialectics" were incompatible, but said it could not "forget the exigencies of the moment for our ideals in the far future"; [30] the Right held that religion really was a private matter, that socialism was nothing but "the name for an epoch of civilization," and that something must be done to stop this charge of atheism which was cutting the Socialist vote.[31] On the one hand, socialism was a world-wide movement which could not be limited to materialism. Only "modern cosmic theism" adequately expressed the philosophy of socialism.[32] On the other hand, religions may have had their origin in material reality, but today they are only remotely

[27] *Ibid.,* pp. 194–95.  [28] *Ibid.,* p. 197.
[29] C. H. Vander Porten in *ibid.,* p. 204.
[30] Ernest Untermann in *ibid.,* p. 194.
[31] Victor Berger in *ibid.,* pp. 203–4. Apparently Berger was the member of the committee who submitted the plank on religion (*ibid.*).
[32] Mila Tupper Maynard of Colorado in *ibid.,* pp. 192–93.

connected "with the ways in which we make our living." [33] Morris Hillquit held that the fact that the Socialist Party had both Christians and agnostics among its membership proved that religion had nothing to do with socialism.[34] A. M. Simons pointed out that great scientists like Lord Kelvin had reconciled religion and science to their own satisfaction. As for himself, said Simons, "I am now truly an agnostic in science, in religion and in Socialism." [35]

The debate was settled when National Secretary J. Mahlon Barnes stated that unless one of the resolutions was passed, the present convention discussion on religion would be used against the party.[36] Some members of the Center faction then recanted. Austin Morrow Lewis of Illinois, who had been the first speaker against the planks, said that after a conference with Berger, Hillquit, and John Work he had been convinced that the resolutions did not mean that "the materialist attitude toward religion" could not be explained from the lecture platform. Since, as Barnes had pointed out, this discussion on religion might be misinterpreted, Lewis asked those who had supported his position to vote for the plank.[37] On a vote by show of hands, the Hillquit substitute was adopted, 79 to 78.[38]

The Socialist Party was careful to design its program and activities so as to win votes from Christians in general as well as from small businessmen, professionals, college students, and craft unionists. But it found no need to engage in propaganda or organizational work among the millions of foreign-born who had poured into the United States in the late nineteenth and early twentieth century and who had formed their own socialist organizations on a national scale. Nonetheless, the rapid growth of the party between 1910 and 1912 was in part due to the affiliation of thousands of members of these groups. Among the most important were the Finnish, Bohemian, Lithuanian, Italian, Norwegian, Polish, and Slavic.[39] Some of these organizations sent representatives to the 1904 Socialist Party Convention. They pointed out that their organizations were more closely affiliated with socialism in their for-

---

[33] J. Mahlon Barnes in *ibid.*, pp. 199–200.
[34] *Ibid.*, p. 193.     [35] *Ibid.*, pp. 204–5.     [36] *Ibid.*, pp. 199–200.
[37] *Ibid.*, pp. 201–2.     [38] *Ibid.*, p. 205.
[39] Letter from National Secretary J. Mahlon Barnes to the National Executive Committee, Nov. 30, 1906, *Socialist Party Weekly Bulletin*, Nov. 30, 1906.

mer homelands than in America, and asked for a procedure whereby they might aid the American socialist movement.

The 1904 convention took no action on this friendly overture, but passed it on to the National Executive Committee. The committee, in October of the year, suggested that if foreign-language organizations wanted to help the American party their locals should join the Socialist Party's state organizations and pay state dues. And the committee added that if these organizations wanted to participate in national party affairs, they would have to pay national dues in addition to state dues.[40] The foreign-language socialist federations were thus given the choice of abandoning their work and joining the party, or joining the party and raising additional funds to maintain their own organization. They did neither.

In 1906 the Finnish Socialist Federation, whose 73 locals with between two thousand and three thousand members made it the largest of these groups,[41] again appealed to the Socialist Party and offered to affiliate with it by establishing a National Translator's Office at party headquarters. This office was to purchase monthly-dues stamps for five cents apiece and sell them through the Finnish Federation's state secretaries to its membership for ten cents apiece. The state secretaries would keep half of the revenue, and remit half to the National Translator for the maintenance of his office. The National Translator would serve as executive secretary for the Finnish Federation and as its liaison with the Socialist Party. This proposal in effect gave the national Socialist Party five cents a month for each Finnish Federation member, without entailing any obligation on the party, but gave the Finnish Socialists no voice in the party because they did not belong to its state organizations. The National Executive Committee, therefore, graciously accepted the Finnish offer.[42]

Many Finnish locals soon affiliated with the party's state organizations and thus became full-fledged party locals who maintained in addition their own national organization.[43] The Socialist Finnish Federation translated party directives and propaganda for

40 *Ibid.*
41 *Ibid.;* J. Maki, "The Finnish Socialist Federation," in *American Labor Year Book,* 1916, pp. 130–32.
42 *Socialist Party Weekly Bulletin,* Nov. 30, 1906.
43 Socialist Party, *Proceedings of the First National Congress, 1910,* p. 261.

its membership, published literature, kept two full-time organizers in the field, and directed all propaganda activities among Finnish-Americans. Many branches owned their own halls and organized orchestras and dramatic, singing, and gymnastic societies. The larger branches presented plays, concerts, and socials, and held propaganda meetings weekly.[44] In 1908 the Federation was operating on a budget of over seven thousand dollars a year,[45] and by 1912 the Federation had a membership of almost twelve thousand, approximately 10 percent of the total Socialist Party strength.[46]

The success of the Finnish Federation encouraged the Socialist Party to make similar arrangements with the other foreign-language socialist organizations. At the 1910 Socialist Congress the party constitution was amended to permit any foreign-language Federation with a membership of at least five hundred to establish a National Translator's Office at party headquarters. The federation was to pay the party five cents a month for each of its members, and the party in turn would pay the translator a salary not to exceed twenty-five dollars a week. Establishment of a Translator's Office automatically brought the Federation's membership into the party, but did not entitle them to a voice in party affairs. For full-fledged membership privileges, Federation branches would have to pay state dues, and through the state organizations, additional national dues. Moreover, all political and propaganda activities of the Federation branches, even if they did not join the state parties, were to be under the direct control of party state organizations.[47]

National Secretary Barnes admitted that this arrangement would compel foreign-language-speaking Socialists to pay more for the privilege of joining the party than English-speaking Socialists, and that many Federation branches who could not afford to pay extra dues would put themselves in the position of paying five cents a month for the privilege of losing all control over their

44 "Report of J. W. Sarlund, Finnish Translator-Secretary, to the 1912 Socialist Party Convention," Socialist Party, *Proceedings of the National Convention, 1912,* pp. 237–39; J. Maki, "The Finnish Socialist Federation," in *American Labor Year Book,* 1916.

45 "Report of Victor Watia, National Finnish Translator-Secretary, to the 1908 Socialist Party Convention," Socialist Party, *Proceedings of the National Convention, 1908,* pp. 315–17.

46 *American Labor Year Book,* 1916, pp. 130–32; *New York Call,* Jan. 2, 1912.

47 Socialist Party, *Proceedings of the First National Congress, 1910,* pp. 259–60.

activities. But "if the foreign comrades understand that and accept it, it is all right." [48] The "foreign comrades" were willing to meet the Socialist Party more than halfway, and by the end of 1912 the Bohemian, Finnish, Hungarian, Italian, Jewish, Polish, Scandinavian, and South Slavic Socialist Federations maintained National Translator Offices at party headquarters.[49] These Federations increased party strength by some twenty thousand members.[50]

Comparatively few of the twenty thousand were entitled to participate in party decisions, however, because most of the branches decided that they could not afford to pay double dues and therefore did not affiliate with party state organizations.[51] Although the Finnish Federation had been comparatively successful in getting its branches to affiliate with state organizations, one of its members charged at the 1912 Socialist Party convention that the state organizations made little effort to contact Federation branches: "In many cases the American comrades seem to have the idea that these comrades are a different sort of people, having nothing to do with the American people." [52] The Finnish Translator-Secretary recommended to the 1912 Socialist convention that Federation financial and affiliation arrangements be modified so as to assure full membership for all foreign-language-speaking Socialists,[53] but the convention failed to take any action. Since the great majority of the Federations' members held positions on party policy extremely critical of Right-wing ideology and practice, the failure to grant them full membership rights seriously weakened Left-wing strength in the never-ending struggle to determine party policy.

The Lithuanian Federation, the only one of the foreign-language Federations which could claim that all its branches were affiliated with party state organizations, denounced party policy

48 *Ibid.*

49 *Socialist Party Monthly Bulletin,* Jan., 1913.

50 According to the *Proceedings of the National Convention, 1912,* pp. 237–48, membership in the various Federations in May, 1912, was: Bohemian, 1,164; Finnish, 11,483; Italian, 1,200; Polish, 4,000; Scandinavian, 1,000; South Slavic, 1,266; Lettish, 983. A Jewish group was organized in July, 1912.

51 Socialist Party, *Proceedings of the National Convention, 1912,* pp. 86–91.

52 *Ibid.,* 89.

53 "Report of J. W. Sarlund, Finnish Translator-Secretary, to the 1912 Socialist Party Convention," Socialist Party, *Proceedings of the National Convention, 1912,* p. 239.

in virtually every field at the same convention. It charged that the party had surrendered almost without a struggle to the "agents of the Civic Federation" in the unions. In place of the "two armed labor movement" it proposed that Socialists run for union office and work for industrial unionism. The party should restore its demand for social ownership of all land. And, "in order to put a check upon the deadly influence of the teachings of the church upon men's minds" and to eliminate superstition in party ranks, all Socialists should be instructed in natural science. Finally, the Lithuanian Federation demanded that the party return to its former position that election campaigns were primarily a means of propaganda. Instead of devoting its energies to the pursuit of political office, the party should adopt a program of militant mass action in support of all working-class struggles.[54]

Even though the Federations doubled their memberships between 1910 and 1912,[55] the Socialist Party did not make great inroads in the ranks of the newly arrived immigrants. One student of American immigration suggests that "probably more immigrant Socialists were lost to the cause in the United States than were won from the ranks of the newcomers." [56] The neglect of propaganda and organizational work among the foreign-born was in large part due to the growth of chauvinism in the Center and Right-wing party ranks, and to a desire to placate American Federation of Labor leaders at all costs.

The original attitude of the party toward the problem of immigration had been that it was a "fake issue" invented by the capitalist parties just as they had invented the issues of tariff, free silver, and anti-imperialism. The only task of the party, therefore, was to expose it as a diversion.[57] By 1904, however, the growing desire on the part of some Socialist leaders to win American Federation of Labor votes for Socialist candidates led the American delegate to the International Socialist Congress, Morris Hillquit, to join the Dutch and Australian delegations in sponsoring a resolu-

---

[54] "Report by the Executive Committee, National Lettish Organization, Socialist Party," Socialist Party, *Proceedings of the National Convention, 1912,* pp. 244–48.

[55] See the reports of the translator-secretaries to the 1912 Socialist Party convention, in Socialist Party, *Proceedings of the National Convention, 1912,* pp. 237–48.

[56] Hansen, *The Immigrant in American History,* p. 95.

[57] *The People* (Williams St.), Jan. 7, 1900.

tion calling for restriction of immigration from "backward races." The resolution was defeated.[58]

Between 1904 and 1907 the virulence of the attacks on Chinese and Japanese immigration in the West Coast socialist press had risen to such heights that the Japanese Socialist Party appealed to American party leaders "to be true to the exhortation of Marx— 'Workingmen of all countries, unite.' "[59] There is no record of a reply being sent to Japan. But in March, 1907, the National Executive Committee passed an immigration resolution, later adopted by the National Committee, and instructed the delegates to submit it to the coming International Socialist Congress at Stuttgart. The resolution called on all Socialist parties to educate immigrants in the principles of socialism and trade unionism, but at the same time "to combat with all means at their command the willful importation of cheap foreign labor calculated to destroy labor organizations, to lower the standard of living of the working class, and to retard the ultimate realization of Socialism."[60]

Hillquit, who again was to be on the American delegation, explained his position, and the meaning of the executive committee resolution, as one which did not completely agree with the trade union analysis as to the permanently harmful effects of immigration. He and the resolution opposed "artificially stimulated" immigration as well as the immigration of workers from industrially backward countries "who are incapable of assimilation with the workingmen of the country of their adoption." Thus, said Hillquit, the Chinese would be excluded, and the exclusion of other races would be decided as the question became pertinent.[61]

The Stuttgart International Socialist Congress, however, rejected the American resolution and instead passed one condemning all measures designed to restrict freedom of immigration on racial or national grounds as reactionary and of no benefit to the working class. The resolution recognized that mass immigration often

[58] Lenz, *Rise and Fall of the Second International*, p. 68.

[59] "A Letter from Japanese Socialists to Their Comrades in the United States," *Socialist Party Weekly Bulletin*, Jan. 19, 1907.

[60] "Minutes of the National Executive Committee, March 2, 1907," *Socialist Party Official Bulletin*, March, 1907; *Socialist Party Official Bulletin*, April, 1907.

[61] Morris Hillquit, "Immigration in the United States," *International Socialist Review*, VIII (Aug., 1907), 73–75.

caused hardships to those workingmen who had succeeded in raising their standards of living. The only way to overcome those hardships, said the Stuttgart resolution, was through organizing the immigrants and through securing legislation granting them equal political and economic rights. Such activities, coupled with the passage of legislation for minimum wages, maximum hours, and regulation of sweated industries, would eliminate most of the difficulties. The Congress did favor, however, prohibiting the import and export of contract labor.[62]

The Right wing and sections of the Center and Left were outraged at the Stuttgart resolution. Victor Berger immediately denounced the American delegates to the Congress, Hillquit, Algernon Lee, and A. M. Simons, as a group of "intellectuals" who had betrayed the American proletariat by permitting passage of a resolution which would admit "Jap" and "Chinaman" coolies into the United States. If we are ever to have socialism in America and Canada, said Berger, we must keep them "white man's" countries.[63] Ernest Untermann, of the Center faction, considered by many to be the leading Marxist theoretician in America, held that the race question would continue long after the class struggle was ended. "The question as to what race shall dominate the globe must be met as surely as the question as to what class shall own the world." [64] Herman Titus, of the party Left wing, wrote with the prejudice of many West Coast Socialists that racial incompatibility was a fact, and "no amount of Proletarian Solidarity or International Unity can ignore it. We must face facts." [65]

At the December, 1907, National Executive Committee meeting, Berger and Untermann moved to reject the Stuttgart resolution and readopt the March Executive Committee statement as official party policy. Berger warned that we would soon have five million "yellow men" invading the country every year. We already have one race question, said Berger, and if something was not done at once, "this country is absolutely sure to become a black-and-

[62] Socialist Party Official Bulletin, March, 1907.

[63] Victor L. Berger, "We Will Stand by the Real American Proletariat," Social-Democratic Herald, Oct. 12, 1907.

[64] Letter from Ernest Untermann to Herman F. Titus, April 9, 1908, The Socialist (Seattle), April 18, 1908.

[65] Herman F. Titus in The Socialist (Seattle), Dec. 7, 1907.

yellow country within a few generations." [66] Both Berger and Untermann agreed to accept a substitute motion by Algie Simons
declaring that the International Congress had no power to determine the tactics of the national parties and that the American
Socialist Party "at the present time, must stand in opposition to
Asiatic immigration." Hillquit was absent, and the motion was
adopted unanimously.[67]

In February, 1908, the National Committee rejected this resolution,[68] but the next month reversed itself and by a vote of 26 to 11,
with 27 abstentions, endorsed the executive committee resolution
in so far as it applied to laborers "coming from Oriental countries,
or others backward in economic development, where the workers of
such countries have shown themselves, as a body, to be unapproach-
able with the philosophy of Socialism." [69] This resolution set the
pattern for all resolutions designed to restrict immigration and
yet absolve the party from the charge of betraying international
socialism.

The 1908 Socialist convention provided the opportunity for the
first full-scale debate on immigration. It came comparatively early
in the convention when the delegates were still fresh, and it was
long and bitter. The resolutions committee reported that they had
been able to agree on a compromise statement: The controlling
principle of the Socialist movement was the interest of the working
class, and to deny the right of the American working class to protect its standard of living from the competition of "imported foreign laborers" was "to set a bourgeois Utopian ideal above the
class struggle." Therefore, the Socialist Party opposed all immigration "subsidized or stimulated by the capitalist class" although
the party was not yet committed to any "attitude" toward legislation designed to exclude particular races. The committee did not
feel itself competent to speak definitively on the subject of racial
differences as a basis of exclusion, and recommended the appointment of an investigating committee to report to the next convention.[70]

[66] "Minutes of the National Executive Committee Meeting, December 14, 1907,"
*The Socialist Party Official Bulletin,* Dec., 1907.
[67] *Ibid.*
[68] *The Socialist Party Official Bulletin,* Feb., 1908.        [69] *Ibid.,* March, 1908.
[70] Socialist Party, *Proceedings of the National Convention, 1908,* p. 105.

The resolution was a "compromise" which did not endorse exclusion openly but placed undesired immigration under the heading of "capitalist stimulated." It was attacked by those who favored exclusion and those who opposed all restrictions, and was supported by some in both groups who thought the resolution could be interpreted to support their position rather than that of their opponents. On one point many were agreed: to permit the "hordes of either Europe or Asia" to invade the country was to lower American civilization. Biological facts could not be ignored. "No mere sentiments or ideals of the present can wipe out the result of centuries of blood and thought and struggle." [71] The class struggle was going on now, and the party could not waste time with ideals.[72] "The brotherhood of man has no place in a capitalist society." [73]

Some delegates favored an immediate end to all immigration,[74] but Ernest Untermann brought the debate back to the race question by holding that exclusion should not be solely on economic grounds because that would exclude some desirable whites. "I am determined that my race shall be supreme in this country and in the world." [75] Berger again warned that the white race could not hope to compete in a propagation contest with the yellow, and reminded his comrades that their first duty was to their class and family.[76] In answer to the reminder that all the delegates were themselves immigrants or descendents of immigrants,[77] it was replied that the descendents of white immigrants were working to raise standards of living while the "yellow races" were not.[78]

By this time opponents of immigration were so impressed by their own analysis that they decided to change their tactics. They introduced an amendment holding that "pending the success of the economic revolution on the political field" it might be "wise and necessary" to exclude all immigration from the Orient.[79] To one Wisconsin delegate even this did not go far enough, and he

71 A. Grant Miller (Colorado) in *ibid.*, pp. 106–7.
72 Gustave Hoehn (Missouri) in *ibid.*, pp. 107–8.
73 Alfred Wagenknecht (Washington) in *ibid.*, pp. 108–9.
74 Daniel Young (Pennsylvania), in *ibid.*, pp. 108–9; Alfred Wagenknecht (Washington) in *ibid.*, pp. 108–9.
75 Ernest Untermann in *ibid.*, pp. 110–11.    76 Victor Berger in *ibid.*, p. 111.
77 G. W. Woodby (California) in *ibid.*, p. 106.
78 Mark Peiser (New York), in *ibid.*, pp. 112–13.
79 A. Grant Miller (Colorado) in *ibid.*, p. 113.

spoke against the amendment because it referred to exclusion as only probably wise.[80] Finally, Max Hayes of the A.F. of L. Typographical Union demanded immediate exclusion and referred deprecatingly to Marx's "Workingmen of the world, unite." After all, said Hayes, Marx wrote that sixty years ago and knew nothing of conditions on our Pacific Coast.[81]

Those delegates who supported the resolution because of their opposition to exclusion did so on the basis of the reasoning advanced in the committee statement.[82] Those who opposed the resolution as a specious defense of restrictive immigration held that it was ridiculous to speak of any workers coming to America of their own free will.[83] Immigration was a product of capitalism. American imperialism made a decent standard of living in the Orient impossible, but when Oriental workers came to America to seek work, "we good, honest Americans, and even some Socialists, want to starve them." The only solution to the problem was achievement of socialism through industrial unionism.[84]

To the opponents of all restrictions on immigration, standards of living were being lowered in America for skilled workers not because of immigration but because of technological advances.[85] The enemy of the American worker was capitalism, not immigrants, who should be organized into militant fighters for socialism.[86]

The idea of equality for all men regardless of race can only be accomplished by the Socialist party. (Applause.) But if we permit ourselves to go to work and tack amendments to the proposition of "Workingmen of all countries unite"—if you tack amendments to that, then tack a clause to the name of the Socialist party, the words, "A d—— lie." [87]

The amendment upholding a policy of immediate exclusion was easily defeated.[88] The committee resolution was then adopted, the

[80] Howard Tuttle (Wisconsin) in *ibid.*, p. 117.
[81] Max Hayes (Ohio) in *ibid.*, pp. 120–21.
[82] Arthur Morrow Lewis (Illinois) in *ibid.*, pp. 109–10; John Slayton (Pennsylvania) in *ibid.*, pp. 111–12.
[83] Barney Berlin (Illinois) in *ibid.*, pp. 113–14.
[84] Ester Nieminen (Minnesota) in *ibid.*, pp. 114–15.
[85] S. A. Knopfnagel (Illinois) in *ibid.*, pp. 115–16.
[86] Solomon Fieldman (New York) in *ibid.*, pp. 119–20.
[87] Barney Berlin (Illinois) in *ibid.*, pp. 113–14.
[88] *Ibid.*, pp. 118–19.

Washington, Ohio, and New Jersey delegations requesting to go on record as voting no, but for different reasons.[89]

The growth of chauvinism among many Socialist leaders kept pace with their growing opportunism. At the 1910 Socialist Party Congress a majority [90] of the Committee on Immigration submitted a resolution calling for the "unconditional exclusion" of all Mongolian races, not for racial reasons but because they were so backward that they constituted a menace to "the most aggressive, militant and intelligent elements of our working class population." The resolution said that America was already afflicted with a Negro race problem, and any additional intensifying of racial conflict by Oriental immigration would relegate "the class war to the rear by weakening the political and economic labor organizations and substituting an Asiatic middle class with a lower standard of living than the American."

Having elevated the "coolie labor" which, according to the 1908 Socialist analysis, threatened to destroy the American working class, to the rank of middle class, the resolution hastened to assure delegates that the policy of exclusion did not apply to other races and nations having a long history of struggle in behalf of labor. The committee resolution gently reminded Socialists that refusal to exclude certain races and nationalities "would place the Socialist Party in opposition to the most militant and intelligent portion of the organized workers of the United States, those whose assistance is indispensable to the purpose of elevating the Socialist Party to political power." Finally, the committee recommended its own continuance because the subject of immigration and racial restriction had yet to be exhausted.[91]

John Spargo began his minority report by quoting the Stuttgart resolution on immigration. He then pointed out that the American proletariat differed from that of other countries in that it was made up of many races and nationalities, and called on the labor movement and the Socialist Party to make every effort to organize

---

[89] *Ibid.*, pp. 121–22.

[90] The three-man majority of the four-man committee was made up of Ernest Untermann, chairman, Victor Berger, and Joseph Wanhope (New York). The minority was John Spargo. (Socialist Party, *Proceedings of the First National Congress, 1910*, p. 75.)

[91] Socialist Party, *Proceedings of the First National Congress, 1910*, pp. 75–77.

the immigrant worker. The minority report took issue with the Stuttgart resolution for prohibiting exclusion because of race under all circumstances. At present, Asiatic immigration into the United States was so small as to constitute no menace to the American working class; but should it ever reach such proportions as to threaten the workers' standard of living, then the class struggle would necessitate Socialist support for exclusion legislation. At any rate, concluded the report, Asiatic labor was contract labor, and contract labor was opposed in the Stuttgart resolution. Therefore, the party could support the position of the International Socialist Congress and still oppose Asiatic immigration.[92]

The debate lasted two full days. Untermann was granted an hour to explain his resolution—the majority report. He began by stating that the immigration question gave the party an opportunity to show their European comrades that it was able to apply Marxist principles to the American situation. The law of self-preservation required the defense of American citizenry rather than the emphasis on "some ultimate ideal." Untermann granted that Marx had called on all workingmen to unite, but that did not mean they must all come to the United States. Asiatic immigration caused unemployment on the West Coast and was responsible for the increase in migratory labor. When workers were forced to leave their homes they lost their right to vote and soon deserted party locals for reactionary syndicalism.

Untermann insisted that racial differences were a product of evolution. If the different races were compelled to amalgamate, evolution would again reproduce exactly the same races "struggling with each other for survival." American experience with Negroes in the South proved that white Socialists could not work with Asiatics. "Wherever the negroes get control they stand aloof from the white men and will not work with them." Any attempt to combat "race prejudice" would be a betrayal of socialist principles.[93]

Spargo's reply to Untermann was less compromising than his resolution. He pointed out that the Industrial Workers of the World had been founded in the Midwest, not on the Pacific Coast. Wages on the West Coast were higher than on the East. If the ma-

<hr>

[92] *Ibid.*, pp. 77–80.          [93] *Ibid.*, pp. 83–92.

jority report was really concerned about immigrant economic competition, it should have recommended the exclusion of those who really "compete" with American labor in the mining, cigarmaking, and garment industries—the Italians, Sicilians, Russians, and Jews. But this was all nonsense, Spargo said. All immigrants were at first compelled to work for low wages. Revolutionary ardor was not limited to those whose forefathers landed at Plymouth Rock. "Big Bill" Haywood had told him that the experience of the Western Federation of Miners proved that the Japanese make fighting trade unionists. Let us put class consciousness above race consciousness, Spargo concluded: "If the Jap will carry the highest standard of civilization, if he will carry the Socialist banner where the white man fails, all hail the Jap; let him carry it for me." [94]

Morris Hillquit then rose and objected to the minority report because its principles were really the same as those of the majority. He pointed out that although the two reports disagreed as to the necessity of exclusion at present, both considered exclusion on the basis of race an acceptable principle. He therefore offered a substitute:

The Socialist Party of the United States favors all legislative measures tending to prevent the immigration of strike-breakers and contract laborers, and the mass immigration of workers from foreign countries brought about by the employing classes for the purpose of weakening of American labor, and of lowering the standard of life of American workers. [95]

Hillquit explained that restrictions on immigration should be based on potential harm to the labor movement and not on race, religion, or nationality. "Flights of imagination" such as future race wars should be left to Jules Verne. Hillquit concluded that since most Asiatic immigration was stimulated by capital, his resolution would automatically restrict it. [96]

The convention now found itself faced with three resolutions: a majority report openly calling for exclusion; a minority report holding that exclusion and immigration restriction were unnecessary because Asiatic immigration was small, but defending the principle of exclusion when necessary; a substitute denouncing the

[94] *Ibid.*, pp. 93–8.        [95] *Ibid.*, p. 98.        [96] *Ibid.*, pp. 98–100.

principle of racial exclusion but defending the practice on non-racial grounds. Spargo offered to withdraw his minority report in favor of Hillquit's substitute, but the chair ruled that it was the property of the convention.[97]

The debate was at least as bitter as that of the 1908 convention and lasted twice as long. Hillquit's substitute was immediately criticized by some members of the party Left wing as a specious attack on racism by "an intellectual attorney." These critics said the substitute really called for greater restrictions on immigration than did the minority report, which specified only contract labor as restrictable. It was a further betrayal of the working class to the reactionary policies of the American Federation of Labor.[98] A representative of one of the Scandinavian branches demanded to know whether, after party leaders had betrayed the principles of international brotherhood and the rights of man, rank and file Socialists were expected to remain in the party for the privilege of voting them into political office.[99] Thomas J. Morgan of Chicago charged that supporters of the majority report had encouraged Hillquit to prepare his substitute when they saw they could not pass their own resolution.[100]

Robert Hunter said he opposed further immigration because the party must always side with the working class. Nevertheless, he favored the Hillquit substitute because it "practically reaffirms the international position, yet enables us to do whatever is necessary to protect the class interests of the workers of America." [101] Meyer London of the New York Jewish Section, however, favored the Hillquit substitute because it rejected race as a basis for exclusion; racial exclusion violated an elementary principle of international socialism and in effect put the American party in a position of saying that those principles were correct in Germany, "the country of Marx, but . . . not good enough in the country of Berger, and Untermann and Wanhope. . . . Do not be such little politicians, in Heaven's name." [102]

[97] *Ibid.,* pp. 100–101.
[98] Fred H. Merrick (Pennsylvania) in *ibid.,* pp. 103–5; Tom Lewis (Oregon) in *ibid.,* pp. 141–42; Frank Cassidy (New York) in *ibid.,* pp. 126–27. Cassidy was a member of the A.F. of L. (*ibid.*).
[99] N. F. Holm (Scandinavian branch, Chicago) in *ibid.,* pp. 138–39.
[100] *Ibid.,* pp. 142–44.        [101] *Ibid.,* pp. 115–17.        [102] *Ibid.,* pp. 126–28.

Victor Berger defended the majority report. Hillquit, he said, was just "hiding behind a phrase." Berger insisted that Asiatic immigration was not merely a question of economics. All civilization was at stake. In this great issue, vowed Berger, "I will fight for my wife and children; I will fight for my neighbor's wife and children; I will fight for all your wives and children against this immigration." [103] Winfield Gaylord of Wisconsin added the plea of the practical politician to Berger's call to the defense of American womanhood. The standard of living, said Gaylord, could be raised only by correct use of the ballot, and correct use of the ballot meant voting the straight Socialist ticket. The purpose of this convention was to build a successful political party, and a successful political party must have homogeneity. Therefore, foreigners must be kept out.[104]

Algernon Lee of New York offered an amendment to Hillquit's substitute to the effect that since there was virtually no voluntary immigration of Asiatic workers, the American working class was justified in excluding them.[105] Hillquit denounced the amendment because it admitted the principle of racial exclusion. He confessed to having favored that principle himself at one time, but claimed to have been enlightened on the subject at the Stuttgart Congress. He then amended his own substitute so that support of legislation to prevent capitalist-encouraged "mass immigration" was changed to "mass importation," a change Thomas Morgan had challenged him to make. Hillquit then insisted that his substitute motion was nothing more nor less than a summary of the Stuttgart resolution.[106]

Spargo replied that Hillquit's motion emasculated the Stuttgart resolution and that in 1909 only four thousand Asiatics entered the country in contrast to hundreds of thousands of Europeans.[107] Untermann concluded the debate with a violent attack on the Industrial Workers of the World, whose supporters in the convention had led the fight against the majority report. All backward races must be excluded, said Untermann. As for the Asiatics who had already gotten in, they should "get out of America and give it back to the Americans." [108]

[103] *Ibid.*, pp. 118–21.　　[104] *Ibid.*, pp. 131–33.　　[105] *Ibid.*, p. 106.
[106] *Ibid.*, pp. 156–58.　　[107] *Ibid.*, pp. 158–62.　　[108] *Ibid.*, pp. 162–67.

Lee's amendment to Hillquit's substitute was overwhelmingly defeated on a roll call vote, 99 to 6.[109] The Hillquit resolution was then adopted, 55 to 50. A study of the vote indicates that defeat of the Lee amendment caused a number of the majority report supporters to vote for the Hillquit substitute as one which favored restricting immigration in practice even if rejecting exclusion in principle. On the other hand, many opponents of restriction and exclusion in both principle and practice voted against the Hillquit motion, apparently preferring Spargo's minority report, which accepted exclusion in principle but offered the least support to restrictions for the present.[110]

Eugene Debs was not a delegate to the 1910 Congress, but his bitter denunciation of all proposals to limit immigration received wide publicity in preparation for the next contest. Debs held that "if Socialism, international, revolutionary Socialism, does not stand staunchly, unflinchingly and uncompromisingly for the working class and for the exploited and oppressed masses of all lands, then it stands for none and its claim is a false pretense and its profession a delusion and a snare." He labeled the restriction and exclusion proposals as unsocialistic, reactionary, and outrageous, and suggested that, if any discrimination had to be shown in the question of immigration, it should be in favor of those races which have been most exploited. Exclusion, an obvious betrayal of socialist principles, would destroy the faith of the working class in the Socialist Party. "Upon this vital proposition I would take my stand against the world and no specious argument of subtle and sophistical defenders of the civic federation unionism who do not hesitate to sacrifice principle for numbers and jeopardise ultimate success for immediate gain, could move me to turn my back upon the oppressed." [111]

The Left wing of the party had not come to the 1910 Congress with an immigration resolution of its own. But the unsatisfactory alternatives presented to it by the Right wing caused the Left to resolve to settle the issue once and for all at the 1912 convention.[112]

---

[109] *Ibid.*, p. 167.  [110] *Ibid.*, p. 168.

[111] Letter from Eugene V. Debs to George D. Brewer, *International Socialist Review*, XI (July, 1910), 16–17.

[112] William English Walling, "Crisis in the Socialist Party," *The Independent*, LXX (May 6, 1912), 1047–51.

At that convention the majority [113] of the Committee on Immigration, with Untermann still acting as chairman, brought in a resolution which made the 1910 majority report seem pro-Asiatic in comparison. It called for the strengthening and strict enforcement of existing exclusion laws. It said race feeling was a product of biology and therefore could not be eradicated. Racial antagonism would persist under socialism and play an important part in economic life. "If it should not assert itself in open warfare under a Socialist form of society, it will nevertheless lead to a rivalry of races for expansion over the globe as a result of the play of natural and sexual selection." [114] Spargo's minority report simply called for an endorsement of the Stuttgart International Socialist Congress resolution on immigration.[115]

For the first time the issue was fairly drawn. But it was not to be decided. The resolutions were introduced in the closing hours of a convention in which the Right wing had won adoption of a constitutional amendment designed to bring about elimination of the entire Left wing. Non-Left wing supporters of the minority resolution found that the support they had given the opportunists on every other issue before the convention made it impossible to rally their forces for a last minute principled stand against chauvinism. Over the bitter protests of John Spargo and the Left-wing delegates, the Right wing voted to accept both reports and to continue the committee on which they had a majority. The 1910 resolution therefore remained the official party policy.[116] Spargo had sowed the winds of opportunism and reaped the whirlwind of chauvinism.

[113] The majority consisted of Untermann, Wanhope, J. Stitt Wilson (California), and Robert Hunter. The minority consisted of Spargo, Leo Laukki (Minnesota), and Meyer London (New York).

[114] Socialist Party, *Proceedings of the National Convention, 1912,* pp. 209–10.

[115] *Ibid.,* p. 211.          [116] *Ibid.,* pp. 166–67.

# XIV

# The Attack on
# Constructive Socialism

THE IMPETUS given to the growing unity of the Center
and Right-wing Socialist Party factions by the disappointing 1908
election returns was sufficiently great to put the new Right wing
or "constructive" faction in control of the national and a majority
of state party organizations by early 1909. But this victory of
constructive over revolutionary socialism did not produce the increase in Socialist strength and votes that its proponents so confidently expected. The Socialist vote continued to drop in the 1909
spring and fall elections.[1] And while membership increased slightly
during the first six months of 1909, it fell by one thousand during
the last six months. For the first time in party history both membership and receipts showed a decline.[2]

The sudden drop in membership was merely the culmination of
a long trend. The Center's practice of uttering revolutionary
slogans while engaging in opportunist tactics had begun to show
a marked increase as early as 1905. As party control shifted into
the hands of the Right wing, party locals found it increasingly
difficult to hold their membership. Algie Simons confessed that
thousands were attracted to the party by its propaganda but only
hundreds were held by its work.[3] Although about 150,000 people
were recruited between 1905 and 1909, party membership in 1909
stood at 41,000.[4]

[1] "Lack of Confidence," *New York Call*, Nov. 24, 1909.
[2] "Report of National Secretary Barnes to the National Executive Committee,"
*Socialist Party Official Bulletin*, Dec., 1909; "Annual Report of the National Secretary of the Socialist Party, January 1 to December 31, 1909," *Socialist Party Official Bulletin*, Jan., 1910.    [3] Quoted in *The Interior*, XL (Nov. 4, 1909), 1488.
[4] *Ibid.;* "What Is the Matter with the Socialist Party?" *International Socialist
Review*, X (Nov., 1909), 449–51.

The slump had been preceded by steady decline in party activity. Lethargy was temporarily overcome during the 1908 presidential campaign, but the failure to increase the Socialist vote returned most locals to an advanced stage of stagnation. If local activity was to consist of literature distribution in order to acquire votes, and if elections failed to produce those votes, local activity appeared to be pointless. Given the party's assumption that the real measure of success was election victory, comparatively feeble efforts in the direction of Socialist Sunday and Rand schools, intercollegiate societies, Christian Socialist Leagues, and attacks on immigration and the Industrial Workers of the World as goodwill gestures toward craft unionism could hardly compensate for a drop in election returns.

During 1909 and the first few months of 1910 the party press was flooded with articles and letters demanding to know "What's the matter with the Socialist Party?" [5] The *New York Call* placed the blame on the membership's "lack of confidence" in its leadership and in itself.[6] Party leaders attributed all difficulties to a lack of imagination and organization in the distribution of literature.[7] Proposals for constitutional reform as the path to renewed party vigor were legion. One national committeeman even suggested abolition of both the National and National Executive committees and the transaction of all national business through referendums as the means to democratize and invigorate the party.[8] Another attributed the lethargy to the "non-acquaintance of the Party membership with the doings and needs of the Socialist Party." She suggested that the national office publish an account of the activities of the various locals as a source of inspiration to the membership.[9] But when the *Weekly Bulletin* began to publish that information, the paucity of activity could hardly be described as an

---

[5] Letter from George Goebel (member of the National Executive Committee) to J. Mahlon Barnes, Feb. 24, 1910, *Socialist Party Weekly Bulletin*, Feb. 26, 1910.

[6] "Lack of Confidence," *New York Call*, Nov. 24, 1909.

[7] See above, p. 243–44.

[8] Letter from W. J. Bell to the *International Socialist Review*, X (Oct., 1909), 276–79. This proposal received sufficient local support to be put to a national referendum. It was defeated 9,318 to 2,334 (*Socialist Party Weekly Bulletin*, Feb. 11, 1910).

[9] Letter from National Committeewoman Carrie C. Block, Oklahoma, to J. Mahlon Barnes, April 23, 1910, *Socialist Party Weekly Bulletin*, April 30, 1910.

inspiration. Not one of the hundreds of articles, directives, and pleas that poured from the pens of Right-wing party functionaries suggested that it might take more than the written and spoken word of Socialist leaders to convince American voters that corruption could be ended and economic reforms enacted by throwing electoral support to the small Socialist Party rather than to the growing progressive wings of the Democratic and Republican parties.

The completion of the Right-Center alliance and the growing stagnation of party activity brought a renewed Left-wing attack on step-at-a-time socialist theories. Until 1908 the party Left wing was seriously handicapped by its lack of a press; the only newspaper of any importance through which it could express its views was *The Socialist*. The paper originated in Seattle in 1900 on a capital of $13 and with Herman Titus, a Seattle physician, as editor. For the first three years of its existence Titus served without pay and personally met all deficits.[10] By 1903 the circulation was 7,000, but Titus was bankrupt. For a time, shortages were covered by contributions from supporters in the Western Left-wing state and local organizations which had named it their official organ.[11] But in 1904 *The Socialist* attacked the "impossibilists" in the party as the other side of the opportunist coin and that group withdrew its support.[12]

*The Socialist* was forced to suspend at the end of 1904, but in March, 1905, publication was resumed in Toledo, Ohio, under the direction of Titus and William Mailly. Titus and Mailly insisted that American workers could not be tricked into voting for socialism. Only when they understood the theories of scientific socialism and realized that all capital was unpaid labor would they "rush together in an organization to gain possession of their own, the Machines of Production."[13]

Throughout its career *The Socialist* attacked Right-wing policies of diluting Marxian principles in an effort to win votes. Supported by the Left-wing Ohio locals, the paper rebuilt its circulation to 5,000. Economic difficulties continued to plague it, however,

[10] *The Socialist* (Seattle), May 24, 1903.
[11] *Ibid.*, July 19, 1903.
[12] "Shall 'The Socialist' Live or Die?" *The Socialist* (Seattle), June 26, 1904.
[13] Herman F. Titus, "Five Years of 'The Socialist,'" *The Socialist* (Toledo), Sept. 16, 1905.

and in 1906 Mailly, who suffered from ill health, left to become drama critic for the *New York Worker*. Titus then moved the paper to Idaho, where it took the lead in arousing the Socialist and labor movements against the threatened frame-up in the Moyer-Haywood-Pettibone kidnapping.[14] In 1907 *The Socialist* was back in Seattle where it continued as a spokesman for the Left until Titus and the Washington Left wing left the party in 1909.[15]

The paper struggled valiantly to give voice to Left-wing protests against the party's growing opportunism, but it had neither the funds nor the location essential to mass circulation. The periodical which finally became the national organ of the Left wing was a ten-cent monthly magazine published by Charles H. Kerr, the *International Socialist Review*. Kerr, the son of a University of Wisconsin professor of Greek literature,[16] was majority stockholder in Charles H. Kerr and Co., one of the two major socialist publishing houses.[17] He began publishing the *Review* in 1900. At that time Kerr believed that "the problems of social evolution must be deliberated on in advance by a select few of superior brain power, who should later on diffuse the results of the deliberations among the common masses." [18]

With A. M. Simons as editor, the *Review* was published to "educate the educators." [19] It quickly achieved a circulation of 4,000, comprising 3,000 subscriptions and 1,000 newsstand sales, and maintained that circulation for eight years.[20] In policy, the *Review* followed the changing ideology of its editor. Beginning with publication of theoretical articles by writers affiliated with the Center faction of the Socialist movement in Europe and America, the editorial line gradually shifted to the right until in January, 1908, its three major articles were "The Element of Faith in Marxian Socialism," "Economic Determinism and Martyrdom," and "Plan-

---

[14] See below, pp. 323–25.          [15] See below, pp. 373–74.
[16] Chaplin, *Wobbly*, p. 71.
[17] The other important publisher was the *Appeal to Reason*.
[18] Kerr in the *International Socialist Review*, IX (Jan., 1909), 559.
[19] "What the Review Has Done," *International Socialist Review*, XI (July, 1910), 46.
[20] Charles H. Kerr, "Help Make a Better Review," *International Socialist Review*, VIII (Feb., 1908), 510–11.

lessness of Production [and not surplus value] the Cause of Panics." [21]

While Simons was moving from the Center to the Right, his publisher was moving to the Left. Kerr "came to realize that the industrial wage-workers arrive from their daily experience at a clearer view of the class struggle than any mere theorist can possibly reach." [22] He determined to make the *Review* a magazine "of, by and for the working class" [23] and use its pages to spread "the propaganda of the revolution and the new industrial unionism." [24]

The growing disagreements between Simons and Kerr brought about the former's resignation in January, 1908. Kerr acted as his own editor for a short time,[25] and then turned the job over to Mary and Leslie Marcy. Mary Marcy had been private secretary to one of Chicago's big meat packers. Her *Letters of a Pork Packer's Stenographer*, published during the investigation of the packing industry which followed publication of *The Jungle*, brought her an immediate reputation as a muckraker. Her husband was a professional journalist.[26] Together they turned the *Review* into a militant Left-wing monthly which was in the thick of every major industrial dispute.

The *Review* urged two devices to end party lethargy: (1) put the party in the forefront of the fight for industrial unionism and all other economic struggles of the workers; (2) instruct members who won political office that their major job was "to hamper the ruling class in the war it will be waging on the revolutionary unions. With tactics like these, apathy will disappear, and the Socialist Party will for the first time become a vital force in the struggle between the capitalists and the wage-workers." [27] Within a year of

---

[21] *International Socialist Review*, VIII (Jan., 1908).

[22] "What the Review Has Done," *International Socialist Review*, XI (July, 1910), 46.

[23] *Ibid.*

[24] "What Is the Matter with the Socialist Party?" *International Socialist Review*, X (Nov., 1909), 451.

[25] Charles H. Kerr, "Help Make a Better Review," *International Socialist Review*, VIII (Feb., 1908), 510.

[26] Chaplin, *Wobbly*, p. 101; "What the Review Has Done," *International Socialist Review*, XI (July, 1910), 55.

[27] "What Is the Matter with the Socialist Party?" *International Socialist Review*, X (Nov., 1909), 451.

Simons's resignation *Review* circulation had leaped 300 percent.[28] By July, 1910, it had climbed to 27,000 and the format was changed to that of the popular illustrated magazines of the day.[29] In June, 1911, the *Review* had 60 pages, was selling 40,000 copies a month, and its circulation was still climbing.[30] Clearly, there were many who agreed with the *Review* that the Socialist Party and reform movements should differ over more than academic predictions concerning the nature of society in the next century.

According to the Left wing, the fundamental principle of the socialist movement was the class struggle.[31] The Left charged that the Socialist Party gave little more than lip service to that struggle. Even Right-wing leaders admitted, on occasion, that the party treated the class struggle as a mere phrase and failed to lead the workers in their daily battles.[32] The Left held that this failure would result in a sharp decline in party membership and vote as soon as middle-class supporters discovered that they could win their reforms through reform parties, and working-class members discovered that the party was of no use to them in their fight for better wages, hours, and working conditions. Massachusetts Socialists, who had seen their 1902 Congressional vote of 35,000 drop to less than 11,000 in 1908,[33] were told: "You are too tame, the spirit of '76 has departed from you. You submit, you don't fight, the Capitalists are not afraid of you and therefore your Proletarian army is not recruited." [34]

It was noted with considerable disgust by the Left that mention of the class struggle was avoided by virtually every leader who replied to the *Saturday Evening Post*'s query on how the party intended to achieve socialism.[35] Herman Titus estimated that not

[28] *International Socialist Review*, IX (Jan., 1909), 559.
[29] *Ibid.*, XI (July, 1910), 55.        [30] *Ibid.*, XII (July, 1911), 1.
[31] "Resolution of Marion County, Indiana Socialist Party Central Committee," *The Socialist Party Official Bulletin*, Feb., 1907; *The Socialist* (Seattle) Feb. 17, 1906.
[32] A. M. Simons, "Some General Tendencies," *International Socialist Review*, VIII (Sept., 1907), 180–81. Simons wrote this article on his return from the 1907 International Socialist Congress.
[33] "Socialist Gains and Losses," *International Socialist Review*, IX (Jan., 1909), 533.
[34] Herman F. Titus in *The Socialist* (Seattle), Nov. 21, 1908.
[35] Robin Ernest Dunbar, "A Conflict among Leaders," *International Socialist Review*, X (Aug., 1909), 149–51.

one third of the membership had any understanding of the principles of scientific socialism.[36] In August, 1909, the *New York Call* printed in its "letters to the editor column" a full-scale discussion as to the meaning of the class struggle. Most of the writers held that the class struggle was a social "fact" but denied that this entailed encouraging or teaching hatred. A minority suggested that recognition of this "fact" should not be a prerequisite to membership in the Socialist Party.

Louis Boudin, a New York attorney, replied for the Left wing. Marxian socialist parties, he wrote, cannot be satisfied "with a mere recognition of the class struggle," but must apply their understanding of this basic social force in leading the workers in their everyday struggles.[37] Frank Bohn of the I.W.W. and *International Socialist Review* was less gentle in his criticism of the constructive Socialists:

Some of our Socialists go into their closets and pray for a system of society the direct opposite of all that capitalism stands for, and then, coming into the open, drag out the decayed carcass of our Constitution and law, clothe it in the robes of divine right, and worship the rotten fabrics which a century and a quarter of American capitalism has despised and spit upon.

The interest of the working class, and the working class alone, must be the sole sanction of all party activity, said Bohn.[38]

The Left wing differed sharply with the Right over the question of constructive or step-at-a-time socialism. Herman Titus denounced the "holiday Socialism" of the Right wing, which emphasized the need to end "disproportionate fortunes" and planned to use the party to reconstruct "the proportionate fortunes" of the middle class. Titus held that socialism would not be won by making public servants of the proletariat as on Prussian railroads and in Russian tobacco factories, "but by the Proletarian constituting itself the Public Master and distributing wealth and power accord-

[36] Herman F. Titus, "Present Danger to Socialism," *The Socialist* (Seattle), Sept. 7, 1907.

[37] Louis B. Boudin, "The Class Struggle and the Mission of the Working Class," *New York Call*, Sept. 21, 1909.

[38] Frank Bohn, "The Future of the Socialist Party in the Light of the Milwaukee Victory," an address delivered at the Collectivist Society Dinner, New York City, May 26, 1910, *New York Call*, May 29, 1910.

ing to its own will." [39] C. W. Barzee, Left-wing National Committeeman from Oregon, declared that America could not "have Constructive Socialism as long as a *profit* system instead of a *use* system continues to order our social relations." Step-at-a-time socialism under capitalism was a contradiction in terms, said Barzee. Before construction of a socialist society could begin,[40] workers, acting through the Socialist Party, would have to seize the powers of government and end the profit system.

Louis Boudin attacked the foundation of all Right-wing socialist theory. Constructive Socialists, he wrote, assumed that the working class was already in possession of full political power because of its right to participate in the election of government officials. Therefore, they believed that all the party had to do was to coax workers to use their political power for the purpose of nationalizing the great monopolies. This would constitute the gradual coming of socialism.

Such theory was superstitious nonsense, according to Boudin. In his opinion the capitalist class owned full title to the state. It used all state powers, and particularly the courts which had usurped the right to judge the constitutionality of legislative enactments,[41] to continue its rule. The working class, therefore, must not simply be urged to use the political powers it already had in democratic theory, but must be led by the Socialist Party in a fight for overthrow of capitalist institutions and for possession of real political power. This fight for power would be carried on to some extent in parliamentary assemblies, Boudin granted. But extra-parliamentary struggle would be necessary to provide the force to back up electoral decisions. Until the party divested itself of its superstitious belief that the capitalist state had already endowed the working class with full political powers which that class had only to use in order to mount the steps to socialism, the Socialist

[39] Herman F. Titus, "Bourgeois Socialism," *The Socialist* (Seattle), Jan. 16, 1909. Titus' article was in reply to an outline of the methods and goals of constructive socialism as presented in Charles Edward Russell's "The Growing Menace of Socialism," *Hampton's Broadway Magazine*, XXII (Jan., 1909), 119–26.

[40] C. W. Barzee, "Revolutionary Program," *The Socialist* (Seattle), May 8, 1909.

[41] Some twenty years later Boudin published his two-volume *Government by Judiciary* (New York, William Godwin, Inc., 1932), a study designed to prove his early hypothesis that American courts had usurped political power.

Party would be unable to mobilize and lead the proletariat in its fight for freedom.[42]

The relation of the state to foreign policy was apparently of no concern to Right-wing Socialists, and received little more attention from the Left. In the days when the Spanish-American war and possession of the Philippines were being debated by McKinley and Bryan, socialist literature made an occasional reference to imperialism as an inevitable capitalist drive for markets and raw materials. But after the 1900 election even Theodore Roosevelt's Big Stick failed to elicit any response from the party. Imperialism and war apparently were considered insignificant next to such burning socialist questions as graft, vice, and corruption.

At the 1910 International Socialist Congress, a resolution was adopted instructing the International Bureau to take any steps necessary to unite working-class action in the threat of war. French and English socialists, supported by Bill Haywood of the Left wing, sought to amend the resolution to include a recommendation of the general strike as a means of resistance to war. The amendment was killed by opposition of the German delegation.[43] Since Victor Berger supported Germany's opposition to the amendment, Haywood demanded to know whether he represented the American or German working class. What Berger replied is unknown, but after the first World War Haywood commented that Berger "might have answered 'neither' quite truthfully." [44]

In April, 1911, the Socialist Party took one of its rare looks at American foreign policy when its executive committee passed a resolution entering "public and emphatic protest" against government support of the Mexican dictatorship of Porfirio Diaz.[45] Seventeen months later Bill Haywood, as a member of the National Executive Committee, noted the worsening relations between the

---

[42] Louis B. Boudin, "The Political Situation in the United States and the Socialist Party," New York Call, Oct. 24, 31, 1909.

[43] Emil Stultz, "The Eighth International Socialist Congress," International Socialist Review, XI (Oct., 1910), 231–32; William E. Bohn, "The International Congress," International Socialist Review, XI (Oct., 1910), 234–39; Haywood, Bill Haywood's Book, 232–33.

[44] Haywood, Bill Haywood's Book, pp. 232–33.

[45] "Proclamation by the National Executive Committee of the Socialist Party of America," International Socialist Review, XI (April, 1911), 585–88.

United States and Mexico and introduced a resolution calling on
the party to mobilize the working class, including preparations
for a possible general strike to prevent a war designed to suppress
"fellow revolutionists." Haywood charged that Mexican revolutionaries "might be in a far better position today if the Socialist
Party had not steadily refused to do its duty." He asked that the
party expel any member who participated in an aggressive war,
including military campaigns against Mexico and Nicaragua.

Hillquit opposed the resolution as devoid of substance, loose in
reasoning, and false in its recital of facts. He was opposed to a
general strike in principle, and even if this were not the case, the
Mexicans could not be considered fellow revolutionaries because
many of them were reactionary. John Spargo added his protest
against Haywood's "monstrous" and "unwarranted attack" on
the party. He pointed out that in the preceding five years "several
ringing resolutions" against war had been adopted by various Socialist bodies. He suggested that it was time to stop "those who
continuously slander and misrepresent the party from the inside."
Haywood's resolution was defeated, three to two, with two abstentions.[46]

Among those who engaged in "monstrous" attacks upon the
party policy of winning political office so that the state could conduct the gradual inauguration of socialism, few were as effective
between 1905 and 1910 as Jack London. London first achieved national Socialist prominence in 1903 when *Wilshire's Magazine* ran
his *The People of the Abyss* in serial form.[47] At first, Right-wing
leaders pointed with pride to this prominent writer who belonged
to the Socialist Party. But in 1906 London began a nation-wide
lecture tour of colleges, universities, and public rallies under the
auspices of the Intercollegiate Socialist Society.[48] His lecture
was entitled "Revolution," and its vigorous attack on capitalism,
coupled with its emphasis on the primary role of the working class
and the secondary role of the middle class, brought rising protests
from constructive socialists.[49] These ranged from J. G. Phelps

[46] Letter from National Secretary John Work to the National Executive Committee, Sept. 26, 1912, *The Socialist Party Monthly Bulletin,* Oct., 1912.

[47] Philip Foner, *Jack London,* p. 52.

[48] *Ibid.,* pp. 72–73, 77–78.

[49] Letter from Jack London to H. Gaylord Wilshire, *Wilshire's Magazine,* X

Stokes's introduction of London at a large New York rally with the comment that he and other Socialists did not agree with London's analysis,[50] to the *Social-Democratic Herald*'s edict that London should stop foaming at the mouth.[51] Right-wing criticism did not stop London from continuing to give the lecture, or prevent the Left wing from making it one of its most popular pamphlets.[52]

Perhaps the Left wing's most effective single piece of propaganda was London's novel, *The Iron Heel*, first published in 1907. The novel purports to be a manuscript discovered in the Fourth Century of the Era of Brotherhood. It describes the efforts of its hero, Ernest Everhard, to convince his fellow socialist leaders that while they talked of victory at the polls a capitalist oligarchy, the Iron Heel, was destroying American democracy. The Socialist leaders remain unconvinced and in 1912 the Iron Heel begins its destruction of the labor movement, the Socialist Party, and all democratic institutions. London's "manuscript," a remarkable precursor of the rise of fascism, breaks off in 1932 at a time when the Iron Heel has successfully crushed the first socialist revolution, but with a second revolt already in the process of organization.

As might be expected, London's novel did not meet with critical acclaim in the non-Socialist press. But its reception by Right-wing Socialist leaders was also less than lukewarm.[53] John Spargo expressed the viewpoint of constructive socialism when he granted that the book was an "ingenious and stirring romance." But Spargo said he could not agree with the (Left-wing) Socialists who hailed it as a "great addition to the literature of Socialist propaganda." The trouble with *The Iron Heel*, according to Spargo, was that it painted a picture

well calculated . . . to repel many whose addition to our forces is sorely needed; it gives a new impetus to the old and generally discarded cataclysmic theory; it tends to weaken the political Socialist move-

---

(April, 1906), 6; letter from Allan L. Benson to the *Social-Democratic Herald*, Feb. 10, 1906.

[50] Foner, *Jack London*, p. 77.

[51] *Social-Democratic Herald*, Feb. 3, 1906.

[52] It was this lecture which popularized the custom among party members of beginning their letters with "Dear Comrade" and closing them with "Yours for the Revolution."

[53] Foner, *Jack London*, pp. 95–96.

ment by discrediting the ballot and to encourage the chimerical and reactionary notion of physical force, so alluring to a certain type of mind.[54]

A few years later London answered his Right-wing critics by re-affirming his belief in political campaigns as a means of educating workers. But, he continued, "history shows that no master class is ever willing to let go without a quarrel. The capitalists own the government, the armies and the militia. Don't you think the capitalists will use these institutions to keep themselves in power? I do." [55]

London's last contribution to the Left wing was his "Dream of Debs," published by the *International Socialist Review* in 1910 and then issued as one of the most widely circulated of all socialist pamphlets.[56] It is the story of a successful nation-wide general strike as seen through the eyes of the rich. Since, in the "Dream of Debs," the American Federation of Labor has been destroyed by its reactionary leaders and the strike is won by an industrial union modeled after the I.W.W., London's point was not difficult to grasp.

The Left wing vigorously protested what they considered the abandonment of revolutionary socialism by Right-wing leaders in their efforts to win votes and elect candidates. Debs charged that Socialist principles were being diluted and that party propaganda was being designed as a "bait for votes" instead of as a means of educating the working class in principles of revolutionary socialism.[57] "Voting for socialism," said Debs, "is not socialism any more than a menu is a meal." [58] The Left wing viewed the prospect of Socialists winning political office "by an opportunist and muddle-headed vote" as the worst calamity that could befall the party.[59] Socialism could not replace capitalism while workers supported a profit economy, no matter who might be elected to office; "nei-

[54] John Spargo in the *International Socialist Review*, VIII (April, 1908), 629.
[55] Quoted in Foner, *Jack London*, p. 96.
[56] *International Socialist Review*, IX (Jan.–Feb., 1910), 481–89, 561–70.
[57] Eugene V. Debs, "Danger Ahead," *International Socialist Review*, XI (Jan., 1911), 413.
[58] *Ibid.*, p. 414.
[59] *Wage Slave* (Michigan), quoted most unfavorably by the *Social-Democratic Herald*, Nov. 14, 1908.

ther capitalism nor collectivism is an automatic machine independent of people's feelings and wishes. The workers will not take control of industry until they desire to do so." [60] Capitalism could not be overthrown by Socialists who won elections on platforms calling for nationalization of the railroads and an end to graft and corruption.[61] And while the party wasted its energies in electioneering that promised an easy, inevitable, and imperceptible "transition into the Millennium," [62] it neglected the economic struggles of the workers. It was no wonder, said the Left, that the party was without close ties to the labor movement.[63]

Debs publicly commented that he was unsuited for political office and would not run for President if there were the slightest chance of being elected. "We want a majority of Socialists, not of votes," he told Lincoln Steffens. "There would be no use getting into power with a people that did not understand; with a lot of office-holders undisciplined by service in the party; unpurged, by personal sacrifice, of the selfish spirit of the present system." [64] The Socialist Party should seek only the votes of those who knew they were voting for revolutionary socialism, the Left said. When the party had educated the workers in principles of scientific socialism and organized them into industrial unions, then and only then would it be ready to take power.[65] And that Socialist victory would not be just another step forward along the path of social progress, a step so small and taken so gradually that few would even notice that it had occurred, said Herman Titus. It "will be a revolution that will even disturb our Capitalist or Puritan grandmothers in their very graves." [66]

Of course, many Right-wing Socialists now accepted Carl Thompson's definition of socialism as simply public ownership of

[60] "Educate, Organize," *International Socialist Review*, IX (Aug., 1908), 141.

[61] Louis B. Boudin, "Prospects of a Labor Party in the United States," *International Socialist Review*, X (April, 1910), 919–20.

[62] Herman F. Titus, "Bourgeois Socialism," *The Socialist* (Seattle), Jan. 16, 1909.

[63] Louis B. Boudin, "Prospects of a Labor Party in the United States," *International Socialist Review*, X (April, 1910), 919–20.

[64] Eugene Debs quoted by Lincoln Steffens, "Eugene V. Debs on What the Matter Is in America and What to Do about It," *Everybody's Magazine*, XIX (Oct., 1908), 458.

[65] Eugene V. Debs, "Danger Ahead," *International Socialist Review*, XI (Jan., 1911), 414–15.

[66] Herman F. Titus, "Bourgeois Socialism," *The Socialist* (Seattle), Jan. 16, 1909.

public utilities and the progressive improvement of conditions of mental and manual labor.[67] Therefore, they could not understand the Left wing's insistence that socialism could not be brought by a capitalist government through piecemeal purchase of the natural monopolies and passage of social-reform legislation. Among the steps toward public ownership already taken in America, Thompson listed the post office, public school system, roads, bridges, parks, life-saving stations, armies, navies, courts, police and fire departments.[68] The Left wing sarcastically described these socialist steps as

succeeding each other in a helter-skelter, ambling over hurdles, breasting storms, fording rivers, tripping over swamps and spinning over mountain peaks, . . . while state, federal and foreign governments vie with each other in establishing public ownership, better wages, and shorter workdays, all serenely innocent of the fact that they are hastening the dawn of Socialism.[69]

Thompson's inclusion of the army, navy, courts, and police as socialist establishments indicates the unbridgeable gap between the revolutionary and constructive wings of the party.

The Left wing sharply criticized the 1912 railroad nationalization bill introduced by Victor Berger, then Congressman from Milwaukee. Berger's plan provided for purchase of the nation's railroads at a physical valuation to be determined by twelve Congressmen. The Left held that these measures were designed to "unload" unprofitable trusts, sell profitable ones at high prices, or bring lower prices to small businessmen. Since striking against government-owned or controlled railroads, mines, and other heavy industries would be characterized as treason, nationalization would cripple the labor movement in just those industries in which a strike "would be most injurious to all capitalists." [70]

[67] Thompson, *Constructive Program of Socialism*, p. 8. Thompson's book received the unofficial endorsement of the party's national office when *Socialist Party Official Bulletin* gave it advertising and publicity—thus breaking its practice of never giving support to propaganda not published or commissioned by the national organization (*Socialist Party Official Bulletin*, March, 1908).

[68] Thompson, *Constructive Program of Socialism*, p. 19.

[69] Joseph E. Cohen, "Constructive Socialism," *International Socialist Review*, IX (Aug., 1908), 85.

[70] William English Walling, "Government Ownership," *International Socialist Review*, XII (April, 1912), 652–54.

The constructive Socialists cited the lower gas rates the Socialist administration had brought to Haverhill, Massachusetts, some ten years before.[71] The revolutionaries replied that since the Socialists had been thrown out of office in two years, despite this "marvelous victory" against the gas company, such examples might better be used as "meat for another chapter on the ingratitude of republics" than as a guide for party tactics.[72] The Left wing granted that national and municipal ownership was more efficient than a system of privately owned monopolies. But nationalization was a step which the capitalists themselves were quite competent to take. The question of concern to the Socialist Party was not how to get the government to purchase trusts, but how to lead the working class in the struggle for political power.[73]

Although they always emphasized that no reform would eliminate surplus value,[74] a majority of the revolutionary wing of the party did not oppose the listing of or fighting for "immediate demands" as such. But they rejected nationalization, trust regulation, and honest government as immediate demands of no concern to the working class.[75] Left-wing city and state platforms made clear their position that socialism could not be won piecemeal. But they frequently listed a series of demands designed to aid the working class in its struggles against its employers. The 1908 Washington state platform, for example, called for abolition of labor injunctions, an eight-hour day and a 44-hour week, abolition of child labor, reduction of residence requirements for voting, the initiative and referendum, freedom of speech and press, and equal suffrage for men and women.[76]

The Left wing contended that reforms of value to the workers could not be won by watering down the Socialist program so as to

[71] Thompson, *Constructive Program of Socialism*, p. 18.

[72] Joseph E. Cohen, "Constructive Socialism," *International Socialist Review*, IX (Aug., 1908), 85.

[73] "Winning Socialist Tactics," *International Socialist Review*, XIII (Dec., 1912), 495–96.

[74] *International Socialist Review*, XI (Sept., 1910), 180.

[75] C. W. Barzee, "Revolutionary Program," *The Socialist* (Seattle), May 8, 1909; Henry L. Slobodin, "What's the Matter with Wisconsin?" *International Socialist Review*, X (Feb., 1910) 688; Herman F. Titus, "Convention Notes," *The Socialist* (Seattle), May 23, 1908; Joseph E. Cohen, "Constructive Socialism," *International Socialist Review*, IX (Aug., 1908), 82.

[76] *The Socialist* (Seattle), July 10, 1908.

elect Socialist officials with middle-class votes. Rather, they could be attained only through organizing industrial unions and educating the working class to register a protest vote for socialism. This growing protest vote would force concessions from the capitalist political parties.[77] The Left wing pointed out that in Cleveland, Ohio, where the party followed the principles of revolutionary socialism, more legislation favorable to labor had been passed than in Milwaukee.[78] Wisconsin, despite the fact that it led the country in electing Socialist aldermen and members of the state legislature on the basis of pledges of middle-class reform, did not enforce employer's liability, limit the "fellow servant" doctrine, restrict company stores, void contracts which waived employee's rights to damages for personal injuries, set maximum hours and minimum wages on public works, provide workmen's compensation for government employees, require the union label on government printing, or provide time for workers to vote. Henry Slobodin of the New York Left wing commented: "We all want practical results. . . . Measured and tested before the forum of results, the Wisconsin ideas and methods are the most impractical, the most visionary, ever promulgated by a responsible Socialist organization." [79]

Not all revolutionary Socialists considered it worthwhile for the party to concern itself with day-to-day interests of the working class. And some Left wingers who were prominent in the fight for higher wages, maximum hours, and labor legislation, on occasion dismissed all activity on behalf of better working and living conditions under capitalism as a waste of time. The *International Socialist Review*, for example, saw no contradiction in giving militant support to all labor struggles while at the same time printing editorials holding that wages must rise and fall with the cost of living.[80] The *Review* also periodically reminded its readers that no reform could be of much use to the working class. The *Review* said

[77] Eugene V. Debs, "What a Million Votes for the Socialist Party Will Mean," pp. 5–9; C. W. Barzee, "Revolutionary Program," *The Socialist* (Seattle), May 8, 1909; Joseph E. Cohen, "Constructive Socialism," *International Socialist Review*, IX (Aug., 1908), 91; *International Socialist Review*, XI (Sept., 1910), 180.

[78] Joseph E. Cohen, "Constructive Socialism," *International Socialist Review*, IX (Aug., 1908), 82.

[79] Henry L. Slobodin, "What's the Matter with Wisconsin?" *International Socialist Review*, X (Feb., 1910), 687–88.

[80] "Suppose Everything Were Reformed!" *International Socialist Review*, XI (Oct., 1910), 241.

the party should devote itself to teaching the theory of surplus value so that workers will not be diverted by political battles staged to determine whether large or small capitalists would keep the wealth created by labor. Once workers grasped the theory of surplus value, they would use their industrial unions and Socialist Party to take possession of all products of social labor.[81]

One working-class Socialist, speaking for a usually inarticulate section of the Left wing, insisted that proletarian Socialists, in contrast to their middle-class comrades, had only one immediate demand—abolition of capitalism. "We proletarians have no time to waste on" women's suffrage, three-cent fares, and public work for the unemployed. "We proletarians are tired; we want a rest; we want to stop feeding, clothing and sheltering those ingrates who murder, starve and jail us outlawed proletarians . . . we want Socialism." [82] The number of Left-wing Socialists who proposed to work for nothing short of the immediate triumph of socialism was probably small. Most revolutionary Socialists, however, thought that improved conditions for the workers could be won through industrial unions rather than through parliamentary action.[83] And while the Washington state platform listed legislative demands, the Left-wing San Francisco and Oregon platforms followed the more common revolutionary Socialist practice of simply pledging to use the city and state governments to support the working class in all its struggles.[84]

The Left wing insisted that their emphasis on revolutionary principles was not only vital to future Socialist victory, but frequently brought immediate returns in the form of a high, uncompromising Socialist vote. Thus, after the disappointing 1908 election in which many former Socialist Party supporters had switched to Bryan, the Left was quick to point out that those states which had made the most strenuous efforts to attract the reform vote had either seen their vote drop sharply, as in Massachusetts, Illinois,

[81] "Stick to the Main Issue," *International Socialist Review,* IX (April, 1909), 803–4.
[82] Charles O. Kohler, "Serious Thoughts," *International Socialist Review,* IX (June, 1909), 1013.
[83] See below, pp. 312–17.
[84] "Oregon State Platform," *The Socialist* (Seattle), April 11, 1908; "Municipal Platform of Local San Francisco," *International Socialist Review,* X (Oct., 1909), 375–76.

Iowa, Kansas, and Nebraska, or had barely held their own, as in Wisconsin. On the other hand, those states which had emphasized the revolutionary nature of the Socialist program—Pennsylvania, Michigan, Minnesota, Idaho, and Colorado—had made the greatest electoral gains.[85] The Left claimed that this applied to agricultural as well as industrial states, mentioning the proportionately high vote registered in Texas, Oklahoma, and Arkansas after a Left-wing election campaign.[86] Moreover, in the state of Washington, where the national office was backing Right-wing attempts to expel Titus and the Left-wing majority,[87] the party had again polled the highest Socialist vote in proportion to population—8.8 percent.[88] Finally, the Left pointed with considerable triumph to the figures released at the end of 1908 which indicated that Left-wing states had scored the greatest increases in party membership.[89]

The emphasis placed on recruiting small businessmen, professionals, and ministers and the leading roles assigned to members of these groups in the party organization were sharply criticized by the revolutionary Socialists. Since the party was anxious to establish its respectability as a prerequisite to winning middle-class votes, it publicized the conversion of writers, lecturers, ministers, and lawyers. This publicity was followed by paid lecture and writing assignments for the new recruits. Then, when elections to city, state, and national party committees took place, it was only natural that the membership elected their most famous recruits. Consequently, the party of the working class was increasingly represented on its policy-making bodies by professionals whose

[85] A comparison of 1904 and 1908 Socialist vote is taken from *The Worker*, Feb. 19, 1905, and the *Social-Democratic Herald*, March 15, 1913:

|               | 1904   | 1908   |              | 1904   | 1908   |
|---------------|--------|--------|--------------|--------|--------|
| Massachusetts | 13,604 | 10,781 | Wisconsin    | 28,270 | 28,164 |
| Illinois      | 69,225 | 34,711 | Colorado     | 4,954  | 6,400  |
| Iowa          | 14,847 | 8,287  | Idaho        | 4,304  | 7,974  |
| Kansas        | 15,494 | 12,240 | Michigan     | 8,911  | 11,586 |
| Nebraska      | 7,412  | 3,524  | Pennsylvania | 21,863 | 38,913 |

[86] "Socialist Gains and Losses," *International Socialist Review*, XI (Jan., 1909), 533–34; *The Socialist* (Seattle), Dec. 19, 1908.

[87] See below, pp. 373–74.

[88] *The Socialist* (Seattle), Dec. 19, 1908.

[89] Arthur Jensen, "Come On Up, Wisconsin," *The Socialist* (Seattle), Jan. 16, 1909.

comparatively recent conversion to socialism had been accomplished through propaganda stressing devotion to reform.[90]

Many of these middle-class Socialist leaders, labeled "intellectuals" by the Left wing, found that their prominence in the party at a time when the progressive movement was on the rise in America enhanced rather than diminished their popularity as lecturers, magazine writers, and after-dinner speakers. Few took any part in the routine work of the locals, but they soon came to look upon themselves as the master strategists of the socialist movement. When their plans were challenged or rejected, they attacked their opponents as working-class "chumps" who failed to recognize that college-trained intelligence and "efficient brains" were necessary for leadership in the Socialist Party.[91]

The arrogance displayed by the "intellectuals" toward the working class members of the party, the triumphant claims made by Right-wing leaders that professionals and small businessmen were "represented very largely" among the party membership,[92] and the candid opportunism of party policy convinced the Left wing that party membership and policy must be revamped from top to bottom. The revolutionaries were willing to grant that middle-class Socialists were intelligent. But, they held, this intelligence was employed to further middle-class, not working-class, interests. The Left said the place for middle-class reformers engaged in the hopeless task of trying to preserve their privileges in a monopoly economy was in the camp of Tom Watson, William Jennings Bryan, and William Randolph Hearst.[93] Those who had learned that re-

[90] Letter from Henry L. Slobodin to the *New York Call*, Nov. 28, 1909; letter from Robert Hunter to the *Social-Democratic Herald*, Dec. 9, 1911.

[91] Letters from W. J. Ghent to *The Worker*, Nov. 23, Dec. 14, 1907; letter from Morris Hillquit to *The Worker*, March 14, 1908; letter from Frances M. Gill, member of the New York General Committee, to *The Worker*, Nov. 30, 1907; "Resolution of Local New York General Committee," *The Worker*, Dec. 21, 1907; Charles Dobbs, "Brains," *International Socialist Review*, VIII (March, 1908), 533–37; Robert Rives LaMonte, "Efficient Brains versus Bastard Culture," *International Socialist Review*, VIII (April, 1908), 634–37; letter from Henry L. Slobodin to the *New York Call*, Nov. 28, 1909; Carl D. Thompson, "Who Constitute the Proletariat?" *International Socialist Review*, IX (Feb., 1909), 603–11.

[92] Spargo, *Socialism*, 1913 ed., p. 169.

[93] Louis Duchez, "The Proletarian Attitude," *International Socialist Review*, IX (April, 1909), 788; Fred L. Schwartz, "A Proletarian Movement," *International Socialist Review*, IX (Feb., 1909), 627; Charles H. Kerr, "The Work of the Convention," *International Socialist Review*, VIII (May, 1908), 701; "Socialism Becoming Respectable," *International Socialist Review*, IX (June, 1909), 995–97.

form was hopeless might join the Socialist Party, but to learn, not to teach. "One cannot in an instant or a year rid oneself of the mental habits ingrained by a lifetime of sycophancy and vampiredom." [94]

The Left said the Socialist Party must be a working-class political organization. Its aim was to educate and organize the proletariat for the winning of political power. It was the political expression of the class struggle, not of Christian brotherhood or "good government." [95] Local Duluth, Minnesota, charged that as things now stood the Socialist Party was

being "Catspawed" and "Lickspittled" by every leech and parasite who has found ingress into the organized political movement that is supposed to represent the working class. Unfrocked priests, pulpitless ministers, quack doctors, clientless lawyers, bankrupted business men, plagiaristic litterateurs, and plain and easy spongers are fast making the movement famous as the hope and sinecure for freaks and fakers of every description and class.[96]

The brotherhood-of-man propaganda and the party policies of municipal reform and trust nationalization were neither bringing socialism nor attracting the support of the industrial proletariat, the Left claimed. They had been formulated by businessmen anxious to protect their capital, reformers unable to break with bourgeois ideals, editors bent upon increased circulation and salaries, and party functionaries craving the rewards of political office.[97] Party leaders strutted "about in Middle Class plumage as if the Proletariat were only common barnyard fowl to lay eggs for bourgeois roosters to cackle over." [98]

The Left declared that the proletariat would furnish its own political and intellectual leaders. They might not have the questionable advantage of a college education, but they would have

[94] Robert Rives LaMonte, "The American Middle Class," *The Arena,* XXXIX (April, 1908), 439.

[95] Charles E. Ruthenberg in the *New York Call,* July 30, 1912.

[96] "Resolution of Local Duluth, Minnesota, December 19, 1911," *The Socialist Party Monthly Bulletin,* Jan., 1912.

[97] Louis Duchez, "The Proletarian Attitude," *International Socialist Review,* IX (April, 1909), 792; "Socialism Becoming Respectable," *International Socialist Review,* IX (June, 1909), 995–97.

[98] Herman F. Titus, "Socialism Harnessed or Unharnessed," *The Socialist* (Seattle), Aug. 22, 1908.

learned from their daily life the facts of the class struggle and economic determinism.[99] Every day they witnessed unemployment and poverty contrasted with overproduction and wealth and therefore needed no metaphysical investigation of the truths of scientific socialism in which intellectual leaders were perpetually engaged. The revolutionaries found that socialist propaganda written by intellectuals concerned itself with answering the objections of members of their own class. They claimed that the proletariat was not interested in whether socialism would end graft, kill incentive, break up the family, or destroy religion. Nor was it concerned about the "spiritual significance of socialism." [100] Proletarian propaganda would be directed at arousing class consciousness and strengthening class solidarity in the industrial unions and the Socialist Party.[101]

Some members of the Left wing reacted so strongly to the growing middle-class character of the party that they proposed to limit membership to the proletariat. The class struggle was the basic fact of life. Historical materialism meant that capitalists and workers stood with "hands raised with daggers to plunge in each others breasts on the economic field"; [102] it was ridiculous to expect them to unite on the political field. "The millionaire, petty bourgeois and ministers" joined the party for two reasons only: either they hoped "to sidetrack the revolutionary proletarian" or they were moved by some vague feeling of sympathy. The "sidetrackers" were obviously not qualified for membership, and the "sympathizers" should not have voice or vote "in the councils of the revolutionary movement." [103]

Even this limitation was not enough for Thomas Sladden, state secretary of the party in Oregon. Obviously influenced by the migratory workers of the Northwest, Sladden defined proletariat

[99] Robert Rives LaMonte, "Efficient Brains versus Bastard Culture," *International Socialist Review*, VIII (April, 1908), 634–37.

[100] A reference to a series of lectures delivered by John Spargo in the Christian Socialist tradition. They were published as *The Spiritual Significance of Modern Socialism.*

[101] Louis Duchez, "The Proletarian Attitude," *International Socialist Review*, IX (April, 1909), 788–93; Charles E. Ruthenberg in the *New York Call*, July 30, 1912.

[102] Thomas Sladden, "The Revolutionist," *International Socialist Review*, IX (Dec., 1908), 425.

[103] Fred L. Schwartz, "A Proletarian Movement," *International Socialist Review*, IX (Feb., 1909), 627–28.

to exclude everyone but the unskilled laborer. The skilled worker was really an artisan because he owned his skill. The proletarian, on the other hand, "has no shops, mills, mines, factories or farms. He has no profession, no trade and no property. He has no home— no country—no religion. He has little education, no manners, and little care for what people think of him. . . . But upon his shoulders rests the problem of freeing society." [104]

Comparatively few members of the Left wing were willing to accept Sladden's definition.[105] But all were agreed that there were too many ministers, intellectuals, professionals, and businessmen in positions of leadership in the socialist movement.[106] The question was how to get them out. The looseness of the national structure, the privately owned press, the practice of admitting everyone to party membership who applied regardless of his interpretation of socialist principles, and the firm grip of the Right wing on the party machinery would have made it difficult to transform the party even if the revolutionaries had the support of a majority of the membership, which they apparently did not.

Herman Titus, as a result of his experiences in Washington factional fights, began to formulate a theory of party organization in 1908 which would have prevented members from riding their individual hobby horses down the road to socialism. He held that the purpose of the party was to secure united action, and that the present loose organization did not meet the requirements of a successful revolutionary socialist movement. It was ridiculous, he said, to permit the Chicago revolutionary and constructive Socialists to engage in continuous civil war while the movement collapsed. The party must decide whether it would base itself on a reform or revolutionary program, and then build an organization that acted on its principles. This, he said, was the reason for the success of both

[104] Thomas Sladden, "The Revolutionist," *International Socialist Review*, IX (Dec., 1908), 423–30.

[105] Herman Titus, under whose guidance Sladden had developed, considered Sladden's article a good antidote for the reform theories that dominated the party. But as for his definition of proletariat, Titus held "the limitation of this term to 'Unskilled Labor' to be un-Marxian, unscientific, confusing and tending to introduce new and unwarranted factions into our ranks." (Herman F. Titus in *The Socialist* [Seattle], Dec. 19, 1908.)

[106] Letter from William C. Green, former state secretary of Florida, to *The Socialist* (Seattle), Feb. 20, 1909.

the Washington and Wisconsin parties.[107] Right-wing party leaders apparently agreed within limits, for they succeeded in eliminating a good part of the Washington Left wing early in 1909.

Other demands by revolutionary locals for a tighter structure which would enforce principles of scientific socialism were ignored.[108] Left-wing Socialists realized that as the program veered more and more toward reform, middle-class recruits would increase in numbers.[109] They consoled themselves, however, with the thought that "captains of industry are making revolutionists faster than professors and editors can make reformers. And when revolutionists shape the policy of the Socialist Party, reformers will find little in it to attract them." [110]

[107] Herman F. Titus in *The Socialist* (Seattle), Aug. 1, 1908; Herman F. Titus, "Our Ninth Year," *The Socialist* (Seattle), Aug. 15, 1908; Herman F. Titus, "Socialist Organization," *The Socialist* (Seattle), Aug. 29, 1908.

[108] "Resolution of Local Duluth, Minnesota," *The Socialist Party Monthly Bulletin,* Jan., 1912.

[109] Letter from Charles E. Ruthenberg to the *New York Call,* July 30, 1912.

[110] "Socialism Becoming Respectable," *International Socialist Review,* IX (June, 1909), 997.

# XV

# Industrial Socialism

SINCE MIDDLE-CLASS "REFORMERS" controlled the party machinery by 1909, the Left wing formulated a theory and program which by its very nature would be outside the scope of direct middle-class influence. All differences between Socialist reformers and revolutionaries in regard to the class struggle, elections, immediate demands, the state, craft unions, nationalization, municipal reform, and step-at-a-time socialism were incorporated in the conflict over industrial socialism.[1]

Most of the theoretical exposition had been worked out by the Left wing between 1904 and 1905 in the discussions which led to organization of the Industrial Workers of the World. But the I.W.W.'s bitter factional fights, its rapid loss of membership,[2] and its comparative inactivity between 1905 and 1908 had caused many of the Left wing to lose their early enthusiasm.[3] Several factors now served to bring about an immediate revival of their interest: the consolidation of the Right wing's control of the national party organization; party indifference toward industrial unionism in the American Federation of Labor; and the effective leadership given by the I.W.W. in the 1909 steel strikes in McKees Rocks, Butler, and New Castle, Pennsylvania.[4]

[1] William E. Bohn, "Reformer and Revolutionist," *International Socialist Review*, X (Sept., 1909), 204–11.

[2] Brissenden, *The I.W.W.*, pp. 211–17; Hillquit, *History of Socialism*, 1910 ed., p. 338. Brissenden says that the 1907 panic almost wiped out the I.W.W., and Hillquit estimates their dues-paying membership in 1907–8 as about five thousand.

[3] Charles H. Kerr, "Socialist Unity in the United States," *International Socialist Review*, VIII (Dec., 1907), 325–29; Charles H. Kerr, "Unionism, Utopian and Scientific," *International Socialist Review*, VIII (March, 1908), 557; "The Industrial Workers of the World," *International Socialist Review*, X (Oct., 1909), 359–60.

[4] "Revolutionary Unionism," *International Socialist Review*, X (Sept., 1909), 266–68; Louis Duchez, "The Strikes in Pennsylvania," *International Socialist Review*, X (Sept., 1909), 193–203; Louis Duchez, "Victory at McKees Rocks," *International Socialist Review*, X (Oct., 1909), 289–300; "The Industrial Workers of the World,"

The basic tenets of industrial socialism were set forth in the *International Socialist Review* and in *Industrial Socialism*, a pamphlet by Bill Haywood and Frank Bohn.[5] Their analysis ran as follows: in every society prior to capitalism, economic and political power were openly united in the hands of the ruling class. When feudalism was being overthrown, however, the bourgeoisie needed the support of the common people. In order to get this support and yet retain control, they set up parliaments which were given formal political power. Real social power, however, continued to reside in economic control. With the rise of trusts, that power became concentrated in the hands of a few men.[6]

According to the industrial Socialists, trusts were the government of industry. Workers had nothing to say about the affairs of that government, and the profits made by their employers were nothing but a tax collected without representation. The real government of America resided in Wall Street. The trusts controlled the political government—schools, press, theater, church, army, and navy.[7] Obviously, the political state was nothing but the tool of the industrial state. Those "who think all we need is votes expect the tool to wield the user, the shadow to change the reality, the servant to command the master." [8]

The industrial Socialists reasoned that since the source of the capitalists' power was their control of industry, the fight to break that control must be waged in the shops. Election campaigns to win the political state were merely echoes of the real battles which were taking place in every factory, mine, and railroad.[9] Working-class votes cast at the ballot box could do no more than gain con-

---

*International Socialist Review*, X (Oct., 1909), 374–75. The party Right wing apparently recognized the possibility that the I.W.W. victories against the Pressed Steel Car Co. in Pennsylvania might revive party enthusiasm for that union. The *New York Call* greeted the successful conclusion of the strike with an editorial warning that only the regular trade unions and the Socialist Party could effectively combat capitalism ("The M'Kees Rocks Victory," *New York Call*, Sept. 9, 1909).

5 Haywood and Bohn, *Industrial Socialism*.

6 William E. Bohn, "Reformer and Revolutionist," *International Socialist Review*, X (Sept., 1909), 204–6.

7 Haywood and Bohn, *Industrial Socialism*, pp. 36–39.

8 William E. Bohn, "Reformer and Revolutionist," *International Socialist Review*, X (Sept., 1909), 209.

9 Connolly, *Socialism Made Easy*, pp. 55–56; "What the Review Stands For," *International Socialist Review* (Sept., 1909), p. 271.

trol of a political state that did not possess real authority. The place where a vote would really count was in the shop where it would challenge the employers at the seat of their power.[10]

It was ridiculous for a working-class party to advance a program of immediate demands in the hope of winning middle-class votes.[11] The immediate demands that concerned workers were shop demands, and step-at-a-time victories would have to be shop victories.[12] Debs said it was of far greater importance for the Socialist Party to aid in the economic organization of workers than to devote its energies to winning meaningless middle-class votes for socialism. When workers were organized in their shops they would inevitably vote the Socialist ticket, and not before.[13]

The only form of working-class economic organization that met the requirements of a trust economy was the industrial union, the Left wing insisted. Craft unions did not fight employers but attempted to organize job trusts to protect the higher wages of a limited number of skilled workers from the competition of those who wanted to break into the craft. But craft unions were doomed to extinction because that "great leveler," the machine, was rendering skills obsolete.[14]

The Left said that industrial unions would be organized on the basis of the products manufactured, not the tool used. Their motto would be, "One union of all workers in an industry; all industries in one union." [15] Their major weapon would be the general strike in the industry, community, and, ultimately, the nation. It was meaningless to argue that a general strike had never been successful, because the correct conditions for such a strike had never existed.[16] By the enfranchisement, through their industrial union, of all workers in the shop, including Negroes, women, and children,

10 Haywood and Bohn, *Industrial Socialism*, pp. 47–48, 50.

11 "What the Review Stands For," *International Socialist Review*, X (Sept., 1909), 270–71.

12 Frank Bohn, "The Ballot," *International Socialist Review*, X (June, 1910), 1120.

13 Eugene V. Debs, "Danger Ahead," *International Socialist Review*, XI (Jan., 1911), 414–15; William Chaney, "Working Class Politics, from Debs' Chicago Speech," *International Socialist Review*, XI (Nov., 1910), 257–61. This speech by Debs was the opening gun of the 1910 Chicago election campaign and was devoted almost entirely to the prime importance of industrial unionism.

14 Haywood and Bohn, *Industrial Socialism*, pp. 43–44.

15 *Ibid.*, pp. 45–46.

16 *Ibid.*, p. 47.

and by the refusal of the union to sign agreements that would permit employers to close factories but prevent workers from striking for better conditions, the working class would be enabled to win control of the industrial government and establish socialism.[17]

Contrary to the belief of clergymen, college professors, and lawyers, socialism was not government ownership. The capitalist government, of course, was simply an organization to protect private property and rule the workers. But, said the Left, *all* political government was administration from the top. Socialism was industrial *democracy*, administration by the rank and file. The institution of government ownership by Socialists elected to political office could not, therefore, be socialism. If the government owned the railroads, for example, "it would have to rob the railroad workers and turn over the stolen money to the idle government railroad bondholders." [18] A government constructed to aid in exploitation of workers could not be converted into a government of, by, and for the workers. "A wise tailor does not put stitches in rotten cloth." [19] In place of the gradual socialization of the economy through government ownership, as conceived by the constructive Socialists, the revolutionary Socialists offered the syndicalist solution. The industrial unions would not only unite the workers for their struggle against capitalism but would form the framework of the society of the future.[20]

In view of the primary role assigned to industrial unions in overthrowing capitalism and building socialism, Left-wing Socialists were faced with the problem of finding a role for their own organization, the Socialist Party. Its most important task, of course, would be to aid in organization of industrial unions.[21] But a political party should have some political function. The revolutionary Socialists found three essential, if secondary, duties for it to perform. In the first place, while the state itself could not be used to inaugurate socialism, it was a deadly anti-union weapon in the

[17] *Ibid.*, pp. 43–48; William E. Bohn, "Reformer and Revolutionist," *International Socialist Review*, X (Sept., 1909), 210–11.

[18] Haywood and Bohn, *Industrial Socialism,* pp. 50–51.

[19] *Ibid.,* p. 51.

[20] *Ibid.*, pp. 49–52; Connolly, *Socialism Made Easy,* pp. 43–44; William E. Bohn, "Reformer and Revolutionist," *International Socialist Review*, X (Sept., 1909), 211.

[21] William E. Bohn, "Reformer and Revolutionist," *International Socialist Review*, X (Sept., 1909), 211.

hands of the capitalists. As the class struggle increased in intensity
in the shops, the employers would use their government to crush the
industrial unions. If the unions were to be free to fight the capitalists on the industrial field, the Socialist Party would have to win
elections in order to prevent use of police, courts, and military
against the workers and their leaders.[22] Therefore, despite Left-
wing contempt for the Milwaukee constructive Socialists, the *International Socialist Review* hailed the 1910 election victory as an
opportunity to organize that city's workers without interference
from the police and courts.[23] And the *Review* was as enthusiastic
over the great gains made by the party in the 1910 Congressional
elections as were the most ardent supporters of step-at-a-time socialism.[24]

Secondly, the party was assigned the task of educating the working class in principles of scientific socialism. If workers were to use
their unions effectively, they must understand the philosophical
and economic theories of Marx and Engels, with particular emphasis on the class struggle, surplus value, and economic determinism.
Political campaigns should be used to publicize these principles,
and political victories would be of great value in arousing the curiosity of the workers about socialism.[25] Finally, municipal victories
would enable the Socialists to use the cities' social services—fire
department, water works, public schools, parks, and public health
—in the interest of the working class.[26]

While these three party functions were indispensable to the victory of the proletariat, the revolutionary Socialists warned it must
never be forgotten that the party existed to aid the industrial union,
and not vice versa.[27] Socialists were to participate in elections to
help the unions in their fight to abolish virtually all political offices,

---

[22] Haywood and Bohn, *Industrial Socialism*, pp. 53–55; Frank Bohn, "The Ballot,"
*International Socialist Review*, X (June, 1910), 1120; "Revolutionary Unionism,"
*International Socialist Review*, X (Sept., 1909), 267; "Politics and the Proletariat,"
*International Socialist Review*, IX (Dec., 1908), 464–65.

[23] Mary E. Marcy, "The Milwaukee Victory," *International Socialist Review*, X
(May, 1910), 991–92.

[24] *International Socialist Review*, XI (Dec., 1910), 364.

[25] Haywood and Bohn, *Industrial Socialism*, pp. 55–58; "Revolutionary Unionism," *International Socialist Review*, X (Sept., 1909), 268; Frank Bohn, "The
Ballot," *International Socialist Review*, X (June, 1910), 1120.

[26] Haywood and Bohn, *Industrial Socialism*, pp. 58–59.

[27] Frank Bohn, "The Ballot," *International Socialist Review*, X (June, 1910), 1120.

not in order to fill those offices with Socialists. Since there would be
no rich to oppress the workers under socialism, government would
be industrial, not political. A socialist government would legislate
for the individual only in regard to shop problems. Legislatures
would be made up of representatives of various branches of industry and they would concern themselves only with improving
production and conditions of labor and minimizing the expenditure
of labor power.[28] Recognition of this proper relationship between
the party and the union would prevent the party from abandoning
its revolutionary program for the sake of reform policies designed
to win votes and the spoils of office.[29]

A minority of the Left, while agreeing that industrial unionism
was essential to the overthrow of capitalism, did not accept all of
this basically syndicalist analysis. The spokesmen of the group were
Eugene Debs and two New York attorneys, Henry L. Slobodin
and Louis Boudin. They conceded that organization of a militant
industrial union was the immediate task of the party. Like other
Left wingers, they agreed that it was ridiculous to expect the capitalist state gradually to transform itself into the co-operative commonwealth. But they refused to dismiss the political state as a mere
shadow of capitalist industry and therefore of little consequence
in the struggle for socialism. They held that since the state was
used to oppress the workers, the proletariat must win political
power by seizing control of the state. Then the workers would use
the state to wipe out capitalism. Through the unity and class consciousness developed in the industrial union, workers would be
taught to vote the Socialist ticket. When the Socialist Party had
swept the national elections, the industrial union would compel
capitalists to accept the Socialist decision at the ballot box.[30]

This variant of the Left-wing position had little support in the
party. The membership increasingly tended to polarize itself

[28] Haywood and Bohn, *Industrial Socialism*, pp. 55, 61–62.
[29] "Revolutionary Unionism," *International Socialist Review*, X (Sept., 1909),
267–68.
[30] Louis Boudin, "The Political Situation in the United States and the Socialist
Party," *New York Call*, Oct. 24, 31, 1909; Henry L. Slobodin, "Politics, Parliaments and the State," *International Socialist Review*, X (April, 1910), 884–88;
Debs, "Danger Ahead," *International Socialist Review*, XI (Jan., 1911), 414–15;
Elias Tobenkin, "Interview with Debs," *New York Call*, June 25, 1911; Eugene V.
Debs, "Party Organization," *Appeal to Reason*, Jan. 20, 1912.

around the two extremes of reform socialism and syndicalism. Boudin and Slobodin were important members of the Left wing in New York, but had no national support for their position. Herman Titus's position closely resembled that of Boudin and Slobodin,[31] but he left the party early in 1909 and from then on pursued his own increasingly sectarian path.[32] Eugene Debs, who might have been able to slow the syndicalist tide, contented himself with general statements on the importance of both economic and political action. And because a majority of the party accepted elections as the core of all Socialist activity, Debs usually stressed the importance of industrial unionism.[33] In fact, although Debs repeatedly affirmed his belief. that socialism would come through an election victory backed by the power of the industrial unions, he endorsed Haywood and Bohn's *Industrial Socialism* as a "splendid pamphlet" that set forth the "true revolutionary attitude of the working class." [34] Rank and file Socialists would have to choose between the opportunism of the reformists and the dual union sectarianism of the syndicalists.

When the Left wing revived its interest in industrial socialism in the fall of 1909, it did not stop to reconsider its earlier decision that industrial unionism must be built outside the already established trade unions. The 1904 American Labor Union charge that the American Federation of Labor was being transformed by Right-wing Socialists at a rate comparable to the growth of a coral reef,[35] and the 1905 Debs epigram that attempts to reform the "rotten graft-infested" craft unions were as "vain and wasteful of time as to spray a cesspool with attar of roses" [36] were accepted by all revolutionary Socialists as self-evident truths. Moreover, mere reorganization of the A.F. of L. along industrial lines would not have satisfied the Left wingers. An industrial union, they insisted, must be a revolutionary union consciously based on the class struggle. It must recognize that its goal was the overthrow of capitalism

31 Herman Titus, "Portland Strike Edition," *The Socialist* (Seattle), March 16, 1907; Herman Titus, "Open Letter to Members of the A.F. of L. in Portland," *The Socialist* (Seattle), March 23, 1907; Herman Titus in *The Socialist*, May 11, 1907.
32 Foster, *From Bryan to Stalin*, pp. 36–38.
33 Elias Tobenkin, "Interview with Debs," *New York Call*, June 25, 1911.
34 *International Socialist Review*, XII (Nov., 1911), front cover.
35 "A Pickwickian Socialist," *American Labor Union Journal*, Dec., 1904.
36 Letter from Eugene V. Debs to the *Chicago Socialist*, Dec. 23, 1905.

and the triumph of the co-operative commonwealth. Thus, unions like the United Mine Workers were industrial in form but not in content. They could not organize the proletariat to strike for its own emancipation.[37]

The Left wing seemed to assume that given militant leadership and the correct organizational forms, the American working class would accept revolutionary slogans and syndicalist theories and abandon their established unions with sufficient rapidity to make possible the creation of revolutionary industrial unions.[38] It took only the 1909 victory at McKees Rocks, Pennsylvania, to convince the revolutionary Socialists that the Industrial Workers of the World was the union that offered "the best available rallying point for socialists on the economic field and it is on that field that the main battle must be fought and won before capitalism will end." [39] The Left wing was committed to dual unionism, and no mere stubborn refusal of workers to join the I.W.W. could shake them in their conviction that they had discovered the royal road to socialism.

The generally unenthusiastic reception given revolutionary unionism by American workers was not the only setback. The chosen economic instrument, the Industrial Workers of the World, took an official stand against political action. And the secondary role assigned political action by Left-wing Socialists themselves made their ranks an easy prey to raids by I.W.W. supporters who insisted that the industrial union must be the *only* form of working-class organization. An attempt was made at the 1907 I.W.W. convention to delete from the preamble the exhortation that "all the toilers [must] come together on the political as well as on the industrial field." It was defeated overwhelmingly, 113 to 15.[40]

At the 1908 convention, however, the 26 delegates who represented the depleted ranks of the Industrial Workers included a

[37] Letter from Justus Ebert to the *New York Call*, Oct. 17, 1909.

[38] "The rank and file of the working class is revolutionary enough to bring about a social revolution next week. What is necessary is the machine through which this revolutionary energy can manifest itself in unionism." (Louis Duchez, "Victory at McKees Rocks," *International Socialist Review*, X [Oct., 1909], 299.)

[39] "The Industrial Workers of the World," *International Socialist Review*, X (Oct., 1909), 360.

[40] *Proceedings of Third Convention of the Industrial Workers of the World*, Official Report No. 3, p. 5; Brissenden, *The I.W.W.*, pp. 188–89.

strong Pacific Coast contingent. These migratory workers joined with the anarchists to support the move to expunge all reference to political action. The preamble was amended to read: "Between these two classes a struggle must go on until the workers of the world organize as a class, take possession of the earth and the machinery of production and abolish the wage system." Daniel De Leon and his supporters withdrew and set up their own industrial union with headquarters in Detroit, and the Industrial Workers of the World was left in control of the syndicalists headed by Vincent St. John and William Trautmann.[41]

Despite this victory of the antipolitical actionists, the revolutionary Socialists were still an important section of the I.W.W., and in many communities the party and the I.W.W. worked in close co-operation.[42] Bill Haywood, who was that union's most important and effective organizer, was one of the leading theoreticians of industrial socialism and was rapidly rising to leadership in the Socialist Party. The election in the spring of 1911 in Butte, Montana, indicates that all Wobblies did not reject voting as useless. The party and the I.W.W. combined forces against the political machines controlled by the Amalgamated Copper Company and won a resounding Socialist victory.[43] And the high vote polled in states under Left-wing leadership in the 1910 and 1912 elections shows that revolutionary Socialists did not neglect political action.[44] One Wobbly has expressed an attitude which was perhaps fairly common among members of the I.W.W.: "Whenever election time came around, I was a good political actionist. I would cling to every straw of encouragement while ballots were being cast and fight desperately against the inevitable let down when the ballots were counted." [45] Furthermore, unless political activity is defined so as to limit it to elections, the Wobblies, through their un-

[41] Brissenden, The I.W.W., pp. 221–31; Henry Kuhn, "Reminiscences of Daniel De Leon," in Daniel De Leon, p. 51.

[42] Frank Bohn, "The Failure to Attain Socialist Unity," International Socialist Review, VIII (June, 1908), 755; Louis Duchez, "The Strikes in Pennsylvania," International Socialist Review, X (Oct., 1909), 193–203; "The Flying Squadron," International Socialist Review, X (Oct., 1909), 374–75. The last article is a description of I.W.W. and Socialist Party co-operation in New Castle, Pennsylvania.

[43] Jack Keister, "Why the Socialists Won in Butte," International Socialist Review, XI (June, 1911), 731–33.

[44] American Labor Year Book, 1916, pp. 99–100.

[45] Chaplin, Wobbly, p. 83.

ceasing struggle for civil rights, engaged in many militant political campaigns.[46]

These political activities, of course, did not change the basic nature of the Industrial Workers of the World. This was a syndicalist organization and most of its members held the Socialist Party and all its works in contempt.[47] The Left wing refused to be discouraged, however. They said the I.W.W. was soundly organized on the economic field. They warned that it could not fulfill its historic mission without ridding itself of its antipolitical fanatics.[48]

Meanwhile, these same antipolitical fanatics were busy undermining the Left-wing position in the party. Not all members of the I.W.W. devoted themselves to union organization. Many were simply ideological syndicalists whose contribution consisted of attacks on the Socialist Party. Some Left-wing Socialists who had rejected political action quit the party and appointed themselves propagandists for the I.W.W.

The trouble was that these ex-Socialists carried their propaganda not into the factories but into Socialists branches. They denounced constructive socialism as the single greatest foe of revolutionary unionism and set out to eliminate as many locals as they could. Their object was conversion of Socialist locals into "mixed" or propaganda locals of the I.W.W. Since charges that the party was a worthless reform movement run by "sky pilots," lawyers, and

[46] Brissenden, *The I.W.W.*, pp. 260–64. In his autobiography Haywood comments: "The history of the I.W.W. has shown the significance of political action. While there are some members who decry legislative and congressional action and who refuse to cast a ballot for any political party, yet the I.W.W. has fought more political battles for the working class than any other labor organization or political party in America. They have had one battle after another for free speech. They have fought against vagrancy laws, against criminal syndicalism laws, and to establish the right of workers to organize. They have gone on strike for men in prison. It is to the ignominy of the Socialist Party and the Socialist Labor Party that they have so seldom joined forces with the I.W.W. in these desperate political struggles." (Haywood, *Bill Haywood's Book*, pp. 221–22.)

[47] Williams, *Eleven Blind Leaders;* Foster, *Pages from a Worker's Life,* pp. 272–74.

[48] Frank Bohn, "Is the I.W.W. to Grow?" *International Socialist Review,* XII (July, 1911), 44. Debs, in one of his rare statements about the I.W.W., said in 1914 that if it had not been "converted . . . into an anti-political machine, it would today be the most formidable labor organization in America, if not the world." (Eugene V. Debs, "A Plea for Solidarity," *International Socialist Review,* XIV [March, 1914], 536–37.)

small businessmen could influence only Left-wing members and Left-wing Socialist locals, it was they who deserted the party. Having joined the I.W.W. propaganda locals, so the revolutionary Socialists charged, they were soon to be "found gathered about a spittoon deciding how the social revolution will finally take place, what is to be done with the political state, etc." [49] Left-wing Socialists who were attempting to convert the party to industrial socialism and support of the I.W.W. thus found their ranks undergoing steady depletion through raids conducted by members of the organization they were doing their best to support.[50]

The emphasis placed by the revolutionary Socialists on industrial unionism did not mean that they limited their activities to supporting the Industrial Workers of the World. Their locals engaged in party organizational, propaganda, and electioneering activities with at least the same enthusiasm as their Right-wing rivals. The nature of the propaganda differed of course. Instead of graft the Left emphasized exploitation of the working class, and instead of votes for reform they asked for votes to aid the unions. But their propaganda and appeals for votes were coupled with militant campaigns for free speech, demonstrations against unemployment, union organization, agitation for the eight-hour day, support of strikes, and defense of the rights of labor.[51] The Right wing, on the other hand, seldom took the lead in such campaigns.[52]

[49] Frank Bohn, "Is the I.W.W. to Grow?" *International Socialist Review,* XII (July, 1911), 42–44.

[50] *Ibid.;* Socialist Party, *Proceedings of the National Convention, 1912,* pp. 71–72; "Socialist Unity in America," *International Socialist Review,* XII (July, 1911), 47–48; Austin Lewis, "A Positive Platform," *International Socialist Review,* XII (April, 1912), 664.

[51] "In Colorado," *The Worker,* Jan. 17, 1904; "A Notable Triumph for Free Speech in Los Angeles," *The Arena,* XL (Oct., 1908), 350–51; "Resolution of New York State Executive Committee," *Socialist Party Official Bulletin,* Jan., 1910; "Mills Supports Wappenstein," *The Socialist* (Seattle), Sept. 14, 1907; *The Socialist* (Seattle), Oct. 12, 1907; *Socialist Party Weekly Bulletin,* Oct. 19, 1907; *The Socialist* (Seattle), March 21, 1908; Herman Titus, "Portland Strike Edition," *The Socialist* (Seattle), March 16, 1907; "Resolution of the Structural Building Trades Alliance of Portland, Oregon," *Socialist Party Official Bulletin,* October, 1908; Anna A. Maley, "One Wyoming Mining Town," *International Socialist Review,* XI (July, 1910), 20–21; *Socialist Party Monthly Bulletin,* May, 1912; "Minutes of the National Executive Committee, May 10, 1912," *Socialist Party Monthly Bulletin,* June, 1912; "Tom Lewis in Jail," *International Socialist Review,* XI (Feb., 1911), 503–4.

[52] Virtually the only action initiated by the Right wing in defense of anyone's right to self-expression, if, indeed, this instance can fall into that category, were two editorials defending Bernarr Macfadden when he was fined $2,000 for publish-

While labor unions and revolutionary Socialists engaged in strikes, demonstrations, and court battles, the constructive Socialists issued proclamations reminding them that their only hope lay in election of Socialists to office. The party's work in the Moyer-Haywood-Pettibone kidnaping and trial and in the Lawrence textile strike reveal much about its approach to Socialist activity.

Frank Steunenberg was elected governor of Idaho in 1896 with the assistance of the Western Federation of Miners. But when the Coeur d'Alene strike occurred in 1899, Steunenberg supported the mine owners by inaugurating a reign of violence, martial law, bull pens, mass arrests, deportations, and blacklists seldom equaled even in a region notorious for its brutal suppression of organized labor. Thanks to the financial support given him in his land speculations by the mine owners, Steunenberg left the governorship in 1901 a wealthy man.[53] The Western Federation of Miners hailed the retirement of this "filthy reptile" with the suggestion that his political tombstone should be inscribed with the words, "Here lies a hireling and a traitor." They predicted that he would sink into obscurity, "damned for the outrages he committed upon the workingmen of the Coeur d'Alene during the past twenty months." [54]

Steunenberg had no chance to sink into obscurity. On December 31, 1905, he was killed by a bomb attached to the gate of his home in Caldwell, Idaho. The Mine Owners Association immediately dispatched James McParland, the labor spy who had destroyed the Molly Maguires and who was now head of the Denver office of the Pinkerton Agency, to assist the Idaho authorities. McParland quickly obtained a confession from one Harry Orchard, a labor spy and *agent provocateur* for the Mine Owners Association. Before he began to work for that organization, Orchard had already committed virtually every crime in the book: larceny, fraud, desertion, bigamy, arson, burglary, and murder. While working for the mine owners he added sabotage and dynamiting to this impressive list.

Prodded by McParland, Orchard confessed to an orgy of crimi-

---

ing an obscene serial. Macfadden, Socialists were informed, had restored health to thousands and everyone should subscribe to his *Physical Culture Magazine*. (*Wilshire's Magazine*, XII [Jan., 1908], 4; *Social-Democratic Herald*, Feb. 13, 1909.)

[53] Stone, *Clarence Darrow for the Defense*, pp. 192–94.

[54] *The Miners' Magazine*, II (Jan., 1901), 7–8.

nal activity, culminating with the murder of Steunenberg at the instigation of the Western Federation of Miners as revenge for the terror of the Coeur d'Alene strike six years before.

On February 17, 1906, Denver authorities aided Idaho officials in kidnaping Charles Moyer, president of the miners' federation, Bill Haywood, its secretary-treasurer, and George Pettibone, former union official, and in transporting them from Denver to an Idaho penitentiary. The three union officials spent the next eighteen months in prison awaiting trial, while the state bribed, intimidated, and framed witnesses, and used ministers, psychologists, and the press to paint a picture of Orchard as a murderer who had been converted to Christianity by McParland. Clarence Darrow was secured for the defense.[55]

The response of the Left wing was immediate. The kidnaping and the Idaho governor's boast that Moyer, Haywood, and Pettibone would not leave the state alive [56] constituted a threat not only to the Western Federation of Miners, the Industrial Workers of the World, and the Socialist Party, but to all organized labor as well. The imprisoned men were leaders in all three organizations, and their conviction would brand the unions and the party as gigantic murder rings. As soon as word of the kidnaping leaked out, the I.W.W. threw all its energies into organizing defense committees, holding protest rallies, and raising defense funds.[57] Within three days of the arrest, the Illinois District convention of the United Mine Workers, under Left-wing leadership, contributed $5,000 to the defense.[58] Eugene Debs wrote a widely circulated appeal, "Arouse, Ye Slaves!" in which he called on workers and Socialists to prepare to defend their comrades with force, if necessary. If the Plutocracy carried out its threat to kill the union leaders, warned Debs, "the governors of Idaho and Colorado and their

---

[55] "Confession of Harry Orchard," *Current Literature*, XLIII (July, 1907), 1–5; "Mollie Maguires in the West," *The Independent*, LX (March 8, 1906), 536; "History of the Case," *Current Literature*, XLII (June, 1907), 587–95; "The Confession and Autobiography of Harry Orchard," *McClure's Magazine*, XXIX (July, 1907), 794–306; "The Acquital of William D. Haywood," *The Arena*, XXXVIII (Sept., 1907), 332–33; Stone, *Clarence Darrow for the Defense*, pp. 185–218.

[56] Quoted by Stone in *Clarence Darrow for the Defense*, p. 191.

[57] *The Chicago Socialist*, Feb. 24, 1906; Brissenden, *The I.W.W.*, pp. 171–72, 175–76.

[58] See sources cited in Note 57.

masters from Wall St., New York to the Rocky Mountains had better prepare to follow them." [59]

The first task of the defense was to discover what actually had occurred and to spread that information throughout the nation. First reports from Colorado and Idaho told little more than the fact of the kidnaping. Herman Titus left at once for Idaho, and for the next three months the Toledo *Socialist* was devoted in large part to publication of his reports on the background of the case and the plans of the prosecution. It was these stories that provided the basis for the work of the first defense committees. In addition to his reporting, Titus took the lead in forming local defense committees and toured the state speaking for the indicted men. In June, *The Socialist* moved to Caldwell, Idaho, so that there would be a local paper to present the workers' side of the story. [60]

In sharp contrast was the reaction of the Right-wing press. Only the *Appeal to Reason* gave the case full and continuous publicity. The *Chicago Socialist*, while calling for protest meetings, from the first assumed that the three men would be executed. [61] By March 10, 1906, only two and a half weeks after the story broke, the *Chicago Socialist*'s coverage had declined to an editorial admonition that workers who wanted to save Moyer, Haywood, and Pettibone should elect 36 Socialists in next month's aldermanic elections. [62] On March 17 the paper announced that the "Socialist party, through its national and local organization and its weekly press, is doing all that is within its power to reveal to the public the iniquitous and desperate character of these outrages." [63] But the March 24 issue did not mention the affair, and, from then on, because of the spring and fall elections and the conversion to socialism of Joseph Medill Patterson, coverage of the case was reduced to passing mention and an occasional short article.

The April, May, and June, 1906, issues of *Wilshire's Magazine* demanded protest meetings from Maine to California and a general strike if the men were convicted. [64] Having sounded this trumpet call, the magazine dropped the subject until the trial began a year later.

---

[59] *Appeal to Reason*, March 10, 1906.     [60] *The Socialist*, March 3–June 2, 1906.
[61] *The Chicago Socialist*, Feb. 24, March 3, 1906.
[62] *Ibid.*, March 10, 1906.              [63] *Ibid.*, March 17, 1906.
[64] *Wilshire's Magazine*, X (April, 1906), 3.

The *Social-Democratic Herald* was one of the few party papers that reported the death of Steunenberg before the kidnaping of the union leaders occurred. The *Herald* hastened to assure its readers that although a worker had killed the former governor, "the working class as a whole is possessed of immense patience, which is an augury that when the labor question is finally settled it will have been settled right." [65] On March 3 the *Herald* printed a short article on the kidnaping which predicted that the mine workers' officials would be executed.[66] The March 10 issue failed to mention the case, and that of March 17 printed a short paragraph on the back page noting that the national office of the party had asked that meetings demanding a fair trial be held "where possible." [67] On March 24 the paper again printed a back-page paragraph explaining that the Milwaukee party would hold a mass meeting a few days after the city's spring elections. "As the kidnapped men are not in immediate need of funds, thanks to the Miners' munificent donation, there will be nothing lost by the short delay." [68] The March 31 issue printed a resolution passed by the Milwaukee Federated Trades Council, but that of April 7 was devoted to celebrating the 7 percent increase in the city's Socialist vote and did not mention any projected mass meeting. The issues of April 14 and 21 each buried a short paragraph on the kidnaping, but at no time did the *Herald* print an article which outlined the whole story. The mass meeting was not held.

Finally, on April 28, Victor Berger explained the rationale behind the Milwaukee party's lack of activity in defense of the three union leaders. Berger said this case differed from that of the Molly Maguires or the Haymarket affair. The Molly Maguires were led by "Irish saloonkeepers and other doubtful elements" and the anarchists had brought on Haymarket by their wild talk. In both instances the capitalist class considered itself threatened as a class. But the Moyer-Haywood "episode" was viewed by the capitalists as a border feud between Western mine owners, "many of whom were themselves prospectors but yesterday," and a group of hardy frontiersmen. According to Berger, the union leaders already had

65 *Social-Democratic Herald*, Jan. 6, 1906.
66 *Ibid.*, March 3, 1906.                    67 *Ibid.*, March 10, 17, 1906.
68 *Ibid.*, March 24, 1906.

the best legal talent available. They would be freed if the Socialist Party and organized labor would act with sufficient restraint as not to arouse the entire capitalist class.[69] The *Herald* did its bit to lull the unnecessary fears of employers by virtually ignoring the case from that time on. The paper held its silence on the kidnaping for yet another reason. Its editor, Frederic Heath, believed the union leaders guilty and feared that support of them, followed by a conviction, would prove embarrassing.[70]

One last point on the handling of the Moyer-Haywood case by the Right-wing Socialist press is worthy of note. While insisting that the men were the innocent victims of a frame-up, the Socialist papers always referred to them as officials of the Western Federation of Miners or of the Industrial Workers of the World. Almost never was it noted that the union leaders were also prominent in the Socialist Party.[71]

The national organization of the party confined itself mainly to appeals for funds, to issuing resolutions, and to making periodic requests to its locals to take action. Two days after Moyer, Haywood, and Pettibone were kidnaped, National Secretary Barnes sent them the following reassuring telegram: "The purchased confession, the secret special train makes the conspiracy of capitalism complete. Russian methods make pertinent the question: Is Colorado in America? Rockefeller reported successfully evading summons. Platt and Depew safe in the Senate!" [72] Three weeks later the National Executive Committee released a circular letter to all its locals instructing them to unite with labor organizations in protest meetings, to send any money raised to national headquarters, and to remember that only by electing Socialists to office could outrages against labor be prevented.[73] At the end of March the executive committee recommended that "wherever practicable" May Day celebrations lodge protests against the Idaho kidnaping.[74] In

[69] Victor L. Berger, "They Cannot Repeat 1886," *Social-Democratic Herald*, April 28, 1906.

[70] Letter from Frederic Heath to Henry E. Allen, cited in *Appeal to Reason*, Jan. 12, 1907.

[71] See, for example, *The Worker*, April 7, 1906.

[72] *Socialist Party Official Bulletin*, Feb., 1906.

[73] *Ibid.*, March, 1906.

[74] "Minutes of the National Executive Committee, March 29, 1906," *Socialist Party Official Bulletin*, March, 1906.

December the national office printed and distributed leaflets publicizing the dissent of Justice McKenna against the Supreme Court decision which denied the imprisoned men's appeal for a writ of habeas corpus.[75]

Nine months after the imprisonment, when the opening of the trial was still in the distant future, the National Executive Committee moved to organize a national conference and co-ordinated movement to free the mine workers' leaders. Signatures were secured from about two dozen local and national A.F. of L. leaders for a petition asking the executive board of that union to call a national conference.[76] William Mailly presented the petition to Gompers, who said he would take the matter up with his board.[77] The board decided against any action.

Three months later, in March, 1907, the party National Executive Committee defeated six to one a motion to organize a national conference of Socialists and organized labor.[78] And in May, as the trial was at last getting under way, the National Committee defeated by 35 to 10 a motion instructing the Executive Committee to consider means of saving the union leaders from execution in the event they were convicted. Those who voted "No" did so on the ground that defense of the men was a trade union matter. If the unions took the lead, the Socialists would tender their support.[79]

As for financial support to defend the miners, money collected by the national Socialist Party, which had almost thirty thousand members, totaled $4,000 in 1906 [80] and $11,000 in 1907.[81] In contrast, the Industrial Workers of the World, whose dues-paying

[75] "To Hell With The Constitution! Says Major McClellan—What Says the Supreme Court of the United States," (Chicago, National Headquarters, Socialist Party); letter from National Secretary J. Mahlon Barnes to members of the National Executive Committee, Dec. 10, 1906, Socialist Party Official Bulletin, Dec., 1906.

[76] "Minutes of the National Executive Committee, December 17, 1906," and letter from J. Mahlon Barnes to Samuel Gompers, Dec. 17, 1906, Socialist Party Official Bulletin, Dec., 1906.

[77] Letter from William Mailly to J. Mahlon Barnes, Dec. 21, 1906, Socialist Party Official Bulletin, Dec., 1906.

[78] "Minutes of the National Executive Committee, March 3, 1907," Socialist Party Official Bulletin, March, 1907.

[79] Socialist Party Official Bulletin, May, 1907.

[80] "Annual Report of the National Secretary of the Socialist Party, January 15, 1907," Socialist Party Official Bulletin, Jan., 1907.

[81] American Labor Year Book, 1916, p. 122.

membership by 1907 was down to about five thousand unskilled and migrant workers, collected $11,000.[82] Small wonder that Tom Sladden, Left-wing state secretary for the party in Oregon, charged that "the Socialist Party has been skulking in its tents while others bore the brunt of the battle." He suggested that something more than resolutions of sympathy were necessary and demanded to know why the party had not voted a direct assessment of one dollar a member: "If I belong to an organization I want to have some assurance that the body behind me has some force. I would hate to have my neck in a noose and my party depending upon raising funds in a basket like the Salvation Army on a street corner raising funds to save the unwashed." [83]

Fortunately for the campaign to save Moyer, Haywood, and Pettibone, not all Socialists were so limited in their activities as was the national organization. Debs toured the country making hundreds of speeches in defense of the union leaders.[84] The Left-wing Colorado party nominated Haywood for governor in the 1906 elections. Haywood accepted from prison, writing, "Principles can not be arbitrated. Let the campaign slogan be, 'There is nothing to arbitrate.' The class struggle must go on as long as one man eats bread in the sweat of another man's face." [85]

The National Committee of the party voted to send four organizers to Colorado for the Haywood campaign, and Right-wing members suggested that they be men of the caliber of Max Hayes and Ben Hanford. The revolutionary Socialists immediately objected to sending "pure and simplers" to a state with a sound revolutionary movement; [86] men should be sent "who are in sympathy with the Socialist movement as expressed in both the political party and in its supporting industrial organization." [87] Max Hayes in particular was anathema. He was "opposed to the working class. He

---

[82] Brissenden, *The I.W.W.*, pp. 171–72.

[83] Thomas A. Sladden, "A Few Words with the Socialists," *The Socialist* (Seattle), Aug. 10, 1907.

[84] Ginger, *The Bending Cross*, pp. 247–48.

[85] Letter from William D. Haywood, Ada County Jail, Idaho, to the State Committee, Socialist Party of Colorado, July 14, 1906, *Social-Democratic Herald*, Aug. 11, 1906.

[86] *Socialist Party Official Bulletin*, Aug., 1905.

[87] Letter from Ward T. Mills (Texas) to J. Mahlon Barnes, *Socialist Party Official Bulletin*, Aug., 1905.

lives and does for the American Federation of Labor. . . . It practically teaches the identity or at least the community of interest between the robber and the robbed." [88] Hayes and Hanford were not assigned the job. Haywood polled 16,000 votes, eight times the 1904 Socialist gubernatorial vote.[89] The Milwaukee Socialists, however, protested the national support given Colorado where the situation was "picturesque but unsubstantial." It recommended that in the future such support be given to communities like Milwaukee which had a chance of electing men to office.[90]

The main vehicles for mobilizing public support for the union leaders were the Moyer-Haywood conferences formed by members and locals of the Socialist Party, the I.W.W., the American Federation of Labor, the Socialist Labor Party, and dozens of independent community groups. Rallies, demonstrations, and parades were held, millions of pieces of literature were circulated, and tens of thousands of dollars were collected. In many of the conferences, members of the Socialist Party played a leading role. In others, their contribution was sporadic, coming to an almost complete halt in the months before the elections in the fall of 1906 and the spring of 1907. And in a few conferences, the Right-wing city and state leadership tried to stop their more militant members from participating at all.[91]

The action of the Cook County (Chicago) executive committee provides the most glaring example of Right-wing refusal to co-operate with other groups in defense of the imprisoned mine leaders. Immediately after the kidnaping the I.W.W. invited the Chicago Socialists along with a number of other radical organizations to participate in the first mass meeting of protest.[92] The Cook County committee responded by sending a letter to all its affiliated locals advising them that "in view of the party's position in the

[88] Letter from National Committeeman Smith (Louisiana) to the National Committee, *Socialist Party Official Bulletin*, Sept., 1906.

[89] *Appeal to Reason*, Dec. 1, 1906.

[90] *Social-Democratic Herald*, Nov. 17, 1906.

[91] *Appeal to Reason*, July 6, 1907; *The Worker*, 1906–7; A. M. Simons, "A Victory Gained," *International Socialist Review*, VIII (Aug., 1907), 110; letter from J. Mahlon Barnes to members of the National Executive Committee, Socialist Party, Dec. 10, 1906, *Socialist Party Official Bulletin*, Dec., 1906.

[92] Letter from William E. Trautmann, secretary of the I.W.W., to the Cook County Committee of the Socialist Party, Feb. 22, 1906, *The Chicago Socialist*, March 17, 1906.

matter of trade unionism" it is "deemed wise not to comply with the request." [93] Instead, the committee called its own meeting for the same day. The rally sponsored by the I.W.W. was attended by 1,500 persons and raised over two hundred dollars. The *Chicago Socialist* neglected to mention how many persons attended the party-sponsored rally at which Seymour Stedman told the audience "We must accept their [the capitalists'] rules" and work for a bigger vote. The sum raised was less than fifty dollars.[94]

The Cook County committee did not stop at merely attempting to sabotage one meeting. When the I.W.W. again took the initiative to call a city-wide meeting to set up a Moyer-Haywood Defense League, the party committee again warned its locals not to attend.[95] The Chicago League, therefore, did not have the support of the Chicago Socialist Party, although individual members and Left-wing locals were very active in the League.[96]

The comparatively negligible contribution of the national organization of the Socialist Party and the sporadic publicity given the protest movements by the Right-wing socialist press did not prevent national party leaders from claiming a major share of the credit for the nation-wide demand for a fair trial for the miners' leaders.[97] At any rate, when Haywood was finally brought to trial in the summer of 1907, the protests had been sufficiently long and loud to ensure him as fair a hearing as could be had in a community bordering on hysteria. Haywood was acquitted. A second trial freed Pettibone, and Moyer was released without further prosecution.[98]

The Socialist support given the Lawrence, Massachusetts, textile strike in 1912 in contrast to the fitful assistance rendered Moyer and Haywood in 1906–1907 is indicative of the increasing influence

[93] Letter to all locals of the Socialist Party from Charles L. Breckon, Secretary, Cook County Executive Committee, *The Chicago Socialist,* March 17, 1906.

[94] *The Chicago Socialist,* March 10, 1906.

[95] Letter to all locals of Cook County Socialist Party from Charles L. Breckon, executive secretary, Cook County Executive Committee, *The Chicago Socialist,* March 17, 1906.

[96] *The Chicago Socialist,* April 14, 1906.

[97] International Socialist Congress, *Recent Progress of the Socialist and Labor Movements in the United States,* p. 32; letter from J. Mahlon Barnes to the members of the National Executive Committee, Dec. 10, 1906, *Socialist Party Official Bulletin,* Dec., 1906; A. M. Simons, "A Victory Gained," *International Socialist Review,* VIII (Aug., 1907), 110, 112; Hillquit, *History of Socialism,* 1910 ed., p. 347.

[98] Stone, *Clarence Darrow for the Defense,* pp. 224–47.

of the Left wing and the growing militancy of the party. Although the conflict between the constructive and revolutionary Socialists was to reach a climax within a few months of the end of the strike, the Right wing supported the Left's leadership of the Lawrence workers.[99] The textile strike was called in January, 1912, in answer to a series of sharp cuts in wages that were already below subsistence level. The cuts were ordered by the absentee owners of the Lawrence mills. The I.W.W., which had greatly increased its strength during 1911, sent Joseph Ettor and Arturo Giovannitti to lead the strike. When they were arrested following the murder of a striker during a parade, they were replaced by the redoubtable "Big Bill" Haywood, who had recently been elected to the National Executive Committee of the Socialist Party.[100]

Of Lawrence's total population of 86,000, at least fifty thousand consisted of strikers and their dependents. The need for funds for food was desperate.[101] In January the National Executive Committee adopted unanimously a motion by Haywood calling on the party to raise funds and tender all other possible assistance to the strikers.[102] The locals pushed the program vigorously and raised $40,000,[103] $18,000 of this sum through the national office.[104]

On February 5 the Italian Socialist Federation proposed the removal of Lawrence children to sympathetic families in other cities —an expedient of the sort had been used successfully in Belgium, France, and Italy. The *New York Call* published an appeal for volunteers to accept the children and received four hundred offers in three days. Committees of Socialist women were appointed to check the proffered homes both before and after the children arrived. On February 10 the first group of 119 children arrived in New York to be greeted by crowds of sympathizers. One week later another 150 were sent to New York and Barre, Vermont.[105]

[99] Ray Stannard Baker, "The Revolutionary Strike, a New Form of Industrial Struggle as Exemplified at Lawrence, Massachusetts," *The American Magazine*, LXXIV (May, 1912), 30B; Leslie H. Marcy and Frederick Sumner Boyd, "One Big Union Wins," *International Socialist Review*, XII (April, 1912), 613–30.
[100] Yellen, *American Labor Struggles*, 185–86.
[101] *Ibid.*, pp. 183–89.
[102] *Socialist Party Official Bulletin*, March, 1912.
[103] Leslie H. Marcy and Frederick Sumner Boyd, "One Big Union Wins," *International Socialist Review*, XII (April, 1912), 619.
[104] *American Labor Year Book*, 1916, p. 122.
[105] Yellen, *American Labor Struggles*, pp. 189–91.

Preparations were then made to remove another two hundred children. But the Lawrence authorities and the Massachusetts press, fearful of the attendant publicity, attacked the project as a plan to exploit the children to publicize the strike. The strikers replied that the children were receiving better care than they did in Lawrence, and that concern might better be shown over exploitation of the children in the mills. The city officials ordered an end to the exodus. When an attempt was made on February 24 to send forty children to Philadelphia, the police attacked them and their parents. Women and children were beaten and clubbed. Thirty adults were arrested on charges of "congregation," and fourteen of the children were sent to the city farm. The country was outraged. Protests poured into Lawrence. The authorities capitulated, and the emigration was resumed.[106]

Haywood appealed to Victor Berger, then serving his first term in Congress, for an investigation of the Lawrence strike. Berger obtained a series of hearings before the House Rules Committee and the resultant publicity did much to aid the strikers.[107] In addition to raising money and caring for children, the Socialist Party through its press and through demonstrations and rallies gave invaluable leadership in the movement to arouse public pressure so as to force the textile mills to capitulate.[108]

In the united effort to win the Lawrence strike factional differences were almost forgotten. There were notable exceptions, however. One such was the attempt of the Central Committee of Local New York to remove Haywood from the party National Executive

[106] C. C. Carstens, "The Children's Exodus from Lawrence," *The Survey*, XXVII (April 6, 1912), 1792; U.S. Congress, House of Representatives, *The Strike at Lawrence, Mass.* Hearings before the Committee on Rules, 62d Cong., 2d Sess., House Doc. 671 (Washington, Government Printing Office, 1912), p. 24.

[107] Haywood, *Bill Haywood's Book*, pp. 249–50; U.S. Congress, House of Representatives, *The Strike at Lawrence, Mass.* Hearings before the Committee on Rules, 62d Cong., 2d Sess., House Doc. 671 (Washington, Government Printing Office, 1912). Berger had aided the I.W.W. once before. In 1911 a Seattle Federal judge had denied a man citizenship because of his membership in the I.W.W. Haywood asked Berger for his aid and the latter secured a Congressional investigation of the judge's activities on the bench which brought about his resignation. (*Bill Haywood's Book*, pp. 249–50.)

[108] Ray Stannard Baker, "The Revolutionary Strike, a New Form of Industrial Struggle as Exemplified at Lawrence, Massachusetts," *The American Magazine*, LXXIV (May, 1912), 19–30C; Leslie H. Marcy and Frederick Sumner Boyd, "One Big Union Wins," *International Socialist Review*, XII (April, 1912), 613–30.

Committee in the middle of the strike.[109] Another was the refusal
of the National Executive Committee to send Left-winger Robert
Rives LaMonte to Lawrence as an organizer for the Socialist
Party. Spargo, in voting no, held that organizers must be selected
with care because the situation was "fraught with danger." [110] The
Right wing's fear of sending one Left winger to Lawrence at a time
when 30,000 strikers were being led by Haywood and the I.W.W.
is somewhat amusing. Of course, the socialist press seldom noted
the fact that the strike was being led by the I.W.W. Still, in the
matter of co-operation, the almost complete lack of which characterized Left-Right relationships, the Lawrence strike was a notable
improvement. When the strike was won, Haywood enthusiastically
reported that

though in the past there has been bitter acrimony between the industrial Socialists and those whose leanings were strongly political, both
factions—if they may so be referred to—have worked shoulder to
shoulder in presenting the facts to the world and in assisting the
Lawrence textile workers to win their fight.[111]

But at the Socialist Party convention less than two months later,
the constructive Socialists moved to expel all the revolutionaries,
with elimination of Haywood not the least of their goals. Consequently, when the Ettor-Giovannitti Defense Committee was organized to defend the two Lawrence leaders who were being tried
as accessories before the fact in the murder of a Lawrence striker,
Right-wing Socialists declined to participate. Although the Committee, with Haywood as chairman, organized Defense Conferences
in all the major cities, carried on activities rivaling the earlier
Moyer-Haywood Conferences, and raised $60,000,[112] the national
organization of the Socialist Party managed to raise only $400 for
the defense of the I.W.W. leaders.[113] Lawrence was both the beginning and the end of united Socialist participation in the economic battles of the working class.

[109] See below, pp. 389–90.
[110] *Socialist Party Monthly Bulletin,* March, 1912.
[111] Quoted in Leslie H. Marcy and Frederick Sumner Boyd, "One Big Union
Wins," *International Socialist Review,* XII (April, 1912), 619.
[112] Yellen, *American Labor Struggles,* pp. 200–201.
[113] *American Labor Year Book,* 1916, p. 122.

# XVI

# The Peak of Socialist Power

THE SOCIALIST PARTY reached the zenith of its power, prestige, and influence between 1910 and 1912. In dues-paying membership, in national and local union influence, in votes polled, and in members elected and appointed to political office the party attained new and sudden stature, stature which was lost almost as quickly as it was achieved.

The causes for this rapid growth after a period of comparative stagnation were probably fourfold. First was the tremendous upsurge of the progressive movement, which culminated nationally in the split of the Republican Party and the election of Woodrow Wilson. Yet previous experience of the Socialist Party indicates that the competition of reform candidates, as in the local and Congressional elections of 1906 and the Presidential election of 1908, reduced rather than increased its vote. That this decline did not continue between 1910 and 1912 despite the growing number of reform candidates was probably the peculiar product of two congruous developments united with a contradictory one. On the one hand the Socialist Party took on new drive and militancy under the spurs of Left-wing criticism and activity. On the other, Right-wing Socialist devotion to a theory of gradual but uninterrupted social change made reform the official basis of party campaigns and propaganda.

At the same time, ordinary reform organizations repeatedly had failed to satisfy the desire for greater economic and social opportunity and honest government which formed the basis of the progressive movement. Consequently, many union members, professionals, and small businessmen decided to give the revitalized Socialist Party a chance to prove its case.[1] It is ironic that the

[1] "The Tide of Socialism," *The World's Work*, XXXIII (Jan., 1912), 252-53;

renewed vigor which won Socialist votes from a million voters, many of whom were interested in comparatively mild reform, was in large part the product of the militancy of the revolutionary Socialists, who viewed craft unionism, trust regulation and nationalization, and "good government" as devices for the preservation of a hated economic system.

The greatly increased strength of Socialists in the American Federation of Labor, however, can be attributed at best only indirectly to the work of the Left wing. Many Left-wing Socialists, of course, continued to work within the A.F. of L. Despite their allegiance to revolutionary unionism, they remained members of the unions which had organized their skills and industries. Moreover, Left-wing criticism of the constructive Socialists' indifference to union work probably spurred Right wingers to greater activity. Outweighing these considerations, however, was the open hostility displayed by the great majority of the Left toward all participation in the affairs of the "reactionary" American Federation of Labor. Since it was the revolutionary Socialists who insisted on the importance of economic organization of the working class, and the constructive Socialists who viewed the unions largely as recruiting grounds for Socialist votes, the concentration of the revolutionists on building the hopelessly small and sectarian I.W.W. left the American Federation of Labor with a generally nonmilitant Socialist core.

Although the constructive Socialists considered the A.F. of L. leadership as "too conservative," at no time did they advance "fundamental criticisms against" that union.[2] The Right wing said industrial strife could at best bring "slight and transitory benefit to the workers." United political action was the only road to lasting social improvement. Therefore, the constructive Socialists said they could not risk dividing the workers at the polls by advocating industrial in place of craft unionism.[3]

In 1909 the Socialist Party inaugurated a short-lived attempt

---

Ira B. Cross, "Socialism In California Municipalities," *National Municipal Review,* I (Oct., 1912), 611–19.

[2] Hillquit in Hillquit, Gompers, and Hayes, *Double-Edge of Labor's Sword,* p. 46.

[3] "Resolutions of the Rhode Island Socialist Party Convention, January 5, 1908," *Socialist Party Weekly Bulletin,* Jan. 18, 1908. These resolutions were adopted by the overwhelming vote of 75 to 2.

to invigorate its propaganda in the unions. Two national organizers were assigned to spend about two months each in addressing locals of the machinists' and molders' unions on the benefits of joining the Socialist Party and voting the Socialist ticket. Although one of the organizers reported that the greatest handicap to Socialist influence in the labor movement was the refusal of many Socialists to participate in union work,[4] the National Executive Committee considered the general response to the agitation excellent.[5] The party therefore organized a trade union department in the national office, which was in charge of organizers sent out to carry the message of socialism to union workers. In 1911, however, the trade union department was dissolved. The national office conceded that it obtained good results; "but," said National Secretary Barnes, it "could not do otherwise than result in unwarranted interference in the internal affairs of the unions." Henceforth, unions would be brought the truths of socialism by their own Socialist members without assistance from the national party.[6]

Socialist Party support of strikes between 1910 and 1912 was considerably greater than in the earlier years. This support almost invariably took the form of publicity in the socialist press designed to counteract stories printed in nonsocialist papers and of financial contributions to the striking unions.[7] There were, of course, exceptions to this general practice. One was the support women Socialists gave the New York bakers in 1910. For weeks they visited apartments on the upper West Side urging boycott of bread that did not have the union label.[8] Another exception was the assistance given to the garment workers. These workers had been led by socialists since the mid-1890s and their bitter and long-drawn strikes in 1909 and 1910 brought them not only publicity and

[4] "Report of John Collins to the National Executive Committee, Minutes of the National Executive Committee, December 11, 1909," *Socialist Party Official Bulletin*, Dec., 1909.

[5] "Minutes of the National Executive Committee, December 11, 1909," *Socialist Party Official Bulletin*, Dec., 1909.

[6] "Annual Report of the National Secretary of the Socialist Party, January 1 to December 31, 1911," *Socialist Party Monthly Bulletin*, Jan., 1912.

[7] *Socialist Party Weekly Bulletin*, June 9, 1910; "Annual Report of the National Secretary of the Socialist Party, January 1 to December 31, 1910," *Socialist Party Official Bulletin*, Jan., 1911; *American Labor Year Book*, 1916, p. 122.

[8] Carrie W. Allen, "The Bakers' Strikes vs. the Bread Trust," *International Socialist Review*, XI (July, 1910), 7–10.

financial assistance from the party, but Socialist personnel to aid in the conduct of the strikes.[9] The constructive Socialist leaders of that union gladly accepted the loss of the right to strike provided in the "Protocol of Peace" which ended the 1910 cloakmakers' strike. They considered the strike an outmoded weapon, and by glossing over the no-strike feature of the agreement, they sold the Protocol to the militant union membership who had forced the strike on them in the first place.[10]

The record of the national party's financial contributions to important strikes indicates the greater support given unions between 1910 and 1912. In 1902 the still infant Socialist organization had managed to raise $10,000 to aid the anthracite strikers. No other contributions are recorded until 1906–1907 when the party, with more than three times its 1902 membership, managed to raise $15,000 in two years to assist the defense of Moyer, Haywood, and Pettibone. No funds were raised for any union purpose in 1908. In 1909 the party contributed $6,000 to aid the great strike taking place in Sweden. But in 1910–1911 almost $11,000 were poured into the garment workers strike, and in 1912 $18,000 went to Lawrence and $2,000 more to smaller strikes.[11] There is no way of estimating what additional funds were given by local Socialist organizations to assist union activities in their communities.

An exact determination of the amount of Socialist influence in the labor unions is probably impossible. There are no data available on the number of trade unionists who joined the Socialist Party or voted the Socialist ticket. There is information, however, on Socialists elected to union office, the passage of "socialistic" resolutions, the attitude of labor papers, union financial support of the party, and the discussions and votes at national American Federation of Labor conventions. Such evidence indicates considerable and rapidly growing support for Socialists and their program.

By 1907, national and international unions representing some three hundred and thirty thousand members had endorsed the Socialist program, usually through passage of resolutions or consti-

[9] Levine, *Women's Garment Workers*, pp. 44–195; *New York Call*, Nov. 28, 1909.
[10] Levine, *Women's Garment Workers*, pp. 198–200.
[11] *American Labor Year Book*, 1916, p. 122.

tutional amendments. Among these unions were the machinists, patternmakers, metalworkers, boilermakers, engineers, brewery workers, boot and shoe workers, textile workers, woodworkers, flint-glass workers, and, of course, the Western Federation of Miners.[12] During the 1908 election campaign the national organization of the American Federation of Labor supported the Democratic Party. But the Wisconsin Federation of Labor, the Toledo Central Labor Union, the Bakery and Confectionary Workers, the United Brewery Workers, the Western Federation of Miners, and many locals of the United Mine Workers, carpenters, and switchmen endorsed the Socialist ticket.[13] In 1909 the United Mine Workers called for nationalization of the great trusts.[14] And craft unions like those of the printers and carpenters had strong Socialist minorities.[15]

Local unions purchased 50 percent of the stock that financed the *New York Call* and the *Chicago Daily Socialist*, and 550 local unions bought subscriptions to *Appeal to Reason* for their 40,000 members. One leading Socialist organizer estimated that 35 percent of the party's annual campaign funds were contributed by the trade unions.[16] By 1907 at least fourteen national or central labor union papers endorsed the Socialist Party.[17] And when the party was at the peak of its power in 1912, resolutions that were passed and Socialists who were elected to top union positions indicate that the party had the official support of the Brewery Workers, Bakery Workers, Cloth Hat and Cap Makers, Ladies' Garment Workers, Fur Workers, Machinists, Journeymen Tailors, and Western Federation of Miners.[18] In addition, there were large contingents of supporters among the coal miners, flint-glass workers, painters,

[12] John Curtis Kennedy, "Socialistic Tendencies in American Trade Unions," *Journal of Political Economy*, XV (Oct., 1907), 482–83.

[13] Robert Hunter, "The Socialist Party in the Present Campaign," *The American Review of Reviews*, XXXVIII (Sept., 1908), 299.

[14] Hillquit, *History of Socialism*, 1910 ed., p. 354.

[15] John Curtis Kennedy, "Socialistic Tendencies in American Trade Unions," *Journal of Political Economy*, XV (Oct., 1907), 483.

[16] *Ibid.*, pp. 484–85.

[17] *Ibid.*, p. 484. Among these papers were the *Cleveland Citizen, The Labor World* (Columbus, Ohio), *St. Louis Labor, Social-Democratic Herald* (official journal of the Milwaukee Trades Council), the *Brewers' Journal, Bakers' Journal, The Glass Worker*, and *The Miners' Magazine*.

[18] Saposs, *Left Wing Unionism*, p. 33; Hunter, *Labor in Politics*, p. 152.

carpenters, cigarmakers, brick, tile, and terra cotta workers, electrical workers, and printers.[19]

Despite these indications of growing support in the craft unions, Socialists offered little opposition to the conservative leadership and policies of the American Federation of Labor until the 1912 convention. Whatever criticism Socialists may have planned to present at the 1907 Federation Convention was quickly abandoned when Gompers announced that he had refused an offer by the National Association of Manufacturers of a "competence" for the remainder of his life.[20] The twenty Socialist delegates [21] decided to give their complete support to the union president. Berger explained that "this was one of the occasions when we had to follow the dictates of our class consciousness regardless of any politics." [22] Besides, they feared that opposition to Gompers would open the party to charges of being used as dupes or allies of labor's enemies.[23] At the following annual convention, Socialist activity was limited to criticism of Federation support of the Democratic Party and to a futile attempt to force an investigation of Gompers's charge that the Socialist propaganda train, the Red Special, was financed by big business.[24]

Socialist tactics at the 1909 A.F. of L. convention were dictated by the same considerations that determined their course in 1907. This time President Gompers and Vice-President Mitchell were under indictment in the Bucks Stove and Range Case. Although the Socialists estimated that a debate on their standard resolution on the benefits of political action and government ownership would have won the support of from 10 percent to 25 percent of the delegates, they decided not to introduce it or any other motion critical of Federation policies and leadership in the interest of presenting

---

[19] Hunter, *Labor in Politics*, p. 182.

[20] Gompers, *Seventy Years of Life and Labor*, II, 207–10.

[21] *The Worker*, Nov. 23, 1907.

[22] Victor L. Berger, "Would Be Folly to Be Sly!" *Social-Democratic Herald*, Dec. 14, 1907.

[23] Max S. Hayes, "The World of Labor," *International Socialist Review*, VIII (Dec., 1907), 371–74.

[24] *Report of Proceedings of the Twenty-Eighth Annual Convention of the American Federation of Labor* (Washington, National Tribune Co., 1908), pp. 226–28; Max S. Hayes, "World of Labor," *International Socialist Review*, IX (Dec., 1908), 469–71.

a solid front to the common enemy.[25] The *New York Call* did note, however, that Gompers, Mitchell, and several members of the Executive Council were leaving for New York after the convention to attend a dinner of the Civic Federation.[26]

Socialists attending the 1910 Federation convention met and decided neither to offer resolutions nor to participate in any debates. This decision was reached for a number of reasons. For one thing, the Federation leadership was still embroiled in the Bucks Stove Case.[27] For another, they did not wish to encourage reports that they were planning to capture the union.[28] Indeed, the only action taken by the Socialists consisted of circulating a statement insisting that the party would not participate in determining union policies in the "industrial struggle." [29] A third reason advanced by the Socialist delegates for standing aloof from all convention discussions was fear that the certain defeat of their resolutions would furnish "the capitalistic politicians of the country, who are being driven to distraction by the rampant dissatisfaction that confronts them on every hand, with a few crumbs of comfort and an opportunity to claim that the tide had turned against radicalism." [30] Finally, in view of the greatly increased Socialist vote in the 1910 elections, they did not want to precipitate a debate that might lead to further discussion of the desirability of a labor party.[31] The Socialist delegates followed their caucus decision and maintained a discreet silence.[32]

As the 1911 A.F. of L. convention approached, the Socialist trade unionists showed signs that they were affected by the growing militancy of their party. They outlined a five-point program which

[25] Max S. Hayes, "World of Labor," *International Socialist Review*, X (Jan., 1910), 649.

[26] *New York Call*, Nov. 21, 1909.

[27] Victor L. Berger, "We Must Present a Solid Front to the Enemy," *Social-Democratic Herald*, Dec. 3, 1910.

[28] *Ibid.;* Max S. Hayes, "World of Labor," *International Socialist Review*, XI (Jan., 1911), 435–36.

[29] Victor L. Berger, "We Must Present a Solid Front to the Enemy," *Social-Democratic Herald*, Dec. 3, 1910.

[30] Max S. Hayes, "World of Labor," *International Socialist Review*, XI (Jan., 1911), 435–36.

[31] *Ibid.*, 436–37.

[32] *Report of Proceedings of the Thirtieth Annual Convention of the American Federation of Labor* (Washington, D.C., The Law Reporter Printing Co., 1910).

they intended to advance at the convention: (1) election of all
Federation officials by a referendum vote of the membership; (2)
passage of a resolution denouncing the National Civic Federation;
(3) securing of a maximum of financial aid for the McNamara
brothers who had been indicted for dynamiting the Los Angeles
*Times* building; (4) conducting a propaganda campaign to lead
to replacement of the union's craft structure with industrial unions; and (5) running Socialist candidates against the Gompers
slate.[33] About forty of the delegates to the convention were members of the Socialist Party.[34]

A majority of the convention resolutions committee reported unfavorably on the motion to elect Federation officers by referendum.
A minority report called for study of the proposition by the Federation Executive Council and its adoption if practical in operation.
Gompers and the Socialists spoke for the minority report, and it
was adopted.[35] More than two thirds of one day was devoted to debating the three resolutions condemning the National Civic Federation and instructing all Federation officials to sever their connections with it. The Socialist side of the debate was led by Duncan
McDonald of the United Mine Workers. His union, at the instigation of the Socialists, had passed a similar resolution.[36] In answering Socialist attacks on the Civic Federation, Gompers was unkind
enough to note that Socialist leaders seized every opportunity to
dine and associate with capitalists.[37] The resolutions were defeated,
12,000 to 5,000.[38]

The convention sent a telegram of support to the McNamara
brothers, endorsed the appeal for financial aid which the Executive
Council had made shortly after the union leaders' arrest, and instructed all Federation employees to contribute one week's wages
to the McNamaras' defense.[39] In answer to a request of the executive committee of the Socialist Party for aid in the Los Angeles
election which was taking place at the same time as the McNamara

---

[33] J. L. Engdahl in the *New York Call*, Nov. 19, 1911; *New York Call*, Nov. 26,
1911.

[34] See sources cited in Note 33.

[35] *Report of Proceedings of the Thirty-First Annual Convention of the American
Federation of Labor*, pp. 206–8.

[36] *Ibid.*, pp. 217–55.                      [37] *Ibid.*, p. 254.

[38] *Ibid.*, p. 255.                          [39] *Ibid.*, pp. 141, 282, 296–97.

trial, the convention unanimously adopted the following resolution: ". . . the candidate of the workers and the progressive,
liberty loving people of Los Angeles is expressed in the nomination
for the mayoralty of Los Angeles of [Socialist candidate] Job
Harriman. This convention urges the citizenship of Los Angeles,
without regard to sex or station in life . . . to vote for Job Harriman and his associates." All workers were called upon to give the
Harriman campaign both moral and financial support.[40]

Socialists introduced a resolution recording a "pronounced feeling of dissatisfaction" among members of the Federation's Federal
Unions with regard to the policy of promoting the organization
of skilled mechanics in craft unions unable to cope with the new
industrial conditions. The resolution urged a propaganda campaign designed to bring "common workers" into Federal Unions
in such numbers as "to enable this class of workers to assume their
logical position as the most powerful factor within the economic
and political labor movement of the future." [41] The resolutions
committee recommended that the resolution be referred to the Executive Council as an organizational problem. Gompers commented
that there were few Federal Unions because regular craft unions
were recruiting the "less skilled workmen." No one spoke in defense
of industrial unionism and the committee recommendation was carried.[42] The Socialists abandoned their plans to run Socialists
against administration candidates for Federation office, and all
officers—Gompers, eight vice-presidents, a secretary, and a treas-
urer—were elected without opposition.[43]

The Socialists went into the 1912 American Federation of Labor
convention determined to make a militant fight against pure and
simple craft-union policies. They were inspired by the large 1912
party vote and by the presence of 100 Socialist delegates, who
represented one fourth the total attendance.[44] Perhaps they were
goaded as well as inspired by the impressive victories scored during
the year by the Industrial Workers of the World. They even spoke
of running William Johnston, Socialist leader in the International

[40] *Ibid.*, pp. 180–90, 307–8.     [41] *Ibid.*, pp. 186–87.
[42] *Ibid.*, p. 187.
[43] *Ibid.*, pp. 343–44; *New York Call*, Nov. 26, 1911.
[44] *New York Call*, Nov. 11, 1912.

Association of Machinists, for vice-president of the Federation.[45] The Socialist delegates quickly organized their caucus under the chairmanship of J. Mahlon Barnes.[46] When they were not in caucus or on the convention floor, they held noonday rallies at the Rochester, New York, factory gates.[47] They were soon so enthusiastic over their new-found strength and militancy that they spoke of putting "up a strong fight for the control of the convention." [48]

The convention resolutions committee again reported against the motion to elect Federation officers by referendum. This time, however, there was no minority report. The debate was long and bitter, and in the course of it Gompers made a vitriolic attack on the Socialists. The motion was defeated, 193 to 57.[49]

The United Mine Workers delegation [50] introduced a resolution which called attention to the sharpening struggle between labor and capital. It moved that the Federation's officers be instructed to use their influence to reorganize the union along industrial lines.[51] A compromise motion was offered which resolved

that where practical one organization should have jurisdiction over an industry, and where in the judgment of a majority of the men actually involved it is not practical, then . . . they [should] organize and federate in a department and work together in such manner as to protect, as far as possible, the interests of all connecting branches.[52]

The Socialists accepted this compromise motion. The debate lasted an entire day. On a roll call vote, it was defeated, 11,000 to 6,000.[53]

When nominations for president of the Federation were in order, the Socialists put forward the name of Max Hayes of the typographers' union to run against Gompers. Hayes won all the votes of five international unions—Bakery Workers, Cloth Hat and Cap Makers, Machinists, Shingle Weavers, and Western Federation

---

[45] Ibid.
[46] New York Call, Nov. 13, 1912.
[47] Ibid., Nov. 13, 14, 1912.
[48] Ibid., Nov. 14, 1912.
[49] Report of Proceedings of the Thirty-Second Annual Convention of the American Federation of Labor (Washington, D.C., The Law Reporter Printing Co.), pp. 363–73.
[50] The six members of the seven-man U.M.W. delegation who introduced the motion were William Green, Frank J. Hayes, John Mitchell, Duncan McDonald, J. H. Walker, and John P. White. The seventh member was Tom L. Lewis (ibid., p. 265).
[51] Ibid., p. 265.
[52] Ibid., pp. 265–66.
[53] Ibid., pp. 309–12.

of Miners. He also received the votes of six of the seven United Mine Workers delegates, three fifths of the Brewery Workers, two thirds of the Journeymen Tailors, one half of the Painters and Decorators, and one half of the Quarry Workers, as well as scattered support from other unions. Gompers won, 12,000 to 5,000.[54]

Even more impressive was the Socialist showing in the balloting for third vice-president. The Socialists ran William Johnston of the machinists against the administration candidate, James O'Connell of the same union. O'Connell won, 10,800 to 6,200.[55] It is little wonder that the *New York Call* concluded that "it was the most encouraging convention the American Federation of Labor has yet had. . . . There is no chance of going backward." [56]

Great as was the elation felt by most Socialists at the impressive showing made by Max Hayes at the A.F. of L. convention, it was the remarkable rise in the party vote in political elections that convinced constructive and many revolutionary Socialists that they had really arrived as a political force. Even before the votes were cast in the 1910 Congressional elections, National Secretary Barnes noted that the party had taken on renewed vitality. For the first time in years a good proportion of the membership took an active part in the campaign.[57] And when the vote was tallied, Socialist returns, which had remained stationary or declined for six years, showed a 50 percent gain. The 1908 Presidential vote of some four hundred thousand had increased to over six hundred thousand.[58]

Equally exciting was the news that the party had at last elected a candidate to Congress. Victor Berger had won 38 percent of the vote in a three-way race for the Congressional seat from the northern half of Milwaukee and its adjoining county.[59] Moreover, the party had elected 19 members to various state legislatures, carried five counties, and won control in 12 cities and towns.[60] Truly, things were looking up.

[54] *Ibid.*, pp. 374–75.          [55] *Ibid.*, pp. 375–76.
[56] "The Rochester Convention," *New York Call*, Nov. 24, 1912.
[57] J. Mahlon Barnes in the *Socialist Party Weekly Bulletin*, Oct. 29, 1910.
[58] *American Labor Year Book*, 1916, pp. 97–98.
[59] *Social-Democratic Herald*, Nov. 12, 1910. Berger received 13,417 votes, his Republican opponent 13,094, and his Democratic opponent 8,397.
[60] *Socialist Party Weekly Bulletin*, Nov. 12, 1910. States with Socialist members of the legislature were California, Massachusetts, Minnesota, and Pennsylvania.

But even these impressive victories faded into insignificance as reports on 1911 local elections poured in. By October, at least 435 Socialists from 33 states held elected offices in over one hundred and sixty municipalities and election districts.[61] When the November and December election results were in, the party found itself with more than one thousand of its members elected to political office in 337 towns and cities.[62] These included 56 mayors, 305 aldermen and councilmen, 22 police officials, 155 school officials, and four poundkeepers.[63]

In the spring elections of 1911, Socialist victories were concentrated in the Middle West, where 50 percent of the contests were won, on the Pacific Coast, and in the mining regions of the West and Northwest. Although most Socialists were elected to office in comparatively industrialized areas, agricultural communities contributed a good proportion of the victories. Few Socialists were elected to office from large urban areas. Although Milwaukee alone elected one eighth of all Socialists to win office, only a third of the victories were scored in communities of over ten thousand, and almost half in communities with a population of less than five thousand.[64]

The fall elections showed a considerable shift in the nature of the vote. The center of gravity shifted eastward, with the Left-wing states and counties of Ohio and Pennsylvania setting new records for party success. This shift is accountable in part, however, by the lack of elections in the old Socialist strongholds in the Middle

---

Counties carried were Lake and Cook in Minnesota, Milwaukee in Wisconsin, Franklin in Ohio, and Marshall in Oklahoma. Cities and towns with Socialist administrations were Grand Salem, Texas; Havelock, Nebraska; East Liverpool, Ohio; Columbus, Ohio; Haverhill, Massachusetts; Carlton, Minnesota; Glen Carbon, Herron, and Dalzell, Illinois; Hamilton, Iowa; Brantwood, Wisconsin; and Two Harbors, Minnesota.

[61] Charles Edward Russell, "Socialism: Just Where It Stands To-Day," *Hampton's Magazine*, XXVII (Jan., 1912), 754; Robert F. Hoxie, "The Rising Tide of Socialism: a Study," *Journal of Political Economy*, XIX (Oct., 1911), 610.

[62] Charles Edward Russell, "Socialism: Just Where It Stands To-Day," *Hampton's Magazine*, XXVII (Jan., 1912), 754; "Annual Report of the National Secretary of the Socialist Party, January 1 to December 31, 1911," *Socialist Party Monthly Bulletin*, Jan., 1912.

[63] "Annual Report of the National Secretary of the Socialist Party, January 1 to December 31, 1911," *Socialist Party Monthly Bulletin*, Jan., 1912.

[64] Robert F. Hoxie, "The Rising Tide of Socialism: a Study," *Journal of Political Economy*, XIX (Oct., 1911), 611, 613.

West. While victories in the spring elections were widely scattered, 42 percent of the 650 new offices won in the fall were in Ohio and Pennsylvania. Farm communities accounted for 45 percent of Socialist triumphs in the spring, but for only 14 percent in the fall.[65] With the Socialist Party in control of the governments of many cities and towns and furnishing a highly vocal minority opposition in hundreds of others, it is little wonder that popular magazines erupted in a barrage of articles on the seemingly irresistible advance of socialism in the United States.[66]

Few of these local victories were won on the issue of capitalism versus socialism. In fact, this issue was usually kept well in the background. The great majority of Socialists elected to office between 1910 and 1912 were ministers and professional men who conducted their successful campaigns on reform questions that appeared crucial in their own communities: local option, prohibition, and liquor law enforcement; corruption, inefficiency, maladministration, graft, and extravagance; bipartisan combination, boss and gang rule, and commission government; public improvements, aid to schools, playgrounds, and public health; municipal ownership, franchises, and equitable taxation; and, in a small minority of the elections, industrial depression and labor disputes.[67]

In California, for example, not one successful Socialist campaign could be described as anything more than a contest between reformers and old-line party bosses.[68] J. Stitt Wilson, who scored the greatest party victory in that state, was elected mayor of Berkeley with the support of the local newspaper, whose editor had turned against the local machine when it excluded him from its key committee. Wilson had a long-established reputation as a well-

[65] Robert F. Hoxie, "The Socialist Party in the November Elections," *Journal of Political Economy*, XX (March, 1912), 207–11.

[66] "Advance of Socialism in the United States," *The Chautauquan*, LXIV (Sept., 1911), 18–19; "The Tide of Socialism," *The World's Work*, XXIII (Jan., 1912), 252–53; "The Warning of Socialism," *Century Magazine*, LXXXIII (Jan., 1912), 472–73; Harry Farrand Griffin, "The Rising Tide of Socialism," *The Outlook*, C (Feb. 24, 1912), 438–48.

[67] Robert F. Hoxie, "The Rising Tide of Socialism: a Study," *Journal of Political Economy*, XIX (Oct., 1911), 620; Hoxie, "The Socialist Party in the November Elections," *Journal of Political Economy*, XX (March, 1912), 213–19; "The Tide of Socialism," *The World's Work*, XXIII (Jan., 1912), 252–53.

[68] Ira B. Cross, "Socialism In California Municipalities," *National Municipal Review*, I (Oct., 1912), 615.

educated, moderately progressive minister and public speaker, and the main election issue was overthrow of machine politics. The Socialist Party increased its strength in minor elections which followed Wilson's victory. None of the election campaigns mentioned the class struggle or suggested that the working class should gain control of the government for even the most moderate of ends. Socialist leaders in Berkeley pointed with pride to the fact that wealthy districts of that city cast at least as high a proportion of votes for their party as did the working-class areas. A writer in the *National Municipal Review*, after a careful study of the Socialist campaign and administration in Berkeley, concluded that "certainly the Socialist Party in Berkeley is not a very revolutionary organization, to be feared by business or the good government forces." [69]

If this was true for Berkeley, it was also true for the great majority of the local Socialist parties which scored election victories. Hundreds of thousands of moderately liberal citizens came to look upon a vote for the Socialist Party as a vote for a specific reform or against corrupt machine politics. As *The World's Work* analyzed the meaning of the support given by middle-class voters to Socialist-sponsored reform measures:

. . . it is silly to maintain that such helpful public acts commit a community to the state ownership of all productive industries. . . . Such protests have a humanizing and liberalizing influence ; and it may very well be that for this reason the Socialists are playing and will play a good part in preventing the fossilization of the old parties. This, in fact, is the reason why many men who utterly reject the creed see the party win minor victories with complacency—the reason why, too, the word "Socialism" no longer frightens them. [70]

The most important of the Socialist municipal election campaigns, one that had tragic consequences for all the major participants—the labor movement, the Socialist Party, the two men on trial for their lives, and their attorney—was the Los Angeles campaign of 1911. Los Angeles was probably the most notorious open-shop city in the country. The Merchants and Manufacturers Association, under the command of General Harrison Gray Otis,

[69] *Ibid.*, p. 616.
[70] "The Tide of Socialism," *The World's Work*, XXIII (Jan., 1912), 252–53.

publisher of the Los Angeles *Times*, enforced the open shop on labor and business alike. Otis viewed his fight against union labor as a military campaign, and his Merchants and Manufacturers Association employed strikebreakers, detectives, thugs, and city government to break unions with every weapon up to and including armed violence. Businessmen who hesitated about joining the Association found themselves subjected to the irresistible economic and social pressure of the entire banking, manufacturing, and merchandising community. As a result, virtually every entrepreneur belonged to the Association. Wages in open-shop Los Angeles were 30 percent below those in the strong union city of San Francisco.[71]

On May 1, 1910, the Los Angeles metalworkers, organized into the International Association of Bridge and Structural Iron Workers, went out on strike. Since 1906 this union had been engaged in virtually open warfare with the National Erectors' Association, a monopoly embracing almost every firm building with steel and which had as one of its basic tenets the enforcement of the open shop.[72] The Los Angeles City Council promptly passed a drastic antipicketing ordinance. Union lines and parades were broken with guns and clubs. The city jails were filled to overflowing with strikers and their supporters.[73] Early on the morning of October 1, the fortress-like building that housed General Otis's Los Angeles *Times* was destroyed by two explosions. The managerial and editorial staff had already left, but 21 workers were killed by falling walls and the fire that followed the explosions.[74] The *Times* immediately charged that the building had been destroyed by the "anarchic scum" of organized labor.[75]

April of the following year saw the beginning of a series of

[71] "For Nation-wide Free Industries," Los Angeles *Times,* Dec., 1912, pp. 3–5, 24–27; "The Arrest of McNamara," *Current Literature,* L (June, 1911), 569; Mayo, *Los Angeles,* pp. 139–43, 148, 151.

[72] Grant, *National Erectors' Association,* pp. 5–120; Harvey J. O'Higgins, "The Dynamiters, a Great Case of Detective William J. Burns," *McClure's Magazine,* XXXVII (Aug., 1911), 348–54.

[73] Peter Clark McFarlane, "What Is the Matter with Los Angeles?" *Collier's,* XLVIII (Dec. 2, 1911), 28; Harvey J. O'Higgins, "The Dynamiters, a Great Case of Detective William J. Burns," *McClure's Magazine,* XXXVII (Aug., 1911), 355; Mayo, *Los Angeles,* pp. 151–53.

[74] "The Los Angeles Atrocity," *The Independent,* LXIX (Oct. 6, 1910), 780–81; "The Arrest of McNamara," *Current Literature,* L (June, 1911), 571; Mayo, *Los Angeles,* pp. 155–57.

[75] Los Angeles *Times,* Oct. 2, 1911.

events which bore a striking similarity to the attempt, five years earlier, of the mine owners' association to convict Moyer, Haywood, and Pettibone and destroy the Western Federation of Miners. James B. McNamara, brother of the secretary-treasurer of the Structural Iron Workers Union, and one Ortie McManigal were arrested with the aid of Burns private detectives in Detroit on charges of safeblowing; they were moved without warrants to a police sergeant's house in Chicago and held incommunicado until extradition papers arrived from Los Angeles. After four days of this secret confinement, McManigal, apparently with the assistance of the Burns Detective Agency which had been retained for some years by the National Erectors' Association to fight the Structural Workers' Union, confessed to numerous dynamite bombings under union pay and direction. However, he denied any part in the Los Angeles *Times* explosion.[76]

James McNamara was promptly shipped to Los Angeles without regard for the laws governing extradition. His brother John was arrested in the union's offices in Indianapolis and dispatched to Los Angeles with such a flagrant denial of his legal rights that both detective William J. Burns and the Los Angeles assistant district attorney were indicted by an Indianapolis grand jury. The McNamara brothers were indicted for murder.[77] The American Federation of Labor secured a most reluctant Clarence Darrow for the defense.[78] Like the Moyer-Haywood-Pettibone case, the Los Angeles tragedy had a long history of open warfare between labor and capital, the activities of a labor-spy detective agency, an explosion, the confession of one man after his secret detention and questioning by private detectives, the illegal extradition of the principals, the determination of the employers to use the case

[76] McManigal, *The National Dynamite Plot;* Burns, *The Masked War,* pp. 125–61; Harvey J. O'Higgins, "The Dynamiters," a Great Case of Detective William J. Burns," *McClure's Magazine,* XXXVII (Aug., 1911), 354–61; "How Burns Caught the Dynamiters," *McClure's Magazine,* XXXVIII (Jan., 1912), 352–59.

[77] Burns, *The Masked War,* pp. 162–210; Grant, *National Erectors' Association,* p. 121; Harvey J. O'Higgins, "The Dynamitors, a Great Case of Detective William J. Burns," *McClure's Magazine,* XXXVII (Aug., 1911), 361–62; "The Arrest of McNamara," *Current Literature,* L (June, 1911), 570, 572–73; "The McNamara Case," *American Review of Reviews,* XLV (Jan., 1912), 9; Mayo, *Los Angeles,* pp. 163–64.

[78] Stone, *Clarence Darrow for the Defense,* pp. 258–63.

to break the union, the conviction of the unions that the entire affair was a frame-up aimed at organized labor, and a defense attorney who was probably the greatest criminal lawyer in America. But the Haywood trial had almost broken Clarence Darrow, and he entered this case with a foreboding that amounted to virtual conviction that given the background and the Los Angeles situation the outlook was almost hopeless.[79]

When the *Times* building was destroyed, Eugene Debs immediately charged that that newspaper and "its crowd of union-haters" were themselves the instigators or perpetrators of the bombing. Debs based his accusation on the theory that those who have most to gain by a crime are the ones most apt to have a hand in its commission. He outlined his case as follows: (1) the class war was reaching a climax in Los Angeles; (2) the resistance of organized labor was rising and the Socialist campaign was at its height; (3) the *Times* was organized labor's most venomous enemy with a record indicating that no crime was too abhorrent for its commission; (4) the *Times* admitted to having expected a bombing and had therefore had a reserve press and labor force in readiness; (5) Los Angeles newspaper articles indicated that the capitalists were growing desperate; (6) bombs were discovered near the homes of prominent members of the Merchants and Manufacturers Association, each before it had exploded. "The bomb that did explode blew up the wage-slaves of the Times only; the bombs that did not explode did not blow up any of the aristocratic owners and managers. There is a peculiar bomb-consciousness in evidence here that clearly draws the line between capitalists and wage workers." [80] The Left-wing *International Socialist Review* agreed with Debs's analysis, adding as an alternative theory that the explosion might have been caused by leaking gas.[81] But as months passed with no arrests, the matter was quickly forgotten by the Socialists.

When news of the transportation of the McNamara brothers to Los Angeles became public at the end of April, 1911, the National

[79] *Ibid.*, pp. 263–64.

[80] Eugene V. Debs, "The Los Angeles Times—Who Committed That Crime," *Appeal to Reason*, Oct. 15, 1910.

[81] "The Los Angeles Conspiracy Against Organized Labor by 'Unionist,'" *International Socialist Review*, XI (Nov., 1910), 262–66.

Executive Committee of the Socialist Party immediately pledged its support to the Structural Iron Workers unions.[82] The committee also adopted a resolution calling on all party locals to form joint committees with the labor unions to raise funds for the defense of the McNamaras and to publicize the frame-up character of the arrest and prosecution. Furthermore, Socialist locals were to raise funds to aid the Socialist campaign in California, and particularly in Los Angeles.[83] Until Darrow's arrival on the Pacific Coast, the defense was directed by the veteran Socialist attorney, Job Harriman. In May the Los Angeles Socialist Party nominated Harriman for mayor and set up headquarters in the city's labor temple.[84] The national Socialist office set up a press service in Los Angeles, the Socialist press gave the case consistent front-page publicity, Debs went on a nation-wide lecture tour, and Big Bill Haywood arrived in California to aid the election campaign by comparing his trial with the McNamaras'.[85]

Even the most optimistic Socialists were surprised at their showing in the first test of strength. The Los Angeles party was campaigning on its usual reform platform—honest government, a single telephone system, completion of a deepwater harbor, municipal ownership of public utilities, and a graduated tax system.[86] But organized labor was aroused as seldom before. And regardless of the reform platform, everyone knew that the real issue was the recently begun McNamara trial.[87] The primaries were held on October 31. The candidate backed by the Good Government Organization and the Merchants and Manufacturers Association re-

[82] Telegram from J. Mahlon Barnes to Frank M. Ryan, President, International Association Bridge and Structural Iron Workers, Indianapolis, April 30, 1911, *Socialist Party Official Bulletin*, May, 1911.

[83] "Minutes of the National Executive Committee, April 30, 1911," *Socialist Party Official Bulletin*, May, 1911.

[84] *Appeal to Reason*, June 3, 1911.

[85] Circular letter from J. Mahlon Barnes to editors of the Socialist press, May 27, 1911, *Socialist Party Weekly Bulletin*, May 27, 1911; Ginger, *The Bending Cross*, p. 305; Stone, *Clarence Darrow for the Defense*, p. 279. William J. Burns replied to the Socialist campaign to free the McNamaras by informing an audience at Columbia University that Debs had employed no less than two hundred men to assassinate him (Coleman, *Debs*, p. 252).

[86] Peter Clark Macfarlane, "What Is the Matter with Los Angeles?" *Collier's*, XLVIII (Oct. 2, 1911), 30–31.

[87] *Ibid.*; *New York Call*, Nov. 12, 1911; Stone, *Clarence Darrow for the Defense*, pp. 278–79; *Appeal to Reason*, May 6, 1911.

ceived 16,000 votes, various minor candidates accumulated 8,000, and Harriman polled over 20,000.[88] Moreover, two Socialist-backed Constitutional amendments—woman suffrage and the initiative, referendum, and recall—were voted into law. The Socialists made no secret of their intention of using the recall to remove the McNamara trial judge, the same jurist who the year before had issued the antipicketing injunctions.[89]

Almost for the first time it dawned on the Socialists that they really had a chance of sweeping the city.[90] The National Executive Committee which had lapsed into its customary lethargy after its first resolutions of support for the McNamaras [91] came to sudden life. Money, literature, and organizers poured into the campaign.[92] As the selection of the jury dragged through November, labor support for the Socialist candidates rose rapidly. Unfortunately, Harriman was so occupied with the campaign that he was completely unaware of the negotiations between Darrow and the prosecution that were to result in disaster for all concerned.[93]

Darrow had taken up the defense of the McNamaras with little hope for success. But once in Los Angeles he had thrown himself into the case with his customary vigor and thoroughness. Law offices were set up, local attorneys added to the defense staff, and private detectives hired to check all evidence. In a few weeks the staffs of both Darrow and the prosecuting attorney were honeycombed with each others' agents reporting on every new discovery, revealing every proposed maneuver. It was not long before the prosecution had located witnesses who were willing to testify that James B. McNamara and two other men had committed a series of acts in and around Los Angeles that tied them to the *Times* explosion. Darrow became convinced both of the guilt of his clients and their inevitable conviction.[94]

---

[88] Peter Clark Macfarlane, "What Is the Matter with Los Angeles?" *Collier's*, XLVIII (Oct. 2, 1911), 28.

[89] *Appeal to Reason,* June 3, Oct. 21, 1911.

[90] Morrow Mayo in *Los Angeles* (p. 169) writes that the probability of Harriman's election was apparent by the middle of August.

[91] "Minutes of the National Executive Committee, August 14–15, October 5, 1911," *Socialist Party Official Bulletin,* Aug., Oct., 1911.

[92] *Socialist Party Weekly Bulletin,* Nov. 7, 1911; A. W. Ricker, "Socialism at Work," *Appeal to Reason,* Nov. 25, 1911.

[93] Stone, *Clarence Darrow for the Defense,* p. 293.

[94] *Ibid.,* pp. 270–83.

At this crucial period, while jury lists were being exhausted in the search for unbiased citizens, Lincoln Steffens returned from Europe and appeared on the scene. While in Europe Steffens had become convinced that the McNamaras were guilty as charged. He hoped to get the brothers to plead guilty and then write a series of articles showing how capital had driven labor to the use of violence in self defense. While thus justifying the use of force, Steffens planned at the same time to usher in a period of brotherhood and love in Los Angeles by convincing the Merchants and Manufacturers Association to accept a compromise in the McNamara case. He sold this idea to Darrow who was frantically searching for some way to save the lives of his clients.[95]

Darrow then informed the brothers that their conviction and execution were certainties. He proposed that they plead guilty in exchange for the following terms: the release of union secretary John McNamara who had not been in California at the time of the explosion and who had no connection with the dynamiting; a life sentence for James McNamara; abandonment of the hunt for his two alleged accomplices. Darrow argued that this arrangement would not only save their lives but, since James McNamara did not belong to the Structural Workers, would also prevent persecution of the union and prosecution of dozens of men under the charges contained in the McManigal confession. After hours of pleading, the brothers finally consented. Darrow then sent one of his colleagues in the case, an attorney who was also a Good Government candidate for office in the December elections, to negotiate with the prosecution and the Merchants and Manufacturers Association. They agreed, provided that John McNamara accepted a sentence of ten years instead of acquittal, and provided that the confession and pleas of guilty were made before the election of December 5.[96]

Darrow returned to his clients. John McNamara was willing to accept this new arrangement to save his brother's life, but James had agreed to the settlement in the first place only to free John and clear the union. After hours of further pleading, James finally

[95] Steffens, *Autobiography,* pp. 658–72.
[96] Stone, *Clarence Darrow for the Defense,* pp. 292–93.

agreed. But even this modification of the original terms was not the end. Just before the plea was made, the judge insisted on fifteen years for John McNamara. This, too, was accepted. On December 1, five days before the election, while thousands of workers displayed buttons reading "McNamaras Not Guilty! Vote For Harriman!" Darrow took his clients into court and pleaded them guilty.[97] The evidence indicates that James McNamara had participated in numerous dynamitings over a six-year period in retaliation for the employers' violent open-shop campaign. No one had been killed in any of these bombings, thanks to the precautions taken by the dynamiters. The charge set at the Los Angeles *Times* building was not large, but subsequent explosions of barrels of printer's ink had wrecked the building and killed 21 workers. John McNamara and the union had had nothing to do with the *Times* dynamiting.[98]

What Darrow and Steffens planned as a negotiated peace turned into a rout and unconditional surrender. The American Federation of Labor immediately denounced the McNamaras and their attorney and insisted that it was innocent of everything but credulity.[99] Right-wing Socialists frantically pointed out that the McNamaras were not Socialists but Democrats and Catholics who used capitalist methods of violence.[100] A. M. Simons even denied that the party had ever called for contributions for their defense. They had simply attempted to carry California for Socialism, and it was this campaign that had brought about the confessions. Therefore, said Simons, "the Socialists alone come out of all this mess with unsmirched character."[101]

Job Harriman, who had not heard of the confession until he had read it in the triumphant newspaper headlines, issued a public statement pointing out that he had not participated on the defense

[97] *Ibid.*, pp. 293–94, 299–301.

[98] Grant, *National Erectors' Association*, pp. 122–23.

[99] Los Angeles *Times*, Dec. 2, 1911; "Statement of McNamara Ways and Means Committee, December 9, 1911," *Report of Proceedings of the Thirty-Second Annual Convention of the American Federation of Labor*, pp. 142–44.

[100] "The Failure of Capitalist Methods," *New York Call*, Dec. 3, 1911; *Appeal to Reason*, Dec. 9, 1911; A. M. Simons in the *Appeal to Reason*, Dec. 16, 1911; Gaylord, *Socialism Is Coming—Now*, p. 26.

[101] A. M. Simons in *Appeal to Reason*, Dec. 16, 1911.

legal staff since the primaries. "The McNamara case," said Harriman, "has never been an issue in the campaign and cannot be an issue now." [102] Harriman could hardly have believed his own statement. Certainly the voters did not. The streets of Los Angeles were strewn with Socialist buttons.[103] Harriman was defeated, 87,000 to 50,000.

The Socialist failure was only one of many blows. Steffens, after a conference with the judge, had reported to Darrow that the court would handle his clients gently and make every effort to quiet the bitterness that was sweeping the city.[104] Instead, Darrow found himself standing between the brothers on election day while the judge denounced them as "murderers at heart." [105] The warrants for James McNamara's alleged accomplices were not dropped. The men were hunted for five years and then convicted with the aid of the McNamara confession. Moreover, McManigal's confession, written in the flowery language of William J. Burns, and the prosecution's charges against the union, both of which Darrow had promised the McNamaras would not be used against organized labor, were all publicized in the later trials. Thirty-two union members and leaders were convicted of participation in dynamite conspiracies and sentenced to prison.[106] The Los Angeles Structural and Iron Workers strike was abandoned.[107] The unions turned from their campaign of defense for those whom they had described as victims of class justice to frantic denials that all labor leaders were murderers.

And what of Clarence Darrow? In 1894 he had given up the Northwestern Railroad as a client in order to defend Eugene Debs from the General Managers Association. But after seventeen years of experience in labor defense cases he had still believed that a real compromise could be worked out with Otis and his associates. Darrow found himself indicted and tried on a charge of jury-bribing and subornation of perjury, charges apparently framed by the

[102] Social-Democratic Herald, Dec. 9, 1911.
[103] Steffens, Autobiography, p. 688.          [104] Ibid., pp. 686–87.
[105] Los Angeles Times, Dec. 6, 1911.
[106] Mayo, Los Angeles, p. 185; Stone, Clarence Darrow for the Defense, p. 306.
[107] Report of Proceedings of the Thirty-Second Annual Convention of the American Federation of Labor (Washington, D.C., The Law Reporter Printing Co.), p. 20.

Merchants and Manufacturers Association before and during the time he was negotiating with them.[108]

Only the Left wing of the Socialist Party refused to surrender. Debs defended the McNamaras as brave but misguided men who had fought back with "the brutal methods of self-preservation which the masters and exploiters of their class have forced upon them." [109] Frank Bohn insisted that the brothers had been misguided only in the sense that John Brown had been misguided. "The hearts of the McNamaras were right. It was their heads which were in error." [110] And, of course, Bill Haywood refused to budge an inch. "I'm with the McNamaras and always will be. You can't view the class struggle through the eyes of capitalist-made laws." [111]

No other Socialist campaigned for office under circumstances approaching the McNamara case. Most election campaigns were fought along the lines of reform versus graft and privilege, and the conduct of successful Socialist candidates in office was in keeping with their campaign pledges. The implementation of the program of constructive socialism can be studied only on the state and municipal level, for during the period under consideration Victor Berger was the lone Socialist elected to Congress.

Berger's Congressional activities during 1911–1912 throw some light on step-at-a-time socialism, however. Beyond two effective investigations in the Lawrence strike and the removal of a prejudiced judge from the Federal bench, his work was largely devoted to introducing measures he viewed as bricks in building the new social order. These included about twenty bills ranging from repeal of the antitrust law and nationalization of certain natural monopolies to old age pensions, abolition of the Senate and the Presidential veto power, regulation of woman and child labor, woman suffrage, local home rule for the District of Columbia, creation of a public store in Washington for civil service employees, and erection of a

---

[108] Stone, *Clarence Darrow for the Defense,* pp. 283–87, 295–98, 307–43. Steffens conceded that his "experiment" was a failure. (Steffens, *Autobiography,* p. 689.)

[109] Eugene V. Debs, "The McNamara Case and the Labor Movement," *International Socialist Review,* XII (Jan., 1912), 400.

[110] Frank Bohn, "The Passing of the McNamaras," *International Socialist Review,* XII (Jan., 1912), 404.

[111] Los Angeles *Examiner,* Dec. 5, 1912.

post office in Waukesha, Wisconsin. Berger also voted for the following bills: Canadian reciprocity, farmers' free list, admission of Arizona along with its constitutional provision for recall, and reduction of tariff duties on steel, wool, and cotton. He voted against a treaty of extradition with Russia.[112]

Between 1898 and 1912 the Socialist Party succeeded in electing about sixty of its candidates to various state legislatures. With the exception of Wisconsin, however, no state ever had more than one or two Socialists in the assembly or senate in any one session.[113] In the years under study, Socialist state legislators introduced some 520 bills,[114] and succeeded in getting the high proportion of 143 enacted into law.[115] Almost all Socialist state assemblymen and senators followed the legislative example set by the Wisconsin party, both because the theory of constructive socialism had received its earliest and most forthright expression in that state and because of the comparatively great electoral success scored by the Wisconsin party.[116]

The Wisconsin Socialists raised the practice of supporting all measures of immediate benefit to the working and middle class to the level of a theory of the gradual coming of socialism. But the pattern of that support was set by the Massachusetts Social Democratic Party in 1899, six years before the Wisconsin party elected a man to the legislature. The two Massachusetts Social Democrats who served from 1899 to 1903 introduced bills for shorter hours, employer liability, municipal home rule, easing provisions for municipal purchase of electric light and gas plants, and the initiative, referendum, and recall.[117]

The first five Socialists elected to the Wisconsin legislature in 1905 introduced more than twenty-four measures, all of which

[112] Social-Democratic Vest Pocket Manual, 1912 Fall Campaign, pp. 21-26; American Labor Year Book, 1916, pp. 101-2.

[113] Ethelwyn Mills, Legislative Program of the Socialist Party, pp. 5-6. States with Socialist legislators were Massachusetts (one from 1898 to 1903, another from 1899 to 1902, and a third elected in 1912); New York (one in 1911); Pennsylvania (one in 1910); Minnesota (one in 1910 and another in 1912); Rhode Island (one in 1911); Kansas (three in 1912); Nevada (two in 1912); California (one in 1912); Illinois (one in 1912); Montana (one in 1912); Washington (one in 1912); Wisconsin (five in 1905, five in 1907, three in 1909, fourteen in 1911). (Ibid., pp. 5-6, 10-11.)

[114] Ibid., p. 10.    [115] Ibid., p. 48.    [116] Ibid., p. 10.

[117] Ibid., p. 5; "Socialist Unity Convention Indianapolis, 1901," typescript in Harper Library, University of Chicago, p. 190.

were defeated. In 1907 they advanced 72 bills, and obtained passage for 15 of them. The 1909 legislative record reflected the decline in Socialist activity. Forty-two measures were introduced by the Socialists, but only two much-amended bills became laws. But in 1911, after the victory in Milwaukee, the 14 Socialist legislators introduced 260 bills, and 67 of them were passed. Moreover, a number of measures introduced by the Socialists over the previous six years had been made part of Democratic and Republican platforms, and they were adopted with Socialist support.[118]

Wisconsin Socialists divided their bills into two categories, those that aided labor and were indirect steps in the direction of socialism, and those directly aimed at increasing the degree of socialism in what they regarded as the mixed capitalist-socialist American economy.[119] Among the former were measures for shorter hours, higher wages, better working conditions, employer liability, regulation of women's, children's and convicts' labor, restraints on use of the injunction, and memorials on restricting immigration. Among the latter were bills for municipal home rule, easing restrictions on municipal ownership, regulation of public utilities, and municipal initiative, referendum, and recall.[120] Equal justice for both rich and poor was to be achieved through a measure calling for a public defender in every county and a memorial demanding election of federal judges.[121] The liberal magazine, *The Independent*, found that Wisconsin citizens did not consider their Socialist legislators as "remarkably radical. Really they are the advance guard of a great civic movement. . . . In its entity theirs is a protest against misgovernment." [122] The legislative department of the party, however, held that if so few Socialists could secure passage of 141 reform measures in 12 years, "then surely the future of the socialist movement is secure." [123]

Milwaukee Socialists set the pattern for Socialist municipal

---

[118] Carl D. Thompson, "Social Democratic Program in the Wisconsin Legislature," *American Political Science Review*, I (May, 1907), 457–65; Ethelwyn Mills, *Legislative Program of the Socialist Party*, pp. 7–10.

[119] Ethelwyn Mills, *Legislative Program of the Socialist Party*, p. 10.

[120] *Ibid.*

[121] Carl D. Thompson, "Social Democratic Program in the Wisconsin Legislature," *American Political Science Review*, I (May, 1907), 464–65.

[122] Fred L. Holmes, "Socialist Legislators at Work," *The Independent*, LXX (March 23, 1911), 594.

[123] Ethelwyn Mills, *Legislative Program of the Socialist Party*, pp. 48–49.

administrations just as they had worked out the tactics for Socialist state legislators. *The Independent* evaluated this program in much the same light as they had viewed the work in Wisconsin : "If this is all the Socialists hope to do it would seem that any progressive and honest Republican or Democrat might approve of the program." [124] Even the far more conservative *Saturday Evening Post* noted that "Berger's party in Milwaukee and Wisconsin, while nominally Socialistic, was really civic and social reform. It was mild and gentle and uplifting and thoroughly housebroken." Victor Berger, said the *Post*, was the "bossiest boss in the state." He had recognized that his party could never win office if it stressed its radicalism. So he had compelled his followers to tone down their socialism to the point where even municipal ownership was barely mentioned. Berger was "a versatile person, with an eye to the main chance and with whom the end always justifies the means." [125]

The Milwaukee Socialists gave their city two years of honest, reform government.[126] Following the lead of Robert La Follette, who had utilized the intellectual resources of the University of Wisconsin in administering the state, they organized a Bureau of Economy and Efficiency under the direction of Professor John R. Commons. The Bureau secured the services of experts in the fields of organization, health and sanitation, engineering, accounting, social work, finance, and taxation. Due in part to a restricted municipal autonomy, little progress was made in extending the city's functions. The record in this direction included only the establishment of a municipal quarry and public comfort station and speeding the work on construction of a city lighting plant.[127]

In other areas, however, the Socialists scored gains that put its two-year term on a level with the best of reform administrations. The Department of Public Works was reorganized, direct employment on municipal projects replaced the contract system, and the cost of asphalt paving was reduced from $2.40 to $1.35 a square yard. The chaotic city budget was replaced with a scientific one.

124 "Milwaukee," *The Independent*, LXVIII (April 14, 1910), 819.

125 "A Neat Minority," *Saturday Evening Post*, CLXXXIII (Dec. 31, 1910), 23.

126 John Collier, "The Experiment in Milwaukee," *Harper's Weekly*, LV (Aug. 12, 1911), 11.

127 *Ibid.*; Graham Romeyn Taylor, "The Socialists in Milwaukee," *The Survey*, XXVII (March 30, 1912), 1997.

Collection of property taxes was enforced. A vigorous campaign to reduce infant mortality was inaugurated, and commissions on tuberculosis and child welfare were created. Ordinances were passed requiring sanitary toilets in factories, safeguarding the health of school children, and limiting sidewalk sweeping to certain hours. Wages of the lowest-paid city employees were raised somewhat,[128] and the Left wing of the party noted with pride that Milwaukee's mayor, Emil Seidel, ordered the chief of police to halt all interference with legal activities of strikers.[129]

While most outside reformers conceded that Milwaukee Socialists had done an outstanding job, the party did not escape criticism within the city. It was accused of raising tax rates, appointing party members to city posts without due regard for ability, and making municipal decisions in party caucus. The party replied that previous budgets carried concealed shortages which had to be replaced, that the old civil service lists were fraudulent, and that opposition threats to eliminate every Socialist from public office did not indicate a devotion to civil service reform. The Socialist record may have been outstanding and its answers to critics conclusive, but this did not prevent the Democratic and Republican parties from uniting in an attempt to overthrow the Socialist interlopers. They nominated a physician who had made an excellent record as health commissioner, raised the slogan of "Redeem Milwaukee," and waged their campaign almost entirely around the issue of antisocialism.[130]

Emil Seidel had been elected mayor in 1910 by polling 27,000 votes out of a total of 60,000. In the April, 1912, elections he polled 30,000 votes, but the "non-partisan" Democratic-Republican candidate polled 43,000.[131] The Milwaukee Socialists claimed that their defeat was really a victory because they had forced the capitalist parties to unite, and because the 1910 victory had been in large part a product of a "protest vote" while the increased 1912

[128] John Collier, "The Experiment in Milwaukee," *Harper's Weekly,* LV (Aug. 12, 1911), 11; Graham Romeyn Taylor, "The Socialists in Milwaukee," *The Survey,* XXVII (March 30, 1912), 1997–98.

[129] "The Struggle of the Garment Workers," *International Socialist Review,* XI (Jan., 1911), 428–29.

[130] Graham Romeyn Taylor, "The Socialists in Milwaukee," *The Survey,* XXVII (March 30, 1912), 1996, 1998–99.

[131] *Social-Democratic Herald,* April 13, 1912.

vote "was a class conscious vote of the workers." [132] The Left-wing *International Socialist Review* agreed that a great victory had been scored in forcing the Democratic and Republican parties to unite. But it warned that the emphasis on middle-class reform, the concern for the interests of Milwaukee's property holders, and the failure to educate the working class in the theories of surplus value and the class struggle would prevent real Socialist victories.[133] Milwaukee Socialists remained unconvinced.

The first Socialist administration of Butte, Montana, 1911–1913, was a small-scale model of the first in Milwaukee. The mayor of Butte listed as the major accomplishments of his first term the reestablishment of the city's credit from its previous bankrupt condition, improved sanitation which lowered the death rate by 3.5 percent, an end to interference with union pickets, and driving the liquor traffic out of the red-light district.[134]

The one important Eastern city won by the Socialists was Schenectady, New York. Schenectady's Republican administration had been under fire for years as the corrupt tool of the "paving gang." In December, 1909, the Democrats won the city elections on pledges to wipe out the paving gang. Once in office, however, they established the same mutually profitable relationship with contractors that their predecessors had enjoyed. During 1911, led by the Reverend George R. Lunn, pastor of the People's Church and editor of the local Socialist newspaper, a vigorous campaign was devoted to exposing inequalities in tax assessments and operations of the paving gang. The Socialists claimed they could operate the city government at a saving of $100,000 a year.

In December, 1911, the voters decided to give the third party a chance; they swept Lunn and virtually every candidate on the Socialist ticket into office.[135] Mayor Lunn promptly announced that while he could not bring socialism in its entirety to Schenectady,

[132] *Ibid.;* the *Milwaukee Leader,* quoted in "Milwaukee's Socialist Reverse," *The Literary Digest,* XLIV (April 13, 1912), 740.

[133] "A Defeat That Is a Victory," *International Socialist Review,* XII (May, 1912), 775.

[134] Walling, *The Socialism of To-Day,* 566–69.

[135] W. W. Campbell, "The Preacher-Socialist Who Made Himself Mayor," *Harper's Weekly,* LV (Dec. 23, 1911), 18.

his administration would make a good start. "We can save money to the people of our city and give them a more efficient administration." [136] During their two years in power the Schenectady Socialists cut the budget while raising the wages of city laborers, reorganized milk inspection, improved street cleaning and repairing, and established a garbage-disposal plant. [137]

Mayor Lunn and his administration came under sharp attack from both his Socialist secretaries, Walter Lippmann and John Macy. Lippmann served during the first six months of Lunn's term in office and resigned in disgust. He charged that the Schenectady Socialists were doing nothing that could not be duplicated in twenty cities with reform administrations. "Socialist rule," wrote Lippmann, "must be described as pretty 'good government.' Timidity of action, the lack of a bold plan, a kind of aimlessness is the reality behind revolutionary speeches." Lippmann pointed out that Schenectady Socialists would be writing slashing attacks on the reforms backed by the present administration if not for the fact that they themselves were the reform government. "Reform under fire of radicalism is an educative thing; reform pretending to be radicalism is deadening." [138]

Mayor Lunn's second secretary, John Macy, was similarly sharp in his criticism. He charged that the only measure adopted by the Socialist administration "for which capitalist society had to spank them" was the establishment of a municipal coal and ice service. The state courts killed the measure with an injunction. Macy granted that any Socialist administration was limited in the scope of its activities. But he argued that Schenectady's Socialists failed to take advantage even of their limited opportunities. They had failed to convert the public schools from instruments of capitalist propaganda into vehicles of Socialist propaganda. They had failed to bond the city to the limit and raise taxes for public improvements. "Instead . . . they adopted the short-sighted policy of economy and low taxes, partly because it was necessary to bid for the support of the property owner and partly because some of the

[136] George R. Lunn quoted in *ibid.*
[137] Walling, *The Socialism of To-Day*, pp. 570–72.
[138] Walter Lippmann, "Schenectady the Unripe," *New York Call*, June 9, 1912.

Socialists themselves were little property owners with the habits of mind of the middle class." [139]

The Left wing of the party was unmerciful in its criticism of constructive Socialist electioneering and reform policies.[140] And the Right wing was equally critical of industrial socialism. But for a few years the tireless activities of both factions in behalf of their own programs resulted in a great but short-lived increase in party membership. In 1904 the dues-paying membership totaled 20,000. For the next three years party rolls grew by only 3,000 a year, standing at 29,000 in 1907. The enthusiasm of the 1908 election campaign brought in over 12,000 new members. But the growing lethargy of the party was reflected in 1909 by a small drop in membership for the first time in the party's history.[141]

The renewed militancy of the revolutionary Socialists which began in the fall of 1909 and the growth of the progressive movement throughout the United States in 1910 brought an immediate spurt in Socialist Party recruiting. Party membership in 1909 stood at 41,000. It jumped to 58,000 in 1910.[142] In the three months following the November, 1910, elections it grew by another 20,000 [143] and membership lists for 1911 averaged 84,000. The party's participation in the labor struggles of 1912, coupled with the election fever of that year, brought enrollment to its all-time high of 150,000 by the May, 1912, party convention.[144]

Membership growth in some states was phenomenal. The Oklahoma party grew from 1,800 in 1909 to 5,800 in 1910.[145] Ohio increased its membership from 2,500 in 1909 to 8,000 in 1911. And Pennsylvania became the state with the largest party membership when it quadrupled its ranks from 3,200 in 1909 to 12,000 in 1912.[146]

The growth in party membership was accompanied by an equal

[139] Macy, *Socialism in America*, pp. 84, 88–89.
[140] Hughan, *Facts of Socialism*, pp. 153–54.
[141] "Annual Report of the National Secretary of the Socialist Party, January 1 to December 31, 1911," *Socialist Party Monthly Bulletin*, Jan., 1912; *American Labor Year Book*, 1916, pp. 94–95.
[142] *Socialist Party Weekly Bulletin*, Jan. 4, 1911.
[143] *Ibid.*, April 1, 1911; *New York Call*, Oct. 8, 1911.
[144] *New York Call*, May 8, 1912.
[145] *Socialist Party Weekly Bulletin*, Jan. 3, 1910, Jan. 4, 1911.
[146] *Socialist Party Weekly Bulletin*, Jan. 3, 1910; *Socialist Party Monthly Bulletin*, January, 1912.

growth in the party budget. Dues continued to provide 60–70 percent of all party income, but the national office budget rose from $36,000 in 1909 [147] to $98,000 in 1912.[148] Income other than dues payments came from the sale of literature, campaign contributions, donations to strike and political refugee funds, and lecture receipts.[149] Expenditures were largely for salaries and operating expenses of the national office.[150] In the election year of 1912, however, a special campaign committee was appointed. The committee raised $23,000 in contributions from "one day's wages" and assessment stamps, $15,000 from the sale of literature and other campaign supplies, and $15,000 from admissions and contributions at party rallies. It spent $66,000 on the campaign: $24,000 on literature, $17,000 on speakers, $21,000 on advertising, stationery, and rent, and $4,000 in appropriations to various states and local districts.[151] As always, the bulk of election expenditures and work was provided by the state and local party organizations.

The Socialist Party entered the 1912 Presidential elections at the height of its power. The Right wing made a concerted effort to stop the nomination of Debs at the May party convention, but was again defeated. It did succeed, however, in nominating as Debs's running mate Emil Seidel, the former Socialist mayor of Milwaukee.[152] Debs's swing through the country on behalf of the party was a tremendous tour de force.[153] He later observed to a friend:

Some thought I was not physically able to make a campaign and to prove it they planned a speaking tour for me the like of which no Presidential candidate has ever made in the history of the United

---

[147] "Annual Report of the National Secretary of the Socialist Party, January 1 to December 31, 1909," *Socialist Party Official Bulletin*, Jan., 1910.

[148] "National Office Financial Report for Year 1912," *Socialist Party Monthly Bulletin*, Jan., 1913.

[149] "Annual Report of the National Secretary, January 1 to December 31, 1909," *Socialist Party Official Bulletin*, Jan., 1910; "Annual Report of the National Secretary, January 1 to December 31, 1910," *Socialist Party Official Bulletin*, Jan., 1911; "Annual Report of the National Secretary, January 1 to December 31, 1911," *Socialist Party Official Bulletin*, Jan., 1912; "National Office Financial Report for Year 1912," *Socialist Party Monthly Bulletin*, Jan., 1913.

[150] See sources cited in Note 149.

[151] "Audit of Campaign Committee Accounts by Ernest Reckett and Co., November 13, 1912," *Socialist Party Monthly Bulletin*, Dec., 1912.

[152] See below, p. 406.

[153] Ginger, *The Bending Cross*, pp. 311–12.

States. I spoke for sixty-eight consecutive days, sometimes five and six times a day, without rest. There were times when I thought I would drop in my tracks, but I kept on determined to fulfill the expectations of the comrades throughout the country.[154]

The Socialist election platform contained a lengthy preamble condemning the capitalist system as outmoded, incompetent, and corrupt. It described the nature of the class struggle and characterized the Socialist Party as "the political expression of the economic interests of the workers." It called on class-conscious workers to use their economic and political organizations "to break the fetters of wage-slavery, and fit themselves for the future society." The preamble was followed by a working program of some fifty demands, including public ownership of the banking and currency system, the means of transportation and communication, natural resources, and grain elevators; conservation of natural resources, public works for unemployed relief, wages and hours laws, and an end to child labor; women's suffrage and a graduated income tax; abolition of the Senate and the Presidential veto power, elimination of the power of the Supreme Court to pass on the constitutionality of legislation, abolition of the federal district courts and circuit court of appeals, curbing the power of injunction, and the calling of a Constitutional convention.[155]

The campaign was complicated by the New Freedom platform of Woodrow Wilson and the Progressive campaign of Theodore Roosevelt. The Progressive Party platform presented no small ideological and propaganda problem to the constructive Socialists, for the Progressives had adopted wholesale many of the immediate demands of the Socialist Party. Of course, the Socialists had been denouncing Roosevelt as an insincere tool of big business for eleven years.[156] And Berger had defined a Progressive as "60 per cent of old disgruntled politician; thirty per cent clear hypocrisy; nine per cent nothing, and 1 per cent Socialist. Put in a bottle and shake

---

[154] Quoted in Herbert Morais and William Cahn, *Gene Debs, the Story of a Fighting American* (New York, International Publishers, 1948), p. 87.

[155] Socialist Party, *Proceedings of the National Convention, 1912*, pp. 102–12, 196–98.

[156] *Social Democratic Herald*, Sept. 28, 1901; *Missouri Socialist*, Oct. 5, 1901; Painter, *That Man Debs*, p. 90; A. M. Simons, "Roosevelt's Muck Rake," *The Chicago Socialist*, April 14, 1906; *The Worker*, June 9, 1906.

well before using and you will have a so-called 'progressive.' " [157]
The Socialists may have destroyed the Progressive ideology and
leadership to their own satisfaction, but they were still forced to
concentrate most of their fire on the Progressive candidate for
President.[158]

Eugene Debs, of course, was not faced with the problem of explaining why reforms advocated by Progressives were not as good
as the same reforms advocated by Socialists. As a revolutionary
Socialist he rejected the theory that capitalism was reforming itself
into socialism. In his campaign he conceded that Roosevelt, Taft,
and Wilson differed on political issues such as direct legislation,
recall of public officials, and direct election of Senators. But they
were of one mind on the paramount economic issue: preservation
of the capitalist system. The Socialists, said Debs, worked to overthrow the present economic order. Moreover, his political party did
not pretend to serve both the capitalists and 'the workers. It appealed to the world's workers on the basis of their class interests.
As for the Roosevelt and Wilson controversy on the best way of
meeting the problem of monopoly, both "control of corporations
and the enforcement of the penal clauses of capitalist anti-trust
legislation, by capitalist politicians, are twin frauds in the program of capitalism's efforts to fool the people." America's capitalist
government was controlled by corporate wealth, said Debs. "Until
*corporate wealth* is supplanted by *common* wealth in the ownership
of this nation," the capitalist government "will continue to write
our laws and to enforce them or not, as best pleases its owners." [159]

The Socialist Party confidently predicted two million votes and
the election of twelve Congressmen.[160] They polled 900,000.[161] Not
only did they fail to elect any new Congressmen, but Victor Berger
lost his seat in the House of Representatives. For while the party
as a whole had increased its 1908 vote by 112 percent, Wisconsin

---

[157] Quoted in Walling, *Socialism as It Is,* p. 181.

[158] "Won't Bite at Bull Moose Bait," *New York Call,* Oct. 30, 1912; Coleman,
*Debs,* p. 263.

[159] Eugene V. Debs, "The Socialist Party's Appeal," *The Independent,* LXXIII
(Oct. 24, 1912), 950–52.

[160] J. Mahlon Barnes, manager, Socialist Campaign Committee, quoted in the
*New York Call,* Oct. 10, 1912.

[161] The Socialist Labor Party polled 30,000 votes (*Social-Democratic Herald,*
March 15, 1913).

Socialists had increased theirs only 21 percent.[162] Again the Left wing of the party was able to point to the elections as proof that their policy of throwing all their strength "into the daily warfare of the workers against the capitalist class" paid off in votes.[163] In Allegheny County, Pennsylvania, where the party had participated in union activity and strikes, the Socialist vote had increased by 300 percent. The solidly Left-wing state of Ohio had polled 90,000 votes, a 190 percent increase over 1908 and the highest state vote in the country. And striking West Virginia miners who had been aided by the revolutionary Socialists expanded the party's vote by 300 percent.[164] On the other hand, such important Right-wing states as Massachusetts, Wisconsin, New York, and New Jersey had increased their vote by the relatively smaller margins of 17–65 percent.[165]

Whatever may have been the disappointment at the failure to poll two million votes and elect a vocal minority to Congress, the Socialist vote was impressive. Competition for reform votes by all parties had been keen. And still the party had managed to more than double its previous Presidential poll. Colonel Harvey, the editor of *Harper's Weekly* and the man who had done much to move Woodrow Wilson into the political limelight, estimated that without the competition of the Progressive Party Debs would have received an additional five hundred thousand votes.[166] The Left wing rejoiced that the party vote had been largely revolutionary, since those who favored reform would have voted for Roosevelt or Wilson.[167] The Right wing forgot for the moment how hard it had worked for reform votes and boasted that "every vote cast for the Socialist ticket this year is a straight vote for the Cooperative Commonwealth." [168] It was "the strongest, straightest, cleanest, most

---

[162] *American Labor Year Book*, 1916, pp. 99–100; *Social-Democratic Herald*, March 15, 1913.

[163] "The Election," *International Socialist Review*, XIII (Dec., 1912), 462.

[164] *Ibid.*, pp. 462–463; *American Labor Year Book*, 1916, pp. 99–100; *Social-Democratic Herald*, March 15, 1913.

[165] *Ibid.*

[166] "The Socialist Vote in the United States," *The Chautauquan*, LXIX (Jan., 1913), 135.

[167] "After the Battle," *International Socialist Review*, XIII (Dec., 1912), 495; Eugene Debs quoted in the *New York Call*, Nov. 7, 1912.

[168] Charles Edward Russell quoted in the *New York Call*, Nov. 7, 1912.

uniform vote we have ever had." [169] Debs predicted the momentary demise of the Republican Party and the rapid disintegration of the Progressives.[170] And the *New York Call* announced "power is in sight. Prepare for it by increasing the party strength." [171]

But instead of increasing party strength, constructive Socialists prepared a coup which they expected would eliminate for all time the revolutionists who were frightening off middle-class supporters.

[169] *New York Call,* Nov. 7, 1912.
[170] Eugene Debs quoted in the *New York Call,* Nov. 7, 1912.
[171] *New York Call,* Nov. 7, 1912.

# XVII

# Factionalism

As THE SOCIALIST PARTY GREW in member-
ship, militancy, and vote, factionalism multiplied rather than diminished. Constructive Socialists denounced Left wingers as syndicalists who believed in guerrilla warfare, chicanery, and violence.[1]
They denied that the revolutionaries were entitled to call themselves
Socialists since they rejected two fundamental Socialist concepts:
use of American democratic institutions to control the economy [2]
and recognition that the world process is evolutionary, not cataclysmic. "Socialism has come to build, not to destroy," [3] Morris Hillquit declared. Right wingers invited those who did not accept the
theory of evolutionary socialism "to clear out of the party as
quickly as possible." [4]

Because the Industrial Socialists were determined to turn the
party into a working-class organization designed to assist the revolutionary unions in their struggle for emancipation, they were
deeply concerned when growing numbers of revolutionary Socialists accepted the Right-wing invitation and left in disgust.[5] The
resolution accompanying the resignation of the entire third-ward
branch of Local Denver, Colorado, bears extensive quotation for
it expresses the disillusion and contempt felt by these Left-wing
deserters toward the policies and tactics of the organization they
had worked so hard to build.

The resolution charged that the party was no longer a revolutionary working-class organization based on principles of scientific

[1] Hillquit, *Socialism Summed Up*, p. 54.
[2] Spargo, *Syndicalism, Industrial Unionism, and Socialism*, pp. 188–89.
[3] Hillquit, *Socialism Summed Up*, p. 55.
[4] *Social-Democratic Herald*, March 20, 1909.
[5] "Socialist Unity in America," *International Socialist Review*, XII (July, 1911),
47–48; Austin Lewis, "A Positive Platform," *International Socialist Review*, XII
(April, 1912), 664.

socialism. It was now "a stamping ground for faddists, careerists and notoriety seekers bent upon obtaining pelf and power at the expense of an already overburdened class." Virtually all official positions had been "usurped by as conscienceless a crew of bourgeois buccaneers as ever practiced piracy on the high seas of Liberty, Equality and Fraternity." Proletarian leadership had been replaced by a

cockroach element, composed of preachers without pulpits, lawyers without clients, doctors without patients, storekeepers without customers, disgruntled political coyotes and other riff-raff. . . . In their mad scramble for votes, these muddle-headed marauders of the middle class have seen fit to foist upon the Socialist Party, in the name of the working class, such infamies as "Craft Unionism," "Anti-Immigration," "State Autonomy," and a series of ludicrous and illogical "Immediate Demands." [Therefore, we] fifty-five proletarian members . . . do reaffirm our allegiance to the principles of SCIENTIFIC SOCIALISM and to the cause of OUR class, and do hereby withdraw from the organization falsely called "The Socialist Party of the United States." [6]

Left-wing Socialists who remained in the party redoubled their attacks on step-at-a-time socialism. In January, 1911, the *International Socialist Review* published one of Eugene Debs's rare statements on party factionalism. In an article entitled "Danger Ahead," Debs warned that too many influential Socialists were willing to sacrifice the party's revolutionary principles for votes and office. It was both useless and dangerous, said Debs, to elect Socialists to public office while the party and its supporters were economically and politically unprepared to overthrow capitalism and establish the co-operative commonwealth. Opportunist tactics pursued by the Right-wing leadership were attracting middle-class reformers who were destroying the party's working-class character and corrupting its revolutionary spirit. Debs warned that the Socialist movement could save itself only if it concentrated on organizing the workers into industrial unions.

Not for all the vote of the American Federation of Labor and its labor-dividing and corruption-breeding craft unions should we com-

---

[6] "Resolution of the Third Ward Branch of Local Denver, Socialist Party of Colorado, September 23, 1909," *International Socialist Review*, X (Nov., 1909), 450.

promise one jot of our revolutionary principles; and if we do we shall
be visited with the contempt we deserve by all real socialists who will
scorn to remain in a party professing to be a revolutionary party of
the working class while employing the crooked and disreputable
methods of ward-heeling politicians to attain their ends.[7]

During the 1908 Presidential campaign the Right-wing-
controlled National Executive Committee indicated their determination to eliminate revolutionary Socialists from all positions
of leadership. Alfred Wagenknecht, a leading West Coast party
organizer, applied for a position as a national organizer. For the
first time the executive committee rejected such an application on
openly ideological grounds. Protests from Socialists all over the
country forced the committee to reverse its decision. But as soon
as the election was over, it aroused another political storm when
it canceled the appointment. The committee claimed that Wagenknecht had been employed only for the duration of the campaign,
a claim the record does not support.[8] The fight over the appointment was perhaps the first shot indicating that the struggle between
Right and Left wings had changed from guerrilla to organized
warfare. Within six months constructive and revolutionary Socialists were at each other's throats in virtually every state in the country.[9]

The Socialist civil war quickly developed a pattern of expulsions, campaigns for control of key committees, formation of dual
state and local organizations, and intervention by the Right-wing
national office.[10] In some of the local organizations the controversies
were so prolonged, involved, and bitter that it is almost impossible
to distinguish between various factions. The Cleveland *Citizen* ac-

[7] Eugene V. Debs, "Danger Ahead," *International Socialist Review,* XI (Jan.,
1911), 413–15.

[8] "Minutes of the National Executive Committee, July 11, 1908," *Socialist Party
Official Bulletin,* July, 1908; *Socialist Party Weekly Bulletin,* Aug. 8, Sept. 9, 12,
1908; "Minutes of the National Executive Committee, August 16, 1908," *Socialist
Party Weekly Bulletin,* Aug. 18, 1908; *Socialist Party Weekly Bulletin,* Oct., 1908.

[9] "Annual Report of the National Secretary of the Socialist Party, January 1 to
December 31, 1909," *Socialist Party Official Bulletin,* Jan., 1910; "Minutes of the
National Executive Committee, December 11–13, 1909," *Socialist Party Official Bul-
letin,* Dec., 1909; Bill Haywood quoted in *The Socialist* (Seattle), June 12, 1909;
"Resolution of Local Tyler, Texas," *Socialist Party Weekly Bulletin,* Oct. 23, 1909.

[10] "Minutes of the National Executive Committee, December 11–13, 1909," *Socialist Party Official Bulletin,* Dec., 1909.

curately described the situation in Chicago with the comment that "if there is any organization of human beings in Chicago—political, industrial, fraternal, religious or otherwise—in which there isn't at least one factional scrap, nobody has ever heard of it." [11] In California, the Right wing won control of the state organization after a two-year orgy of expulsions, election of dual local and state officials, and intervention by Wisconsin Socialist organizers.[12] The new Right-wing state committee, headed by Job Harriman, promptly forbade Eugene Debs and Bill Haywood to appear before any Socialist local in the state.[13]

In proportion to population the Left-wing Washington Socialist Party had the highest membership and second highest vote in the country.[14] Late in 1906 the Washington Right-wing Socialists invited Walter Thomas Mills to leave Chicago and take charge of their campaign to gain control of their state's party.[15] When Mills arrived, he suggested that a "good government" campaign be offered in place of the Left wing's effective fight for free speech, relief for the unemployed, and union organization. All efforts should be concentrated on getting the support of "solid, earnest citizens." Furthermore, said Mills, acceptance of Socialist ideology need not be a requirement for party membership. Everyone who voted the Socialist or Socialist-supported reform ticket should have a voice in party decisions.[16] The resultant factional fight was bitter, accompanied by numerous suspensions, expulsions, and referendums.[17] At the July, 1909, state convention the Right wing was in

11 Quoted in the *New York Call*, Jan. 10, 1912.

12 Letter from Maynard Shipley to the *International Socialist Review*, X (Sept., 1909), 281–82; letter from William McDevitt, National Committeeman for California, to J. Mahlon Barnes, March 17, 1910, *Socialist Party Weekly Bulletin*, March 23, 1910; *Socialist Party Official Bulletin*, March, 1910; *Socialist Party Weekly Bulletin*, April 30, 1910.

13 *New York Call*, June 11, 1911.

14 "Minutes of the National Executive Committee, December 18, 1908," *Socialist Party Official Bulletin*, Dec., 1908.

15 *Saturday Evening Tribune* (Seattle), May 4, 1907; *The Socialist* (Seattle), April 14, 1907; Seattle *Post-Intelligencer*, Sept. 4, 1907. The *Saturday Evening Tribune* was published in Seattle by W. T. Mills.

16 Seattle *Post-Intelligencer*, Sept. 9, 1907; *Saturday Evening Tribune*, May 25, Aug. 31, Sept. 14, 1907; *Socialist Party Weekly Bulletin*, Oct. 19, 1907; *The Socialist* (Seattle), Sept. 14, Oct. 12, 1907, March 21, 1908.

17 *The Socialist* (Seattle), April 11, 20, May 4, June 15, July 27, Aug. 17, 24, 31, Sept. 7, Nov. 16, 1907, June 27, Nov. 21, 1908, March 27, May 1, July 3, 1909; *Saturday Evening Tribune*, May 4, 25, Aug. 31, Sept. 14, 1907; *The Worker*, May 18,

the majority for the first time in the state's history. The Left
charged the Right with unconstitutional conduct at the convention's opening sessions, walked out of the convention, and held one
of their own.[18] A referendum of the state's membership was held
to determine which of the two state committees had the support of
a majority of the Socialists. Before the referendum could be completed, the National Executive Committee declared it illegal and
recognized the organization of the constructive Socialists.[19] Herman Titus and other Left-wing leaders in the state promptly abandoned the party as unworthy of their further support.[20]

When the members of the Missouri Socialist Party voted in 1910
to revoke the charter of Local St. Louis for fusion tactics in the
1909 election, both the National Executive Committee and Right-
wing organizers from Wisconsin attempted to intervene. Only a
resolution by the National Committee and a referendum of the
party membership prevented the executive committee from up-
setting the decision of the Missouri Socialists.[21]

Right-wing-controlled Local Omaha seceded from the Left-wing
controlled Nebraska state organization and set up a rival state
committee. The new committee was supported by three locals, the
old by eighteen. The National Executive Committee ruled that
the entire state should be reorganized and employed the leader of
Nebraska's Right-wing faction to do the job. Within two months
the National Committee had voted down twenty-five different mo-

---

1907; letter from Ira Wolfe, Secretary, Provisional Committee, Socialist Party of
Washington to E. Stephens, March 16, 1908, *The Socialist* (Seattle), April 4, 1908;
letter from E. Backus to Frederic Heath, July 14, 1908, *Social-Democratic Herald,*
Aug. 15, 1908; letter from Emil Herman to Frederic Heath, Aug. 21, 1908, *Social-
Democratic Herald,* Sept. 12, 1908; *Social-Democratic Herald,* Dec. 26, 1908; So-
cialist Party, *Proceedings of the National Convention, 1908,* pp. 38–61; Frederic
Heath, "The National Convention," *Social-Democratic Herald,* May 23, 1908.

[18] *The Socialist* (Seattle), July 10, 17, 1909; letter from A. H. Barth to Members
of the Socialist Party of Washington, *The Socialist* (Seattle), July 17, 1909. Barth
was a leader of the Right wing.

[19] *Socialist Party Weekly Bulletin,* Aug. 21, Sept. 11, 1909.

[20] *The Workingman's Paper,* Oct. 30, 1909.

[21] Letter from R. R. Ristine, State Secretary of Missouri Socialist Party to
J. Mahlon Barnes, Aug 11, 1910, *Socialist Party Weekly Bulletin,* Aug. 20, 1910;
"Minutes of the National Executive Committee, Dec. 11, 1910," *Socialist Party
Official Bulletin,* Dec., 1910; "Minutes of the National Executive Committee, Febru-
ary 6, 1911," *Socialist Party Official Bulletin,* Feb., 1911; *Socialist Party Weekly
Bulletin,* July 18, Sept. 16, 23, Dec. 9, 1911; *Socialist Party Monthly Bulletin,*
Jan., 1912.

tions aimed at supporting one or the other of the warring state committees. The controversy lasted for more than a year, but since the national office had the final word in determining which state committee and locals it would recognize as legal, the Right wing emerged victorious.[22]

Before November, 1906, factionalism in New York City was at a minimum. Almost all members and leaders belonged to the Center and Left factions, and there was comparatively little disagreement as to program and tactics. In the fall elections, however, the Hearst Municipal Ownership Party cut deeply into the Socialist vote and Morris Hillquit was defeated as a Congressional candidate on New York's East Side. The Center faction, led by Hillquit, Algernon Lee, and William J. Ghent, concluded that more than a modicum of opportunism was necessary for electoral success. Using the Rand School and the Collectivist Society, an unofficial organization of the party's intellectual elite, as their base, Hillquit, Lee, and Ghent moved to gain control of party committees and *The Worker*. Since working-class members of the Left wing already had elected the better-known and more articulate middle-class Socialists to the key policy committees, it was a comparatively simple matter for the increasingly opportunist Center to convert the tactics and ideology of the New York party to step-at-a-time socialism.[23]

In 1908 the New York Left wing organized the "Proletarian Society" for the purpose of "internal propaganda." [24] Hillquit immediately charged the Left with planning to incite one part of

[22] *The Socialist Party Official Bulletin,* April–Dec., 1907; "Resolution of Local South Sioux City, Nebraska, November 1, 1907," *The Socialist* (Seattle), Nov. 23, 1907; "Minutes of the National Executive Committee, December 15, 1907," *Socialist Party Weekly Bulletin,* Dec. 16, 1907; letter from Emil Herman to J. Mahlon Barnes, *Socialist Party Weekly Bulletin,* Jan. 4, 1908; letter from Leonard DeVore, National Committeeman of Nebraska to J. Mahlon Barnes, Jan. 13, 1908, *Socialist Party Weekly Bulletin,* Jan. 18, 1908; letter from Fred L. Schwartz to J. Mahlon Barnes, July 1, 1908, *Socialist Party Weekly Bulletin,* July 3, 1908; "Minutes of the National Executive Committee, May 18, 1908," *Socialist Party Official Bulletin,* May, 1908; "Minutes of the National Executive Committee, July 10, 1908," *The Socialist Party Official Bulletin,* July, 1908.

[23] Letter from Morris Hillquit to *The Worker,* Feb. 8, 1908; letter from E. S. Egerton to *The Worker,* Feb. 9, 1908; letter from Moses Oppenheimer, Member, Executive Committee, Local New York, to *The Worker,* Feb. 22, 1908; letter from William Kohn, chairman, General Committee, Local New York, to *The Worker,* Feb. 29, 1908; letter from William Mendelson to the *New York Call,* Dec. 5, 1909.

[24] *The Worker,* Feb. 1, 1908.

the membership against the other and suggested that a "real strong movement" be built "before we commence to worry about the preservation of its purity." [25] The Left replied that the opportunists and so-called intellectuals had started the factionalism and that no party could be strong without being pure.[26] But the revolutionary Socialists had roused themselves too late. The party's reform ideology and tactics attracted more middle than working class recruits. And while a number of the most active New York locals, such as Brooklyn's Branch Five, were solidly Left wing, Hillquit's control was never seriously threatened.[27]

The battle between Right and Left-wing factions quickly moved from the local to the national level. The National Executive Committee was the most important national Socialist body. It consisted of seven Socialists elected annually by the party membership voting through their locals. Since nomination by only one local was required in order to place a name on the ballot, each Socialist had to cast his votes for seven of more than one hundred and fifty candidates. In the January, 1909, elections, for example, 13,000 of the party's 41,000 members attended local meetings and cast ballots for 7 of 200 candidates. About half of the votes were scattered among 190 nominees, who were virtually unknown outside of their own states. Consequently, the successful candidates were the nationally famous Socialist writers, lecturers, and editors. Since these categories were filled by members of the middle class, the Left wing of the party, whose leaders were known only in the local areas in which they worked, failed to elect a single member of the executive committee. The vote for the successful candidates ranged from 6,000 down to 3,000.[28]

Most of the legislative and administrative powers exercised by the National Executive Committee had been acquired by default.

[25] Letter from Morris Hillquit to *The Worker*, Feb. 8, 1908.

[26] Letter from Frances M. Gill to *The Worker*, Feb. 15, 1908; letter from Moses Oppenheimer to *The Worker*, Feb. 29, 1908.

[27] Letter from A. Mayell to the *New York Call*, Dec. 29, 1911; letter from Karl Heidermann and F. Sumner Boyd to the *New York Call*, June 8, 1912.

[28] *Socialist Party Weekly Bulletin*, Feb. 15, 1909; *Socialist Party Official Bulletin*, Feb., 1909; *International Socialist Review*, IX (March, 1909), 722. Members of the National Executive Committee for 1909 in order of their vote were Victor Berger, Morris Hillquit, Robert Hunter, A. M. Simons, John Spargo, John Work, and A. H. Floaten (Colorado).

The party constitution assigned them to the National Committee. Each state was represented on this latter committee by one member, plus an additional member for every two thousand members or major fraction thereof. The executive committee was designed as an administrative body of the National Committee. But since the latter conducted all its business by mail and never met, and since the former was elected independently of the latter, the executive committee quickly acquired most of the powers formally bestowed upon the National Committee. The delegates to the 1908 Socialist convention attempted to return the executive committee to its constitutional place and to prevent a minority of the party from electing all seven members of that body. They amended the constitution to provide for its election by the National Committee instead of by a membership referendum.[29] The Right-wing Socialists, however, secured passage of a motion delaying the operation of this amendment until after the election of the 1909 executive committee. And early in 1909 a national referendum conducted on the issue of democracy in the party repealed the amendment.[30]

By January, 1910, the procedure for executive committee elections had been changed yet again. The committee was to be elected for a two-year term by a national referendum. A preferential system of balloting was to be used, in which each voter placed a number from one to 27 in order of preference before the names of the 27 candidates. The seven candidates receiving the lowest total would be elected. The number of names appearing on the ballot had dropped sharply, because a candidate was now required to have his nomination seconded by five Socialist locals.[31]

Electioneering by both factions reached new heights.[32] The *International Socialist Review* suggested that those who favored a revolutionary party might well put a high numeral next to the name of Victor Berger.[33] William English Walling sent out a

[29] Socialist Party, *Proceedings of the National Convention, 1908*, pp. 246–55.

[30] "Report of the National Secretary to the National Congress of the Socialist Party, May 15, 1910," Socialist Party, *Proceedings of the First National Congress, 1910*, p. 24.

[31] *Socialist Party Official Bulletin*, Nov., 1909; *Socialist Party Weekly Bulletin*, Dec. 14, 1909.

[32] *Socialist Party Weekly Bulletin*, March 12, 21, April 2, 9, 1910.

[33] "A Step Backward: Shall We Take It?" *International Socialist Review*, IX (June, 1909), 998–99.

circular letter urging the defeat of Berger, Hillquit, Hunter, Simons, and Spargo, all members of the 1909 committee.[34] Berger, who was conducting a vigorous campaign for re-election, pointed out that intellectuals were in the majority of every party executive board in Europe. He warned that the only danger facing the party was the possibility that the revolutionists might gain control of the executive committee. If the present leadership were continued in office, Berger promised, the American party would be the strongest Socialist organization in the world by 1920. "Woe to him who stands in the way!" [35]

The Left wing had obtained passage of a National Committee motion which provided that occupations of candidates for the executive committee be printed on the ballot.[36] But neither this device, designed to expose the middle-class nature of Right-wing candidates, nor preferential voting could overcome the Left wing's lack of nationally known candidates. Five of the seven committeemen elected were leaders of the constructive Socialist faction.[37] The other two, Lena Morrow Lewis of California and James F. Carey of Massachusetts, were not consistent members of either faction and were elected with Left-wing support.[38]

Revolutionary Socialists took what consolation they could from the recriminations flung back and forth between two of the constructive Socialists elected to the executive committee. Personal differences between George Goebel, a national organizer for the party, and John Spargo, perhaps the party's best-known writer and lecturer, led to a public exchange of charges and countercharges. Spargo accused Goebel of using his position as a paid employee of the national office to win both his position on the executive committee and a trip to Europe in an *Appeal to Reason* subscription contest.[39] Goebel in turn accused Spargo of unethical

---

[34] E. H. Thomas, "Attempt to Capture Socialist Party!" *Social-Democratic Herald,* Dec. 25, 1909.

[35] Victor L. Berger, "Plain Words for Plain Socialists," *Social-Democratic Herald,* Dec. 25, 1909.

[36] *Socialist Party Weekly Bulletin,* March 10, 1909.

[37] The five in order of selection were Robert Hunter, Victor Berger, Morris Hillquit, John Spargo, and George H. Goebel (New Jersey). (*Socialist Party Weekly Bulletin* [Feb., 1910].)

[38] *Ibid.;* "Socialist Party Election," *International Socialist Review,* X (March, 1910), 855–56.

[39] Letter from John Spargo to J. Mahlon Barnes, March 4, 1910, *Socialist Party*

electioneering tactics. He further charged that Spargo neither knew nor cared about organizational problems and used his position on the executive committee for the exclusive purpose of securing lecture engagements and furthering the sales of his books.[40]

A special target was J. Mahlon Barnes, who had used his office as national secretary to aid the constructive Socialists in their battles with the revolutionaries. One Left-winger characterized Barnes as "very clever and very cautious. He would commit himself to nothing and to everything, to nobody and to everyone, but be right there doing business all the time. He undoubtedly has the clerical ability of a good secretary, and no matter how he appears, lines up with the opportunists on all organization matters." [41] But since it was virtually impossible to find a candidate for national secretary as well known as the incumbent, Barnes seemed destined to hold his office for the rest of his life.

It was not the revolutionary Socialists but the effects of personal jealousies, his own indiscreet conduct, and the enmity of the Christian Socialists which finally succeeded in ousting the national secretary. In the summer of 1910 an old-time Chicago Socialist, Thomas J. Morgan, published a series of charges against Barnes in his privately printed weekly paper, *The Provoker*. Morgan had been retained by Mother Jones, the almost legendary organizer of the mine workers, to compel Barnes to repay a loan she had made to him. In the process of forcing payment, Morgan accused Barnes of dishonesty, incompetence, drunkenness, and practicing free love with national office employees. A former employee of the national office wrote to the National Executive Committee documenting the charges from personal experience. When the executive committee refused to place the matter before the National Committee, a number of locals passed resolutions calling for the executive committee's resignation. In the meantime, Reverend Edward E. Carr, editor of the *Christian Socialist*, had taken up the attack. In December, the executive committee capitulated and arranged for the election

*Weekly Bulletin*, March 12, 1910; letter from John Spargo to J. Mahlon Barnes, March 25, 1910, *Socialist Party Weekly Bulletin*, April 2, 1910.

[40] Letter from George H. Goebel to J. Mahlon Barnes, March 18, 1910, *Socialist Party Weekly Bulletin*, March 21, 1910; letter from George H. Goebel to J. Mahlon Barnes, April 2, 1910, *Socialist Party Weekly Bulletin*, April 9, 1910.

[41] J. B. Osborne, "Convention Notes," *The Socialist* (Seattle), June 13, 1908.

of a National Committee investigating body. The investigators reported their conclusions in February, 1911. They held both Barnes and the executive committee innocent of all misconduct.[42]

The executive committee refused to publish the testimony taken by the investigators. Instead, they obtained passage of a National Committee motion accepting their conclusions. But within two weeks many of the national committeemen who had supported the motion were demanding publication of the testimony.[43] The controversy raged for another six months. Finally, in August, the National Executive Committee met and heard the testimony of some of the witnesses against Barnes. At the conclusion of the hearings the committee reported that Barnes had placed the mother of his illegitimate child on the party payroll and deducted two dollars weekly from her pay check as payment for a thirty-dollar loan he had made to her. It held that Barnes's conduct in this matter was a "grave indiscretion" and reluctantly accepted his resignation. On the other charges against the national secretary the committee maintained a discreet silence.[44]

The revolutionary Socialists quickly discovered that they had no cause to celebrate the removal of the man who had helped arrange for the suspension and expulsion of numerous Left-wing locals. The National Executive Committee announced that it had elected John M. Work, a member of the extreme Right wing, to replace Barnes as national secretary.[45]

The Left wing scored its first major victory in a national party election in the summer of 1910. Bill Haywood had earned a national reputation as a result of his effective leadership of the Western Federation of Miners and Industrial Workers of the World and his tireless work during local and national Socialist election campaigns. But he had stubbornly refused to stand for party office. Finally, in 1910 he was prevailed upon to run for delegate to the forthcoming International Socialist Congress. Of the eight delegates elected, Berger scored the highest vote, polling almost ten

[42] *Socialist Party Official Bulletin*, Aug., 1910–Feb., 1911; "Report of the Investigating Committee, Sub-Committee of the National Committee, February 28, 1911," *Socialist Party Official Bulletin*, Feb., 1911.

[43] *Socialist Party Official Bulletin*, March–April, 1911.

[44] "Minutes of the National Executive Committee, August 11–13, 1911," *Socialist Party Official Bulletin*, Aug., 1911.

[45] *Ibid.*

thousand votes. Second, with just two hundred votes less than Berger, was Haywood. The third-place delegate, Robert Hunter, ran three thousand votes behind Haywood, and the fourth-place delegate, Morris Hillquit, ran a thousand votes behind Hunter.[46] At last the Left wing had a candidate who could compete with the most famous among Right-wing lecturers, writers, and editors.

However, revolutionary Socialists could not use Haywood to blast their way into the National Executive Committee at the end of 1910 because the committee chosen at the beginning of that year had been elected for a two-year term. They therefore decided to use their growing strength in an attempt to eliminate all Right-wing executive committee incumbents who had dominated that body for some years. In March, 1911, the Left wing initiated a national referendum on a constitutional amendment providing that all national officers should be elected annually and that no Socialist should hold the same office for longer than two years. The Right wing was taken by surprise and the amendment was adopted by a vote of 9,000 to 8,500.[47] By this coup the Left had made the top Right-wing vote-getters, Berger, Hillquit, Spargo, and Hunter, ineligible for re-election. But the executive committee elections were still seven months away. Constructive Socialists recovered from their shock and in July initiated a referendum calling for repeal of the amendment. The repeal was carried, 11,000 to 7,500.[48]

When Haywood accepted nomination to the National Executive Committee in November, 1911, he said that he did not want anyone to vote for him without understanding his position. He therefore issued a public statement outlining his views. The executive committee, wrote Haywood, must abandon its practice of acting as a supreme court in all local matters. It must also cease appropriating to itself the power to legislate in all party affairs. The role of the committee should be to guide the propaganda work of the party. This propaganda should be directed at educating the working class toward the end of political and industrial solidarity.[49]

Morris Hillquit led the attack on Haywood's candidacy. In a

[46] *Socialist Party Weekly Bulletin,* June 8, 1910.
[47] *Ibid.,* April 22, 1911.
[48] *Socialist Party Weekly Bulletin,* Aug. 12, 1911.
[49] William D. Haywood, "To the Members of the Socialist Party," *International Socialist Review,* XII (Dec., 1911), 375.

widely reprinted letter to the *New York Call*,[50] Hillquit quoted the following passage from Haywood's *Industrial Socialism:* When the worker comes to understand the meaning of economic determinism,

he retains absolutely no respect for the property rights of the profit takers. He will use any weapon which will win this fight. He knows that the present laws of property are made by and for the capitalists. Therefore he does not hesitate to break them. He knows that whatever action advances the interests of the working class is right, because it will save the workers from destruction and death.

Hillquit charged that this statement was anarchistic and opposed to the Socialist doctrine of economic determinism. Socialists, said Hillquit, believed that modern law was largely class law, but favored change "by the regular and lawful methods established for that purpose. To preach to the workers lawbreaking and violence is ethically unjustifiable and tactically suicidal." America was a political democracy and the minority would have to convert the majority to its view. Hillquit argued that Socialists would expect obedience to working-class laws when they were in power. Therefore, it was only fair to obey capitalist laws when the latter were in power. If capitalists refused to obey Socialist laws, then Socialists would "fight like tigers" from the barricades. But any violation of law at the present time would make Socialists nothing more than "petty criminals and sneak thieves." Hillquit explained that he was writing this letter because "capitalist agencies" watched every party statement. "Any indiscreet remark or expression is sure to be quoted against us forever and ever." [51]

Haywood replied promptly. He said everyone agreed that the ballot was important and effective. But, he asked, does Hillquit propose "to stand behind a barricade of lawbooks firing a series of well-written briefs at the advancing army of capitalistic minions?" He demanded that Hillquit name an instance in which the capitalists had failed to violate their own laws when they stood in

---

[50] Letter from Morris Hillquit to the *New York Call*, Nov. 20, 1911.

[51] *Ibid.* Hillquit failed to explain why he had waited over a year to answer Haywood's "indiscreet" remarks. "Hillquit waited until 30,000 copies had gone out to poison the minds of the American working people and then . . . on November 14, four days after its authors had accepted nominations for the National Executive Committee he selected a single sentence to furnish a basis for his theoretical attack." (Letter from Frank Bohn to the *New York Call*, Feb. 25, 1911.)

the way of further exploitation of the working class. "Is it necessary to build the barricades on the asphalt pavement before the door of the building where his law offices are located before he will be brought to a realization of the fact that the fight is now on?" The capitalist legal system could not be used to bring socialism, Haywood insisted. On the contrary, that legal system would collapse only after private ownership of the means of production had been abolished.[52]

The Hillquit-Haywood exchange precipitated a year-long discussion of the use of force and violence. The discussion began over the executive committee elections. But it was continued because of the hysteria the McNamara confession aroused among Right-wing leaders,[53] and because of their determination to break the back of their Left-wing opposition. Henry L. Slobodin, who twelve years before had been Hillquit's right-hand man in the Socialist Labor Party civil war, at once came to Haywood's defense. He said that if Hillquit had had the temerity to present such an analysis of socialist ideology a few years earlier it would have "astounded the Comrades." Now it would astound no one because the "reformist and legitimist view" was held by most party leaders; "A policy of extreme parliamentarianism invited corruptionists and breeds corruption."

Slobodin said that in effect Hillquit denied that the disrespect shown for the rights of private property during a strike had anything to do with economic determinism. If Hillquit's thesis that all laws must be obeyed until they were changed by established legal processes was correct, then the working class should not have organized unions or conducted strikes when such acts were criminal nor should they now engage in secondary boycotts. Slobodin charged that Hillquit was unable to distinguish between "antisocial and pro-social crimes." Both sides carried on the class struggle with whatever means lay at hand. If, as Hillquit suggested, it was worth fighting to preserve socialism, it was worth fighting to get it:

Every act that furthers the interests of the working class is sane and wise, law or no law. Socialism stands within the capitalist made legal

[52] Letter from William D. Haywood to the *New York Call*, Nov. 28, 1911.
[53] *New York Call*, Dec. 3, 1911.

system so long as it has no other means to attack, to abolish and over-throw it. Given the means, the Socialist party will overthrow the entire system of private property, law or no law.[54]

In support of his candidacy for the executive committee, Hill-quit noted that two extreme wings had developed in the party "of late," the opportunist [55] and the revolutionary or impossibilist. Both sought immediate results, and both were incorrect. But, said Hillquit, they were not an equal threat to the Socialist movement. Political opportunism appeared only "sporadically and shame-facedly" and was quickly checked. "The Socialist party of the United States is probably the most uncompromising Marxian party in the world." Impossibilism, on the other hand, was on the increase and constituted "the most serious menace to the progress and triumph of Socialism in this country." [56]

John Spargo announced that he had agreed to run for re-election as "a duty I owed the party." He would not abandon the struggle against the "pernicious influence of the *International Socialist Review* and its hired representatives," Haywood and Frank Bohn. These latter two, said Spargo, echoing the charge made against him by George Goebel two years before, were running for office only in order to secure "fat and profitable contracts" for the *Review*.[57]

The battle to keep Haywood off the executive committee raged with unprecedented fury. The preferential ballot had been abandoned, and party members were instructed to vote for seven of the 48 candidates. Victor Berger polled the highest vote, followed by Job Harriman who had achieved temporary fame as attorney for the McNamaras and candidate for mayor of Los Angeles while the executive committee balloting was taking place. In third place was "Big Bill" Haywood, two thousand votes ahead of Morris Hillquit, and four thousand votes ahead of John Spargo, who had barely managed to win the seventh seat on the committee. The high vote polled by Frank Bohn did little to quiet Right-wing

[54] Letter from Henry L. Slobodin to the *New York Call*, Nov. 30, 1911.

[55] By "opportunist" Hillquit probably meant those willing to reach campaign agreements with other political parties.

[56] Letter from Morris Hillquit to the *New York Call*, Nov. 27, 1911.

[57] Letter from John Spargo to the *New York Call*, Nov. 30, 1911.

concern over the growing strength of the revolutionary Socialists.[58]

While the executive committee election was taking place, the
*New York Call* was being flooded with letters on the question of
obedience to established law. This controversy had been precipitated by the Hillquit attack on Haywood and had grown in intensity after the McNamara confession. Defenders of Hillquit
pointed to the McNamara case as an example of the harmful effects
violence brought to the Socialist movement. Socialists, they held,
must show themselves to be possessed of greater virtue than all
other groups, and must therefore oppose all violence. Defenders
of Haywood replied that American Socialists must greet capitalist
laws with the same scorn German Socialists had shown for Bis-
marck's Socialist Exception Laws. The German Socialists had
declared on the floor of the Reichstag: "We spit on your law!" [59]

A few days after the executive committee election, Local New
York held a mass meeting at Cooper Union, at which Haywood
was the main speaker. To a cheering audience that was following
the heated discussion on the question of obedience to law then
raging in the letters columns of the *Call*, Haywood announced that
he would discuss the class struggle in terms so simple that even a
lawyer would be able to understand it. He said the class struggle
could not be viewed through the stained-glass windows of a cathe-
dral or the spectacles of capitalist law. Opportunists and Christian
Socialists, said Haywood, had grown drunk on religious fanati-
cism and were trying to sober up on economic truth. When they got
about half sober they began to think they could convert the capitalist to the brotherhood of man, and that once converted he would
quietly turn over his property to the working class. "To understand
the class struggle you must go into the factory and you must ride
on top of the boxcars or underneath the box cars. You must go into
the mills."

Haywood then recounted the story of the bloody struggles of the
Western Federation of Miners. He pointed out that despite nu-

[58] *Socialist Party Monthly Bulletin,* Jan., 1912. Those elected in order of total
vote polled were Berger, Harriman, Haywood, Hillquit, Alexander Irvine (Los
Angeles, also a product of McNamara trial publicity), Kate Richards O'Hare (St.
Louis), and Spargo.
[59] *New York Call,* Dec. 1–29, 1911.

merous election promises and victories, the miners had won the eight-hour day only after a long and murderous strike. And when the eight-hour day had been won through economic action, it had proved to be "court-decision proof." On the other hand, said Haywood, the experiences of the miners had shown how important was the control of the police and militia. When the Socialists had won political office they would use the powers of government to protect strikers. "That's about as far as I can go on political action. But that's a long way."

Capitalist law and captialist government, charged Haywood, had been used to murder miners and their wives and children. "Do you blame me when I say that I despise the law (tremendous applause and shouts of 'No!') and I am not a law-abiding citizen. (Applause.)" Socialism would be won when industrial unions, after first winning better wages, hours, and working conditions, finally locked out their employers. Haywood held that Socialists "despise covering up their aims and purposes. We should say that it is our purpose to overthrow the capitalist system by forcible means if necessary." [60]

The *New York Call* buried an emasculated, half-column story on Haywood's speech on its second page under the misleading heading, "Conditions Make for Lawlessness." [61] Other New York papers were not so reluctant to quote Haywood. The *Tribune* story said that he had announced himself as opposed to law and order.[62] The *Times* headlines read: "Haywood Declares an Industrial War; Man Accused of Idaho Dynamiting Urges Socialists to Prepare for Conflict; Defends the McNamaras; Thinks Conditions Justify All Kinds of Violence on the Part of Workers." [63] The *Times* story quoted extensively from the section of Haywood's speech dealing with his disrespect for law and order. The next day the *Times* ran an editorial in which it held that Haywood had been acquitted of murder by a jury "generally believed to have been intimidated."

[60] William D. Haywood, "Socialism the Hope of the Working Class," *International Socialist Review*, XII (Feb., 1912), 461–71. This is a stenographic report of the Haywood speech at Cooper Union.

[61] *New York Call*, Dec. 22, 1911.

[62] New York *Daily Tribune*, Dec. 22, 1911.

[63] New York *Times*, Dec. 22, 1911.

In his Cooper Union speech, said the editorial, he "practically declared himself guilty, and gave the lie to the jury." The paper went on to say that men like Haywood and Debs did great harm to the labor movement. It was ridiculous of them to talk about industrial democracy. "What have we now, in every state of the Union, but an 'industrial democracy?' " [64]

This publicity was not to the liking of New York's reform Socialists. The day after the *Times* and *Tribune* stories appeared, the *New Yorker Volkszeitung*, which had led the attack on De Leon in 1899, printed an editorial expressing regret that Haywood had not spoken so clearly before the executive committee elections. For if he had, said the Socialist German-language daily, he would never have been elected to the top council of the party. The editorial charged that Haywood had spoken not as a Socialist but as an anarchist and anti-parliamentarian syndicalist: "Much as we may regret it, it is our positive conviction that William D. Haywood . . . has severed the connecting link between himself and the Socialist Party." [65] The following day the *New York Call* reprinted the *Volkszeitung* editorial.[66]

Left-wing Socialists rallied to Haywood's defense. One indignant *Call* subscriber demanded to know why he had to go to the New York *Times* for quotations from the speech of an executive committee member made at a meeting sponsored by Local New York. "Is the *Call* afraid of Haywood and his ideas?" [67] Courtenay Lemon, at one time the leading editorial writer for the *Call*, emptied the vials of Left-wing wrath. He charged that the paper's handling of Haywood was in keeping with the cowardly response of party leaders to the McNamara confession. That confession, wrote Lemon, had placed

the whole "slush-mush-gush" school of Socialists, the "humanitarians" whose message vacillates between a slobber and a stutter, those whose Socialism is "constructive" (like those "constructive recesses" of Congress), the almost-Comrades, near Socialists, pink tea Social-

---

[64] "Haywood and Others," New York *Times,* Dec. 23, 1911.

[65] "Once More—Clearness is a Necessity," *New Yorker Volkszeitung,* Dec. 23, 1911.

[66] *New York Call,* Dec. 23, 1911.

[67] Letter from E. W. Waldron to the *New York Call,* Dec. 29, 1911.

ists, one-step-backwards-at-a-time Socialists—in short, the whole horde of bourgeois pseudo Socialists . . . in a plight. What an embarrassing time these people will have explaining [the McNamaras and Haywood] to their friends—what a "spiritual struggle" they will once more have to go through to decide whether they can still identify themselves with the labor movement.

Lemon added that votes and office were not the be-all and end-all of socialism. Regardless of what ultraparliamentarians thought, anyone who believed that political action had any value at all, even only educational value, belonged in the Socialist Party. After all, said Lemon, it was only a question of present tactics. "After the Revolution, we are all Anarchists." Anarchism had far more in common with revolutionary socialism than the Right wing's Fabianism. Syndicalism served a valuable function in bridging the gap between socialism and anarchism. The working class, argued Lemon, had no use for "a frock-coated Socialist movement with a prayer book in one hand and a law volume in the other." The working class would have to fight for socialism, and the Socialist Party needed "a little more class hatred—yes, hatred—h-a-t-r-e-d, hatred. Class hatred is class consciousness in its fighting clothes." Men in battle had no time to waste on the ethical mysticism of loving the capitalist while hating capitalism. "Whatever they may be as fathers and husbands and after-dinner speakers, the capitalists as capitalists are wild beasts—and against wild beasts any weapon is justifiable." [68]

Early in January, 1912, New York Socialists arranged a debate in Cooper Union between Hillquit and Haywood on "What Shall the Attitude of the Socialist Party Be toward the Economic Organization of the Workers?" Haywood told the audience that New York Socialists should not be sitting by waiting for the next election but should be out aiding the laundry workers who were on strike. The American Federation of Labor was too reactionary to reform and the capitalist system too rotten to change a step at a time. He charged that Hillquit had abandoned the class struggle when he helped negotiate the garment workers' agreement that eliminated the right to strike. Finally, he insisted that Hillquit did not understand the meaning of the term "industrial unionism" be-

[68] Letter from Courtenay Lemon to the *New York Call*, Dec. 31, 1911.

cause he viewed it as a sort of enlarged craft unionism. "I . . . say . . . that industrial unionism comprehends all that· Socialism comprehends, and that industrial unionism is Socialism with its working clothes on."

Hillquit replied that everyone agreed that industrial unionism was superior to craft organization. But "it is not within the province of the Socialist Party to make special propaganda for the industrial form of organization or for any form of organization of labor." Hillquit conceded that American Federation of Labor leaders were reactionary, but the only task of the Socialist Party was to teach the rank-and-file of labor to vote the Socialist ticket. It would be a serious mistake for the party to aid a second labor organization. "I assure you that within five years and no longer the American Federation of Labor and its rank and file will be socialistic." [69]

Two weeks after the debate Haywood left for Lawrence to take charge of the great textile strike. In the middle of the strike, when Haywood was appealing to Socialists for aid for the starving workers, the *New York Call* decided to revive its attack upon him. It denounced Haywood as a man who had never learned how to think, a pseudo "intellectual worker" who was a "soft handed, soft sitting, non-productive member of society." [70] As the strike reached its climax early in March, Local Yuma, Arizona, somehow got wind of a rumor that in an unreported speech asking New York Machinists for support for the Lawrence strikers, Haywood had spoken deprecatingly of the effectiveness of the ballot. Local Yuma immediately called for a national referendum on the removal of Haywood from the executive committee. [71]

Since the Yuma motion required the endorsement of locals representing 5 percent of the membership before it could be submitted to a referendum vote, it was necessary to get the support of some of the large locals. Just before the close of the March 9 meeting of the New York Central Committee, a motion was introduced to support the Yuma resolution. Discussion was cut off, and the motion

[69] "Stenographic Report of the Hillquit-Haywood Debate," *New York Call*, Jan. 14, 1912.

[70] "The New Utopianism," *New York Call*, Feb. 11, 1912.

[71] "Minutes of Central Committee, Local New York, March 23, 1912," *New York Call*, April 3, 1912.

adopted, 14 to 11.[72] On March 13 the Lawrence strike ended in an overwhelming victory for the workers. Haywood was the hero of the hour.[73] On March 23 the New York Central Committee met again, decided that it had acted with unseemly haste, and withdrew its endorsement of the referendum to recall Haywood.[74] The Local Yuma motion died for want of a second.[75]

Haywood remained in Lawrence to lead the fight in the eight mills which had refused to capitulate. From there he went to take charge of the textile strikes in Lowell, Massachusetts, and Passaic, New Jersey. During April and May, Haywood and the Left wing were engaged in organizing defense committees for Ettor and Giovanitti, the Lawrence strike leaders who were being tried for murder because they led a union parade in which one of the paraders was killed. In the meantime, Right-wing Socialist leaders laid plans to eliminate Haywood and his supporters at the May, 1912, Socialist convention.[76]

[72] "Minutes of Central Committee, Local New York, March 9, 1912," *New York Call*, March 14, 1912; letter from Moses Oppenheimer, member of the Central Committee, to the *New York Call*, March 12, 1912.

[73] *New York Call*, May 22, 1912.

[74] "Minutes of Central Committee, Local New York, March 23, 1912," *New York Call*, April 3, 1912.

[75] *Socialist Party Monthly Bulletin*, March–April, 1912.

[76] "A Crisis in the Socialist Party," *The Masses*, III (Feb., 1912), 3; "Keep Step, or Fall Out," *The Masses*, III (June, 1912), 3; John Spargo in the *New York Call*, April 23, 1912; A. M. Simons, " 'My Big Brother Can Lick Ye,' " *Social-Democratic Herald*, May 4, 1912.

# XVIII

# The Recall of Bill Haywood

A S THE MAY, 1912 Socialist convention approached, the personal attacks on Haywood and the revolutionary Socialists reached new heights.[1] Algie Simons ignored the fact that while Haywood was in jail in 1906 he had been the Socialist candidate for governor of Colorado on a program of "No Compromise and Nothing to Arbitrate." Simons charged that while the party was working to save his life, Haywood "was working in the Boise jail to elect Democratic politicians." [2] The Right wing claimed that the Lawrence strike and all other successful I.W.W. battles had really been won by the Socialist Party. "Everywhere this terrible new revolutionary organization has played the part of the small boy that runs around spitting in people's faces and then yelling for his big brother to come and do the fighting." [3]

The constructive Socialists said that sabotage was a weapon of the slum proletariat, not of the class-conscious workers. They charged that sabotage and direct action meant personal violence, and any attempt on the part of the syndicalists to deny this definition was "plain lying." The Right wing claimed that revolutionary Socialists opposed majority rule and believed in propaganda of the deed and group ownership of industry. Those who accepted this combination of anarchism and syndicalism did not belong in the Socialist movement.[4]

*The Masses* prayed that the coming party convention would remove Haywood from the executive committee.[5] John Spargo set the main convention task as elimination of all anarchist influence,

[1] *New York Call,* March 13, 27, 28, April 8, May 21, 1912.

[2] A. M. Simons, " 'My Big Brother Can Lick Ye,' " *Social-Democratic Herald,* May 4, 1912.

[3] *Ibid.*

[4] *Ibid.;* Spargo, *Syndicalism, Industrial Unionism, and Socialism,* p. 177.

[5] "Direct Action," *The Masses,* III (March, 1912), 3.

and happily reported that "there is no very general demand apparently for Debs." [6] On the eve of the convention Berger stated that the party was about to enter a new epoch in its history. Agitational work was about to give way to the standard activities of a major political party. The convention would have to amend the party constitution so as to protect the organization from cranks, freaks, and impossibilists who were harming the Socialist cause. Berger said the party was now in a position to elect a number of Congressmen and therefore it must adopt a program which, while it did not forget the final aim of abolishing capitalism, would "appeal to every man and woman working with brains or brawn." [7]

The Left wing was as determined as the Right to force a showdown at the 1912 convention. The Left said that the Lawrence victory proved that "winning tactics" had been discovered. Industrial unionism was no longer an untested theory, but had been proven in battle. It was about to sweep both the labor movement and the Socialist Party.[8] The *International Socialist Review* called upon all "clear-headed" revolutionists who had left the party in disgust or who had hesitated to join what they considered a vote-getting, office-seeking machine to enroll at once so that the party might be set upon the road of revolutionary socialism.[9]

The Left was hard pressed to answer charges that it advocated terrorism and murder. The cruelest blow at the Left was struck by a leading member of its own faction, Eugene Debs. In February, 1912, Debs entered the controversy raging around the paragraph from Haywood and Bohn's *Industrial Socialism* that Hillquit had quoted in an attempt to prevent the election of Haywood to the executive committee.[10] Debs wrote that he found that paragraph "entirely sound." He had no respect for capitalist laws designed to enslave and rob the working class. But, continued Debs, he was opposed to sabotage and direct action because physical force, when applied by the individual worker, harms the proletariat instead of

---

[6] Interview with John Spargo, *New York Call*, April 23, 1912.

[7] United Press interview with Victor L. Berger, *New York Call*, May 9, 1912.

[8] "The Victory at Lawrence," *International Socialist Review*, XII (April, 1912), 679.

[9] "The Socialist Party of America," *International Socialist Review*, XII (April, 1912), 679–80.     [10] See above, pp. 381–84.

the capitalist. Furthermore, these "guerrilla" tactics violated working class psychology and had prevented the growth of the Industrial Workers of the World. "I am opposed to any tactics which involve stealth, secrecy, intrigue, and necessitate acts of individual violence for their execution." The workers could be emancipated only through the exercise of their collective will, and that will and its inherent power could be developed only through education, enlightenment, and self-imposed discipline.

Debs said the Socialist Party should eliminate intellectuals from all official positions. And it should endorse industrial unionism, encourage the organization of a new revolutionary union, and, although it could not hope to be too successful, bore from within the craft unions. But, at the same time, concluded Debs, "I hope to see the Socialist party place itself squarely on record at the coming national convention against sabotage and every other form of violence and destructiveness suggested by what is known as 'direct action.'" [11]

The *International Socialist Review*, which published Debs's article, promptly denied that the phrase "direct action" had anything to do with the individual action of the bomb thrower. It recalled the statement in the party's 1908 Declaration of Principles that "the Socialist party is primarily an economic and political movement." The economic movement, explained the *Review*, meant direct action, and it regretted that Debs had accepted the false definition of that phrase invented by enemies of industrial unionism. Dynamite, concluded the *Review*, was the weapon of the craft unionist who was "vainly seeking to oppose modern capitalism with an outgrown and dying form of organization." [12]

Immediately before the opening of the May, 1912, Socialist convention, the *Review* published Frank Bohn's definitions of some key Left-wing terms. A socialist was anyone who favored common ownership and democratic control of industry, no matter what means he advocated to achieve that goal. Belief in political action was not a prerequisite to being a Socialist. Political action was any activity designed to gain control of the powers of the political state

[11] Eugene V. Debs, "Sound Socialist Tactics," *International Socialist Review*, XII (Feb., 1912), 481–86.
[12] *International Socialist Review*, XII (Feb., 1912), 505.

through use of the machinery provided by the state. Direct action was "any action taken by the workers directly at the point of production with a view to bettering their conditions." Opposition to direct action, therefore, was opposition to all labor unionism. Sabotage meant "strike and stay in the shop." This enabled striking workers to draw pay and keep out scabs while fighting their employers. It did not necessarily mean destruction of property, although workers always had and always would engage in such destruction as long as the class struggle continued. Sabotage included anything which obstructed the regular conduct of industry, including the limitation of output.

Bohn defined a social revolutionist as one who believed that the working class would take possession of "the means of power" and would socialize industry within a comparatively short revolutionary period. The opportunist believed that socialism was coming over a long period of time, during which the forces of social control would gradually pass from the capitalist to the working class. In practice, the opportunist was a reformer to whom socialism was the sum total of all reforms. Since he was usually a member of the middle class he tended "to ignore the mass action of labor," overemphasize political action, measure Socialist success by the size of the vote, compromise with capitalist parties, and make office-seeking a profession. Impossibilism was "a term of reproach hurled by the office seekers upon the heads of those who claim that Socialist education is the most important feature of the movement." However, the term could be used legitimately to describe those Socialists who limited their activities to criticizing "politicianism," and who make "a trade of criticism and bitter invective."

Bohn said an industrial union was a union of all who worked in the same industry. A revolutionary unionist was one who planned to use the industrial union and the Socialist political organization to overthrow capitalism and establish "an industrial democracy." The revolutionary unionist also held that the union "is, or should become, the fundamental revolutionary Socialist organization. . . . If the revolutionary unionist advocates political action, as most of them do, it is chiefly for the purpose of preventing the destruction of the union by the capitalist political power." And finally, syndicalism and revolutionary unionism were synonymous.[13]

Seven months before the May, 1912, Socialist convention the Right-wing party leaders had concluded that the growing influence of industrial socialism could best be checked by destroying the magazine which served as its organizational and propaganda medium, the *International Socialist Review*. In the middle of the hotly contested National Executive Committee elections of December, 1911, Robert Hunter moved that the committee request the National Committee to investigate the affairs of Charles H. Kerr and Co. In making his motion, Hunter charged that Kerr ran the concern as a dictatorship, and was building a machine for the purpose of subverting the Socialist Party. "It has sneered at Political Action, advocated rival unionism, and vacillated between Anarchism and Proudhonism. The constant emphasis THE REVIEW lays on Direct Action and its apparent faith that a revolution can be evoked by Will or Force is in direct opposition to our whole philosophy." [14] The executive committee carried Hunter's motion by a vote of five to one,[15] and the National Committee accepted the recommendation by a vote of 34 to 22.[16]

Winfield Gaylord of Wisconsin, Clyde A. Berry of Missouri, and Stephen M. Reynolds of Indiana were selected to conduct the investigation. Gaylord did not serve because of a meeting of the Wisconsin legislature. The investigating committee was to make its report a week before the Socialist convention, and the Right wing apparently believed its disclosures would be the first shot in the expected convention battle. The committee report, however, was not what had been expected. The committee found that Kerr had started his business in 1886, and had reorganized it as a corporation in 1896. Kerr had owned $9,500 of the company's $10,000 capital stock. In 1904 the capital stock had been increased to $50,000. In 1912 3,600 shares of stock at ten dollars a share were outstanding, and of these, Kerr owned 1,100. At the January, 1912, company meeting, Kerr had had the proxies for an additional

[13] Frank Bohn, "Some Definitions," *International Socialist Review*, XII (May, 1912), 747–49.
[14] *Socialist Party Weekly Bulletin*, Nov. 23, 1911.
[15] *Ibid.*, Dec. 7, 1911.   [16] *Ibid.*, Jan., 1912.

1,200. Therefore, concluded the committee, the stockholders "are not hostile to the ideas of Comrade Kerr so far as the business of the company is concerned." [17]

The committee reported that the receipts for Kerr and Co. during 1911 had totaled $63,000: from the sale of books, $39,000; from the *Review*, $22,000; and from advertising $2,000. Profits had amounted to $2,200. Kerr received $1,500 a year in salary, and Mary Marcy received $1,000. The company's ten to fifteen employees worked an eight-hour day, were paid time and a half for overtime, and received a week's vacation with pay. The *Review* had subscriptions totaling 17,000, and sold an additional 32,000 copies a month in bundles.

Having stated the facts in the case, the committee turned on those who had instigated the investigation. They reported that Hunter had become a stockholder in Kerr and Co. in 1900. If he had wanted to check the books and records of the company he had been free to do so at any time. There had been no need to call on the party to investigate a private stock company. The Kerr Co. had met promptly every request of the committee, and "we believe that no Socialist publishing house has more open methods of conducting the publishing business than this one." [18]

Although the attack on the *Review* had misfired, control of the party machinery and press gave the constructive Socialists a resounding victory in the elections for delegates to the 1912 Socialist convention.[19] An analysis of the background of the 293 delegates who assembled in Indianapolis in May reveals much about the character of party leadership. Native-born Americans were in the great majority. The average age of the party leadership had increased noticeably over earlier conventions: more than a third of the delegates were over forty-five years old, more than half were over forty, and only 31 were under thirty.[20]

---

[17] "Report of Clyde A. Berry and Stephen M. Reynolds to the Comrades of the Socialist Party of America, May 5, 1912," *Socialist Party Monthly Bulletin*, June, 1912.

[18] *Ibid.*

[19] A. M. Simons, "The Everlasting Union Question," *Social-Democratic Herald*, May 11, 1912; Henry L. Slobodin, "What The National Convention Should Do," *New York Call*, April 26, 1912.

[20] In contrast, a majority of the delegates to the founding convention of the party in 1901 were in their twenties and thirties (see above, p. 104).

In terms of occupations, the largest groups were made up of 32 newspapermen, 21 lecturers, 20 lawyers, 12 mayors, and 11 full-time party functionaries. Categories such as manufacturers, real estate brokers, retail merchants, authors, ministers, physicians, and dentists provided another 60 delegates. There were also 11 white collar workers, ten farmers, and seven housewives. Of the rest, the great majority were skilled workers such as carpenters, machinists, and electricians. Fewer than thirty delegates could be characterized as unskilled or semiskilled workers. About half of the delegates were party officials in one capacity or another. Only four had been members of the party for less than three years, and only 23 for less than four years. Clearly, the unskilled workers who had joined the Left wing after 1909 were not at the convention in force.[21]

No sooner had the convention been organized than the day's chairman, J. Mahlon Barnes, announced that he was in possession of a telegram from one of the branches of Local Denver challenging the right of one member of the National Executive Committee to a seat on the floor since he was under charges in that branch. It was an open secret that the committeeman referred to was Bill Haywood. By a vote of 128 to 50 the delegates voted to table the telegram without reading it. Barnes promptly released the telegram to the press which used it as its main convention story.[22]

The next day Haywood rose on a point of personal privilege to give his unchallenged version of the charges against him. During the Lawrence strike he had gone to Bridgeport, Connecticut, to raise money for the textile workers. He was scheduled to speak under the auspices of the Lawrence Strikers Aid Committee, which had as one of its sponsors the Brotherhood of Machinists, the I.W.W. rival of the International Association of Machinists. The Bridgeport Socialist local promptly warned Haywood that they would prefer expulsion charges against him if he spoke as scheduled. Haywood had replied that he saw nothing wrong in speaking before a union organized to rival the local Association of Machinists since its officers were members of the anti-Socialist Militia of Christ. He urged Local Bridgeport to forget factional quarrels for the moment and join in sponsoring the rally. Instead, Right-wing

21 *New York Call*, May 5, 1912.
22 Socialist Party, *Proceedings of the National Convention, 1912*, pp. 31, 58.

Socialists organized a rival meeting to be held the same night as the Haywood rally. They raised a total of twelve dollars for the Lawrence strikers and then turned the money over to the Lawrence American Federation of Labor which was co-operating with the mill owners in an effort to break the strike. Following the Haywood rally, Local Bridgeport had communicated with the Right-wing branch in Denver which had sent the telegram to the convention. The delegates again tabled the telegram, and instructed convention officials not to release communications to the press before they had been read to the convention.[23]

The second skirmish between the Right and Left wings followed hard on the first. A month before the convention opened, Haywood had called the attention of the executive committee to conditions in San Diego, California, where the I.W.W., A.F. of L., and the Socialist Party were engaged in a free speech fight with city authorities that was assuming aspects of open warfare. He moved that the party give a maximum of moral and financial aid. Berger, over Haywood's protests that the need was urgent, amended the motion to request an investigation by the California state committee of the party. The amendment was carried and three weeks passed before a majority of the executive committee concluded that the free speech fight was a legitimate one.[24] Despite John Spargo's insistence that the free speech fighters were "a vicious element with criminal faces," [25] the committee sent the California party $250 to use in San Diego.[26]

When the national party convention convened a few days later, the Left wing moved that telegrams of support and protest be sent to the groups engaged in the San Diego struggle. The Right wing amended the motion to instruct the executive committee to investigate the situation in California and report its recommendations to the convention. The amended motion was carried.[27] The executive committee brought in a report suggesting that telegrams be sent to all groups engaged in the San Diego fight, with the exception of

[23] Ibid., pp. 40–41.

[24] Socialist Party Monthly Bulletin, May, June, 1912.

[25] "The National Socialist Convention of 1912," International Socialist Review, XII (June, 1912), 807–8.

[26] Socialist Party Monthly Bulletin, June, 1912.

[27] Socialist Party, Proceedings of the National Convention, 1912, pp. 60–63.

the I.W.W. The Left protested that the Industrial Workers were leading the struggle. The Right replied that the I.W.W. was implicitly recognized because a telegram was to be sent to the Free Speech League on which the I.W.W. was represented. The revolutionary Socialists insisted that it was high time the party explicitly recognized the existence of a labor organization entitled the Industrial Workers of the World. A majority of the delegates agreed, and the Socialist Party established diplomatic relations with the revolutionary union to the extent of one telegram.[28]

The Right wing countered this minor victory for the Left by calling on an honored guest to address the convention. Karl Legien was the secretary of the German General Federation of Labor Unions and Right-wing leader of the German Social-Democratic Party. He was in the United States on a lecture tour arranged for him by Samuel Gompers.[29] When Legien arrived in New York in April his greeting to trade union and Socialist delegations which met the boat was a statement attacking strikes as beneficial only to employers. He also suggested that the I.W.W. dissolve itself and turn its membership over to the A.F. of L.[30] In May, Legien obtained Gompers's permission to cancel a number of lecture engagements so that he might accept an invitation to attend the Socialist convention to "help prevent the introduction and passage of a resolution hostile to the trade union movement." [31]

Legien began his address to the convention by telling the delegates that he had been informed by prominent members of the party that the convention was about "to decide most delicate and important questions." The German party, said Legien, had repeatedly emphasized the necessity of a politically neutral trade union movement which was to be left free to choose its own tactics. His party, continued Legien, had expelled all those who refused to join the neutral unions. "In our German movement we have no room for sabotage and similar syndicalist and destructive tenden-

[28] *Ibid.*, pp. 70–72. Party recognition of the I.W.W. in the Lawrence strike had been implicit rather than explicit, because the Socialist press and national organization seldom referred to any possible relation between that union and the striking textile workers.

[29] Gompers, *Seventy Years of Life and Labor*, II, 35.

[30] *New York Call*, April 17, 1912.

[31] Samuel Gompers in Hillquit, Gompers, and Hayes, *Double-Edge of Labor's Sword*, pp. 51–52.

cies." The German Social-Democratic Party had always co-operated with the trade unions to suppress dual unions. And, Legien pointedly concluded, this policy of support of the established trade union movement was one of the main reasons that at the last election his party had polled 4,500,000 out of a total of 15,000,000 votes.[32]

By this time rumors of the controversy in the Committee on Labor Organizations and Their Relation to the Party were sweeping the convention. There were stories of various majority reports, one of which was supposed to give outright endorsement to the American Federation of Labor. The committee "reds," represented by "the three Toms," Tom Clifford of Ohio, Tom Hickey of Texas, and Tom Lewis of Oregon, were said to be holding out for endorsement of industrial unionism as the highest expression of socialism on the economic field.[33] It came as something of a shock, therefore, when the committee brought in a unanimous report. The committee resolution found both political and economic organization equally necessary for working-class emancipation. It pointed out that the labor movement had made great progress, including the organization of new trades, the amalgamation of related trades into "federations and industrial unions," and the opening of union meetings and journals to the discussion of social and political problems.

The resolution held that only those engaged in the union movement could solve the problem of the correct form of organization, and the party "therefore reaffirms the position it has always taken with regard to the movement of organized labor": (1) the party has neither the right nor the desire to interfere in the question of union tactics or organization forms; (2) the Socialists "call the attention of their brothers in the labor unions" to the importance of organizing the unorganized, particularly the unskilled and immigrant workers; (3) the party was duty-bound to give moral and material support to the unions; (4) Socialists were to join and participate in the unions in which they were eligible for membership.[34]

The resolution was clearly a compromise. The Right had avoided

---

[32] Socialist Party, *Proceedings of the National Convention, 1912*, pp. 58–60.
[33] "The National Socialist Convention of 1912," *International Socialist Review*, XII (June, 1912), 821.
[34] Socialist Party, *Proceedings of the National Convention, 1912*, p. 195.

the specific endorsement of industrial unionism, while the Left was content to accept its implicit recognition.[35] Bill Haywood held that he could now

go to the working class, to the eight million women and children, to the four million black men, to the disfranchised white man who is disfranchised by industrial depression, the men who have no votes, and . . . carry to them the message of Socialism. I can urge them, and do it from the Socialist platform, to organize the only power that is left to them, their industrial power.[36]

The Right wing, of course, did not accept this interpretation of the committee report. The *New York Call* viewed it as a triumph for the constructive elements in the party because it avoided the "dogmatic assertion that we must be industrialists, when industrialism has yet to prove its organizing and constructive ability." [37] Since the resolution meant many things to many men, it was adopted unanimously.[38]

The convention's Committee on Platform also brought in a unanimous report. The Left wing was so pleasantly surprised by the emphasis placed on the class struggle in the platform's lengthy preamble that they did not bother to challenge the fifty-odd immediate demands of the working program. The preamble was adopted without dissent and only Berger's plank calling for tariff reduction was challenged and eliminated as irrelevant to the Socialist movement.[39]

The sixth day of the convention opened with still another victory for the Left. With the draft of a new party constitution about to be discussed, constructive Socialists divided their support between two Right-wing candidates, and the revolutionists elected Lewis J. Duncan of Montana chairman for the day.[40] Up to this point Right-wing leaders had handled themselves quite badly. Although the great majority of the delegates were professionals, businessmen, and leaders in the craft unions, Socialists whose sympathies were

---

[35] *Ibid.*, p. 99.                    [36] *Ibid.*, p. 100.
[37] "A True Unity Convention," *New York Call*, May 18, 1912.
[38] "The National Socialist Convention of 1912," *International Socialist Review*, XII (June, 1912), 823.
[39] Socialist Party, *Proceedings of the National Convention, 1912*, pp. 102–12, 196–98. For a summary of the platform see above, p. 366.
[40] Socialist Party, *Proceedings of the National Convention, 1912*, p. 113.

with the program of constructive rather than revolutionary socialism, the Left had won most of the victories. Haywood had been
seated, a telegram of support had been sent to the I.W.W., a trade
union resolution implicitly recognizing the advantages of industrial unionism had been passed, and a platform with a revolutionary
preamble had been adopted. Berger's *Social-Democratic Herald*
commented:

It was only necessary to watch the early proceedings of the Indianapolis convention to see how the direct actionists have spread their
poison in our movement. The first few days' deliberations were a
shameful spectacle, giving the capitalistic enemy good opportunity
to connect up our people with the Los Angeles murders and murderers,
and especially since the convention took place at the scene of the Mc-
Namaras' labors.[41]

Constructive Socialist leaders had to find an issue upon which
they could unite their followers. The basic difference between the
two factions was that the Left wanted the party to be a revolutionary propaganda organization which took the lead in developing
mass struggles, particularly in the field of industrial unionism. The
Right wanted a party organized to win votes, elect Socialists to
office, and secure reform legislation which, it claimed, would increase the socialist content of the national political and economic
life. Although the Left was unable to convince a majority of the
membership that all political reforms were a waste of time, its criticism of "vote-catching" opportunism and its leadership in the fight
for industrial unionism and civil liberties was winning it growing
support. The Right wing, in the face of rising labor militancy and
reform-party competition, found it increasingly difficult to attack
the specific labor and civil liberty campaigns advanced by the revolutionists. If it was to score a decisive victory at the 1912 convention, it would have to avoid the questions of opportunism and industrial unionism and concentrate its fire against a Left-wing
theory which could not help but be anathema to middle-class convention delegates.

Immediately following adoption of the platform and the labor
union resolution, Berger, Hillquit, Spargo, and Harriman called

[41] *Social-Democratic Herald,* May 25, 1912.

a caucus of Right-wing leaders. The caucus decided to advance a constitutional amendment designed to eliminate Haywood and the Left.[42] The Committee on Constitution, consisting of the party's leading lawyers with Hillquit as chairman, made its report the next day. At the 1908 Socialist Convention, the constitution had been amended so that Article II, Section 6, provided for expulsion of all party members who opposed "political action as a weapon of the working class." [43] But since industrial socialists advocated political action for the purpose of gaining control of the police powers of the state, that constitutional provision could not be used against them.

The 1912 Committee on Constitution recommended that Article II, Section 6, be changed to provide for expulsion of anyone "who opposes political action or advocates crime against the person or other methods of violence." The section was immediately amended from the floor so that it read: "Any member of the party who opposes political action or advocates crime, sabotage, or other methods of violence as a weapon of the working class to aid in its emancipation, shall be expelled from membership in the party." Hillquit announced that the Committee on Constitution accepted the amendment unanimously.[44] And so as to leave no doubt in the minds of the delegates as to what was involved, Reverend Winfield Gaylord of Wisconsin informed them that acceptance of the platform and trade union resolution the day before had been "too smooth." Gaylord announced that the Wisconsin delegation was not going to leave the platform and trade union resolution open to the interpretation that the party advocated "crime of any kind." [45] Fred Merrick of Pennsylvania moved to delete the entire section. He pointed out that the sentence was open to numerous interpretations and begged the delegates not to destroy the unity that had been achieved

[42] Ginger, *The Bending Cross*, p. 309; "The National Socialist Convention of 1912," *International Socialist Review*, XII (June, 1912), 824.

[43] Socialist Party, *Proceedings of the National Convention, 1908*, pp. 238–39. This clause was adopted by a vote of 82 to 48, with the Left warning that in France political opportunism had driven the working class to anarchism. (*Ibid.*, pp. 239–43.)

[44] Socialist Party, *Proceedings of the National Convention, 1912*, pp. 122, 134. This Socialist constitutional provision bears a striking similarity to the criminal syndicalist laws passed in the United States during the first World War.

[45] *Ibid.*, p. 122.

the day before. His remarks were interrupted with the cry, "The syndicalists must go," and the great debate was launched.[46]

Proponents of the section against violence, sabotage, and crime held that belief in political action meant acceptance of existing legal definitions of crime. Until enough Socialists had been elected to office to change the laws, the present social order would have to be preserved.[47] The Right wing said that sabotage meant the bomb, the dagger, murder, and every other form of violence.[48] Property was the product of human labor and the Socialist Party could never advocate its destruction.[49] In answer to the Left wing's citation of the Boston Tea Party, the Right replied that the dumping of the tea had been nothing but an outburst by "John Hancock and a band of smugglers who used their own selfish interests to accomplish their purpose." [50]

Hillquit explained that while it would have been interference with the trade unions to instruct Socialists to work for industrial unonism, it was not interference to forbid Socialists to advocate sabotage in their union meetings.[51] Berger made his annual threat to pull Wisconsin out of the party unless the constitution was amended to prevent the anarchists from using "our political organization" as a cloak for direct action, sabotage, syndicalism, and other forms of violence.[52] Hillquit concluded for the Right wing. It had taken the Socialist movement thirty-five years to reach the point where they were a real political power, "and, I say, if there is one thing in this country that can now check or disrupt the Socialist movement, it is not the capitalist class, it is not the Catholic Church, it is our own injudicious friends from within." [53]

The revolutionary Socialists thus found themselves attacked on an issue they found almost impossible to explain to a middle-class delegation. The industrial Socialists had borrowed the theory of sabotage from the French trade unionists. Under the most propitious circumstances it would have been difficult to convince a

[46] Ibid.
[47] Statement by Winfield Gaylord in ibid., p. 123.
[48] Statement by Victor Berger in ibid., p. 130; statement by James Oneal (Indiana) in ibid., pp. 132–33.
[49] Statement by Winfield Gaylord in ibid., p. 123.
[50] Statement by Charles Dobbs (Kentucky) in ibid., p. 128.
[51] Ibid., p. 135.      [52] Ibid., p. 130.      [53] Ibid., p. 135.

group of small businessmen and professionals that the class
struggle must and should result in limiting production and damag-
ing property. The McNamara case and the loss of the Los Angeles
election made the circumstances anything but propitious.

The Left wing began their reply by charging that the question
of violence was a false issue. The real question, it said, was whether
the party should adopt the progressive policy of industrial socialism or continue the reactionary policy of "monkeying with the old,
outworn machinery" of the capitalist state.[54] No one wanted violence, the revolutionary Socialists insisted. If the party constitution must contain an answer to every charge made by enemies of
socialism, then it should include provisions for expelling anyone
who favored larceny, polygamy, free love, breaking up the home,
and destroying incentive.[55]

The Left charged that the step-at-a-time or "yellow" Socialists
spoke and acted as though violence in American class struggles
began with and continued because of the Industrial Workers of the
World.[56]

It would seem that some of you in this convention think it is the duty
of the working class to permit the capitalist class to interfere with
your property, . . . to reduce the part of the produce of your labor
that you get . . . [to the point] that you suffer, and that in place
of going back at them and protecting yourselves you should just
calmly submit to it and let them grind you down without using any
opportunity you have at your hands to defend your property.[57]

The courts, said the "reds," were constantly adding to the list of
union activities to be judged destructive of property rights. They
demanded to know whether striking workers convicted by such
courts would be expelled from the party.[58] The Socialist Party,
they insisted, must be an organization for establishing a new social
order, not for suppressing crime.[59]

A roll-call vote was demanded. While the tellers totaled the vote,

[54] Statement by J. O. Bentall (Illinois) in *ibid.*, p. 128.
[55] Statement by Dan Hogan (Arkansas) in *ibid.*, pp. 130–31; statement by William Bessemer (Ohio) in *ibid.*, p. 132.
[56] Statement by William Bessemer in *ibid.*, p. 132.
[57] *Ibid.*
[58] Statement by Marguerite Prevey (Ohio) in *ibid.*, pp. 127–28.
[59] Statement by Tom Clifford (Ohio) in *ibid.*, p. 133.

delegates sang "The Marseillaise" and "The Red Flag." [60] The motion to delete Article II, Section 6, was defeated, 191 to 90.[61]

Flushed with victory, the Right wing interrupted further consideration of the constitution to consider nominations of party candidates for President and Vice President of the United States. States were called upon alphabetically, every delegate having the right to nominate. At the end of the roll call, three candidates had been nominated, Eugene Debs of Indiana, Emil Seidel of Wisconsin, and Charles Edward Russell of New York. A delegate demanded to know whether there was any truth in the rumor that had been circulated throughout the convention that Debs was too ill to run for office.[62] Hillquit asked permission to discuss the qualifications and shortcomings of the nominees. The Left-wing chairman, Lewis Duncan, ruled him out of order on the ground that convention rules prevented nominating speeches. Hillquit appealed the ruling, but the Chair was sustained.[63]

Someone demanded to know whether Debs would accept. The Chair replied he would, according to people "who claim to know what they are talking about." Victor Berger challenged the Chair with "Do they?" The Chair replied "They do," and ordered the roll call vote.[64] Seidel, supported by the extreme Right of the West and Middle West, polled 56 votes; Russell, supported by the extreme Right of the Eastern states, 54. Debs was nominated with 156, an absolute majority.[65] Three delegates accepted nomination for Vice President, Dan Hogan of Arkansas for the Left wing, and John Slayton of Pennsylvania and Emil Seidel for the Right. Seidel won the nomination with 159, Hogan receiving 73 and Slayton 24. Some Left-wing delegates voted for Seidel for the sake of a unity slate.[66]

For the first time the Right wing had been able to muster 40 percent of the vote in opposition to Debs and select as his running mate a Socialist affiliated with the extreme Right wing of the party. After passage of Article II, Section 6, of the constitution and the

[60] New York Call, May 18, 1912.
[61] Socialist Party, Proceedings of the National Convention, 1912, pp. 136–37.
[62] Ibid., p. 137.          [63] Ibid., pp. 137–38.          [64] Ibid., p. 138.
[65] Ibid., pp. 138–41.          [66] Ibid., pp. 141–43.

nominations of Debs and Seidel, delegates began to straggle home. The next day the convention refused to endorse the international socialist position on immigration and then adjourned.[67]

The nonsocialist press greeted the adoption of the anticrime, sabotage, and violence clause with unprecedented enthusiasm for the party and its works. The independent Providence *Journal* and the Republican Springfield *Union* congratulated the party on its wise decision to stand for law and order.[68] The Baltimore *American* hailed the victory of "conservative socialism" over "the more radical outcroppings of the party." [69] The Republican Pittsburgh *Leader* predicted added power and influence for the Socialists now that they had rejected "all means but regular parliamentary action." [70] The formerly anti-Socialist *Nation* now found that the Socialist Party had too much at stake to risk the desperate tactics of syndicalism.[71] And the *Outlook* declared that victory of the "level-headed" Socialists "will be welcome to Americans without regard to party." [72]

The Left wing advised its supporters to ignore the sabotage amendment as preposterous.[73] Debs, who had again refused to attend the convention, reaffirmed his opposition to "anarchistic tactics" but objected to expulsion as a punishment for differences of opinion.[74] Courtenay Lemon characterized the amendment both as "the desire of small-spirited opportunists to vote themselves a schoolboy's certificate of good behavior for vote-catching purposes" and as "a ready weapon for use against all who dare criticize their compromises or oppose their policies." [75] But the *New York Call* urged the party members to vote for the amendment in the referendum about to take place. "The attempt to force the

---

[67] *Ibid.*, pp. 166–67. See above, pp. 287–88.

[68] Quoted in "Socialists Rebuking Violence," *The Literary Digest*, XLIV (June 1, 1912), 1144–45.

[69] *Ibid.*                [70] *Ibid.*

[71] "Socialism and Syndicalism," *The Nation*, XCIV (May 30, 1912), 534.

[72] "The Socialist Platform and Candidates," *The Outlook*, CI (June 1, 1912), 235.

[73] Henry L. Slobodin, "Some Opinions," *International Socialist Review*, XII (June, 1912), 831; "A History-Making Convention," *International Socialist Review*, XII (June, 1912), 874–75.

[74] Eugene V. Debs, "This Is Our Year," *International Socialist Review*, XIII (July, 1912), 16–17.

[75] Letter from Courtenay Lemon to the *New York Call*, June 3, 1912.

party into an attitude of endorsement of certain trade union tactics," said the *Call*, "is an attempt to dominate the party itself." [76]

Only 11 percent of the membership participated in the referendum on the new constitution. Article II, Section 6, was adopted, 13,000 to 4,000. [77]

Bitterness engendered by the antisabotage amendment now threatened to wreck the Presidential campaign. In the closing hour of the convention, Hillquit, as chairman of the Committee on Constitution and as a member of the National Executive Committee, moved that former National Secretary J. Mahlon Barnes be appointed campaign manager. Hillquit added that he thought "this convention and this party owes a reparation to Comrade Barnes because of the campaign of slander instituted against him." He gave the impression that the nomination of Barnes came with the unanimous recommendation of the constitutional and executive committees. Barnes was elected to the post. [78]

Immediately after the convention the Christian Socialist Fellowship attacked the Barnes appointment because of the latter's alleged immorality. [79] The *International Socialist Review* joined in the attack and circularized Left-wing locals calling for a referendum. The *Review* charged that Hillquit had misrepresented the attitude of the executive committee on the convention floor. The basic issue was not the question of Barnes's moral fitness, said the *Review;* "The question is this: Shall the Socialist party stand for the brand of bossism that has so long prevailed in the old capitalist political parties as exemplified in the forcing of J. Mahlon Barnes upon the party as campaign manager. . . . The issue is Hillquitism." [80] The party's Right-wing leaders replied that the *Review*

[76] "Section 6, Article II," *New York Call*, July 7, 1912.

[77] *New York Call*, Aug. 13, 1912.

[78] Socialist Party, *Proceedings of the National Convention, 1912*, pp. 164–66; letter from William E. McDermut (stenographic reporter, 1912 Socialist convention) to John Spargo, July 25, 1912, *Socialist Party Monthly Bulletin*, Sept., 1912.

[79] "Statement of Campaign Manager J. Mahlon Barnes to the Members of the Socialist Party, Aug. 6, 1912," *Appeal to Reason*, Aug. 17, 1912; Ginger, *The Bending Cross*, p. 310.

[80] "Shall Bossism Prevail in the Socialist Party?" *International Socialist Review*, XIII (July, 1912), 77–78.

and its supporters were "deliberately engineering a move to cripple the campaign." [81]

By the middle of June the executive and campaign committees were compelled to hold a joint meeting to discuss the Barnes appointment. Debs told the committees that he was being flooded with letters from members and locals threatening to withdraw support from the campaign unless Barnes was removed. Debs held that Barnes should be forced to resign. Spargo, Berger, and Hillquit replied that those who refused to work with Barnes should get out of the party. Debs launched a blistering attack on Hillquit and informed him that those who objected to Barnes were just as good Socialists as Hillquit. Haywood and Kate Richards O'Hare forced Hillquit to admit that the National Executive Committee had not only failed to recommend the appointment of Barnes, but had not even formally discussed the question of whether to employ a campaign manager. The meeting adjourned without taking decisive action.[82]

Motions and endorsements for a national referendum on the removal of Barnes poured into the national office. Debs and Barnes issued public statements attacking one another's positions.[83] Berger attacked the referendum as an attempt to disrupt the party by the advocates of "anarchism, free love, direct action, and sabotage." Debs's opposition to Barnes, said Berger, was just another example of his "unduly inflated ego." [84] The question of what Hillquit actually told convention delegates about the executive committee's attitude toward the Barnes nomination was debated on all sides. The Left forced the convention stenographer to admit that, after the Barnes controversy developed, the Right-wing members of the executive committee had convinced him that he had made an

[81] Letter from Algernon Lee, Gustave A. Strebel, William E. Duffy, Charles J. Ball, Jr., Meyer London, and U. Solomon to the *New York Call*, July 2, 1912.

[82] "Minutes of Joint Session of the National Executive Committee and Campaign Committee, June 16, 1912," *Socialist Party Monthly Bulletin*, July, 1912; Ginger, *The Bending Cross*, pp. 310–11.

[83] Eugene V. Debs, "Statement of Presidential Candidate to the Members of the Socialist Party," *Appeal to Reason*, July 20, 1912; "Statement of Campaign Manager J. Mahlon Barnes to the Members of the Socialist Party," *Appeal to Reason*, Aug. 17, 1912.

[84] Victor L. Berger, "Their Purpose Is All Too Plain in the Barnes Case," *Social-Democratic Herald*, Aug. 10, 1912.

error in his stenographic report. Therefore, he had changed the official version of the convention proceedings.[85]

In an effort to stop the national referendum, the executive committee ordered an investigation of the Texas local whose motion was the basis of that referendum. Charles E. Russell was sent from New York to Texas, but when he reported that the charges against the local were groundless, the executive committee repudiated his investigation. The committee issued a public denunciation of the referendum "as a fraud and imposition upon the Socialist Party," and delayed its operation so that the final vote was not counted until the end of September.[86] With the election only a month away the party membership voted 19,000 to 11,500 to continue the Barnes appointment through the campaign.[87]

The Left wing's attack on Barnes was not the only quarrel to disrupt the election campaign. Factionalism had gained so much momentum that nothing could slow it down. Having passed a constitutional provision against sabotage and violence, the Right wing resumed its propaganda barrage against Haywood. The *Social-Democratic Herald* repeated the charge against him made by the New York *Times* six months earlier. Haywood, said the *Herald*, was a coward who, when on trial for his life, "hid his belief in murder; but once out of danger he not only publicly applauded the crimes of the McNamaras but has tried his best to turn Socialists into emissaries of murder and violence, backed up by the anarchistic intellectual, C. H. Kerr and his anarchistic *Review*." [88]

The Right wing moved from an attack on revolutionary Socialist ideology to a general assault on the Left wing's labor defense and free speech campaigns. The charge that party "reds" believed in murder and violence was of more than academic significance. Haywood and the Left were concentrating most of their energies in

[85] Letter from William E. McDermut (stenographic reporter, 1912 Socialist convention) to John Spargo, July 25, 1912; "Minutes of the National Executive Committee, August 18, 1912," *Socialist Party Monthly Bulletin*, Sept., 1912.

[86] "Minutes of the National Executive Committee, August 17–18, 1912," *Socialist Party Monthly Bulletin*, Sept., 1912; letter from William D. Haywood to the National Executive Committee, *Socialist Party Monthly Bulletin*, Oct., 1912.

[87] *Socialist Party Monthly Bulletin*, Oct., 1912.

[88] *Social-Democratic Herald*, May 25, 1912.

organizing committees for the defense of Ettor and Giovannitti, the two Lawrence strike leaders facing trial for murder.[89] The Left viewed the public charges of advocacy of violence and murder made by constructive Socialists as a "stab in the back at the men who were facing trial." [90] On September 30, the opening day of the trial, 15,000 Lawrence workers staged a 24-hour protest strike. When the millowners fired and blacklisted some two thousand of the workers who participated in the strike, Haywood and the I.W.W. threatened a mass exodus of textile workers from Lawrence. The *New York Call* promptly labeled the plan as an "asinine" attempt to "migrate from the class struggle." [91] The Lawrence millowners did not agree with the *Call.* The blacklist was abandoned and all the strikers were rehired.[92]

The constructive Socialists condemned the Left-wing free speech fights and unemployed demonstrations as "frame-ups." The Right said they were of no benefit to the labor movement, and were conducted for the sole purpose of milking funds from the Socialist Party. "The Socialist movement is tired of being panhandled by these professional panhandlers. . . . Let the disorder boys and gurleys [I.W.W. organizer Elizabeth Gurley Flynn] depend on their own crowd for their sustenance, and by all means let our movement get down to its own work in the good old international way." [93]

In August, the National Executive Committee, goaded into action by Haywood, issued an appeal for funds to aid the I.W.W. Timber Workers who were being beaten and jailed in Louisiana. But Spargo announced that as far as he was concerned this was the last time the party would aid the I.W.W. as long as that union refused to use its funds for political purposes.[94] And the following month, when Haywood criticized the executive committee for not organizing aid for the Mexican revolutionaries, Spargo announced that "the time has come when we must call halt to those

[89] Yellen, *American Labor Struggles*, pp. 200–201.

[90] Haywood, *Bill Haywood's Book*, p. 258.

[91] "Why Precipitate a Tragedy?" *New York Call*, Oct. 6, 1912.

[92] Yellen, *American Labor Struggles*, p. 202.

[93] *Social-Democratic Herald*, May 25, 1912.

[94] "Minutes of the National Executive Committee, August 17, 1912," *Socialist Party Monthly Bulletin*, Sept., 1912.

who continuously slander and misrepresent the party from the inside." [95]

New York's militant five hundred-member Branch Five was sharply criticized for having Haywood as its main speaker at a Socialist rally. Branch Five was informed that Haywood's election to the executive committee had been due to a "misunderstanding." [96] The *New York Call*, in describing Haywood's activities on behalf of Ettor and Giovannitti and his leadership of the Little Falls strike, always referred to him as "an organizer for the Industrial Workers of the World," virtually never as a Socialist. [97] The executive committee of Local New York requested its branches to cease circulation of the *International Socialist Review*. [98] And when some New York Socialists attempted to sell the *Review* at the Debs Madison Square Garden rally in September, the rally's arrangements committee sent the police to stop them. [99]

Haywood was not one to meet these attacks in silence. When the New York *Tribune* asked him whether it was true, as rumored, that he had played an important part in drawing up the platform of the Progressive Party, Haywood charged that this "perfectly preposterous fairy tale" had been circulated by the Right wing. Haywood told the reporter that since Hillquit, Berger, and Spargo had failed to oust him at the 1912 Socialist convention, they were now trying to discredit him by implying that he was "flirting with our great national mountebank and with the authorized representative of big finance." He added that Right-wing leaders

are delightful opportunists who pose as deadly enemies of capitalism and then feel immensely flattered when they are invited, as Morris Hillquit was recently, to "perform" at pink teas at Fifth Avenue mansions. They wish to crown themselves with the halo of a Socialist apostle, but they do not care to face the music and to bear the opprobrium which attaches to the name in capitalist quarters. [100]

[95] *New York Call*, Sept. 18, 1912.

[96] Letter from I. M. Rubinow to the *New York Call*, June 2, 1912. Branch Five replied that it had distributed at least seven times as much literature and engaged in more political activity than any other New York branch. The great majority of its members had voted for Haywood and intended to do so again. (Letter from Karl Heidemann and F. Sumner Boyd to the *New York Call*, June 8, 1912.)

[97] *New York Call*, Nov. 7, 1912.

[98] "Minutes of the Executive Committee, Local New York, July 23, 1912," *New York Call*, July 25, 1912.

[99] Letter from Charles Rice to the *New York Call*, Oct. 24, 1912.

[100] New York *Daily Tribune*, Sept. 14, 1912.

On November 26 Ettor and Giovannitti were found not guilty.[101] Five days later the Left-wing Branch Seven of the New York Socialist Party sponsored a victory rally at Harlem Casino which was attended by three thousand people. The main speakers were Joseph Ettor and Bill Haywood. A two-column story on the affair was carried in the *New York Call*. The presence of Haywood was not mentioned until the last paragraph, which read as follows:

William D. Haywood, national organizer of the I.W.W. spoke last. He said that while it has become more difficult to convict leaders of the working class than it was twenty-five years ago, the capitalists have a new scheme of putting the strike leaders in jail for a long period and trying them afterwards. He said that a man who speaks for liberty in the United States speaks for a jail sentence.[102]

The next day, however, the *Call* ran a story noting that "surprise has been expressed in Socialist circles over some of the statements that were made by William D. Haywood, member of the National Executive Committee of the Socialist Party and general organizer of the I.W.W." at the Ettor meeting. This surprise, said the *Call*, was occasioned by the fact that a member of the executive committee "made recommendations" that had been repudiated by the last Socialist convention. The *Call* then proceeded to quote some of Haywood's remarks, "for the benefit of those who may have overlooked" them:

Well, direct action is the shortest way home. It is the surest way, particularly for the women and children, the black men and especially for the disfranchised American workingman. . . . And I believe in sabotage, that much misunderstood word. . . . There is no revolutionary action that can be too strong if we will only throw the capitalistic class back. . . . The jails all over the country are filled with many of the working class this very day. But they are not filled by political Socialists, but are filled by the men and women Socialists of the Industrial Workers of the World.[103]

The same day that the *Call* noted that Haywood's remarks had caused "surprise," the *New Yorker Volkszeitung* demanded to know how it was possible "that such an ignorant phrasemonger"

[101] *New York Call*, Nov. 27, 1912.          [102] *New York Call*, Dec. 2, 1912.
[103] "Haywood Causes Surprise," *New York Call*, Dec. 3, 1912.

had ever been elected to the executive committee. It charged that
in his speech Haywood had boasted that he had never asked any
workingman for his vote and had always advocated direct action
and sabotage. The *Volkszeitung* concluded that Haywood did not
belong in the party or on its executive committee. And since he did
not have the integrity to resign, the party would have the "unpleasant obligation" to remove him. The *New York Call* immediately reprinted the *Volkszeitung* editorial [104] and ran one of its own
which repeated the charge that Haywood had said that he had never
advocated political action or asked workers for their votes.[105]

There is no transcript of what Haywood really said at the Harlem Casino. He unquestionably did advocate sabotage and labor
union or direct action. But belief in sabotage did not necessarily
mean encouraging violence. At Lawrence, for example, violence
was almost eliminated after Haywood and Ettor took charge of
the strike. [106] It is highly doubtful that Haywood claimed that he
had never advocated political action or asked workers to vote the
Socialist ticket. It is perhaps significant that the *Call* story, which
quoted disconnected sentences from his speech in an attempt to
put his remarks in contradiction to party policy, did not quote anything about political action and voting. Furthermore, the *Call*
editorial, which denounced the speech, criticized him for saying
that he would not waste his time talking about ballots to voteless
foreigners and women and children.[107] This is in keeping with Haywood's previous position on voting and probably was the basis for
the charge that he claimed to oppose political action and never
asked workers for their votes.

At the 1912 Socialist convention, Haywood had praised the
labor union resolution because it would enable him to carry the
message of socialism to the voteless Negroes, foreigners, women
and children, and unemployed. He had added, "I have likewise
urged that every worker that has a ballot should use that ballot to
advance his economic interest. In Lawrence, Massachusetts, while
only fifteen per cent of the workers had a vote before the strike,
since the strike we have taken into the Socialist party as many as

104 *New York Call*, Dec. 4, 1912.
105 "Haywood as a Reactionist," *New York Call*, Dec. 4, 1912.
106 Brissenden, *The I.W.W.*, pp. 287–88.
107 "Haywood as a Reactionist," *New York Call*, Dec. 4, 1912.

one hundred members at a meeting." [108] On another occasion Haywood remarked, "I advocate the industrial ballot alone when I address the workers in the textile industries of the East where the great majority are foreigners without political representation. But when I speak to American workingmen in the West I advocate both the industrial and political ballot." [109]

A few days after the Harlem Casino meeting, Haywood told another rally that "I do believe in political action, because it gives us control of the policeman's club." He added that political action was also invaluable as an educational device.[110] One version of the Harlem Casino meeting had Haywood saying, "I have never asked a worker for his vote—particularly women, children, the disfranchised and foreign-speaking workers. Instead I have taught them the class struggle." [111] But the meaning of this quotation, even if accurate, is not clear. Many Socialists refused to "ask for votes" because they wanted votes only from those who were "straight Socialists," not mere reformers. Votes, they said, would automatically follow an understanding of Socialist principles.[112] Thus, Presidential candidate Debs at the height of the 1912 campaign told his audiences: "The capitalist politician appeals to you for your votes. We ask you only to think, for if we know that you think, we know how you will vote. I am the only candidate for President who is not asking for your votes." [113] Finally, it is difficult to believe that Haywood, who was one of the most vigorous and effective party campaigners in the 1904 and 1908 national and Congressional elections, who was his party's candidate for governor in 1906, and who had spent the fall of 1911 campaigning for Harriman in Los Angeles, would say that he had never advocated political action or wanted the votes of the working class.

Shortly after his week of New York speeches, Haywood left for Chicago to participate in the I.W.W. organizing drive in the stock-

[108] Socialist Party, *Proceedings of the National Convention, 1912,* p. 100.
[109] Quoted in Macy, *Socialism in America,* pp. 164–65.
[110] Quoted in Mary Brown Sumner, "The Parting of the Ways in American Socialism," *The Survey,* XXIX (Feb. 1, 1913), 625.
[111] *Ibid.*
[112] Letter from Rose Pastor Stokes and J. G. Phelps Stokes to the *New York Call,* Dec. 30, 1912; letter from Ida Crouch Hazlett to the *New York Call,* Jan. 8, 1913.
[113] Quoted on the cover of the *International Socialist Review,* Vol. XIII (Nov., 1912).

yards.[114] But two days after the Harlem Casino speech, the executive committee of Local New York declared that in view of his opposition to political action and to the platform and declaration of Socialist principles, Haywood would not be permitted to speak for Local New York or any of its branches again. The committee also decided to prefer charges against him.[115] Within two weeks the New York State Committee had voted, 31 to 4, to inaugurate a national referendum to recall Haywood from the National Executive Committee.[116] Even before the state committee had voted on the motion, the state secretary sent a copy of the resolution to the New Jersey State Committee suggesting that it take similar action. This was done by a vote of 10 to 8.[117] Both the New York and New Jersey state committees defeated motions requesting an explanation from Haywood before voting on the motion for his recall.[118]

National Secretary John Work promptly announced that the New York and New Jersey state organizations represented over 5 percent of the party membership and that he was mailing out "Referendum D, 1912" on the recall of Haywood from the National Executive Committee. It was established practice in the party that referendums would not contain charges and arguments which might prejudice the vote. If this procedure had been followed in Referendum D, the ballot would have had printed at the top the simple question: "Shall William D. Haywood be recalled from the National Executive Committee?" Instead, the ballot was headed with the following resolution:

WHEREAS, W. D. Haywood, a member of the National Executive Committee, has stated in public meetings in New York City that he never advocated the use of the ballot by the workers, and instead advised them to use direct action and sabotage, a violation of Article 2, Section 6, of the National Constitution; therefore, be it

---

[114] New York Call, Dec. 14, 1912.

[115] "Minutes of the Executive Committee of Local New York, December 3, 1912," New York Call, Dec. 6, 1912.

[116] New York Call, Dec. 10, 18, 1912.

[117] "Minutes of the State Committee of New Jersey, December 8, 1912," New York Call, Dec. 15, 1912.

[118] Letter from William Walker, member, New Jersey State Committee, to the New York Call, Dec. 20, 1912; letter from Milo C. Jones, recording secretary, New Jersey State Committee, to the New York Call, Dec. 25, 1912; "The Motion to Recall Haywood," International Socialist Review, XIII (Feb., 1913), 625.

*Resolved,* By the state Committee representing the Socialist party of the State of New York, that W. D. Haywood, is unworthy to remain any longer a member of the National Executive Committee, and the committee therefore initiates a motion for his recall from the National Executive Committee as provided by the National Constitution.[119]

The National Constitution, of course, provided for expulsion from the party for violation of Article II, Section 6, not for recall from the executive committee. There were no charges that Haywood had been derelict in his duties as a member of that body. Haywood was given no opportunity to reply to the charges through official party channels.[120] The *International Socialist Review* denounced the referendum for carrying "a preamble falsely charging Haywood with saying things he never said." [121] But the Right-wing Socialist press was closed to such denials. One month after the referendum closed the National Committee of the party, by a vote of 41 to 7, with 33 not voting, instructed the National Secretary to refrain from printing comments or preambles on national referendums. Members of the committee held that the membership had been misled in the Haywood case, and that the preamble to Referendum D assumed that Haywood was guilty as charged and then asked the party membership whether or not he should be recalled.[122]

In January, while the vote was being taken, Haywood spoke before a Socialist rally in Denver. He urged the workers to organize industrial unions and to join and support the political activities of the Socialist Party.[123] The balloting closed February 26. About 25 percent of the membership participated. Haywood was recalled from the National Executive Committee by a vote of 22,000 to 11,000.[124]

Once again the Socialist Party came in for unqualified praise from the non-Socialist press. Its editorials congratulated the party for repudiating anarchism, sabotage, and violence.[125] The New

---

[119] *Socialist Party Monthly Bulletin,* Jan., 1913.
[120] *Ibid.,* March–April, 1913.
[121] "The Motion to Recall Haywood," *International Socialist Review,* XIII (Feb., 1913), 625.
[122] *Socialist Party Monthly Bulletin,* March–April, 1913.
[123] Letter from Una G. Roberts, Denver, Colorado, to the *New York Call,* Jan. 19, 1913.
[124] *Socialist Party Monthly Bulletin,* March–April, 1913.
[125] *The Survey,* XXIX (March 29, 1913), 909.

York *World* announced that Socialists now could "honestly appeal to public opinion as a party that recognized the rules of orderly government and rejects the theory that the lawless shall gain power by intimidation and terrorism." [126] And the Detroit *Tribune* hailed the elimination of Haywood as proof that the party was openly "opportunist" and favored "progressive or evolutionary Socialism." [127]

The newspapers' enthusiasm for the recall of Haywood was not accompanied by a growth in party membership, activity, or vote. Shortly before the May, 1912, convention, party membership had reached 150,000.[128] Yet, despite the enthusiasm engendered by a Presidential campaign, enthusiasm which in the past had enormously increased recruiting, party membership for the year 1912 averaged 118,000.[129] This drop must be explained at least in part by the disaffection of Left-wing members following the adoption of Article II, Section 6, of the party constitution. While the vote on Referendum D was taking place, revolutionary Socialists were threatening to resign if the motion carried.[130] After Haywood was recalled, the decline in membership was precipitous. Haywood, himself, refused to renew his membership.[131] Thousands of Left-wing Socialists followed his lead. Within four months party enrollment had dropped another 40,000.[132]

Socialist support of and influence in the unions also took a sharp decline. The national party had contributed over $21,000 in 1912 in support of strikes and labor defense cases. In 1913 the amount was only $400, and by 1914 it had dropped to zero.[133]

At the 1912 American Federation of Labor convention the Socialists had led an all-day fight for reorganization of the union along industrial lines and on a roll-call vote had won 35 percent of the votes for their position. At the same convention they had fought for election of Federation officers by referendum vote. Their candidate for president of the Federation had received almost one

---

[126] Quoted in *ibid.*          [127] Quoted in *ibid.*
[128] *New York Call,* May 8, 1912.
[129] *Socialist Party Monthly Bulletin,* Jan., 1913.
[130] "The Motion to Recall Haywood," *International Socialist Review,* XIII (Feb., 1913), 625.
[131] Haywood, *Bill Haywood's Book,* pp. 259–60.
[132] *The Party Builder,* June 28, 1913.
[133] *American Labor Year Book,* 1916, p. 122.

third and their candidate for third vice-president more than one third of the votes cast.[134] But at the 1913 Federation convention, the Socialists made no mention of election by referendum. They introduced a watered-down motion on industrial unionism but did not speak in support of it. The motion was dismissed without even a roll-call vote.[135] No candidate was put up against Gompers and he was elected unanimously. William Johnston, the Socialist leader in the machinists, again ran for vice-president against O'Connell of the machinists, and again polled more than one third of the vote.[136]

At the 1914 Federation convention the resolution on industrial unionism was introduced by a delegate of the Illinois Federation of Labor on instructions from that body. Again no one spoke in its defense, and again it was defeated without a demand for a roll-call vote.[137] No candidate was run against Gompers, and Johnston, instead of running as Socialist candidate for vice-president, nominated his former opponent, O'Connell. All administration candidates were elected without opposition.[138] At the 1915 convention a resolution to investigate the feasibility of industrial unionism was defeated without debate, 181 to 31.[139] Gompers and the rest of the administration candidates were unopposed.[140] By the 1916 convention, Socialist influence in the national Federation had virtually disappeared. There was no resolution on industrial unionism, and if the Socialist delegates to the convention conducted any activity in line with party policy it is not disclosed by the convention *Proceedings*.[141]

Nor did the party fare any better at the polls. In the 1916 elections the Right wing at last selected one of its leaders as candidate for President. He polled 585,000 votes, a third less than Debs had

[134] See above, pp. 343–45.

[135] *Report of Proceedings of the Thirty-Third Annual Convention of the American Federation of Labor*, p. 377.

[136] *Ibid.*, pp. 384–86.

[137] *Report of Proceedings of the Thirty-Fourth Annual Convention of the American Federation of Labor*, p. 353.

[138] *Ibid.*, pp. 457–59.

[139] *Report of Proceedings of the Thirty-Fifth Annual Convention of the American Federation of Labor* (Washington, D.C., The Law Reporter Printing Co., 1915), p. 299.

[140] *Ibid.*, pp. 447–48.

[141] *Report of Proceedings of the Thirty-Sixth Annual Convention of the American Federation of Labor.*

won in 1912. And since the size of the total vote cast in the 1916 Presidential election had increased considerably over that of 1912, the percentage of the total vote polled by Socialists dropped even more sharply. Debs had won 6 percent of the total vote in 1912; Allan Benson won 3 percent of it in 1916.[142]

Despite these losses, the party maintained enough of an organization and membership to remain the unchallenged leader of the socialist movement in the United States for a few more years. Many revolutionary Socialists refused to abandon the struggle,[143] and in 1915 they united as a party caucus under the name Socialist Propaganda League.[144] The final split and deterioration of the party awaited several events: the support accorded the First World War by a majority of the parties affiliated with the Socialist International; the Russian Revolution; the formation of the Communist International; and the expulsion of the Left and now majority wing of the party by the constructive Socialists in 1919.

[142] Morison and Commager, *Growth of the American Republic*, II, 741–42.
[143] Hughan, *Facts of Socialism*, p. 162.
[144] Foster, *From Bryan to Stalin*, p. 290.

# XIX

# Conclusion

THE SOCIALIST PARTY was organized in 1901 by American Marxists convinced that capitalism had outlived its usefulness and was now destroying the nation's comparative economic equality and corrupting its democratic heritage. The Socialists were not alone in recognizing the growing dichotomy between American democratic theory and practice. The progressive movement sought to meet monopoly limitations on equality of opportunity with a program that ranged from honest city government to regulation and destruction of trusts. The Socialist Party, on the other hand, argued that such reforms could never end the basic contradictions which were responsible for the decline in liberty and equality. The Socialists held that freedom and capitalism, particularly in capitalism's monopoly phase, was a contradiction in terms. And they insisted that monopoly was not just an accidental variant of a normally competitive economy, but an inevitable development which could not be stopped within the system which gave it birth. If monopoly was to be eliminated, capitalism would have to be eliminated. Social ownership and democratic management of the means of production would not only refurbish fading American ideals but would also provide economic, social, and political opportunities impossible even in the days of Jefferson and Jackson.

There was much in American society to confirm the Socialist analysis. Neither antitrust laws nor government regulation appreciably retarded the centralization and concentration of wealth and power. The activities of farmers, workers, and small businessmen, whether expressed in Granger laws, Farmers' Alliances, the Populist Party, craft unions, or the progressive movement, did little to alter the developing pattern of American monopoly capitalism. Campaign promises of political reformers were legion. But farms continued to be foreclosed, tenancy increased, strikes were broken, businesses were bankrupted. America was still the land of opportunity when compared with Europe. But it was also increasingly the land of tenant and bare subsistence farming, unemployment, poverty, slums, corruption, and economic oligarchy. Growing numbers of Americans wondered whether there was anything in the system of free enterprise worthy of preservation.

In the twelve years from the time of its organization, the American Socialist Party grew from considerably less than ten thousand to 150,000 dues-paying members. It increased its electoral strength tenfold, from 95,000 to 900,000. It elected well over two thousand of its members to public office. It secured passage of hundreds of reforms, and contributed to the adoption of many times more. It won position and influence in the American Federation of Labor and led in the organization of a small but militant revolutionary union. It publicized inequities in American economic, social, and political life, and participated in the struggle to restore substance to the nation's democratic ideals. Clearly, whatever may have been the objective difficulties in advocating socialism in the wealthiest and most democratic capitalist country in the world, the Socialist Party had achieved some notable successes.

Yet within another ten years the party was through as a positive force in American political life. What can account for this rapid decline? If, at the height of what was later called American "normalcy," socialism could make such impressive gains, why did it not continue to do so? Or at the very least, why did it fail to hold what it had already won? One answer might be that the Socialist Party went the way of the entire progressive movement. But that would still beg the questions of what happened to the progressive movement and what there was about the Socialist Party that tied its fate so closely to that of the progressives. An analysis of the character of the Socialist movement might help explain the collapse of the programs designed to stop the growing power of corporate enterprise and the comparatively easy triumph of American monopoly during and after the First World War.

While accomplishments of the Socialist Party in twelve short years appear impressive, it can hardly be argued that the party made the most of its opportunities. As a national organization it consistently refused short-run co-operation with groups which refused to accept its entire program. It opposed the formation of a labor party. It gave less than halfhearted assistance to labor unions. It did not fight for civil rights. It shared and furthered the racial and national prejudices of the most conservative American Federation of Labor leaders.

From its formation, the Socialist Party was torn by factionalism. The Left wing consisted of militant fighters for better working conditions, industrial unionism, and civil rights. But after 1905, "revolutionary Socialists" neglected political action and insisted upon complete acceptance of their ultraleftist, sectarian analysis as a precondition to any organized activity. Thus, they quickly abandoned work for industrial unionism within the American Federation of Labor not only because they held there was little hope of converting that union to an industrial form, but also because they insisted upon a union which from its inception would have as its primary goal the overthrow of capitalism. Comparatively few American workers in 1905 had already concluded that a socialist society offered them the best chance for economic and social well-being. Yet, Left-wing Socialists operated on the theory that the mere existence of the Industrial Workers of the World would cause workers still convinced that there was hope for independence and prosperity under capitalism suddenly to understand the nature of the class struggle, surplus value, and the general strike, and join the I.W.W. in sufficient numbers to build a successful revolutionary union.

Even if American workers had been as class conscious and revolutionary as Left-wing Socialists assumed they were, syndicalism offered no real answer to the question of how to win socialism. Revolutionary Socialists viewed political power and the state as of little importance—mere reflections of the real world of factories, railroads, and mines. In so far as they were concerned with gaining control of the state, it was only to prevent use of troops and police against striking workers. Right-wing Socialists believed they could use the existing state apparatus to bring about the gradual growth of socialized production. Left-wing Socialists believed they could immobilize the state apparatus through election of Socialists to public office and then use the revolutionary union and the general strike to lock out employers, seize industry on the shop level, and set up a trade union state. It is difficult to decide which of the two programs is the more naive.

Political action played such a small part in revolutionary Socialist theory that even if the Left wing had been in control of the party it is highly doubtful that the party would have played a permanent role on the American scene. In theory, since the revolutionary union was to be the real fighting organization of the working class, all the Socialist Party was expected to do was prevent government strike-breaking and educate workers in the syndicalist version of the theories of Marx and Engels—although workers were already assumed to be sufficiently versed in those theories to join the revolutionary I.W.W. In practice, the Left acted as though the real purpose of the party was to serve as a propaganda and fund-raising wing of the revolutionary union. Successful political parties whose members consider the acquisition of wealth as the party's main function are not unknown to American history. But a successful political organization devoted to raising money and promoting public relations for the revolutionary activities of an industrial union has yet to make its appearance.

There is no denying the courage and devotion to the welfare of American labor of the Left-wing Socialists. Bill Haywood and Eugene Debs contributed much to the struggle for a truly democratic America. The revolutionary Socialists through the Socialist Party and the Industrial Workers of the World organized semi-skilled and unskilled workers, led strikes, pushed the theory of industrial unionism, fought for civil rights, and established a tradition of militant union activity which has exerted an influence far beyond those immediately affected. And it was while the Left wing was most active in the party, from 1909 through 1912, that the Socialist movement achieved its greatest strength and influence.

But the record of the revolutionary Socialists is not without serious blemishes. Their sectarianism and syndicalism, their refusal to work within the A.F. of L., their dual unionism and their neglect of political activity all served to isolate them from the rank and file of American labor. Consequently, when the labor unions were subjected to an all-out attack after the First World War, the Left-wing Socialists were in no position to organize and lead mass resistance. They fought valiantly where they could. But the great body of American workers found themselves in battle under the weak-kneed direction of the conservative officials of their craft unions, officials whose leadership had never really been challenged because the Left-wing Socialists refused to contaminate themselves and their ideals by working within the American Federation of Labor and the railroad brotherhoods. The strikes were broken, the unions decimated, and American labor left to the tender mercies of the "business unionism" of the 1920s.

The shortcomings of the Left wing were serious enough. But major responsibility for the failure of the movement must rest upon the Right wing. It was the "constructive Socialists" who controlled the party and determined policy and activity. And it was they who turned the party into what they themselves called an opportunist political organization devoted to winning public office for its leaders.

When the Socialist Party was formed in 1901, most of its leaders and the great majority of its members belonged to the Left and Center factions. They held that socialism would be ushered in only after the working class had gained state power through Socialist control of a majority of national and local offices. To bring about that victory the party was to educate the workers in the principles of scientific socialism and aid the unions in their economic struggles with capital. Progress was to be measured by the growth of the Socialist vote in elections. But the purpose of election campaigns, except for the final one in which the Socialists would win complete victory, was primarily educational. A small Right wing argued that socialism was coming into the capitalist economy a step at a time, that the country was already partly socialist, and that the Socialist Party should devote itself to winning elective office and securing passage of reform legislation. This legislation would increase the socialist content of American life.

The Center and Right wings were made up of small businessmen, professionals, and craft union leaders. Both wings claimed to look forward to the day when America would be socialist. But the program of the Right differed little in content from that of reform parties and the progressive movement—political reform, an end to vice and corruption, trust regulation and nationalization. For the first few years the Center attacked the Right's program as a non-Socialist plan to preserve the dying middle class. However, the early successes of the party—100,000 votes in 1900, 200,000 in 1902, and 400,000 in 1904—were followed by a sharp drop in the Socialist vote, due in large part to the competition of reform parties in 1905 and 1906. The Center concluded that it would be easier to win early election victory through appeals to middle-class progressives than through the difficult and thankless task of organizing and educating workers. With political office seemingly within grasp, the temptation proved too great. The Center adopted the Right-wing program, allied itself with Victor Berger's step-at-a-time Socialists, and made opportunism and election victory the principles of Socialist Party activity. The Left wing countered this move by helping to organize and support the nonpolitical Industrial Workers of the World.

The new and enlarged Right wing limited its union activity to convincing members of craft unions that they should vote Socialist at elections. In an effort to placate A.F. of L. officials, industrial unionism was dropped and opposition to many of the worst features of craft unionism was abandoned. Under Right-wing leadership, the Socialist Party not only refused to fight for equal rights for Negroes and immigrants, but displayed a chauvinism seldom equaled by the most conservative A.F. of L. officers. Many Socialists used the party as a political machine to secure positions of income and power within the craft unions. Once in power, they, no more than their "pure and simple" colleagues, cared to risk their "pie cards" by reorganizing their unions along industrial lines or leading them in militant struggles for better wages, hours, and working conditions. Thus, Right-wing Socialists in the unions strengthened rather than fought those characteristics of craft unionism which made it timid, conservative, and of little use to the great majority of nonskilled workers. It is small wonder that Socialist trade unionists in the 1920s swallowed the "business unionism" and greater productivity propaganda of the trusts they had once organized to fight.

In order to win votes and office from middle-class Americans convinced that comparatively moderate reforms would make the country once again a land of opportunity, Right-wing Socialists repeatedly diluted their party's program until by 1912 it could be described as the left wing of the progressive movement. The state ceased to be an instrument of capitalist rule and became an impartial body which was gradually, very gradually, inaugurating a socialist society. But that society was now little more than government ownership of the great public utility trusts. The profits of other businesses were no longer a product of the exploitation of labor, but a just income earned by the initiative and effort of their owners. Vote Socialist! And Socialist officials would enact legislation to protect little business, adjust tax rates, end corruption, and bring new opportunities to professionals.

Right-wing Socialists insisted they were interested in elections, not strikes. Middle-class America could vote the Socialist ticket and be sure that its vote would contribute nothing to the "unreasonable" demands of labor. Constructive Socialists viewed economic and political activity as irrevocably separated. The trade unions handled economic matters. The Socialist Party was engaged in politics. Moreover, Socialist trade unionists would be reasonable in their demands on employers, for they understood the limitations of the capitalist system. As Victor Berger broadly hinted during Milwaukee municipal elections, a vote for socialism was a vote against strikes. Apparently everyone had something to gain from step-at-a-time Socialist victories except the worker, and he should vote Socialist because the party claimed to represent his interests. Some day in the far future, America would be socialist. And then even the worker would benefit, for, according to those Socialist pamphlets aimed at labor instead of the middle class, socialism was a worker's society. Peculiarly enough, American workers soon concluded that little was to be gained through votes and contributions in support of the Socialist ticket.

With such a program, the Socialist Party quickly degenerated into a vote-getting machine. The majority of party members still hoped for socialism. But Right-wing leaders hoped for political office. Constructive Socialists sabotaged organization of labor parties and refused to co-operate with other reform movements. Since only straight Socialist votes could bring the rewards of political life, almost all party activity was limited to propaganda, spoken and written, designed to convince everyone to vote Socialist.

The party as an organization refused to participate in labor's day-to-day struggles. And only rarely was the Left wing able to push the party into halfhearted support of major strikes and labor defense cases.

As prospects for electoral success seemed to grow, Right-wing Socialist leaders dumped increasingly large sections of the program in a desperate effort to win votes. Was middle-class America frightened by strikes, industrial unionism, free speech campaigns? Left-wing members of the party were expelled, industrial unionism dismissed as unimportant, imprisoned labor leaders abandoned. Were some Americans prejudiced against Negroes and the foreign-born? Negroes were attacked as "lynchable degenerates," and immigrants as saboteurs of America's high standard of living. Did little businessmen hesitate to vote for a party that pledged social ownership of all means of production and distribution? Socialism was redefined to mean public ownership of public utilities. Was socialism itself a word which terrorized reformers still devoted to free enterprise? Socialism was dismissed as a social form still generations away.

The Socialist Party, organized to bring real democracy to America, itself became one of the most undemocratic of political organizations. Elections to party office continued to be held, but the democratic forms lacked all democratic content. Rank and file Socialists received information on party activity and policy through the party press, lectures, and national office. And Right-wing party editors, speakers, and officials made sure that only their point of view was presented. When control of almost all avenues of communication failed to quiet rank and file unrest, control of party machinery made expulsion a simple matter. The party of the working class became largely middle class in membership and orientation, ruled by a small group of lawyers, writers, ministers, editors, businessmen, and craft union leaders. The goals of the party became power, public and trade union office, and financial reward for those in control.

For a short time, the militancy of the Left-wing Socialists and the failure of more openly conservative reform movements brought some electoral success. But votes for Socialism brought neither a better life for workers nor an end to monopoly pressure on the middle class. There was little reason for Americans interested in reform to accept the campaign promises of Victor Berger and Morris Hillquit rather than those of Woodrow Wilson, Theodore Roosevelt, and Robert La Follette. On the contrary, there was every reason to vote for those most likely to be elected to positions where they could write into law those reforms expected to restore opportunity and morality to America. Workers and middle-class reformers alike quickly deserted the party. Whatever may have been the contribution of constructive Socialists to the general sentiment for reform and to the passage of reform legislation, they did not change the United States from a capitalist to a socialist society. And that, after all, was their avowed purpose.

The Socialist Party conducted only one more major campaign after the expulsion of the Left wing in 1919. In 1920 Eugene Debs, once again in prison, this time for opposition to American participation in the First World War, received 900,000 votes from an electorate considerably enlarged by the enfranchisement of women. But Socialist leaders recognized that vote as one of loyalty to Debs, not to socialism and the Socialist Party. By 1921 membership had dropped to 13,500,[1] a few thousand more than had originally organized the Socialist Party.

During the "normalcy" of the 1920s, Right-wing Socialists went the way of most of the rest of the progressive movement. They concluded that American big business was here to stay, and that more was to be gained by working under it than fighting it. What was left of the party was predominantly middle class. And if the middle class thought it could make money, thanks to monopoly organization of the economy, there was little reason for the old socialist reforms designed to eliminate monopoly from American life.

The Socialist Party had been organized to combat the institutions, practices, and values of monopoly capitalism. Instead, it had been corrupted by them. Like other movements sworn to change the American economy, it had proven too willing to settle for a few favors and promises from the dreaded enemy. Whatever the future of socialism in America, it no longer lay with the Socialist Party.

[1] Madison, *Critics and Crusaders,* p. 461.

# Bibliography

The source materials listed below are to be found in the following special collections and libraries:

## SPECIAL COLLECTIONS

De Leon Collection. Wisconsin State Historical Library, Madison, Wisconsin.

Labadie Collection. University of Michigan, Ann Arbor, Michigan.

Lloyd, Henry D., Papers. University of Illinois, Urbana, Illinois.

Morgan, Thomas J., Collection. University of Illinois, Urbana, Illinois.

## LIBRARIES

General Library, University of Illinois, Urbana, Illinois.

General Library, University of Michigan, Ann Arbor, Michigan.

General Library, University of Wisconsin, Madison, Wisconsin.

Harper Library, University of Chicago, Chicago, Illinois.

John Crerar Library, Chicago, Illinois.

Newberry Library, Chicago, Illinois.

Wisconsin State Historical Library, Madison, Wisconsin.

## PRIMARY SOURCES: OFFICIAL DOCUMENTS AND NEWSPAPERS

Advance, 1896–1901. Published by San Francisco Socialists, this was the official organ of Pacific Coast members of the Socialist Labor Party and, later, of the Social Democratic Party.

American Federationist, The, 1894–1913. Published monthly by the American Federation of Labor.

American Labor Union Journal, The, 1902–1904. Published as a weekly by the American Labor Union prior to July, 1904, when it became a monthly.

Appeal to Reason, 1895–1912. Published weekly in Girard, Kansas.

Chicago Daily Socialist, The, 1907–1912.

Chicago Record-Herald, The, 1901–1912.

Chicago Socialist, The, 1899–1907. Published weekly. Named The Workers' Call from March, 1899 to March, 1902.

Chicago Tribune, The, 1897–1912.

Cleveland Citizen, The, 1893–1912. Published weekly by the Central Labor Union of Cleveland. Max S. Hayes was the editor and it was avowedly pro-Socialist Party.

Common Sense, 1902–1909. Published weekly by Los Angeles Socialists.

Comrade, The, 1901–1905. An illustrated Socialist monthly, absorbed by the International Socialist Review, May, 1905.

Industrial Workers of the World. Proceedings of the First Convention . . . June 27–July 8, 1905. New York, Labor News Company, 1905. The Labor News Company was the publishing house of the Socialist Labor Party, not the Socialist Party.

International Socialist Congress, Stuttgart, Germany, Aug. 18, 1907. Recent Progress of the Socialist and Labor Movements in the United States. Report of Morris Hillquit. Chicago, C. H. Kerr and Company, 1907.

International Socialist Review, 1900–1913. Published monthly in Chicago by Charles H. Kerr and Company.

Knights of Labor. Proceedings of the General Assembly . . . 1893. Philadelphia, Journal of the Knights of Labor, 1893.

Los Angeles Times, The, 1910–1911. For material on the McNamara case.

Masses, The, 1911–1912. Published monthly.

Milwaukee Journal, The, 1900–1912. For material on the Wisconsin Social Democratic Party.

Milwaukee Leader, The, 1911–1912. Daily newspaper started by Milwaukee Socialists after they won the city election in 1910.

Miner's Magazine, The, 1900–1912. A monthly published by the Western Federation of Miners.

Missouri Socialist, The, 1901–1902. During the first year of the Socialist Party, when its national office was in St. Louis, this weekly served as the unofficial voice of the national board (the Local Quorum).

National Rip Saw, The, 1912. Published monthly in Girard, Kansas.

New Jersey Socialist Unity Conference. Proceedings . . . 1905–1906. Conferences held by members of the Socialist and Socialist Labor parties in an attempt to work out a program which would lead to unification of the two parties.

New Time, The, 1902–1906. Published weekly in Spokane, Wash. A Right-wing Socialist paper addressed mainly to the farm vote.

New York Call, The, 1909–1913. Published daily.

New York Socialist, The, 1899–1908. Published weekly. Appeared July, 1899 to April 21, 1901 as *The People,* published by the Hillquit-led faction of the Socialist Labor Party, and then by the Social Democratic Party. Called *The New York Worker* from April 28, 1901 to March 28, 1908, when it became the *New York Socialist*. Replaced by *The New York Call,* a daily.

New York Times, The, 1897–1912.

New York Daily Tribune, The, 1894–1912.

New Yorker Volkszeitung, 1896–1902, 1911–1912. German-language daily. Played leading role in splitting the Socialist Labor Party, 1898–1899, and in defeating the Socialist Party Left wing in 1912–1913.

New York Worker, The. *See* New York Socialist, The.

Party Builder, The, 1912–1913. Official national bulletin of the Socialist Party, published weekly. The fact that control of the *Builder* was in the hands of the Socialist Party Lyceum Department indicates the type of party-building activity the national leadership thought most important by 1912.

People, The, 1893–1900. Official organ of the Socialist Labor Party; Daniel De Leon was editor. Published weekly. Contains minutes and reports of all official party business. Between July, 1899 and April, 1901 the Hillquit faction of the Socialist Labor Party published a weekly paper also called *The People*. The De Leon paper was published from offices on Beekman St., the Hillquit paper from offices on Williams St. The Williams St. *People* became successively the *New York Worker* and the *New York Socialist*.

"Proceedings of Socialist Unity Convention." Stenographic report of the proceedings at Indianapolis in 1901. Typescript in Harper Library, University of Chicago.

Railway Times, The, 1896–1897. Published in Chicago by the American Railway Union, this paper became the *Social Democrat* in July, 1897, immediately after the formation of the Social Democracy of America.

Social Crusader, The. *See* Socialist Spirit, The.

Social Democrat, The, 1897–1898. Published weekly in Chicago by the Social Democracy of America as the continuation of the *Railway Times*. Contains minutes and reports of party business.

Social-Democratic Herald, The, 1898–1913. Published in Chicago, 1898–1901, as the official organ of the Social Democratic Party with head-quarters in Chicago. After the formation of the Socialist Party, the paper was moved to Milwaukee where it became the party's leading advocate of step-at-a-time socialism. The title also appeared without the hyphen, as *Social Democratic Herald*.

Social Democratic Party. "Report of the Secretary of N.E.B. of S.D.P., June 1898–January, 1900." Typescript in John Crerar Library, Chicago. Report of Seymour Stedman, Secretary, Social Democratic Party with headquarters in Chicago.

Socialist, The, 1900–1909. Published in Seattle, Washington, as a weekly by Herman Titus and the Left-wing Washington Socialists. In 1905–1906 it was published in Toledo, Ohio, under the joint editorship of Titus and William Mailly, but in 1907 moved back to Seattle.

Socialist Alliance, The, 1896–1898. Published by the Socialist Trade and Labor Alliance.

Socialist Labor Party. Proceedings of the Ninth Annual Convention . . . 1896. This is the convention which endorsed the Socialist Trade and Labor Alliance.

Socialist Labor Party. Socialistische Arbeiter-Partei, Platform, Constitution und Beschlusse, welche von dem 26, 27, 28, 29, 30, und 31, Decem-

Socialist Labor Party (*Continued*)
ber 1877 zu Newark, N. J. Cincinnati, 1878. Organization convention of the Party.

Socialist Labor Party of the United States. Report . . . to the International Congress Held in Stuttgart, August 18–25, 1907.

Socialist Party. Information Department and Research Bureau . . . 111 N. Market St., Chicago, November 15, 1912—May 1, 1913. Chicago, Socialist Party National Office, 1913. Lists services performed by and available through this department.

Socialist Party. Proceedings of the First National Congress . . . Chicago, May 15–21, 1910. Chicago, Socialist Party, 1910. Called a "congress" instead of a "convention" because no candidates for political office were nominated.

Socialist Party. Proceedings of the National Convention . . . Chicago, May 1–6, 1904. Chicago, National Committee of the Socialist Party, 1904.

Socialist Party. Proceedings of the National Convention . . . Chicago, May 10–17, 1908. Chicago, Socialist Party, 1908.

Socialist Party. Proceedings of the National Convention . . . Indianapolis, Indiana, May 12–18, 1912. Chicago, Socialist Party, 1912.

Socialist Party Monthly Bulletin, The, 1912–1913. Published by the national office of the Socialist Party as the party's official bulletin, it was the continuation of the Socialist Party Official Bulletin (1904–1912). Issue for Feb., 1912 lists the three hundred-odd periodicals which endorsed the Socialist Party.

Socialist Party Official Bulletin, The, 1904–1912. Published monthly by the national office of the Socialist Party to inform party officials on party business. Contains printed minutes of committee meetings, correspondence with the national office, and reports of party activities. In Jan., 1912, become *The Socialist Party Monthly Bulletin*.

Socialist Party of the United States of America. Report . . . to the International Socialist and Trades Union Congress, Amsterdam, Holland, August 14–20, 1904. Chicago [Socialist Party], 1904.

Socialist Party Weekly Bulletin, The, 1903–1911. Mimeographed reports from the Socialist Party's national secretary to state and local officials. Material was similar to that published in the *Official Bulletin,* but was frequently more detailed and controversial.

Socialist Spirit, The, 1898–1903. Began publication as *The Social Crusader,* "a messenger of brotherhood and social justice," and became the *Socialist Spirit* in 1901. Published monthly. Franklin H. Wentworth was editor.

Socialist Teacher, The, 1903. The three issues of this monthly were published in Kansas City by Walter Thomas Mills in connection with his International School of Social Economy.

Socialist Trade and Labor Alliance of the United States and Canada.
Constitution . . . Adopted at Its First Convention, Held in New York
City, June 29 to July 2, 1896. New York, 1896.

U.S. Congress, House of Representatives. The Strike at Lawrence, Mass.
Hearings before the Committee on Rules. 62d Cong., 2d Sess., House
Doc. 671. Washington, Government Printing Office, 1912.

U.S. Congress, Senate. Report on the Chicago Strike. Senate Executive
Documents, 53d Cong., 3d Sess., Appendix A. Washington, Government
Printing Office, 1894. A report on the Debs-led Pullman strike of
1894.

U.S. Congress, Senate, Privileges and Elections Committee. Hearings
before a Sub-Committee on Campaign Contributions. 62d Congress, 3d
Session, 1913. Washington, Government Printing Office, 1913.

Voice of Labor, The, January–June, 1905. Published in Chicago by the
American Labor Union while waiting for the formation of the Industrial
Workers of the World.

Wayland's Monthly, Girard, Kansas, Nos. 1–100, 1899 [?]–1908. A
monthly series of pamphlets, rather than a periodical.

Western Federation of Miners of America. Official Proceedings of the
Tenth Annual Convention . . . 1902. Colorado, Colorado Chronicle,
1902.

Wilshire's Magazine, 1901–1912. Published by Gaylord Wilshire successively in Los Angeles, New York, Canada, and London. A monthly.

Workers' Call, The. See Chicago Socialist, The.

Workingmen's Party of the United States. Proceedings of the Union Congress, July 19–22, 1876. New York, Social Democratic Printing Association, 1876. In the Harper Library, University of Chicago.

OTHER PRIMARY SOURCES

Abbott, Leonard D., "The Socialist Movement in Massachusetts," The
Outlook, LXIV (Feb. 17, 1900), 410–12. Largely devoted to the Socialist Party in Haverhill and to the state's Socialist legislators.

"Acquittal of William D. Haywood, The," The Arena, XXXVIII (Sept.,
1907), 332–33. Concerns Haywood's trial for murder of Governor
Steunenberg.

Address by Teller County Locals of the Socialist Party to the Socialists
of Colorado, Setting Forth the Reasons for the Complete and Immediate Reorganization of the Socialist Party in Colorado. Cripple
Creek, Colorado, 1903. An attack on Right-wing Socialists in Colorado
and on the Social Crusade.

"Advance of Socialism in the United States," The Chautauquan, LXIV
(Sept. 1911), 18–19. Records the growing number of Socialist election
victories.

American Labor Year Book, The, 1916. New York, The Rand School of

American Labor Year Book, The, 1916 (*Continued*)

Social Science, 1916. Prepared by the Department of Labor Research of the Rand School. Contains historical sketches and reports dealing with various phases of the American socialist movement.

"American Socialism," *The Independent*, LII (Dec. 13, 1900), 3004. Discussion of the Socialist vote in the 1900 national and local elections.

Andrews, E. F., "Socialism and the Negro," *International Socialist Review*, V (March, 1905), 524–26. Socialism will solve the "Negro problem" by means of segregation.

"Antagonism between Christianity and Socialism, The," *The Literary Digest*, XXVIII (June 11, 1904), 853. Summary of speech delivered at Harvard University by Anatole Leroy-Beaulieu.

"Arrest of McNamara, The," *Current Literature*, L (June, 1911), 569–76. Background of the bombing of the Los Angeles *Times* and the detective work which led to the arrest of the McNamaras.

Aterbury, Ben. An Open Letter to the Average American Workman. Social Democratic Party Leaflet No. 2. Issued before the 1900 presidential election by the National Campaign Committee of the Social Democratic Party with headquarters in Chicago.

Avery, Martha Moore, "Socialist Sunday School," *The National Civic Federation Review*, III (May, 1908), 16. An attack on the Socialist Sunday Schools.

Baker, Ray Stannard, "The Debs Co-operative Commonwealth," *The Outlook*, LVI (July 3, 1897), 538–40. A fairly sympathetic report of the formation of the Social Democracy of America and its plans to colonize a western state.

——— "The Revolutionary Strike, a New Form of Industrial Struggle as Exemplified at Lawrence, Massachusetts," *The American Magazine*, LXXIV (May, 1912), 19–30C. In addition to giving a report of the Lawrence strike, Baker notes the growing conflict between reform and revolutionary socialism.

"Barbarous Spokane," *The Independent*, LXVIII (Feb. 10, 1910), 330–31. Describes the suppression of civil liberties in Spokane, Wash.

Beaumont, Saul, "Zionism or Socialism: Which Will Solve the Jewish Question?" *The Arena*, XXXIX (Jan. 1908), 54–58. Socialism, not Zionism, is the only remedy for the long-persecuted Jews.

Benson, Allan Louis. Socialism Made Plain. Why the Few Are Rich and the Many Poor. Milwaukee, Milwaukee Social-Democratic Publishing Company, 1904. Hailed by the party Right wing as the best propaganda exposition of socialism.

——— The Truth About Socialism. New York, B. W. Huebsch, 1913. Benson replaced Spargo as the most popular of Right-wing Socialist propagandists and was chosen as the party's candidate for President of the United States by a national referendum in 1916 after Debs and Charles Edward Russell had declined to run.

Beresford, Thomas. Tactics and Strategy. San Francisco, 1903. Privately printed and distributed by the author. A Left-wing exposition of Socialist principles and tactics. The Seattle *Socialist* referred to it as "a book all Socialists should read."

Berger, Victor L., "What is the Matter with Milwaukee," *The Independent,* LXVIII (April 21, 1910), 840–43. Berger holds that only businessmen who insist upon increasing their profits through government corruption have anything to fear from a Socialist victory in Milwaukee.

———— "Socialism, the Logical Outcome of Progressivism," *The American Magazine,* LXXV (Nov., 1912), 19–21. Berger contends that those who really want progressive reforms should vote the Socialist ticket.

Bernstein, Edward. Evolutionary Socialism. London, Independent Labour Party, 1909. Bernstein's revisions of Marxism had considerable influence on American Right-wing Socialists.

"Better than Socialism," *The Outlook,* LXX (Jan. 25, 1900), 213–14. Reforms are better than socialism because socialism would end individual liberty.

"Bishop Quigley's Attack upon Socialism," *The Literary Digest,* XXIV (Jan. 12, 1902), 508. Bishop Quigley says that socialism is the enemy of religion, morality, and private property.

Blatchford, Robert. Merrie England, a Plain Exposition of Socialism. New York, Commonwealth Company [1896?]. This book was published in England about 1894. Its combination of reform and utopian socialism made it one of the most popular propaganda volumes on socialism.

Bloor, Ella Reeve. We Are Many. New York, International Publishers, 1940. The autobiography of a woman who was an active Socialist organizer in Ohio and who engaged in the campaign for woman suffrage during the period under study.

Bohn, Frank, "The Ballot," *International Socialist Review,* X (June, 1910), 1120. The only victories which can be won a step at a time are union victories in the shop.

———— "The Passing of the McNamaras," *International Socialist Review,* XII (Jan., 1912), 404. Bohn says the McNamaras are not to be blamed. Their hearts were right, but they were only acquainted with "capitalist methods" of combat.

———— "Some Definitions," *International Socialist Review,* XII (May, 1912), 747–49. Left-wing definitions of key terms in socialist theory.

Bohn, William E., "Reformer and Revolutionist," *International Socialist Review,* X (Sept., 1909), 204–11. Industrial socialism versus reform socialism, from the point of view of the former.

Bondy, Joseph, "Thurber Answered, the Trend against Corporate Greed Not a Trend towards Socialism," *Moody's Magazine,* I (April, 1906), 571–75. An answer to an article published in the preceding issue of this magazine by F. B. Thurber, president of the U.S. Export Association,

Bondy, Joseph (*Continued*)
which argued that the progressive attack on big business was part of an evil trend toward socialism.

Boudin, Louis B., "Prospects of a Labor Party in the United States," *International Socialist Review,* X (April, 1910), 919–20. Boudin concludes that fortunately the prospects are dim.

Bouquet of Epigrams Culled From the Speeches of Eugene V. Debs. Social Democratic Leaflet No. 6. Issued for the 1900 presidential campaign by the National Campaign Committee of the Social Democratic Party with headquarters in Chicago.

Boyle, James. What Is Socialism? New York, The Shakespeare Press, 1912. An unsympathetic analysis from the A.F. of L. point of view.

Braden, Lincoln, "A Socialist Criticism of Milwaukee's Socialist Program," *The American Review of Reviews,* XLII (Nov. 1910), 601. Milwaukee Socialists cannot hope to succeed with their program because they ignore the economic truths discovered by Malthus.

Bryan, William Jennings, "Individualism versus Socialism," *Century Magazine,* LXXI (April, 1906), 856.

Burns, William J, The Masked War. New York, George H. Doran Company, 1913. The story of the McNamara case from the point of view of the private detectives involved.

Campbell, W. W., "The Preacher-Socialist Who Made Himself Mayor," *Harper's Weekly,* LV (Dec. 23, 1911), 18. About George D. Lunn, who had just been elected mayor of Schenectady, N.Y.

Capitalist's Union or Labor Unions: Which? Chicago, C. H. Kerr and Company, 1904. Pocket Library of Socialism No. 40. Issued by Union 7386, A.F. of L. Holds that unions must support Socialist candidates because rise of trusts, "the capitalist's union," necessitates political action.

Casson, Herbert N., "Socialism, Its Growth and Its Leaders," *Munsey's Magazine,* XXXIII (June, 1905), 290–97. Describes the growth of "practical socialism," largely in terms of Berger and the Wisconsin party.

"Catholic Campaign against Atheistic Socialism, A," *The Literary Digest,* XXXII (June 9, 1906), 875. Summarizes the Catholic campaign to combat the rise of socialism by arousing Christian forces to work along Christian Democratic lines.

Chaney, William, "Working Class Politics, from Debs' Chicago Speech," *International Socialists Review,* XI (Nov., 1910), 257–61. Debs, making the opening speech in the Chicago Socialist campaign in the fall of 1910, called on the party to devote less time to vote-catching and more time to helping the cause of industrial unionism.

Chaplin, Ralph. Wobbly. Chicago, The University of Chicago Press, 1948. The autobiography of a Wobbly and Left-wing Socialist who was connected with the *International Socialist Review.*

Chase, John C., "Municipal Socialism in America," *The Independent*, LII (Jan. 25, 1900), 249–51. Chase was elected Socialist mayor of Haverhill, Mass. in December, 1898. He outlines the possibilities and limitations of municipal socialism.

"Cheerful Destroyers," *The Nation*, LXXXVIII (May 27, 1909), 527–28. Notes the increasing moderation and "good taste" of the socialist program.

"Christian Injunctions against Socialism," *The Literary Digest*, XXXIV (May 5, 1907), 716. A series of quotations from the Bible on obeying masters, respecting authority, etc. Taken from the *Catholic Standard and Times*, Philadelphia.

"Church and Socialism, The," *The Arena*, XL (Sept., 1908), 243–44. Growing number of ministers joining the socialist movement.

"Church's Growing Sympathy with Socialism, The," *Current Literature*, XLIII (Nov., 1907), 537–39.

Clark, Calvin M., "A Socialist Mayor in Haverhill, Mass.," *The Independent*, L (Dec. 29, 1898), 1926–27. The election of John Chase.

Cline, Charles E. The Socialist Catechism. Chicago, C. H. Kerr and Company, 1904. Pocket Library of Socialism No. 41. Questions and answers on the Socialist Party.

Clinton, DeWitt. How, When, and Where to Inaugurate Socialism or Universal Co-operation. Los Angeles [1902?]. Socialism should be inaugurated city by city through step-at-a-time purchase of industry and extension of municipal construction and banking.

Coates, D. C., "The Struggle in Colorado," *The American Labor Union Journal*, Sept. 3, 1903. Deals with the strikes of the Western Federation of Miners.

Cohen, Joseph E., "Constructive Socialism," *International Socialist Review*, IX (Aug., 1908), 85. An unsympathetic analysis of step-at-a-time socialism.

——— Socialism for Students. Chicago, C. H. Kerr and Company, 1910. Socialist theories from a Left-wing point of view.

——— "Socialist Ideology," *International Socialist Review*, X (Aug., 1909), 874–75.

Coler, Bird S. Socialism in the Schools. New York, The DeVinne Press, 1911. The facts that schools now teach children how to sew and cook and that the state doctor looks after the children's health are warnings that atheism and socialism are entering all public schools. This tendency must be stopped and the family once again left to look after children.

Collier, John, "The Experiment in Milwaukee," *Harper's Weekly*, LV (Aug. 12, 1911), 11. The first year of Milwaukee's Socialist administration. Rather sympathetic.

"Compromises of the Socialist Convention, The," *The Independent*, LXXII (May 30, 1912), 1181–82. Discussion of the factional fights at the 1912 Socialist national convention.

"Confession and Autobiography of Harry Orchard, The," *McClure's Magazine,* XXIX (July, 1907), 294–306. Orchard was the confessed murderer of Governor Steunenberg, claiming he killed him under instructions from the Western Federation of Miners.

"Confession of Harry Orchard," *Current Literature,* XLIII (July, 1907), 1–5.

Connolly, James. Socialism Made Easy. Chicago, C. H. Kerr and Company, 1909. Revolutionary socialist theory discussed by the Irish revolutionary leader.

"Constructive Socialism," *The Independent,* LXVI (June 10, 1909), 1304–06. Favorable editorial comment on the answers given by constructive Socialists to the article, " 'Practical' Socialism, Is There Any Such Thing?" in *The Saturday Evening Post,* CLXXXI (May 8, 1909), 8–9, 55.

Cook, Waldo Lincoln, "The Shadow of Socialism," *Annals of the American Academy of Political and Social Science,* XVIII (Sept., 1901), 212–25. Largely a discussion of the relationship between socialism and opposition to imperialism in Europe.

Corbin, Caroline. Socialism and Christianity, with Reference to the Woman Question. Chicago, 1905. Issued by the Illinois Association Opposed to the Extension of Suffrage to Women. The author opposes woman suffrage because it is "the corner stone of socialism."

Cross, Ira Brown, "Socialism in California Municipalities," *The National Municipal Review,* I (Oct., 1912), 611–19. Cross finds all the successful Socialist campaigns to have been waged around issues of immediate reform, not of socialism, and that Socialist office holders advocate only the mildest of reforms.

"Currents in American Socialism," *The Nation,* XCII (June 15, 1911), 594–95. Notes with approval the growth of constructive socialism.

Daniel De Leon, the Man and His Work, a Symposium. New York, National Executive Committee, Socialist Labor Party, 1920. A series of essays on De Leon and the history of the Socialist Labor Party by men who had worked with him.

Davis, John. Public Ownership of Railroads. Girard, Kansas, J. A. Wayland, 1902. Studies in Socialism No. 20. The advantages of socialism shown by describing the benefits which would follow nationalization of railroads.

Debs, Eugene V. The American Movement. Terre Haute, Indiana, Standard Publishing Company, 1904. A history of the American socialist movement from utopian beginnings to the formation of the Socialist Party.

—— "The Anthracite Arbitration," *The American Labor Union Journal,* Jan. 18, 1903. Criticizes the United Mine Workers for not calling a general coal strike to aid the anthracite workers.

—— The Children of the Poor. Chicago National Office of the Socialist Party.

——— "Danger Ahead," *International Socialist Review,* XI (Jan., 1911), 413. Debs warns the Socialist Party that its growing opportunism, as expressed in abandoning its revolutionary program in the pursuit of votes, will make it impossible for it to lead the fight for socialism.

——— "How I Became a Socialist," *The Comrade,* I (April, 1902), 147–48.

——— Industrial Unionism. New York, Labor News Company, 1911. An address delivered at Grand Central Palace, New York City, December 10, 1905. Favors industrial unionism and the Industrial Workers of the World.

——— The Issue. Girard, Kansas, J. A. Wayland, 1908. The only issue is capitalism versus socialism.

——— "The McNamara Case and the Labor Movement," *International Socialist Review,* XII (Jan., 1912), 400. Debs defends the McNamaras, holding them to have been sincere but misguided.

——— "Social Democracy," *The National Magazine,* IX (Oct., 1898), 54–58. Description of the Social Democratic Party and its program.

——— "The Social Democratic Party," *The Independent,* LII (Aug. 23, 1900), 18–21. Reasons for voting the Social Democratic ticket.

——— "The Social Democratic Party's Appeal," *The Independent,* LVII (Oct. 13, 1904), 835–40. An appeal for support in the 1904 election.

——— "Socialist Ideals," *The Arena,* XL (Nov., 1908), 432–34. End of struggle for bread will permit development of mind and soul.

——— "Socialist Party's Appeal," *The Independent,* LXV (Oct. 15, 1908), 875–80. An appeal for support in the 1908 election.

——— "Socialist Party's Appeal," *The Independent,* LXXIII (Oct. 24, 1912), 950–52. An appeal for support in the 1912 presidential election.

——— "Sound Socialist Tactics," *International Socialist Review,* XII (Feb., 1912), 481–86. Debs wants elimination of "intellectuals" and "reformers" from party leadership, but also wants a party declaration against "direct action," which he defines as personal violence.

——— Unionism and Socialism, a Plea for Both. Terre Haute, Indiana, Standard Publishing Company, 1904. The need for industrial union organization and socialist activity in order to win the co-operative commonwealth.

——— "The Western Labor Movement," *International Socialist Review,* III (Nov., 1902), 258. A defense of the American Labor Union and industrial unionism.

Debs: His Life, Writings and Speeches, with a Department of Appreciations. Girard, Kansas, The Appeal to Reason, 1908.

"Debs, Seidel and the Socialist Dissensions," *Current Literature,* LIII (July, 1912), 35–38. A discussion of socialist factionalism as revealed at the May, 1912 Socialist convention.

"Defeat for Socialism, A," *The Literary Digest,* XXI (Dec. 15, 1900), 724. Defeat of John Chase for re-election as mayor of Haverhill, Mass.

De Leon, Daniel. Reform or Revolution. New York, 1934. Attacks reform socialism and develops the theory of industrial unions as the fighting arm of the socialist movement.

——— Speeches and Editorials. 2 vols. New York, New York Labor News Company, 1918.

Dietzgen, Eugene. Lese Majesty and Treason to the "Fakirs" in the Socialist Labor Party. Chicago, March 6, 1899. A pamphlet issued by Dietzgen as part of the factional fight against De Leon in the Chicago Socialist Labor Party.

Downing, George W., "Planlessness of Production the Cause of Panics," *International Socialist Review,* VIII (Jan., 1908), 414–15. Argues that surplus value bears little if any relation to depressions in the era of monopoly.

"Dream of Young Socialists," *The Nation,* LXXXII (March 8, 1906), 192. Socialism can't be stopped by appeasing it with socialistic legislation.

"Droning Young Socialist, A," *The North American Review,* CLXXXIII, (Sept. 21, 1906), 563–65. An attack on Joseph Medill Patterson, who had recently joined the Socialist Party.

Duchez, Louis, "The Proletarian Attitude," *International Socialist Review,* IX (April, 1909), 788. Duchez insists that the proletariat has no use for reform legislation such as that advocated by the Right wing of the Socialist Party.

——— "The Strikes in Pennsylvania," *International Socialist Review,* X (Sept., 1909), 193–203. These were the I.W.W.-led strikes which rearoused the enthusiasm of the Left wing of the Socialist Party for the I.W.W.

——— "Victory at McKees Rocks," *International Socialist Review,* X (Oct., 1909), 289–300. Argues that the effectiveness of the I.W.W. in these Pennsylvania strikes demonstrates that correct Socialist Party policy must be aimed at building revolutionary unionism through the I.W.W.

Dunbar, Robin Ernest, "A Conflict among Leaders," *International Socialist Review,* X (Aug., 1909), 149–51. A Left-wing Socialist attack on the answers contributed by Right-wing Socialist leaders to the article, " 'Practical' Socialism, Is There Any Such Thing?" *The Saturday Evening Post,* CLXXXI (May 8, 1909), 8–9, 55.

Dvorak, Robert, "The Garment Workers Strike Lost, Who Was To Blame?" *International Socialist Review,* XI (March, 1911), 550–56. Dvorak was the *Chicago Daily Socialist* reporter assigned to cover the strike. He accuses Right-wing Chicago Socialist leaders of betraying support of the strike in order to win favor with the city's conservative A.F. of L. leaders.

Elliot, Francis M., "Socialism and Public Ownership," *International Socialist Review,* VI (June, 1906), 732–35.

Ely, Richard T., "Socialistic Propaganda," *The Chautauquan,* XXX (Jan., 1900), 381–82. Concerned entirely with the European socialist movement.

Ely, Richard T., and Thomas K. Urdahl, "Progress of Socialism since 1893," *The Chautauquan,* XXX (Oct., Dec., 1899), 77–84, 294–99. Deals primarily with the European socialist movement.

"Encyclical on Socialism, The," *Public Opinion,* XXX (Feb. 7, 1901), 178. The Associated Press summary of the Pope's encyclical.

England, George Allen, "Milwaukee's Socialist Government," *The American Review of Reviews,* XLII (Oct., 1910), 445–55. A description of the first few months of the Socialist administration.

Ensor, R. C. K., ed. Modern Socialism as Set Forth by Socialists in Their Speeches, Writings, and Programmes. New York, Harper and Brothers, 1910. A source book of selections describing socialism in various European countries.

Flower, B. O., "Socialism in Europe and America," *The Arena,* XXV (April, 1901), 442–47. Predicts that American socialism will appeal increasingly to man's spiritual side.

———— "Union of Socialistic Forces," *The Arena,* XXVI (Oct., 1901), 430–31. Sympathetic treatment of formation of the Socialist Party. Flower particularly likes the "immediate demands" of the platform.

For Nation-wide Free Industries. Dec., 1912. A thirty-two page supplement published by the Los Angeles *Times,* recounting its battle against labor unions and in the McNamara case.

Foster, William Z. The Crisis in the Socialist Party. New York, Workers Library Publishers, 1936. Includes a history of factionalism and Socialist Party policy, 1900–1912.

———— From Bryan to Stalin. New York, International Publishers, 1937. Foster was associated with Herman Titus and the Washington Socialist Party until that group left the party in 1909. This volume, together with *Pages from a Worker's Life,* comprises his autobiography.

———— Pages from a Worker's Life. New York, International Publishers, 1939.

Founding of the First International. New York, International Publishers, 1937. Contains letters and documents pertaining to the founding of the first socialist international, including correspondence with American socialists.

Frank, Henry, "The Meaning of the Invasion of European Socialism," *The Arena,* XXXVIII (Sept., 1907), 277–84. The growth of European, i.e., Marxist, socialism in the United States indicates that we, too, have a class society. ·

French, W. E. P., "A Socialism in Our Midst," *The Arena,* XXXII (July, 1904), 32–39. Captain French, of the U.S. Army, maintains that the Army is a good example of socialism. He holds that Americans should

French, W. E. P. (*Continued*)

encourage, as constructive, an evolution toward socialism, but oppose all revolution as destructive.

"Gains of the Socialists, The," *Public Opinion,* XXXIII (Nov. 20, 1902), 647. The newspapers quoted are impressed by the increase in the Socialist vote in the 1902 congressional elections in Massachusetts, Ohio, Illinois, and Colorado, but are divided as to the possibilities of further growth of the socialist movement.

Gaylord, Winfield R. Socialism Is Coming—Now. St. Louis, Labor Publishing Company, 1912. An exposition of step-at-a-time socialism by one of the leaders of the Wisconsin Social-Democratic Party.

Ghent, William James, "The 'Appeal' and Its Influence," *The Survey,* XXVI (April 1, 1911), 24–28. An analysis of the growth and circulation of The *Appeal to Reason.*

———— Mass and Class. New York, The Macmillan Company, 1904. When the ethics of the "producing classes" triumph, justice will reign.

———— Our Benevolent Feudalism. New York, The Macmillan Company, 1902. An attack on capitalist society by a writer connected with the Center faction of the Socialist Party.

———— Socialism and Success, Some Uninvited Messages. New York, John Lane Company, 1910. Uninvited messages pointing out the errors of their ways to reformers, "retainers of capitalists," and Left-wing Socialists.

———— "Why Socialists Are Partisans," *The Independent,* LIX (Oct. 26, 1905), 967–71. The Socialist Party refuses to work or amalgamate with reform parties because the middle class seeks to use the workers only for middle-class ends.

Gladden, Washington, "The Spread of Socialism," *The Outlook,* LXII (May 13, 1899), 116–22.

Goldman, Emma. Living My Life. 2 vols. New York, Alfred A. Knopf, 1931. Autobiography of an anarchist leader.

Gompers, Samuel, "Debs, the Apostle of Failure," *The American Federationist,* XV (Sept., 1908), 737. An attack on Debs in connection with the A.F. of L. support of William Jennings Bryan in the 1908 presidential campaign.

———— Seventy Years of Life and Labor. 2 vols. in 1. New York, E. P. Dutton and Company, 1943. Considerable space is devoted to the author's conflicts with Socialists.

Gordon, F. G. R. Panics: Cause and Cure. Girard, Kansas, J. A. Wayland, 1901. Wayland's Monthly No. 12. Socialism is the only cure for depressions.

Grant, Luke, "Haywood Trial, a Review," *The Outlook,* LXXXVI (Aug. 24, 1907), 855–62. The trial of Bill Haywood for the murder of Governor Steunenberg.

———— The National Erectors' Association and the International Association of Bridge and Structural Ironworkers. U.S. Commission on Industrial Relations. Washington, Government Printing Office, 1915. A study of the conflict between capital and labor which led to the bombing of the Los Angeles *Times* and the McNamara case.

Green, William C. Some Reasons Why Farmers Should be Socialists. Girard, Kansas, J. A. Wayland, 1903. Wayland's Monthly No. 43.

Grifflin, Henry Farrand, "The Rising Tide of Socialism," *The Outlook,* C (Feb. 24, 1912), 438–48. Deals mainly with the Socialist victory in Schenectady, N.Y.

"Growth of Socialism," *The American Review of Reviews,* XX (Aug., 1899), 221–22. The article finds few signs of growing socialism in the U.S., and is mainly devoted to Europe.

"Growth of Socialism, The," *Gunton's Magazine,* XVII (July, 1899), 6–15. Holds that the real socialist danger is from the "unintelligent crusade against wealth"—i.e., the crusade led by those favoring anti-trust legislation and municipal ownership and control.

"Growth of Socialistic Sentiment," *The Literary Digest,* XVIII (April 29, 1899), 480–82. The American press considers the increasing sentiment for municipal ownership a sign of the growth of socialism.

"Growth of the Socialist Vote," *Public Opinion,* XXVIII (May 10, 1900), 584. Predicts the Socialists will get 100,000 votes in the 1900 presidential election.

Hagerty, Thomas J. Economic Discontent and Its Remedy. Terre Haute, Indiana, Standard Publishing Company, 1902. Hagerty was a former Catholic priest who became a Socialist organizer. In 1905 he played a leading part in organizing the Industrial Workers of the World.

—— "The Function of Industrial Unionism," *The Voice of Labor,* III (March, 1905), 5. The industrial union is to be the fighting, revolutionary organization. One of a series of articles laying the ideological groundwork for the I.W.W.

Hall, Thomas C., "Socialism as a Rival of Organized Christianity," *The North American Review,* CLXXVIII (June, 1904), 915–26. The strength of socialism is in its faith. It can be met only by the revitalized faith of Christianity.

Hanford, Benjamin. Fight for Your Life. New York, Wilshire Books, 1909. A short biography and selected writings of the Socialist leader.

—— The Labor War in Colorado. Volkszeitung Library, Vol. 6, No. 4. History of the struggles of the Western Federation of Miners.

—— Railroading in the United States. New York, Socialistic Cooperative Publishing Association, 1904. The advantages to railroad workers and users which would follow the establishment of socialism.

Hard, William, "The Making of a Socialist," *The World To-day,* XI (Aug., 1906), 851–55. Describes the history and theory of a lawyer who had joined the Socialist Party. The lawyer claimed never to have read a book on socialism. He held that socialism was inevitable, that it

Hard, William (*Continued*)
was simply a case of the trusts vs. the public interest. The child-labor
law was an example of the entering wedge of socialism.

Haywood, William D. Bill Haywood's Book. London, Martin Lawrence,
Limited. Haywood's autobiography.

———— "Industrial Unionism," *Voice of Labor,* III (June, 1905), 2.
Socialism can be won only through the organization of a revolutionary
industrial union.

———— "Socialism the Hope of the Working Class," *International Socialist
Review,* XII (Feb., 1912), 461–71. Stenographic report of Haywood's
speech at Cooper Union, December, 1911, in which he held that workers could not be expected to respect capitalist laws made for the
purpose of exploiting them.

———— "To the Members of the Socialist Party," *International Socialist
Review,* XII (Dec., 1911), 375. Campaign statement made during the
December, 1911 elections for the National Executive Committee, Social-
ist Party.

Haywood, William D., and Frank Bohn. Industrial Socialism. Chicago,
C. H. Kerr and Company, 1911. States the theoretical position of the
Left wing of the Socialist Party after 1909.

Hearst Ticket, The. New York, New York Socialist Party, 1906. An
election leaflet attacking middle-class reforms.

Herron, George D., "The Social Opportunity," *International Socialist
Review,* IV (April, 1904), 589–90. The Socialist Party will gain victory by combining moral appeal and Marxian analysis.

———— Why I Am a Socialist. Chicago, C. H. Kerr and Company, 1900.
Pocket Library of Socialism No. 20.

Hillquit, Morris. History of Socialism in the United States. New York,
Funk and Wagnalls, Company, 1903. Useful mainly for information on
socialist activities prior to the formation of the Socialist Party. The
1903 edition was published so soon after formation of the Socialist
Party that Hillquit, probably for the sake of party unity, glossed over
the conflicts which attended the formation of the party. The 1910 edition contains some useful material on the party's history.

———— Loose Leaves from a Busy Life. New York, Macmillan Company,
1934. Hillquit's autobiography.

———— Socialism in Theory and Practice. New York, Macmillan Company, 1909.

———— Socialism Summed Up. New York, H. K. Fly Company, 1913. This
volume, together with *Socialism in Theory and Practice,* outlines Hillquit's theories of constructive socialism.

———— "The Socialist 'Plan' of Wealth Distribution," *Putnam's Magazine,* IV (April, 1908), 54–57. Hillquit's interpretation of the Socialist
plan for ownership of means of production and the distribution of
material reward in socialist society.

Hillquit, Morris, Samuel Gompers, and Max J. Hayes. Double-Edge of Labor's Sword. Chicago, Socialist Party National Office, 1914. Discussion, testimony, and cross-examination before U.S. Committee on Industrial Relations.

Hillquit, Morris, and John A. Ryan. Socialism: Promise or Menace? New York, Macmillan Company, 1914. A debate between Hillquit and Ryan, a Catholic leader active in social reform movements. Reprinted from seven articles which appeared in *Everybody's Magazine*.

"History, of the Case," *Current Literature*, XLII (June, 1907), 587–95. The trial of Haywood for the murder of Governor Steunenberg.

Hitchcock, C. C. The Ethics of Socialism. Girard, Kansas, J. A. Wayland, 1901. Wayland's Monthly No. 17.

Holmes, Fred L., "Socialist Legislators at Work," *The Independent*, LXX (March 23, 1911), 592–94. Description of the activities of Wisconsin's Socialists in the state legislature.

How a Socialist Local or Branch Should be Conducted. Chicago, National Headquarters, The Socialist Party [1904?].

"How Burns Caught the Dynamiters," *McClure's Magazine*, XXXVIII (Jan., 1912). A description by William J. Burns of the detective work involved in trapping the McNamara brothers.

Howe, Frederic C., "The Peaceful Revolution," *The Outlook*, XCIV (Jan. 15, 1910), 115–19. Description of the European socialist movement.

Hoxie, Robert F., "The Convention of the Socialist Party, 1908," *The Journal of Political Economy*, XVI (July, 1908), 442–50. Very sympathetic to the Right wing of the Socialist Party.

—— "The Rising Tide of Socialism," *The Journal of Political Economy*, XIX (Oct., 1911), 609–31. An analysis of local Socialist political campaigns and victories.

—— "The Socialist Party and American Convention Methods," *The Journal of Political Economy*, XX (July, 1912), 738–44.

—— "The Socialist Party in the November Elections," *The Journal of Political Economy*, XX (March, 1912), 205–23. A further analysis of Socialist election tactics and victories.

Hunter, Robert. Labor in Politics. Chicago, The Socialist Party, 1915. History of socialist work with labor unions.

—— "The Socialist Party in the Present Campaign," *The American Review of Reviews*, XXXVIII (Sept., 1908), 293–99. An analysis of the Socialist Party campaign in the 1908 presidential election.

—— Socialists at Work. New York, Macmillan Company, 1908. Deals almost entirely with the European socialist movement.

Hyde, Henry M., "Socialists at Work," *The Technical World Magazine*, XVI (Feb., 1912), 621–29. Deals mainly with the successes and failures of Milwaukee's first socialist administration.

Industrial Crises: Cause and Cure. Social Democratic Party Leaflet No. 5. Issued for the 1900 presidential election by National Campaign Committee of the Social Democratic Party with headquarters in Chicago.

"Industrial Workers of the World, The," *International Socialist Review,* X (Oct., 1909), 359–60. Beginning of the revival of Left-wing Socialist interest in the I.W.W.

"Information Department and Research Bureau," *National Municipal Review,* II (July, 1913), 500–501. Description of the Socialist Party bureau which was designed to explore the road of step-at-a-time socialism.

"Intercollegiate Socialism," *Public Opinion,* XXXIX (Nov. 4, 1905), 592–93. Formation of the Intercollegiate Socialist Society.

"Is Socialism Anti-Christian?" *The Literary Digest,* XXIV (Jan. 11, 1902), 51–52. The negative replies of Thomas McGrady, J. Stitt Wilson, Robert Rivés LaMonte, and George D. Herron.

Johnston, Charles, "Socialism and the American Farmer," *The North American Review,* CXCVI (Sept., 1912), 305–11. Socialist work among farmers.

Jones, Ellis O., "The Parlor Socialists," *International Socialist Review,* VIII (Oct., 1907), 214–22. The growing number of middle-class or "parlor" Socialists is a sign of the Americanization of the Socialist Party.

―――― "Some Unique Features of the Socialist Party," *The Arena,* XXXVIII (Oct., 1907), 423–26. The Socialist Party is not a militant but an educational organization. Socialism is inevitable, but without the Socialist Party it would take a little longer to come.

―――― "Why I Am a Socialist," *The Arena,* XXXVII (Jan., 1907), 45–47. Jones was head of the Intercollegiate Socialist Society and a member of the Socialist Party.

Jones, George D., "Why I Am Not a Socialist," *The Arena,* XXXVII (March, 1907), 274–75. He is not a socialist because socialism is too vague, and is the enemy of family life, the home, and individual liberty. But he favors municipal ownership of public utilities.

Kampffmeyer, Paul. Changes in the Theory and Tactics of the (German) Social-Democracy. Translated by Winfield R. Gaylord. Chicago, C. H. Kerr and Company, 1908. Circulated by the Right wing of the American Socialist Party to show that the American party should also turn to constructive socialism.

Keister, Jack, "Why the Socialists Won in Butte," *International Socialist Review,* XI (June, 1911), 731–33. Analysis of the victory in mayoralty elections in Butte, Montana which was won by Left-wing Socialists and members of the I.W.W.

Kelly, Edmond. Twentieth Century Socialism: What It Is Not; What It Is; How It May Come. New York, Longmans, Green, and Company, 1913. Favors evolutionary, rather than revolutionary, socialism.

Kennedy, John Curtis, "Socialistic Tendencies in American Trade Unions," *The Journal of Political Economy,* XV (Oct., 1907), 470–88.
An analysis of Socialist Party influence in the trade unions.

Kerby, William J., "Catholicity and Socialism," *The American Catholic
Quarterly Review,* XXX (April, 1905), 225–43. Catholic opponents of
socialism must make a greater effort to understand the appeal of socialism to workers. They must attack it not merely on grounds of atheism
and free love but must combat it on a higher spiritual level.

———— "Aims in Socialism," *The Catholic World,* LXXXV (July, 1907),
500–511. Kerby now holds that the Catholic Church should not be too
hasty in condemning socialism since the Socialists may have legitimate
proposals for solution of some of the world's problems.

Kerr, Charles H. Morals and Socialism. Chicago, C. H. Kerr and Company, 1899. Pocket Library of Socialism No. 10.

Kerr, May Walden. Socialism and the Home. Chicago, C. H. Kerr and
Company. Pocket Library of Socialism No. 28. Socialism will protect,
not destroy, the home.

Kohler, Charles O., "Serious Thoughts," *International Socialist Review,*
IX (June, 1909), 1013. The revolutionary proletariat must insist upon
nothing short of an immediate revolution.

"Labor Party, A," *International Socialist Review,* X (Jan., 1910), 594–
606. An exposé of the secret proposals at the meeting of the National
Executive Committee of the Socialist Party to support the formation
of a labor party.

Ladoff, Isador. The Passing of Capitalism, and the Mission of Socialism.
Terre Haute, Indiana, Debs Publishing Company, 1901. Ladoff and
Berger were among the earliest theorists of step-at-a-time socialism.

LaFollette, Robert M. LaFollette's Autobiography: a Personal Narrative
of Political Experiences. Madison, Wis., The Robert M. LaFollette
Company, 1919. Written as part of the progressive movement's attempt
to win the Republican presidential nomination for LaFollette in 1912.

LaMonte, Robert Rives, "The American Middle Class," *The Arena,*
XXXIX (April, 1908), 436–39. The middle class cannot hope to preserve itself from monopoly domination through the passage of reform
legislation.

———— "Efficient Brains versus Bastard Culture," *International Socialist
Review,* VIII (April, 1908), 634–37. An attack on the Right-wing position that party leadership must remain in the hands of middle-class
intellectuals.

———— Science and Socialism. Chicago, C. H. Kerr and Company, 1901.
Pocket Library of Socialism No. 22. Marxian exposition of theories of
historical materialism, surplus value, and class struggle by a Left-wing
Socialist.

———— "Socialism and the Trade Unions," *International Socialist Review,*
V (July, 1904), 12–17. LaMonte suggests that all trade unions are or-

LaMonte, Robert Rives (*Continued*)
ganizations to gain advantages for one group of workers against the rest of labor. This is the position of the "impossibilities" in the Socialist Party.

Langdon, Emma F. The Cripple Creek Strike, 1903–1904. Victor, Colorado, 1904. Written from the miners' point of view.

Leffingwell, William H. Easy Lessons in Socialism. Chicago, C. H. Kerr and Company, 1904. Pocket Library of Socialism No. 38.

——— "The Socialist Local," *Wilshire's Magazine,* XIII (March, 1909), 15. Advice to Socialist locals on how to conduct their activities.

Lewis, Arthur Morrow. Evolution, Social and Organic. Chicago, C. H. Kerr and Company, 1908. An attempt to correlate biological and social evolution.

——— "A Positive Platform," *International Socialist Review,* XII (April, 1912), 664–65. Lewis proposes a revolutionary Socialist platform which combines political and industrial union action in order to stop the degeneration of the party and the desertion of its members.

"Liberal Socalism," *The Independent,* LV (Aug. 27, 1903), 2067–68. The present Socialist leadership has a peasant and artisan background and is therefore against liberty. A movement that will combine socialism and individual liberty is wanted.

Lloyd, Henry D., "The Socialistic Regime," *The Independent,* LIV (July, 1902), 1069–72. Points out that the growing concentration of wealth in private hands necessitates the coming of socialism, which is described as "the same old democracy with a new motto."

London, Jack, "The Dream of Debs," *International Socialist Review,* X (Jan., Feb., 1910), 481–89, 561–70. Story of an imaginary general strike won by a revolutionary union patterned after the I.W.W. after the craft unions had betrayed the workers.

——— The Iron Heel. New York, Macmillan Company, 1908. London's novel of the coming triumph of a capitalist oligarchy. An attack on evolutionary socialism.

"Los Angeles Atrocity, The," *The Independent,* LXIX (Oct. 6, 1910), 780–81: Story of the bombing of the Los Angeles *Times* building.

"Los Angeles Conspiracy, The, against Organized Labor by 'Unionist,'" *International Socialist Review,* XI (November, 1910), 262–66. The article charges that the bombing of the Los Angeles *Times* building was probably no bombing at all, but an explosion caused by leaking gas, and that it is being used as part of the open-shop campaign in Los Angeles.

Lynch, Daniel. Socialism and Trade Unionism. Chicago, C. H. Kerr and Company, 1900. Pocket Library of Socialism No. 17. Lynch, the president of Union No. 11, Boston Brotherhood of Painters and Decorators of America, suggests that Socialists must take the lead in trade-union struggles.

MacFarlane, Peter Clark, "What Is the Matter with Los Angeles?" *Col-*

*lier's,* XLVIII (Dec. 2, 1911), 28, 30–31. Events leading to the trial of the McNamaras.

McGrady, Thomas, "The Catholic Church and Socialism," *The Arena,* XXXVIII (July, 1907), 18–27. The Catholic Church will be defeated only when society is reduced to two classes, workers and a few billionaires, and the Church is forced to expose its procapitalist position. At present, the leadership of the Socialist Party is too stupid to win Catholic support.

McGregor, Hugh, "Words of Warning," *The American Federationist,* XII (Aug., 1905), 514–15. Warns the Socialist Party that in aiding the formation of the Industrial Workers of the World it is fighting organized labor.

Machine Production: Where the Profits Go. Social Democratic Leaflet No. 3. Issued for the 1900 presidential campaign by the National Campaign Committee of the Social Democratic Party with headquarters in Chicago.

MacKaye, James, "Democracy and Socialism," *The Arena,* XXXVII (June, 1907), 579–96. Those who favor democracy must support socialism and the Socialist Party.

McManigal, Ortie E. The National Dynamite Plot. Los Angeles, The Neale Company, 1913. McManigal confesses to participating in many bombings allegedly ordered by the International Association of Bridge and Structural Iron Workers in their struggle against the National Erectors' Association. It was this confession which led to the McNamara trial. Probably written with the assistance of William J. Burns.

Macy, John Albert. Socialism in America. New York, Doubleday, Page and Company, 1916. Macy was a member of both the Socialist Party and the Industrial Workers of the World. Highly critical of step-at-a-time socialism.

Malkiel, Theresa, "Where Do We Stand on the Woman Question?" *International Socialist Review,* X (Aug., 1909), 159. Accuses the Socialist Party of fostering a belief in male supremacy.

Marcy, Leslie H., and Frederick Sumner Boyd, "One Big Union Wins," *International Socialist Review,* XII (April, 1912), 613–30. Story of the strike at Lawrence, Mass.

Marcy, Mary 'E., "The Milwaukee Victory," *International Socialist Review,* X (May, 1910), 991–92. Socialist victory in Milwaukee should be used to further the organization of labor in that city.

Marx, Karl, and Frederick Engels. Selected Correspondence, 1846–1895. New York, International Publishers, 1942. Contains Engels's letters on the American socialist movement.

Meily, Clarence, "Economic Classes and Politics," *International Socialist Review,* V (July, 1904), 21–28. Relationship of economic classes and American political parties.

Mills, Ethelwyn. Legislative Program of the Socialist Party. Chicago, The Socialist Party National Office, 1914. The record of the work of Socialists in state legislatures, 1899–1913.

Mills, Walter Thomas. How To Work for Socialism. Chicago, C. H. Kerr and Company, 1900. Pocket Library of Socialism No. 22. Visit your friends; don't antagonize them; join the Socialist Party so that you may be more effective in your conversations with your friends.

———— The Struggle for Existence. Chicago, International School of Social Economy, 1904. An early exposition of constructive socialism, widely used in socialist lectures and educationals.

———— What Is Socialism? Girard, Kansas, J. A. Wayland, 1901. Wayland's Monthly No. 19. Exposition of constructive socialism.

"Milwaukee," The Independent, LXVIII (April 14, 1910), 819–20. Socialist victory in Milwaukee provides opportunity for a valuable experiment.

Ming, John Joseph. The Characteristics and the Religion of Modern Socialism. New York, Benzinger Brothers, 1908. Attack on socialism by a member of the Society of Jesus.

"Moderate Socialists, The," The Nation, LXXXVII (Sept. 24, 1908), 280–81. The American Socialist Party is becoming more moderate, is willing to compromise.

Molle, Jessie M., "The National Convention and the Woman's Movement." International Socialist Review, VIII (May, 1908), 690. Discussion of action taken at Socialist convention and desire of Socialist women for equality in the Socialist Party.

"Mollie Maguires in the West," The Independent, LX (March 8, 1906), 536. Story of the murder of Governor Steunenberg.

Moyer, H. P. A B C of Socialism. Girard, Kansas, J. W. Wayland, 1903. Wayland's Monthly.

Municipal Campaign Book. Milwaukee, County Central Committee, Social-Democratic Party, 1912. Contains expositions of theory and accomplishments of constructive Socialists in the U.S., with emphasis on Milwaukee.

"Murder Charge at a Labor Union's Door," Harper's Weekly, LI (May 25, 1907), 762–65. Trial of Haywood for murder of Steunenberg.

"National Socialist Convention of 1912, The," International Socialist Review, XII (June, 1912), 807–24.

"Neat Minority, A," The Saturday Evening Post, CLXXXIII (Dec. 31, 1910), 23. Article on Berger, the "boss" of reform socialism.

"Notable Triumph for Free Speech in Los Angeles, A," The Arena, XL (Oct., 1908), 350–51. Story of free-speech fight in Los Angeles.

Noyes, William H. The Evolution of the Class Struggle. Chicago, C. H. Kerr and Company, 1899. Pocket Library of Socialism No. 2. The class struggle from the point of view of a Left-wing Socialist.

O'Higgins, Harvey J., "The Dynamiters, a Great Case of Detective William J. Burns," *McClure's Magazine*, XXXVII (Aug., 1911), 346–64. Story of arrest of McNamara brothers.

"Oklahoma Encampment, The," *International Socialist Review*, X (Sept., 1909), 278–79. Propaganda encampment for farmers.

O'Neill, James M., "Western Federation of Miners," *The American Labor Union Journal*, Sept. 3, 1903.

"Opportunism, Good and Bad," *The Independent*, LIX (Oct. 26, 1905), 995–96. Good opportunism in the American Socialist Party.

"Oregon-California Encampment, The," *International Socialist Review*, XI (Aug., 1910), 107–9. Socialist propaganda encampment for farmers.

"Origins of American Labor Union," *The American Labor Union Journal*, Sept. 3, 1903.

Orth, S. P. Socialism and Democracy in Europe. New York, Henry Holt and Company, 1913. Contains a bibliography classified by countries and copies of documents pertaining to the European socialist movement.

Parce, Lida, "Woman and the Socialist Philosophy," *International Socialist Review*, X (Aug., 1909), 125–28. Attacks male supremacy in the Socialist Party.

"Parlor Socialists," *The Independent*, LXIV (April 9, 1908), 821. Defense of middle-class reformers who joined the Socialist Party.

"Parlor Socialists," *The Living Age*, CCLXII (July 3, 1909), 52–55. An attack on the Socialist Party, inspired by Theodore Roosevelt's attack on Parlor Socialists.

"Party Owned Press, A," *International Socialist Review*, X (July, 1909), 68–70. The *Review* is opposed to a party-owned press because it will permit greater Right-wing control of party policy.

Patterson, Joseph Medill. Confessions of a Drone. Chicago, C. H. Kerr and Company, 1905. Pocket Library of Socialism No. 45. Patterson confesses the source of his unearned income, etc.

——— The Socialist Machine. Chicago, C. H. Kerr and Company, 1905. Pocket Library of Socialism No. 45. A description of the national organization and its propaganda methods.

Payne, Edward B., "What Shall Society Do To Be Saved? The Socialist's Answer," *Overland Monthly*, XXXV (June, 1900), 530–34. One step toward saving society is to end America's competitive economy and replace it with a co-operative one.

"Pickwickian Socialist, A," *The American Labor Union Journal*, Dec., 1904. An attack on Right-wing Socialists for supporting the American Federation of Labor.

Poole, Ernest, "Harnessing Socialism." *The American Magazine*, LXVI (Sept., 1908), 427–32. Discusses theories of the constructive Socialists whom he encountered at the 1908 Socialist Party convention.

Poole, Ernest, "Abraham Cahan: Socialist-Journalist-Friend of the Ghetto," *The Outlook,* IC (Oct. 28, 1911), 467–68. Cahan was editor of the Jewish Socialist newspaper, *Forward.*

Powderly, Terrence V. The Path I Trod. New York, Columbia University Press, 1940. Autobiography of the leader of the Knights of Labor.

" 'Practical' Socialism, Is There Any Such Thing?" *The Saturday Evening Post,* CLXXXI (May 8, 1909), 8–9, 55. Ten Socialists discuss how socialism will come to the United States.

"Professional Assassin," *The Outlook,* LXXXVI (June 15, 1907), 303–4. The assassin is Harry Orchard, who confessed to murdering Governor Steunenberg.

"Propaganda of Socialism, A," *The Nation,* LXXXI (Oct. 5, 1905), 272–73. Socialism is foreign and despotic.

"Ravishing of the Socialist Party, The," *The Independent,* LXXIII (Aug. 29, 1912), 506–7. Discusses the theft of the Socialist Party's immediate demands by the newly-formed Progressive Party.

"Real Danger of Socialism, The," *The World's Work,* IX (Dec., 1904), 5670. Agrees with President Eliot of Harvard that conservative elements in the trade unions must be strengthened so as to fight the Socialists.

"Recall of Haywood, The," *The Independent,* LXXIV (March 6, 1913), 490. Story of recall of Haywood from the National Executive Committee of the Socialist Party.

"Recall of William D. Haywood," *The Survey,* XXIX (March 29, 1913), 909–10.

" 'Red' Sunday-Schools and Child Socialists," *The American Review of Reviews,* XXXVIII (July, 1908), 112–13. Views with alarm.

"Revoluntionary Unionism," *International Socialist Review,* X (Sept., 1909), 266–68. Beginning of revival of Left-wing Socialist enthusiasm for the Industrial Workers of the World.

Richardson, Noble A. Industrial Problems. Chicago, C. H. Kerr and Company, 1910. "Intended for use in the general propaganda work of the Socialist party." Largely an indictment of capitalism.

——— Introduction to Socialism. Girard, Kansas, J. A. Wayland, 1903. Wayland's Monthly No. 37.

——— Methods of Acquiring National Possession of Our Industries. Girard, Kansas, J. A. Wayland, 1903. Wayland's Monthly No. 38. Four possible methods—confiscation, competition, purchase, and pension of the owners.

Robbins, I. M., "The Economic Aspects of the Negro Problem," *International Socialist Review,* X (June, 1910), 1006–17. Left-wing Socialist analysis of the sources of discrimination against Negroes.

Russell, Charles Edward, "The Growing Menace of Socialism," *Hampton's Broadway Magazine,* XXII (Jan., 1909), 119–26. Right-wing predictions of the coming success of the Socialist Party.

—————— Why I Am a Socialist. New York, Hodder and Stoughton, 1910. Russell was a popular magazine writer and one of the leaders of the Right-wing Socialists in New York.

"Scabbing after Election," *The American Labor Union Journal,* Oct., 1904. The scabbing consists of supporting craft unions after having voted the Socialist ticket.

"School for Socialism," *Public Opinion,* XXXIX (Oct. 28, 1905), 562. Story of the endowment of the Rand School.

Schwartz, Fred L., "A Proletarian Movement," *International Socialist Review,* IX (Feb., 1909), 627. A Left-wing Socialist's insistence that the party represent the interests of the working class, not the middle class.

Scudder, Vida D. Socialism and Character. Boston, Houghton Mifflin and Company, 1912. Christian Socialist approach.

—————— "Socialism and Sacrifice," *The Atlantic Monthly,* CV (June, 1910), 836–49. Spiritual aspects of the socialist movement.

"Senator Hanna on Labor Unions and Socialism," *The Literary Digest,* XXVIII (Jan. 30, 1904), 136–37. Senator Hanna holds that trade unions are becoming more conservative and that the Socialists will never win their support.

Simons, A. M. The American Farmer. Chicago, C. H. Kerr and Company, 1902. An analysis of the problems of the farmer and the benefits which socialism will bring him. Simons was generally considered by Center Socialists to be the party's leading expert on the farm problem.

—————— "The Chicago Conference of Industrial Unions," *International Socialist Review,* V (Feb., 1905), 496–99. Favorable report on the conference which led to the formation of the I.W.W.

—————— "Industrial Workers of the World," *International Socialist Review,* VI (Aug., 1905), 66. Favorable report on formation of the I.W.W.

—————— The Man under the Machine. Chicago, C. H. Kerr and Company, 1899. Pocket Library of Socialism No. 8.

—————— The Philosophy of Socialism. Chicago, C. H. Kerr and Company, 1904. Pocket Library of Socialism No. 35.

—————— Single Tax vs. Socialism. Chicago, C. H. Kerr and Company, 1899. Pocket Library of Socialism No. 6.

—————— Socialism. Girard, Kansas, J. A. Wayland, 1900. Studies in Socialism No. 5.

—————— "Socialism and the Trade Union Movement," *International Socialist Review,* III (July, 1902), 46–49. Trade unions are for ameliorative action in the economic field. But only the Socialist Party can end exploitation of labor.

—————— "Socialist Movement in America, The," *The World To-Day,* V (July, 1903), 935–40. Status of Socialist Party as of 1903.

—————— The Socialist Program. Chicago, National Headquarters, Socialist

Simons, A. M. (*Continued*)

Party, 1908. Discussion of the immediate demands of the 1908 platform.

—— What the Socialists Would Do If They Won in This City. Chicago, C. H. Kerr and Company, 1901. Pocket Library of Socialism No. 24. The Socialists would institute reforms to help the working class prepare for the eventual seizure of power.

Sinclair, Upton, "The Message of Socialism to Collegians," *The Independent*, LXIX (Aug. 18, 1910), 353–58.

—— Our Bourgeois Literature: the Reason and the Remedy. Chicago, C. H. Kerr and Company, 1904. Pocket Library of Socialism No. 43. First published in *Collier's Weekly*, Oct. 8, 1904.

—— "The Socialist Party," *The World's Work*, XI (April, 1906), 7431–32. Description of party organization and work.

Skelton, Oscar Douglass. Socialism: a Critical Analysis. Boston, Houghton Mifflin Company, 1911. Largely an attack on socialist theory, not on activities of the Socialists.

Sladden, Tom, "Mixers," *The Socialist Party Weekly Bulletin*, Feb. 8, 1908. An attack on John Work's platform proposals for the 1908 Socialist convention.

—— "The Revolutionist," *International Socialist Review*, IX (Dec., 1908), 423–30. The Socialist Party should accept only proletarians (defined as unskilled workers) as members.

Slade, Edward, "The Socialist Programme," *The Arena*, XXXV (June, 1906), 597–600. An attempt to synthesize various European and American Socialist programs.

Slobodin, Henry L., "What's the Matter with Wisconsin?" *International Socialist Review*, X (Feb., 1910), 688. Slobodin accuses step-at-a-time socialism of having failed to achieve the minimum health and safety programs for labor which have been obtained in states which did not boast a healthy constructive socialist movement.

—— "Politics, Parliaments and the State," *International Socialist Review*, X (April, 1910), 884–88. The industrial union will educate the workers to vote the Socialist ticket and force acceptance of the workers' pro-Socialist vote at the polls.

—— "Get-Rich-Quick-Schemes," *International Socialist Review*, XI (Feb., 1911), 486–87. An attack on those who used the Socialist Party to advance questionable business propositions for their own advantage, with emphasis on Wilshire's gold-mine-stock deal.

Smith, Clarence, "Wanted—Real Hard Work by Every Friend of Western Unionism," *The Miner's Magazine*, II (Feb., 1901), 31–32. A plea for support for the Western Federation of Miners and the Western Labor Union.

Smith, D. M., "An 'Impossibilist' Position," *International Socialist Review*, V (July, 1904), 46–48. A statement of "impossibilist" theories by a supporter.

"Social Democracy of America, The," *The Literary Digest*, XV (July 3, 1897), 274. Announcement of its formation and its program.

Social Democracy Red Book. Terre Haute, Indiana, Debs Publishing Company, 1900. Contains histories of the Social Democracy of America and Social Democratic parties and biographical sketches of socialist leaders.

Social Democratic Party. Boston, Social Democratic Party, 1900. Issued by the party with headquarters in Springfield as part of the 1900 presidential campaign.

Social Democratic Party. New York, Social Democratic Party, 1904. The New York state organization of the Socialist Party was still known as the Social Democratic Party. It changed its name under pressure from the Democrats in 1906. This pamphlet was issued during the 1904 presidential campaign and describes the work and program of the party.

Social-Democratic Vest Pocket Manual, 1912 Fall Campaign. Milwaukee, Milwaukee County Social-Democratic Party, 1912. A handy volume of campaign facts and arguments for the Socialist propagandist.

"Socialism and Religion," *The Independent*, LXIV (June 11, 1908), 1360. Agrees with the 1908 Socialist convention position that religion has nothing to do with socialism.

"Socialism and Sex Relations," *The Living Age*, CCLV (Dec. 21, 1907), 759–60. Socialism as a threat to morality in sex relations.

"Socialism and Socialism," *The Independent*, LVII (Dec. 8, 1904), 1337–38. If socialism is to come to America, the Socialist Party must be more than a wage-workers' party, because America is not a class society.

"Socialism and Syndicalism," *The Nation*, XCIV (May 30, 1912), 533–34. Report on the anti-sabotage resolution at the 1912 Socialist convention.

"Socialism and the Home," *The Arena*, XXXVII (March, 1907), 2–4. Editorial holding that five out of six American Socialists are not opposed to the concept of the home.

"Socialism as Religion," *The Independent*, LV (Dec. 12, 1903), 397–99. Socialism is too often a religion of hate. Should be an altruistic program of municipal ownership.

"Socialism in the New York Campaign," *The Outlook*, LXXXIV (Nov. 3, 1906), 541–42. Competition of Hearst and the Socialist Party.

"Socialism in the United States," *The Independent*, LII (Jan. 25, 1900), 266–67. Distinguishes between evolutionary and revolutionary socialism. The former is government ownership of natural monopolies and is popular. The latter is Marxian socialism.

"Socialism in the United States," *The Independent*, LIV (Nov. 27, 1902), 2850–51. Analysis of the 1902 election returns.

"Socialism in the United States," *Yale Review*, XV (May, 1906), 1–6. Attack on socialism and defense of capitalism. Criticizes Sinclair's *The Jungle*, holding that the novel's hero, Jurgis, was given great op-

"Socialism in the United States" (*Continued*)
portunities which he failed to use, and was therefore responsible for his own downfall.

Socialist Almanac and Treasury of Facts, The. New York, 1898. Prepared by Lucien Sanial for the American Socialist Labor Party.

Socialist Campaign Book. Ed. Carl D. Thompson. Compiled under the direction of the National Campaign Committee of the Socialist Party. Chicago, National Headquarters, Socialist Party, 1912. Published for the 1912 presidential campaign.

Socialist Campaign Book of 1900, The. Edited under the supervision of the National Campaign Committee of the Social Democratic Party. Chicago, C. H. Kerr and Company, 1900. This campaign book was the work of the Social Democratic Party with headquarters in Springfield, Massachusetts.

Socialist Campaign Book, 1902, Containing Arguments Advanced in the Interest of the Socialist Party. Issued by the Socialist Party of Toledo, Ohio.

Socialist Collection. Ninety-one pamphlets bound in nine volumes, most of which were published before 1900. Harper Library, University of Chicago.

"Socialist Defeat at Haverhill, The," *The Outlook*, LXVI (Dec. 22, 1900), 958. Defeat of Chase in his campaign for re-election as mayor of Haverhill, Mass.

"Socialistic Symposium, A," *Harper's Weekly*, L (Sept. 29, 1906), 1378–79. The contributors agree that before society can be changed, there must be a spiritual change in human nature. Material things are of little concern.

"Socialist Mayor, A," *The Outlook*, LX (Dec. 17, 1898), 939. Election of Chase as mayor of Haverhill, Mass.

"Socialist Mayor's Inaugural, The," *The Outlook*, LXI (Jan. 14, 1899).

"Socialist Mayor's Program, A," *The Literary Digest*, XVIII (Jan. 14, 1899), 34–35. Program of Mayor Chase of Haverhill, Mass.

"Socialist Municipal Office Holders," *National Municipal Review*, I (July, 1912), 492–500. Analysis of positions held by Socialists, 1908–1912.

"Socialist Party, The," *The Arena*, XXXII (Sept., 1904), 315–17. Praises the party's 1904 "working programme," i.e., the immediate demands of the platform.

Socialist Party Municipal Platform of New York City. New York, Socialist Party, 1909.

Socialist Party, The: National Platform, Resolutions at National Convention, National Constitution, Directory of Socialist Locals. Chicago, C. H. Kerr and Company, 1904. Pocket Library of Socialism No. 33.

Socialist (Perpetual) Campaign Book. Compiled under the direction of the National Executive Committee by Joseph Medill Patterson. Chicago,

National Headquarters, Socialist Party, 1908. This is the campaign
book for the 1908 presidential election.

"Socialist Platform, The," *The Outlook,* LXXXIX (Aug. 25, 1908),
974–76. Criticizes the 1908 Socialist platform for favoring substitution
of collective for private ownership and for ending controls on the
majority.

"Socialist Platform and Candidates, The," *The Outlook,* CI (June 1,
1912), 235.

"Socialist Politics," *The Nation,* XCVIII (Feb. 12, 1914), 155–56. Notes
sharp drop in party membership between March, 1912 and June,
1913.

"Socialist Reverses, The," *The Independent,* LV (Nov. 26, 1903), 2823.
Attributes drop in Socialist vote in some areas to neglect of principles
for personal political advantage.

"Socialist Rule of Milwaukee, The," *The Independent,* LXIX (July 21,
1910), 148–49.

"Socialists, The," *The Independent,* LVII (Nov. 17, 1904), 1165–66.
The increased Socialist vote is explained in terms of the party's attrac-
tion for socially-minded people of other than the working class.

"Socialists and Syndicalism," *The Chautauquan,* LXX (May, 1913),
256–57. Recall of Haywood from the National Executive Committee
of the Socialist Party.

"Socialist Showing, The," *The Nation,* LXXXVII (Dec. 3, 1908), 540–41.
If the Socialists hope to increase their vote they must offer voters more
immediate benefits in place of a future utopia.

"Socialists Rebuking Violence," *The Literary Digest,* XLIV (June 1,
1912), 1144–45. Favorable newspaper comment on the 1912 Socialist
constitutional amendment against sabotage and other crimes.

"Socialist Vote," *The Literary Digest,* XLV (Nov. 23, 1912), 943–44.

"Socialist Vote in the United States," *The Chautauquan,* LXIX (Jan.,
1913), 135–36.

Spargo, John. The Common Sense of Socialism—a Series of Letters Addressed to Jonathan Edwards of Pittsburgh. Chicago, C. H. Kerr and
Company, 1908. Answers the standard objections to the socialist solution.

——— Forces That Make for Socialism in America. Chicago, C. H.
Kerr and Company, 1905. Spargo was the most popular theorist of
step-at-a-time socialism.

——— "The Influence of Karl Marx on Contemporary Socialism," *The
American Journal of Sociology,* XVI (July, 1910), 21–40. Marx was
utopian in his theoretical analysis, but scientific in his opportunist
tactics. The modern socialist movement rejects Marx's mistaken theories,
but accepts his opportunist tactics.

——— Karl Marx: His Life and Work. New York, B. W. Huebsch, 1910.
Spargo holds that Marx's contribution to the socialist movement was

Spargo, John (*Continued*)

not his theory, which has been demonstrated to be inaccurate, but his opportunist tactics.

———— "Private Property and Personal Liberty in the Socialist State," *The North American Review,* CLXXXIX (June, 1909), 844–56. In the socialist state, only the great trusts will be publicly owned, and there will be more personal liberty than ever before.

———— Sidelights on Contemporary Socialism. New York, B. W. Huebsch, 1911.

———— Socialism: a Summary and Interpretation of Socialist Principles. New York, Macmillan Company, 1906. The 1913 edition of this work shows further compromises with reform and additional dilution of Marxist theory, which Spargo still claimed to accept in part.

———— The Socialists, Who They Are and What They Stand For: The Case for Socialism Plainly Stated. Chicago, C. H. Kerr and Company, 1906.

———— The Spiritual Significance of Modern Socialism. New York, B. W. Huebsch, 1908. At about this time, Spargo began to emphasize the Christian values to be obtained through socialism, in contrast to his previous emphasis on social and economic gains.

———— The Substance of Socialism. New York, B. W. Huebsch, 1909. An exposition of the moral values of socialism and socialist teaching.

———— Syndicalism, Industrial Unionism, and Socialism. New York, B. W. Huebsch, 1913. An attack on revolutionary socialism and the I.W.W.

———— "Woman and the Socialist Movement," *International Socialist Review,* VIII (Feb., 1908), 449–55. Criticism of male supremacy in the Socialist Party.

Spargo, John, and G.B.L. Arner. Elements of Socialism. New York, Macmillan Company, 1912.

"Split in the Socialists' Ranks, The," *Public Opinion,* XXIX (July 19, 1900), 70–71. Reprint of articles by Imogene C. Falion in *The Coming Nation* which accuses Debs and the Social Democratic Party of deliberately betraying the socialist movement by refusing to unite with the Hillquit faction of the Socialist Labor Party.

Steffens, Lincoln. The Autobiography of Lincoln Steffens. New York, Harcourt Brace and Company, 1931.

———— "Eugene V. Debs on What the Matter Is in America and What to Do About It," *Everybody's Magazine,* XIX (Oct., 1908), 455–69. Besides the interview with Debs, the article contains an interesting passage at arms between Debs and Berger, who was present at part of the interview.

"Stick to the Main Issue," *International Socialist Review,* IX (April, 1909), 803–9. The Socialist Party should concentrate its efforts on teaching the proletariat the theory of surplus value.

Stokes, J. G. Phelps, "Reasons for Supporting Debs," *The Outlook,* XC (Oct., 1908), 378–81.

Stultz, Emil, "The Eighth International Socialist Congress," *International Socialist Review*, XI (Oct., 1910), 231–32.

Sumner, Mary Brown, "The Parting of the Ways in American Socialism," *The Survey*, XXIX (Feb. 1, 1913), 623–30. A detailed account of the issues which led to the move to recall Haywood from the National Executive Committee of the Socialist Party. Pro-Haywood in orientation.

Taylor, Graham Romeyn, "Socialists in Milwaukee," *The Survey*, XXVII (March 30, 1912), 1996–99. An evaluation of Mayor Seidel's administration.

Teller, Charlotte, "The National Socialist Convention," *The Arena*, XL (July, 1908), 26–39.

"This Is Not Socialism," *The Outlook*, LXXXII (Feb. 24, 1906), 391–92. Control of railroads and municipal ownership of utilities are necessary reforms, but are not socialism.

Thompson, Carl Dean. The Constructive Program of Socialism as Illustrated by Measures Advanced by Socialists in Municipal, State, and National Legislation. Milwaukee, Social-Democratic Publishing Company, 1908.

———— "The Need of Cooperation of the Rochdale Type in and about Chicago." Unpublished Master's thesis, Department of Sociology, University of Chicago, 1902. Thompson holds that co-operatives will help ameliorate depressed social conditions, but will contribute nothing to the solution of the basic social problem. Eight years later, however, he was insisting that co-operatives will help usher in socialism.

———— The Principles and Program of Socialism. What It Is, What It Is Not, How to Inaugurate It: Briefly Stated with References on Each Point to the More Extensive Literature Where Full Treatment May Be Found. Denver, Colorado, Social Crusade, 1904. The Social Crusade was made up in large part of ministers who were advancing the cause of constructive as against revolutionary socialism in the Socialist Party.

———— The Rising Tide of Socialism. Chicago, National Office of the Socialist Party, 1911. A leaflet describing the growing electoral and legislative success of the party.

———— "Social Democratic Program in the Wisconsin Legislature," *The American Political Science Review*, I (May, 1907), 457–65. By one of the leaders of the Wisconsin Socialist Party.

———— "A Socialist's Definition of Socialism," *The Arena*, XXXIX (May, 1908), 564–69. Socialism is public ownership of utilities plus democracy.

———— "Who Constitute the Proletariat?" *International Socialist Review*, IX (Feb., 1909), 603–11. An answer to Tom Sladden's "The Revolutionist," *International Socialist Review*, IX (Dec., 1908), 423–30. Thompson classifies as proletariat anyone who works with brains or hands. Furthermore, the capitalist class has provided the American Socialist Party with some of its finest leadership.

Thurber, F. B., "The Socialist Trend," *Moody's Magazine,* I (March, 1906), 416–21. Thurber, president of the U.S. Export Association, finds all attempts to regulate corporations to be signs of the threatening advance of socialism.

"Tide of Socialism, The," *The World's Work,* XXIII (Jan., 1912), 252–53. Typical of the magazine articles noting the sudden increase in Socialist electoral success.

"Time Serving Diplomacy," *Voice of Labor,* Feb., 1905. The diplomats discussed are the Socialist leaders who compromise their principles in order to win the votes and support of the craft unions.

Titus, Herman F., "A.B.C. of Socialism," *The Socialist* (Toledo), April 8, 1905. Short exposition of revolutionary socialist theory.

Toilers of America Vote For Your Freedom, by An American Miner. Social Democratic Leaflet No. 4. Issued for the 1900 presidential campaign by the National Campaign Committee of the Social Democratic Party with headquarters in Chicago.

To Unorganized Socialists. Social Democratic Leaflet No. 1. Issued for the 1900 presidential campaign by the National Campaign Committee of the Social Democratic Party with headquarters in Chicago. An appeal to ex-members of the Socialist Labor Party and non-party socialists to vote for Debs.

"Trouble in Los Angeles, The," *The American Review of Reviews,* XLV (Jan., 1912), 8–12. The McNamara case.

"Two Socialist Mayors in Massachusetts," *The Outlook,* LXIII (Dec. 16, 1899), 904. The mayors are in Haverhill and Brockton.

"United Socialists, The," *The Outlook,* LXIV (April 7, 1900), 750. The unity negotiations between the Social Democratic Party and the Hillquit faction of the Socialist Labor Party. The description of "unity" turned out to be premature by more than one year.

Untermann, Ernest. How To Get Socialism. Girard, Kansas, J. A. Wayland, 1903. Achieve socialism by joining the Socialist Party and helping sweep a national election.

———— Marxian Economics—a Popular Introduction to the Three Volumes of Marx's "Capital." Chicago, C. H. Kerr and Company, 1907.

———— The Municipality from Capitalism to Socialism. Girard, Kansas, The Appeal to Reason [1902?]. The role of the municipality in a socialist society.

———— Science and Revolution. Chicago, C. H. Kerr and Company, 1905. Untermann was considered by many Socialists to be the leading Marxist theorist in the U.S. He belonged to the Center faction, and like most of the Center, became a member of the Right wing.

———— "The Trade Union Resolution and the Working Program," *American Labor Union Journal,* May 19, 1904. An attack on the trade union resolution for favoring craft unionism and opposing industrial unionism.

Vail, Charles H. The Mission of the Working Class. Chicago, C. H. Kerr and Company, 1899. Pocket Library of Socialism No. 9. Largely a paraphrase of Frederick Engels's *Socialism: Utopian and Scientific.*

———— Modern Socialism. New York, Commonwealth Company, 1897. The Reverend Vail became the first national organizer of the Social Democratic Party with headquarters in Springfield, Mass. This book is an exposition of Marxian socialism.

———— Principles of Scientific Socialism. Chicago, C. H. Kerr and Company, 1899.

Van Rensselaer, James T., "The Identity of Socialism and Christianity," *The Arena,* XXXIV (July, 1905), 39–44. Van Rensselaer was editor of *Common Sense,* the Los Angeles Socialist paper, and was the son of a minister.

Vidrine, Eraste, "Negro Locals," *International Socialist Review,* V (Jan., 1905), 389. A criticism of the failure of the Socialist Party to fight for rights of Negroes.

Walling, William English, "A Crisis in the Socialist Party," *The Independent,* LXII (May 16, 1912), 1047–51. History of the controversy on Asiatic exclusion in the Socialist Party.

———— "Government Ownership," *International Socialist Review,* XII (April, 1912), 652–54. Walling holds that government ownership under capitalism is not a step toward socialism, nor is it of any benefit to the working class.

———— Socialism as It Is: a Survey of the World-Wide Revolutionary Movement. New York, Macmillan Company, 1912. Walling belonged to the Left wing of the American Socialist Party.

———— The Socialism of To-Day. New York, Henry Holt and Company, 1916. A source book designed to show recent developments and present positions of European and American socialist parties.

"Warning of Socialism, The," *The Century Magazine,* LXXXIII (Jan., 1912), 472–73. The growing Socialist vote means that the Democratic and Republican parties must support reform measures and combat graft.

Wayland, Julius Augustus. Leaves of Life: a Story of Twenty Years of Socialist Agitation. Girard, Kansas, The Appeal to Reason, 1912. Contains an autobiographical sketch of the publisher of the *Appeal to Reason* and a biography of Wayland by A. W. Ricker of the *Appeal* staff. This book was not sold, but distributed free to the "Appeal Army" of subscription salesmen.

"Way to Encourage Socialism, The; the Wrong Way To Do an Important Thing," *The World's Work,* VII (Nov., 1903), 4054–55. The only way to stop growth of socialism is to end the abuses of the privileged classes of society.

Webster, Robert W. The Kingdom of God and Socialism. Chicago, C. H. Kerr and Company, 1904. Pocket Library of Socialism No. 37. Reverend Webster was minister of the Church of the Commonwealth, Los Angeles.

Webster, Robert W. (*Continued*)
  The pamphlet holds that socialism is the working out of God's divine
  plan on earth.
"What Is Socialism?" *The Outlook,* LXXXIV (Sept. 1, 1906), 10. Socialism is state ownership and the destruction of individual liberty.
"What Is the Matter with the Socialist Party?" *International Socialist
  Review,* X (Nov., 1909), 451. The party is not growing because it
  has become a vote-catching machine and has ceased to fight for the rights
  of the working class. Must support industrial unionism.
"What Socialism Is Not," *The Independent,* LIX (Dec. 21, 1905),
  1487–88. Now that socialism wants only ownership of mines, railroads,
  and street franchises, it no longer means slavery. At last it is presenting
  an acceptable program.
What the Social Democratic Party Is. Chicago, National Headquarters,
  1900.
"What the Socialist Vote Means," *Public Opinion,* XXXVII (Nov. 17,
  1904), 617. Newspaper opinion on the increased 1904 Socialist vote
  varies between dismissing it as just the reaction of disgruntled radical
  Democrats and an indication of the need for drastic reform in America
  to stop further increases in Socialist success.
"Which—Socialism or Co-operation?" *The Outlook,* LXXXIII (Aug. 4,
  1906), 808–10. Instead of socialism, Americans should favor co-operation and labor should get a larger share of the produce under capital-
  ism.
"Why I Left the Ministry for Socialist Propaganda, by Another Socialist,"
  *The Independent,* LVIII (June 8, 1905), 1284–88.
Why Join the Socialist Party? Chicago, C. H. Kerr and Company, 1902.
  Join the party so that you may make a greater contribution to political
  campaigns.
Why Socialists Pay Dues. Chicago National Committee of the Socialist
  Party. Everyone pays dues so that no small group can control the
  party.
"Why the Catholic Church Opposes Socialism, by a Leading Socialist,"
  *The Arena,* XXXVII (May, 1907), 520–24. Because it is a wealthy,
  exploiting institution, because socialism stands for separation of church
  and state, and because socialism is an ideal attracting the Irish who
  were formerly attracted by the ideals of the Church.
Will, Thomas E., "Individualism through Socialism," *The Arena,* XXXVI
  (Oct., 1906), 359–63. A reply to an article by William J. Bryan, "Individualism versus Socialism," *Century Magazine,* LXXI (April, 1906),
  856.
Williams, Benjamin H. Eleven Blind Leaders of "Practical Socialism"
  and "Revolutionary Tactics" from an I.W.W. Standpoint. New Castle,
  Pennsylvania, Press of the I.W.W. Publishing Bureau, 1911. An attack on the position of Socialist Party leaders expressed in " 'Practical'

Socialism, Is There Any Such Thing?" *The Saturday Evening Post,* CLXXXI (May 8, 1909), 8–9, 55.

"Will Syndicalism Supplant Socialism?" *Current Literature,* LIII (Sept., 1912), 317–19. Theoretical exposition of syndicalism.

Wilshire, Gaylord, "Class vs. Class: Resultant," *Wilshire's Magazine,* VI (Nov., 1904), 3–4. The resultant will be the elimination of classes in socialism.

———— "The Death of the Democratic Party," *Wilshire's Magazine,* VI (Dec., 1904), 3. Defeat of Bryan and increased Socialist vote mean that the Socialist Party is about to replace the Democratic Party as the second American political party.

———— "Reno and the Negro Problem," *Wilshire's* XIV (Aug., 1910), 6–7. Since the Negro does not have any respect for property, the Socialist Party should stand for his complete disfranchisement.

———— The Significance of the Trust. New York, Wilshire's Magazine [1903?]. Trusts significant as harbingers of socialism, under which they will be democratized.

———— Socialism Inevitable. New York, Wilshire Book Company, 1907. A second volume of editorials from *Wilshire's Magazine.*

———— "Vote-Chasing and the Revolution," *Wilshire's* XVI (June–July, 1912), 4. Wilshire discovers that he has never believed that elections would bring socialism. Now believes that syndicalism is the only road to socialism.

———— Why a "Workingman" Should Be a Socialist. New York, Wilshire's Magazine, 1903. Wilshire Leaflet No. 1. This leaflet was written in 1890. By 1903 its total printing was three million.

———— Wilshire Editorials. New York, Wilshire Book Company, 1906. A reprint of editorials which first appeared in *Wilshire's Magazine.*

Wilshire, Gaylord, and E.R.A. Seligman. Debate on Socialism, Wilshire-Seligman, Cooper Union, N.Y.C., January 16, 1903. Wilshire Leaflet No. 3, 1903. Seligman argued, among other points, that capitalism was not torn by contradictions because depressions were getting less and less severe.

Wolfe, Ira. The Cause of the Factional Fight in the Socialist Party of Washington. Seattle, Wash., 1907. Circulated in Washington to influence state Socialist referendum on question of expelling Local Seattle for condoning fusion with nonsocialist parties. Printed by the Right wing of the party.

Wood, Eugene, "The Red Dawn, Recollections of the Socialist Convention of 1908," *Wilshire's Magazine,* XII (July, 1908), 7–8.

Wood-Simons, May. Socialism and the Organized Labor Movement. Chicago, C. H. Kerr and Company, 1904. Pocket Library of Socialism. Historical Sketch of growth of unions, concluding with a plea for union members to support the candidates of the Socialist Party.

Wood-Simons, May. Woman and the Social Question. Chicago, C. H. Kerr and Company, 1899. Pocket Library of Socialism No. 1. Advantages of Socialism to women.

Work, John M. What's So and What Isn't. Girard, Kansas, J. A. Wayland, 1905. Wayland's Monthly No. 59. Presents Socialist answers to common objections to socialism.

Yarros, V. S., "Socialist Tendencies in Anglo-Saxon Countries," *Self Culture,* XI (March, 1900), 13–17. Notes a dangerous tendency toward "municipal socialism" which will end traditional Anglo-Saxon liberty.

SECONDARY SOURCES

Bliss, William D. P. Handbook of Socialism. New York, Charles Scribner's Sons, 1907. Bibliography and bibliographical notes on socialist writers and leaders of all countries. Chronological chart showing development of socialism in the nineteenth century by countries.

Brissenden, Paul Frederick. The I.W.W.; a Study of American Syndicalism. New York, The Columbia University Press, 2d ed., 1920.

——— The Launching of the I.W.W. Berkeley, The University of California Press, 1913.

Brooks, John Graham. The Social Unrest: Studies in Labor and Socialist Movements. New York, Macmillan Company, 1903. Exposition of reform socialism, with emphasis on Belgium and Germany. Attacks revolutionary socialism and many Marxist theories.

——— American Syndicalism: the I.W.W. New York, Macmillan Company, 1913.

Carrol, Mollie May. Labor and Politics. Chicago, The University of Chicago Libraries, 1920.

Chamberlain, John. Farewell to Reform. New York, The John Day Company, 1933. A study of the Progressive Movement.

Coleman, McAlister. Eugene V. Debs, a Man Unafraid. New York, Greenberg, 1930. A biography of Debs.

Commons, John R., and Associates. History of Labour in the United States. 4 vols. New York, Macmillan Company, 1918–1935.

Cox, Ora Ellen. The Socialist Party in Indiana since 1896. Chicago, 1916.

Cross, Ira Brown. The Essentials of Socialism. New York, Macmillan Company, 1912. A summary of various socialist theories and policies.

Destler, Chester McArthur, "Western Radicalism, 1865–1901: Concepts and Origins," *The Mississippi Valley Historical Review,* XXXI (Dec., 1944), 335–68. For western radical influence on the Populist Movement and Bellamy's Nationalist Movement.

Dutt, R. P. The Two Internationals. London, George Allen and Unwin, 1920.

Ely, Richard T. Recent American Socialism. Baltimore, Johns Hopkins University, 1885.

—————— Socialism and Social Reform. New York, Thomas Y. Crowell and Company, 1894.

Faulkner, Harold U. The Quest for Social Justice, 1898–1914. New York, Macmillan Company, 1931.

Fine, Nathan. Labor and Farmer Parties in the United States, 1828–1928. New York, The Rand School of Social Science, 1928. The author is more than a little sympathetic to evolutionary socialism.

Foner, Philip S. Jack London, American Rebel. New York, The Citadel Press, 1947. Contains some of the social writings of London and a long biographical essay on London by Foner.

—————— History of the Labor Movement in the United States. New York, International Publishers, 1947.

Ginger, Ray. The Bending Cross, a Biography of Eugene Victor Debs. New Brunswick, New Jersey, Rutgers University Press, 1949. The best of the biographies of Debs.

Graham, William. Socialism, New and Old. New York, D. Appleton and Company, 1901. Traces development of socialist philosophy. The author is not a Marxist.

Hansen, Marcus Lee. The Immigrant in American History. Cambridge, Harvard University Press, 1940.

Haynes, Fred E. Social Politics in the United States. Boston, Houghton Mifflin Company, 1924. Has three chapters on the socialist movement in the United States.

Hicks, John Donald. The Populist Revolt. Minneapolis, The University of Minnesota Press, 1931.

Hughan, Jessie Wallace. American Socialism of the Present Day. New York, John Lane Company, 1911. The author's sympathies are with evolutionary socialism.

—————— The Facts of Socialism. New York, John Lane Company, 1913.

Karsner, David. Debs: His Authorized Life and Letters from Woodstock Prison. New York, Boni and Liveright, 1919.

Kirkup, Thomas, and Edward R. Pease. A History of Socialism. London, A. and C. Black, 1913. For material on the Second International.

Lenz, J. The Rise and Fall of the Second International. New York, International Publishers, 1932. The author is sympathetic to the Left-wing position in the International.

Levine, Louis. The Women's Garment Workers. New York, B. W. Huebsch, Inc., 1924. The women's garment workers' union was socialist-led during the period under study.

Madison, Charles A. Critics and Crusaders. New York, Henry Holt and Company, 1948. Contains two good chapters on Debs and the Socialist Party.

Mayo, Morrow. Los Angeles. New York, Alfred A. Knopf, 1933. For material on the bombing of the Los Angeles *Times* building and the McNamara trial.

Morison, Samuel E., and Henry Steele Commager. The Growth of the American Republic. Vol. II. New York, Oxford University Press, 1942.

Obermann, Karl. Joseph Weydemeyer. New York, International Publishers, 1947. A sympathetic biography of this early German-American Marxist.

Olin, Charles Henry. Socialism. Philadelphia, Penn Publishing Company, 1914. Simplified and frequently inaccurate summary of various socialist positions.

Painter, Floy Ruth. That Man Debs, and His Life Work. Bloomington, Indiana, Indiana University Graduate Council, 1929. A biography of Debs.

Perlman, Selig. A History of Trade Unionism in the United States. New York, Macmillan Company, 1922.

Pierce, Bessie Louise. A History of Chicago. 4 vols. New York, Alfred A. Knopf, 1937–.

Pringle, Henry. Theodore Roosevelt. New York, Harcourt Brace and Company, 1931.

Quint, Howard H. "Julius A. Wayland, Pioneer Socialist Propagandist," The Mississippi Valley Historical Review, XXXV (March, 1949), 585–606.

Rae, John. Contemporary Socialism. London, Swan Sonnenschein and Company, 1901.

Saposs, David J. Left Wing Unionism: a Study of Radical Policies and Tactics. New York, International Publishers, 1926.

Schlesinger, Arthur M. The Rise of the City. New York, Macmillan Company, 1940.

Shannon, David A., "The Socialist Party Before the First World War: an Analysis," The Mississippi Valley Historical Review, XXXVIII (Sept., 1951), 279–88.

Shannon, Fred A. The Farmer's Last Frontier. New York, Farrar and Rinehart, 1945.

Stoddart, Jane T. New Socialism: an Impartial Inquiry. London, Hodder and Stoughton, 1909. Contains a chapter (pp. 233–42) summarizing Werner Sombart's "Warum gibt es in den Vereinigten Staaten keinen Sozialismus?"

Stone, Irving. Clarence Darrow for the Defense. New York, Garden City Publishing Company, 1943.

Wachman, Marvin, "History of the Social-Democratic Party of Milwaukee, 1897–1910." Urbana, University of Illinois, 1943. Abstract of thesis.

Yellen, Samuel. American Labor Struggles. New York, Harcourt Brace and Company, 1936. For material on the strike in Lawrence, Mass.

Zimand, Savel. Modern Social Movements. New York, H. W. Wilson Company, 1921. Contains short descriptive summaries and bibliographies.

# Index